Macromedia® Flash™ MX Professional 2004 for Server Geeks

NATE WEISS

www.newriders.com

800 East 96th Street, 3rd Floor, Indianapolis, Indiana 46240

An Imprint of Pearson Education

Boston • Indianapolis • London • Munich • New York • San Francisco

Macromedia Flash MX Professional 2004 for Server Geeks

International Standard Book Number: 0-7357-1382-0

Library of Congress Catalog Card Number: 2003113740

Printed in the United States of America

First printing: December, 2003

08 07 06 05 04   7 6 5 4 3 2

Interpretation of the printing code: The rightmost double-digit number is the year of the book's printing; the rightmost single-digit number is the number of the book's printing. For example, the printing code 04-1 shows that the first printing of the book occurred in 2004.

Trademarks

Warning and Disclaimer

PUBLISHER
Stephanie Wall

PRODUCTION MANAGER
Gina Kanouse

SENIOR ACQUISITIONS EDITOR
Linda Anne Bump

DEVELOPMENT EDITOR
Jill Batistick

SENIOR PROJECT EDITOR
Lori Lyons

COPY EDITOR
Jill Batistick

INDEXER
Larry Sweazy

PROOFREADERS
Jeanette Lynn
Ben Lawson
Linda Seifert

COMPOSITION
Amy Hassos

MANUFACTURING COORDINATOR
Dan Uhrig

INTERIOR DESIGNER
Wil Cruz

COVER DESIGNER
Aren Howell

MEDIA DEVELOPER
Jay Payne

MARKETING
Scott Cowlin
Tammy Detrich
Hannah Onstad Latham

PUBLICITY MANAGER
Susan Nixon

Contents at a Glance

Introduction   xix

PART I: A CRASH COURSE IN FLASH

1 Getting Acquainted with Flash   3

2 Your First Flash Interface   23

3 Digging a Bit Deeper   79

PART II: KEY FLASH CONCEPTS FROM A DEVELOPER'S PERSPECTIVE

4 ActionScript: A Primer   115

5 Movie Clips as Objects   181

PART III: GETTING CONNECTED TO YOUR DATA

6 Connecting to Servers with Plain Text   231

7 Connecting to Servers with XML   271

8 Connecting to Servers with Flash Remoting   315

9 Connecting to Servers with Web Services   379

PART IV: USING FLASH FOR DATA COLLECTION

10 Flash and Sessions   439

11 Building Better Forms with Flash   489

PART V: APPENDIXES

A Notes on Building the SimpleBarChart Component   551

B Cross-Domain Data Access Policies in Flash Player 7   583

Index   591

To the cities of New York and Seattle, and to one of their late residents.

Table of Contents

PART I   A CRASH COURSE IN FLASH

Chapter 1	**Getting Acquainted with Flash**	3
	Why Flash?	4
	What's in It for You?	4
	How Flash Connects to Servers	5
	The Languages You'll Use	6
	A Quick Vocabulary Lesson	7
	Flash's Evolution over the Years	10
	Quick Tour of the Flash IDE	11
	First Looks	12
	The Timeline	14
	The Tools Bar	15
	The Stage	16
	Components Panel	16
	Actions Panel	17
	Properties Panel	18
	Help Panel	18
	Setting Up Your Server for This Book's Examples	19
	Setting Up the Database	19
	Setting Up Your Server Software of Choice	20
	Putting the Example Files in Your Web Server's Document Root	22
	Summary	22
Chapter 2	**Your First Flash Interface**	23
	Getting Ready: Supplying Data to Flash	24
	Encoding Data as Simple "Variables" for Flash	25
	Doing It with ColdFusion	26
	Doing It with ASP.NET	28
	Doing It with Java	30
	Building the Flash Interface	31
	Adding the Visual Elements	31
	Using ActionScript to Fetch and Display Data	35
	Publishing and Testing the Interface	42
	Accessing a Movie Clip from the Main Timeline	44
	Creating Navigation with Buttons and XML	46
	Supplying Information to Flash as XML	46
	Supplying XML from ColdFusion	47
	Supplying XML from ASP.NET	48
	Supplying XML from Java	50
	A Quick Introduction to Flash's XML Object	51
	Viewing Output Generated by trace *Statements*	54

Loading an External SWF at Runtime   56
Creating Simple Rollover Buttons   59
Adding ActionScript for Button Events   63
Creating an ArtistButtonClip for Each Artist at Runtime   65
Testing It Out   68
Adding the Interface to a Web Page   69
Copying and Pasting the HTML   70
Relative Versus Absolute URLs for Fetching Server Data   74
Hey, Check Out That File Size!   75
That Wasn't So Bad, Was It?   76
Summary   76

Chapter 3 Digging a Bit Deeper   **79**
Understanding the Library and Symbols   80
Symbols and Instances   80
Other Features Available in the Library Panel   84
Understanding the Timeline   86
The Timeline in the Flash IDE   87
Using the Timeline to Add Animation   87
Controlling Animation Playback with ActionScript   92
Jumping to Frames by Name Rather Than by Number   95
Easing the Tweened Motion for a More Natural Effect   96
Deciding Which Frame to Jump to at Runtime   97
Understanding More About Buttons   98
Changing a Button's Appearance on Rollover   99
Button Events   100
Invisible Buttons and the Hit Frame   103
Understanding More About Movie Clips   104
The Main Timeline Versus Movie Clip Timelines   104
Timelines as State Mechanisms   105
Target Paths, Parents, and Children   106
A Few Words About the this *Keyword*   109
Movie Clip Events   109
Understanding What Components Are   110
Moving On   111
Summary   111

PART II   KEY FLASH CONCEPTS FROM A DEVELOPER'S PERSPECTIVE

Chapter 4 ActionScript: A Primer   **115**
About ActionScript   116
ActionScript's Relationship to JavaScript and ECMAScript   117
A Brief History   118
What's New in ActionScript 2.0   118
Making the IDE Work for You   119
Positioning and Activating the Actions Panel   119
Actions Panel Tools   121

Helping the Actions Panel Understand the Types
   of Your Variables 125
Actions Panel Preferences 128
The Help Panel 129
Basic Language Elements 130
  Using Comments 130
  Syntax Basics 131
  Variables 133
  Conditional Statements 137
  Expressions 140
  Loops 143
Fun with Datatypes 146
  Numbers 146
  Strings 147
  Dates 148
  Arrays 149
  Associative Arrays 150
Creating Your Own Functions 151
  The Basics 152
  Arguments 152
  Returning Values from Functions 154
  Strict Typing 155
  Storing Functions in Separate ActionScript Files 156
Creating Your Own Classes 157
  Ways to Create New Classes 158
  Inheritance 172
Responding to Events 174
  Responding to Events Using the Classic Event Model 175
  Responding to Events Using the Listener Event Model 178
Summary 180

Chapter 5 Movie Clips as Objects **181**
The *MovieClip* Class 182
Learning by Example: A Gesture-Based Scroller Widget 190
  Building a Simple Example That Uses the Scroller 191
  The Handmade Members of the GestureMovieClip Class 197
  Reviewing the Code for GestureMovieClip 200
Movie Clips in the Library 202
  About Specifying ActionScript 2.0 Classes for Library Symbols 202
  Attaching Movie Clips from the Library Using
    Linkage Identifiers 206
  Changing the Appearance and Position of a Clip 209
  Removing Clips 211
Responding to Mouse Movements 212
  A Quick Tangent: Scheduling Method Calls with setInterval() 213
  Looking at the Current Mouse Position 214
  Reflecting Changes to a Clip Right Away with updateAfterEvent() 217

Adding Content to Movie Clips at Runtime   218
Drawing Lines and Shapes Programmatically   219
Creating Mask Clips Programmatically   221
Turning Clips into Components   223
Summary   227

PART III   GETTING CONNECTED TO YOUR DATA

Chapter 6 **Connecting to Servers with Plain Text**   **231**
Using the *LoadVars* Class   231
  Retrieving Structured Data   234
  Showing Structured Data in a Sliding Ticker   244
  Examining the newsTicker.fla Example Document 245
  Intercepting and Parsing Raw Text Data Yourself 252
  Round Trips: Sending Variables to the Server 258
Other Means of Sending and Loading Variables   269
Summary   270

Chapter 7 **Connecting to Servers with XML**   **271**
Using the XML Class   272
  Quick Review of Basic XML Terminology   272
  XML Class Members   275
  Typical Usage Pattern   280
  Populating a Gesture-Driven Scroller with XML 281
Using XPath in Flash   299
  Making the XPathAPI Class Available to Your Document 300
  XPathAPI *Usage Basics*   301
  A Concrete Example   303
Using the *XMLConnector* Component   308
Summary   313

Chapter 8 **Connecting to Servers with Flash Remoting**   **315**
Introducing Flash Remoting   316
  Flash Remoting Versus Web Services   316
  Which Application Servers Are Supported?   318
  Some Remoting Terminology   319
Getting Set Up   320
  Installing the Client-Side Components to the Flash IDE 320
  Installing the Server-Side Components   322
Your First Remoting Project   323
  The Server-Side Code   324
  The Client-Side Work   328
  Some More Details About Gateway URLs   333
  More Details About Responder Functions   336
  More Details About Responding to Status Events 338
Using the Special Flash Remoting Debugger   339

Remoting Classes: A Mini-Reference   340
   The NetServices *Class: Connecting to a Remote Server*   341
   The NetConnection *Class: Connecting to a Specific Service*   341
   The RecordSet *Class: Accessing Query Results*   342
A More Sophisticated Example   345
   On the Server   347
   On the Client   349
Flash Remoting and Data Binding   361
   Using RecordSet and DataSet Together   362
   Introduction to the DataSet *Component*   363
   Adding Databound Components to the Song Rater Example   364
   Basic DataSet *Class Members*   372
What You Haven't Learned About Flash Remoting   374
   Incrementally Loading Recordsets   374
   Server-Side Details   375
   Arrays and Other Datatypes   376
   Client-Side Recordset Filtering and Sorting   376
Open Source Remoting, Alternative Implementations,
  and Other Third-Party Tools   377
Summary   378

Chapter 9 Connecting to Servers with Web Services   **379**
Overview of Flash's Support for Web Services   380
   What Are Web Services?   380
   How Does One Create a Web Service?   381
   Some Quick Definitions   381
   Flash as a Web Service Client   383
   Options for Connecting to Web Services   383
Using the *WebServiceConnector* Component   385
   The Server-Side Code   386
   Components Used in the Rating Chart Example   404
   WebServiceConnector *Component Reference*   406
   Basic Usage of the WebServiceConnector *Component*   409
   A Few Words About the SimpleBarChart *Component*   413
   The ActionScript Code   415
The Web Services Panel   420
Viewing Trace Statements from the Data Logger   422
Connecting to a Web Service Using Script Alone   423
Web Services and Data Binding   428
   The Server-Side Code   428
   WebServiceConnectors, DataSets, and UI Controls   429
   Changes to the ActionScript Code   430
Flash's Security Policies and Third-Party Web Services   434
Summary   435

PART IV   USING FLASH FOR DATA COLLECTION

Chapter 10	**Flash and Sessions**	**439**
	Session State Concepts—A Quick Recap	440
	Passing URL and Form Variables	441
	Step 1: Passing the Variables to Flash	442
	Step 2: Passing the Variables Back to the Server	445
	Sharing Session Variables with Flash	449
	Making Flash a Participant in the Session	449
	Maintaining Session State Without Cookies	451
	Sharing Cookies with Flash	453
	Persisting Data with Local Shared Objects	454
	The SharedObject Class	455
	Basic SharedObject Usage	456
	Allowing SWFs to Share the Same Local Shared Objects	457
	Local Shared Objects and Size Limitations	458
	Putting It Together: Tracking User Logins	459
	The Server-Side Code	461
	The Client-Side Code	475
	Testing it Out	487
	Summary	488
Chapter 11	**Building Better Forms with Flash**	**489**
	Flash as Form Presentation Engine	491
	Advantages and Disadvantages of Flash-Based Forms	491
	Controls at Your Disposal	493
	Rich Internet Applications	495
	Basic Form Submissions	495
	Introducing Form Screens	497
	The Two Types of Screen-Based Documents	498
	Creating Screen-Based Documents	499
	Scripting Form Screens	504
	Attaching ActionScript Code to Screens	511
	Some Thoughts on Form Validation	515
	Simple Script-Based Validation	516
	Databound Validation	520
	Realtime Server-Side Validation	526
	The Customer Entry Example	527
	Loading External Content into Screens	542
	Specifying External Content at Design Time	543
	Loading External Content via ActionScript	544
	Accessing the External Content After It Loads	544
	Adding a ProgressBar Component	544
	Summary	548

PART V   APPENDIXES

Appendix A   **Notes on Building the *SimpleBarChart* Component**   **551**

About Flash MX 2004 Components   552

Differences Between Components and Ordinary Movie Clips   553

About the *SimpleBarChart* Component   554

SimpleBarChart Reference   555

Creating the *SimpleBarChart* Component   557

What to Look for in the Source Document   557

Required Elements in a Component's ActionScript File   560

Marking Properties as Inspectable   562

ActionScript Source Code for SimpleBarChart   563

Recompiling the Component After Making Changes   579

Summary   581

Appendix B   **Cross-Domain Data Access Policies in Flash Player 7**   **583**

How the Policy Is Enforced   584

Creating a Cross-Domain Policy File   585

Issues to Keep in Mind   588

General Policy File Considerations   588

Policy Files and Flash Player Versions   589

Index   **591**

About the Author

 **Nate Weiss** has been building commercial applications with various web server technologies for 7 or 8 years now (that's around 20 in geek years). Recently, these applications have used an increasing amount of Flash-based widgets to increase the usability and compatibility of select user interfaces.

Nate has spoken at Macromedia developer conferences and user group meetings on a number of topics ranging from XML to scripting. He was a member of the Team Macromedia peer-to-peer support group for several years, and he contributed the SDK to the Open WDDX project. He contributed to a number of Ben Forta's best-selling books about ColdFusion, and often makes components and other coding experiments available at his website, www.nateweiss.com. Nate can be reached at nate@nateweiss.com.

About the Technical Reviewers

These reviewers contributed their considerable hands-on expertise to the entire development process for this book. As each chapter was being written, these dedicated professionals reviewed all the material for technical content, organization, and flow. Their feedback was critical to ensuring that the text—and the Flash, ActionScript, ColdFusion, ASP.NET, and Java files that accompany it—fit our readers' need for the highest-quality technical information.

 **John Grden** is the Lead Macromedia Flash Developer for Zing.com as well as founder/owner of AcmeWebWorks.com. Zing.com is the leading 3D interactive chat site on the web today. Zing's interface is done completely in Flash and works in concert with a few server-side technologies such as Flash Communication Server MX, ASP, and Java. Along with moderating one of the largest Macromedia-related user lists on the Internet, John spends most of his Flash development time creating some of the most engaging Flash games on the web today. Currently, he's engaged in re-creating specific games based on a popular movie series' battles and events that are not only available on his site, but also will soon be available at www.TheForce.net. John is certified as a Macromedia Flash Designer. You can find out what he's been up to at AcmeWebWorks.com.

 **Kathy Hester** spends most of her time as a trainer for web designers and developers. When not involved with training sessions, Kathy works as an independent contractor doing design. In her spare time, she manages the New Orleans ColdFusion User Group and works with Hal Helms teaching Fusebox methodology. Kathy can be reached at kathyhes@realsheep.com.

Acknowledgments

Okay, I'll try to do this in chronological order.

First, I must thank Charlie Arehart for not only coming up with the original vision for this book, but also for turning the project over to me. This must be what it's like to be a Hollywood director who's been asked to adapt a beloved novel by a great modern writer: The director tries to be faithful to the spirit of the original, but in the end, the audience ends up shrugging their shoulders, unimpressed. ("Yeah, it was okay. But the book was better.") Or the uncle in the city who's been asked to take care of his brother's teenager for the summer. ("What happened to my kid? You let him get those tattoos? Do you *have* a shower in this apartment? And what's that in his nose?") Anyway, Charlie, I hope this is basically what you had in mind. Thanks again.

I must also thank Ben Forta, that Godfather of Macromedia-related publishing, for helping out Charlie and me with the initial ideas for the book, answering my questions, and patiently hooking me up with information. As I was writing this thing, there was often a miniature Conscience of Ben hovering over my left shoulder (scary thought—and I guess it was Linda over my right shoulder, ha), encouraging and inspiring me through example to try just a little harder and explain just a little more clearly.

Thanks to Angela Kozlowski, Robin Dennis, and Sara Hohn for taking the time to give me their advice and professional opinions about this book before I started writing.

Thanks to my aunt and uncle, Gigi and Don Spates, for their company and use of their pond, porch, and home while I wrote the first few chapters of this book, out on the lovely North Fork of Long Island.

The middle chapters of this book were written in the cool and beautiful city of Seattle, Washington, where I managed to have a great time even though I was working more or less non-stop. I wouldn't have been able to do it without the companionship of Heather Greene and Matt Gershoff, my awesome, unbelievably supportive friends and traveling companions. Showers of thanks to Pam Robertson for putting me up, putting up with me, and generally being cool, positive, and supportive, and for having red hair. Thanks also to Apple and Tucker Martine, to Keith, Eric, Floyd, the Nineteen Pound Hammer, Jen, Calla, and that awesome dude in the yellow shirt for making the whole experience so much fun. To Amanda Wilde, John in the morning, and the other DJ's at KEXP (www.kexp.org) for providing the soundtrack. Oh, and cafes Vita, Vivace,

Ladro, and Bauhaus, where I spent whole days drinking the best lattes in the history of ever.

Back in New York, I'd like to thank Jeanmarie and Stan Williams for their unfailing support while I finished this thing upstairs. And to all my NYC comrades for their support and friendship, and for generally remembering that I existed even though I was holed up in my apartment for months: Heather Greene and Matt Gershoff (again), Liz and Andy Gershoff, Melissa Caruso and John Scott, Jenny Turner, Jason Stover, Jason Weeden, Desia and Brian Zumhagen, Rebekkah Linton, Shira Machleder, Dawne Eng, Jennifer Sainato, Lisa, Lars, Lucas, and Lea Blackmore, Lee Gregory, Mary Godinho, and Stephanie Hawkins. I am also in debt to some great public spaces in Manhattan: The Rose Reading Room at the New York Public Library on 42nd Street, the Cafe at HERE, and the Starbucks on Astor Place (where I was one of several freaky-looking late-night regulars). In Brooklyn: the Flying Saucer Café, Ozzie's on 5th, and the hip new Tea Lounge on Union.

Thanks to the virtual company of Miss Jen deHaan, who had so many beta-forum-reading, ActionScript-writing, scrollbar-wanting, confidentiality-agreement-having, red-blooded developer and designer geeks downloading her messages on one hot summer evening that the power went out from New York City to the great plains of Ohio.

Thanks, of course, to my mother Sally, to my sister Liz, my cousin Carrie, and to my sister's friend Ken for their support. You may not realize it, but you all really helped me with this. Thanks also to my brother Jon and my father, George, for being with me in spirit.

Thanks to my absolutely fabulous technical editors, Kathy Hester and John Grden, for all their help, guidance, and patience as I explored the nooks and crannies that they already knew so well. In particular, John, you have been absolutely great—and a whole book on Flash later, I am no closer to understanding how you pulled off those amazing Star Wars games.

Perhaps most of all, I want to thank the good people at New Riders who got this book into your hands. Some people talk a good game about teamwork and support, but these goddesses of technical publishing take the phrase "group effort" to a whole new level. A thousand thanks to my publisher, Stephanie Wall, for believing in the project, pushing me forward on the phone, and cutting me some slack here and there. A bizillion truly heartfelt thanks to my editor, Linda Bump, for her unbelievable, unwavering support and understanding, and generally motivating and accommodating spirit all through this process.

And countless thanks to my development and copy editor, Jill Batistick, for so carefully reviewing my use of language, always being in my corner, and putting up with my silly insistences and inconsistencies about certain phrases.

And thanks to you, kind reader and fellow server geek—whoever and wherever you are. If you have problems, questions, or comments, feel free to write to me at nate@nateweiss.com. I may not be able to answer or respond to every question, but I'll do my best.

—Nate

Tell Us What You Think

As the reader of this book, you are the most important critic and commentator. We value your opinion and want to know what we're doing right, what we could do better, what areas you'd like to see us publish in, and any other words of wisdom you're willing to pass our way.

As the Senior Acquisitions Editor for New Riders Publishing, I welcome your comments. You can fax, email, or write me directly to let me know what you did or didn't like about this book—as well as what we can do to make our books stronger. When you write, please be sure to include this book's title, ISBN, and author, as well as your name and phone or fax number. I will carefully review your comments and share them with the author and editors who worked on the book.

Please note that I cannot help you with technical problems related to the topic of this book, and that due to the high volume of email I receive, I might not be able to reply to every message.

Fax: 317-428-3382

Email: linda.bump@newriders.com

Mail: Linda Bump
            Senior Acquisitions Editor
            New Riders Publishing
            800 East 96th Street, 3rd Floor
            Indianapolis, IN 46240 USA

INTRODUCTION

Dear Reader:

At the beginning of this year, I got an interesting telephone call. It was my esteemed colleague Charlie Arehart on the phone. He provides consulting and training for all sorts of web developers—especially those who work for companies that use Macromedia technologies. Charlie explained that he was getting more and more requests all the time for information and training about tying Flash front ends to databases and other backend systems. And the requests weren't coming from long-time Flash users. They were coming from ColdFusion enthusiasts, ASP.NET developers, and Java programmers.

The problem, Charlie explained, was that there weren't enough books about Flash to which a web developer could relate. Sure, there were lots of general-interest Flash books, and most of them had a chapter or two about server integration at the end. There were a few books that were all about specific server integration technologies such as Flash Remoting and Flash Communication Server, but they tended to assume that the reader already knew Flash. Books about Flash programming with ActionScript tended to make the same assumption.

Because there weren't any books written just for them, web developers had to buy many different books, reading a few chapters from each, or just try to teach themselves. Many bits and pieces of information were available online in the form of tutorials, knowledge base articles, user forums, user group websites, and even print magazines, but it takes time to find all that information—time that many developers just don't have.

So, Charlie's idea was to create a book about Flash that would treat the web developer as a first-class citizen. The book would get developers "over the hump" without forcing them to wade through a bunch of information about drawing and animation and design. The book wouldn't try to be all things to all people. Instead, it would focus on those aspects of Flash most likely to be of interest to developers.

Was I in?

Sure, I was in. It was the book I'd wanted when I was learning Flash myself. Speaking of which....

My Own Experience with Flash

A few years ago, I realized that I wanted to use Flash in the dynamic web application on which I was working. The project's requirements called for tricks that were going to be a royal pain using the usual client-side scripting and HTML techniques. I knew hardly anything about Flash, but I had been keeping an eye on the technology for a while. I knew that more and more people were using it to collect and present live information from databases and so on. Thus, I figured it wouldn't be too hard to get Flash to do what I needed.

And it *wasn't* too hard. Problem was, it wasn't particularly easy either. As I worked, I couldn't shake off the feeling that I was out of my home territory. The Flash authoring interface was clearly for artists and graphic designers—and seemed to be obsessed with abstract notions, such as gradient colors and time-lines, for which I had no use. I felt like I was crashing a party at an art school—a lovely and interesting place to visit, but not a place where my talents were going to get me anywhere.

Aside from the general sense of feeling out of place, there was also the fact that the parts of Flash that would help me talk to my server were a bit lacking. Sure, I could make calls to my server and exchange data, but the process felt a bit cobbled together. There didn't seem to be a clean, structured model for building the kinds of interfaces I wanted for my users.

All this happened quite some time ago, back when Flash 4 was the current version. Things have come a long way since then. Most of the things that used to be hard have gotten easier, and the features for connecting to servers have become more and more sophisticated with each new version. Today's Flash is truly a tool for application development as much as it is for design, if you know how to use it. It's a great product, capable of an astonishing variety of things, and you're going to enjoy getting familiar with it.

Who Is This Book For?

This book was written for web application developers who don't know Flash, but who want to use it in their Internet/intranet/extranet applications. Ideally, you are less interested in creating huge "pure Flash" sites that use Flash to bypass the browser experience and more interested in using Flash here and there to solve specific problems that can't be easily solved with traditional HTML and scripting techniques.

To get the most out of this book, you need to be familiar with at least one of the following: ColdFusion MX, ASP.NET, or Java/JSP/J2EE development. If you use PHP, Perl, or another web application environment for your work, this book will still help you, but you'll have to adapt the server-side code to work with your environment. (Adapting shouldn't be too hard, as the server-specific code has been kept as simple as possible.)

Who Is This Book Not For?

Good question. The way I see it, this book is *not* for you if any of the following is true:

- **You don't know servers.** This book is written for people who understand ColdFusion, ASP.NET, or J2EE-style application development. People who use Perl or PHP also might be interested because most of the examples can be translated pretty easily. However, most of the examples will confuse you if you don't know anything about server-side development.

- **You want to learn everything about Flash.** This book intentionally avoids teaching you everything you need to know about Flash. The product is just too big to explain completely without getting off topic. Instead, the focus is on those features that you are likely to need right away so that you can feel comfortable enough to start building data-enabled Flash applications. If you want to learn Flash inside and out, you'd be better off with a different book.

- **You are using an older version of Flash and don't want to have to adapt any of the examples.** Although the general principles discussed in this book are mostly applicable to earlier versions, many of the specific examples depend on features in the MX 2004 release. In general, Chapters 1 through 8 are applicable to any reasonably recent version of Flash (version 5 and later). Chapters 9 through 11 are applicable only to the Professional version of Flash MX 2004. (Jump ahead to Chapter 1, "Getting Acquainted with Flash," if you want details about what's new in Flash MX 2004.)

Assuming that you aren't in one of the preceding groups, I invite you to flip through some of the chapters now, glancing at the figures and example code along the way. If they seem adaptable to the problems you need to solve, buy this book and let's get started. If not, perhaps it's best for us to part ways (but you can keep the book in mind for someone else!).

In Closing...

If you choose to use this book, I believe that you will be well on your way to making Flash a part of your new and existing web applications. Good luck, and have fun.

—Nate Weiss

PART I
A CRASH COURSE
IN FLASH

1   Getting Acquainted with Flash   3

2   Your First Flash Interface   23

3   Digging a Bit Deeper   79

CHAPTER 1

GETTING ACQUAINTED WITH FLASH

Presumably, you've picked up this book because you are a seasoned web developer who's interested in learning how to work with Macromedia Flash. You already know your way around the server side of web application development, how to create dynamic pages that interact with databases, and what's generally involved in creating sites that use a combination of HTML, CSS, images, live data, and perhaps a bit of XML. You might be coming from a Microsoft ASP or ASP.NET background, a Java/J2EE background, or a ColdFusion background. Or, if you're like many people, you might come from a mix of these backgrounds.

What you like to use on the server side doesn't matter so much to me. What *does* matter is that you are curious about incorporating Flash into your dynamic, data-aware, server-driven web applications. You have likely heard how recent versions of Flash have included more and more features that are focused on application development, as opposed to design, art, and animation. You also might have heard that this version of Flash—Macromedia Flash MX 2004—is the most developer-friendly version yet. You even might have played around a bit with Flash on your own. Great.

This book is designed to help people like you get into Flash development without learning a lot about how to do design-related tasks, such as drawing and animation. We'll touch on that stuff in a bit, but the idea is to really concentrate on just those aspects of Flash that work with your server. This first chapter introduces you to some basic concepts and terminology, setting you up for the hands-on crash course you are going to take in Chapter 2, "Your First Flash Interface," and Chapter 3, "Digging a Bit Deeper."

Why Flash?

Why indeed. You already know that pages that do just about anything can be built using server-side logic alone. Data sits in a database, or maybe in XML files or some other source, gets processed by some kind of middleware layer, and ends up in the user's browser window in the form of HTML. It's simple and relatively clean. If you want to provide something interactive, you just use JavaScript and DHTML to create pages that morph and unfold before the user's eyes. And, um, at least in theory, you have no browser compatibility issues to worry about because you're using standards-based technologies.

Okay, that line of thinking makes sense a lot of the time. It might even make sense most of the time. But let's face it—there are often a bunch of nooks and crannies within a web application where the basic mechanisms provided by HTTP and HTML just aren't good enough. No matter how lean and efficient your code, no matter how pristine everyone's Net connection is, the tried-and-true approach to drilling in on data (view, click, redraw, view, click, redraw) can be a slow bore for your users and is often a strain on your server's resources.

Flash can often be a great solution for any application that needs—or wants—to present information with a flair, without needing to redraw the whole page each time the user wants to change the window into the data.

What's in It for You?

Good question. The fact that you've already had some success come your way as a server-side web developer is proof that you don't really *need* to know Flash. Heck, it might even be true that no one in the world *really* needs to know it. However, utilized in the right places, it can make your life easier—and it can make your users' lives easier too. Really.

At the least, you'll have another bullet point on your resume and another tool in your toolbox, ready for use in unusual situations. You'll understand when it makes sense to use Flash and when you should leave it alone. If asked to produce a data-aware widget for a new project, you can whip up a quick prototype in Flash, hook it up to data and logic on your server, and then pass it off to that designer with the cool glasses to make it pretty.

At the most, you can author a whole new set of web applications and pages. Each will be twice as clean, twice as elegant, and twice as fun as its predecessor. You'll be the life of the party, getting your freak on with the hippest, least geeky creatures in town, impressing devotees and critics alike with your ability to marry form to function with such grace.

Actual mileage may vary.

How Flash Connects to Servers

You can use Flash with a wide variety of server-side environments. This book's examples only show Flash being used with ColdFusion, ASP.NET, and Java, but you can use it in other environments as well, including PHP, Perl, home-grown CGI or ISAPI/NSAPI code, or whatever so-called middleware you feel comfortable with.

Within each server-side environment, you can integrate your systems with Flash using any combination of the following:

- **By passing values back and forth as CGI-style name/value pairs.** This is similar conceptually to how you work with forms and URL parameters today, but without sending the page on a round trip to the server. You will get a taste of this in Chapter 2 and learn more about it in Chapter 6, "Connecting to Servers with Plain Text."
- **By passing information back and forth between Flash and your server in the form of XML.** This enables you to easily exchange multifaceted, arbitrarily complex data with your server—quite possibly reusing work you have done elsewhere. You get a taste of this in Chapter 2 and learn more about it in Chapter 7, "Connecting to Servers with XML."
- **By having Flash talk to a Flash Remoting Gateway on your server.** This is often the easiest, fewest-lines-of-code way to go. If you use ColdFusion or JRun, you already have access to Flash Remoting. It's included in the box. If you use ASP.NET or J2EE, you just need to get a Flash Remoting license and install the gateway on your server. You learn about this stuff in Chapter 8, "Connecting to Servers with Flash Remoting."

- **By having Flash talk to Web Services.** Each Web Service might be on one of your own servers, or it might be a publicly available service run by a third party. In either case, you can choose to have Flash talk directly to the service, or you can use your server as a go-between. You learn about these options in Chapter 9, "Connecting to Web Services."

Again, this book focuses on ColdFusion, ASP.NET, and Java. However, with the exception of the Flash Remoting option, any application capable of exchanging XML or plain text data over HTTP can be integrated with Flash using the basic techniques discussed in this book. You can even have Flash fetch static XML or plain text documents from your server (you would just update those files manually or through some kind of batch process).

The Languages You'll Use

As you work through this book, you will see a variety of different languages in use. Most examples involve three or four different languages at the same time. Sound like a bit much? Well, I'm not just talking about programming or scripting languages. I'm also talking about markup languages and the visual elements you add to your Flash files.

You'll encounter the following languages:

- **Your server-side language of choice.** Of course, the server-side part of your work will be written in whatever language you use today. You'll continue to use the Java language (or JSP tags, perhaps) if you're using a J2EE server. You'll continue to use C# or VBScript (or another supported scripting language) if you're using ASP.NET. And you'll continue to use CFML if you're using ColdFusion.
- **ActionScript.** A modern, flexible scripting language, ActionScript is what you use within Flash to do things such as performing an interaction with your server, changing what information is displayed to the user, or moving things around on the screen. It's based on the same standard that JavaScript is based on, so it looks familiar if you've done client-side browser scripting in the past. (As of this version of Flash, there are now two slightly different versions of ActionScript that you can mix and match as you wish—this book uses both.)

- **Visual language elements.** One of the interesting aspects of Flash work is that visual items (images, buttons, slides, and animations) can be thought of as programming objects that have their own functions, scriptable properties, and so on. Thus, visual items can actually be thought of as pieces of a visual programming language (or at least as parts of a visual vocabulary). At the very least, they are pieces of the same puzzle.

- **XML.** It's not a programming language, of course, but XML *is* a language. You won't be required to use XML to incorporate Flash into your web applications, but you will probably want to after you see how easy it is to exchange structured data and instructions between your server and Flash.

- **SQL.** Assuming that some of the information you would like to present in a Flash-powered interface is stored in a database, you will continue to use SQL to fetch and update your data tables. However, rather than displaying the fetched data only as HTML, you will send some of your data to the Flash client sitting within your pages.

- **HTML.** Yes, HTML is still involved. This book isn't trying to rewrite the rules about anything. I'm not going to encourage you to rewrite all—or even many—of your pages as "pure Flash" pages. Thus, your applications can still involve as much traditional HTML work as you want them to. (You will also use HTML to embed your Flash work within your pages, just as you use it to embed images today.)

A Quick Vocabulary Lesson

Like most software, Flash has a set of key concepts and vocabulary words that appear throughout its documentation, dialog boxes, and other screens. The following are the most important terms and ideas for you to get a handle on:

- **Movie.** The presentations that you create with Flash are called *movies*. Don't worry: Just because something is called a "movie" doesn't mean that you have to create characters that move around or tell a story. The term stems from Flash's roots as an animation tool and doesn't have much meaning to you and me. Just accept that the files you create with Flash to be shown on the web are always called movies, even if they look and behave more like stock tickers, data-entry forms, or interactive navigation widgets. I often use the term "interface" rather than movie, just to emphasize the fact that this book is more interested in data than it is in motion. That said, the fact that motion, animation, and other movie- or cartoon-like functionality is available to you when you need it is a big plus.

- **Flash.** The term "Flash" is used most often to refer to the product called Macromedia Flash, which is the development environment (or, if you prefer, the programming environment or design environment) that you use to create Flash movies for display on the web. Because it includes drawing tools, Flash is similar to design environments such as Adobe Photoshop or Macromedia's own FreeHand product. However, because it is also a scripting or programming environment, it is also comparable to programming environments such as Microsoft Visual Studio, Borland's Delphi product, and the like. The term "Flash" sometimes gets confusing because people sometimes say "Flash" when they are actually talking about the Flash Player (next). Some other times, they are talking about the collective concept as a whole: the Flash IDE, the Flash Player, Flash movie files, and so on. Just to reduce any potential confusion, this book usually uses the term "Flash IDE" to refer to the development environment.

- **Flash Player.** The Flash Player is what your users need to have installed on their computers to see the Flash movies (or user interfaces, or presentations, or whatever you want to call them) that you create with the Flash IDE. Whereas the Flash IDE is something that you have to buy from Macromedia, the Flash Player is distributed free of charge. What's more, the vast majority of browsers come with a relatively recent version of the Flash Player already installed, which means that you can reasonably assume that most users can view the Flash content that you create. If not, they need only install the Flash Player, which is a relatively small and quick download for most people. Most Flash Players are installed on computers with web browsers, but players also exist for other devices, such as handheld organizers, certain cell phones, and WebTV consoles.

- **SWF.** When you create a movie with the Flash IDE, the end result is a file with a .swf extension. This is the actual movie or presentation file that the Flash Player displays to your users. People often call these SWF files or SWFs (pronounced "*swiffs*"). Optimized for delivery over the web, SWFs can be very small in size (depending, of course, on what you do with them).

- **FLA.** As you just learned, SWF files are the end result of your work with Flash; they are what is delivered to the Flash Player for playback. FLA files, on the other hand, are the files that you work with in the Flash IDE to produce your SWFs. If you think of SWFs as being like a compiled program (an .exe or .dll file, say, or a compiled Java class), then FLAs can be thought of as source code (like C++ code, or an uncompiled .java file). SWFs aren't meant to be editable files—if you want to make a change to a SWF, you need to go back to the original FLA and edit it in the Flash IDE. Then you compile—or publish—the changes as a new SWF.

- **Publish.** The process of creating a SWF from an FLA file is called *publishing*. As I mentioned, this idea of publishing is roughly analogous to compilation. This step is quick and easy in Flash. You just choose File > Publish in the Flash IDE and voila! Your SWF is created in the same folder as your source .fla file.

- **Movie clip.** Any Flash movie might actually be made up of any number of smaller parts, called *movie clips*. Movie clips might contain data-entry elements, navigation elements, animations, artwork, and the like. Each movie clip is a separate visual object and can be controlled through ActionScript. Just as classes are the central organizing principle of Java programming—or just as data tables are the organizing principle of relational database design—so, too, are movie clips the organizing principle of most Flash work. Your ActionScript code is executed within the context of a movie clip, data from your server is fetched by or loaded into movie clips, and so on. The movie clip is the basic building block of Flash development, at least for us geeks.

- **Timeline.** If you have peeked over a designer's shoulder as he or she was working in the Flash IDE, or if you've flipped through any other books about Flash, you've probably seen or heard reference to the timeline. As its name implies, the timeline represents the flow of time in your Flash movies. Like a CD or DVD player, the timeline can be started and stopped, and individual moments in time can be jumped to or looped repeatedly. For designers or animators, the timeline is generally about making things move around. For programmers, the timeline is more often used to jump from one visual state to another, like jumping from one paused scene to another on a DVD.

Flash's Evolution over the Years

This book concentrates on the feature set in the most recent version of Flash (Macromedia Flash MX 2004). That said, many of the techniques and examples in this book work with older versions of the Flash IDE and Player with little modification. The following is a quick rundown of the various versions of the product to help you understand a bit about how the product has evolved and when key developer features were introduced:

- Early versions of Flash were targeted mostly at graphic designers. The product first appeared on the market as a lightweight, low-bandwidth-friendly cousin of Macromedia's popular Shockwave product. The Shockwave environment used metaphors from movie productions (you had a "Stage," a "Cast," "Characters," "Scenes," and so on). Some of those metaphors still exist in today's Flash, but the product has grown away from the film-studio analogy over the years. These early versions—through Flash 3, released in 1998—made it increasingly possible to create and deliver exciting, colorful, motion-rich presentations. Flash movies started appearing on the front pages of websites everywhere, sometimes to emphasize brand or company identity, and sometimes just to add a bit of "eye candy" to otherwise-static pages.

- Flash 4, released in 1999, was the first version of Flash that really addressed the possibilities of tying Flash work to a server in more or less real time. Key scripting functionality, such as the `loadVariables()` and `duplicateMovieClip()` functions, made it possible to create Flash movies that reflected the state of server-side data, and the guts of the product continued to move toward an object-oriented paradigm (where the central "object" was a movie clip). People started experimenting with using Flash as a more important part of their dynamic web applications rather than using it only for splash pages and other purely visual flourishes.

- Flash 5, released in 2000, was the first version of the product that could be said to be fully programmable. Prior versions had supported some simple scripting features, but Flash 5 introduced ActionScript, a full-fledged, modern scripting language that was as mature, feature-rich, easy to use, and familiar to web developers as the language on which it was based: JavaScript. For the first time, programmers had access to real OOP-style objects to control what appeared on the screen, real string-manipulation functions, real variable scopes, and so on. The Flash IDE also got real script-editing features, such as code completion and syntax coloring. Features related to XML were also added at this time.

- Flash MX, released in 2002, was another release that offered a lot to developers. Nearly all of Macromedia's most important products—Flash, ColdFusion, Fireworks, and Dreamweaver—were updated to "MX," with an emphasis on integration between the products and a consistent message about enabling what Macromedia calls Rich Internet Applications (RIAs). In Flash, this plays out most obviously with new features related to Web Services and Flash Remoting (which integrates Flash with ColdFusion and other server products in the most seamless way yet). Support for video playback and the loading of external sound and image files make it even easier to create Flash presentations that change over time on their own. The Flash Player also obtains access to the user's camera and microphone in support of Macromedia's Flash Communication Server product, which enables the creation of online games, chat, conferencing, and other peer-to-peer applications with Flash.

- Flash MX 2004 is the most recent version of Flash as of this writing. Again, the product contains a host of developer-friendly features and continues Flash's evolution as a product that is truly part design tool and part developer tool. In fact, for the first time, two different versions of the product exist: one aimed a bit more at web application developers (Flash MX Professional 2004) and one aimed at artists and designers (Flash MX 2004). Brand new features in the Professional version—such as Screens and a new set of data-bound Components—make it easier than ever to "draw" data and entry mechanisms. The ease is reminiscent of classic client-server data-access features from products such as Visual Basic, Delphi, PowerBuilder, and the like, but with all of Flash's visual flair, lightweightness, and ubiquity.

Quick Tour of the Flash IDE

You're almost ready to start working with Flash. In Chapter 2, you build your first Flash movie—or, if you prefer, interface—that fetches and displays information from your server. You will, of course, be using the Flash IDE to build that first example, so let's take a few moments now to get you familiarized with the development environment.

> **NOTE**
>
> I am assuming that you have already installed Flash MX 2004—preferably the Professional version—on your computer. If you don't have Flash, you can purchase it from a software retailer or buy it online from Macromedia or a third party. If you want to try Flash before buying it, you can download a 30-day trial version from `www.macromedia.com`, which should be more than enough time to work through the examples in this book. The trial version is a full-featured version of Flash; the only difference is that it ceases to work after 30 days. You can always buy a license online from Macromedia at the end of your 30-day trial (and you don't have to reinstall the software).

First Looks

I'd like you to show you around the Flash IDE:

1. Launch Flash MX 2004.

2. If you have changed the positions of any of the panels in the past, choose Window > Panel Sets > Default Layout if you want your screen to match up to the figures in this section. If you just installed Flash, you can skip this step.

3. Take a quick look around. Notice that the Flash IDE is separated into a number of different *panels* (see Figure 1.1). The Timeline panel is across the top of the screen, a Properties panel is at the bottom of the screen, a Tools panel is docked along the left edge, and Components and Behaviors panels are docked along the right edge.

4. If you take another, closer look, you'll see other panels that are visible but minimized. For instance, above the Properties panel along the bottom, you can see a Help panel and then an Actions panel just above it. If you click the title bar for a panel, you will expand or minimize it. Go ahead and sneak a quick peak at some of the minimized panels now if you feel like it.

5. Right-click the title bar for the Projects panel and choose Close Panel to get rid of it for now. Do the same for the Color Mixer and Behaviors panels.

6. Expand the Component Inspector panel. Your workspace should now look something like Figure 1.2. This is a good starting point for the type of work we are going to be doing in this book.

7. Choose Window > Save Panel Layout. Then type **My Development Layout** in the Save Panel Layout dialog box and click OK to save the layout.

8. Now that you've saved this new panel set, you can fool around with the panels as much as you want, knowing that you can quickly return to the basic layout shown in Figure 1.2. Just choose Window > Panel Sets > My Development Layout.

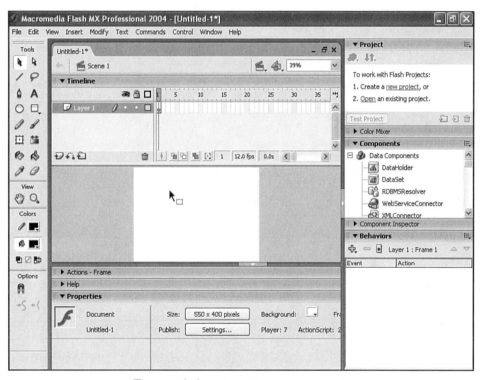

FIGURE 1.1   The default panel layout.

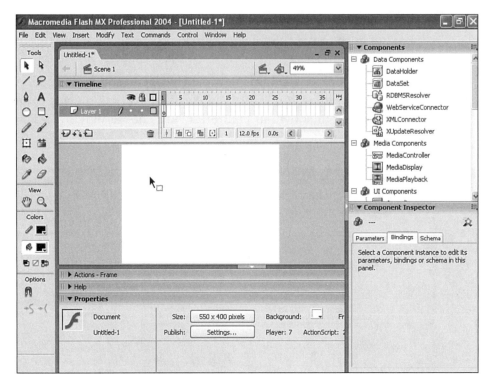

FIGURE 1.2   A better starting point for developers.

The Timeline

Take a look at the Timeline panel, at the top edge of the Flash IDE (see Figure 1.3). The left part of the timeline shows the *layers* in your document (right now there's only one layer); you can use layers to determine which objects show up in front of others.

The right side of the timeline shows the *frames* (the series of small, white and grey squares, marked 1, 5, 10, and so on). Frames represent individual moments in time. If you tell your movie to "play," the timeline begins advancing through the frames at regular intervals. Each frame can contain different objects or the same objects in different places; as the frames change, the objects will appear, disappear, or move around. Each frame can also contain ActionScript code that causes the Flash movie to do something, such as communicate with your server, enable or disable something, ask the user for some kind of response, or perform whatever action you need to take.

FIGURE 1.3   The Timeline panel.

The Tools Bar

The Tools bar, docked by default along the left edge of the screen, provides tools for drawing and selecting visual objects (see Figure 1.4). The most important tool is the Selection tool at top left (the black arrow). Other important tools are the Text tool, which can be used to create static text or dynamic text fields; the Oval and Rectangle tools, which can be used to draw buttons; and the Fill tool, which is used to fill areas with color or gradients. You will use some of these tools in Chapter 2.

FIGURE 1.4   The Tools bar.

The Stage

The white area in the center of the screen is known as the Stage (see Figure 1.5). Whatever you place on the Stage is visible when the movie appears in the Flash Player on the user's machine. Items placed in the gray area that surrounds the Stage won't be visible, but you can have them move onto the Stage (and thus into view) in response to something the user does or when some kind of information is received from your server.

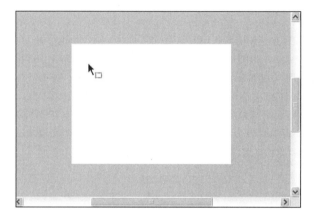

FIGURE 1.5   The Stage.

Components Panel

Flash MX 2004 comes with an all-new set of components, represented in the Components panel (see Figure 1.6). Most of the components are user interface elements that you can use to create data entry forms, scrolling display panels, and other commonly needed items. You can download and install more components from the Macromedia Flash Exchange online; you can also create your own.

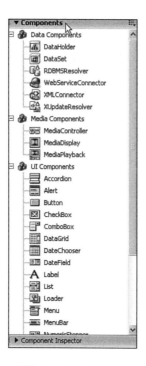

FIGURE 1.6   The Components panel.

Actions Panel

Finally, someplace to type code! Yes, the Actions panel is where you add the ActionScript code that makes your Flash interface do whatever it is designed to do (see Figure 1.7). It can interact with your server, move things around, and create stuff out of thin air. The Actions panel includes the syntax-coloring and code-completion features that you'd expect from a modern code editor. You'll add some code using this panel as you build your first Flash interface in Chapter 2.

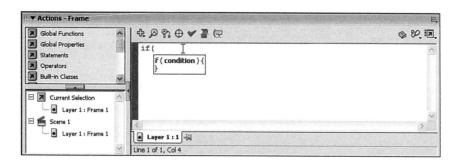

FIGURE 1.7   The Actions panel.

Properties Panel

The Properties panel, docked by default along the bottom edge of the screen (see Figure 1.8), changes depending on what object is currently selected on the Stage or timeline. If you select a frame in the timeline, the Properties panel shows the options available for the frame. If you select a button on the Stage, the panel shows the options available for buttons, and so on. You will use this panel a number of times in Chapter 2 as you work with various objects.

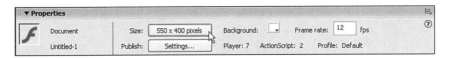

FIGURE 1.8   The Properties panel.

Help Panel

The Help panel (see Figure 1.9) is always available to help you find out more about how to use Flash. It contains the full Flash documentation set—including the ActionScript Reference Guide and ActionScript Dictionary, which you will refer to often as you write ActionScript code. You can browse through the documentation section by section, or you can search it by typing keywords.

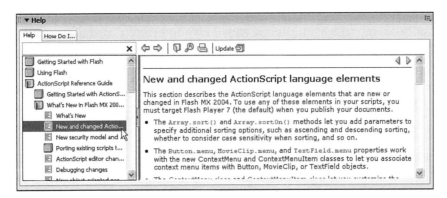

FIGURE 1.9   The Help panel.

Setting Up Your Server for This Book's Examples

> **NOTE**
>
> Download the example files for this book from `www.flashforservergeeks.com`. The files are provided as a single .zip archive that includes all the code listings, example database, and other supporting files.

The Flash examples in this book can connect to servers running ColdFusion MX, ASP.NET, or Java. You can use all three if you wish. You just need to install the appropriate server software on your local machine (or whatever machine you want), and then set up your server to use the example database in this book.

> **NOTE**
>
> For Java, this book usually uses JSP pages and servlets as examples for simplicity's sake. For the most part, other J2EE elements could work with Flash using the same basic data-exchange techniques.

Setting Up the Database

This book's examples use a database called VenueDB, which is the database for a fictional music venue. The database contains the following tables:

- Articles (where each record represents an article page)
- Artists (information about musical artists)
- Customers (with username and contact information)
- Events (musical events taking place at the venue)
- PageComments (comments from users about pages in the site)
- SongRatings ("love it" or "hate it" ratings for songs)
- Songs (information about MP3 recordings of songs)
- Users (credentials and rights for intranet users)

Populated versions of the example database are provided for the following database systems:

- Access 2000 (just use the VenueDB.mdb file)
- MySQL (run the VenueDB.sql script to create the database)
- SQLServer 2000 (just attach the VenueDB.mdf file)
- Oracle (run the VenueDB.sql script to create the database)

In general, the easiest thing is to use the Access version of the database. You don't have to bother setting up a database server. If you are on an operating system that can't use Access databases, however, or if you want to use one of the other database systems just to be difficult (just kidding!), be my guest.

In any case, the examples in this book assume that the example database can be reached using an ODBC datasource called VenueDB. I realize that you probably wouldn't use ODBC in practice (you would use one of the other System.Data providers under ASP.NET, a "pure" JDBC driver under Java, or one of the built-in drivers if using ColdFusion), but it works well for the purposes of this book. The particulars of how your middleware connects to databases isn't what we're concerned with here anyway.

NOTE

You can skip the ODBC part if you are using only ColdFusion. Just get the database set up.

To create the ODBC datasource in Windows, you use the Data Sources applet (which is located either in the Control Panel or in Administrative Tools, depending on your version of Windows). Use whatever driver (Microsoft Access or whatever) is appropriate for the version of the example database you've decided to use. Just make sure you're creating a System DSN (not a User or File DSN), and make sure to name it VenueDB.

Setting Up Your Server Software of Choice

This section briefly describes what you need to do to prepare your server software of choice (ASP.NET, Java/J2EE, or ColdFusion) to work with this book's examples. None of this is likely to be new to you at all. It's the same kind of thing you would do when setting up any data-aware application with your server.

Setting Up ASP.NET

If you want to use this book's ASP.NET examples:

1. You need to have ASP.NET installed and configured properly on your server. That generally means installing the .NET Framework, unless you are using a version of Windows that includes the framework.

2. Your .NET installation needs to include Data Provider for ODBC (that is, the System.Data.ODBC namespace). The easiest way to get this is to make sure you're using the .NET Framework 1.1 or later. If you don't want to use version 1.1, you can download the Data Provider for ODBC separately from Microsoft's site.

3. You need to create an ODBC datasource called VenueDB that points to the example database for this book.

Setting Up Java

If you want to use this book's Java examples:

1. You need to have some kind of server software installed that is capable of serving JavaServer Pages (JSP) and hosting Java servlets. (If you are also working with the ColdFusion examples, you can use just ColdFusion MX 6.1 or later for both.)

2. You need to create an ODBC datasource called VenueDB that points to the example database for this book. The examples will use the sun.jdbc.odbc.JdbcOdbcDriver driver included in the Java SDK to connect to the ODBC datasource, using a connection URL of jdbc:odbc:VenueDB.

Of course, you are free to use a different JDBC driver; you'll just have to adjust the driver and connection URL in the Java examples accordingly. In addition, you'll have to do the same if you're using a platform that doesn't support ODBC.

Setting Up ColdFusion

If you want to use this book's ColdFusion examples:

1. You need to have ColdFusion MX installed on your server. If you don't own ColdFusion, you can obtain a 30-day trial version from www.macromedia.com. (The trial version reverts to a developer mode after 30 days, which means you can keep using it for development and learning, but others won't be able to access the server over the network.)

2. Use the ColdFusion Administrator to create a datasource called VenueDB that points to the example database for this book. Make sure that the new datasource connection verifies correctly.

3. Make a note that if you are using the standalone version of ColdFusion, you probably need to add the usual reference to port 8500 in each URL to the .cfm page found throughout this book.

Putting the Example Files in Your Web Server's Document Root

> **NOTE**
>
> Download the example files for this book from www.flashforservergeeks.com. The files are provided as a single .zip archive that includes all the code listings, example database, and other supporting files.

Now all you need to do is place the example files in the correct place. The example files are all contained within a folder called `venue`; within the venue folder are folders for each chapter (`chapter02`, `chapter03`, and so on). Just place the venue folder within your server's document root. The files in the `chapter02` folder, for instance, should now be accessible at URLs starting with `http://localhost/venue/chapter02`.

> **NOTE**
>
> Of course, the `localhost` part is correct only if your server software is installed on your local workstation. If your server is on another machine, just use that machine's hostname or IP address instead. You will, however, need to place a cross-domain policy file on the server if it is not located on your local machine. See Appendix B for details.

Summary

This chapter started out by providing a bit of background about Flash and related terminology. It then took you on a very brief tour of the Flash IDE and explained how to configure your server to work with this book's examples. Now you're all ready to get your hands dirty in Chapter 2, where you'll start creating Flash interfaces that integrate with data on your server.

CHAPTER 2

YOUR FIRST FLASH INTERFACE

In Chapter 1, "Getting Acquainted with Flash," you learned a bit about Flash, what it can mean for you as a web developer, and a bit about the development environment. Chapter 2 builds on that by showing you how to build a simple-but-functional Macromedia Flash interface that displays information that it retrieves from your server at runtime. Along the way, you'll learn a bit about ActionScript, movie clips, variable scopes, and other Flash concepts and terminology.

Our first Flash interface displays information about musical artists from the Venue example database. First, we'll put together simple server-side code that "supplies" information about artists to Flash. Then we'll put together a simple user interface that displays that information in the Flash Player.

We're jumping off the deep end here. Okay, maybe not the deep end (the flashy high dives and swift cannonballs come later). But don't worry if you feel like you're in a bit over your head as you read this chapter. The idea here is just to get you immersed as quickly as possible—the details come later. To put it another way: Come on in, the water's fine!

Getting Ready: Supplying Data to Flash

In this book, we're mostly thinking about Flash as the "client" part of a loosely defined client/server type of application. You have information or logic that sits on your server, and you want to use Flash to expose that information to your users in some kind of interesting or convenient way. Therefore, most of the Flash projects in this book require a certain amount of server-side code (written in whatever language is appropriate for the application server you favor), plus some client-side scripting that interacts with the server-side code to retrieve, update, or otherwise interact with the data available to the server-side part.

At this point, you probably have lots of questions, like "How exactly do I supply data to Flash?" and "What format does it need to be in for Flash to be able to understand it?" and "When Flash has some information, how do I go about showing it to the user?" Hey, those are great questions. I can give you some short answers right now. (The long answers, of course, make up much of the rest of this book.)

You can supply data to Flash using any of the following techniques:

- **As plain text.** Your server supplies text that represents name/value pairs, using the same & and = format used in the "query string" portion of URLs. Flash retrieves the text and makes each name/value pair available to ActionScript as a simple string variable.

- **As XML.** Flash retrieves the XML from your server, parses it, and makes the various elements and attributes in the XML available to ActionScript as objects. If it helps, you can think of the XML functionality as being similar conceptually to the SAX or DOM-style interfaces provided by other XML parsers.

- **Through Flash Remoting.** Flash Remoting makes it even easier to exchange data between your server and Flash. Flash Remoting is included in ColdFusion and JRun; if you use .NET or another J2EE server, you must purchase the server-side portion from Macromedia (it's very reasonably priced for what you get).

- **Through a Web Service.** If your language or programming environment of choice provides an easy way to create Web Services, you can create a service that exposes whatever data is appropriate. Flash can call the service's methods just like any other consumer of the service.

Each technique gets its own chapter in Part III, "Getting Connected to Your Data," of this book. For now, we're going to concentrate on the first method because it's the simplest and thus lets you start seeing results right away—no matter what application server you use. The other techniques will be easier to understand after you see how this stuff works.

Encoding Data as Simple "Variables" for Flash

As you just learned, you can supply data to Flash as plain text, as XML, or through Remoting or Web Services. This section is going to look at the first option, where information is made available by the server using a very simple "plain-text" format. If a page on your server knows how to return data in this format (as opposed to what your pages normally return, which is probably HTML or XHTML), Flash can easily grab the text and make it available to your users.

Let's get more specific. This special "plain-text" format that I've been speaking about is simply the same format that you already use to supply URL parameters or variables to your dynamic web pages. You know how that works: anything after the ? in a URL is called the *query string*. Within the query string, any number of name/value pairs can be provided, where the name and value are separated by = signs, and the pairs are separated from each other by & signs. Within a value, any "funny" characters (such as spaces, slashes, and so on) are escaped using character codes and the % sign.

NOTE

Again, you probably know all this by heart already, so I won't beat it to death here. This was all determined a long time ago, back when the HTTP and CGI specifications were created. If you want to find out more about the particulars, go online and run a quick search for the application/x-www-urlformencoded standard format.

Because this is the format one uses to supply values *to* a web page, it makes some sense that Macromedia allows you to use this same format to pass values *from* a page as well. Here's a simple scenario: you have a page on your server that accepts a musical artist's ID number as a URL parameter and then responds with information about that artist. The URL you use to request the information from the server might look like this:

```
http://www.mycompany.com/mypage.jsp?idArtist=5
```

Your server-side code would use the ID number to retrieve information about the artist from a database. Then it might respond with the name and age of the artist, plus the type of music he or she plays, like so:

```
artistName=Natalie%20Weiss&artistAge=19&musicType=Pop
```

If the Flash Player was told to fetch this line of text from your server, the end result would be the creation of three variables:

- `artistName` (which would hold the value "Natalie Weiss")
- `artistAge` (which would hold the value "19")
- `musicType` (which would hold the value "Pop")

Remember, the server-side code would be responding with *only* this line of name/value pairs. The page wouldn't return any HTML or anything else that would normally make any sense to display in a browser. To put it another way, URLs that supply data to Flash aren't meant for end users to see. They are for Flash's eyes only.

NOTE

All variables exchanged using the plain-text mechanism are received by ActionScript as string variables (specifically, instances of the `String` class, as you will learn more about in Chapter 4, "ActionScript: A Primer") out of the box. If you want the rest of your code to interpret one of these variables as a number, Boolean, date, or other datatype, you will need to perform the type conversion yourself (it's easy, don't worry about it). You will learn more about this in Chapter 4.

Doing It with ColdFusion

Now let's take a look at the simple code needed to supply data in the plain text format we just discussed. I'll start with ColdFusion (for no particular reason). If you prefer ASP.NET or Java, feel free to skip ahead to Listings 2.2 and 2.3 now. All three listings are extremely simple and are basically just simple transliterations between the languages.

Take a look at Listing 2.1. As you can see, there isn't much to this listing at all. Please note that it's assumed that you have already used the ColdFusion Administrator to create a datasource named VenueDB that points to the example database for this book. (Refer back to the end of Chapter 1 for instructions about setting up the datasource if you haven't set it up already.)

LISTING 2.1   artistVarSource.cfm—Supplying Name/Value Pairs from ColdFusion

```
<!--- This page requires an "idArtist" parameter in the URL --->
<cfparam name="URL.idArtist" type="numeric">

<!--- Simple query to fetch Artist info from database --->
<cfquery name="ArtistQuery" datasource="VenueDB">
 SELECT sArtistName, sImageName, sDescription
 FROM Artists
 WHERE idArtist = #URL.idArtist#
</cfquery>

<!--- Omit debug info, and anything not in <cfoutput> blocks --->
<cfsetting showdebugoutput="No" enablecfoutputonly="Yes">

<!--- Set the MIME content-type of our response to "text/plain" --->
<cfcontent type="text/plain" reset="yes">

<!--- Output the information --->
<!--- (code on multiple lines here, but output is on one line) --->
<cfoutput>artistName=</cfoutput>
<cfoutput>#URLEncodedFormat(ArtistQuery.sArtistName)#</cfoutput>
<cfoutput>&imageName=</cfoutput>
<cfoutput>#URLEncodedFormat(ArtistQuery.sImageName)#</cfoutput>
<cfoutput>&description=</cfoutput>
<cfoutput>#URLEncodedFormat(ArtistQuery.sDescription)#</cfoutput>
```

The <cfparam> declares that this page requires a URL variable named idArtist. That value is used in a <cfquery> that retrieves information about the corresponding artist record in our example database. At the bottom, simple <cfoutput> blocks are used to output the name/value pairs. Note that ColdFusion's URLEncodedFormat() function is wrapped around each value, which takes care of escaping any special characters (such as spaces or slashes) in the values.

The <cfsetting> and <cfcontent> tags are optional in this case, but it's a good idea to include them in this fashion in pages that supply name/value pairs to Flash. The <cfsetting> tag turns off ColdFusion's debugging output for this page if it happens to be turned on at the server level because this page should generate only the name/value pairs, not any HTML or additional text such as debugging messages. It also tells ColdFusion to output text only between <cfoutput> tags, which avoids any issues regarding generated whitespace. The <cfcontent> tag sets the content type of this page's response to text/plain rather than to the default text/html content type. Flash actually wouldn't mind if this step was omitted, but it makes sense to set the content type to `text/plain` because the page's output doesn't contain any HTML markup.

Go ahead and visit this page with a browser with an `idArtist=1` in the URL and check out the results (Figure 2.1). Depending on the browser you are using, the content might appear in your default text editor, or you might be prompted to save the content to a file (different browsers deal with `text/plain` content differently). None of that matters much. The point is that you should be able to see a line of text with the artist information in a name/value pair. If you get some kind of error message, you probably just need to correct something about the datasource for the example database.

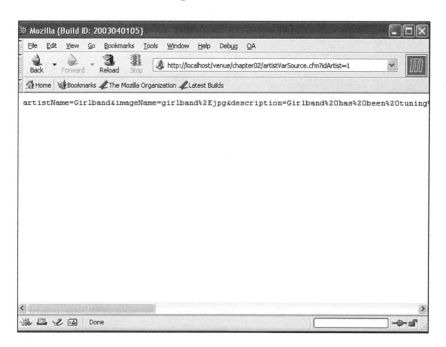

FIGURE 2.1   Checking the name/value pairs in a browser.

Doing It with ASP.NET

If you prefer to work with ASP.NET, Listing 2.2 is the equivalent version of Listing 2.1. It's assumed that you have already created an ODBC datasource named VenueDB that points to the example database for this book. You should be able to test this listing out by passing it an `idArtist=1` parameter in the URL (as shown in Figure 2.1).

> **NOTE**
>
> This example relies upon the `System.Data.ODBC` namespace, which is included with version 1.1 of the .NET Framework. If you are using version 1.0 of the framework, you will need to download the `System.Data.ODBC` package from Microsoft's website for this listing to work without modifications.

LISTING 2.2   artistVarSource.aspx—Supplying Name/Value Pairs from ASP.NET

```
<%@ Page Language="vb" Debug="true" %>
<%@ Import Namespace = "System.Data.ODBC" %>

<script runat="server">
 Sub Page_Load
  ' Define database connection
  Dim ConnStr as String = "DSN=VenueDB"
  Dim conn as OdbcConnection = new OdbcConnection(ConnStr)

  ' Set up query
  Dim CmdStr as String = "SELECT * FROM Artists " _
   + "WHERE idArtist = " + Request.Item("idArtist")
  Dim cmd as OdbcCommand = new OdbcCommand(CmdStr, conn)

  ' Establish connection and perform query
  conn.Open()
  Dim reader As OdbcDataReader = cmd.ExecuteReader()

  ' Fetch first (and only) line of data
  reader.Read()

  ' Set the MIME content-type of our response to "text/plain"
  Response.ContentType = "text/plain"

  ' Output the information
  ' (code on multiple lines here, but output is on one line)
  Response.Write("artistName=" _
   + Server.URLEncode(reader.Item("sArtistName")))
  Response.Write("&imageName=" _
   + Server.URLEncode(reader.Item("sImageName")))
  Response.Write("&description=" _
   + Server.URLEncode(reader.Item("sDescription")))
 End Sub
</script>
```

> **NOTE**
>
> Of course, this is just one of many different ways to code this example. Naturally, the same example could be transliterated into JScript or C#, and you might choose to use the data objects and methods from the `System.Data.OleDb` or `System.Data.SqlClient` namespaces rather than the `System.Data.ODBC` namespace. The example is written this way just to keep things clear, relatively independent of database type, and interoperable with the other server types covered in this book. Feel free to change the scripting language or data-fetching specifics as you see fit.

Doing It with Java

Last, but certainly not least, Listing 2.3 shows a JavaServer Pages (JSP) page that can be used interchangeably with Listing 2.1 or Listing 2.2. You should be able to test this listing out by passing it an `idArtist=1` parameter in the URL (as shown back in Figure 2.1).

LISTING 2.3   artistVarSource.jsp—Supplying Name/Value Pairs from JSP

```
<%@ page
  import="java.sql.*,java.net.URLEncoder"
  contentType="text/plain"
%>

<%
  // This is the SQL query statement we will use to fetch data
  String sql = "SELECT * FROM Artists "
    + "WHERE idArtist = " + request.getParameter("idArtist");

  // Execute the SQL query against the example database
  Class.forName("sun.jdbc.odbc.JdbcOdbcDriver");
  Connection con = DriverManager.getConnection("jdbc:odbc:VenueDB");
  ResultSet rs  = con.createStatement().executeQuery(sql);

  // Get the index positions of the columns we want to output
  int colArtistName = rs.findColumn("sArtistName");
  int colImageName = rs.findColumn("sImageName");
  int colDescription = rs.findColumn("sDescription");

  // Clear any whitespace, to ensure our output is on first line
  out.clear();

  // Send the name/value pairs to the output stream
  while ( rs.next() ) {
    out.print("artistName=");
    out.print(URLEncoder.encode(rs.getString(colArtistName)));
    out.print("&imageName=");
```

```
    out.print(URLEncoder.encode(rs.getString(colImageName)));
    out.print("&description=");
    out.print(URLEncoder.encode(rs.getString(colDescription)));
  }
%>
```

Building the Flash Interface

Now that you have the pages that supply the plain text data in place, you can move on to creating a simple Flash interface that displays the information. This part of the chapter will show how easy it is to fetch information from a web server and display that information to your users. You'll also learn how to have the Flash Player display images on-the-fly. Along the way, you will learn a few things about ActionScript.

Adding the Visual Elements

The first thing to do is to create a new Flash document, as follows:

1. In Flash, choose File > New from the main menu. The New Document dialog box appears (see Figure 2.2).

2. Make sure Flash Document is selected under Type, and then click OK. (You'll learn about using some of the other document types later in this book.)

3. Choose File > Save to save the document, using artistWidget.fla for the file name.

NOTE

Again, I'm assuming that you are saving your work for this chapter in the venue/chapter02 folder within your web server's document root. Normally, you wouldn't keep your Flash document (.fla) files in a folder that's accessible by your web server (because they are your "source code"), but it makes sense to do so now while learning.

---

4. Choose Preview Mode > Outlines from the View menu. This makes it easier to work with the elements you'll be adding to the interface. As a developer, you'll often want to use this Preview mode because you'll often be working with elements that don't show any interesting content at design time (as opposed to runtime, when they are filled with information from your server).

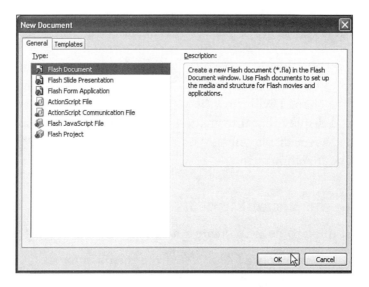

FIGURE 2.2   Creating a new Flash document.

Now add the visual elements to the new document by following these steps:

1. In the Components panel, locate the Loader item in the tree of components (see Figure 2.3). If you don't see the Components panel, choose Window > Development Panels > Components to make it visible.

2. Use your mouse to drag a Loader component from the tree to the top-left corner of the Stage (the white area of your new movie). This Loader component will be used to display a photo of each artist.

3. With the Loader selected, take a look at the Properties panel. (If you don't see the Properties panel, choose Window > Properties to make it visible—or press Ctrl+F2.) Just for fun, click the Parameters tab at the top right corner of the Properties panel. You will see several parameters related to the display of visual content (`autoLoad`, `contentPath`, and `scaleContent`). Just take a look—you don't have to change any of the parameters now (though you will be changing the `contentPath` parameter through script later).

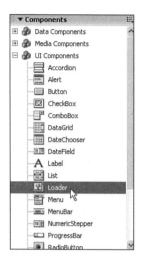

FIGURE 2.3   The Components panel.

4. Still in the Properties panel, type `ldrPhoto` in the Instance Name field (see Figure 2.4). You can use this name to refer to this Loader object in ActionScript code. Instance names are case-sensitive, so be careful about lowercase and uppercase letters.

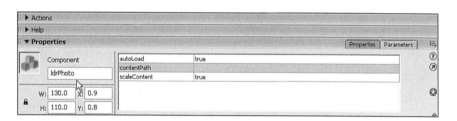

FIGURE 2.4   Adjusting the properties of the Loader component.

5. In the Tools panel, select the Text tool, and then click once on the Stage, just to the right of the Loader you just created (see Figure 2.5) to create a new text field. This text field will be used to display the name of each artist.

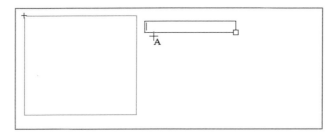

FIGURE 2.5   Adding a text field to the document.

6. With your new text field selected, use the Properties panel to set the Text type to Dynamic Text (as opposed to Static Text), if necessary, and then set the Instance Name to `txtArtistName`.

7. Repeat Steps 5 and 6 to create another text field with an Instance Name of `txtDescription`. Also using the Properties panel, set the Line type to Multiline (as opposed to Single Line). Finally, double-click the field and drag the square at the bottom corner to resize the field so that it holds multiple lines of text. If you haven't done so, double-click the txtArtistName text box and drag its width to match that of the txtDescription text box.

8. Now that you have all the elements on the Stage, try to make them look reasonably nice by arranging them with your mouse. You can resize the Loader by right-clicking on it, choosing Free Transform, and then dragging its bottom-right corner. You can also resize it by typing a new width and height into the Properties panel.

9. If you wish, use the Properties panel to choose a large font size for the first text field (the artist name), and a small font size for the second field (the description). I used a font size of 12 for the former and 9 for the latter. I also selected the bold option for the artist name to make it stand out a bit more. When you are finished, your interface should look something like mine (see Figure 2.6), but don't obsess too much about the looks. We're just trying to make something that works for now.

10. Use File > Save to save your work.

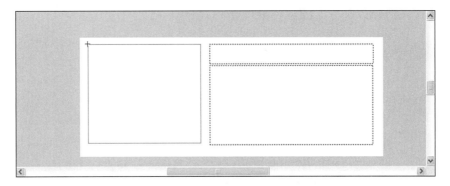

FIGURE 2.6   Empty elements for displaying text and an image.

Using ActionScript to Fetch and Display Data

So far, you have a simple user interface with three empty elements: a Loader component where a photo will appear, and two text fields where the artist's name and a description appear. Now you can add the ActionScript code that gets the appropriate information into these empty elements.

NOTE

The current version of Flash provides a number of different ways to accomplish this same type of operation, some requiring more lines of code, others requiring hardly any. I've chosen a sort of classic technique for this chapter because it is simple and adaptable to many different types of situations. You will learn more about other ways to fetch and display information throughout this book.

Turning Your Display Elements into a Movie Clip Object

The first thing you're going to do is to turn the three elements into a movie clip. Making the elements into a movie clip serves two purposes: first, you can then treat the movie clip as a visual "object" that can be moved around as a single item on the Stage; second, the movie clip serves as a programming "object" that contains code specific to the elements it contains. In short, the clip becomes an container for the visual elements and related code, enabling you to think of the elements and code together in an object-oriented fashion.

To create the movie clip, follow these steps:

1. With the document from the last section still open, select the three empty elements: the Loader component and the two text fields. (You can do this by clicking the elements while holding the Shift key, or by choosing Edit > Select All.)

2. With the three elements still selected, choose Modify > Convert to Symbol. The Convert to Symbol dialog box appears.

3. In the Name field, type `ArtistDisplayClip` (see Figure 2.7).

4. Make sure the Behavior option is set to Movie Clip, and then click OK.

FIGURE 2.7   Converting content into a movie clip symbol.

At first, it looks like nothing has changed. However, if you experiment a bit, you will find the three empty elements are now accessible as a group, as follows:

First, if you *single-click* one of the three empty elements, you will actually be selecting the new movie clip on the stage. The clip can be moved around, resized, or cut-and-pasted as a single object.

If you *double-click* one of the three empty elements, you will be "brought into" a special mode in which you can edit the movie clip. In this mode, you can move or resize the individual elements, or add code to the movie clip. We'll call this mode *Symbol Edit mode.*

After you are in Symbol Edit mode, you can double-click any other area of the Stage (the blank white area) to get yourself out of Symbol Edit mode.

NOTE

Other ways exist to navigate between the editing modes. You can select the movie clip, and then choose Edit > Edit Selected to enter Symbol Edit mode, and Edit > Edit Document to return to the Normal mode. Or you can use the Edit Symbol button at the right side of the Edit bar (which appears above the timeline, and can be toggled with Window > Toolbars > Edit bar) to navigate between the various movie clips in your document; you can use the Scene 1 button on the same bar to return to the main document.

Go ahead and experiment a bit with switching back and forth between editing the movie clip symbol and editing the main part of the new document. Don't be afraid to move things around. You can always undo your changes with Edit > Undo, or by loading the finished version of the document from this chapter's example files.

> **NOTE**
>
> You can also open the Library panel with Window > Library and then double-click your new movie clip's icon in the Library to edit it. Using the Library panel is handy if your Flash documents get complicated with lots of different movie clips and other elements involved.

Adding the ActionScript Code

Okay, now that you've created a movie clip, it's time to add the ActionScript code that makes it behave as expected. Please follow these steps:

1. If you're not in it already, double-click the movie clip to get into Symbol Edit mode.

2. Click the first frame in the timeline, as shown near the top of Figure 2.8.

3. Take a look at the Actions panel (if you don't see the Actions panel, use Window > Development Panels > Actions to show it). The tab at the bottom of the Actions panel should be labeled Layer 1 : 1, and the status bar at the bottom of the panel should read Line 1 of 1, Col 1. If not, click once on the Stage. (If still not, then you're in the wrong place—choose Edit > Edit Document to zoom back out to the main document and try again.)

4. Type the code shown in Listing 2.4 into the Actions panel (visible in Figure 2.8). This code creates two functions, `loadArtist()` and `onArtistVarsLoaded()`, which we discuss in the next section.

5. Use File > Save to save your work.

> **NOTE**
>
> If you don't want to type this code in yourself, you can copy and paste it from the ArtistDisplayCode1.txt file included with this chapter's examples. This text file is provided only for that purpose. It doesn't need to be present in your site directory for the example to work.

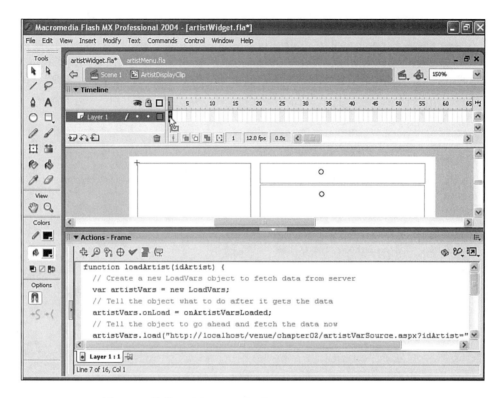

FIGURE 2.8   Adding ActionScript code to a movie clip.

LISTING 2.4   Code in Frame 1 of the `ArtistDisplayClip` Movie Clip

```
function loadArtist(idArtist) {
  // Create a new LoadVars object to fetch data from server
  var artistVars = new LoadVars;
  // Tell the object what to do after it gets the data
  artistVars.onLoad = onArtistVarsLoaded;
  // Tell the object to go ahead and fetch the data now
  artistVars.load("http://localhost/venue/chapter02/
  ➥artistVarSource.aspx?idArtist=" + idArtist);
}

function onArtistVarsLoaded() {
  // Populate text fields with values retrieved from server
  txtArtistName.text = this.artistName;
  txtDescription.text = this.description;
  // Load appropriate artist photo into Loader object
  ldrPhoto.contentPath = "../images/artists/" + this.imageName;
}
```

Of course, if you are using ASP.NET or Java, you should change the ".cfm" in this listing to ".aspx" or ".jsp," respectively.

NOTE

Okay, quick sanity check time. If you're at all familiar with JavaScript syntax—or even C or Java syntax—the code in Listing 2.4 shouldn't be too scary. If, on the other hand, the basic form of the code (the concept of a function, the use of parentheses, curly braces, semicolons, and so on) looks like a completely foreign language that makes absolutely no sense to you, you might want to skip ahead to Chapter 4 or check out a JavaScript tutorial online.

A Quick Introduction to the LoadVars *Object*

The code you just added to the document uses the `LoadVars` object, which is a special utility object exposed at runtime by the Flash player. As the name implies, the `LoadVars` object provides a means for retrieving variables (that is, name/value pairs) from a web server. Basically, this just means that the object knows how to connect to a URL through HTTP, parse the retrieved text into name/value pairs, and make the pairs available as variables, which you can use in whatever way you see fit.

You're going to learn far more about all this stuff in Chapter 6, "Connecting to Servers with Plain Text". For now, it's enough to know that most uses of the `LoadVars` object involve four basic steps:

1. Creating an instance of the `LoadVars` object, using the `new` keyword.

2. Setting the new instance's `onLoad` property to the name of a function (that you write yourself) that should be called when the variables are successfully retrieved from the URL. For lack of a better term, let's call it a *responder function*.

3. Calling the instance's `load()` method, which is what tells the Flash player to actually contact your web server.

4. Using the retrieved values by referring to them by name within the responder function.

In the code you just added (Listing 2.4), the first three steps occur in the function called `loadArtist()`. The fourth step occurs within the responder function, which, in this case, is called `onArtistVarsLoaded()`.

By the way, it's important to understand that the actual retrieving of variables by the `LoadVars` object's `load()` method is *asynchronous*. What this means is that the Flash player does not wait for the name/value pairs to be retrieved from the URL. Therefore, your code cannot safely refer to the retrieved variables until the responder function is called. Of course, this is for a good reason: it enables your movie to work on other things (perhaps displaying an animation) while information is being downloaded. It also enables your movie to fetch variables from more than one URL at the same time (if you wish).

Providing a Way for the User to Select an Artist

Okay—you've created the visual elements, put them in a movie clip, and added the script needed to fetch and display information from your server. It sure seems like the information should be displayed when the `loadArtist()` function is called (see Listing 2.4).

Unfortunately, that function isn't called by anything yet, so nothing's ever going to happen. We'll do something more sophisticated in a bit; for now, let's just make a simple spin control that enables the user to choose which artist to display. Whenever the user changes the value in the spin control, information about the corresponding artist will be shown.

To add the spin control, perform the following steps:

1. If you're not in it already, enter Symbol Edit mode for your movie clip by double-clicking one of the empty visual elements.

2. Drag a NumericStepper component from the Components panel onto the Stage ("NumericStepper" is Flash's name for a spin control). Because you're in Symbol Edit mode, you're adding the component to the movie clip, rather than the main part of the document.

3. Use View > Preview Mode > Full to turn off the Outline Preview mode you turned on earlier. Note that you can now see the little up and down arrows in the new NumericStepper component, but it's a little harder to keep track of where the Loader is. Use whichever Preview mode you prefer from here on out.

4. Make sure the new NumericStepper is selected, and then use the Properties panel to set the `minimum` property to 1, the `maximum` property to 5, and the `value` property to 1. In other words, we want the user to be able to choose a number from 1 through 5, and we want the initial value to be 1.

5. With the NumericStepper still selected, type the following code into the Actions Panel (see Figure 2.9):

```
on(change) {
  _parent.loadArtist(this.value);
}
```

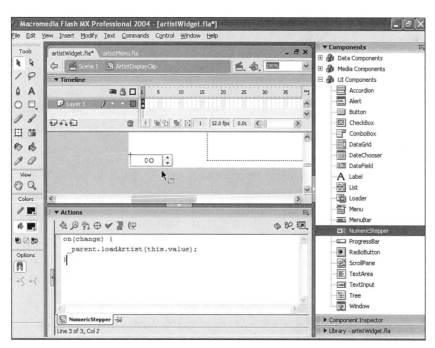

FIGURE 2.9   Adding code that fires when the spin control is edited.

In plain English, this code basically means "when the user changes the value of the spin control, call the `loadArtist()` function, passing the user's chosen value as the function's `idArtist` argument." You can learn more about the `on(change)` syntax shown here in Chapter 4. For now it's enough to understand what's probably already obvious: any code between the curly braces is executed whenever the spin control's value is changed.

Within the `on(change)` block, we call the `loadArtist()` function that was created in Listing 2.4. The current value of the spin control is available from the `this.value` property, which means that if the user has just changed the control's value to say, 2, then 2 is passed as the desired artist ID to the `loadArtist()` function.

Also, note the use of the `_parent` keyword in this `on(change)` block. Within an event handling block for a component, any references to functions or variables are assumed to be methods or properties of the component itself, rather than items in the document you are creating. To refer to items within the document, you need to use `_parent` (which, roughly translated, means "the parent movie clip or document that is containing this component"). The next chapter discusses these concepts in more depth.

Cool. Everything should be set up now. Let's test it out!

Publishing and Testing the Interface

Now all we have to do is *publish* the movie that contains your new interface. Publishing basically turns your Flash document (the .fla file you've been working on) into a much smaller, streamlined file that the Flash player can understand. This new file will have a .swf extension. These files are generally called SWFs (pronounced "swiffs").

To publish your movie, simply choose File > Publish or press Shift+F12. A progress meter appears momentarily while the Flash IDE compiles and streamlines the movie's content. That's it!

Now you can test your interface out by viewing it on a web page. For your convenience, Flash created a simple HTML page for testing purposes when you published the movie. You should be able to visit this page right now using the following URL:

```
http://localhost/venue/chapter02/artistWidget.html
```

> **NOTE**
>
> Of course, if your web server (the one with ColdFusion, ASP.NET, or a JSP engine installed) is not on your local workstation, you'll need to replace the `localhost` part of this URL with whatever server name is appropriate. You will also need to change the URL reference shown in Listing 2.4.

When you visit this URL in a web browser, it looks like a mostly empty page except for the presence of the spin control (see Figure 2.10). That should change, however, if you adjust the value of the spin control. If you change the value to 2, you should see a name, description, and photo for the artist with ID number 2; if you change the value to 3, you should see artist number 3, and so on.

FIGURE 2.10   Testing the retrieval of data from your server.

Clearly, this is an imperfect use of the spin control as a navigation element. For one thing, the range of possible values has been hard-coded into the movie. If the number of available artists changes, the movie has to be republished. Also, this use of the spin control assumes that the artists' ID numbers are consecutively numbered, starting with one, and that the user would be interested in viewing the artists in ID-number order. If an artist was deleted, or if the user wanted to view the artists in a more intuitive order (say, alphabetically), this facile technique would cease to work properly.

That said, I want you to perform one other experiment with the spin control before we replace it with more sensible navigation.

Accessing a Movie Clip from the Main Timeline

Right now, the spin control the user can use for navigation is part of the `ArtistDisplayClip` movie clip. However, if you think about the movie clip as a sort of object—meant to encapsulate the idea of displaying information about a single artist—then the spin control seems a little out of place because it's about moving between records rather than displaying the current record. Conceptually, it would be a bit more consistent to have the spin control sit outside the movie clip.

This is by no means a grave problem at this point because we've already established that the spin control has to go pretty soon anyway. But just to see what's involved, let's move the control out of the movie clip and have it sit within the main document—also called the *main timeline*—instead. This won't change the movie visually; the interface will look exactly the same when it is published. The only difference will be a subtle change in how the objects and code in the movie are organized.

To make this change, perform the following steps:

1. If you're not in it already, enter Symbol Edit mode for the movie clip by double-clicking one of the visual elements.

2. Select the spin control by single-clicking it. Make sure it's the only thing selected. You may need to click once on a blank area of the Stage first, and then click the spin control.

3. Cut the control to the Clipboard by using Edit > Cut from Flash's main menu, or by right-clicking the control and choosing Cut from the context menu. You can also use the customary Ctrl+X keyboard shortcut.

4. Exit Symbol Edit mode by double-clicking an empty area of the Stage.

5. Paste the spin control back in by choosing Edit > Paste in Place.

Okay, the spin control is now sitting in the main timeline, rather than sitting within the main movie clip. Everything looks pretty much the same, but if you were to publish and test the movie right now, you would find that it doesn't work properly.

Why? Well, if you recall, the code that executes when the spin control is edited looks like this:

```
_parent.loadArtist(this.value);
```

This line used to work back when the spin control and the `loadArtist()` function were sitting in the same conceptual place: the movie clip (represented here by the `_parent` keyword). Now that the spin control and the function it wants to call are in different places, you need to change the code slightly to "target" the function within the clip.

To make this change, just do the following:

1. Make sure you are *not* in Symbol Edit mode, and then select the movie clip on the Stage by single-clicking the photo loader or one of the text fields. Don't double-click; that brings you to Symbol Edit mode.
2. Using the Properties panel, set the Instance Name to `mcArtistDisplay`. This gives the clip a name that can be referred to in ActionScript.
3. Select the spin control, and then add the `mcArtistDisplay` name between `_parent` and the `loadArtist()` function, using dot notation. The code should now look like this:

```
on(change) {
  _parent.mcArtistDisplay.loadArtist(this.value);
}
```

4. Now republish the movie (using File > Publish or Shift+F12) and test it again. It should now work just as it did before.

So, what have you learned by moving the spin control from one place to another? Well, you've learned that functions defined in a movie clip are considered to be part of that clip object. Each movie clip has its own *scope* for things such as variables, functions, and visual objects. Within a clip, you can refer to one of its functions using just the function name. However, if you want to refer the same function from the main document (or, for that matter, another movie clip), you must use the clip's instance name in addition to the function name.

Okay, that's enough talk of scopes and targeting for now. You'll learn lots more about this stuff in later chapters. Now let's see what's involved in building a better navigation system for users to view movies.

Before you continue, go ahead and remove all traces of the NumericStepper by deleting the symbol from your document's Library. Just follow these steps:

1. Display the Library panel (Window > Library).
2. Right-click the `NumericStepper` symbol, and then choose Delete from the context menu.
3. Note that all instances of the symbol (in this case, there was only one) have been removed from the document, regardless of where the individual instances may have appeared.

It generally makes sense to remove symbols from the Library that aren't being used anymore. You'll learn more about the Library in Chapter 3, "Digging a Bit Deeper," and Chapter 5, "Movie Clips as Objects."

Creating Navigation with Buttons and XML

So far, we have created a simple interface for displaying information about a single artist. It gets its information from the server in the form of simple text variables. Now we'll create another Flash interface that provides a rollover button for each artist. As the user rolls his or her mouse over each button, information about that artist is shown, courtesy of the example you just built. And rather than getting the information from the server in the form of simple text variables, Flash will retrieve the information in the form of XML.

By the time we're done, you will have learned a bit about creating buttons, attaching ActionScript code to specific events (such as a mouse rollover), loading movies within other movies, and a few other Flash concepts such as the use of layers. Heck, we'll even throw in a simple animation effect, just so you can see how all that works.

Supplying Information to Flash as XML

Once again, we'll start this second example on the server side, taking a look at the ColdFusion, ASP.NET, and Java code that's needed to generate the XML that this second Flash example consumes. Just for consistency's sake, I'm going to start with the ColdFusion version of the code. You are free to jump ahead to the ASP.NET or Java version as you wish. All three of these examples are going to be pretty simple.

First, let's take a quick look at the XML that each of the three server-side scripts are going to produce. Listing 2.5 shows the XML code that will be generated by any of the subsequent three listings, assuming that the Artists table still has the original five records in it.

LISTING 2.5   artistsXmlSample.xml—Sample XML Encoding of Artist Information

```
<?xml version="1.0" encoding="UTF-8"?>
<artists>
    <artist id="1">
     <name>Girlband</name>
    </artist>
    <artist id="5">
     <name>Nervous Men</name>
    </artist>
    <artist id="3">
     <name>Room by River</name>
    </artist>
    <artist id="4">
     <name>Swim</name>
    </artist>
    <artist id="2">
     <name>The New Oldies</name>
    </artist>
</artists>
```

Supplying XML from ColdFusion

Listing 2.6 is the simple ColdFusion code that will be supplying the XML for use by our simple Flash-based navigation interface.

LISTING 2.6   artistsXmlSource.cfm—Generating XML About Artists with ColdFusion

```
<!--- Retrieve information about artists from database --->
<cfquery name="ArtistQuery" datasource="VenueDB">
 SELECT idArtist, sArtistName
 FROM Artists
 ORDER BY sArtistName
</cfquery>

<!--- Compose XML document --->
<cfxml variable="ArtistXML">
 <artists>
  <cfoutput query="ArtistQuery">
   <artist id="#idArtist#">
```

continues

LISTING 2.6   artistsXmlSource.cfm—Generating XML About Artists with ColdFusion (Continued)

```
    <name>#XmlFormat(sArtistName)#</name>
  </artist>
 </cfoutput>
 </artists>
</cfxml>

<!--- Omit debug info, and anything not in <cfoutput> blocks --->
<cfsetting showdebugoutput="No" enablecfoutputonly="Yes">

<!--- Set the MIME content-type of our response to "text/xml" --->
<cfcontent type="text/xml" reset="yes">

<!--- Output the XML code --->
<cfoutput>#ToString(ArtistXml)#</cfoutput>
```

As you can see, there really isn't much to this listing. It's quite similar in structure to the first ColdFusion example (Listing 2.1). The most important difference, of course, is the inclusion of the `<cfxml>` tag, which is a quick and easy way to create properly formatted XML documents.

I think you'll find this listing to be mostly self-explanatory. As in Listing 2.1, the `<cfsetting>` and `<cfcontent>` tags could be omitted in most cases, but it can't hurt to include them.

> **NOTE**
>
> Instead of using the `<cfxml>` tag, you could use the `XmlNew()` function and build the XML document more programmatically. When you choose to use `<cfxml>`, make sure to use the `XmlFormat()` function because you are including character data that might contain angle brackets, quotation marks, or other characters considered special to XML.

Supplying XML from ASP.NET

As you probably know, there are many ways to generate an XML document on the fly using the various resources available in a typical .NET installation. Listing 2.7 uses the `XmlTextWriter` object and methods available in the .NET Framework's `System.Xml` namespace. You could alternatively use the MSXML parser through COM (especially if you wanted to maintain compatibility with ASP versions prior to .NET), or use a third-party or custom object of some kind.

LISTING 2.7　artistsXmlSource.aspx—Generating XML About Artists with ASP.NET

```
<%@ Page Language="vb" Debug="false" %>
<%@ Import Namespace = "System.Data.ODBC" %>
<%@ Import Namespace = "System.Xml" %>

<script runat="server">
 Sub Page_Load
   ' Define database connection
   Dim ConnStr as String = "DSN=VenueDB"
   Dim conn as OdbcConnection = new OdbcConnection(ConnStr)

   ' Set the MIME content-type of our response to "text/plain"
   Response.ContentType = "text/xml"

   ' Set up query
   Dim CmdStr as String = "SELECT idArtist, sArtistName " _
     + " FROM Artists ORDER BY sArtistName"
   Dim cmd as OdbcCommand = new OdbcCommand(CmdStr, conn)

   ' Establish connection and perform query
   conn.Open()
   Dim reader As OdbcDataReader = cmd.ExecuteReader()

   ' Begin XML document
   Dim w As XmlTextWriter = New XmlTextWriter(Response.OutputStream,
 ➥Nothing)
   w.Formatting = Formatting.Indented
   w.WriteStartDocument()

   ' Add document root element
   w.WriteStartElement("artists")

   ' For each record returned by query...
   While reader.Read()
    w.WriteStartElement("artist")
    w.WriteAttributeString("id", reader.Item("idArtist"))
     w.WriteStartElement("name")
      w.WriteString(reader.Item("sArtistName"))
     w.WriteEndElement()
    w.WriteEndElement()
   End While

   ' Close document root
   w.WriteEndElement()
   w.Close()
 End Sub
</script>
```

I believe this listing is largely self-explanatory. The first half of the listing fetches information from the database; the second half creates the XML document using the `WriteStartDocument()`, `WriteStartElement()`, and related methods. The code in the `While` block does most of the work of producing the actual XML, which is easy to see if you compare the tag and attribute names in the `While` block with the resulting XML (which you saw back in 2.5). See your .NET documentation for details.

Supplying XML from Java

Finally, Listing 2.8 shows the Java version of the XML-producing page. Of course, this is just one of many possible ways that this code could be structured. There are many different ways to connect to a database and many different ways to produce XML on-the-fly. I chose to write the listing this way mainly so that it would be simple and self-explanatory.

LISTING 2.8   artistsXmlSource.jsp—Generating XML About Artists with Java Server Pages

```
<%@ page
   import="org.w3c.dom.*,javax.xml.parsers.*,javax.xml.transform.*,
   javax.xml.transform.dom.*,javax.xml.transform.stream.*,java.sql.*"
   contentType="text/xml"
%>

<%
   // This is the SQL query statement we will use to fetch data
   String sql = "SELECT idArtist, sArtistName " +
    "FROM Artists ORDER BY sArtistName";

   // Execute the SQL query against the example database
   Class.forName("sun.jdbc.odbc.JdbcOdbcDriver");
   Connection con = DriverManager.getConnection("jdbc:odbc:VenueDB");
   ResultSet rs  = con.createStatement().executeQuery(sql);

   // Get the index positions of the columns we want to output
   int colID = rs.findColumn("idArtist");
   int colName = rs.findColumn("sArtistName");

   // Clear any whitespace, to ensure our output is on first line
   out.clear();

   // Create a new XML document
   DocumentBuilderFactory df = DocumentBuilderFactory.newInstance();
   DocumentBuilder builder = df.newDocumentBuilder();
   Document doc = builder.newDocument();
```

```
// Compose XML document
Element elArtist, elName, elRoot;
elRoot = doc.createElement("artists");
doc.appendChild(elRoot);

// For each record returned by the database
while ( rs.next() ) {
  // Create and attach <artist> element node
  elArtist = doc.createElement("artist");
  elArtist.setAttribute("id", rs.getString(colID));
  elRoot.appendChild(elArtist);

  // Create and attach <name> element node
  elName = doc.createElement("name");
  elName.appendChild(doc.createTextNode(rs.getString(colName)));
  elArtist.appendChild(elName);
}

// Send XML document to output stream
TransformerFactory tf = TransformerFactory.newInstance();
Transformer trans = tf.newTransformer();
trans.transform(new DOMSource(doc), new StreamResult(out));
%>
```

In actual practice, you would most likely write the code a bit differently, using more classes or beans, taking advantage of the higher-level database connectivity support in the newer `javax.sql` package, and so on. You might also choose to write the code as a servlet rather than a JSP page. Any Java-based construct that can expose XML through an http:// URL will do.

A Quick Introduction to Flash's XML Object

In the first example in this chapter (Listing 2.4), we used the `LoadVars` object in ActionScript code to retrieve simple name/value pairs from a web server. Flash also provides a similar object called XML, which can be used to retrieve XML data from a web server. Typical coding steps for using the XML object for this purpose are similar to the steps used for `LoadVars`. First the `onLoad` event handler is attached to a custom function that processes or displays the information after it is received; then the `load()` method is used to start the actual fetching process.

> **NOTE**
>
> The XML object is capable of a lot more than what we're going to use it for in this step sequence. You'll learn more about it in Chapter 7, "Connecting to Servers with XML."

The first thing we'll do is to create a new Flash document for this example. Then we will add some simple ActionScript code to handle the XML retrieval. Just follow these steps:

1. Create a new Flash document using File > New.
2. Click Frame 1 in the timeline, and then type the ActionScript code shown in Listing 2.9 into the Actions panel.
3. Save your work.

> **NOTE**
>
> Of course, the file extension in the URL provided to the `load()` method in this listing depends on whether you are using ColdFusion, ASP.NET, or Java. Just change the last few characters of the URL as appropriate.

LISTING 2.9   Code in Frame 1 of artistMenu.fla

```
// Kick off the XML process
loadArtists();

function loadArtists() {
 var artistsXml = new XML;
 artistsXml.ignoreWhite = true;
 artistsXml.onLoad = onArtistsXmlLoaded;
 artistsXml.load("http://localhost/venue/chapter02/
 ➥artistsXmlSource.aspx");
}

function onArtistsXmlLoaded() {
 // Grab array of child nodes of the root node
 // (we expect children to be <artist> elements)
 var arArtistNodes = this.firstChild.childNodes;

 // For each child node...
 for (var i = 0; i < arArtistNodes.length; i++) {
  // Grab artist ID number and name from current child node
  var currentID = arArtistNodes[i].attributes.id;
  var currentName = arArtistNodes[i].firstChild.firstChild;
```

```
// Show the ID number and name in trace statements,
// just to prove that we retrieved the information
trace("Artist " + currentID + ": " + currentName); }
}
```

This code creates two functions: `loadArtists()` and `onArtistsXmlLoaded()`. They are similar to the `loadArtist()` and `onArtistVarsLoaded()` functions, respectively, from Listing 2.4. In fact, the first function is nearly identical to its predecessor. The only real differences are the names of the variables and the line about setting the XML object's `ignoreWhite` property to `true`. You will learn more about the `ignoreWhite` property and other XML object functionality in Chapter 7. For now, it's enough to know that you will generally want to set `ignoreWhite` to `true` when working with XML that represents a data structure (as opposed to XML that represents a document, such as XHTML).

As you can see, the `onArtistVarsLoaded()` function is also pretty simple. It uses a number of methods and properties that you don't know about yet. Again, you'll learn this all in more depth later, but I've provided a quick explanation of the most important points in Table 2.1.

TABLE 2.1 A Quick Explanation of Key Elements in Listing 2.9

ELEMENT	DESCRIPTION
`this`	Within the body of this function, `this` keyword always refers to the XML object that just finished retrieving data from your server. You can use this to refer to any of the XML object's methods and properties.
`this.firstChild.childNodes`	After XML has been retrieved, the `firstChild` property refers to the root node of the XML document. In this case, it is the `<artists>` element shown in Listing 2.5. The `childNodes` property of the root node, as the name implies, returns all of the root node's immediate children (in this case, the `<artist>` tags for each artist). The child nodes are returned as an array, which can be looped over using a `for` loop.

continues

TABLE 2.1   A Quick Explanation of Key Elements in Listing 2.9 (Continued)

ELEMENT	DESCRIPTION
`arArtistNodes[i]`	Within the `for` loop, the "current" artist node can be accessed as the current position in the array that was returned by the `childNodes` property.
`arArtistNodes[i].attributes.id`	Each XML element node has an `attributes` property that can be used to access that element's attributes by name.
`arArtistNodes[i].firstChild.firstChild`	The `firstChild` property of the `<artist>` element contains the `<name>` element for that artist. The `firstChild` element contains the actual string (in XML terms, the text node) between the `<name>` tags.
`trace`	The `trace` statement isn't specific to the XML object, but it's a useful tool when testing or debugging code that accesses XML information. Whatever expression you supply to the `trace` statement is displayed in a special window within the Flash IDE, as explained in the "Viewing Output Generated by Trace Statements" section, next.

So, in broad strokes, the `onArtistVarsLoaded()` function gets a list of `<artist>` elements within the XML document and places them in an array called `arArtistNodes`. Then a `for` loop is used to loop over the contents of the array, placing the values of the `id` attribute and the `<name>` element into the `currentID` and `currentName` variables, respectively. Right now, the only thing that's done with these values is to display them in the Flash IDE using the `trace` statement. We'll do something more useful with the values as we move forward with this example.

Viewing Output Generated by *trace* Statements

Right now, you should be able to prove to yourself that the XML document is able to be retrieved and parsed by the ActionScript code you just created. Simply choose Control > Test Movie from Flash's main menu. This puts your Flash document into a special "testing," or "preview," mode. The preview should include an Output window that contains the results of the trace statement from Listing 2.1. The output proves that the ActionScript code you added in the last section is looping over the <artist> elements in the XML document returned by your server, and successfully pulling out the ID number and name of each artist (see Figure 2.11).

FIGURE 2.11   The text generated by trace statements becomes visible in the Output window.

Flash's Test Movie mode is used by designers to preview visual things like animations, and by developers for debugging purposes (of course, lots of people wear both hats to some degree). As it stands right now, nothing visual has been added to this new movie, so the only thing you're going to see is the output generated by the trace statement in Listing 2.9. I think you get my point here. Trace statements are a quick and easy way to verify that the expected information has been successfully retrieved from your server.

While in Test Movie mode, you might want to explore some of the menu items and other special functionality available to you while testing, in particular:

- You can choose View > Download Settings > DSL (or any of the other speeds listed) and then View > Simulate Download to see how long it will take a SWF to appear over a typical DSL connection.
- The Debug > List Objects and Debug > List Variables options provide a quick way to "dump" the current contents of a SWF to the Output window for debugging and testing purposes.
- Within the Output window, the Panel menu at the top-right corner (where the mouse cursor is in Figure 2.11) provides options for turning word wrapping on and off, finding a word in the generated output, and saving or printing the current contents of the Output window.

When you're done testing, you can return to your work document (the .fla file) by doing any of the following while in Test Movie mode:

- Choose File > Close.
- Click the customary X-shaped Close icon at the top-right corner of the movie preview.
- Use the Ctrl+W keyboard shortcut.
- Click the tab for the .fla file above the movie preview. The tabs allow you to switch back and forth between your FLA and the preview SWF.

Loading an External SWF at Runtime

Okay, so far we know we're retrieving artist information from the XML supplied by your server. Now we want to get the artist-display widget SWF to display within the new document, so that it can display information about the bands listed in the XML. The first thing to do is to create an empty movie clip that will be used to load the artist-display SWF into our new movie. You have already created movie clips earlier in this chapter by converting something visual into a new movie clip. Now you'll be creating a clip that doesn't contain anything at all until runtime.

To create this empty movie clip, do the following:

1. If it's not showing already, make the Library panel visible by choosing Window > Library.
2. Click the Panel menu (the icon at the top-right corner of the panel, to the right of the word Library), and then choose New Symbol (see Figure 2.12).
3. Type `ArtistWidgetLoaderClip` for the name, make sure Movie Clip is selected for the Behavior, and then click OK. There should now be an entry in the Library panel for the `ArtistWidgetLoaderClip` movie clip symbol that you just selected, and you will be in Symbol Edit mode for the new clip.
4. Choose Edit > Document to exit Symbol Edit mode, which will return you to the main document.
5. Create a new instance of the new clip by dragging the entry from the Library onto the Stage, positioning it somewhere near Stage center. You'll note that the new clip is represented onscreen by a small white circle.

FIGURE 2.12   Creating a new, empty symbol in the Library.

6. With the new clip selected on the Stage (single-click the clip to select it if it's not already), use the Properties panel to set its instance name to `mcArtistWidgetLoader`.

7. Click once on the Stage and look at the Actions panel. You should see the code that you added previously (from Listing 2.9). If you don't, click once on an empty area of the Stage, or on Frame 1 in the timeline. Add the following lines just above the existing code (see Figure 2.13):

```
// Execute onThisMovieLoaded() when this SWF loads in Flash Player
this.onLoad = onThisMovieLoaded;

function onThisMovieLoaded() {
 // Load the movie artistWidget movie into this movie,
 // using the mcArtistWidgetLoader clip as a "container"
 mcArtistWidgetLoader.loadMovie("artistWidget.swf");

 // Kick off the XML process
 loadArtists();
}
```

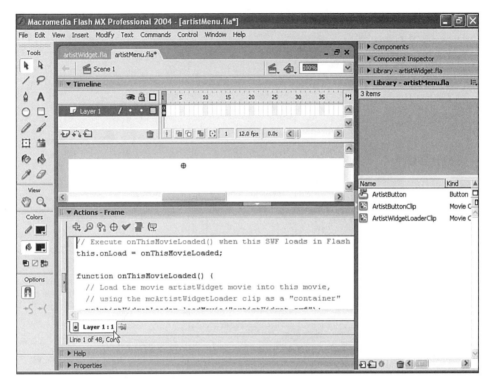

FIGURE 2.13   Attaching code to the SWF's `onLoad` handler.

This code shows you how to do two things. First, it shows you how to create a chunk of code that executes only once, when a movie first loads in the Flash Player. Simply create a function that contains whatever initialization code you want to execute when your SWF first loads. Then assign the new function to the main movie's `onLoad` event. After the Flash Player loads your movie, it will fire the `onLoad` event, which in turn will execute your initialization code.

> **NOTE**
>
> The name of your initialization function can be anything you want, but it's helpful to use a consistent name for this purpose throughout your Flash movies so that it's easy to keep track of what's going on. The `onThisMovieLoaded` function name used in this example is one suggestion; another sensible convention would be `thisMovie_Load` or `this_Load`.

Secondly, this new code shows you how the `loadMovie()` method of Flash's `MovieClip` object can be used to load an external SWF file into the currently-showing movie. In this case, the external movie appears in the currently showing movie at the spot defined by the position of the `mcArtistWidgetLoader` movie clip instance (in other words, where the small white circle is on the Stage).

Creating Simple Rollover Buttons

Now let's see what's involved in creating a rollover button for each artist in the XML data. This is going to require two basic steps:

1. Creating a single button, which then is placed into a movie clip that can be referred to by name in ActionScript.
2. Adding ActionScript code within our `onArtistsXmlLoaded()` function to create new copies (or instances) of the button for each artist at run-time.

So, the first thing to do is to create the button. Button creation is something that is well documented in the Flash documentation and any number of online tutorials and Flash books, so I'm going to keep this fairly brief. It's important for you to know how to create buttons, but I'm not going to get into creating really pretty, animated ones right now. We'll just create something simple that works.

Just follow these steps:

1. Make sure you are not in Symbol Edit mode by choosing Edit > Document if it is available. In addition, make sure you can see the Stage properly. This might mean minimizing the Actions panel or changing the zoom level by choosing View > Magnification > Fit in Window.
2. If it's not selected already, choose View > Preview Mode > Full. This mode is handier for drawing than the Outlines mode you were using when working with the empty data-display elements earlier.
3. Using the Tools panel, select the Rectangle tool. Also, make sure the Fill Color and Stroke Color (that is, the line color) are set to a combination of colors that you like. I chose a black stroke color and a bluish fill color.

4. Draw a rectangle on the Stage by clicking and dragging with your mouse (see Figure 2.14). You want the rectangle to be fairly wide and not very tall; according to the Properties panel, mine is about 175 pixels wide and about 18 pixels tall, but don't worry too much about the exact size. If you mess up, just delete what you've done and try again. (You can also stretch or resize the rectangle by selecting it, choosing Modify > Transform > Free Transform from the main menu, and then dragging the black stretch handles around.)

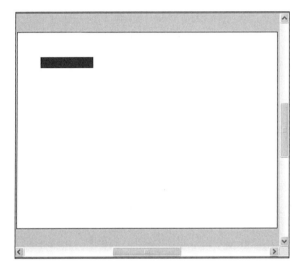

FIGURE 2.14   Drawing a new button shape on the Stage.

5. Make sure the rectangle you just drew is selected. You can do that by switching back to the Selection tool and double-clicking the rectangle, dragging the Selection tool with your mouse, or by choosing Edit > Select All from the main menu. Consult the Flash documentation for more details about selecting items on the Stage.

NOTE

The first time you click the interior of a rectangle, you select only its fill (the area within the lines). To select the lines and the fill—which is what you want to do 99 percent of the time—you need to double-click the interior of the rectangle.

6. With the rectangle still selected, choose Modify > Convert to Symbol or simply press F8. The Convert to Symbol dialog box appears. (You used this dialog box earlier to create a movie clip symbol. This time, you'll use it to create a button symbol.)

7. Type **ArtistButton** in the Name field, and then select Button for the Behavior option (see Figure 2.15). Click OK to create the new button.

FIGURE 2.15   Converting the shape to a button symbol.

8. Use the Text tool to add a new text field to the stage, and then position it right on top of the button you just created (see Figure 2.16). If you need to resize the text field, double-click it and drag the white handle at the bottom-right corner of the field.

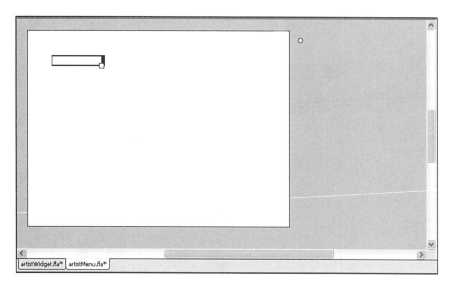

FIGURE 2.16   Placing a text field on top of the button.

9. Use the Properties panel to set the Text Type to Dynamic Text and to give it an Instance Name of txtArtistName. Also make sure that the Line Type is set to Single Line and that the Selectable option (located to the right of the line type) is turned off.

10. Double-click the text field and type the words **Artist Name** into the field. This is where the actual artist's name will appear at runtime. Use the Properties panel to change the Text Color and Font Size to something that makes the text visible over the background of the button.

11. Select both the button and text field, either by selecting the Selection tool and dragging your mouse around the whole area, or by choosing Edit > Select All. You're now going to turn both elements into a single movie clip.

12. Choose Modify > Convert to Symbol again. In the Convert to Symbol dialog box, type **ArtistButtonClip** in the Name field and select Movie Clip for the Behavior option.

13. Still in the Convert to Symbol dialog box, click the Advanced button (visible previously in Figures 2.7 and 2.15) to reveal the symbol's linkage options.

14. Check the Export for ActionScript option. As you do so, Flash fills in the Identifier field to match the symbol's name (ArtistButtonClip), as shown in Figure 2.17.

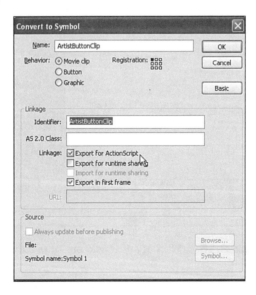

FIGURE 2.17   Placing a text field on top of the button.

As you're learning, much of Flash development has to do with creating movie clip symbols. They are the significant objects in the world of a Flash movie. Basically, just about anything visual that you want to be able to control through script should be turned into a movie clip. You will see this process happening over and over again throughout this book; it will soon become second nature to you. Chapter 5 is dedicated to movie clips and their planetary role in Flash's programmatic universe.

Adding ActionScript for Button Events

Next you can add ActionScript code that makes your new button do what it is supposed to do: display information about an artist, using the artist-display widget you created in the first part of this chapter. We're going to do this by writing some code for the button's rollOver event.

> **NOTE**
>
> Every button exposes a number of useful events to which you can attach ActionScript code. In this chapter, you're going to see only the rollOver event in action, but you will learn about other button-related events (such as rollOut and press) in Chapter 3.

The easiest way to add ActionScript code to a button-related event is to follow this basic form, where *event_name* is any of the valid button events (such as rollOver):

```
on(event_name) {
  ...code to execute...
}
```

In this case, we want to call the loadArtist() function from the artistWidget.swf interface that you created in the first part of this chapter. Follow these steps to add the appropriate code to your rollover button symbol:

1. Enter Symbol Edit mode for the ArtistButtonClip movie clip symbol. Make sure that you're editing the ArtistButtonClip symbol (which is a movie clip), not the ArtistButton symbol (which is a button).

2. Select the ArtistButton instance that's sitting within the movie clip by single-clicking it. (If you find that you keep selecting the txtArtistName text field rather than the button, try locking the text field by selecting it, and then choosing Modify > Arrange > Lock. This

makes the text field unselectable, which means that the button behind it is easy to select. See the Flash documentation for details about locking objects on the Stage.)

3. With the button selected, look at the Actions panel. The tab at the bottom of the panel should read `ArtistButton`, indicating that the code you're about to add is attached to the button.

4. Type the following ActionScript code into the Actions window:

```
on(rollOver) {

  _parent.mcArtistWidgetLoader.mcArtistDisplay.loadArtist(this.idArtist);
}
```

You might notice that this code is very similar to a line of code you added earlier to the first interface you created in this chapter. That example contained a spin control that called the `loadArtist()` function whenever its value was changed. Here's that code, for comparison's sake:

```
on(change) {
  _parent.mcArtistDisplay.loadArtist(this.value);
}
```

There are only a few differences between these two snippets of code. The first is the event to which the code reacts. Rather than reacting to the `change` event of the spin control, the snippet you just added reacts to the user rolling over the artist button. The second difference is the inclusion of the `mcArtistWidgetLoader` movie clip instance. Because this movie clip loads and contains the artistWidget.swf movie at runtime, you can call any of its functions as if they were methods of the loader clip. This makes sense if you continue to think of movie clips as containers for code and visual content.

NOTE

You can continue to "drill in" as far as you need to access functions or variables that currently occupy any of the movie clips in your SWF, any movie clips that those clips might contain, and so on. Just use dot notation to specify the "path" to the function or variable you want, where each dot essentially represents a level of movie clip nesting. We'll examine these concepts in more detail in Chapter 3.

The third difference is the value passed to the `loadArtist()` function. To understand the difference, keep in mind that the `this` keyword (in ActionScript and JavaScript) always refers to the current object, whatever that object might be (in Flash, such objects are most likely to be movie clips or non-visual objects such as `LoadVars` or the `XML` object). In the original snippet, the `this` keyword referred to the spin control, and `this.value` referred to its current value. In the new snippet, the `this` keyword refers to the `ArtistButtonClip` movie clip, and `this.idArtist` refers to...what, exactly? There isn't anything named `idArtist` in this movie clip.

Well, keep in mind that we intend to make copies of this movie clip at runtime, such that there is an instance of the `ArtistButtonClip` for each artist. With that in mind, it would obviously make sense for `this.idArtist` to hold the ID number of the artist. Well, it turns out that every movie clip instance has its own *variable scope*, which just means that each instance can keep its own local variables. You can access the variables in a clip's variable scope from outside the clip using dot notation. Within the clip, local variables are available in the `this` scope. Thus, if while we are creating the copies of `ArtistButtonClip` for each artist we set a variable called `idArtist` in each copy's scope, we should be all set. We could refer to `this.idArtist` within the clip to get the ID number, which means we can pass the ID number to the `loadArtist()` function, as shown in the first snippet in this section.

Creating an *ArtistButtonClip* for Each Artist at Runtime

Now that `ArtistButtonClip` has been created and contains the appropriate ActionScript code on the button it contains, our last task is to write some code to create a copy of each clip for each artist when the XML information is received from the server. We'll use the `attachMovie()` function for this purpose, which creates new instances of movie clip symbols from the Library.

To add the appropriate code to your document, follow these steps:

1. If you're not there already, return to the main timeline by choosing Edit > Edit Document.
2. Assuming that you created the `ArtistButtonClip` symbol, the original instance of the symbol is still on the Stage. Delete the instance. Note that the symbol remains in the Library even though no instances currently remain on the Stage.

3. Look at the Actions panel. You should see the code from Listing 2.9 that you added at the beginning of this section. If not, click once on a blank area of the Stage on Frame 1 in the timeline.

4. Find the line of code with the `trace` statement in it. Remove that line (and the comments that went along with it) and replace it with the following code:

```
// Create new copy of mcArtist movie clip,
// then place reference to it in newClip variable
_root.attachMovie("ArtistButtonClip", "mcArtist" + i, i);
var mcNewClip = _root["mcArtist" + i];

// Position the just-added copy
mcNewClip._x = 10;
mcNewClip._y = 30 * i;

// Place the name and ID into the just-added copy
mcNewClip.txtArtistName.text = currentName;
mcNewClip.idArtist = currentID;
```

First, the `attachMovie()` method is used to create a new copy of the `mcArtist` movie clip (remember, `mcArtist` is the name of the instance of `ArtistButtonClip` that's sitting on the Stage). We discuss this method in more detail in Chapter 3, but for now, just accept the idea that this method creates a fresh instance of the clip and places it on the Stage at the same exact spot as the original. The method can be called on any movie clip, or on the special keyword `_root`, which is a reference to the main document in the current SWF. (Actually, `_root` refers to the main document of the SWF that was originally loaded in the Flash player, which is a distinction that becomes important when you load SWFs within other SWFs.)

Note that the `attachMovie()` method takes three arguments. The first argument is the Linkage Identifier for the desired movie clip symbol, which you assigned earlier (see Figure 2.17). The second argument is the instance name for the new clip, and the third argument is a number that displays the display *depth*. Each clip that you add to a movie at runtime must be given a different depth number. The Flash Player uses the depth number to determine which clip appears over the other when two clips are occupying the same physical location. The clip with the higher depth number appear to be "on top," obscuring clips at lower depths from view. So, in this case, the first artist gets a clip named `mcArtist1` at depth 1, the second artist gets a clip named `mcArtist2` at depth 2, and so on.

NOTE

If, when adding a clip, you use a depth number that is already in use, the new clip replaces the existing one. That's why it's important to give each attached clip instance a different depth number, which is easily accomplished in this situation by using the current value of `i`). We'll discuss this in more detail in Chapter 3. If the nature of your code is such that you cannot be sure which depth numbers have been used previously, you can use the `MovieClip.getNextHighestDepth()` method to supply the value for `attachMovie()`'s third argument; this is discussed in Chapter 5.

Next, a variable named `mcNewClip` is created that holds a reference to the just-added movie clip. Because the just-added clip has a dynamic name, we need to use the `_root` keyword again to grab a reference to the `MovieClip` object that represents the new clip. Don't worry about the specifics of `_root` too much at this point. For now, it's enough to understand that using `attachMovie()` and `_root` together in this basic form is a sensible way to create and then manipulate a new movie clip instance. The result is a variable that is a `MovieClip` object and thus provides all of `MovieClip`'s methods, properties, and events. You will learn more about the power of `MovieClip` objects in Chapter 3, and much more about them in Chapter 5.

NOTE

Alternatively, you can use `_level0` instead of `_root`. The difference between the two is usually not important for the kind of work we will be doing in this book, but there can occasionally be a subtle difference between them in situations where SWFs are loading other SWFs at runtime through the `loadMovie()` method. I recommend that you use `_root` instead of `_level0`, unless you find yourself in a specific situation where `_root` is treating you badly. If it is, look up `_level0` in the Flash documentation for an explanation of how it differs from `_root`.

The next few lines of code position the new clip by setting its `_x` and `_y` properties, which of course control the clip's horizontal and vertical position (relative to the upper-left corner of the Stage). You can experiment with these values to cause the rollover buttons to be arranged differently on the Stage at runtime. For instance, the number 30 on the right-side of the expression for the `_y` value represents the amount of vertical space (measured in pixels) between the buttons. Increasing the number causes the buttons to have more vertical space between them; decreasing the number causes them to be closer together.

The name of the current artist is displayed visually on the button within the new clip, by setting the text property of the txtArtistName text field (which, as you'll recall, is sitting on top of the button, within the ArtistButtonClip movie clip) to the value of the currentName variable. Finally, the ID number of the current artist is placed into the new movie clip with a variable name of idArtist. This is what enables the code attached to the button within the clip—which you added in the previous section—to refer to this.idArtist when calling the loadArtist() function.

Testing It Out

You should now be able to test out the completed interface by publishing the movie (File > Publish) and then visiting the chapter02/artistMenu.html page with your web browser. If you prefer, you can also test the movie within the Flash IDE using Control > Test Movie. In any case, when the movie appears, you should see buttons that display the name of each artist, and details about that artist should be displayed when you roll your mouse over the button area (see Figure 2.18).

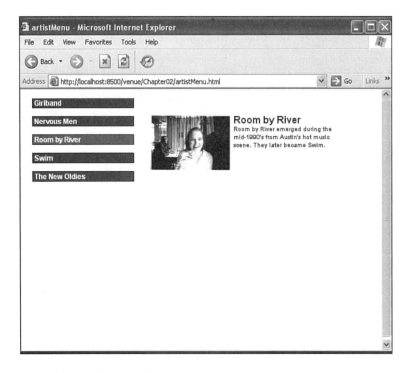

FIGURE 2.18   Testing the new buttons.

> **NOTE**
>
> If the buttons don't appear exactly where you want them to, just adjust the `_x` and `_y` parts of the code that you added in the last section. If the artist-detail information doesn't appear where you want it to, just move the `mcArtistWidgetLoader` movie clip (represented by the small white circle on the Stage). Then republish or retest your movie.

Congratulations. It's not particularly fancy or visually impressive, but you've created a user interface with Flash that does the following:

- Retrieves name/value pairs from your server in real time.
- Retrieves and parses XML supplied by your server, also in real time.
- Uses movie clips and rollover buttons to provide a browsing interface for navigating amongst records in the database.
- Displays text and image data about individual records.

Not bad, considering that you're only on the first hands-on chapter of this book.

Adding the Interface to a Web Page

So far, you have only seen our example Flash interfaces being displayed in the bare-bones HTML pages that Flash creates automatically when you publish a movie. You might be wondering what's involved in adding a SWF to one of your own pages.

Turns out that it's pretty easy and conceptually similar to adding an image to a web page. You just need to make sure that the .swf file is accessible via your web server. Then you just add some markup to your HTML that tells your browser to display the SWF wherever you want it to appear. This simple process is conceptually similar to using an `<img>` tag to display a simple GIF or a JPEG image. Instead of `<img>`, you use a set of nested `<object>`, `<param>`, and `<embed>` tags. The syntax is not quite as straightforward, mainly because of compatibility issues that arose out of the so-called browser wars back in the day, but it's still fairly easy after you have seen an example or two.

NOTE

Just before this book went to press, Microsoft announced that upcoming versions of its Internet Explorer will enforce new policies when Flash content (and many other types of plugin-style content) is displayed on a web page. In a nutshell, the new policies will result in the user being prompted before each Flash movie is displayed within a web page. The prompt will read "Press OK to continue loading the content of this page." To get rid of the prompt, you will need to use slightly different HTML syntax than is shown and discussed in the remainder of this chapter. The new policies are in response to a patent dispute; it was somewhat unclear at press time whether the new policies will actually take effect. It appears that Macromedia will make some free tools available to automate the appropriate changes to any existing web pages that include Flash content. At the time of this writing, detailed information about this issue was available from Microsoft at `http://msdn.microsoft.com/ieupdate/` and from Macromedia at `http://www.macromedia.com/devnet/activecontent/`.

Copying and Pasting the HTML

The easiest way to get the appropriate HTML for displaying your movie in a web page of your own is to let Flash generate the set of HTML tags for you. Then you just copy and paste them into whatever web pages you want, adjusting the relative URL to the .swf file as necessary. The basic steps are as follows:

1. Use File > Publish to generate the compiled SWF and test HTML page for your movie, and then pull the HTML page up in your browser. If you want, you can use File > Publish Preview > HTML to publish the files and pull them up in your browser in one step.

2. Use your browser's View Source command to view the test HTML code that Flash generated for you.

3. Copy and paste the HTML code into your own web page, and then add whatever relative path information is appropriate to the `src` and `movie` parameters. Just use the same dot and slash syntax that you would use for images in `<img>` tags.

NOTE

Of course, if you are using Dreamweaver, you can just drag a .swf file from the Assets panel into your web pages. Other web page editors provide you with similar niceties. Use whatever HTML tools you wish.

As an example, Listing 2.10 shows the HTML code the Flash generated when I published the artistWidget document. As you can see, most of the parameters are repeated twice; both sets of syntax are needed to support the various versions of Netscape and Microsoft browsers out there.

LISTING 2.10 HTML Snippet from Flash's Auto-Generated Movie Testing Page

```
<OBJECT
  classid="clsid:D27CDB6E-AE6D-11CF-96B8-444553540000"  codebase=
➥"http://download.macromedia.com/pub/shockwave/cabs/flash/
➥swflash.cab#version=7,0,0,0"
WIDTH="350"
HEIGHT="132"
ALIGN="middle"
id="artistWidget">
<PARAM NAME="movie" VALUE="artistWidget.swf">
<PARAM NAME="quality" VALUE="high">
<PARAM NAME="bgcolor" VALUE="#FFFFFF">
<PARAM NAME="enableScriptAccess" VALUE="sameDomain">

<EMBED
  WIDTH="350"
  HEIGHT="132"
  ALIGN="middle"
  NAME="artistWidget"
  src="artistWidget.swf"
  quality="high"
  bgcolor="#FFFFFF"
  enableScriptAccess="sameDomain"
  TYPE="application/x-shockwave-flash"
  PLUGINSPAGE="http://www.macromedia.com/go/getflashplayer">
</EMBED>
</OBJECT>
```

> **NOTE**
>
> For clarity's sake, I've added whitespace and indentation and reordered some of the attributes. The code that Flash generates is formatted more compactly on just a couple lines.

HTML <object> and <embed> Parameters

Table 2.2 provides a quick rundown of the parameters that appear in Listing 2.10. You can get more information about these parameters in the Flash documentation set (see the Publishing topic in the *Using Flash* portion of the Flash documentation). The only information you absolutely have to provide is src and `movie`, but in practice you will at least want to provide the `width` and `height` parameters as well.

TABLE 2.2 Parameters Available for Use

PARAMETER	DESCRIPTION
src / movie	The filename of the compiled movie (.swf), including whatever relative or absolute path information is necessary. The paths work just like the `src` attribute of an HTML `<img>` tag. Note that this parameter is called `src` in the `<embed>` syntax, but `movie` in the `<param>` syntax.
width	The width of the movie, expressed either as a number of pixels or as a percentage of the horizontal space available on the page. In either case, this parameter works just like the `width` attribute of an HTML `<img>` tag.
height	The height of the movie, also expressed as pixels or a percentage.
quality	The display quality of the movie. You will rarely want to change this from its default value of `high`.
align	The alignment of the movie on the page. This parameter works like the `align` attribute of an HTML `<img>` tag.
bgcolor	The background color of the movie, expressed as a hex value (just like the `bgcolor` attribute for the HTML `<body>` or `<td>` tags).
id / name	Assigns a name to the instance of the Flash Player that is playing your movie in the browser at runtime. This name is available to JavaScript; you can use JavaScript commands to start and stop the movie, advance the timeline to particular frames, and so on. Note that this parameter is called `id` in the `<embed>` syntax, but `name` in the `<param>` syntax. Interactions with JavaScript are not discussed specifically in this book; consult the Flash documentation about `FSCommand` for details.
allowscriptaccess	When the movie is being controlled by JavaScript in the surrounding web page, this attribute controls what exactly is enabled. The idea is to cut down on potential security exploits through scripting. The default `sameDomain` value makes sense in most situations. Interactions with JavaScript are not discussed specifically in this book; consult the Flash documentation for details.

PARAMETER	DESCRIPTION
play	Determines whether the movie will be playing when it appears in the browser. If set to `true` or omitted, the main timeline immediately begins advancing through its frames. If set to `false`, the main timeline is frozen when the movie first appears and does not begin advancing through its frames until it is specifically started through script.
loop	Determines whether the movie's main timeline loops indefinitely, like a film loop. If set to `true` or omitted, the main timeline loops back to Frame 1 after the last frame has been reached. If set to `false`, the main timeline stops after it reaches its last frame.
menu	Determines whether a context menu with options for zooming, printing, player settings, and display quality shows up if the user right-clicks the movie. If set to `true` or omitted, the context menu includes these items. If set to `false`, an abbreviated context menu is shown, which includes options only for player settings and the about page for the Flash Player. It is also possible to add your own context-sensitive items to the right-click menu, or to remove Flash's built-in menu items; see the `ContextMenu` and `ContextMenuItem` classes in the Flash documentation for details.
devicefont	In certain situations, you might want the Flash Player to use *device fonts* when displaying text fields, especially when using small font sizes. Issues regarding fonts and font substitutions aren't within the scope of this book; please consult the Flash documentation for details.

> **NOTE**
>
> You'll notice that a few attributes in Listing 2.10 are not shown in this table (`classid` and `codebase` in the `<object>` syntax; `type` and `pluginspage` in the `<embed>` syntax). These values are just part of the mechanics of telling the browser that the Flash Player should be used to render the SWF content (as opposed to some other plug-in). You generally don't need to change these values.

About the play *and* loop *Parameters*

As described in Table 2.2, the play and loop parameters can be used to determine whether the main timeline of a movie plays over and over, plays just once, or doesn't play at all until told to do so by a script. Regarding this issue, it's important to understand the following:

- The play and loop parameters affect only the main timeline in the actual SWF. The timelines of any movie clips within the SWF are unaffected.

- Neither the play nor the loop parameters have any actual effect if the main timeline contains only one frame. Movies (or movie clips) that have only one frame in their timelines don't advance.

- Setting the play parameter to false is functionally equivalent to putting a stop() ActionScript command in the first frame of the main timeline. You might want to consider using the stop() approach in the SWF, rather than relying on the correct HTML tags being used each time the movie is placed on a web page.

- Setting the loop parameter to false is equivalent to putting a stop() command in the *last* frame of the main timeline. Again, using ActionScript rather than the loop parameter in your HTML tags might be preferable because it keeps the SWF in charge of itself.

Relative Versus Absolute URLs for Fetching Server Data

The examples in this chapter use the LoadVars.load() and XML.load() methods to connect to your web server for current information from a database. As the examples stand right now, the load() method is being given fully-qualified URLs (including the http:// protocol part, server name, and so on). Using the fully-qualified URLs makes development easier because the movies have enough information to contact your server even when you're testing them within the Flash IDE (using Control > Test Movie or File > Publish Preview).

After you're done with the initial development, though, or if you plan to always test your movies in the context of one of your own web pages (as opposed to the ones Flash generates when you publish), it generally makes sense to use relative rather than absolute URLs. For instance, because the server-side pages that supply XML are currently in the same folder as the SWFs themselves, you can change this line:

```
artistsXml.load("http://localhost/venue/chapter02/artistsXmlSource.aspx"
);
```

to this:

```
artistsXml.load("artistsXmlSource.aspx");
```

Hey, Check Out That File Size!

One interesting thing to note at this point is the relative file sizes of your Flash IDE documents (the .fla files) and the compiled files for the Flash Player (the .swf files). My uncompiled .fla files for this chapter's examples turned out to be around 50–70KB each. Whether that's something that you would consider to be a large file depends on your point of view, but the important thing to realize is that the size of the .fla files have no bearing to the users of your application. Your users never have to download the .fla at all; you can keep the .fla anywhere you want, well outside of your web server's document root. Only the compiled .swf is ever delivered to the Flash Player for viewing, and it's the only file that needs to be in a location that's accessible through your web server.

The compiled .swf files for this chapter's examples are small. The artistMenu.swf file is less than 1K, and the artistWidget.swf file is just a bit over 30K. So, in terms of total download size and time, adding this chapter's movies to one of your web pages would cost you almost nothing. Of course, it makes sense to also consider the size of the XML and name/value data that the SWFs then retrieve from the server. The download for the XML data is pretty small too—less than 1K presently. Of course, this would increase as more artist records were added to the database. In addition, the name/value data that supplies the detail information about each artist is also very small, and it is fetched from your server only when it is actually needed. This keeps the initial load on the server down and ensures that your Flash UI scales reasonably well as more and more records are added to the database.

> **NOTE**
>
> Of course, because this SWF displays JPEG images for each artist, you need to consider the size of those files as well when thinking about network traffic and bandwidth usage and so on. Flash is neither more nor less efficient than a regular web browser when it comes to downloading external images.

That Wasn't So Bad, Was It?

This chapter got you started on the road toward creating Flash user interfaces that talk to your web server. If you're like me, though, some huge and nagging questions are bouncing around in your head right now: "What's the point?" and "Yes, we were able to create a Flash movie that displayed information from our database, but why? Is it really better than just creating an HTML page that displays information about artists?" and "Why go through all this trouble to learn Flash if the resulting interface isn't any more useful for users? What is its *raison d'etre*?"

Well, one could argue that while this chapter's examples aren't exactly exciting or pretty, they are already somewhat useful. You could easily adapt them to many situations where you want to present a master/detail interface that enables your users to sift through a set of records—without reloading the page for each record, and without using frames, pop-up windows, or tedious cross-browser DHTML techniques.

To put it another way, I didn't want to start off with a "Hello, World" example. I wanted to give you something real, while at the same time introducing you to the basic building blocks of a typical Flash interface. Looking back on this chapter, I think you'll agree that you've learned a lot and can see that Flash definitely has potential for you as a web developer.

However, this is obviously just the beginning. As our examples get more complex in chapters to come, the advantages of creating certain portions of your applications with Flash become more and more self-evident. They are more dynamic, more responsive, and more fun to use.

Summary

The first part of this chapter walked you through the creation of your very first Flash interface, called artistWidget.swf. That SWF connects to your server through the `LoadVars` object and displays artist information in text fields and artist photos in a Loader component. The second example, called artistMenu.swf, connects to your server via the `XML` object and displays information about each artist in response to mouse rollover events.

I realize that some of the details may still seem a bit sketchy. This chapter had a lot of ground to cover in a short amount of time. The idea was for you to get your feet wet right away, even if that meant skipping over some theory along the way. In Chapter 3, you will take a closer look at some of the issues and concepts that were skipped over (or only touched on briefly) in this chapter. Chapters 4 and 5 then back up to provide a conceptual overview of key ActionScript and MovieClip concepts, thus completing your introduction to Flash. Chapters 6–9 continue your training by providing detailed discussions of the various methods of interacting with servers.

CHAPTER 3

DIGGING A BIT DEEPER

In Chapter 2, "Your First Flash Interface," you created a Macromedia Flash interface that retrieved some information from your server and displayed it to your users in the form of a useful—but, let's face it, somewhat clunky—user interface. This chapter refines the simple examples from Chapter 2, making them just a bit more interesting. Specifically, we do the following:

- Add some animation and control it programmatically.
- Dress up the buttons to make them feel more interactive.

At the same time, we will take a closer look at a number of concepts that were only touched on in Chapter 2. Specifically, you will learn more about:

- **Timelines.** How they work with animations, how they can be controlled programmatically, and how they relate to your movie clips, variables, and functions.
- **Buttons.** What they are, how they work, and how they relate to ActionScript.
- **Movie clips.** What they mean to you and why they are so important.

- **The Library and symbols.** How you can use both to your advantage.
- **Components.** How to work with them, how to think about them, and how to obtain and install new ones.

Let's get started.

Understanding the Library and Symbols

In Chapter 2, you used the Library panel in the Flash IDE to create a new, empty movie clip for loading an external SWF. You also learned that you could use the Library panel as a way to quickly enter Symbol Edit mode for a movie clip.

At a high level, the Library can be thought of as your home base for the creation and management of buttons, movie clips, and more. Everything that participates in your Flash movie—movie clips, buttons, and so on—appears in the Library, regardless of whether it is currently visible on the Stage.

> **NOTE**
>
> If you use Dreamweaver, you can think of the Library as being somewhat like the Assets panel in Dreamweaver. It's the place where you can see all the items that participate in your project in an organized, sorted list—instead of having to find the items as they are strewn about your web pages.

Symbols and Instances

Think of the Library as your home base for working with *symbols*. You already heard the word "symbol" a few times in Chapter 2; now it's time for a proper explanation. Basically, the notion of a symbol is Flash's main metaphor for enabling you to create reusable objects.

Designers often get introduced to symbols with an explanation like the following: If you are going to have five or six star shapes as visual decoration in a movie, you can create one star symbol and place visual copies of it on the Stage. The copies are called *instances*, and each instance can be messed around with a bit (its size can be stretched, its color can be tinted, it can be moved around, and so on). By using symbols and instances rather than drawing five or six separate stars, a certain amount of drawing work is saved, and the shapes are automatically kept consistent with one another. In addition, the file size of the compiled SWF is generally smaller because the symbol needs to be included in the actual file only once. The larger or more complex the artwork, the greater the benefit.

As a developer, these notions of symbols and instances probably sound a whole lot like the notions of classes and instances involved in object-oriented programming (OOP). Symbols would be like classes, and instances of symbols on the Stage would be like instances of classes in OOP-style code. Just as OOP classes usually represent a type of real-world object (a car or a person, say, or a database connection), a Flash symbol might represent a type of visual widget (a button or a star). In addition, just as instances of OOP classes might represent specific, real-world cars or people (my 1985 Chevy Nova hatchback, say, or Liz Phair), instances of Flash symbols are the actual buttons and stars that are visible to your users.

You get the idea. This is not the time or the place to worry a whole lot about whether Flash symbols strictly adhere to OOP principles (for instance, whether they support polymorphism and so on). For now, let's just agree that it makes sense to think about them as being object-like. Later chapters—especially the conspicuously titled Chapter 5, "Movie Clips as Objects"—explore the concept in greater detail.

In any case, symbols are reusable "things," and the Library is where you see the definitions of those things. You can see the symbols defined in the artistMenu.fla document right now, by opening the file and then looking at its Library panel (Window > Library). The `ArtistButton`, `ArtistButtonClip`, and `ArtistWidgetLoaderClip` symbols that you created in Chapter 2 are all listed there.

The artistMenu.fla document instantiates the three symbols in different ways. Just one instance of the `ArtistWidgetLoaderClip` symbol is used—the instance on the Stage named `mcArtistWidgetLoader`—and it was created at design time, by placing the instance on the Stage visually. The `ArtistButtonClip` symbol is instantiated at runtime through the ActionScript's `attachMovie()` method.

Regardless of how your symbols are instantiated, each instance can be controlled through script using its instance name. Following the object-oriented analogy, the instance names are similar conceptually to the names of variables that hold class instances—objects—in an OOP-style language such as Java (or ActionScript).

The Three Types of Symbols

Flash supports three different types of symbols, two of which you've seen already. When you begin the task of creating a new symbol, you are asked which of these three types you want to create:

- **Movie clips.** This is the most common type of symbol. It's also the most scriptable and flexible, which makes it the most interesting type of symbol for us developer types. Movie clips can load external SWFs or images, can be created, duplicated, and removed at runtime, can be moved around on the Stage through the use of script, and much more. Every movie clip has its own timeline and its own local variable scope. It addition, clips very often contain significant chunks of ActionScript code. Movie clips are complex and chameleon-like beasts that serve many purposes and are very, very important for any Flash designer or developer.

- **Buttons.** Buttons are also very important, and you can see them in most of this book's examples, but their mission in life is much simpler and tightly defined than the mission of movie clips. As such, there is less to talk about. Like a movie clip, each button has a timeline, but it's a strange timeline that doesn't advance automatically over time. See "Understanding More About Buttons," later in this chapter for more details.

- **Graphics.** Graphic symbols are the least interesting type of symbol as far as the scope of this book goes. Graphics are similar to movie clips, but they don't play in their own timeline, don't have their own variable scope, and generally can't be manipulated through script. You'll see many graphic symbols as you work with Flash (they might decorate the movie clips or buttons with which you are working), but they won't be much of a focus throughout this book.

NOTE

Actually, there are two other types of symbols—font symbols and video symbols—but they are used differently and aren't covered in this book. See the Flash documentation for details about embedding font and video symbols in your movies.

Symbol Names, Instance Names, and Linkage Identifiers

Every symbol has a name, called the *symbol name*. Each instance of the symbol that you place on the Stage may also be given a name, called the *instance name*. You can use the instance name in ActionScript to move the symbol around, make copies of it at runtime, change its appearance, and so on.

You assign the symbol name when you create the symbol, whether you create a symbol from scratch (as you did with `ArtistWidgetLoaderClip`) or convert existing visual content to a symbol (as you did with `ArtistButton`). If you want to change the name of the symbol later, you can do so by right-clicking the symbol in the Library and choosing Rename. Symbol names are for your use and organization as a developer. You never refer to them in your script code, so you can rename them at any time without affecting how your movie behaves.

Instance names are different, in that their main purpose is to make the instance accessible to ActionScript. Therefore, changing an instance's name will affect how a movie behaves, unless you make the change throughout all script code that interacts with the instance. You can use Flash's Find and Replace tool (on the Edit menu) to help find where you need to make those changes. If you create new instances of a symbol at runtime (for instance, using the `attachMovie()` method as you did in Chapter 2), you provide the instance name in your script code. For instances created at design time, you provide the instance name in the Properties panel.

If you want to be able to create new instances of a symbol at runtime with the `attachMovie()` method, you need to give the movie a *linkage identifier*. To assign or change the identifier, you right-click on the symbol in the Library and choose Linkage from the context menu. (You can also choose Properties, then Advanced, as described in Chapter 2).

NOTE

The most common reason to give a symbol a linkage identifier is to make it available to `attachMovie()`. That being said, you will also need to provide a linkage identifier if you want to specify the symbol as the `icon` property of a Button component, as the `contentPath` for a Loader component, or as the `contentPath` for a form or slide screen (see Chapter 11, "Building Better Forms with Flash," for information about form and slide screens).

By default, the linkage identifier is the same as the symbol name, but they can be different if you wish. Keep in mind that while the symbol name is for organizational purposes only (and thus has no bearing on your scripting), the linkage identifier does affect your scripting, so make sure to adjust any relevant `attachMovie()` calls if you change a symbol's identifier.

> **NOTE**
>
> By the way, instance names are case-sensitive. In general, you should consider just about everything in Flash to be case-sensitive. The rules about case-sensitivity were somewhat less strict in previous versions of Flash, but with the advent of ActionScript 2.0 and the Flash Player 7, you should keep your mind in a case-sensitive mode from here on out.

Symbol Naming Conventions

You may have noticed that I have been using a bit of a naming convention for symbols and symbol instances in this book. For instance, I use the word "Clip" at the end of each movie clip symbol's name (`ArtistButtonClip` or `ArtistWidgetLoaderClip`). For instance names, I have been using the same name—without the `Clip` part—and appending "`mc`" to each instance name (`mcArtistButton`, `mcArtistButton1`, `mcArtistButton2`, and `mcArtistWidgetLoader`). Of course, you don't have to use these conventions in your own movies, but you might want to come up with some kind of system for naming your symbols and instances and stick to it as much as you can.

> **NOTE**
>
> The Flash IDE tends to encourage a slightly different naming convention for symbol instances, wherein each movie clip instance name ends with `_mc`, each button instance name ends with `_btn`, and so on. See the "Helping the Actions Panel Understand the Types of Your Variables" section in Chapter 4, "ActionScript: A Primer," for details.

Other Features Available in the Library Panel

The Library panel offers lots of additional features that haven't been discussed yet. I have included some of the most important items in the following list. You can read all about the details in the Flash documentation.

- You can drag any symbol from the Library onto the Stage to create a new instance of the symbol.

- You can duplicate an existing symbol by right-clicking it and choosing Duplicate. This does not create a new instance of the symbol; it creates a whole new symbol (which you then can create instances of).

- You can organize your symbols into folders, which can be handy if your Flash projects start to get complicated. To create a new folder, choose New Folder from the panel menu at the top-right corner of the Library. Then you can drag the symbols you want into the new folder. The folders are for organizational purposes only; they do not implicitly define packages. You can name or nest them however you wish.

- You can keep track of how many instances of each symbol are being used with the Keep Use Counts Updated and Update Use Counts Now commands on the Library panel menu. If a symbol's usage count is zero, and you're not going to create instances of it at runtime through script, you should probably delete it from the Library, just to keep it from becoming cluttered.

- You can change a symbol's type. For instance, if a symbol was originally created as a graphic, you might want to change it to a movie clip for additional control. Right-click the symbol, and then choose Properties. You can then change the behavior type.

- You can export or import the symbol for runtime sharing. Runtime sharing enables you to keep your commonly used symbols—animated logos, say, or buttons that perform certain actions—in a shared SWF file. The Flash Player downloads and uses the symbols when your movie is actually viewed (that is, at runtime). Runtime shared objects are not covered explicitly in this book; see the Flash documentation for details.

- You can drag a symbol from one FLA's library onto the Stage of another document. An instance of the symbol appears on the Stage, and the symbol itself appears in the second document's library from that point forward. If the symbol was already present in the second document, Flash will ask you if you want to replace the existing definition with the one you are dragging in (thereby updating the existing symbol's behavior or appearance).

- For symbols that will be used in many different documents, you can keep the symbols in FLAs that you keep in a central, shared location. Then, in each document that needs to use the shared symbol, you use the Source section of the Create New Symbol dialog box to pull the desired symbol in from the shared FLA. If the shared symbol changes, you can update it in the other documents at any time by choosing

Update from the symbol's context menu in the library. You can even have Flash keep the shared symbols updated automatically through the *Always update before publishing* option. See the Flash documentation for details; you may also want to check out the difference between sharing symbols in this fashion (where the sharing happens at design or publication time) versus runtime shared objects (where the sharing happens over the network when the movie is actually played).

- For movie clips only, you can export your symbol to a new SWF file (which you then could load as an external SWF using the `loadMovie()` method you learned about in Chapter 2) or to the new `MovieClipLoader` class in MX2. You can also export the SWF as a compiled SWC file if you are creating a component, or convert it to a compiled clip if it contains a large amount of script code that need not be recompiled each time you publish your movie. SWCs are discussed briefly in Appendix A, "Notes on Building the SimpleBarChart Component"; see the Flash documentation for information about compiled clips. Both are of interest mainly to the development of components, a topic that is outside the scope of this book.

- Also for movie clips only, you can create a component definition for any movie clip, which is a shortcut for allowing the clip to behave like a component. We will experiment a bit with this concept in the "Turning Clips into Components" section in Chapter 5.

Understanding the Timeline

The timeline is one of the Flash concepts that can seem a bit intimidating for us people coming from a server-side background. We're just not used to thinking about the even flow of time on the client. Flash needs to have such a concept, of course, because one of its big jobs is to present streaming, animated, and interactive content. Time is of the essence; it's natural that something to do with time would be a central concept in the Flash vocabulary.

But let's face it: we web-server people are used to thinking about time in a much more fragmented way. A browser contacts the web server in an instant; the server responds a few milliseconds later. After that short burst of activity, there is no interaction between the server and browser until the next page request (if one ever comes). It's almost as if time is frozen between page requests.

The Timeline in the Flash IDE

When people use the word *timeline*, they are often referring to the passing of time and what should happen at various moments as time advances. Other times, they are talking about the Timeline panel in the Flash IDE, which is a clever visual representation of how time passes at runtime. (Think of the Timeline panel as the easy, visual way to create simple animations, tell Flash to execute certain lines of code at certain moments, and so on.)

Using the Timeline to Add Animation

In general, this book isn't going to spend lots of time on how to add visual flourishes, such as animations and fancy artwork, to your Flash user interfaces. Many, many resources are available in book form and online where you can learn all about that stuff. More likely than not, an actual designer with real talent will be creating the look and feel for your interfaces anyway (unless you have such interests and talents yourself, in which case, more power to you).

All that said, it's important for you to know how to create simple animations so that you can see what's involved in making them so that you won't be confused by the movies that designers create. It's also important to understand the relationship that time has to your scripting and server-side processing.

Let's go back to the artistMenu.fla example from Chapter 2 and add a bit of animation. We'll make the details about each artist—that is, the information shown in the `mcArtistWidgetLoaderClip` instance—slide into and out of view as the user rolls over each button. The animation will make the example just a bit more dynamic and interesting.

Take a look at the Timeline panel (if the Timeline panel isn't showing, choose Window > Timeline to display it). The Timeline panel (see Figure 3.1) has two sections. The section on the left is a list of *layers* within your document; right now there is only one layer, named Layer 1. The section on the right, which contains lots of little squares, represents the *frames* in your document.

What are frames, you ask? Think about how a cartoon is created in the real world (um, at least, how animated films used to be made, when they were drawn by hand). To create the illusion of motion, an artist creates a series of images, each one subtly different from the last. When the images are displayed one after another, the eye is deceived into thinking that the images are "moving." Frames in Flash are similar. A single frame represents a single moment in time; a series of frames represents a moving period of time.

FIGURE 3.1   The Timeline panel shows layers on the left and frames on the right.

And what are layers? As the name implies, layers provide a way for certain visual elements to be drawn on top of others. Again, if you think about how a cartoon might be drawn, the background of the cartoon might be thought of as being its own "layer," and the characters in the cartoon might be drawn on sheets of clear plastic that are "layered" on top of the background. As time progresses in the world of the cartoon, the character layers are often animated while the background remains stationery. Likewise, the main purpose of layers is to make it easier to animate some things while leaving other things alone. For instance, in this exercise, we are interested in making the detail-display portion of the interface slide in and out from view, but we want the buttons to remain stationary. Therefore, we put the detail-display widget into its own layer and animate it there; the buttons are isolated from the animation effect. (A secondary purpose of layers is to make certain that items appear to be on top of one another—this trick is usually of more interest to designers and animators than to developers.) This will all make more sense to you after you see it in action.

First, let's place the visual elements on the Stage into their own layers, which makes it easier to animate exactly what we want. To do so, follow these steps:

> **NOTE**
>
> If you don't want to walk through these steps yourself, you can just open up the completed artistMenu.fla document from this chapter's example files.

1. Open the artistMenu.fla document from Chapter 2's example files.

2. Make sure you are editing the main document—as opposed to one of your symbols—by choosing Edit > Edit Document if it's available (if it's not available, then you are already editing the main document).

3. Select the empty `ArtistWidgetLoaderClip` movie clip that's currently on the Stage by selecting the small white circle that represents it.

4. Choose Modify > Timeline > Distribute to Layers. Flash creates a new layer named Layer 2 and places the clip instance into the new layer. You can see the new layer in the list of layers on the left side of the Timeline panel.

NOTE

In general, it makes sense to put any individual element that you want to animate in its own layer.

---

5. Double-click the name of the new layer (Layer 2) in the timeline. The name becomes editable. Change the name to **Detail** (see Figure 3.2) and then press Enter to rename the layer.

FIGURE 3.2 Naming a new layer.

6. Create a new layer by clicking the new layer icon at the bottom left corner of the Timeline panel (visible in Figure 3.2), or by choosing Insert > Timeline > Layer. Change the name of the new layer to **Background**. If necessary, drag the new Background layer down so that it is the bottommost layer in the list.

7. Make sure the Background layer is selected, and then use the Rectangle tool to draw a colored rectangle on the Stage, filled with a light color of some kind (I used a light blue). Adjust the rectangle's position and size so that it takes up the entire width of the Stage and is aligned with the top edge of the Stage. The easiest way to do this is to double-click the rectangle, and then use the Properties panel to set the X and Y position to 0,0, the width to 550, and the height to 250 (or so—the height doesn't matter as much, as you will soon see). Refer to the finished FLA document from this chapter's example files if you get confused about the drawing.

8. If you wish, add some text to the Background layer to show a title or instructions for your users. I placed the words "Artist Menu" in a large bold font, with the phrase "Roll your mouse over the band names... it's fun!" in a smaller font underneath. You can decorate the layer with other shapes or colors if you wish.

9. Change the name of the Layer 1 layer to **Actions**. Note that the layer has a lowercase *a* symbol in its first frame, which indicates that the layer contains ActionScript code.

10. You should now have three layers named Actions, Detail, and Background (in that order, from top to bottom). By clicking the layer names in the Timeline panel, you should be able to verify that the Actions layer contains no visual elements, that the Detail background contains only the `mcArtistWidgetLoader` movie clip, and that the Background layer contains only the light-colored rectangle.

Now you're ready to create the animation. You'll do this by adding some *keyframes* to the Detail layer of the timeline. Keyframes are special frames that contain new, changed, or repositioned content. The simplest way to make an object move around is to create a keyframe a few frames ahead. Then, in the new keyframe, move the object to wherever you want it to end up on the Stage. Think of the first frame as the beginning of the movement and the new keyframe as the end of the movement. Flash takes care of moving the object smoothly between the intervening frames.

Follow these steps to create the animation:

1. Select the `ArtistWidgetLoader` clip (by clicking the small white circle once), and then use the Properties panel to set its X position to 600 and its Y position to 35. This should reposition the clip off the right side of the Stage (so that it is sitting within the gray area outside the Stage, as shown in Figure 3.3). If you wish, you can drag the clip with your mouse to reposition it, instead of using the Properties panel.

2. In the timeline, select Frame 10 in the Detail layer by clicking it once.

3. Choose Insert > Timeline > Keyframe or simply press F6 on your keyboard. You'll notice that Frames 1–10 are now shaded gray, and black dots are in Frames 1 and 10. The dots indicate that Frames 1 and 10 are keyframes.

4. Repeat Steps 2 and 3, this time inserting a keyframe in Frame 20. You should now have three black-dotted keyframes in the Detail layer (see Figure 3.4).

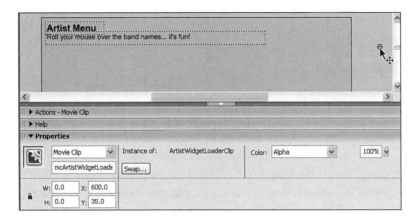

FIGURE 3.3 Moving the loader clip to its initial position off the Stage.

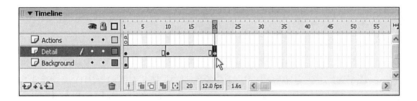

FIGURE 3.4 Adding keyframes to the Detail layer.

5. Click once on the middle keyframe (Frame 10) to select it.

6. Move the `ArtistWidgetLoader` instance in Frame 10 back onto the Stage by selecting it and then using the Properties panel to change its X position to 200. The Y position can remain at 35.

7. In the Timeline panel, right-click Frame 1 in the Detail layer, and then choose Create Motion Tween from the context menu. You'll notice that an arrow is now displayed across the selected frames (visible in Figure 3.5).

8. Repeat Steps 6 and 7, this time right-clicking Frame 10 to create the motion tween.

9. Right-click Frame 20 of the Background layer, and then choose Insert Frame (not Insert Keyframe) from the context menu. Flash responds by filling Frames 1 through 20 with a shaded color (see Figure 3.5), indicating that the same content should be displayed in all 20 frames of this layer. Note that while Frames 10 and 20 of the Details layer contain keyframes (marked with black dots in the timeline), the only keyframe in the Background layer is Frame 1. In other words, Frame 1 is the only frame that contains new or changed content in the Background layer.

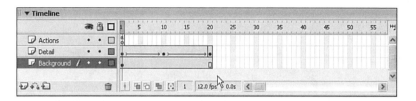

FIGURE 3.5   Adding regular frames to the Background layer.

That was a lot of clicking around and fiddling with layers, all of which may seem like a bunch of abstract and inscrutable nonsense to you at this point. If it helps, think of the timeline adjustments you just made as having the following plain English meaning: "The content in the Detail layer should start off the Stage, move onto the Stage after time has progressed by 10 frames, and then move back to its original position. Meanwhile, the content in the Background layer should remain constant through all 20 frames."

At this point, you could test the movie by publishing it and viewing it in your browser. If you did so, you would see that the detail clip indeed moves around according to the changes you made to the timeline. However, it would not move around in response to a user's actions. Instead, it would just move back and forth, as if it were on an endless loop. You need to add a tiny amount of ActionScript code to start and stop the animation in response to the user's actions.

Controlling Animation Playback with ActionScript

ActionScript provides a number of simple but effective commands for starting and stopping the animation in a movie or movie clip. You can also tell the Flash Player to jump around to specific frames in the timeline, which enables you to cause animations to play—or other visual state changes to take place—when something special happens (a button rollover or mouse click, for instance). Table 3.1 lists the timeline-control commands available to you. You can use these commands to control the main timeline of your Flash movie, or the timelines of any of its movie clips.

> **NOTE**
>
> The "commands" listed in Table 3.1 are actually methods of the `MovieClip` class, which will be covered in greater detail in Chapter 5. For now, just accept that they always control the current timeline when they are used alone. Later, you will see that they can also be called as methods of any `MovieClip` class instance, to control the playback of each movie clip that participates in a SWF.

TABLE 3.1   ActionScript Commands for Controlling Animation Playback

COMMAND	DESCRIPTION
gotoAndPlay(frame)	Moves the playhead to the specified frame and begins playing the movie or movie clip. The frame can be specified by name or by number.
gotoAndStop(frame)	Moves the playhead to the specified frame, while also stopping the movie or movie clip (if it is playing). The frame can be specified by name or by number.
nextFrame()	Advances the timeline ahead by one frame.
play()	Begins playback.
prevFrame()	Rewinds the timeline back by one frame.
stop()	Stops playback.

Let's try adding some of these scripting commands to the artistMenu.fla example so that it responds to button rollovers and rollouts.

1. Right-click Frame 10 of the Actions layer and choose Insert Keyframe from the context menu to create a new keyframe.

2. With Frame 10 still selected, type **stop();** in the Actions panel (see Figure 3.6).

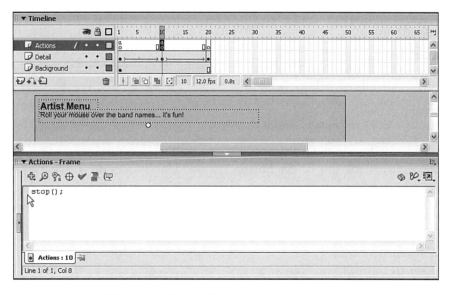

FIGURE 3.6   Adding a stop() command.

3. Repeat Steps 1 and 2, this time adding the `stop()` command to Frame 20 of the Actions layer.

4. Enter Symbol Edit mode for the `ArtistButtonClip` movie clip. Click once on the `ArtistButton` button within the clip to select the button. (If you find that you keep selecting the `txtArtistName` text field accidentally, lock it by single-clicking it and then choosing Modify > Arrange > Lock.) The Actions panel should show the `on(rollOver)` code that you added in the last chapter.

5. Add an `gotoAndPlay()` call to the `on(rollOver)` block, as shown in Listing 3.1.

6. Add an `on(rollOut)` block with a second `gotoAndPlay()` call, as also shown in Listing 3.1.

LISTING 3.1   ActionScript Code Attached to the `ArtistButton` Instance in `ArtistButtonClip`

```
on(rollOver) {
  _parent.mcArtistWidgetLoader.mcArtistDisplay.loadArtist(this.idArtist);
  _parent.gotoAndPlay(1);
}

on(rollOut) {
  _parent.gotoAndPlay(11);
}
```

The first `gotoAndPlay()` command tells the Flash Player to begin the first animation you created in the last section (the one that begins at Frame 1) when the user hovers the mouse over the button. As a result, the user will see the artist's details slide into view. When the timeline gets to Frame 10, the `stop()` command you added to that frame causes the details to remain stationary as long as the user keeps his or her mouse hovered over the button.

The second `gotoAndPlay()` command will be executed when the user moves the mouse back out of the button region. This causes the Flash Player to move to the beginning of the second animation (the one that slides the details out of view) and then play it. After the details have slid out of view, the timeline is stopped once again by the `stop()` command you added to Frame 20.

Note that we need to use the `_parent` keyword to target the timeline that we want to control. The `_parent` keyword always contains a reference to the `MovieClip` object that represents the movie that the current clip is sitting within. Because this `ArtistButtonClip` is sitting directly within the main document, `_parent` refers to the main timeline. If we left out the `_parent` keyword, the `gotoAndPlay()` call would be referring to the `ArtistButtonClip`'s own timeline.

At this point, you can go ahead and test the movie. As you roll over the button for each artist, their details slide into view; when you move the mouse away, the details slide back out of view. This gives the user a sense of something being retrieved. In one sense, the animation is a mere flourish. In another sense, it's a visual cue that something is happening and that the information being presented is current. It also reinforces the (usually subconscious) notion that the user is drilling further into your data.

Jumping to Frames by Name Rather Than by Number

In the last section, you added `gotoAndPlay()` calls that advanced playback to key frames in the movie. You specified the desired frames by number (1 and 11). If you want, you can name the frames that are important to you; you can then use the name with the `gotoAndPlay()` or `gotoAndStop()` commands listed in Table 3.1. To try this out, do the following:

1. In the main document timeline, create a new layer called Labels, under the existing Actions layer.

2. Select Frame 1 in the new layer, and then set the Frame Label field in the Properties panel to **slideDetailsIn**.

3. Add a keyframe at Frame 11 in the new layer, and then set its Frame Label field to **slideDetailsOut** (see Figure 3.7).

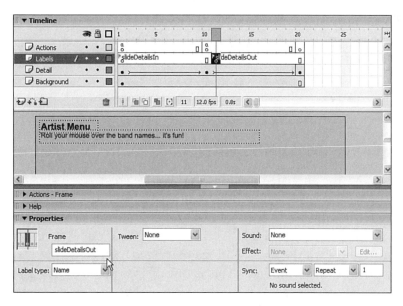

FIGURE 3.7 Giving a frame a label so it can be referred to by name.

4. In the ActionScript code for the `ArtistButton` in the `ArtistButtonClip` movie clip, change the reference to Frame 1 to `"slideDetailsIn"` and change the 11 to `"slideDetailsOut"`. The code should now look like Listing 3.2.

LISTING 3.2 Using Named Frame Labels Rather Than Frame Numbers

```
on(rollOver) {
  _parent.mcArtistWidgetLoader.mcArtistDisplay.loadArtist(this.idArtist);
  _parent.gotoAndPlay("slideDetailsIn");
}

on(rollOut) {
  _parent.gotoAndPlay("slideDetailsOut");
}
```

The behavior of the movie has not changed. However, the use of frame labels can make your ActionScript code easier to follow and maintain. If, say, you decide that you want to have the sliding-out motion begin at Frame 30 instead of Frame 10, you wouldn't have to remember each place within the movie where the frame was referred to by number. As long as you keep the names consistent, your movie can continue to function properly even if the durations or positions of your animated effects change.

> **NOTE**
>
> By the way, there is no rule which says that you must place frame labels in a layer named Labels, or in a separate layer at all. Many people recommend keeping all frame-resident ActionScript code in a layer called Actions, and all labels in a layer named Labels, but other people prefer to keep labels and actions in the same layers as their visual elements. You are free to use as many separate layers for non-visual elements as you wish. Only layers that contain visual elements have any bearing on how the movie looks and behaves at runtime.

Easing the Tweened Motion for a More Natural Effect

Right now, the animated motions that you've created are always moving at the same, constant speed. There's nothing wrong with this, but you might want to experiment with *easing* the motions. You can tell Flash to ease a motion *in* or *out*. If a motion is eased in, that means that the motion starts off slowly and speeds up toward the end. Motions that have been eased out start quickly and slow down toward the end. (This is one of those times when a picture is worth a thousand words; easing is hard to explain but easy to understand after you see it happening.) Often, motions that have been eased have a sense of naturalness to them that just feels right.

To experiment with easing, try the following:

1. On the main timeline, double-click Frame 1. This should select all the frames of the first animation (Frame 1 through Frame 9).

2. In the Properties panel, set the Ease field to 100. The word "Out" appears next to the Ease field to indicate that you have eased the motion out.

3. Now double-click Frame 10 (selecting the frames of the second animation), and then set the Ease field to –100. The word "In" appears next to the Ease field.

When you test your movie now, you'll notice that the motions have a smoother, less machine-like feel to them. Go ahead and experiment with using different ease values for the two motions, just to give yourself a sense of how they affect the feel of the movie.

Deciding Which Frame to Jump to at Runtime

Right now, the sliding-in motion always starts at Frame 1, and the sliding-out motion always starts at Frame 11. This is fine as long as the user keeps the mouse hovered over the button until the sliding-in motion is completed. However, if the user rolls the mouse away from the button before the details have slid in, the fact that the details "jump" straight to the beginning of the easing-out motion seems kind of strange.

Flash provides three properties that provide information about frames and frame numbers (see Table 3.2). You can use these properties for lots of different things. We'll use two of them now to make the sliding-out motion seem less jumpy.

TABLE 3.2   MovieClip Properties Related to Frames and Frame Numbers

PROPERTY	DESCRIPTION
_currentframe	Returns the number of the current frame.
_totalframes	Returns the number of frames in the movie or movie clip.
_framesloaded	Indicates the number of frames that have been loaded. Flash is capable of starting a movie's playback before it has been completely downloaded. This property is commonly used to create reloaders or progress meters that display while a movie is loading.

Right now, your on(rollOut) block looks like this:

```
on(rollOut) {
  _parent.gotoAndPlay("slideDetailsOut");
}
```

Try changing the code to the following:

```
on(rollOut) {
  _parent.gotoAndPlay(_parent._totalframes - _parent._currentframe + 1);
}
```

Now, when you test the movie, you should see that the sliding motions behave more intuitively. If you let the details slide all the way in, then _currentframe is 10 when you decide to roll your mouse out of the button region. Because the total number of frames in the main timeline is 20, the expression within the parentheses evaluates to 11 (20–10+1), which is what you were using before. If you decide to roll your mouse out somewhere in the middle of the sliding-in motion (say, at Frame 4), the expression returns the corresponding frame from the sliding-out part of the animation (Frame 17).

NOTE

It's possible to use this simple math because of the way we set up the animations; because they are "mirrored" around a center frame (Frame 10), it's easy to determine which frame is the counterpart of the other. Other situations might require slightly more complicated math, but the basic idea is clear: you can use _currentframe to determine where the timeline is at any given moment and act accordingly.

Just as before, it's important to include the _parent keyword when referring to the _totalframes and _currentframe properties. If not, they return frame information from the perspective of the current timeline (the ArtistButtonClip, which has only one frame).

Understanding More About Buttons

In Chapter 2, you created simple buttons that display information about individual artists. As it stands, the buttons are extremely simple. I'd like to show you a little more about them so that you can better understand the buttons that you'll find later in this book (and in the wild).

> **NOTE**
>
> The information in this section pertains to button symbols that you create yourself, and which are listed as button symbols in the Library. Flash MX 2004 also includes a separate Button component, which looks like the buttons found in modern operating systems. The Button component is used in several of the examples from the final chapters of this book.

Changing a Button's Appearance on Rollover

Flash makes it very easy to create buttons that change appearance when the user moves the mouse over them. When creating pages with normal HTML, such buttons are usually created by making two versions of an image—the button in its normal state and the button in its hovered-over state—and then switching between the two images through JavaScript. This practice can occasionally be wasteful or a pain to maintain, especially if many such buttons are on your pages.

Flash's built-in concept of a button includes not two but three visual states: the normal state, the hovered-over state, and the pressed-down state. If you want the appearance of the button to change when rolled over or pressed, you can make the change directly in the Flash IDE.

To add rollover and pressed visuals to your Flash document, do the following:

1. Enter Symbol Edit mode for the `ArtistButton` symbol. (Remember that there are several different ways to enter the mode. For instance, you can double-click the symbol in the Library panel, or you can choose ArtistButton from the Edit Symbols drop-down menu on the edit bar above the Stage.)

2. Look at the Timeline panel. You'll notice that the timeline looks a little different when you're editing a button (as opposed to the main document or a movie clip). The part on the left, where the layers are visible, looks the same. However, the part on the right shows only four special frames: Up, Over, Down, and Hit (see Figure 3.8).

3. Right-click the Over frame and choose Insert Keyframe. Flash marks the frame with gray shading and a black dot to indicate that it's now a keyframe (a frame that has content different from the frame that preceded it). Flash also copies the button shape from the first frame—that is, the Up frame—into the new Over keyframe. You can change or decorate this version of the shape in any way you see fit—the Flash player shows it when the user hovers the mouse over the button.

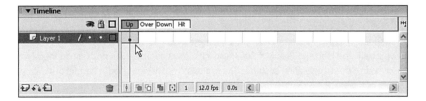

FIGURE 3.8   The special button version of the timeline.

4. Choose a color from the Fill Color palette on the Tools panel. It doesn't matter what color you use for this exercise, though it's pretty traditional to use a color that is a bit lighter than the button's normal state.

5. Select the Paint Bucket tool from the Tools panel, and then click once on your button to change its interior to the new color (see Figure 3.9). Go ahead and experiment with different colors if you wish.

FIGURE 3.9   Changing the rolled-over appearance of a button.

6. Repeat Steps 3–5, this time for the Down frame rather than the Over frame. This is the version of the button's appearance that is shown when a user actually clicks the button. Again, use whatever colors make sense for you.

When you test the example now, you will find that it has the same basic functionality as it did before, except that the buttons for each artist change color.

> **NOTE**
>
> You aren't limited to changing only the color of your button. You can change its size or shape, decorate it with other shapes or images, and add animated movie clips to the Over or Down frames.

Button Events

Now that your button does something special (changes color) when clicked, it would make sense to have something actually happen when a user clicks the button for an artist. Take a moment to glance at Table 3.3. It shows the different events that you can respond to when working with buttons. You have already worked with the onRollOver and onRollOut events, back when you created the `on(rollOver)` and `on(rollOut)` blocks on the `ArtistButton` symbol (refer back to Listing 3.2). In a moment, you can use the `onRelease` event to handle a button click.

TABLE 3.3   Button Events

EVENT	DESCRIPTION
onDragOut	Occurs when the user attempts to start dragging the button.
onDragOver	Occurs when the user attempts to drag something over the button.
onKeyUp	Occurs when the user types (that is, presses and then releases) a key on the keyboard. The button must have the input focus for this event to fire. See the Flash documentation for details.
onKillFocus	Occurs when a button loses focus. See the Flash documentation for details.
onPress	Occurs when the user presses a button (that is, when the user clicks the mouse while hovering over it). If you want the button to perform some kind of action, it is usually more appropriate to use the `onRelease` event rather than this event.
onRelease	Occurs when the user presses and then releases a button. This is usually the event that you want to use to handle what would normally be considered a click.
onReleaseOutside	Occurs when the user presses a button, but then moves the mouse somewhere else before releasing it.
onRollOut	Occurs when the user rolls the mouse out of the button region.
onRollOver	Occurs when a user hovers over the region defined by the Up state of a button (or the Hit state if it's bigger, as discussed in the next section).

Let's say you want to use the buttons for each artist as a sort of navigation tool, providing a way for users to get to non-Flash pages that exist elsewhere on your server. You basically want the button to take the user to a traditional detail-showing type of page, with the ID number of the selected artist included as a URL parameter. In other words, you want the buttons to continue to behave as they are when hovered over, but you want them to behave like normal HTML links when clicked.

To add this simple navigation functionality to the buttons, just do the following:

1. Get yourself to the rollover/rollout code that's attached to the `ArtistButton` instance within the `ArtistButtonClip` movie clip. (Enter Symbol Edit mode for the clip, and then click once on the button.)

2. Add the following `on(release)` block below the `on(rollOver)` and `on(rollOut)` blocks you already have:

```
on(release) {
 var pageUrl = "artistPage.jsp?idArtist=" + escape(this.idArtist);
 getURL(pageUrl, "_blank");
}
```

This particular `on(release)` block handles the button's `onRelease` event; whenever a user clicks this button, any code within the block is executed. Within the block, a string variable called `pageURL` is created. It contains the URL to which the browser should navigate. Flash's `getURL()` function is then used to load the specified page into a new browser window.

You haven't seen the `getURL()` function before, but for now, it's enough to know that you can pass it two arguments, which are basically identical to the first two arguments of the `window.open()` method you use when opening a new window with JavaScript. The first argument is the URL of the page to load, and the second argument (which is optional) is the window-target name that tells the browser whether to open the page in a new window, the current window, or some other window. Here, the "magic" window-target name of `_blank` is used, which means that a new browser window is opened each time the user clicks an artist's button.

You can use the same "magic" window-target names in Flash as you do in HTML. That is, you can use `_blank` to open a new window for every click, `_self` to replace the current browser document with the new URL (which of course means the Flash movie on the current page disappears), `_parent` to target the parent frame, or `_top` to target the outermost frame ("breaking out" of all nested framesets). If you use any other name, a new browser window is opened upon the first click and reused thereafter. Consult any HTML reference or guide for details if this is unfamiliar to you.

You are free to share the same window-target names between your Flash interfaces and your HTML pages; your browser will behave as expected. For instance, you might have already set up a frameset where one of the frames is named `artistFrame` (that is, the `<frame>` tag has a `NAME="artistFrame"` attribute). If you use `"artistFrame"` as the second attribute for `getURL()` in Flash, the requested page appears within the existing frame rather than in a new browser window.

> **NOTE**
>
> Window-target names are case-sensitive, both in the context of HTML pages and in Flash. Make sure to use consistent capitalization throughout.

If you test your movie now by publishing your movie and trying it out in a browser, you will find that you can click a button and be taken to the detail page for the corresponding artist. (Actually, you get a 404 error from your server because we haven't created an artistPage.jsp page, but you get the idea. The page could be written with JSP, ASP.NET, ColdFusion, or anything else, and it would use the passed-in `idArtist` parameter from the URL to look up any needed artist information from the database.) Of course, you are free to use just about any ActionScript code that you want within an `on(release)` block. You aren't restricted to using `getURL()` only.

Invisible Buttons and the Hit Frame

You just learned how to use the Over and Down frames to create different looks for your buttons when the user hovers over or clicks them. What about that other frame, marked Hit (refer back to Figure 3.8)? The Hit frame is generally used to create invisible "hot spots" that respond to mouse hovers or clicks. This enables you to create buttons that appear activated when the user hovers the mouse *near* the visual button, rather than right over it, or to create buttons that aren't visible at all but that still respond to mouse actions.

Try the following:

1. Go back into Symbol Edit mode for the `ArtistButton` symbol.
2. Right-click the Hit frame and choose Insert Keyframe.
3. With the Hit frame still selected in the timeline, double-click the button shape so that its border and fill are selected.
4. Right-click the button shape and choose Free Transform. Use the black handles at the corners to stretch the shape out so that it's somewhat bigger than it was before. If you want, you can compare the shape in the Hit frame with the other frames by clicking the frames in the timeline.

If you test the movie now, you will find that the buttons look exactly the same as before. However, the amount of space on the screen that is actually "hot"— that causes the onRollOver and onRollOut events to fire—is now defined by what's in the Hit frame instead of what is actually visible (that is, what is in the Up frame). Go ahead and experiment with the Hit frame for a while. For instance, try the following:

- Draw some strange shapes in the Hit frame, and then test the movie. You'll find that the shape of the "hot spot" for the button is the same as the shapes you add to the Hit frame.

- Make the shapes in the Hit frame smaller than the other frames. You'll find that *only* the part of the button that has something in the Hit frame is "hot." In other words, when there is a Hit frame, it defines the shape of the button. The normal Up frame is just decoration.

- Delete the Hit frame altogether by right-clicking it in the timeline and choosing Remove Frames. Re-insert it by choosing Insert Keyframe; it should now contain the same shape as the other frames again. Now go to the Up, Over, and Down frames and delete all shapes from each of them. The buttons are now completely invisible to the eye—only the name of each artist is shown, without a surrounding shape—but they behave just as they did before. (Note that you might have to change the text color of the txtArtistName text field in the ArtistButtonClip movie clip so that you can see the artist names.)

Understanding More About Movie Clips

As you are learning, movie clips are extremely important to all types of Flash work, be it design, animation, or application development. You are going to get a whole chapter about movie clip nuances soon enough (Chapter 5), but I'd like to take some time here to flesh out some of the movie clip concepts you were introduced to in Chapter 2.

The Main Timeline Versus Movie Clip Timelines

Flash has a few concepts that are simple and easy to understand, while at the same time being somewhat tricky to explain. Some of these slightly tricky concepts are the relationships between the various timelines involved during the playback of a SWF. They are as follows:

- Every Flash movie (SWF) has its own timeline, generally referred to as the *main timeline*. By default, a movie automatically starts playing when it first appears in the Flash Player.

- Every movie clip within the SWF also has its own timeline, which plays independently of the main timeline. The movie clips might also contain other movie clips, which also have their own, independent timelines.

- Each timeline can be controlled with ActionScript commands such as `gotoAndPlay()` and `stop()`.

- Each timeline also has its own variable scope. Variables set in one timeline are not visible in another timeline without using a target path (details are in the next section, "Target Paths, Parents, and Children").

- The speed at which all timelines move along is determined by the main document's *frame rate*. The default frame rate is 12 frames per second (fps), meaning that the Flash Player attempts to advance to the next frame every 1/12th of a second. You can set the frame rate for each SWF by choosing Modify > Document and then entering a new number in the Frame Rate field.

NOTE

You can make your animations move twice as smoothly by doubling the frame rate and doubling the number of frames over which each motion is tweened.

If the user is using a slow or strained computer, or if the movie hasn't yet finished downloading, there might be a longer delay than 1/12th of a second (or whatever you choose) between some frames. This occurs because Flash never skips frames that contain code to maintain the correct frame rate. Flash considers each code-containing frame to be critical, the content of which absolutely must be displayed or executed, even if that means that the movie takes more time to be displayed than was intended.

This is in opposition to most streaming video formats, for instance, which do just the opposite. They discard frames of video as needed to play back the content at the requested speed. To put it another way, the frame rate for a Flash movie is really the maximum or requested frame rate. The actual frame rate is whatever the Flash Player can pull off at runtime. In practice, most computers don't have much of a problem with reasonable frame rates.

Timelines as State Mechanisms

I like to think of the timeline as a conceptual container for the current *state* of a movie or movie clip. You are probably used to thinking about the notion of state when working with your server-side environment. For instance, most servers provide the notion of session state that gives you a mechanism for associating variables with individual client sessions. Each session gets its own local variable scope, which can be thought of as its own memory space within your server. Depending on the server, the session state also includes a bit of metadata, such as when the session is scheduled to time out. So, in plain English, the session state is a record of what the session is currently up to.

Each timeline within a SWF can be thought of in a similar way: as the current state of the movie or movie clip. In this context, *state* means what the movie or movie clip is up to (that is, its current status). For movies and movie clips, the state information includes the current values of the variables in its local variable scope. The state also includes the current frame number and whether the movie or movie clip is currently playing. You can mess around with a movie or movie clip's state by controlling the timeline with ActionScript commands such as stop() and gotoAndPlay(), or by setting variables in the timeline's local scope.

> **NOTE**
>
> Another term that comes to mind when you are thinking about state is persistence. Flash supports something called a local shared object, which is conceptually similar to the cookies you know and love (or hate) from straight web page development. For details, see Chapter 10, "Flash and Sessions."

Target Paths, Parents, and Children

Every Flash movie represents a tree-like hierarchy of individual movies. You can think of this hierarchy as being somewhat like a set of nested folders on a computer's drive. At the very least, every SWF contains at least the main timeline, which we can think of as being at the root level of the hierarchy. Within the main timeline, there might be any number of movie clips, and any of those movie clips might themselves contain more movie clips, and so on.

Take a look at Figure 3.10. It shows the hierarchy of movies and movie clips (or, if you prefer, the hierarchy of timelines) within the artistMenu.fla example that was created in Chapter 2. You dealt with this hierarchy implicitly all throughout Chapter 2, but you might not have envisioned it as a tree-like structure.

This figure is no great revelation. It simply reflects the fact that there are two movie clip instances on the Stage in the main timeline: mcArtistWidgetLoader (b) and mcArtistButton (e). The mcArtistWidgetLoader clip (b) exists only to load the artistWidget.swf movie, which in turn contains one movie clip on its stage: mcArtistDisplay (c), which in turn includes another clip called mcPhotoLoader (d).

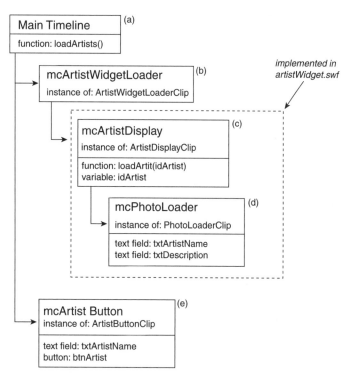

FIGURE 3.10   Clip/timeline hierarchy in artistMenu.fla from Chapter 2.

What the figure should make clear is the implicit parent/child relationship between the various timelines participating in the completed SWF. The two clips within the main timeline (`mcArtistWidgetLoader` and `mcArtistButton`) can be called *children* of the main timeline. Each child, of course, has the main timeline as its *parent*.

If, for whatever reason, you want to refer to one movie clip from ActionScript code in another clip, you need to use a *target path* to specify which clip you want to access or control. If the clip to which you want to refer is a child of the clip for which you are writing the ActionScript code, you can refer to it by its instance name. On the other hand, if the clip to which you want to refer is a parent of the clip for which you are writing the ActionScript code, you can refer to it with its built-in `_parent` property. The `_parent` property is similar conceptually to using `../` in relative URL paths.

If you want to refer to the `loadArtists()` function in (a) from ActionScript code in (d), you could use the following:

```
_parent._parent._parent.loadArtists();
```

To refer to the `txtArtistName` text field in (e) from (d), you could use this:

```
_parent._parent._parent.mcArtistButton.txtArtistName.text;
```

You can also use absolute paths by referring to the `_root` keyword, which holds a reference to the main timeline. Here are some examples:

```
_root.loadArtists();
_root.mcArtistButton.txtArtistName.text;
```

Many people advise against the use of absolute paths (`_root`) over relative paths (`_parent`), even if it means a bit more typing. The reasoning is the same as when considering absolute versus relative paths in URLs. The use of relative paths generally leads to more portable code that can be reused without modification.

However, code that uses `_root` is often easier to read, write, and maintain. The proof is in the pudding: the `_root` lines are much shorter than their `_parent`-based equivalents in the snippets you just looked at. Therefore, there are just as many people that favor this approach to targeting movie clip timelines.

It's possible to create individual documents that make either approach seem easier to work with. In the end, you will just have to use common sense when deciding which approach to use in your Flash projects. In general, relative paths are more impervious to changes in the movie clip hierarchy within a movie, and more exchangeable with other documents without modifications—in other words, they are usually more cleanly abstracted. However, absolute paths are often easier to work with in practice, especially when a document's clip hierarchy is complex.

> **NOTE**
>
> Certain (relatively unusual) circumstances exist in which you might want the `_root` keyword to refer to the main timeline in a given SWF file, even if it has been loaded into another SWF through `loadMovie()`. For instance, you might want to be able to refer to `_root` from within (d) in Figure 3.10 and have it return a reference to (c) instead of to (a). Flash 2004 provides a new `_lockroot` property to address this kind of situation. See the Flash documentation for details about `_lockroot`.

A Few Words About the *this* Keyword

In Chapter 2, you added code that used the `this` keyword to refer to a number of different objects in ActionScript code. The `this` keyword behaved differently according to its context, as follows:

- In the `on(rollOver)` block for the `ArtistButton` instance within `ArtistButtonClip`, `this` was used to refer to the clip's `idArtist` variable (which had been set previously as the XML data about artists that was retrieved from the server).

- In the `on(change)` block for the spin control that was used temporarily in the first example, `this` was used to refer to the current value of the control.

- When responding to the `onLoad` event of the XML object used to retrieve artist information from your server, the `this` keyword was used to refer to the XML object that was doing the retrieving.

- To set up a responder function for the `onLoad` event of the artistMenu movie, `this` was used to refer to the `MovieClip` object that represents the main timeline.

The `this` keyword always refers to the current object, whatever that might be. In code that responds to an event, `this` refers to whatever object fired the event. In other code attached to a frame of a timeline, this refers to the `MovieClip` object that represents the associated movie or movie clip. You can also use `this` to refer to instances of custom objects that you create yourself. You will learn more about `this` in Chapter 4 and Chapter 5.

Movie Clip Events

In Chapter 2, you created a function called `onThisMovieLoaded()` that was then assigned to the `onLoad` event of the main timeline. This causes the `onThisMovieLoaded()` function to execute when the SWF first loads into the Flash Player at runtime. The code within the function performs whatever tasks are necessary to set up the movie for display, such as loading external SWFs into movie clips and fetching an initial chunk of data from the server.

ActionScript's `MovieClip` object provides a number of events, all of which you learn about in Chapter 5. Here's a quick sampling, just to give you an idea:

- `onLoad`, which fires when a SWF is first loaded by the Flash Player. You saw this event in use in Chapter 2.

- `onSetFocus`, which fires when a movie clip receives the input focus. One way a clip would receive the input focus is when the user selects an editable text field.
- `onRollOver`, `onRollOut`, `onRelease`, and other mouse-related events that are similar to the button events listed in Table 3.2.

Understanding What Components Are

In Chapter 2, you used a `NumericStepper` component to create a spin control on the Stage that the user could use to scroll through artists. You will learn more about components in Chapter 11. For now, consider the following:

- Components are special movie clips that encapsulate some kind of functionality. The functionality is usually visual in nature, but some components (such as the `DataHolder` and `WebServiceCall` components) are not visible at runtime.
- Because components are movie clips, you must use `_parent` when handling a component event to refer to the movie or movie clip in which the component is sitting.
- Flash 2004 comes with a number of handy components pre-installed. Many of these components mimic—and extend—the functionality of HTML forms controls (drop-down lists, option buttons, and so on).
- You can download and install other components from the Macromedia Flash Exchange site or from third parties. Once installed, the components appear in the Components panel along with the ones that ship with Flash 2004. To install new components, you use the Macromedia Extension Manager application (version 1.6 or later), which is available for free download from `www.macromedia.com`. The Extension Manager is simple and straightforward to use.

You can also create your own components that you can reuse in your own Flash projects or distribute or sell to other people. As of Flash MX 2004, components can be compiled so that other people can't edit them in the Flash IDE.

Moving On

Chapter 1, "Getting Acquainted with Flash," introduced you to what Flash is all about and took you on a quick tour of the Flash IDE. Chapter 2 walked you through the creation of a simple UI interface for viewing data fetched from the server in the form of plain text and XML. This current chapter fleshed out some of the ideas that were mentioned in passing during Chapter 2 while adding some visual feedback in the form of rollovers and animations.

The good news is that you're now done with the "crash course in Flash" part of this book. The bad news, of course, is that you're done with the "crash course in Flash" part of this book because things get more complicated from here on out.

The intention for these chapters was to get you to learn by example about the basic concepts that you are most likely to need when making the move from server-only development to server-and-Flash development. Of course, you don't know everything that someone who has been using Flash for years knows, but you should know enough not to be totally lost in the Flash IDE. In addition, if you find yourself in a cocktail-party conversation about symbols, timelines, and movie clips, you'll at least be able to follow what everyone is saying.

From this point forward, our examples become more sophisticated and interesting, and there will be less discussion of basic concepts and fewer step-by-step instructions. Of course, I'll help you understand where to look and what to look for in each example.

Summary

This chapter has fleshed out some of the concepts that were introduced while you were building your first two Flash interfaces in Chapter 2. In particular, you learned about the relationship of the Library panel to a movie's symbols, and the relationship of the timeline to a movie's variables. This chapter also explained how to use some additional Flash features to dress up Chapter 2's examples a bit. Specifically, you learned to create animations with the timeline—as well as buttons that respond visually to mouse events such as rollovers.

Chapters 4 and 5 will continue to flesh out your understanding of Flash by focusing on two of its most important facets: ActionScript and movie clips. You can them move on into Chapters 6–9, each of which focuses on integrating Flash with your server using a different means of communication (plain text variables, XML, Flash Remoting, and Web Services).

PART II
KEY FLASH CONCEPTS
FROM A DEVELOPER'S
PERSPECTIVE

4   ActionScript: A Primer   115

5   Movie Clips as Objects   181

CHAPTER 4

ACTIONSCRIPT: A PRIMER

In Chapter 2, "Your First Flash Interface," and Chapter 3, "Digging a Bit Deeper," you created a few different Macromedia Flash interfaces that get information from your server and present that information to your users. At a high level, that's what this book is all about. As you have learned, the scripting language you use to program your movie—to tell it to talk to your server, for instance, or to manipulate what appears on the Stage—is called ActionScript. It's the only language that the Flash Player understands, so you need to know it reasonably well.

This chapter is where we talk about ActionScript as a language. It's not so much about what you can *do with* ActionScript—heck, the whole rest of this book is about what you can do with it. This chapter is more about *how* you do things with ActionScript—what the syntax is, what the rules are, and so on.

NOTE

Look, I'm going to be dead honest with you here. Depending on your background, you might find this chapter to be a complete bore. Please feel free to skip ahead if you don't feel like reading this stuff right now. Just know that it's here to come back to if you get confused about the language, its semantics, how objects or variables behave, or how class or object inheritance works.

About ActionScript

This section provides you with a brief history of the ActionScript language, its relationship to other languages such as JavaScript, and what's new in the most recent version of the language: ActionScript 2.0. Again, I'm going to be talking mostly about ActionScript as a language, not about the fancy tricks you can pull off with it.

Hmm…what exactly do I mean by all this "ActionScript as a language" talk, anyway? Well, when you're using ActionScript, you're almost always working with two different, but related, sets of concepts:

- **First, there's the language itself.** This includes the statements and keywords you can use, such as `if` and `for` and `function`; the operators you can use, such as `*` for multiplication and `==` for testing equality; the datatypes available to you, such as `String` and `Date`; and the way variables are declared and behave.
- **Second, there are the objects you can control with the language.** In Flash, the most important and interesting object classes are the ones—such as `MovieClip` and `Button`—that affect the movie visually at runtime. Of course, there are lots of other interesting objects that don't represent themselves visually, such as `XML` and `LoadVars`.

If you want, think about the first bullet (the language itself) as being like one of those generic, all-purpose remote controls that can be used to control just about any kind of stereo or TV or VCR. Think about the second bullet (the runtime objects) as the devices you happen to own that can be controlled by the remote. Flash provides access to a certain set of objects (in this analogy, the objects are "devices" such as `MovieClip`, `Button`, `TextField`, and so on), but in the future, it might provide access to more objects. As long as the devices know how to respond to the remote control (ActionScript, the language), you don't have to get a new remote.

Okay, the analogy isn't perfect, but you get the idea. *What* you control is different from the *means* to control.

> **NOTE**
>
> This kind of distinction used to drive me nuts. I remember—and I'm showing my age here—reading through the beta discussion lists during Netscape 3.0's development and feeling completely irked and dismissed when someone would point out that a particular bug or problem was a JavaScript issue rather than a browser issue, or vice-versa. I had always thought of the browser and JavaScript as being inexorably linked, part and parcel of the same thing. All I knew was that my script wasn't working, and whether the problem was with the "browser" (whatever that was) rather than the "language" (whatever that was), I felt like someone was just splitting hairs. It's similar with ActionScript—it feels a bit strange to talk about it purely as a language, because the only place you ever use it is within the context of Flash. Still, it's interesting to keep the discussion separate (at least for the span of one chapter) because you'll come away with a better understanding of what's happening behind the scenes as you add ActionScript to your Flash projects.

ActionScript's Relationship to JavaScript and ECMAScript

You've already seen a bit of ActionScript code in Chapters 2 and 3, so you know that ActionScript is a lot like JavaScript. The two languages share a great deal—in fact, they can be said to have been derived from a common source. Here's the deal: JavaScript came first, developed by Netscape in the early years of the Web's influence. The JavaScript language was later standardized by a standards body called the European Computer Manufacturers Association (ECMA); the standardized specification for the language is called ECMAScript. (I'm smoothing the history out a bit here, but you get the basic idea.)

Today, there are a number of different languages that can be said to implement the ECMAScript standard. The most obvious, of course, continues to be JavaScript, which is used mostly in browsers such as Netscape and Opera (although it is also used in a number of other products). Another ECMAScript-based language (historical and compliance details notwithstanding) is Microsoft's JScript language, which is used in Internet Explorer browsers and can also be used in ASP, ASP.NET, and other scriptable products from Microsoft. In addition, we have ActionScript, which is Macromedia's own implementation and is currently used only in the context of Flash SWFs. In practice, the languages are mostly equivalent.

> **NOTE**
>
> Interestingly enough, you can actually use JavaScript (not ActionScript) to script the Flash IDE. This scripting capability is new in Flash MX 2004, and will be of most interest to creators of third-party add-ins for Flash. That said, you can also use the IDE-scripting functionality to create macro-like scripts for automating certain common tasks. This topic is outside the scope of this book, so you will need to consult the Flash documentation for details. Run a quick search for "jsfl" within the Help panel to get started.

A Brief History

Very briefly, ActionScript's history is as follows:

- In version 4 (and earlier versions) of Flash, there was no language called ActionScript. Instead, there was a very basic means to add *actions* to movies. The actions had names like `play()`, `goto()`, and `duplicateMovieClip()`; those actions are still supported in today's Flash for backward compatibility.

- Version 5 of Flash introduced ActionScript 1.0, which was the first time Flash developers had access to a fully featured, JavaScript-like language for controlling movies. This is when the Flash world started needing to think about things such as objects and methods.

- Version 6 of the Flash Player (the version that coincided with Flash MX) didn't update the ActionScript language itself, although it did continue to place more emphasis on scripting than ever before. A number of new scriptable objects were introduced, some visual and some not. These objects include `LoadVars`, `TextField`, and `Microphone`, to name just a few.

- Version 7 of the Flash Player (the version that coincides with Flash MX 2004) introduced version 2.0 of the ActionScript language. ActionScript 2.0 is Macromedia's implementation of the ECMAScript 4 proposed specification. You'll learn about what ActionScript 2.0 offers you in the next section of this chapter.

What's New in ActionScript 2.0

ActionScript 2.0 is all about adding a bit of rigor to the process of writing script code—in keeping with the current direction of the EMCAScript specification—while maintaining compatibility with ActionScript 1.0. The new language firms up some of the mushier concepts in the original version of ActionScript (or JavaScript, or ECMAScript, or however you want to think about it).

Here's what's new in ActionScript 2.0:

- **A formalized means to create new classes (that is, new types of objects).** It was possible to create new classes—or class-like things—previously, using something called an object prototype. Although the old system worked, it had many shortcomings. ActionScript 2.0 adds an actual `class` keyword, and adds a standard way to keep all the code for a class together in a single file. Each class can have any number of methods and properties, each of which can be public or private. You'll learn more about this in the "Creating your Own Classes" section later in this chapter.

- **Formal implementations of other object-oriented concepts, such as inheritance, packages, and interfaces.** We're not going to discuss interfaces in this book, but you will see plenty of examples of class and object inheritance, and a few examples of class packages (especially in Appendix A, "Notes on Building the `SimpleBarChart` Component"). See the "Inheritance" section later in this chapter for more details.

- **Strict data typing.** You can now declare the data type of any variable, using a simple colon syntax. For instance, instead of declaring a variable called age with `var age`, you can specify that the variable always hold a number using `var age:Number` instead. This allows the compiler to look over your shoulder while you are working, making sure that you are matching the datatypes of variables and function arguments correctly. You'll learn more about strict data typing in the "Variables" section later in this chapter.

In general, you don't have to use any of the new ActionScript 2.0 syntax if you don't want to. If you ignore this stuff, you basically end up writing ActionScript 1.0 code, which is fine. That said, it probably makes sense to go ahead and make use of the new features (especially the support for formal OOP-style classes) when you can. Reason? The resulting code will, in general, be easier to maintain over time.

Making the IDE Work for You

I'd like to take a moment to point out some of the features the Flash IDE provides for making your ActionScript-writing tasks easier and how you can customize it a bit to suit your needs. It's helpful to be aware of the facilities built into the Actions panel; it can improve your quality of life as a coder.

Positioning and Activating the Actions Panel

First of all, I suggest experimenting with using the Actions panel in Floating mode, rather than using it in its default position (docked under the Stage). The default location doesn't leave a whole lot of room to type (see Figure 4.1). You might enjoy the extra space you get by undocking it.

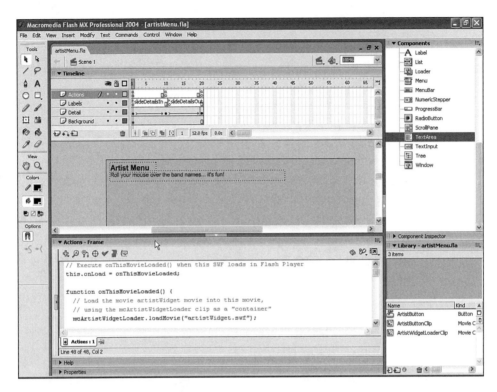

FIGURE 4.1   The default position of the Actions panel leaves it a bit cramped.

Here's how to undock the Actions panel:

1. Make sure the Actions panel is showing; choose Window > Development Panels > Actions if it's not. You can also use F9 as a hotkey for showing/hiding the Actions panel.

2. Using your mouse, grab the Actions panel by its handle (the little dots just to the left of the word "Actions" in the panel's title bar), and drag the panel into the middle of the screen (see Figure 4.2).

3. Resize the Actions panel so that it fills up as much of the screen as you like.

Now the Actions panel will float above the Stage. You can press F9 to make the panel appear and disappear. Soon it will become second nature to press F9 whenever you want to see or hide your code.

If you end up hating this setup, you can always re-dock the panel to its original position or experiment with slightly different setups. In addition, if you find that you like to use different screen configurations for different types of tasks (or at different times of the day, or while listening to different Pink Floyd albums, or whatever), keep in mind that you can save the current panel layout using Window > Save Panel Layout. After it is saved, you can quickly switch to your layout of choice using Window > Panel Sets.

NOTE

If you haven't saved any layouts yet, you can still revert back to the default by using Window > Panel Sets > Default Layout.

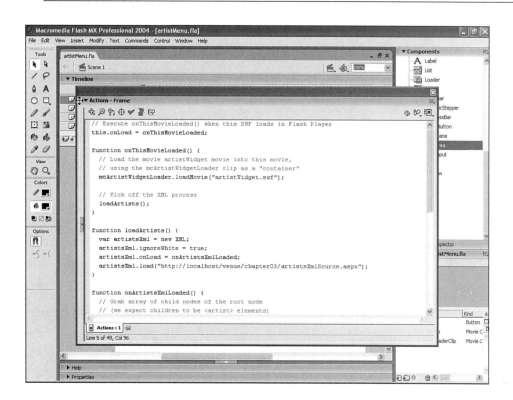

FIGURE 4.2   You have a lot more room to type if you undock the Actions panel.

Actions Panel Tools

The Actions panel includes a number of tools that make it easier to write and maintain your ActionScript code. I'd suggest taking some time to click around, making yourself aware of what the various buttons and menus do. This section points out some of the most helpful features.

Inserting Code

Note the two smaller window areas on the left side of the Actions panel. The one at top left is particularly handy while coding. Part quick-reference guide and part code-typing utility, it shows a tree of all the built-in functions, objects, methods, and other items that you're likely to insert into your code at one time or another. After you've found the item you want, just double-click it to insert the item into your code without having to type it yourself. For instance, say you can't remember what the name of the attachMovie() method is, or you're just not in the mood to type it. Just open the tree to Built-in Classes > Movie > Movie Clip > Methods > attachMovie, and then double-click to insert the method at the current cursor position in the code window (see Figure 4.3). Note that Flash also provides a pop-up code hint in the code window that shows the method's arguments.

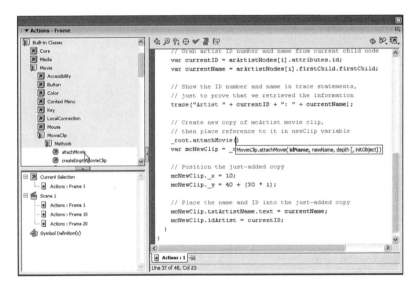

FIGURE 4.3   The reference tree makes it easy to remember and insert items into your code.

The area at bottom left is also handy. You can use it to jump around between frames or movie clips that contain ActionScript code. Open up an existing FLA and play around with this a bit to see how it works.

Except for the figures in this section, this book usually shows the Actions panel with these window areas hidden. That's just to give you a better view of the code in the figures, not because they aren't helpful during development.

You can also use the button marked with a + at the top-left corner of the code window. It provides the same information as the tree shown in Figure 4.3, except as a pop-up menu that doesn't take up any screen real estate. You might want to try hiding the two windows at the left side of the Actions panel (just drag the gray bar that separates them from the actual code window) to give you more space to type in. You can then use the + button to add items to your code (see Figure 4.4).

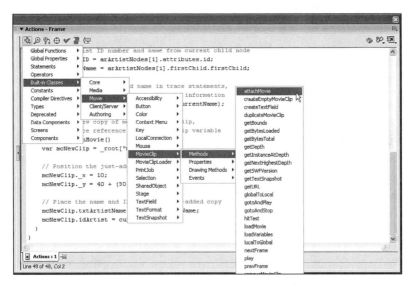

FIGURE 4.4   You can also use this context menu to help you remember and add items to your code.

Other Actions Panel Tool Buttons

Note the six buttons to the right of the + button above the code window (you can see these buttons at the top of Figure 4.4). Take a minute to check them out:

- The Find button is a quick way to get to the Find dialog box. You can also use Ctrl+F as a keyboard shortcut.
- The Replace button takes you to the Replace dialog box, which is used for performing search and replace operations (Ctrl+H is the keyboard shortcut).
- The Target button pulls up the Insert Target Path dialog box, which can sometimes be useful for inserting the name of an item elsewhere in your document (like in another movie clip).

- The Check Syntax button checks your code for syntax errors (or you can use the Ctrl+T keyboard shortcut). Any errors will be shown in the Output panel.

- The Auto Format button will format your code for you, adding or removing indenting and newlines so that all your loops, function blocks, and so on are easy to spot. Note that you can customize how your code gets formatted using the Auto Format Options dialog box (choose Auto Format Options from the context menu at the right edge of the Actions panel's title bar).

- The Show Code Hint button shows a code hint (if available) for the item at the current cursor position, as discussed in the "Using Code Hints" section, which is coming up next.

Using Code Hints

The Flash IDE can provide code hints for you as you type. Similar to the code hint or code-completion features found in other development IDEs, Flash's code hints pop up automatically whenever you're typing something that the Actions panel recognizes. Code hints appear in two different forms:

- If you're typing the name of an object, a drop-down list of methods, properties, and events appears as soon as you type a dot (.) after the object name. Just select the item you want using your mouse or the arrow keys, and then click or press Enter (or Tab) to insert the item into your code (after the dot).

- If you're typing the name of a built-in method (or function), you'll see a yellow hint that shows the names of the method's arguments. You can use this to jog your memory as you type, so you don't have to have the arguments for every function memorized ahead of time.

Both types of code hints appear automatically as you type, after a short delay. You can customize the length of the delay in the Preferences dialog box (see the "Actions Panel Preferences" section for more information).

NOTE

If the hint disappears, you can get it back by pressing Ctrl+T or clicking the Show Code Hint button at the top of the code window.

It's worth noting that the Flash IDE can show the first type of code hint only if it knows the type of object to which you are referring. The next section explains how this works.

Helping the Actions Panel Understand the Types of Your Variables

As I just mentioned, the drop-down list of methods and properties shows up only if you're typing the name of an object that the Flash IDE recognizes. For instance, say you have a variable called mcScroller, which you know will hold a movie clip instance at runtime. It would be nice if the Flash IDE could show the drop-down list of MovieClip members whenever you type the name of this variable. There are three different ways to make this happen, as explained in the next three sections.

Through Strict Variable Typing

The first way is to use ActionScript 2.0's strict variable typing to explicitly declare the type of the variable. For instance, if you put the following line at the top of whatever code or function on which you're working, the design-time Flash IDE will know that mcScroller represents a MovieClip at runtime. You would put this line anywhere a var declaration makes sense (as discussed in the "Variables" section later in this chapter):

```
var mcScroller:MovieClip;
```

Through Naming Conventions

The second way for the Actions panel to know the types of your variables is for you to use consistent naming conventions. For instance, in this book, I usually use a lowercase mc at the beginning of each variable that represents a movie clip. You can teach the Flash IDE about the naming conventions you like to use, which will give it the datatype information it needs to help you out with code hints and the like.

By default, Flash is configured to recognize certain suffixes at the ends of variable names, according to the naming conventions listed in Table 4.1.

TABLE 4.1   Default Naming Convention Suffixes for Built-In Datatypes

DATA OR OBJECT TYPE	NAMING CONVENTION SUFFIX
MovieClip	_mc
Array	_array
String	_str
Button	_btn
TextField	_textfield
TextFormat	_textformat
Date	_date
Sound	_sound
XML	_xml
XMLNode	_xmlnode
XMLSocket	_xmlsocket
Color	_color
ContextMenu	_cm
ContextMenuItem	_cmi
PrintJob	_pj
MovieClipLoader	_mcl
Error	_err
Camera	_cam
LoadVars	_lv
LocalConnection	_lc
Microphone	_mic
NetConnection	_nc
SharedObject	_so
Video	_video

So, in the default configuration, Flash would be able to provide code hints and other context-sensitive help if your MovieClip variables, for instance, end with the mc suffix. Thus, a variable name of scroller_mc would be recognized as a movie clip by the Actions panel. However, mcScroller, as I would normally name the variable, would not.

If you want to use naming conventions other than what's listed in Table 4.1, you can edit the AsCodeHints.xml file, located in Flash's configuration directory on your machine. If you open this file, you'll see that it includes a `<typeinfo>` element for each suffix shown in Table 4.1. For instance, the entry for `MovieClip` looks like this:

```
<typeinfo pattern="*_mc" object="MovieClip" />
```

The AsCodeHints.xml file is in the ActionsPanel folder of Flash's configuration directory, the location of which depends on the operating system you're using. For instance, on my Windows machine, the file is located at C:\Documents and Settings\Administrator\Application Data\Macromedia\Flash 2004\en\Configuration\ActionsPanel (which happens to be a hidden folder, so you have to choose Tools > Folder Options > View > Hidden files and folders in a Windows Explorer window to see it).

The `pattern` attribute indicates the naming convention, where the asterisk (*) character is a wildcard that represents the rest of the variable name. An asterisk at the beginning means that the pattern is a suffix; an asterisk at the end means that the pattern is a prefix. So, if you want to use `mc` as a prefix for MovieClip variables (as in `mcScroller`), you can add a new `<typeinfo>` line that looks like this:

```
<typeinfo pattern="mc*" object="MovieClip" />
```

> **NOTE**
>
> Like most everything in the world of ActionScript, these prefixes and suffixes are case-sensitive.

For example, I like to add the following lines to my AsCodeHints.xml file, which causes Flash to recognize my array variables if I gave them names such as `arChildren` or `arSlides`, and movie clips as if I gave them names such as `mcScroller` or `mcArtist`:

```
<!-- Custom patterns that I created myself -->
<typeinfo pattern="mc*" object="MovieClip" />
<typeinfo pattern="ar*" object="Array" />
<typeinfo pattern="s*" object="String" />
<typeinfo pattern="m*" object="Number" />
<typeinfo pattern="btn*" object="Button" />
<typeinfo pattern="txt*" object="TextField" />
<typeinfo pattern="d*" object="Date" />
<typeinfo pattern="lv*" object="LoadVars" />
```

```
<typeinfo pattern="xml*" object="XML" />
<typeinfo pattern="xn*" object="XMLNode" />
<typeinfo pattern="ti*" object="TextInput" />
<typeinfo pattern="ds*" object="DataSet" />
<typeinfo pattern="ws*" object="WebServicesConnector" />
```

Through Special Comments

The next way for the Actions panel to know the types of your variables is to place special comments in your code. Just create a single-line comment that indicates the datatype, then the variable name, and then a semicolon. Here are two such comments:

```
// MovieClip myClip;
// Array myArray;
```

After you add such a comment to your code, Flash will be able to provide code hints for the specified variable from that point forward. This method comes in handy when, for whatever reason, you want to give a variable a name that doesn't conform to the usual naming convention and also can't easily be declared with a datatype using the strict variable typing syntax discussed previously.

Actions Panel Preferences

You might want to check out the ActionScript tab of Flash's Preferences dialog box (Edit > Preferences). It provides a number of helpful options for tweaking the behavior of the Actions panel (see Figure 4.5).

For instance, I like to do the following:

- Change the Tab Size to 2 rather than 4, so that indented code doesn't get nested too far away from the left margin.
- Change the Delay for Code Hints to 0 seconds, so that code hints appear right away instead of after a short pause.
- Adjust the Syntax Coloring colors, so that comments and other important items really stand out. In particular, I usually set the color for comments to a bright red. Comments are the most important part of my code, after all (hint, hint).

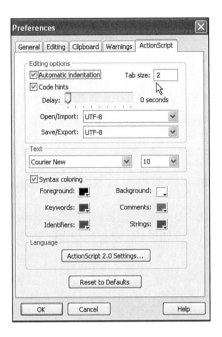

FIGURE 4.5   Flash's ActionScript preferences include helpful options for coding.

The Help Panel

I talked a lot about the Actions panel in this section, but make sure to keep the Help panel in mind too. You can show or hide the Help panel with the F1 key, and you can browse through it in book/chapter form or search it by typing keywords. You'll find a wealth of reference and explanatory information about scripting, working with the drawing tools, creating animations, and more (see Figure 4.6). It's a great place to learn about all the topics that fall outside the purview of this book.

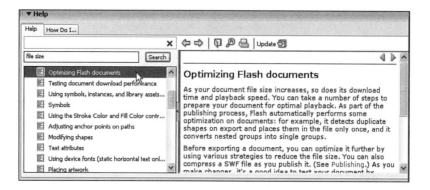

FIGURE 4.6   The Help panel is packed full of great information about using Flash, from both coding and non-coding perspectives.

Basic Language Elements

Okay, now that you've gotten a little bit of the history and background of ActionScript and how to use the tools in the Actions panel to your advantage, it's time to dig right in to the particulars of using ActionScript. This section introduces you to the basic form of the language, such as when to use curly braces and semicolons, how to create loops and conditional statements, and so on.

Using Comments

Comments are as important to ActionScript coding as they are to any type of programming. Sure, they take extra time to write, but it's always worth it to add as many comments to your code as possible while you work. I try to write at least a line's worth of comments for any important line of code. Not only does it make your life easier later, but I personally find that adding them keeps my mind moving, thus speeding up the initial code-writing process as well.

NOTE

Hey, seriously, add comments! Then add some more! I promise you won't ever regret it.

ActionScript supports the same two types of comments that are used in C++, Java, JavaScript, and many other languages:

- Single-line comments, which start with `//` and continue to the end of the line
- Block-style comments, which start with `/*` and end with `*/` and can span any number of lines

The block-style syntax is especially handy for temporarily "commenting out" a block of code.

The first line of the following code is an example of a single-line comment:

```
// This variable contains the current date and time
dCurrentDate = new Date();
```

Here's another example:

```
dCurrentDate = new Date() // Get the current date and time
```

Here's an example of a block-style comment, which might appear at the top of an ActionScript file (especially if the file happened to be written by some self-aggrandizing code geek named Nate Weiss):

```
/*
 GestureMovieClip class: simple "gesture based" scrolling
 Author: Nate Weiss (nate@nateweiss.com)
 Free for commercial, non-commercial, or educational use.
*/
```

Syntax Basics

ActionScript uses curly braces, semicolons, and newlines in the same basic way that other similar-looking languages use them. If you've worked with JavaScript, Java, or C++, you should be in good shape.

Semicolons and Newlines

You can end any line of code with a newline, a semicolon, or both (most people use both). For instance, you would normally put a semicolon and newline after each `var` statement, like so:

```
var age = 34;
var name = "Nate";
```

It's not the usual practice, but you can leave off the semicolons if you wish, like so:

```
var age = 34
var name = "Nate"
```

If, for some reason, you want to put two lines of code on one physical line, you can use semicolons without newlines, like so:

```
var age = 34; var name = "Nate";
```

Curly Braces

Curly braces are used to define blocks of code. They are used in various contexts, whenever a set of code lines should be considered a group. Traditionally, you use them to define loop blocks, conditional blocks, or functions. For instance, here's a conditional block:

```
if (numRecords == 0) {
 txtStatusMessage.text = "No matches found.";
}
```

And here's a function block:

```
function showMessage() {
 if (numRecords == 0) {
  txtStatusMessage.text = "No matches found.";
 }
}
```

You are free to add indentation or newlines as you type your braces. Some people like to place their braces as shown in the preceding code; other people like to put the braces on their own lines, like so:

```
function showMessage()
{
 if (numRecords == 0)
 {
  txtStatusMessage.text = "No matches found.";
 }
}
```

NOTE

The Auto Format Options dialog box provides some options that control whether the braces appear on their own lines, should you decide to have the Flash IDE reformat your code for you. See the "Other Actions Panel Tool Buttons" section earlier in this chapter for more information.

Braces are technically optional when it comes to writing loop and conditional blocks. For instance, the following is perfectly legal, even though no curly braces are used:

```
if (numRecords == 0)
  txtStatusMessage.text = "No matches found.";
```

So is this:

```
if (numRecords == 0) txtStatusMessage.text = "No matches found.";
```

If you leave out the braces, the `if` simply affects the next line of code (which might or might not be on a separate physical line). Any subsequent lines are not affected by the `if` at all; they will always execute, regardless of the conditional statement in question.

By the way, I don't recommend leaving out the braces, because it's easy to get confused about what's going on, and all sorts of seemingly-buggy behavior can result. The curly braces are for your benefit as much as they are for the compiler's.

Whitespace

Aside from the fact that newlines usually appear at the end of a line of code (and, as you just learned, must appear if you don't use semicolons at the ends of your lines), whitespace is of no significance to ActionScript. You can use as many tabs and spaces as you want to indent or organize your code; they will have no effect on runtime behavior or performance.

Variables

As with any type of programming, ActionScript coding relies on the use of variables. It's really easy to use variables in ActionScript because they are as loosely or strongly typed as you want them to be.

Creating Variables and Using the var Keyword

You can create a variable using just its name, an equal sign, and the value that you want to place into the variable, like so:

```
name = "Nate";
```

However, it is almost always preferable to create the variable using the var keyword. Here's an example:

```
var name = "Nate";
```

The var keyword tells ActionScript how you want the variable to be scoped. A var line that appears within a function means that the variable exists only within the context of the function. If you use var outside a function, the variable is scoped globally within the current timeline (that is, the variable exists for all functions and other lines of code that are executed within the context of the current movie or movie clip). On the other hand, if you leave out the var keyword, the variable is always scoped globally throughout the current timeline, regardless of whether the line appears inside or outside a function.

Here's a quick snippet that demonstrates what I'm talking about. Assume that this code is in Frame 1 (or any frame, really) of a Flash movie:

```
// This variable exists throughout the current timeline
var count = true;

function doSomething() {
 // This variable exists only within this function
 var count = 0;

 while (count < 5) {
  count = count + 1;
 }
}
```

There are two separate variables named count here. The first one exists globally for all functions and other lines of code that execute within the context of the current timeline. It's been assigned the Boolean value of true, and is probably meant to represent some kind of option about whether a "hit count" of some kind is meant to be maintained. The second count variable, on the other hand, is local to the doSomething() function, and it is a numeric value that gets incremented in a loop.

With the two `var` lines in place as shown here, the two variables are kept separate. As the `doSomething()` function executes, it does not affect the variable outside the function.

If you were to remove the word `var` from within the function, there would actually be only one variable called `count`. It would start out with the value of `true`, but then as soon as `doSomething()` was called, it would get set to `0`, and then get incremented to `5` as the function executed. Depending on the situation, this could mess up the way the movie behaves, especially if some other code was depending on `count` to hold only a `true` or `false` value. (Will the other code know how to behave properly if it encounters a value of `5`?) This kind of situation is usually called a *name collision*, and it can lead to unpredictable results.

In general, you should always use `var` to identify all variables that get created within a function. Try not to forget the `var`; if you do, you'll accidentally be creating a timeline-scoped variable rather than a function-scoped one. If you need to declare the variable as local, but aren't ready to assign it a value yet, just define it with the `var` keyword and variable name, but leave off the assignment part (that is, the equals sign and value). For instance, the following snippet declares `count` as local to the function with `var`; it then gives it an initial value using conditional logic, and then increments the value in a loop:

```
function doSomething() {
  // This variable exists only within this function
  var count;

  // Later, some kind of condition might set the value:
  if (name = "nate") {
    count = 1;
  } else {
    count = 0;
  }

  while (count < 5) {
    count = count + 1;
  }
}
```

When you declare a variable with `var` but don't give it a value, the variable will hold the special value `null` until you give it another value later. That is, this line:

```
var count;
```

is effectively equivalent to this line:

```
var count = null;
```

Variables and Datatypes

In ActionScript 1.0 (that is, before this release of Flash), all variables were loosely typed. That is, the act of setting a variable to a value implicitly defined its initial datatype, but the datatype could change at any time. For instance, I could define a variable called `myNumber`, which would hold the number 1, like so:

```
var myNumber = 1;
```

Later, I could change the value to "555-1212," which is a string, like this:

```
myNumber = "555-1212";
```

I could even set it to a `MovieClip` instance, using the following line of code. The following line would retrieve whatever clip is at Level 1 in the root time-line, even though the variable name `myNumber` doesn't sound like the variable is going to hold a movie clip:

```
myNumber = _root.getInstanceAtDepth(1);
```

All of this continues to be the case in Flash MX 2004 and Flash Player 7, unless you specify the datatypes of your variables using the new strict variable typing syntax (discussed next).

Strict Variable Typing

ActionScript 2.0 enables you to specify the data type of any variable, using a simple colon syntax. You can use strong typing whenever the datatype—number, string, date, or whatever—isn't going to change as your code does its work. In practice, this means that you can almost always use strong typing if you want to.

The syntax is simple and intuitive. Basically, just put a colon and the desired data type after the variable name as you declare it with `var`, like so:

```
var nyNumber:Number = 1;
```

If you just want to declare the variable and specify its datatype, but don't want to give it a value yet, just leave off the assignment part, like so:

```
var myNumber:Number;
```

Any of the built-in datatypes or class types can be used where the word `Number` appears in the preceding code. We're not going to cover every single one of these in this chapter, but you can learn about the ones you are most likely to encounter in the "Fun With Datatypes" section later in this chapter. Here are some examples that create variables of the `Number`, `String`, and `MovieClip` types:

```
var nMyNumber:Number = 1;
var sMyPhoneNumber:String = "555-1212";
var mcMyScroller:MovieClip;
```

Just like about everything else in ActionScript land, the class or datatype name after the colon is case-sensitive.

The principal benefits of using strict variable typing are as follows:

- It makes your life a bit easier at design time (that is, while you are writing your code) because the Flash IDE will be able to provide you with code hints as you type (see the "Helping the Actions Panel Understand the Types of Your Variables" section earlier in this chapter).
- It makes your code easier to read and maintain by you and other humans. It's like a naming convention policy—except with teeth—because your movie won't compile if you attempt to deviate from the type definitions you've established.

For complete details about the technical benefits of strict variable typing in ActionScript 2.0, see the Flash documentation or the Macromedia website. For our purposes in this book, I use strict typing whenever possible in the examples because it is good coding practice. You can make your own decision about when to use it in your own code.

Conditional Statements

It's hard to imagine any type of programming that doesn't involve `if` and `else` constructs of some kind. ActionScript makes it easy to write `if` and `else` statements that make whatever decisions you need to be made at runtime. You can also use `switch` and `case` statements as an alternative way to choose between a set of different values.

if *and* else *statements*

The `if` statement consists of a condition (between a set of parentheses) and a block of code (between a set of curly braces) that should execute only if the condition is met. Here's an example:

```
if (age > 30) {
  txtStatusMessage.text = "This person can't be trusted!";
}
```

Any `if` statement can be followed by `else`, followed by a block of code that should execute whenever the `if` condition is *not* met. For instance:

```
if (age > 30) {
  txtStatusMessage.text = "This person can't be trusted!";
} else {
  txtStatusMessage.text = "We can trust this person.";
}
```

There is no explicit `elseif` statement, but if you want to evaluate a series of statements, each with their own condition, use an `if` after the `else`, like so:

```
if (age > 30) {
  txtStatusMessage.text = "This person can't be trusted!";
} else if (age <= 16) {
  txtStatusMessage.text = "Too young to sign up.";
} else {
  txtStatusMessage.text = "We can trust this person.";
}
```

It's traditional to always use curly braces when writing an `if` or `else` block, but they are technically optional when there is only one line of code to execute conditionally. In addition, you can indent the braces differently if you wish. See the "Curly Braces" section, earlier in this chapter, for details.

switch *and* case *statements*

Most of your conditional statements will be performed with `if` and `else` statements, but you can sometimes use `switch` and `case` with greater ease. You provide a single expression after the `switch`, then a series of `case` blocks that respond to the various values to which the expression might evaluate.

Each block of case code starts with a colon and ends with the word break, as shown in the next code snippet. You need to end each case block with break, unless you want multiple case blocks to respond to the same value under certain conditions. See the Flash documentation for details.

If you want, you can also provide a default block; it will execute if none of the case blocks turn out to be executed at runtime. It's traditional to put the default block last, but you don't have to. Of course, you might leave out the default block entirely if you don't need it.

Here's an example that assigns different values depending on the value of a fictional variable named personType:

```
switch (personType) {
 case "boss":
  salary = 10;
  salutation = "Dear Sir:";
  break;
 case "coder":
  salary = 5;
  salutation = "Hey, good looking:";
  break;
 case "designer":
  salary = 5;
  salutation = "Hey, you with the cool glasses:";
  break;
 default:
  salary = 0;
  salutation = "[unknown]";
  trace("Unknown person type");
  break;
}
```

The ? and : operators

In many situations, you might find yourself writing if / else code that does just one thing: sets a variable to one value or another depending on a condition. For instance, consider this code:

```
if (firstName == "Nate") {
 myColor = "Purple";
} else {
 myColor = "White";
}
```

In such a case, you can use the special ? and : operators as shorthand, like so:

```
myColor = (firstName == "Nate") ? "Purple" : "White";
```

> **NOTE**
>
> The use of parentheses before the ? is optional, but helps to keep things clear visually.

Expressions

As you've seen, the heart of any `if` statement is the part inside the parentheses, which is the conditional expression to evaluate. You also use expressions when setting variables. The following subsections contain a few details about what you can use in expressions.

Conditional Expressions

Most expressions are made up of three parts: an *operator*, plus items on either side of the operator. Usually, the item on the left side is a variable; the item on the right is usually a constant value or another variable. Here's a list of the most important conditional operators:

- Use == to test for equality.
- Use != to test for inequality.
- Use >= and <= for greater-than or less-than tests.
- Use && to combine two tests using AND logic.
- Use || to combine two tests using OR logic.

The single biggest slip-up many coders (including myself) make is accidentally using a single equal sign (instead of two together) when testing for equality, like so:

```
if (age = 30) {
 txtStatusMessage.text = "Happy thirtieth birthday!";
}
```

Even though it looks correct to our human eyes, this code will not behave as expected because ActionScript always interprets a single equal sign as a request to set a variable, not a request to evaluate a condition. The correct syntax would be this:

```
if (age == 30) {
 txtStatusMessage.text = "Happy thirtieth birthday!";
}
```

Another potential "gotcha" for new ActionScript coders is the fact that you need to use && and || to perform AND and OR operations (as opposed to and or or, neither of which actually exist in the language). Use parentheses to isolate multiple conditions from one another if you need to, like so:

```
if ((gender == "m" && age == 30) || (gender == "f" && age == 36)) {
  txtStatusMessage.text = "Happy thirtieth birthday!";
}
```

Other Operators

There are a whole bunch of other operators that don't make decisions per se. Rather, they perform computations that can be used either to make decisions or to set variables to calculated values.

You can use any of the mathematical operators that you would expect to find in a programming language. Use parentheses to isolate math operations from one another if you need to. Otherwise, rules of operator precedence kick in, which work as they do in algebra or in other programming languages (multiplication is performed before addition and so on). See the ActionScript dictionary in the Flash documentation for details.

Some examples are as follows:

```
var dogYears = humanYears * 7;         // multiply by 7
var dogYears = (humanYears * 7);       // same as above
var dogYears = humanYears * 7 + 1;     // multiply by 7, then add 1
var dogYears = humanYears * (7 + 1);   // multiply by 8
```

true *and* false

ActionScript reserves true and false as keywords, which you can use in conditions. For instance, if you have a Boolean variable called isUnderage, you might use a test like the following:

```
if (isUnderage == true) {
  trace(" This person is underage");
}
```

This statement could also be written as follows:

```
if (isUnderage) {
 trace("This person is underage");
}
```

In either case, the expression inside the parentheses evaluates to true when the person is underage. Some people like the brevity of the second form; others find the explicit reference to true to be more clear. See the Flash documentation for additional details.

null *and* undefined

Two more special keywords are null and undefined, either of which indicate a non-existent, missing, or otherwise "empty" value. If, for instance, you try to refer to a variable that does not exist, the variable will evaluate to undefined.

NOTE

I'm not going to get into the delicate, language-theory semantics of what constitutes a null versus an undefined. Although they are different in theory, they are close to synonymous in practice. For details, see the Flash documentation or the ECMAScript specification.

You can test for undefined using the == or != operators. Here's an example:

```
if (personType == undefined) {
 personType = "normal employee type";
}
```

A variable might, in other situations, evaluate to null. For instance, you might specifically set a variable to null to indicate the lack of a value. For instance, consider the following code:

```
if (personType == undefined) {
 salary = null;
}
```

After a variable has a null value, you can test for it using == or !=, like so:

```
if (salary != null) {
 // Give a 10% raise
 newSalary = salary * 1.10;
}
```

However, `null` and `undefined` are considered equivalent to each other if they are compared with `==` or `!=`, so the following would have the same result:

```
if (salary != undefined) {
 // Give a 10% raise
 newSalary = salary * 1.10;
}
```

> **NOTE**
>
> You might encounter an `undefined` value within the body of one of your own functions. If your function expects an argument, but no argument is provided when the function is called, the value of the argument will be undefined within the body of the function. Similarly, you might explicitly pass `null` to the function if you don't have a specific value to supply as the function's argument. In either case, you can test the argument against `undefined` (or `null`) within the body of the function, perhaps by displaying an error message or skipping some of the function's tasks when a value has not been provided.

Loops

ActionScript supports most of the looping constructs that you have come to expect from other programming languages. Basically, each type of loop involves a condition (which appears in parentheses), followed by a group of lines that should be executed over and over again until the condition is no longer true. The group of lines is traditionally delimited with curly braces.

for *loops*

Here's a simple `for` loop, which executes five times, incrementing the i variable by 1 for each iteration:

```
for (i = 0; i < 5; i++) {
 // The first time through this loop, i will be 0.
 // The second time, it is 1; the fifth and last time it is 4.
}
```

If you're in a function and haven't yet declared the i variable, you can do so inline (within the parentheses that establishes the `for` loop), as follows:

```
for (var i = 0; i < arClips.length; i++) {
 // inside this loop, arClips[i] is "current" item from array
}
```

> **NOTE**
>
> This doesn't mean that the `i` variable exists only within the context of the loop. It just means that the variable is local to the function in which the loop appears; the variable will continue to exist after the loop finishes executing. That is, it's equivalent to using the `var` keyword to declare the `i` variable somewhere above the loop (see "Creating Variables and Using the `var` Keyword" section earlier in this chapter).

for in *loops*

Used much less commonly, ActionScript also provides `for in` loops, which loop over all the members of an object. For instance, say I create an object called `oMyself` and assign it two properties, like so:

```
var oMyself = new Object;
oMyself.firstName = "Nate";
oMyself.age = 34;
```

The following loop would then execute twice, setting the `propName` variable to `firstName` for one of the iterations and to `age` for the other iteration. As you can see, this type of loop is handy when the names of an object's properties might not be known until runtime:

```
for (var propName in oMyself) {
  trace("the value of the " + propName + " property is " +
  oMyself[propName]);
}
```

You would see something like the following in the output window:

```
the value of the name property is nate
the value of the age property is 34
```

> **NOTE**
>
> There is no guarantee that a `for in` loop will process the object's properties in any particular order. It will not, for instance, necessarily process them in the same order that they were added to the object. If order is important, you need to use an array to store the values, not an `Object` instance.

while *loops*

Here's a `while` loop that—like the first `for` loop in the last section—executes five times, incrementing the `i` variable for each iteration. Functionally, this loop works the same way as the first `for` loop that you just saw.

```
var i = 0;
while (i < 5) {
  i++;
}
```

It's possible to accidentally write this type of loop in such a way that it never ends, so be careful. However, if you do so, the Flash Player (or the Flash IDE, if you are playing the movie in Test Movie mode) will allow the infinite loop to run for only 15 seconds. If it takes longer than 15 seconds, the user will be asked if he or she wants the script to be halted. Thus, while you should be careful about making sure not to write infinite loops, you're not going to crash the user's machine if you do make a mistake.

Using break *and* continue

The `break` statement stops execution of the current loop. Code execution continues at the next line of code after the loop block. Consider the following code:

```
// Local variable
var oFoundPerson = null;

// Use loop to attempt to find the person
for (var i = 0; i < arPeople.length; i++) {
  if (arPeople[i].name == "Nate") {
   oFoundPerson = arPeople[i];
   break;
  }
}

// Conditional processing depending on whether person was found
if (oFoundPerson == null) {
  txtStatusMessage = "We found Nate, whew!";
} else {
  txtStatusMessage = "Nate is MIA as usual.";
        }
```

The `continue` statement skips the remainder of the current loop, but allows the rest of the loop iterations to execute normally. For instance, the following loop would execute once for each item in the `arPeople` array, but would skip processing for people named Nate (I mean, who cares about such people anyway?):

```
for (var i = 0; i < arPeople.length; i++) {
 if (arPeople[i].name == "Nate") {
  continue;
 }

 // Any other processing here would be skipped for Nate
}
```

Fun with Datatypes

ActionScript provides a rich set of datatypes, such as `String`, `Date`, `Number`, and `Object`. You'll have to consult the Flash documentation for all the details, but this section will give you a bit of "getting up to speed" information about the most important datatypes.

Numbers

Numbers are pretty simple in ActionScript. There's only one numeric datatype, called `Number` (there's no datatype-level distinction between singles and doubles, for instance, or between integers and reals). The following line creates a variable that holds the number 34:

```
var age = 34;
```

As discussed earlier in this chapter, you can also use strict variable typing to declare a numeric variable, like so:

```
var age:Number = 34;
```

> **NOTE**
>
> Technically, there is a subtle distinction between the `Number` type (which is its own class, which individual number values are considered instances of) and what Flash calls a primitive number value. In practice, the difference doesn't matter much. See the Flash documentation for details.

Strings

In ActionScript, the datatype for handling character data is the `String` datatype. You can create string values using simple assignment statements, like so:

```
var name = "Nate";
```

Although it's traditional to use double-quote characters around string values, you can also use single-quote characters, like so:

```
var name = 'Nate';
```

If you want to embed a literal quote mark within a string, you can use back-slashes to escape the quote marks, like so:

```
var message = "And then I said, \"Hello, World!\"";
```

On the other hand, you can use single quotes around strings that contain dou-ble quotes (or vice versa). If so, you don't need to escape with backslashes (though you may if you want to). Here's an example:

```
var message = 'And then I said, "Hello, World!"';
```

To embed a newline character, you can use \n or \r for character code 10 or 13, respectively. In addition, you can use \t for tab characters (character code 9). Here's an example:

```
var message = "This is on one line\nAnd this is on another";
```

There are lots of handy methods that you can use on strings. Essentially, any string variable implicitly becomes an instance of the `String` class, so you can use any `String` class methods on your string variables. For instance, here's an example that uses the `String.toUpperCase()` and `String.substring()` methods to grab the first character of a string and convert it to uppercase:

```
var firstInitial = name.substring(0, 1).toUpperCase();
```

The length of any string is available through the `String.length` property:

```
var passwordLength = txtPassword.text.length;
```

For more information about the methods and properties of the `String` class, consult the ActionScript dictionary in the Flash documentation.

Dates

In ActionScript, the `Date` datatype always holds a date and time value (consider every date value to represent a moment in history; moments in history occur at a specific date and time, not just a date or just a time). To create a value that contains the current date and time, call the `Date` class's constructor with no arguments, like so:

```
var rightNow = new Date;
```

or

```
var rightNow = new Date();
```

To create a date value that represents 12:00 AM on a specific date, use the following:

```
var myBirthday = new Date(1969, 3, 18);
```

To create a value that represents a specific time on a specific date (in this case, 5:18 in the morning), use the following:

```
var myBirthday = new Date(1969, 3, 18, 5, 18);
```

As usual, you can use ActionScript 2.0's strict variable typing if you wish:

```
var myBirthday:Date = new Date(1969, 3, 18, 5, 18);
```

There are a number of methods available for `Date` values. Examples include `getYear()`, `getMonth()`, and `getDate()`, which return the year, month, and day-of-month component of any `Date` instance (again, where `Dates` are treated like moments in history). Here's an example that uses these methods together:

```
var rightNow = new Date();
var myBirthday = new Date(1969, 3, 18);
var myBirthdayThisYear = new Date(rightNow.getYear(),
myBirthday.getMonth(), myBirthday.getDate());
```

You can compare two dates using the `>`, `<`, `>=`, and `<=` operators, like so:

```
if (myBirthday < rightNow) {
 txtMessage.text = "You already had your birthday this year!";
}
```

Arrays

Arrays are objects that hold any number of values. You access the individual values by index position (that is, by number). To create an empty array, call the `Array` class constructor with zero arguments, like so:

```
var myArray = new Array;
```

or

```
var myArray = new Array();
```

When you have an array, you can add items to it using the `Array.push()` method:

```
arNames.push("Nate");
```

Access the items in an array using square bracket notation, where 0 indicates the first item in the array, like so:

```
// Outputs the first name in the array:
trace(arNames[0]);
// Outputs the second name:
trace(arNames[1]);
```

The number of values in the array is always available through the `length` property:

```
var numberOfNames = arNames.length;
```

The `length` property is commonly used to create loops that perform some kind of processing on each value in the array:

```
for (var i = 0; i < arNames.length; i++) {
 // Within this loop, use arNames[i] to refer to current name
}
```

You can set values (as opposed to reading values) using square-bracket notation too, like so:

```
arNames[1] = "Pamela";
```

Arrays grow in size as needed. Because arrays are zero-indexed, this line:

```
arNames[arNames.length] = "Pamela";
```

is equivalent to this line:

```
arNames.push("Pamela");
```

> **NOTE**
>
> There are lots of other handy Array methods, for sorting, reversing the order of the items, and so on. See the Flash documentation for details.

You can create an array and populate it with values in one step, like so:

```
var arPrimeNumbers = [1, 3, 5, 7, 11, 13, 17];
```

If a function or method is expecting an array as one of its arguments, you can use the same square bracket notation to create the array and pass it in one step:

```
processNumbers([1, 3, 5, 7, 11, 13, 17]);
```

Associative Arrays

ActionScript doesn't have an explicit datatype for *associative arrays* (that is, objects that work like arrays but where the values are referenced by name rather than number—other languages sometimes call these *structures* or *hashtables* or *hashes*). You can, however, use the generic Object class as an associative array. Here's an example:

```
oStates = new Object;
oStates["WA"] = "Washington";
oStates["NY"] = "New York";
oStates["MA"] = "Massachusetts";
```

You can also create objects using a special bracket notation, like so:

```
oStates = {WA:"Washington", NY:"New York", MA:"Massachusetts"};
```

> **NOTE**
>
> Of course, you are not restricted to storing simple strings as the values of the individual properties. The values can be of any datatype—numbers, dates, arrays, even other objects.

After you have created one of these objects, you can access the values (usually called the *properties*) in the object using square bracket notation, like so:

```
stateName = oStates["WA"];
```

You can also use dot notation, like so:

```
stateName = oStates.WA;
```

If the property name is dynamic (that is, if the property to which you are referring is stored in a variable), you must use the square-bracket notation, like so:

```
stateName = oStates[txtStateAbbrev.text];
```

Like most everything in ActionScript, property names are case-sensitive, so the following code would return undefined:

```
stateName = oStates["wa"];
```

See the "for in loops" section, earlier in this chapter, for an example of looping over the properties of an object.

> **NOTE**
>
> In general, it's a good idea to use an associative array (as described in this section) rather than a normal array whenever you will be looking up the values by name. Doing so prevents you from having to loop over an array's contents to find appropriate values over and over again.

Creating Your Own Functions

The simplest way to reuse your code and keep it nice and human-readable is to create your own functions (sometimes called *custom functions* or *user-defined functions*). This section provides an introduction to the topic of creating your own functions. You can find lots of examples of user-defined functions throughout this book.

> **NOTE**
>
> This section will likely provide all you need to know for a while, but there are a few details that I don't have the space to discuss here. In particular, functions are actually special types of objects, which in turn can be assigned to other objects and so on at runtime. When you have a chance, take a look at the Flash documentation for details about the finer points of function creation.

The Basics

At its simplest, ActionScript's function-creation syntax can be thought of as a way to refer to a chunk of code by name. Here's an example:

```
function sayHello() {
 txtStatusMessage.text = "Hello, world!";
}
```

After a function has been created, you execute it just like any of Flash's built-in functions. The `sayHello()` function that was just created could be called using the following line:

```
sayHello();
```

Arguments

In many cases, you will want your function to accept arguments. You create the arguments by listing their names inside the parentheses (after the function name). Within the function itself, refer to the same name to access the argument's value. Here's an example:

```
function sayHello(firstName) {
 txtStatusMessage.text = "Hello, " + firstName;
}
```

You can call this function like so:

```
sayHello("Nate");
```

Separate multiple arguments with commas, as shown in the following code:

```
function sayHello(firstName, lastName) {
 txtStatusMessage.text = "Hello, " + firstName + " " + lastName;
}
```

You can call this function like so:

```
sayHello("Nate", "Weiss");
```

If you call the function without providing one of the arguments, its value will be `undefined` when the function executes. For instance, the following code would cause the `firstName` argument to be set to `Nate` and the `lastName` argument to be set to `undefined`:

```
sayHello("Nate");
```

You can check whether an argument was actually provided to a function when it is called by testing for `undefined` within the body of the function, like so:

```
function sayHello(firstName, lastName) {
 if (firstName == undefined || lastName == undefined) {
  trace("One of the arguments is missing!");
  return;
 };

 // ...rest of function code would go here...
}
```

> **NOTE**
>
> In some situations, you might explicitly pass a value of `undefined` or `null` to a function. For instance, if a person's last name is known but the first name is unknown, you could call the `sayHello()` function as `sayHello(null, "Weiss")`. Internally, the function could test whether the `firstName` argument evaluates to `null` or `undefined`, using a default value such as "Mr. or Mrs." when it does.

You can also access an argument using the `arguments` keyword, which evaluates to an array of the arguments that are actually passed to the function when it is called. Thus, the following function behaves the same way as the previous one:

```
function sayHello(firstName, lastName) {
 txtStatusMessage.text = "Hello, " + arguments[0] + " " + arguments[1];
}
```

> **NOTE**
>
> The `arguments` array comes in handy when you want to create functions that behave differently depending on the number of arguments that are passed to the function. The situation won't come up often, but you might run into the need for it from time to time. See the Flash documentation for details.

Returning Values from Functions

To return a value from a function, use the `return` keyword:

```
function computeAge(dob) {
 var rightNow = new Date();
 var computedAge = rightNow.getYear() - dob.getYear();
 return computedAge;
}
```

You could call this function like so:

```
myDOB = new Date(1969, 3, 18);
myAge = computeAge(myDOB);
```

> **NOTE**
>
> As discussed in the "Variables" section earlier in this chapter, the use of the `var` keyword in the function block means that the `rightNow` and `computedAge` variables are local to the function. They will not collide with other variables of the same name elsewhere, and their values cease to exist after the function has done its work.

I personally like to use the name `result` when creating a variable that I intend to return with the `return` keyword. I find it's easier to remember what the function is up to later if I use this naming convention. I usually declare the variable as local at the top with a `var` line. Of course, I always add comments (hint, hint), like the following:

```
// This function computes a person's age, based on date of birth
function computeAge(dob) {
 // These variables exist only within this function
 var result;
 var rightNow = new Date();

 // Compute the age
 result = rightNow.getYear() - dob.getYear();

 // Return the result
 return result;
}
```

Strict Typing

In ActionScript 2.0, you can use strict typing for the arguments and return value for a function. You do this using colon-based syntax, just as you do for strictly typed variables (see the "Strict Variable Typing" section earlier in this chapter). Because the `computeDate()` function from the last section accepts a date (the date of birth) and returns a number (the computed age), you can define it like so:

```
function computeAge(dob:Date):Number {
  // ...actual code here...
}
```

There are a number of advantages to declaring the types of your arguments and return values. First, it makes the function's intended use and behavior clearer for humans. Secondly, it enables the ActionScript compiler to check for type mismatches when you test (or test the syntax of) your movie. For instance, if you attempt to use the `computeAge()` function using a non-date value for the `dob` argument, you will get an error message from the Flash IDE at compile time. The following function call would throw a type mismatch error when you attempted to publish the movie:

```
computeAge("Younger");
```

You will also get the same error message if you attempt to assign the return value of a function to a variable that has a type other than the declared return type. Thus, the following code would fail to compile:

```
var myAge:String;
myAge = computeAge(myDOB);
```

However, this code would compile without errors:

```
var myAge:Number;
myAge = computeAge(myDOB);
```

The following code would also compile, because it doesn't specify a strict type for `myAge`:

```
var myAge;
myAge = computeAge(myDOB);
```

Storing Functions in Separate ActionScript Files

At any time, you may choose to move any of your ActionScript code into a separate file and then include the file using an #include line. When you do this, your SWF will behave as if the contents of the file actually appear in your Flash document, right where the #include line is. Such files are called ActionScript files, and they traditionally have an .as extension.

> **NOTE**
>
> You can create a new .as file by choosing File > New and then choosing ActionScript File in the Type list. The new file will appear in its own document tab within the Flash IDE. Of course, you are free to create the file using another text editor instead, but the Flash IDE provides such nice syntax coloring, code hints, and other niceties that you might not want to.

For instance, assume that you had an FLA that contained a function—and the code that calls the function—in Frame 1, like this:

```
// Define the function
function computeAge(dob:Date):Number {
 // ...actual code here...
}

// Use the function
var myDOB = new Date(1969, 3, 18);
var myAge = computeAge(myDOB);
```

You could choose to move the function block to a separate file called ageFunctions.as. Such a file is often informally called a *library* of functions or a *library file* (not to be confused with the actual Library panel in the Flash IDE). Then you could change the code in Frame 1 of your FLA to this:

```
// Include library of age-related functions
#include "ageFunctions.as"

// Use the function
var myDOB = new Date(1969, 3, 18);
var myAge = computeAge(myDOB);
```

The main advantage, of course, is that the function(s) in the .as file can now be used in as many Flash projects as you want. If you find a problem with one of the functions, you need only correct it in the .as file (then re-publish the SWFs, of course). Thus, the primary benefit is maintainability. Intelligent use of .as files can also keep the code that remains in your FLAs more concise and easier to read.

NOTE

If you use a source control program such as Visual SourceSafe, the program's Difference and History features provides another great reason to use separate .as files. Your source control program will be able to track and highlight individual changes in an .as file (because it's a plain text file). FLA documents, on the other hand, are binary files—so the source control program will only be able to save each version of your FLAs. It won't be able to show you the differences between them.

You don't have to worry about making the .as file available on your web server so that the Flash Player can download it along with your SWF. The contents of the file get incorporated into the SWF when you publish it. In other words, the #include directive is processed at publish time (compile time), not at runtime.

By the way, I know that I'm making it sound as if only functions are allowed in ActionScript files. In actuality, however, you can put any kind of ActionScript code in an .as file, not just function declarations.

Creating Your Own Classes

As you learned in Chapter 2 and 3—and in this chapter as well—ActionScript provides access to a whole bunch of built-in classes. Some of the classes implement ActionScript's datatypes (such as the String class and the Date class). Other classes represent specific Flash concepts (such as the MovieClip, Button, and LoadVars classes). Each class provides a set of methods, properties, and events that expose useful functionality and that generally are related by a single concept (such as a date, a string, a movie clip, or a button).

As you might expect, ActionScript also enables you to create your own classes. This section introduces you to the ActionScript concepts and syntax related to class creation. I can't teach you everything about the topic in the space I have here, but you will learn enough to be more than on your way.

Ways to Create New Classes

There are two different ways to create classes in today's ActionScript:

- The first way, which has been around forever, is to create a new object and then give it methods and properties by using a special property called `prototype`. I call this the "classic" method of creating classes (um, no pun intended, honest). It's kinda ad-hoc, kinda hacky, kinda loosey-goosey, and kinda confusing sometimes. However, it's also kind of cool and kind of fun. Macromedia generally advises us to consider this method kinda outdated now.

- The second way, which is new for ActionScript 2.0, is to create a special file called a class file. You set up the class's methods and properties within the file, using special keywords such as `class`, `extends`, `public`, `private`, and `static`. This is now generally considered to be the preferred way to create classes.

The following two sections briefly explain how to create classes using each technique. Much more detail is provided for the second technique because it is the preferred method for creating classes now that ActionScript 2.0 has arrived on the scene.

Classic Prototype-Based Classes

To create a class using the classic prototype technique, you create what's called a *constructor function*. There's actually nothing special about a constructor function, or that identifies it as being different from a normal function. The only thing that makes it special is the fact that you plan on using the function as a class rather than as a normal function.

The constructor function for a class can accept any number of arguments, just like a normal function. Within the constructor, you can create the class's properties by assigning values to a special object called `this` (where `this` represents the specific instance of the class when it gets instantiated). You can create as many properties as you want, and name them whatever you want. Typically, at least some of the properties are populated using the arguments that are passed to the constructor function.

Sound confusing? Well, it's a lot easier to understand when you see it in action. The following would create a new class called `Person`. Each instance of the Person class will have three properties: `firstName`, `lastName`, and `dob`.

```
function Person(firstName, lastName, year, month, day) {
  this.firstName = firstName;
```

```
  this.lastName = lastName;
  this.dob = new Date(year, month, day);
}
```

To create an instance of the class, you call the function normally, except you insert the special `new` keyword, like so:

```
var myself = new Person("Nate", "Weiss", 1969, 3, 18);
```

The `myself` variable now holds an instance of the `Person` class. You can access its `firstName` and `lastName` properties by name. These two properties simply contain the same values that were originally passed to the constructor. The `dob` property is a little different because it is a `Date` object that was created from the last three arguments of the constructor. You could, for instance, get the year of this person's birth at any time, using `myself.dob.getYear()`.

To create methods, you assign functions to the constructor function using a special syntax that involves the `prototype` keyword, according to the following basic form:

```
ClassName.prototype.methodName = function(arguments) {
  // function code goes here
}
```

For instance, the following creates a new version of the `Person` class. This one still has the `firstName`, `lastName`, and `dob` properties, but it also has three methods called `setDateOfBirth()`, `getFullName()`, and `getCurrentAge()`. Note that the first method accepts properties, and it is called internally within the constructor.

```
// Constructor: creates new Class called Person
function Person(firstName, lastName, year, month, day) {
  this.firstName = firstName;
  this.lastName = lastName;
  this.setDateOfBirth(year, month, day);
}

// Method: Sets the dob property
Person.prototype.setDateOfBirth = function(year, month, day) {
  this.dob = new Date(year, month, day);
}

// Method: Returns first/last names, concatentated together
Person.prototype.getFullName = function() {
```

```
  return this.firstName + " " + this.lastName;
}

// Method: Returns the current age of the person
Person.prototype.getCurrentAge = function() {
  var rightNow = new Date();
  return rightNow.getYear() - this.dob.getYear();
}
```

With this code in place, you can now create an instance of the class and call its methods, like so:

```
var myself = new Person("Nate", "Weiss", 1969, 3, 18);
mcSomeMovieClip.txtName.text = myself.getFullName();
mcSomeMovieClip.txtAge.text = myself.getCurrentAge();
```

That's as far as I can go with this topic here. You'll find a more sophisticated example of prototype-based object creation in Chapter 7, "Connecting to Servers with XML" (the XMLExtensions.as file).

ActionScript 2.0 Classes

ActionScript 2.0 provides for a new, more cleanly structured way of creating classes. In general, the actual behavior is the same, but the new way of creating classes is easier to understand, more formalized, easier to debug, more declarative, and generally easier to follow.

The Basics

To create a new class using the ActionScript 2.0 technique, you create a new ActionScript file, where the new file has the same name that you want to use for your new class. Thus, for the Person class, you would create a file named Person.as. This book refers to such a file as a *class file*.

NOTE

The filename is case-sensitive. It's traditional to capitalize the first letter of a class name; the name of the corresponding class file should be capitalized to match.

Within the file, you use the `class` keyword to create a block that contains all the code for the class. Within the `class` block, any variables that you create will be the class's properties, and any functions you create will be the class's methods. If you want your new class to have a constructor function, which does any initial processing when instances of the class are created, just add a function with the same name as the class itself. Listing 4.1 provides an example.

LISTING 4.1   Person.as

```
class Person {

 // Properties
 var firstName;
 var lastName;
 var dob;

 // Constructor
 function Person(firstName, lastName, year, month, day) {
  this.firstName = firstName;
  this.lastName = lastName;
  this.setDateOfBirth(year, month, day);
 }

 // Method: Sets the dob property
 function setDateOfBirth(year, month, day) {
  this.dob = new Date(year, month, day);
 }

 // Method: Returns first/last names, concatentated together
 function getFullName() {
  return this.firstName + " " + this.lastName;
 }

 // Method: Returns the current age of the person
 function getCurrentAge() {
  var rightNow = new Date();
  return rightNow.getYear() - this.dob.getYear();
 }
}
```

After this file is in place, you can use its methods and properties just like the ActionScript 1.0 version from the last section. It will behave the same way, but the new version is a lot easier to understand.

> **NOTE**
>
> You will learn where to save your class files in the "The Classpath: Where to Save Your Class Files" section, coming up shortly.

Adding Strict Typing

Within an ActionScript 2.0 class, you can add strict typing to the following:

- The class's properties (the `var` statements within the `class` block but outside any `function` blocks)
- The arguments for each method (that is, each function within the class)
- The return type for each method (except for the constructor, which should not specify a return type)
- The variables used within each `function` block

You'll see an example that uses strict typing in each of these places in the next section. For more information about the benefits of strict variable typing, see the "Strict Variable Typing" section earlier in this chapter.

Public and Private Methods (and Properties)

If you want, you can add the keyword `public` or `private` before each method or property name in a class file. Members marked `public` are meant to be used normally; that is, you can use them outside the context of the class file (most likely in the Actions panel of an FLA). Members marked `private` are for internal use only within the class file itself.

> **NOTE**
>
> Remember that the term "member" is just a generic term that means "method or property" (or event).

Listing 4.2 shows how to add public and private keywords to the code from Listing 4.1. In addition, this version adds the strict typing information that was discussed in the last section.

LISTING 4.2   Person.as (Second Version)

```
class Person {

 // Properties
 public var firstName:String;
 public var lastName:String;
 public var dob:Date;

 // Constructor
 public function Person(firstName:String, lastName:String, year:Number,
month:Number, day:Number) {
   this.firstName = firstName;
   this.lastName = lastName;
   this.setDateOfBirth(year, month, day);
 }

 // Method: Sets the dob property
 private function setDateOfBirth(year:Number, month:Number,
day:Number):Void {
   this.dob = new Date(year, month, day);
 }

 // Method: Returns first/last names, concatentated together
 public function getFullName():String {
   return this.firstName + " " + this.lastName;
 }

 // Method: Returns the current age of the person
 public function getCurrentAge():Number {
   var rightNow:Date = new Date();
   return rightNow.getYear() - this.dob.getYear();
 }
}
```

There are two main benefits of declaring your class's members as public or private:

- They make the intended use and behavior of the class clear to human eyes. One glance is all it takes to know whether a property or method is meant to be used in your normal ActionScript code (public) or is meant for internal use only (private).
- If you use strict variable typing when you actually instantiate and use the class elsewhere in your code, then the compiler will complain when you attempt to publish your movie (or use the Check Syntax button).

Thus, consider the following code:

```
var myself:Person = new Person("Heather", "Greene", 1977, 2, 6);
```

If you use this line to instantiate the `Person` class in some frame of an FLA, you might get an error message from the compiler if you attempt to call the `setDateOfBirth()` function using code like the following (because `setDateOfBirth()` is marked as a private method in Listing 4.2, the idea being that a person's birthday can't be changed after the corresponding object has been constructed):

```
myself.setDateOfBirth(1970, 2, 6);
```

In this version of Flash at least, `private` is just for the purpose of providing this compiler error if you attempt to use a method in a way that it was not meant to be used. It's a helpful hint, intended only to help you keep your code clean and well-defined. It's not about security. All Flash is doing is reviewing your code, based on the fact that you've told it that `myself` is always going to be an instance of `Person` as your code executes. If you don't provide that datatype information, Flash is forced to assume that you might assign `myself` a value of some other type at runtime.

If, however, you instantiated the class without strict variable typing, like the following, then you could call the `setDateOfBirth()` method without problems, regardless of the fact that it's been marked `private`:

```
var myself = new Person("Tucker", "Martine", 1973, 1, 16);
```

At the risk of belaboring the point, it's very important to understand that marking a method or property with `public` or `private` doesn't enforce any kind of runtime security policy. The only service that `private` provides is to cause the compiler to throw an error message if you attempt to use the method or property from outside the class. Because this check kicks in only if you use strict typing when you access the member, you must not think of `private` as a way to create redistributable classes that are protected from unwanted calls to their internal methods. If you sell or distribute a class, its methods are out there in the world and can be called from the Actions panel of any FLAs that use the class. Think of `private` as a way to encourage the correct/intended use of your class, not as a way to keep them secret.

If you don't specify `public` or `private`, a member is assumed to be public. Thus, all the members in the first version of this class (Listing 4.1) were public.

The Classpath: Where to Save Your Class Files

When you create new classes using the new ActionScript 2.0 technique, you save the file somewhere within a special set of folders. This set is called the *classpath*. The notion of a classpath in Flash is similar conceptually to the way the classpath works with Java.

When you attempt to use an ActionScript 2.0 class in a Flash document (an .fla file), the Flash compiler will look for the corresponding .as file in the following locations:

- The current folder (that is, the folder in which your FLA is saved)
- The Classes folder within Flash's configuration directory
- Any other folder that you specify in Flash's classpath preferences

The location of the predefined Classes folder depends on your operating system. On my Windows XP machine, the folder is located at C:\Documents and Settings\Nate\Application Data\Macromedia\Flash 2004\en\Configuration\ Classes. On a Mac, look for the folder at MacintoshHD:Users:(yourname): Library:Application Support:Macromedia:Flash MX2:en:Configuration:Classes. See the Flash documentation for details.

In the case of the `Person` class, the Flash IDE needs to be able to find the Person.as file in the current folder, or in the special Classes folder. If it can't, it will display an error message when you try to publish, test, or syntax-check your movie.

It's up to you whether to store your class files in the current folder or in the special Classes folder. If you expect to use the class only in one movie (or related movies, all of which are in the same folder), it probably makes sense to keep it in the current folder. If you expect to use it in lots of different Flash documents, keep it in the Classes folder. (You can always move the file from one place to another later.)

If you want, you can add an additional folder to the classpath to tell the Flash compiler to look for class files there too. For instance, you might want to add a network folder to the classpath so that your whole team is using the same class files. This setup would have the added benefit of keeping your own classes separate from the ones that Macromedia ships with the Flash product.

To change the classpath, choose Edit > Preferences and then click the ActionScript 2.0 Settings button under the ActionScript tab. This brings you to the ActionScript Settings dialog box, where you can add folders to the classpath using either an actual folder path or a relative path (see Figure 4.7). For instance, you can add ../shared/classes, which would enable you to keep your class files in a folder called shared, which is at the same folder level as the current FLA.

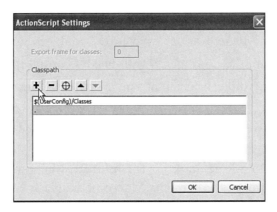

FIGURE 4.7   You can add new folders to the classpath to suit your needs.

NOTE

A similar dialog box exists for adjusting the classpath for an individual FLA rather than for all the FLAs on your machine. You get to this dialog box through File > Publish Settings > Flash. Then, click the Settings button.

Search the Flash documentation for the word **classpath** for details about how Flash finds class files in the classpath.

Class Packages

The ActionScript 2.0 class metaphor also includes the concept of class *packages*, which are sets of classes that are meant to be used together. Thus, you can create a package called venue, which contains all the classes that are meant to be used within the "venue" example application; if the Person class was a part of this package, its full name would be venue.Person. For instance, if my company was called Orange Whip Consulting, I might use owc.venue as the package name; the full name of the Person class might then be owc.venue.Person.

There is no specific `package` keyword in ActionScript. Packages are instead defined implicitly using folder names. To make a class part of a package, do the following:

1. Create a folder with the same name that you want to use for the name of the package. The folder needs to be in the classpath, so it needs to sit within the current folder or the special classes folder (or any classpath folders you've set up yourself). Use nested folders if you want.

2. Place your class file in the new folder.

3. Change the name of the class in the actual class file (which follows the `class` keyword) to its new full name. So, rather than `class   Person`, you might have `class   owc.venue.Person` instead.

Then, to use the class, refer to it by its full name, like so:

```
var myself:owc.venue.Person = new owc.venue.Person("Heather", "Greene",
1977, 2, 6);
```

As an alternative, you can import the class or the whole package using the `import` keyword. For instance, if you put any one of the following lines at the top of the code where you want to use the class:

```
import owc.venue.Person;
import owc.venue.*;
import owc.*;
```

You could then instantiate the `Person` class without having to type the package name, like so:

```
var myself:Person = new Person("Heather", "Greene", 1977, 2, 6);
```

For details about packages and the `import` keyword, see the Flash documentation.

Static Methods and Properties

Most classes represent real-world concepts that are meant to be instantiated before they are used. For instance, the `Person` class represents the idea of a person; you create instances (through the `new` keyword) to represent individual people. The idea is that each instance contains data that is different from person to person. That is, the methods and properties reflect the data for each individual person.

Sometimes, you might want to create a particular method as part of a class, but you don't want the method to change or access any instance-level data. In other words, the function has no need to access the `this` scope. In such a case, you can mark the method as `static` to indicate that its processing always produces the same result (assuming a given set of arguments, of course).

After you've marked a method as `static`, you can call it as a member of the class itself, instead of having to instantiate the class. Some of the built-in ActionScript methods are static. The most obvious example is the `Math` class, which provides a large number of static methods for performing various mathematical operations. You don't create an instance of the `Math` class before using its methods; instead you call the methods directly on the class itself, as in `Math.abs()` or `Math.round()`.

Listing 4.3 shows the code for a class called `RandomUtils`, which provides two methods for creating random integers. The `pickRandomInteger()` method picks a number between 0 and the maximum you specify. The `getRandomSequence()` method returns an array of numbers with the specified length, which contains a set of sequential numbers in a random order. Because both methods are `static`, you call them on the `RandomUtils` class itself, like so:

```
// Get a sequence of numbers, like 5,4,1,3,2 or 2,4,5,3,1
var arSequence:Array = RandomUtils.getRandomSequence(5);
// Get a number between 1 and 10
var myNumber:Number = RandomUtils.pickRandomNumber(9) + 1;
```

LISTING 4.3   RandomUtils.as

```
class RandomUtils {

  // This method picks an integer between 0 and the specified number
  public static function pickRandomInteger(max:Number):Number {
    return Math.floor( (Math.random() * max) );
  }

  // This method returns an array of integers in random order.
  public static function getRandomSequence(length:Number):Array {
    var arResult:Array = new Array;
    var arTemp:Array = new Array;

    // Fill temporary array with values, where values are the same
    // as the index position
    for (var i = 0; i < length; i++) {
      arTemp[i] = i;
    }
```

```
  // While there are values in the temp array...
  while (arTemp.length > 0) {
   // Pick an integer from 0 to the length of the temp array
   var randPos = pickRandomInteger(arTemp.length);
   // Take value at picked temp position and put it in result
   arResult.push( arTemp[randPos] );
   // Remove value from temp array
   arTemp.splice(randPos, 1);
  }

  // Return the result
  return arResult;
 }

}
```

You can also use `static var` instead of `var` when declaring a property to indicate that its value is not meant to change over time. This is a useful way to create a named constant, like `Person.PERSONTYPE_MANAGER` or `Person.PERSONTYPE_UNDERLING`, which might map to arbitrary numeric values. See the Flash documentation for details about `static`. There are also a few examples of static properties in Appendix A.

Getters and Setters

You can create *getter and setter functions* for any or all of a custom class's properties. Getters and setters enable you to specify code that should be executed whenever the property's value is accessed or changed.

The following snippet creates a class called `MyClass`. The class exposes a single property—a string property called `firstName`:

```
class MyClass {
  private var __firstName;

  public function get firstName():String {
    return this.__firstName;
  }

  public function set firstName(val:String):Void {
    this.__firstName = val;
  }
}
```

The following rules and recommendations apply to the creation of getters and setters, as exhibited by the preceding snippet:

- You label a function as a getter or setter by including the `get` or `set` keyword between the `function` keyword and the name of the function.

- A getter function, by definition, must return the value of the property. It's recommended that you specify the datatype of the property using ActionScript 2.0's strict typing feature.

- A setter function must accept exactly one argument—the proposed new value for the property—and should not return anything. It's recommended that you specify the datatype of the incoming argument using strict typing, and specify `Void` as the return type to formalize the fact that the function must not return a value.

- Unfortunately, the name of a getter or setter function cannot be the same as the property it is getting or setting. Therefore, the tradition is to use an internal variable that matches the name of the corresponding getter and setter function, except preceded by one or two underscores (the Flash documentation suggests two).

- Because you don't want the internal variable to be accessed directly without going through the getter or setter, it is traditional to declare the internal variable as `private`.

NOTE

The underscore-based naming scheme is not exactly elegant, but it works—and it helps you easily spot properties that are protected by getters and setters.

As it stands, the preceding snippet would behave exactly like the following, more concise version of the same class declaration:

```
class MyClass {
   public var firstName;
}
```

So, if the addition of getters and setters requires so many more lines of code, why use them? The answer is that you don't have to, unless you want special processing to occur when a property is changed or accessed.

This is one of those concepts that is easier to understand with a simple example. Suppose you wanted to create a new version of the `Person` class, with the following properties:

- `firstName` and `lastName` properties, which are normal, public properties that don't have getters and setters.
- A `fullName` property, which is implemented by a getter and setter that access the values of `firstName` and `lastName` internally, without actually storing a separate piece of data for `fullName`.
- An `age` property, which is implemented by a getter and setter that ensure that an invalid value for the person's age cannot be set.

The following code snippet shows how to create such a class:

```
class Person {
  public var firstName:String;
  public var lastName:String;
  private var __age:Number;

  public function get age():Number {
    return this.__age;
  }

  public function set age(val:Number):Void {
    if (val < 0) {
      trace("Invalid age provided, value was not set");
      return;
    }
    this.__age = val;
  }

  public function get fullName():String {
    return this.firstName + " " + this.lastName;
  }

  public function set fullName(val:String):Void {
    var arWords:Array = val.split(" ");
    if (arWords.length == 2) {
      this.firstName = arWords[0];
      this.lastName = arWords[1];
    }
  }
}
```

> **NOTE**
>
> See the SimpleBarChart.as file from Appendix A's examples for another example of a component class that uses getters and setters for several of its properties. That example also makes the getters inspectable, meaning that the underlying properties can be set in the Flash IDE with the Properties panel or the Component Inspector.

Inheritance

No object-oriented-style class system would be complete without a notion of inheritance. ActionScript enables you to create *subclasses* of any existing class; these subclasses inherit all the members (methods, properties, and events) from the subclass and then add additional functionality. You can create subclasses of built-in classes or of your own classes.

Note the following two methods of implementing inheritance (that is, of creating subclasses) in ActionScript:

- Through the prototype-based system that was introduced in ActionScript 1.0.
- By adding the `extends` keyword to an ActionScript 2.0 style class file.

Classic Prototype-Based Inheritance

It's possible to create subclass-like objects using the ActionScript 1.0 `prototype` technique that was discussed briefly in the "Classic Prototype-Based Classes" section earlier in this chapter. It's a topic with a lot of ins and outs, and it is just too complicated and strange to discuss here with any clarity. Now that ActionScript 2.0 is in place, I would recommend that you use the new `extends` keyword to implement inheritance whenever possible. If you want information about prototype-based inheritance (sometimes called "chaining"), please consult the Flash documentation.

ActionScript 2.0 Inheritance

ActionScript 2.0 makes inheritance clean and simple. To create a subclass of an existing class, you need only use the `extends` keyword after the name of your class in its class file. For instance, to create a subclass of the `Person` class called Manager, you would use the following:

```
class Manager extends Person {
  // Additional members go here
}
```

Any methods or properties you add to this class block will be available to any instances of the new `Manager` class. In addition, the instances will also be able to use the methods and properties of the `Person` class. You can see a good example of a subclass in the form of the `GestureMovieClip` class in Chapter 5, "Movie Clips as Objects."

What We Haven't Covered About the Class System

This section has provided you with a lot of crash-course style information about how classes work, especially when using the new, simplified syntax that was introduced in this version of Flash.

There's a lot that we haven't been able to discuss in this chapter, though. Some items of interest, which you might want to check out in the ActionScript Reference Guide part of the Flash documentation, include the following:

- **The notion of interfaces, which enables you to create miniature "specifications" that certain classes should understand or respond to.** If you're familiar with how interfaces work in other languages, you won't be too surprised at how it's implemented in ActionScript. Search the Flash documentation for the `interface` and `implements` keywords for details.

- **The specific methods and properties provided by the built-in datatype classes such as String, Number, Date, and Array.** The "Fun With Datatypes" section in this chapter provided a few quick examples that showed off a few methods of each class, but you should definitely take a few moments at some point to skim though the members of these classes (in the ActionScript Reference part of the Flash documentation), just so you know what's available.

- **The particulars of creating events.** Your custom classes can throw their own events, using the event listener/dispatch model that was introduced in this version of Flash. Search the Flash documentation for `dispatchEvent()` for details.

- **How to extend the functionality of existing classes.** This is done by adding ad-hoc methods and properties to classes at runtime, rather than creating subclasses (descendants) of the existing classes. Even though it's not quite in the spirit of ActionScript 2.0 principles, it's still a technique that can come in handy. For an example, see the discussion of the XMLExtensions.as script file in Chapter 7.

Responding to Events

Many of the objects that you will be working with in Flash can generate events. The specific events that a particular object will generate varies, of course, depending on what type of object it is. `ButtonClip` objects generate `onClick` and `onRelease` events; `MovieClip` objects generate `onLoad` and `onKeyPress` events (among many others), `XML` objects generate `onData` and `onStatus` events, and so on.

This section will explain what to do when you want your movie to respond in some way when an event occurs. Of course, your movies don't have to respond to every event that an object is capable of firing. You only need to respond to the ones that are important to your application.

This subject would actually be quite simple to explain, if it weren't for one complicating factor: as of Flash MX 2004, there are now two completely different event mechanisms within the product. The two event mechanisms are as follows:

- **Classic event model.** All the classes that were around before Flash MX 2004 fire this type of event. This includes nearly all classes that are not found in the Components panel. The most obvious and commonly used examples are `MovieClip`, `Button`, `TextField`, `XML`, and `LoadVars` (most of which you have already seen in use).

- **Listener event model.** Classes that are new for Flash MX 2004—including all the component and screen-related classes—fire this type of event. It appears that Macromedia is planning on promoting the listener event model on a going forward basis, but for now, you can think about it as being a component-specific feature.

> **NOTE**
>
> The term "classic event model" is my own. You won't find it in the Flash documentation.

There are a number of ways in which the new event model is more sophisticated and flexible. The most important advantage from our point of view is the fact that it allows any given event to cause multiple responder functions to fire. Under the classic model, each of an object's events can be hooked up to only one responder function at a time.

In any case, you need to know how to work with both types of events, because you don't get to choose which one to use (unless you are making up your own events, which is possible but not covered in this book). It is the object you are using that determines which event model is used.

Sound confusing and a bit inconsistent? Fair enough. The good news is that the two event models are not dramatically different to use in actual practice. The next few sections should help you understand how to work with each of them.

Responding to Events Using the Classic Event Model

Up until Flash MX 2004, ActionScript treated events in more or less the same fashion that they had been treated in JavaScript. Responding to an event under this model is quite simple. You simply write a responder function that performs whatever tasks you want to take place when the event fires. The responder function is assigned directly to the object. The object will execute the responder function whenever it is appropriate to do so.

Writing Responders in Two Steps

So far, this book has shown you how to create event responders using two steps. First, the responder function is created with a normal `function` block, just like any other function. Then the responder function is hooked up to the event to which it is meant to respond. Here is a bare-bones example that creates a responder function called `afterEagleClipLoads()` and then hooks it up to the `MovieClip.onLoad` event for a movie clip instance called `eagleClip`.

```
function afterEagleClipLoads () {
   trace("The eagleClip has loaded.");
}
eagleClip.onLoad = afterEagleClipLoads;
```

Some events automatically pass additional information to responder functions they are hooked up to. The additional information is provided in the form of arguments. For instance, the `onLoad` event of the `LoadVars` and `XML` objects pass a Boolean value that indicates whether the object was able to fetch data successfully from the remote URL. For instance, the following code snippet creates an event responder function called `afterDataLoadAttempt` and then hooks it up to the `onLoad` event of a new `XML` object called `myXML`:

```
function afterDataLoadAttempt(success) {
  if (success == false) {
    trace("the data could not be loaded.");
  } else {
    // (normal processing would go here)
  }
}
myXML = new XML;
myXML.onLoad = afterDataLoadAttempt;
myXML.load("myPage.jsp");
```

By the way, the name of the argument (I used the name success) can be anything you like because the event passes the argument to your responder by position (not by name). Alternatively, you could omit the success argument from the function's declaration altogether, instead of referring to the passed-in value as arguments[0] within the body of the function.

Writing Responders in One Step

Event responder functions can also be declared and hooked up in a single step using the alternate function-creation syntax that you saw earlier in this chapter. The following snippet will operate in the same way as the two-step version that you just saw:

```
eagleClip.onLoad = function() {
  trace("The eagleClip has loaded.");
}
```

Within the body of a responder function, the this keyword refers to the object that is firing the event. For instance, you could refer to this._x or this._y to get or set the X or Y position of eagleClip at the moment that the onLoad event fires. This rule applies regardless of whether you use the two-step or one-step syntax for creating the responder function itself.

For events that provide additional information to their responders as arguments, you can provide internal names for the arguments inside the parentheses that follow the word function. For instance, the following snippet is the single-step version of the myXML example from the previous section of this chapter:

```
myXML = new XML;
myXML.onLoad = function(success) {
  if (success == false) {
    trace("the data could not be loaded.");
```

```
  } else {
    // (normal processing would go here)
  }
}
myXML.load("myPage.jsp");
```

Writing Responders Using on(event) Syntax

Wait, there's more! Believe it or not, there is actually a third syntax for responding to events under the classic event model. This means of writing an event handler is often used for button objects, but you can use it for just about any other type of object that appears visually on the Stage.

To respond to an event using on(event) syntax, you follow these steps:

1. Select the object on the Stage.
2. In the Actions panel, type **on(event_name)**—where *event_name* is a placeholder for the name of the event to which you want to respond—followed by a pair of curly braces.
3. Between the curly braces, provide the code you want to execute when the event fires. (Within the curly braces, the this keyword will resolve to the object to which you are attaching the code.)

For instance, you could add the following code to the Actions panel for any button symbol instance on the Stage. It would generate a trace message (which includes the button's instance name) each time the button is clicked:

```
on(release) {
  trace("The button symbol named " + this._name + " was clicked.");
}
```

NOTE

Many experienced developers suggest staying away from the on(event) syntax, except when attaching just a line or two of code to an event. The reason is that it gets hard to keep track of all the code in your projects if it is scattered about in the Actions panels for the various objects that you are using. The alternative is to write event responder functions using either the two-step or one-step syntax described in the previous two sections of this chapter. That way, all your code can stay in one place and can easily be moved to an #include file or ActionScript 2.0 class file.

Responding to Events Using the Listener Event Model

As of Flash MX 2004, the product includes a new event implementation, which the Flash documentation calls the *event listener* event model. Under this new system, you don't attach your responder functions to an object directly. Instead, you hook them up with a new method called `addEventListener()`.

The new `addEventListener()` method is exposed by each component that ships with Flash MX 2004. So, in broad strokes, if you dragged an object onto the Stage from the Components panel (assuming it's one of the objects that shipped with the product), you should use `addEventListener()` to hook your event responder code up to whatever events you want to handle.

> **NOTE**
>
> The new `addEventListener()` method is also exposed by the `mx.screens.Screen`, `Form`, and `Slide` classes that you will learn about in Chapter 11, "Building Better Forms with Flash."

Using addEventListener()

The `addEventListener()` method accepts two arguments. The first argument is the name of the event to which you want to respond; the second argument is the function that you want to execute when the event fires. As an example, the following snippet of code would handle the `click` event fired by a Button component with an instance name of `myButton`:

```
function whenMyButtonIsClicked () {
   trace("The button has been clicked.");
}
myButton.addEventListener("click", whenMyButtonIsClicked);
```

This book often uses a simple naming convention (borrowed from the Flash Remoting Components framework, which you will learn about in Chapter 8, "Connecting to Servers with Flash Remoting") for event responder functions, where the name of the function is made up of the target object's name, followed by the event name. So, instead of being named `whenMyButtonIsClicked`, the responder function would be named `myButton_Click`. This naming convention has no special meaning to Flash. You can choose to use it, or a convention of your own choosing, as you see fit.

> **Note**
>
> Um, not to confuse matters or anything (LOL), but there is also a naming convention that *does* have special meaning to the event-listener runtime implementation, where you append the word `Handler` to the name of the event and use that as the name of your responder function (for instance `clickHandler`). This convention is relatively unlikely to be applicable to your own work anytime soon. See the Flash documentation for details.

Accessing the Event Object

When you create a listener function, you can specify a single argument in the function declaration (the `function` block). At runtime, a special *event object* will be passed to the argument when the function is executed in response to an event.

The event will contain at least two properties, as follows:

- `type`, which contains the name of the event, as a string (the type would be `click`, for instance, when the function is executed in response to a `Button` component's `click` event).
- `target`, which is a reference to the object that fired the event.
- Any other properties specific to the type of event being fired. These properties are explained in the Flash documentation for the event.

The following function skeleton could be hooked up to one or more `Button` components with `addEventListener()`; within the body of the function, `eventObj.type` would evaluate to `click`, and `eventObj.target` would evaluate to the `Button` component itself:

```
function whenButtonIsClicked(eventObj) {
  // your code here
}
```

> **Note**
>
> You can name the argument whatever you want. The Flash documentation sometimes uses `eventObj` as the name; other times it uses `ev` as the name.

Using on(event) *Syntax*

You can the on(event) syntax that was described earlier in this chapter to respond to listener-style events. Thankfully, the on(event) syntax is consistent for the two event models.

As an example, the following code could be added to the Actions panel of a Button component, which would execute when the component was clicked at runtime:

```
on(click) {
  trace("The button symbol named " + this._name + " was clicked.");
}
```

> **NOTE**
>
> Button *components* (which you drag onto the Stage from the Components panel) emit a click event when a user clicks and then releases the button. The equivalent event for a button *symbol* (which you would generally create yourself in the Library) is called onRelease, not onClick. Unfortunately you have to remember the two different event names for the two types of buttons.

Summary

This chapter has covered a lot of ground in a (relatively) short amount of time. You've learned about ActionScript's basic syntax and language elements, the datatypes available to you, how to respond to events, and how to create your own functions and classes. Along the way, you learned a bit about how the language evolved and how to use some of the methods exposed by the built-in datatype classes.

Chapter 5 shows you how to apply much of this newfound knowledge to the most interesting and encompassing object in the ActionScript universe: the built-in MovieClip class. If this chapter was about theory, then Chapter 5 is its empirically-minded doppelganger.

MOVIE CLIPS AS OBJECTS

In the brash, rash, crash course that was Chapters 2 and 3 ("Your First Flash Interface" and "Digging a Bit Deeper," respectively), you learned a bit about how to work with movie clips, which are probably the most important types of objects in Macromedia Flash. Chapter 4, "ActionScript: A Primer," started following up on that crash course by explaining the ActionScript language to you, which is used most often to manipulate movie clips at runtime. This chapter continues the follow-up by filling in the details on movie clips and what they mean to you as a server-side code enthusiast.

First, we take a closer look at the methods, properties, and events supported by the MovieClip class. Then we build a mouse-gesture-powered scrolling interface that you can adapt for use in your own projects. Not only does such a scrolling interface make for a good discussion of many movie clip concepts, but it may come in handy for your own pages as well.

> **NOTE**
>
> The scrolling interface developed in this chapter is revisited in Chapter 7, "Connecting to Servers with XML," where it becomes a consumer and displayer of XML-encoded information provided by a server.

The *MovieClip* Class

First off, let's take a look at the members—that is, the properties, methods, and events—provided by the MovieClip class in this version of Flash. As you're about to see, Flash has many members, some of great interest to people like you and me and some of interest mostly to designers.

I find it somewhat intimidating to look through the ActionScript reference for the MovieClip class because the members seem to represent so many different concepts and ideas. To make it all a bit easier to digest, Tables 5.1 through 5.5 break down the MovieClip's members into functional categories, as follows:

- Appearance and positioning of movie clips on the Stage (Table 5.1)
- Loading and creating movie clips at runtime (Table 5.2)
- Playback and timeline control (Table 5.3)
- Responding to mouse input (Table 5.4)
- Drawing lines and shapes at runtime (Table 5.5)

These tables don't list every single property, method, and event that the MovieClip class offers. Most are listed here, but I have omitted some members that fall outside the scope of this book. Consult the Flash documentation for a complete (if a bit overwhelming) listing.

First, Table 5.1 shows the properties and methods that you use to control the appearance or position of an existing movie clip on the Stage. The clip might be one that you put on the Stage at design time (in the Flash IDE), or it might be one that you created at runtime through attachMovieClip() or a related method (see Table 5.2).

TABLE 5.1 *MovieClip* Class Members Related to Appearance and Positioning on the Stage

METHOD OR PROPERTY	DESCRIPTION
_alpha	Numeric property. The alpha (transparency) value of the clip, where 100 means no transparency and 0 means totally transparent.
_height	Numeric property. The height of the clip, in pixels. You can set this property to change the clip's height at runtime.
_highquality	Numeric property. Controls whether text in the movie might be anti-aliased and font-smoothed. See the Flash documentation for details.
_rotation	Numeric property. The rotation of the movie clip, measured in degrees. You can use this property to turn the clip around on its axis at runtime.
_visible	Boolean property. Whether the movie clip is visible. You can use this property to show or hide the clip at runtime.
_x	Numeric property. The horizontal (left/right) position of the clip, relative to the parent clip's registration point. See the "Changing the Appearance and Position of a Clip" section for details.
_xscale	Numeric property. The current horizontal-scale factor of the movie clip. You can use this property to make a clip skinnier or wider, possibly stretching or skewing its appearance.
_y	Numeric property. The vertical (up/down) position of the clip, relative to the parent clip's registration point.
_yscale	Numeric property. The current vertical-scale factor of the movie clip. You can use this property to make a clip taller or shorter, possibly stretching or skewing its appearance.
getBounds()	Method. Returns information about how the actual content of the movie clip is distributed around its registration point.
globalToLocal(point)	Method. Converts coordinates between the clip's coordinate system and the Stage's coordinate system (or the coordinate system of another clip). This property is used most often by game developers, but you might have cause to use it if you were building an interactive product simulation or something of that nature.

continues

TABLE 5.1   *MovieClip* Class Members Related to Appearance and Positioning on the Stage (Continued)

METHOD OR PROPERTY	DESCRIPTION
hitTest(target)	Method. Determines whether two clips are touching each other. There are several forms of this method; see the Flash documentation for details.
setMask()	Method. Sets a clip as a mask of another clip. See the "Creating Mask Clips Programmatically" section later in this chapter.

Table 5.2 lists the MovieClip members that you use to dynamically load or create other movies, movie clips, or images at runtime via script.

TABLE 5.2   *MovieClip* Class Members Related to Loading and Creating Clips at Runtime

MEMBER	DESCRIPTION
_framesloaded	Numeric property. The number of frames that have been loaded into the current movie. You can use this to determine if a particular frame has been loaded into the Flash Player.
_name	String property. The instance name of the movie clip.
_parent	MovieClip property (returns a MovieClip instance). The parent of the current movie clip.
_target	String property. The target path of the current movie clip.
_totalframes	Numeric property. The total number of frames in a clip's timeline.
_url	String property. The URL of the SWF or JPG file being shown in the movie clip.
attachMovie(idName, newName, depth [,initObject])	Method. Creates a new instance of a movie clip symbol from the Library. This method was used in the artistMenu.fla example from Chapter 2. See the "Attaching Movie Clips from the Library Using Linkage Identifiers" section for further details.
createEmptyMovieClip (instanceName, depth)	Method. Creates a new movie clip without any content. See the "About Subclassed Constructors for MovieClip Symbols" section for an example.

MEMBER	DESCRIPTION
createTextField (instanceName, depth, x, y, width, height)	Method. Creates a new text field with the specified instance name, depth, position, and size. The SimpleBarChart class in Appendix A, "Notes on Building the SimpleBarChart Component," provides an example of using this method, along with the related TextFormat class.
duplicateMovieClip (newName, depth [,initObject])	Method. Duplicates a movie clip instance on the Stage. Similar conceptually to attachMovie(), except that the new clip instance is copied from an existing instance on the Stage, rather than being copied from the Library.
getBytesLoaded()	Method. The number of bytes of the SWF or JPEG file that is currently being loaded into the movie clip. After a call to loadMovie(), you can use this property together with getBytesTotal() to show a status indicator as a movie is loading.
getBytesTotal()	Method. The total size of the SWF or JPEG file that is currently being loaded into the movie clip, in bytes.
getDepth()	Method. The current depth level of a movie clip, which affects how clips are stacked at runtime (their z-order). The depth is initially specified by the attachMovie(), createEmptyMovieClip(), or duplicateMovieClip() methods, and can be changed at runtime via the swapDepths() method.
getSWFVersion()	Method. The version of the Flash Player for which the SWF being shown in the clip was published.
getURL(url [, target, variables])	Method. Instructs the browser to load a URL into the current browser window, or a new or existing browser window as indicated by the target argument. The URL can begin with the javascript: pseudo-protocol to instruct the browser to execute a JavaScript command. Similar conceptually to the LoadVars.send() method, which can be easier to use. This method is discussed briefly at the end of Chapter 6, "Connecting to Servers with Plain Text."

continues

TABLE 5.2   *MovieClip* Class Members Related to Loading and Creating Clips at Runtime (Continued)

MEMBER	DESCRIPTION
`loadMovie(url [,variables])`	Method. Loads a SWF or JPG file into an existing movie clip. You saw an example of this method's use in the artistMenu.fla example in Chapter 2. It's worth noting that while this is the simplest and easiest way to load an external file into a movie clip, the `LoadVars.load()` and `MovieClipLoader.loadClip()` methods provide similar functionality.
`loadVariables(url [, variables])`	Method. Loads variables from a server. In general, the `LoadVars` class provides a cleaner means of exchanging plain text variables with a server, as detailed in Chapter 6.
`onData`	Event. Fires when variables are receives from a server. In general, the `onData` event of the `LoadVars` class does a better job.
`onLoad`	Event. Fires when the content in the current movie clip has been fully loaded.
`onUnload`	Event. Fires when the content of the current movie clip is unloaded by means of `unloadMovie()`.
`removeMovieClip()`	Method. Completely removes the movie clip from the currently playing movie and destroys its `MovieClip` instance. See the "Removing Clips" section later in this chapter for more details.
`swapDepths (depth or target)`	Method. Swaps the depth levels (the stacking order) of two existing movie clips. This method is used by the slide show example in Chapter 6.
`unloadMovie()`	Method. Unloads external content from a movie clip, but leaves the now-empty movie clip in place. Discussed briefly in the "Removing Clips" section later in this chapter.

Table 5.3 lists the `MovieClip` members that you use to control or monitor a movie or movie clip's playback at runtime. You can use the methods in this table to start and stop the playhead that invisibly advances each clip's timeline from frame to frame. For clips that have only one frame, these members have no real effect.

TABLE 5.3 *MovieClip* Class Members Related to Playback and Timeline Control

METHOD OR PROPERTY	DESCRIPTION
_currentframe	Numeric property. The frame number of the current frame in the timeline. This property is read-only; use gotoAndPlay() or gotoAndStop() to change the current frame.
gotoAndPlay(*frame*)	Method. Advances the playhead to the specified frame and tells the timeline to begin advancing from frame to frame at the movie's frame rate. The frame can be specified by number or by name, as discussed in the "Jumping to Frames by Name Rather Than by Number" section in Chapter 3.
gotoAndStop(*frame*)	Method. Advances the playhead to the specified frame and tells the timeline to remain at that frame until further notice. The frame can be specified by number or by name.
nextFrame()	Method. Advances the playhead to the next frame.
onEnterFrame	Event. Fires as the playhead enters a new frame, which means that the event normally fires continuously at the movie's frame rate. Any code you attach to this event will fire before any code that is attached to the frame in the timeline.
play()	Method. Tells the timeline to begin advancing from frame to frame at the frame rate specified by the top-level SWF (the rate is determined by the SWF you actually embed in your web pages, not by clips or movies that you load dynamically at runtime).
prevFrame()	Method. Rewinds the playhead to the previous frame.
stop()	Method. Stops the playhead at its current position (like the pause button on a VCR), so that it no longer advances automatically from frame to frame.

Table 5.4 shows the MovieClip members that your Flash projects can use to respond to the user's mouse movements. The gesture-based scroller example in this chapter uses the _xmouse and _ymouse properties to determine whether to scroll the widget's contents at any given time.

TABLE 5.4   *MovieClip* Class Members Related to the Mouse

PROPERTY	DESCRIPTION
_droptarget	MovieClip property (returns a MovieClip instance). Used for creation of drag-and-drop interfaces. See the Flash documentation for details.
_xmouse	Numeric property. The current horizontal position of the mouse, relative to the current clip's registration point. Discussed in the "Responding to Mouse Movements" section later in this chapter.
_ymouse	Numeric property. The current vertical position of the mouse, relative to the current clip's registration point. Discussed in the "Responding to Mouse Movements" section later in this chapter.
onDragOut	Event. Used for creation of drag-and-drop interfaces. See the Flash documentation for details.
onDragOver	Event. Used for creation of drag-and-drop interfaces. See the Flash documentation for details.
onRelease	Event. Fires when the user presses and then releases the mouse button while hovering over the current movie clip. Similar conceptually to the onRelease event fired by button symbols, which you saw in action in Chapter 3. See also the related onPress, onReleaseOutside, onMouseDown, and onMouseUp events in the Flash documentation.
onRollOut	Event. Fires when the user moves the mouse out of the current clip's boundaries. Similar conceptually to the onRollOut event fired by button symbols, which you saw in action in Chapter 3.
onRollOver	Event. Fires when the user moves the mouse within the current clip's boundaries. Similar conceptually to the onRollOver event fired by button symbols, which you saw in action in Chapter 3.
useHandCursor	Boolean. Determines whether a hand cursor should be used when the mouse rolls over the movie clip. If true (the default), the cursor will change to a hand if the clip is behaving like a button (that is, if its onRelease or related events are being used). If false, a pointer cursor is always used, regardless of whether the clip is behaving like a button.

Finally, Table 5.5 lists one final set of MovieClip members. These methods are a bit different, conceptually, from the ones in the other tables; instead of providing control over clips that presumably already present some kind of visual content, these members enable you to create entirely new content at runtime by drawing brand new lines and shapes via script. The example widget in this chapter uses some of these methods to draw boxes and borders; see the "Drawing Lines and Shapes Programmatically" section of this chapter for details. The `SimpleBarChart` class from Chapter 9, "Connecting to Servers with Web Services," and Appendix A takes things a bit further by using these methods to create simple charts that visualize the state of information on the server.

TABLE 5.5 *MovieClip* Class Methods Related to Drawing Lines and Shapes at Runtime

METHOD	DESCRIPTION
`beginFill([rgb, alpha])`	Indicates the start of a new shape that should be filled in with a solid color. This method is demonstrated in the "Drawing Lines and Shapes Programmatically" section of this chapter.
`beginGradientFill(fillType, colors, alphas, ratios, matrix)`	Indicates the start of a new shape that should be filled in with a gradient color. See the Flash documentation for details.
`clear()`	Erases all shapes and lines that were created in the current clip using the other methods listed in this table.
`curveTo(controlX, controlY, anchorX, anchorY)`	Draws a curved line. See the Flash documentation for details.
`endFill()`	Fills in a shape that was previously started using `beginFill()`. This method is demonstrated in the "Drawing Lines and Shapes Programmatically" section of this chapter.
`lineStyle(thickness [, rgb, alpha])`	Sets the thickness (in pixels), color, and alpha (transparency) of lines subsequently drawn with `lineTo()` or `curveTo()`. A line thickness of 0 indicates that a hairline-width line should be drawn. Hairlines are always represented on the screen using just one pixel, regardless of how the movie clip is scaled or resized. Lines of any other width will change thickness if the clip is scaled or resized (a line that starts out with a thickness of 1 will be shown with a thickness of 5 pixels if the movie clip is scaled to 5 times its original height). For this reason, a thickness of 0 is usually desired when drawing on a clip

continues

TABLE 5.5   *MovieClip* Class Methods Related to Drawing Lines and Shapes at Runtime (Continued)

METHOD	DESCRIPTION
	that might later be resized. This method is demonstrated in the "Drawing Lines and Shapes Programmatically" section of this chapter.
`lineTo(x, y)`	Draws a straight line from the current drawing position to the specified X/Y coordinates. This method is demonstrated in the "Drawing Lines and Shapes Programmatically" section of this chapter.
`moveTo()`	Changes the position of the current drawing position without drawing anything. This method is demonstrated in the "Drawing Lines and Shapes Programmatically" section of this chapter.

Learning by Example: A Gesture-Based Scroller Widget

Now that you've skimmed through the methods, properties, and events supported by the `MovieClip` class, let's jump right in with a relatively complicated example. Although this example doesn't make use of every single `MovieClip` member, it uses enough of them that it will give you a good idea how to work with movie clips in the future.

In your travels throughout the Web, you might have come upon sites that use scrolling interfaces built with Flash, where the content of the interface slides from side to side in response to how you move your mouse. If you're not familiar with what I'm talking about, or if you just want to see the main example for this chapter in action, go ahead and pull up the UseScroller1.html page (included with this chapter's example files) in your browser. You'll see a series of "slides," arranged side by side like a filmstrip (see Figure 5.1).

By placing your mouse over the filmstrip and moving it from side to side, you can scroll the filmstrip to the left or right. Right now the slides are just placeholders, numbered from 1 to 10, but they could display just about any information you wanted them to.

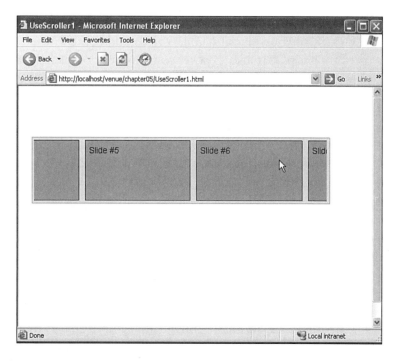

FIGURE 5.1   Users can scroll through the contents of this widget by "gesturing" with the mouse.

NOTE

In Chapter 7, the placeholders will be replaced with dynamic content from your server, retrieved in the form of XML code. You can look ahead to Figure 7.1 in Chapter 7 to see the final results.

People often refer to this type of widget as being "gesture-driven," meaning that it enables the user to gesture with his or her mouse to direct the interface to show specific information. You can use this type of widget whenever you want to show a potentially large amount of images or information in a limited amount of screen real estate.

Building a Simple Example That Uses the Scroller

The scroller functionality is encapsulated by an ActionScript 2.0 class called `GestureMovieClip`. This new subclass is a descendant of the built-in `MovieClip` class, and as such, inherits all the methods, properties, and events listed in Tables 5.1 through 5.5.

The class exposes a few methods (above and beyond the ones exposed by `MovieClip` itself, of course) that enable you to add content (the "slides") to the widget (the "filmstrip"). It also exposes some useful properties that control the filmstrip's width, the speed of the scrolling, and so on. You'll see a listing of these members in Table 5.6; feel free to skip ahead if you want to glance at it now.

> **NOTE**
>
> Later, we'll turn the `GestureMovieClip` into a simple component so that you can set its properties interactively using the Properties panel or the Component Inspector. See the "Turning Clips into Components" section later in this chapter.

Using this chapter's `GestureMovieClip` class involves three basic steps:

1. First, you create movie clip symbols that you want to be shown within the scrolling filmstrip. Just to be clear, I'll call these clips your "*slide clips.*"
2. Next, you create an empty movie clip symbol that is linked to the `GestureMovieClip` class (as opposed to the normal `MovieClip` class) and place an instance of the clip on the Stage, wherever you want the scroller widget to appear at runtime.
3. Finally, you write some simple ActionScript code that adds instances of your slide clips to the scroller widget. When your movie appears in the Flash Player, the scroller should behave as expected.

> **NOTE**
>
> Don't confuse the term *slide clip*, which is just a term I made up for this example, with Flash MX Professional 2004's new *slide screens* feature (discussed in Chapter 11, "Building Better Forms with Flash").

Let's walk through each step in detail. First, to create the slide clips that will be shown in the scroller, do the following:

> **NOTE**
>
> If you don't feel like going through these steps, you can open the finished UseScroller1.fla file that is included with this chapter's example files.

1. Use File > New to create a new Flash Document and save it as UseScroller1.fla.

2. Use Insert > New Symbol to bring up the Create New Symbol dialog box. Type **SlideClip** for the Name and make sure the Behavior option is set to Movie Clip. Click the Advanced button at the bottom of the dialog box, and then check the Export for ActionScript option and confirm that the Linkage Identifier field is also set to SlideClip (see Figure 5.2). Then click OK to create the new symbol.

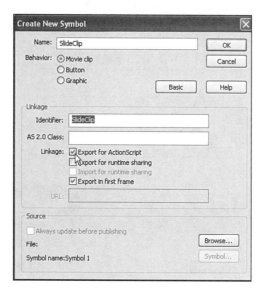

FIGURE 5.2   Creating a new movie clip to display in the scroller.

3. In Symbol Edit mode for the new clip, use the Rectangle tool to create a filled-in box (I made mine purple because I love that color these days) on the clip's Stage.

4. Double-click inside the rectangle to select it, and then use the Properties panel to set its size to a height of 100 pixels and a width of 200 pixels. Also, set the box's X and Y coordinates to 0, which will make the box's top-left corner align precisely to the clip's registration point.

5. Create a new text field within the bounds of the box you just created, and then use the Properties panel to set its Type property to Dynamic Text and its Variable property to slideName (see Figure 5.3). If a variable named slideName is set within this movie clip's timeline at runtime, its value will automatically be displayed in this text field. Also, turn off the text field's Selectable option, and set the Font to _sans.

Now you have a mockup of a slide to display in the scroller. We don't need to place any actual instances of the clip symbol on the Stage; they will be created at runtime through ActionScript. Of course, in actual use, you would have someone create something that looked a bit nicer and that showed some kind of useful information. Figure 7.1 in Chapter 7 shows one way in which actual dynamic content might be displayed in the scroller.

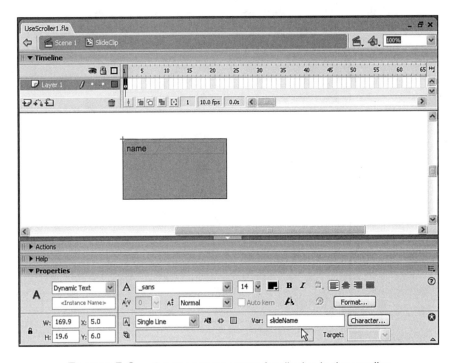

FIGURE 5.3   Creating test content for display in the scroller.

The next step is to create another movie clip symbol. This one represents the scroller widget (the filmstrip) and will actually be placed on the Stage at the spot where you want the scroller to appear.

To create the scroller movie clip, do the following:

1. Use Insert > New Symbol to create another movie clip symbol. Type **ScrollerClip** for the name, check the Export for ActionScript box, and verify that the Linkage Identifier field is set to ScrollerClip.

2. Still in the Create New Symbol dialog box, type **GestureMovieClip** in the AS 2.0 Class field (see Figure 5.4). This tells Flash that you want this clip symbol to inherit the methods, properties, and events of the

`GestureMovieClip` subclass rather than the methods, properties, and events of the standard `MovieClip` class. The source code for `GestureMovieClip` is included with this chapter's example files and is discussed throughout the latter half of this chapter.

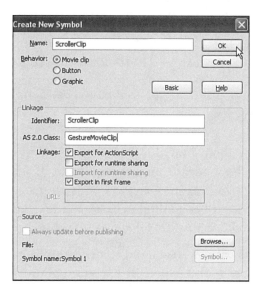

FIGURE 5.4   Creating a symbol of type `GestureMovieClip`.

3. Click OK to create the new symbol.
4. Drag an instance of the new `ScrollerClip` symbol from the Library onto the Stage. Position it somewhere near the left edge of the Stage. Use the Properties panel to give it an instance name of `mcScroller`.

Great! Now you have a blank movie clip that exposes all the members of `GestureMovieClip`. I know you don't know what those members are yet; if that's bothering you, just skip ahead to Table 5.6 for a quick glance at the methods and properties you'll be able to use on this new clip instance.

Now you're ready to add some simple code to the scroller to make it do its actual work. The scroller is really easy to use, so you'll only need to add a couple of lines. If you were a designer that was only interested in using the scroller—rather than understanding how it works internally—this would be the only code in this chapter that you would need to be aware of.

Here's how to add this scroller-usage code to your movie:

1. Click Frame 1 of the main timeline (not the timeline of one of the movie clip symbols).

2. Add the following code to the Actions Panel:

```
// Add some instances of the SlideClip symbol to the scroller
for (var i = 0; i < 10; i++) {
  mcScroller.addClip("SlideClip", {slideName:"Slide #" + (i+1)});
}
// Now that scroller is loaded up, enable its functionality
mcScroller.enableGestures();
```

You'll learn more about how this code works in a moment, but I think you can probably get the basic idea from just looking at it. mcScroller represents the scroller widget, the addClip() method adds an instance of a clip symbol from the Library to the scroller, and enableGestures() turns on the scroller's mouse-gesture functionality.

At this point, you can go ahead and test this movie by means of File > Publish Preview or Control > Test Movie or Ctrl+Enter. Your mcScroller instance appears as a light gray rectangle with a dark gray border. Within the rectangle are 10 instances of your SlideClip symbol, labeled Slide #1, Slide #2, and so on (see Figure 5.5). You can gesture with your mouse to slide the content from left to right.

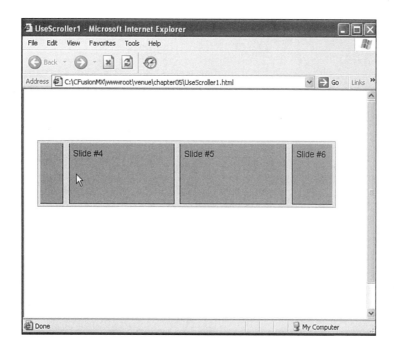

FIGURE 5.5   Here's what this simple demo of the GestureMovieClip looks like.

The Handmade Members of the *GestureMovieClip* Class

Now that you've seen a basic use of the GestureMovieClip subclass, it's time to start looking into its guts, which in turn will help you learn more about the built-in MovieClip class (on which the subclass is based). Let's start by taking a look at GestureMovieClip's public members. The public methods are listed in Table 5.6; the public properties are in Table 5.7.

NOTE

If you're a bit confused about what I mean by "public members" or about why I'm referring to GestureMovieClip as a "subclass" or "descendant" of MovieClip, you need to take a look at the "Creating Your Own Classes" section at the end of Chapter 4.

TABLE 5.6   Public *GestureMovieClip* Methods

MEMBER	DESCRIPTION
enableGestures()	Enables the mouse-gesture scrolling functionality. The functionality is disabled when the scroller first appears, so that you have a chance to add clips to the widget before users can start scrolling through it. When you are done adding clips by means of addClip(), call this method to enable the scroller.
removeAllClips()	Removes all clips from the scroller. Use this method if you want to clear the scroller so that a new set of slides can be added to it. Note that no method is provided for removing one clip at a time (though it wouldn't be so hard to create such a method).
addClip(idName [, initObject, newName])	Adds a slide clip to the scroller. idName is the linkage identifier of the clip in the Library. The optional initObject argument can be used to supply parameters (variables) to the new clip. The optional newName argument is the instance name for the new clip; if this argument isn't provided, a default name is created by concatenating mcSlide with the new slide's index position (mcSlide0, mcSlide1, and so on).
disableGestures()	Disables (turns off) the mouse-gesture scrolling functionality.

TABLE 5.7   Public *GestureMovieClip* Properties

MEMBER	DESCRIPTION
areaWidth	Numeric property. The width of the scrolling area, in pixels. The default width is 500.
areaHeight	Numeric property. The height of the scrolling area. The default height is 100 pixels.
paddingBetweenClips	Numeric property. The amount of space to use between the slide clips as they are added to the scroller. The default padding is 10 pixels.
deadCenter	Numeric property. Defines the amount of space in the center of the scroller that *does not* respond to mouse motions. You can set this value to 0 if you want the whole scroller to be "live" with respect to mouse motions (although this will make it hard for users to keep the slides still when they find

Member	Description
	something interesting). Set it to a high number if you want only the left and right edges of the scroller to be live. The default value is 50 pixels to the left and right of center (for a total dead area of 100 pixels).
maxSpeed	Numeric property. The maximum speed at which the slides can move at any given moment. This property works together with refreshInterval to control how quickly and smoothly the slides scroll. The default maximum is 30 pixels at a time.
refreshInterval	Numeric property. The number of milliseconds that elapse between individual movements of the slides in the scroller. The default interval is 50 milliseconds, which means that the slides can move up to 20 times per second. Increase the number for smoother motion, but keep in mind that a larger number obviously represents more CPU utilization on your users' machines. If you increase this number, you might want to decrease the maxSpeed so that the slides don't move too fast.
drawBorder	Boolean property. Whether to draw a border around the edge of the scroller widget. The default is true.
borderColor	Hexadecimal numeric property. The color of the border, if any. The default is 0xAAAAAA (a medium gray). Other examples of color values would be 0xFF0000 for red, 0x00FF00 for green, 0x0000FF for blue, 0x000000 for black, and 0xFFFFFF for white.
borderWidth	Numeric property. The thickness of the border, if any. The default is 1 pixel. Specify 0 for a hairline-width border.
borderPadding	Numeric property. The space between the active area of the scroller and the border. The default is 5 pixels.
bgColor	Hexidecimal numeric property. The color of the scoller's background. The default is 0x000000 (black).
bgAlpha	Numeric property. The alpha (transparency) value of the background. The default is 10 (very transparent, which makes the background appear as a light gray color).

If you want, you can go ahead and experiment with some of the properties by changing them from their default values. You should set the properties before you call any of the methods (the simple implementation of the class doesn't enable you to change them on the fly without getting inconsistent results, though you could change that as a learning exercise). For instance, to get rid of the border and background and increase the spacing between the individual slides, you could add the following lines to the top of the code you added to Frame 1 of UseScroller1.fla:

```
// Tweak some of the scroller's properties
mcScroller.drawBorderAndBackground = false;
mcScroller.paddingBetweenClips = 50;
```

Reviewing the Code for *GestureMovieClip*

Because the functionality of the scroller widget is encapsulated by the `GestureMovieClip` class, the actual code that makes it work is in an ActionScript file called GestureMovieClip.as. Let's start taking a look at the contents of that file.

> **NOTE**
>
> As discussed in the "Creating Your Own Classes" section of Chapter 4, the GestureMovieClip.as file can be stored in the current folder (that is, the same folder as the FLA that is using the class), the special Classes folder within Flash's configuration directory, or any other folder that you have added to Flash's classpath.

Go ahead and open the file up in Flash now. At the top, you'll see all the properties listed in Table 5.7, followed by `function` blocks for all the public methods listed in Table 5.6. Some of the public methods call private methods internally; the private methods are grouped together at the bottom of the file.

> **NOTE**
>
> Because I wanted to make sure that you had a non-trivial, real-world example to work with in this chapter, the GestureMovieClip.as file turns out to be pretty long (around 250 lines of code, including comments). It's not hard to understand, though, and I encourage you not to feel intimidated by it.

The next few sections of this chapter discuss much of the code in the GestureMovieClip.as file. Note, however, that not every method is discussed line by line (that would get old fast). You will therefore need to spend a bit of time looking through the file on your own, following the flow from method to method.

Here's a typical sequence of events and the methods that are involved in each step:

1. When an instance of the scroller is first instantiated (that is, when it first appears on the Stage), the properties are established and set to their initial, default values (as listed in Table 5.7).

2. Next, the class's constructor is called. This happens automatically; you don't have to call the constructor yourself.

3. Within the constructor, a private method called createMaskClip() is used to create something called a *mask clip*, which creates the effect of the filmstrip being viewed through a rectangular window-like area.

4. Within createMaskClip(), another private method called drawBox() is used to do the actual work of creating the rectangular area in the mask clip.

5. If it wishes, the movie that is using the class (in this case, the UseScroller1.fla document) adjusts any or all of the instance's public properties listed in Table 5.7.

6. The movie that is using the class calls the addClip() method to create instances of slide clips and add them to the scroller interface.

7. When addClip() is called for the first time, a private method called initializeVisuals() is used to draw the scroller's border and fill in the background color, if called for.

8. Within addClip(), the new instance of the desired slide clip is created. The new instance is then passed to a private method called addClipInstance(), which places the clip at the appropriate visual position.

9. After each call to addClip(), the movie that is using the class is free to manipulate or initialize it in whatever way is appropriate, using any of the usual MovieClip members shown in Tables 5.1 through 5.5 (or any subclassed members if the slide is itself an instance of a MovieClip descendant).

10. The movie that is using the class calls the `enableGestures()` method to make the scroller start doing its thing. The method tells ActionScript to execute a private method called `respondToMouseGestures()` repeatedly (many times per second), which "watches" the user's mouse position and responds by scrolling when appropriate.

11. Whenever `respondToMouseGestures()` determines that scrolling actually needs to take place, another private method called `scrollContents()` is called to do the work of changing the filmstrip's position.

12. If the movie that is using the class wishes, it calls `disableGestures()` to stop the repeated execution of `respondToMouseGestures()` and thus stop the scrolling effect.

13. If the movie that is using the class wants to do so, it calls `removeAllClips()` to clear the contents of the scroller.

Again, take a look at GestureMovieClip.as on your own now if you want to see the entire file at once (it's a bit too long for it to appear sensibly in printed form in this book). The next few sections discuss most of the file's contents, one chunk at a time—discussing a number of the most important `MovieClip` members and concepts along the way.

Movie Clips in the Library

You added a few movie clips to the Library panel in Chapter 2, and you created two more movie clips in the Library for the UseScroller1.fla example. Let's talk a bit more about what it means to add a clip to a document's Library.

About Specifying ActionScript 2.0 Classes for Library Symbols

I like to think of each movie clip in the Library as being a special descendant of the `MovieClip` class. Each inherits the methods, properties, and events of `MovieClip`, and each also inherits a blank canvas on which to draw and an empty timeline with which to work. One of the properties that can be overridden by a descendant is the content in its Stage and timeline.

If you accept this way of thinking about clips, the `SlideClip` symbol you created in the Library can be thought of as a descendant of `MovieClip`; the descendant inherits everything about a normal movie clip, and it extends the normal behavior by adding a purple box and a text field. When you create instances of the clip—which you can do at design time by dragging the symbol onto the Stage or at runtime through a script—each clip instance becomes a class instance in the OOP sense. Thus, the instance has access to all the members of the class and also has its own memory space in which to maintain its current state. (The state includes the variables that have been set in the timeline, plus the current position of the playhead in the timeline, plus any child movie clips you might add to the SlideClip instance, and so on.)

> **NOTE**
>
> I'm not trying to suggest that every movie clip you create is or is not a literal descendant of MovieClip. This is just an interesting (and hopefully instructive) way to think about the relationship.

So what happens when you set the AS 2.0 Class field in the Create New Symbol dialog box (as shown back in Figure 5.4) when creating a new movie clip symbol? You're telling Flash that you want the new clip to descend from the specified class rather than the built-in MovieClip class. The idea is that the specified class is itself an official descendant of MovieClip, so at a minimum, it knows how to do everything that MovieClip does. Presumably, the specified subclass also implements some kind of additional functionality that you are interested in using.

So, when you created the ScrollerClip symbol in the last step sequence and set its AS 2.0 Class field to GestureMovieClip, you were telling Flash that you want all instances of the symbol (which, again, are created when you drag the symbol onto the Stage or when you create instances programmatically through script) to inherit all the methods and properties of GestureMovieClip in addition to the usual MovieClip members. That's why you were able to call GestureMovieClip-specific methods such as enableGestures() in the Actions panel.

Let's take a look at the first and most important part of the GestureMovieClip.as class file: the use of the extends keyword to specify the class as a descendant of MovieClip. If you look in the file, you'll see that the whole thing is bracketed by the following class declaration:

```
// This class is a descendant of the built-in MovieClip class
class GestureMovieClip extends MovieClip {
}
```

Not surprisingly, any custom class you specify in the AS 2.0 Class field for a movie clip symbol should extend the MovieClip class.

> **NOTE**
>
> Again, if the class and extends syntax or the other words I'm throwing around here (like descendant and constructor) are unfamiliar to you, please go back and review the "Creating Your Own Classes" section of Chapter 4.

About Subclassed Properties for MovieClip Symbols

Like any class, descendants of MovieClip might add any of their own properties by declaring variables within the class block (but outside any function blocks). The properties will then be known to any instances of symbols that specify the class in their AS 2.0 Class field. For instance, GestureMovieClip contains the following property declarations (the public ones are listed in Table 5.7). When an instance of the symbol is created at runtime, the new instance will be populated with its own copy of each property (each property will get whatever default value is specified after the = sign, if any):

```
// This class is a descendant of the built-in MovieClip class
class GestureMovieClip extends MovieClip {

   // These properties are local to each instance of this subclass
   // These properties can be manipulated to customize its behavior
   public var areaWidth:Number = 500;
   public var areaHeight:Number = 100;
   public var paddingBetweenClips:Number = 10;
   public var deadCenter:Number = 50;
   public var maxSpeed:Number = 30;
   public var refreshInterval:Number = 50;
   // More public properties, related to drawing border/background
   public var drawBorderAndBackground:Boolean = true;
   public var borderColor:Number = 0xAAAAAA;
   public var borderWidth:Number = 1;
   public var borderPadding:Number = 5;
   public var bgColor:Number = 0x000000;
   public var bgAlpha:Number = 10;

   // These are also local to each instance of the subclass,
   // but they are for internal use only
   private var arClips:Array = new Array;
   private var centerPoint:Number;
```

```
   private var intervalID:Number;
   private var mcCanvas:MovieClip;
   private var mcMask:MovieClip; private var initialized:Boolean =
false;
```

About Subclassed Constructors for MovieClip *Symbols*

Also like any class, descendants of MovieClip might implement their own constructor functions. If you want any special processing to take place when a symbol is first created, create a constructor function that contains the appropriate code. If you don't have any such needs, it's up to you whether to just create an empty placeholder constructor or to omit it entirely.

In GestureMovieClip.as, the constructor function looks like this:

```
// Constructor function; gets called when scroller is instantiated
public function GestureMovieClip() {

  // Create new movie clip within this one, where we'll show items
  this.createEmptyMovieClip("mcCanvas", 0);

  // Create a mask clip, which contains just a filled-in black box
  createMaskClip(mcCanvas, "mcMask", -1, -1, areaWidth+1,
areaHeight+1);
}
```

The first line uses the MovieClip.createEmptyMovieClip() method (see Table 5.2) to create a new, empty movie clip symbol with an instance name of mcCanvas. The individual slide clips will be placed onto this "canvas" clip, and then the canvas will be moved back and forth to create the scrolling effect. It's a clip within a clip, the purpose of which is to contain the slide clips so that they can be moved around as a group.

Because the canvas clip is created within the scroller clip, it is represented as a MovieClip variable called mcCanvas within the scroller clip's Timeline variable scope. Within the remainder of the class file, the clip can be referred to as this.mcCanvas, this["mcCanvas"], eval("mcCanvas"), or, because this is always implied within a class file, just mcCanvas.

Because of the strict type checking in place in any ActionScript 2.0 file, you must declare mcCanvas as a property of the class at the top of the class file (you can see it in the first code snippet in this section). Otherwise, you will get an error message when you attempt to compile or syntax check your work. Basically, the rule is that every variable used in a class file must be known as a property of the class, a local function variable, or a property inherited from the superclass.

The other line in the constructor is a call to the class's private `createMaskClip()` method, which creates another clip within the scroller clip for a special purpose. More about this special purpose is in the "Creating Mask Clips Programmatically" section later in this chapter.

Attaching Movie Clips from the Library Using Linkage Identifiers

When you created the `SlideClip` movie clip symbol earlier, you checked the Export for ActionScript check box and specified a *linkage identifier* for the new symbol (refer back to Figure 5.2). As you learned in Chapters 2 and 3, linkage identifiers are special names that you give to symbols that you want to be able to create brand new instances of at runtime. After you've assigned a linkage identifier to the symbol, you can create new instances of it at runtime by means of the `MovieClip.attachMovie()` method (see Table 5.2).

Without the linkage identifier, you can't use `attachMovie()`. As you'll find in your travels through this book and through the Flash universe, `attachMovie()` is an incredibly important method, often at the heart of any Flash project that presents dynamic information, so you'll soon be used to assigning linkage identifiers for many of your clips.

The `GestureMovieClip` example class uses `attachMovie()` in just one place, but it's an important one: within the public `addClip()` method that adds slide clips to the scroller. Here's the code for that method:

```
// This function creates a new clip instance, registers it with
// the scrolling/gesture system, and returns the new instance
public function addClip(idName:String, initObject:Object,
newName:String) : MovieClip {
  // Local variables
  var newDepth:Number;
  var mcNew:MovieClip;

  // If first time, initialize border and other visual aspects
  if (!this.initialized) {
    initializeVisuals();
  }
```

```
// Depth of the new clip
newDepth = this.mcCanvas.getNextHighestDepth();
// Create an instance name for new clip if one isn't provided
if (newName == null) {
  newName = "mcSlide" + newDepth;
}

// Create new movie clip on the internal "canvas" clip
this.mcCanvas.attachMovie(idName, newName, newDepth, initObject);
mcNew = this.mcCanvas[newName];

// Call addClipInstance() to position and register the new clip
addClipInstance(mcNew);

// Return the just-created movie clip instance
return mcNew;
}
```

The first line of this method is a bit of a tangent; it checks whether the private initialized property has been set and calls initializeVisuals() if not. You'll learn more about this method later in the "Drawing Lines and Shapes Programmatically" section. For now, just accept that it executes the first time this method is called for a particular instance.

The next line uses the MovieClip.getNextHighestDepth() method to obtain the next available depth level to use when creating the clip instance that is about to be added to the scroller. As you learned in Chapters 2 and 3, each clip that you add at runtime needs to have its own level number; if you reuse a level number, the new clip replaces the existing one. You can either keep track of which level to use on your own by maintaining an internal counter within your code, or you can use getNextHighestDepth() to get the next available level for you. (Note that getNextHighestDepth() is new for Flash Player 7, which is the version that coincides with Flash MX 2004.)

> **NOTE**
>
> Here's a brain teaser for you: In the just-discussed case, you could use this.arClips.length rather than this.mcCanvas.getNextHighestDepth(). Can you see why? (*Hint:* You'll probably need to look ahead to the code for the private addClipInstance() method in the next section to see why.)

Next, an `if` block is used to assign a default value to the `newName` argument when a value is not specified when the method is actually called. This makes `newName` an optional argument. Whatever coder is using the class can specify an instance name; otherwise, one is created. (The coder can refer to the built-in `_name` property of the movie clip; this function returns to get the assigned name.)

Now it's time to use `attachMovie()` to actually create a new instance of the specified movie clip and add it to the scroller. You'll note that `attachMovie()` is called as a method of the canvas clip within the scroller, not the scroller clip itself. This means that the `_parent` property of the new clip will be set to the canvas clip. The new clip will also be physically attached to the canvas clip (that is, the new clip will move when the canvas clip is moved, which is what we're looking for).

In another situation, you might want to call `attachMovie()` as a method of the class for which you're writing the code. In such a case, you would call `this.attachMovie()` rather than `this.mcCanvas.attachMovie()`.

After `attachMovie()` has been used to create the new slide clip instance, it is set to the local variable `mcNew`, which is just a handy way to refer to the clip that was just added. The expression on the right side of this assignment is `this.mcCanvas[newName]`, which is a convenient way to refer to a variable or property of an object when the actual name of the variable or property is not known until runtime (for details, see the "Associative Arrays" section in Chapter 4).

> **Note**
>
> You could also use `eval("this.mcCanvas." + newName)`, but the square bracket syntax is more direct. In either case, you may leave off the `this` part. I like to include it because I find it emphasizes that I'm referring to a property of the class rather than to a local function variable.

Next, the private `addClipInstance()` method is used to position the new slide clip in the correct spot on the canvas. Finally, the newly created clip is returned as the function's return value.

Initializing Movie Clips with Parameters

If you look back at the `addClip()` method in the last section, you'll see that it accepts an argument named `initObject` (see Table 5.2). This argument is passed directly to the `MovieClip.attachMovie()` method without modification (that is, it's a passthrough for `attachMovie()`'s argument).

You can use the initObject argument when calling attachMovie() to supply parameters to the new clip as it is instantiated. The argument accepts an associative array (that is, an instance of the Object class) that can contain any number of name/value pairs. Flash copies each value into the new clip's timeline as it is created. You can create the associative array using new Object and then pass it to the initObject argument, or you can create and pass the argument inline using curly-brace notation.

For instance, in the simple code you added to UseScroller1.fla, you used curly-brace notation to create a variable named slideName in the new clip's timeline, like so:

```
mcScroller.addClip("SlideClip", {slideName:"Slide #" + (i+1)});
```

You could have done the same thing using two steps, like so:

```
var oClipVars:Object = {slideName:"Slide #" + (i+1)};
mcScroller.addClip("SlideClip", oClipVars);
```

The following would also be functionally equivalent:

```
var oClipVars:Object = new Object;
oClipVars.slideName = :"Slide #" + (i+1);
mcScroller.addClip("SlideClip", oClipVars);
```

For details about these different syntax options, see the "Associative Arrays" section in Chapter 4.

Changing the Appearance and Position of a Clip

After a movie clip has been created using the attachMovie() or createEmptyMovieClip() methods that you have been learning about, you can use any of the various MovieClip members listed in Table 5.1 to change the position of the clip or how it appears on the stage. For instance, you can use the _visible property to show or hide the clip, the _rotation property to turn it clockwise or counterclockwise, or the _xscale and _yscale properties to resize or stretch it. This section shows you how to use the _x property to set a clip's left/right position; you can use the same basic syntax to set any of the other appearance-changing properties.

Changing a Clip's Position

In the last section, you saw that the public addClip() method calls an internal method called addClipInstance() to position each new slide clip on the canvas. Here's the code for that method:

```
private function addClipInstance(mcAdd:MovieClip):Void {
  // Position the new clip at the appropriate spot on the stage
  if (this.arClips.length > 0) {
    var mcPrior:MovieClip = this.arClips[this.arClips.length - 1];
    mcAdd._x = mcPrior._x + mcPrior._width + this.paddingBetweenClips;
  }

  // Add new clip to this timeline's arClips array
  this.arClips.push(mcAdd);
}
```

This code uses two of the properties in Table 5.1 to put the slide in the correct spot. The _x and _width properties are used to determine the position and width of the slide (if any) that appeared just before the one that is being added. A bit of math is performed (based on the width of the previous clip), and then the _x property is used to place the slide in the correct spot.

You'll note that the class's private arClips property is being used here to keep track of all the slide clips as they are added to the scroller. The Array.push() method is used to add the clip instance to the array each time this code is executed; therefore, this.arClips.length always holds the current number of slides in the scroller. This makes it easy to set the mcPrior variable to the previously added slide.

Another strategy would be to forget about the arClips array altogether and just maintain a private property called mcLastSlide. That code might look like this:

```
private function addClipInstance(mcAdd:MovieClip):Void {

  // Position the new clip at the appropriate spot on the stage
  if (this.mcLastSlide != undefined) {
   mcAdd._x = mcLastSlide._x + mcLastSlide._width +
   ➥this.paddingBetweenClips;
  }

  // Remember that this slide is the most recent one
  this.mcLastSlide = mcAdd;
}
```

MOVIE CLIPS IN THE LIBRARY

Understanding the Registration Point

When you are getting or setting the value of the _x property (or the _y property, which works the same way except for the vertical position), the value is always measured relative to the parent clip's registration point. The registration point is represented by a small cross when you are editing a symbol (it's visible at the top-left corner of the rectangle you added in Figure 5.2), and it always represents the X/Y position 0,0.

You can move all the content within a clip (in this case, the rectangle and the text field) in Symbol Edit mode, which is effectively equivalent to moving the registration point. For instance, if you moved the content such that the rectangle was centered over the registration point, the top-left corner of the rectangle would then be at X/Y coordinate –90,–50 (assuming the rectangle was 180 pixels wide and 100 high) rather than at X/Y coordinate 0,0.

To keep the implementation of GestureMovieClip simple, an assumption is made that the content of each slide is positioned such that the registration point is at the upper-left corner of the content. If not, the slides might appear to be positioned incorrectly. If you need to support slide clips that use the registration point differently, you can use the MovieClip.getBounds() method (see Table 5.1) to help compute the appropriate offsets. See the Flash documentation for details.

Removing Clips

Any clips that have been added to a movie using attachMovie() or createEmptyMovieClip() can be removed using the removeMovieClip() method. For instance, our GestureMovieClip example exposes a public method called removeAllClips(), which iterates through the slides in the scroller (that is, the contents of the arClips array property), removing each one as it goes. Here's the code for that method:

```
// This method removes all clips from the interface
public function removeAllClips() {
   while (arClips.length > 0) {
     var mcCurrent = arClips.pop();
     mcCurrent.removeMovieClip();
   }
}
```

First, the `Array.pop()` method is called, which removes the last item from the `arClips` array and returns the item that was removed. Then the `removeMovieClip()` method is used to delete the clip.

By the way, it's important to understand that *removing* a clip is different from *unloading* a clip. As you have already learned in Chapter 2, you can use the `MovieClip.loadMovie()` method to load an external SWF or JPG into the position defined by an existing movie clip. To unload the external SWF or JPG, you use `MovieClip.unloadMovie()`, which unloads the external content but leaves the original movie clip container in place. To destroy the original movie clip, you could use `removeMovieClip()`, but then you would no longer be able to load external movies into it by means of `loadMovie()`.

> **NOTE**
>
> Again, to keep the `GestureMovieClip` example as simple as possible, no method is exposed for removing one clip at a time. You could create one without too much effort; you would just need to make sure to rearrange all the clips visually if one was removed from the middle of the canvas clip.

Responding to Mouse Movements

At this point, you've seen quite a bit of the `GestureMovieClip` class's code, but you haven't yet seen how the core scrolling functionality was implemented. Obviously, to create the scrolling functionality, we need be able to determine the position of the mouse.

Flash provides a few different mechanisms for working with the position of the mouse:

- **The `_xmouse` and `_ymouse` properties that are available for each movie clip instance (including `_root`).** These properties can be used at any time to determine the X/Y position of the mouse.
- **The `onMouseMove` event, which is also available for any movie clip instance (including `_root`).** You can write code that responds to this event so that your movie can perform whatever processing it needs to whenever the user's mouse moves.
- **The built-in `Mouse` object, which also exposes a similar `onMouseMove` event.** The `Mouse` object also provides a number of other methods for responding to the mouse wheel, hiding the mouse pointer from view, or designing new mouse pointers of your own.

The scroller example for this chapter needs to respond continuously to the current position of the mouse, not just when it moves. Thus, it need only use the _xmouse and _ymouse properties of the scroller clip. You can consult the Flash documentation for details about the other, event-driven techniques; they fall a bit outside the scope of this book.

A Quick Tangent: Scheduling Method Calls with *setInterval()*

If you recall, the mouse gesture functionality is disabled when the scroller first appears. To enable the scrolling, the document that is using the scroller needs to call its enableGestures() method. Here's the code for that method, from the GestureMovieClip.as class file:

```
// This function enables the gesture motions by scheduling
// the respondToMouseGestures() function for repeated execution
public function enableGestures() {
   intervalID = setInterval(this, "respondToMouseGestures",
refreshInterval);
}
```

And here's the code for the disableGestures() method, which can be used to turn off the gesture functionality:

```
// This disables gesture motions by stopping scheduled execution
public function disableGestures() {
  clearInterval(this.intervalID);
}
```

The basic idea is this: A private method called respondToMouseGestures() does the work of looking at the current mouse position and scrolling the canvas clip accordingly. We want this method to be called repeatedly, many times per second. ActionScript's built-in setInterval() function is designed for just this kind of situation. It's like an invisible timer that schedules execution of a function at set intervals.

You can use setInterval() in one of two forms, depending on whether you want to schedule execution of an object's method or a standalone function. For a method, you use this form, where object is the object in question, *method_name* is a placeholder for the name of the method you want to call, and interval is the amount of time between executions (in milliseconds):

```
setInterval(object, method_name, interval [, param1, param2...]);
```

For a standalone function, you use this form, where `function` is the function you want to be called every `interval` milliseconds:

```
setInterval(function, interval [, param1, param2...]);
```

In either case, `setInterval()` returns a number called the interval ID, which represents the scheduled job that was just created. You can stop the scheduled executions at any time by passing the interval ID to the `clearInterval()` function, like so:

```
clearInterval(intervalID);
```

As you can see, the `enableGestures()` and `disableGestures()` methods at the beginning of this section are little more than thin wrappers around `setInterval()` and `clearInterval()` that schedule and stop the repeated execution of the private `respondToMouseGestures()` method.

Looking at the Current Mouse Position

Here's the code for the `respondToMouseGestures()` method. It might look a bit complicated at first, but it's pretty simple after you take a close look at it. As you do so, keep an eye on the `scrollBy` variable. It represents the number of pixels that the slides should be moved by. If, at the end of the function, `scrollBy` is still 0, the slides don't need to move. If `scrollBy` is a negative number, the slides should move by that number of pixels to the left; if `scrollBy` is positive, the slides should move to the right.

```
// This function does the work of scrolling the clips
// as the user gestures from side to side with her mouse
private function respondToMouseGestures():Void {

  // These variables are local to this function
  var scrollBy: Number = 0;
  var gestureExtent: Number = 0;
  var curMousePos: Number = _xmouse;
  var isForward: Boolean = curMousePos > centerPoint;

  // Stop now if mouse not currently in enabled area
  if ( _ymouse < 0 || _ymouse > areaHeight || _xmouse < 0 || _xmouse >
areaWidth)
    return;

  // If user is gesturing forward, and is past "dead center" zone,
  // compute the amount, in pixels, that user is gesturing by
  if (isForward && (curMousePos > centerPoint + deadCenter) ) {
```

```
      gestureExtent = curMousePos - (centerPoint + deadCenter);
   }
   // Do the same if the user is gesturing backward
   if (!isForward && (curMousePos < centerPoint - deadCenter) ) {
      gestureExtent = curMousePos - (centerPoint - deadCenter);
   }

   // If we've determined that the user is indeed gesturing
   if (gestureExtent != 0) {
      // Compute how fast we should move the slides
      scrollBy = gestureExtent / 5;

      // Enforce a maximum speed limit
      if (isForward) {
         scrollBy = Math.min(scrollBy, maxSpeed)
      } else {
         scrollBy = Math.max(scrollBy, -maxSpeed);
      }
   }

   // If we've determined to scroll the contents, scroll them now
   if (scrollBy != 0) {
      scrollContents(scrollBy);
   }
}
```

First, the current value of _xmouse is set to the local variable called curMousePos. The xmouse property always holds the X coordinate of the mouse's current position, relative to the scroller clip's registration point. If the mouse is to the left of the registration point (that is, at the top-left corner of the scroller), _xmouse will hold a negative value; if the mouse is to the right, the value will be positive. The _ymouse property works the same way for the Y coordinate.

> **NOTE**
>
> The code in this method creates a local variable called curMousePos to hold a snapshot of the _xmouse position when the method first begins its work. You could just get rid of curMousePos and refer to _xmouse directly throughout, but there would be no guarantee that the value of _xmouse would not change while the method was executing.

The first `if` statement checks whether the mouse is currently positioned over the scroller area. If the mouse's position is to the left or right of the scroller, or above or below it, it's not over the scroller area. This means that the function doesn't need to do anything at the moment, so `return` is used to stop right there.

Assuming that the mouse is somewhere over the scroller clip, execution proceeds to the next two `if` blocks, which calculate a value for the local `gestureExtent` variable. If the user's mouse is beyond the "dead" area to the right of the center of the scroller, `gestureExtent` will be a positive number that indicates the extent of the user's current mouse gesture (the number of pixels beyond the dead area). If the mouse is beyond the dead area to the left, `gestureExtent` will be a negative number. If the user's mouse is currently over the dead area in the center of the scroller, `gestureExtent` will remain 0.

The rest of the code is fairly elementary. Some simple math is performed on the `gestureExtent` value to create a value for the `scrollBy` value. You could use just about any math formula here, as long as it increases `scrollBy` as `gestureExtent` increases, and vice versa. The formula affects how smoothly the slides speed up if the user moves the mouse slowly away from the center of the scroller. (If you're good with trigonometry, you could probably come up with a formula that would create a very smooth, natural slope, but the simple one I have in there now results in relatively smooth-feeling behavior, which is good enough for our purposes.) The final step is to use the built-in `Math.min()` and `Math.max()` methods to apply a "speed limit" to the `scrollBy` variable so that the slides don't move too quickly at any given time.

Assuming that `scrollBy` has been found to be something other than 0, the value is passed to the private `scrollContents()` method, which is where the slides are actually moved to the left or right. Here's the code for that method:

```
private function scrollContents(scrollOffset:Number):Void {

  // Make sure we don't let the clips slide too far forward
  if (scrollOffset > 0 && mcCanvas._x + 0 + scrollOffset > 0) {
    scrollOffset = -mcCanvas._x;
  }

  // Make sure we don't let the clips slide too far backward
  if (scrollOffset < 0 && (mcCanvas._x + mcCanvas._width +
scrollOffset) < areaWidth) {
    scrollOffset = areaWidth - mcCanvas._x - mcCanvas._width;
  }
```

```
  // Move each of the clips by the appropriate amount
  if (scrollOffset != 0) {
    mcCanvas._x += scrollOffset;
    updateAfterEvent();
  }
}
```

The important part of this method is at the end, where the _x position of the canvas clip is moved to the left or right by the value of the scrollOffset argument. Then Flash's built-in updateAfterEvent() method is called to make sure that the display is refreshed right away (more on that in the next section).

The if blocks at the beginning of the function simply test whether moving the canvas by the requested amount will cause the canvas to be too far to the left or right. Without these checks in place, the canvas (and all the slide clips on it) could just slide off into infinity, never to be see again!

By the way, the += operator used here is just a shorthand operator for incrementing the value on the left by the value on the right. So, this:

```
mcCanvas._x += scrollOffset;
```

is equivalent to this:

```
mcCanvas._x = mcCanvas._x + scrollOffset;
```

See the Flash documentation for details about += and other, similar operators.

Reflecting Changes to a Clip Right Away with *updateAfterEvent()*

Normally, the Flash Player refreshes its display twelve times per second, or whatever you set the Frame Rate field to in the Document Properties dialog box (Modify > Document). This makes sense because most Flash documents change only as the playhead moves along the timeline, advancing the state of whatever tweening, animation, or other frame-by-frame changes might be taking place.

This GestureMovieClip example, however, is causing what's shown in the movie to change by the number of milliseconds specified by the class's refreshInterval property. It's possible that some other content within the document is changing according to the document's frame rate, but for the scroller at least, the schedule established by the setInterval() function is essentially overriding the frame rate.

Whenever a piece of code causes a change to what should be displayed in a movie and if the change might occur more frequently than the frame rate, you should call Flash's built-in `updateAfterEvent()` function. This function causes the Flash Player to update the screen right away (as opposed to the next time the current frame advances in the timeline).

Of course, you have to be reasonable in your expectations. The number of screen refreshes per second that will actually be possible at runtime depends on the user's hardware, operating system, available memory, and all the other usual factors. Don't expect that the player will be able to keep up with 10,000 screen refreshes per second or something. If you do happen to call `updateAfterEvent()` more frequently than the player is physically able to keep up with, the player will ignore as many of the calls as it needs to maintain its sanity. On the other hand, if you call `updateAfterEvent()` less frequently than the frame rate, the player will ignore the calls at runtime because they would have no effect anyway. Please see the Flash documentation for all the particulars.

> **NOTE**
>
> The `updateAfterEvent()` function has an effect only if used in the context of an event handler or a function that was scheduled for execution by `setInterval()`. It is silently ignored otherwise.

Adding Content to Movie Clips at Runtime

Whew, we've covered just about everything in `GestureMovieClip`. There's just a couple of things left. The first is the creation of the scroller's border and background. We'll use some of the drawing-related methods listed in Table 5.5 to perform this task.

> **NOTE**
>
> Another completely different strategy would be to forget the drawing methods altogether and instead add a box-like symbol—with a hairline-width line around it—to the Stage and then stretch it to the appropriate size on the fly using its `_width` and `_height` properties (see Table 5.1).

Drawing Lines and Shapes Programmatically

If you recall, a private method called `initializeVisuals()` is called the first time a clip is added to the scroller by means of `addClip()` (refer back to the "Attaching Movie Clips from the Library Using Linkage Identifiers" section for more information). That method calls another private method called `drawBox()`, which does the work of drawing the border and background. Here's what the `initializeVisuals()` method looks like:

```
private function initializeVisuals() {
  // Get X coordinate of center (left/right) of the scrolling area
  this.centerPoint = this.areaWidth / 2;

  // Draw the border and background, if called for
  if (this.drawBorderAndBackground) {
    drawBox(this,
      0-this.borderPadding,                          // x position
      0-this.borderPadding,                          // y position
      this.areaWidth + (this.borderPadding*2),       // width
      this.areaHeight + (this.borderPadding*2),      // height
      this.bgColor,                                  // background color
      this.bgAlpha,                                  // background alpha
      this.borderColor,                              // line color
      this.borderWidth);                             // line width
  }

  // Remember that we've performed this initialization step
  this.initialized = true;
}
```

As you can see, there's barely anything here, except for the call to `drawBox()`. The `drawBox()` method accepts a number of arguments, which describe the position, width, height, border, and background color for the desired rectangle. This code simply passes the various border- and background-related properties of the `GestureMovieClip` class to create the appropriate border and background effect.

NOTE

Because `drawBox()` takes quite a few arguments, I've spread the call over multiple lines to keep the code easy to read. You are free to add as much whitespace as you want between the parentheses of a function call if that helps you read and maintain your code more easily.

Here's the code for the private `drawBox()` method:

```
// This method draws a box within any clip
// (The implementation is generic and could be reused elsewhere)
private function drawBox(mcOn:MovieClip, x:Number, y:Number, w:Number,
h:Number, bgColor:Number, bgAlpha:Number, lineColor:Number,
lineThickness:Number):Void {
  // Coordinates of lower-right corner
  var x2:Number = x + w;
  var y2:Number = y + h;

  // Get ready to start drawing
  mcOn.moveTo(x, y);
  mcOn.lineStyle(lineThickness, lineColor);
  mcOn.beginFill(bgColor, bgAlpha);

  // Draw the four lines
  mcOn.lineTo(x2, y);   // top side
  mcOn.lineTo(x2, y2);  // right side
  mcOn.lineTo(x, y2);   // bottom
  mcOn.lineTo(x, y);    // left side

  // Fill the box in
  mcOn.endFill();
}
```

The `mcOn` argument is the movie clip on which to draw the box; the other arguments are self-explanatory (x and y position, width, height, and so on). Within the method, variables called x2 and y2 are created, which hold the X/Y coordinates of the bottom right corner of the desired rectangle.

Now it's time to use the drawing methods from Table 5.5 to create the actual box. First, `moveTo()` is used to move the invisible "pen" to the spot where the top-left corner of the box is to be. Next, the `lineStyle()` method is used to set the desired thickness and color of the box's outline. Then `beginFill()` is called to set the desired color and alpha (transparency) for the box's fill (background) color.

Drawing the actual box just requires four simple calls to the `lineTo()` method to draw the four lines that define the box. Finally, the `endFill()` method is called to fill in the box we just defined with the desired fill color.

Creating Mask Clips Programmatically

One of the stranger creatures you'll find prowling around in the Flash universe is what's called a *mask*. A mask basically creates a "hole" or "window" through which other content shows.

Here's how I usually explain masks to people: Imagine that you have a piece of construction paper. Now cut a shape—a rectangle, a star, a circle, or whatever—out of the middle of the construction paper. This is your mask. Now place the construction paper on top of this morning's newspaper. You can see only the part of the newspaper that shows through the little window you cut into the construction paper, right? Well, that's exactly how masks work in Flash. You draw a shape on the mask and then use it to show only the identically-shaped part of whatever content lies beneath it.

There are two ways to mask content in Flash:

- You can create a mask layer in the Timeline panel and then use the drawing tools (at design time) to define the shape of the "window" that you want your other content to show through.

- You can create a movie clip (a *mask clip*) that defines the shape of the "window" that you want the contents of some other clip (I call this the *maskee clip*) to show through. Then you use `MovieClip.setMask()` to tell Flash to mask the maskee with the mask clip (say that three times fast!). This is the approach the `GestureMovieClip` class uses.

In either case, you can animate the content of the mask, causing the shape, size, or position of the "window" to change (many cool effects can result). Remember that no one ever sees the mask, so the color and other visual particulars of the mask's content is unimportant. The only thing that matters is the shape of the mask's content.

If you recall, the constructor function for the `GestureMovieClip` class calls a private method called `createMaskClip()`, like so:

```
// Create a mask clip, which contains just a filled-in black box
createMaskClip(mcCanvas, "mcMask", 0, 0, areaWidth, areaHeight);
```

Here's the code for the `createMaskClip()` method:

```
// This method creates a mask clip for any movie clip
// (The implementation is generic and could be reused elsewhere)
private function createMaskClip(mcMaskee:MovieClip,
instanceName:String, x:Number, y:Number, w:Number, h:Number):Void {
  var mcMask:MovieClip;

  // Create a new clip, which will be the mask
  this.createEmptyMovieClip(instanceName, this.getNextHighestDepth());
  mcMask = this[instanceName];

  // Draw black box in new movie clip
  drawBox(mcMask, x, y, w, h, 0x000000, 100);

  // Set the box clip as the canvas clip's mask--the mask behaves
  // as a square window through which canvas clip's contents appear
  mcMaskee.setMask(mcMask);
}
```

As you can see, this method is pretty simple and is just a conceptual wrapper around the notions of creating a new movie clip, drawing a rectangular shape on it, and then setting it as a mask for some other clip. The mcMaskee argument is the movie clip whose content should be masked. The instanceName argument is the instance name for the mask clip that is about to be created.

First, the mask clip is created by means of `createEmptyMovieClip()` (at the next available depth level), and a reference to the resulting movie clip is placed in the mcMask convenience variable. Next, the drawBox() method from the last section is used to draw a black rectangle on the mask clip. Finally, the setMask() method of the built-in MovieClip class (see Table 5.1) is used to set mcMask as a mask clip though which to show the content of mcMaskee.

You might want to try a few experiments to see how the mask clip affects the scroller's appearance. First, try commenting out the call to createMaskClip() in the GestureMovieClip constructor and then test out your movie. You'll see that the slides are now visible at all times, even when they are outside the bounds of the scroller area (see Figure 5.6). Now uncomment that call and comment out the call to setMask() instead (within the body of the createMaskClip() method) so that the mask clip is created but never set as a mask for the scroller. When you test the movie, you'll see a black box where the scroller usually is. This is the shape of your mask. Now uncomment the setMask() call to return the example to its usual working behavior.

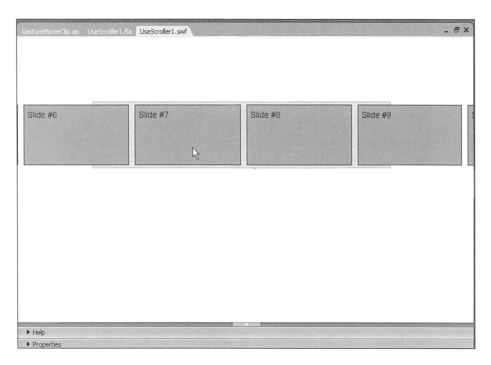

FIGURE 5.6   Without a mask clip, the slides are visible beyond the scroller area.

> **NOTE**
>
> The mask clip for this example is created at runtime by drawing shapes on an empty movie clip, but mask clips can also be created at design time (as movie clip symbols in the Library). Because you can use any of Flash's drawing tools to create the mask clip, you can create some pretty interesting-looking masks. You can move the masks around at runtime—or scale or rotate them—for all kinds of interesting effects. See the Flash documentation for details.

Turning Clips into Components

The UseScroller1.fla document that you created earlier contains a movie clip named ScrollerClip, which is based on the GestureMovieClip class. If you want, you can use the Library panel to quickly turn the ScrollerClip symbol into a component. After you've turned it into a component, you can set its properties interactively through the Properties panel or the Component Inspector. That way, you can set some of its characteristics, such as the size of the scrolling area or the border color, without coding.

NOTE

The instructions in this section use the Library panel's Component Definition dialog box to provide metadata about the new component's properties. While it's quick and easy, and suffices for simple components such as this chapter's scroller example, it is no longer the officially preferred way to create a component. As of Flash MX 2004, the preferred way is to extend one of two special base classes (`mx.core.UIComponent` or `mx.core.UIObject`) and embed the component's metadata within the ActionScript 2.0 class file that implements the component's behavior. While a full discussion of this topic is well beyond the scope of this book, Appendix A provides a reasonable crash course in basic component creation under the new methodology.

To turn the `ScrollerClip` into a component, follow these steps:

1. In the Library panel, right-click the `ScrollerClip` symbol and choose Component Definition. The Component Definition dialog box appears.

2. Click the Add Parameter button (the button with the plus sign on it) at the top-left corner of the Component Definition dialog box. Flash responds by adding a row to the parameters list with a dummy name, value, and type.

3. Change the name of the new parameter to **borderColor**.

4. Change the type of the new parameter to Color. Note that the Value column adjusts itself to show a color picker for choosing color values.

5. Use the color picker in the Value column to set the value to light gray (#CCCCCC).

6. Repeat Steps 2–5 to create another parameter called **borderWidth**. Set the type to Number and the value to 1.

7. Click OK to turn the movie clip into a component (see Figure 5.7). Note that `ScrollerClip` is now listed as a component rather than a movie clip in the Library (see Figure 5.8).

NOTE

For now, don't set the AS 2.0 Class field in the Component Definition dialog box (but remember that the field was set in the symbol's Symbol Properties dialog box). Refer to Appendix A for an example that uses this field to create a component properly from scratch.

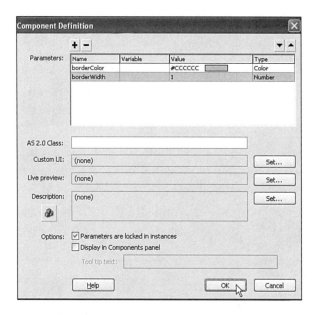

FIGURE 5.7   It's easy to turn a movie clip symbol into a component.

FIGURE 5.8   The symbol now appears as a component in the Library.

Now you can set the border color for each instance of ScrollerClip interactively at design time, using the Properties panel. To test this out, do the following:

1. Select the mcScroller instance of the scroller on the Stage.

2. In the Properties panel, click the Parameters tab (at the top-right corner of the panel). Whoa, check it out...the borderColor and borderWidth parameters you just added are now visible.

3. Use the color picker for the borderColor parameter to change the border color to some other color, like red (see Figure 5.9). Change the border width too if you feel like it.

4. Test out your movie...you'll see that the border has actually been changed. Pretty slick, eh?

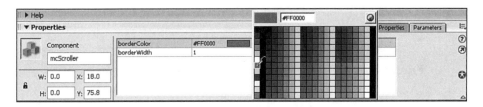

FIGURE 5.9   Now you can adjust the component's properties interactively.

If you open up the UseScroller2.fla file (included with this chapter's examples), you'll see that I've added all the public properties of the GestureMovieClip class (Table 5.7) as components of the ScrollerClip symbol for you. Now you can adjust any of the mcScroller instance's properties using the Properties panel. You can also use the Component Inspector to adjust the same values (see Figure 5.10).

▼ Component Inspector

ScrollerClip, <mcScroller>

Parameters | Bindings | Schema

Name	Value
areaWidth	500
areaHeight	100
paddingBetweenClips	10
refreshInterval	50
maxSpeed	30
deadCenter	50
drawBorderAndBackground	true
borderColor	#0000FF
borderWidth	5
borderPadding	5
backgroundColor	#000000
backgroundAlpha	10

▶ Library - UseScroller2.fla

FIGURE 5.10   You can adjust component properties in the Component Inspector.

Summary

This chapter has reinforced your understanding of the `MovieClip` class and its relationship to Flash and ActionScript development. You have seen how to create descendants of `MovieClip` and use them in your documents, how to create and manipulate new clip instances at runtime, and how to turn class-based movie clip symbols into components. Don't worry—the remaining chapters of this book will continue to use `MovieClip` extensively, so you'll see plenty more examples. In particular, Chapter 7 revisits the `GestureMovieClip` class created in this chapter by hooking it up to XML-encoded data from your server.

PART III
GETTING CONNECTED TO YOUR DATA

6   Connecting to Servers
    with Plain Text   231

7   Connecting to Servers with XML   271

8   Connecting to Servers
    with Flash Remoting   315

9   Connecting to Servers
    with Web Services   379

CHAPTER 6

CONNECTING TO SERVERS WITH PLAIN TEXT

In Chapter 2, "Your First Flash Interface," you created a very simple Macromedia Flash interface that connected to your server to retrieve variables in a simple name/value format. You were introduced to the basics about retrieving values with the LoadVars object and how to display the values to your users. So, you've already learned a lot. This chapter fleshes out your understanding of the LoadVars class and a few other, similar means of retrieving values provided in the form of plain text.

Using the *LoadVars* Class

Table 6.1 shows the members (methods, properties, and events) of the LoadVars class.

TABLE 6.1   *LoadVars* Class Members

MEMBER	DESCRIPTION
addRequestHeader (name, value)	Method. Specifies the name and value of an HTTP header to send to the server along with the name/value pairs currently set on the LoadVars object. The header will be sent when the send() or sendAndLoad() method is next used. You

continues

TABLE 6.1   *LoadVars* Class Members (Continued)

MEMBER	DESCRIPTION
	only need to use this method if your server is expecting some kind of extended information in the form of a custom header. There are certain header names that cannot be sent from Flash; refer to the ActionScript Dictionary for the list of forbidden header names.
getBytesLoaded()	Method. Returns the number of bytes that have actually been received by the server. This number increases during a load() or sendAndLoad() operation; when the operation is complete, this number should equal the number returned by getBytesTotal().
getBytesTotal()	Method. Returns the number of bytes that will be returned by the server during the current load() or sendAndLoad() operation.
load(url)	Method. Begins the fetching of data from a server. The url argument is the URL from which to fetch data. The LoadVars object will continue to fetch the data in a separate thread; the onLoad event will fire when the data has been completely received. If you want, you can monitor the download progress using the getBytesLoaded() method.
send(url, [targetWin, method])	Method. Navigates the browser to a new URL, sending variables to that URL as a part of the process. The url argument is the URL to which to send variables. The method argument might be set to either "POST" (which means that your server will receive the variables as "form" variables) or "GET" (which means your server receives them as "url" variables); if you don't specify a method, the default is POST.
sendAndLoad(url, [targetObj, method])	Method. Silently sends variables to a web server, without navigating the browser to a different page. The url argument is the URL to which to send variables. If you want to receive any name/value pairs with which the server might respond, set the targetObj argument to a second LoadVars object; the onLoad event of the second object will fire when the variables have been received. You will see this in action in the "Round Trips: Sending Variables to the Server" section later in this chapter.

MEMBER	DESCRIPTION
toString()	Method. Returns a url-encoded version of all the variables currently present in the LoadVars object.
decode()	Method (undocumented as of this writing). Accepts a string of name/value pairs and sets properties (variables) on the current LoadVars object that represent each pair. This method is called internally within the default handler for the onData event. Returns nothing.
contentType	Property. The MIME content type that is sent to the server along with the next send() or sendAndLoad() operation. You can use this property to send data to the server in a form other than name/value pairs. You would also have to replace the toString() method with your own custom encoding mechanism.
loaded	Property. After a fetching operation has been started with load() or sendAndLoad(), this property is set to false. It remains false until the data has been fetched completely.
onData	Event. Fires when data has been completely retrieved from the server, but before it has been parsed into name/value pairs. Flash passes one argument to this event, which is the raw text of the server's response (as a String). See the "Intercepting and Parsing Raw Text Data Yourself" section later in this chapter for details.
onLoad	Event. Fires when data has been completely retrieved from the server, and after the LoadVars object has parsed the data into name/value pairs and set corresponding string properties on itself. Flash passes one argument to this event, which is a Boolean value that indicates whether the operation completed successfully. You saw examples that used this event in Chapter 2, and nearly all the examples in this chapter use it as well.

You already know about the typical usage pattern for LoadVars. Just to recap, you will often use it by following these conceptual steps:

1. Create an instance of the LoadVars class.
2. Attach a function to the onLoad event that does whatever you want done with the retrieved data. This function will be called by your LoadVars instance when the data has been retrieved in full.

3. Call the `load()` method. Your `LoadVars` instance begins contacting the server in a separate thread. When the server's response has been received, the name and value of each name/value pair will be exposed to you as a string property of the `LoadVars` instance. The `onLoad` method will be fired when this work is done; in the meantime, your movie can continue displaying other things.

If you would like to review what this basic usage looks like in practice, flip back to the `movieWidget` example in Chapter 2. The remainder of the `LoadVars` discussion in this chapter will focus on slightly more advanced scenarios. Don't worry; none of it is hard.

Retrieving Structured Data

Now you know how to retrieve variables from a server in the form of simple name/value pairs. You might be wondering if it's possible to retrieve more complex information. What about structured data—such as an array, associative array, or object? What about a recordset retrieved from a server-side database?

The simple name/value pair format that the `LoadVars` class expects doesn't support anything like that directly. The value of each variable is assumed to be a simple string. There isn't any built-in support for data types other than strings, and there isn't any support for container-type values, such as arrays or the like.

All is not lost, though. It is pretty easy to create your own little system for getting structured data from a server. This section will build a simple mechanism for retrieving recordsets from the server. You could easily adapt this strategy to support other types of complex information, such as arrays or objects (or structures or associative arrays or whatever your environment calls them).

NOTE

I'm going to use the term "recordset" to refer to the results of a SQL SELECT statement. Depending on what server-side environment you're using, you might be used to calling these things queries, recordsets, rowsets, or some other vocabulary word.

Of course, there are other, less homegrown ways to transfer structured information to Flash. Here are the other strategies discussed in this book:

- **XML.** You got an introduction to using XML for this purpose in Chapter 2. You'll be exploring the nooks and crannies of Flash's XML support in Chapter 7, "Connecting to Servers with XML."

- **Flash Remoting.** If you own the Macromedia Flash Remoting product, you can use its built-in support for structured information, such as recordsets and arrays, instead of the strategy discussed in this section. See Chapter 8, "Connecting to Servers with Flash Remoting," for details.

- **Web Services.** Web Services can return arrays, recordsets, and arbitrarily structured objects. You will learn how to work with Web Services in Chapter 9, "Connecting to Servers with Web Services."

So, with three more modern, sophisticated means of exchanging data at your disposal, why bother thinking about the exchange of structured data with the relatively primitive LoadVars class? Perhaps you're working for a client that doesn't want to use Flash Remoting or Web Services for licensing reasons. If so, that leaves you with the XML or plain text options. XML is certainly more standardized and powerful, but you may run into situations where it isn't particularly easy to return XML from a particular process, or where it feels like overkill. In such a situation, you could consider the techniques discussed in this section.

In any case, digging deeper into the LoadVars class makes for an interesting discussion and a good excuse to learn more about certain ActionScript concepts, such as the extension of built-in classes.

The Basic Idea

There are many ways to approach the problem of retrieving recordset-style information with the LoadVars class. The strategy we're going to employ here is a very simple one. Basically, we're going to use a simple naming convention when creating name/value pairs on the server side. We'll have our server-side code return two special variables that provide our Flash-side code with a bit of metadata about the recordset in question:

- **fieldNames.** This will be a comma-separated list of the recordset's column names.

- **numRecords.** This will be a number that indicates how many rows are in the recordset.

Then we'll have the server return name/value pairs for each row and column in the recordset, using a naming convention of *fieldname_n*, where the *fieldname* part is the name of the column and the *n* part is the row number. For instance, for a recordset that has two columns—name and age—and three rows, the server would send back name/value pairs with these names:

- fieldNames (the value would be "name,age")
- numRecords (the value would be 3)
- name_1
- name_2
- name_3
- age_1
- age_2
- age_3

The Server-Side Code

Listing 6.1, Listing 6.2, and Listing 6.3 show ColdFusion, ASP.NET, and JSP versions of pages that return recordset data in this fashion. Each listing queries the Articles table from this book's example database and returns the headline, summary, and filename for each article.

LISTING 6.1   newsVarSource.cfm—The ColdFusion Version

```
<!--- Retrieve article data from database --->
<cfquery datasource="VenueDB" name="ArticleQuery">
 SELECT * FROM Articles
 ORDER BY dPublishDate DESC
</cfquery>

<!--- Omit debug info, and anything not in <cfoutput> blocks --->
<cfsetting showdebugoutput="No" enablecfoutputonly="Yes">

<!--- Set MIME content-type of our response to "text/plain" --->
<cfcontent type="text/plain" reset="yes">

<!--- Output a name/value pair to report number of records --->
<cfoutput>numRecords=#ArticleQuery.RecordCount#</cfoutput>
<cfoutput>&fieldNames=headline,summary,filename</cfoutput>

<!--- Output name/value pairs for each record --->
<cfloop query="ArticleQuery">
 <cfoutput>&headline_#CurrentRow#=</cfoutput>
 <cfoutput>#URLEncodedFormat(sHeadline)#</cfoutput>
```

```
<cfoutput>&summary_#CurrentRow#=</cfoutput>
<cfoutput>#URLEncodedFormat(sSummary)#</cfoutput>
<cfoutput>&filename_#CurrentRow#=</cfoutput>
<cfoutput>#URLEncodedFormat(sFilename)#</cfoutput>
</cfloop>
```

LISTING 6.2   newsVarSource.aspx—The ASP.NET Version

```
<%@ Page Language="vb" Debug="true" %>
<%@ Import Namespace = "System.Data.ODBC" %>

<script runat="server">
 Sub Page_Load
  Dim ConnStr As String
  Dim conn  As OdbcConnection
  Dim CmdStr As String
  Dim cmd    As OdbcCommand
  Dim reader As OdbcDataReader
  Dim numRecords As Int32 = 0

  ' Set up database connection
  ConnStr = "DSN=VenueDB"
  conn = new OdbcConnection(ConnStr)
  conn.Open()

  ' Insert new comment record into database
  CmdStr = "SELECT * FROM Articles ORDER BY dPublishDate DESC"
  cmd = new OdbcCommand(CmdStr, conn)
  reader = cmd.ExecuteReader()

  ' Set the MIME content-type of our response to "text/plain"
  Response.ContentType = "text/plain"

  While reader.Read()
   numRecords = numRecords + 1
   Response.Write("&headline_" & numRecords & "=")
   Response.Write(Server.URLEncode(reader.Item("sHeadline")))
   Response.Write("&summary_" & numRecords & "=")
   Response.Write(Server.URLEncode(reader.Item("sSummary")))
   Response.Write("&filename_" & numRecords & "=")
   Response.Write(Server.URLEncode(reader.Item("sFilename")))
  End While

  ' Respond with the ID number of the just-inserted record
  Response.Write("&numRecords=" & numRecords)
  Response.Write("&fieldNames=headline,summary,filename")
```

continues

```
 conn.Close()
End Sub
</script>
```

LISTING 6.3   newsVarSource.jsp—The Java Version

```
<%@ page
 import="java.sql.*,java.net.URLEncoder"
 contentType="text/plain"
%>


<%
// This is the SQL query statement we will use to fetch data
String sql = "SELECT * FROM Articles ORDER BY dPublishDate DESC";

// Execute the SQL query against the example database
Class.forName("sun.jdbc.odbc.JdbcOdbcDriver");
Connection con = DriverManager.getConnection("jdbc:odbc:VenueDB");
ResultSet rs = con.createStatement().executeQuery(sql);

// Get the index positions of the columns we want to output
int colHeadline = rs.findColumn("sHeadline");
int colSummary = rs.findColumn("sSummary");
int colFilename = rs.findColumn("sFilename");

// Clear any whitespace, to ensure our output is on first line
out.clear();

// Send the name/value pairs to the output stream
int numRecords = 0;
while ( rs.next() ) {
 numRecords++;
 out.print("&headline_" + numRecords + "=");
 out.print(URLEncoder.encode(rs.getString(colHeadline)));
 out.print("&summary_" + numRecords + "=");
 out.print(URLEncoder.encode(rs.getString(colSummary)));
 out.print("&filename_" + numRecords + "=");
 out.print(URLEncoder.encode(rs.getString(colFilename)));
}

out.print("&fieldNames=headline,summary,filename");
out.print("&numRecords=" + numRecords);
%>
```

At this point, you should be able to test whichever version you want by visiting it with your browser. The server should respond with plain text content that includes the `fieldNames` and `numRecords` variables, plus pairs named `headline_1`, `headline_2`, `summary_1`, `summary_2`, and so on.

Building the LoadVarsExtended Class

On the Flash side, we create a subclassed version of the built-in `LoadVars` class, which we'll call `LoadVarsExtended`. Taking advantage of the new class inheritance model in ActionScript 2.0, this new subclass will inherit all the methods, properties, and events from `LoadVars` (as listed in Table 6.1). In addition, it will have one additional method called `getRecordsetValues()`, which can be called any time after the `onLoad` event fires. This method will return an ActionScript object that contains one property for each column in the original recordset. The value of each property is an array that contains the data (rows) for that column. Thus, if you use this line in your `onLoad` event handler, where `myLVE` is an instance of our new `LoadVarsExtended` class, your code might look like this:

```
myQueryData = myLVE.getRecordsetValues();
```

Because each column is now represented as a native ActionScript array object, you can refer to the data that was originally in the first row of the recordset's age column as `myQueryData.age[0]`, the second row as `myQueryData.age[1]`, and so on. This is a simple but effective API for receiving rows of table-style information from a server.

Listing 6.4 shows the code for the new `LoadVarsExtended` class. This is a good example in two respects: first, it shows you how to reassemble structured information after it has been received as simple text variables from a server; second, it's a good example of creating a new ActionScript 2.0 class that inherits from one of Flash's built-in classes.

> **NOTE**
>
> This file needs to be stored in a location that's accessible via the Flash compiler's classpath. That means either storing it in the same folder as the FLAs that will use the new class or storing the file in a designated classpath folder. See Chapter 4, "ActionScript: A Primer," for details.

LISTING 6.4   LoadVarsExtended.as—The *LoadVarsExtended* Class

```
class LoadVarsExtended extends LoadVars {
 // We expect these variables to be populated after load
 // This is a class definition, so they are "properties")
 var numRecords, fieldNames: String;

 // This function returns an object full of arrays, where
 // each array represents a column full of data (rows).
 // A convenient way to access name/value pairs of data
 function getRecordsetValues() {
  // These variables are local to this function/method
  var fieldName, fieldValue: String;
  var row, i: Number;
  var arFieldData: Array;
  var arFieldNames: Array = this.fieldNames.split(",");
  var result: Object = new Object;

  // Check: Make sure we have fieldNames and numRecords
  if (!this.fieldNames or !this.numRecords) {
   return null;
  }

  // For each field (column name)
  for (i = 0; i < arFieldNames.length; i++) {
   // This is the name of the current field
   fieldName = arFieldNames[i];
   // Create a fresh array to store field's values in
   arFieldData = new Array;

   // Loop from 1 to the number of rows
   for (row = 1; row <= this.numRecords; row++) {
    // Expect variables: "fieldName_1", "fieldName_2"...
    fieldValue = this[fieldName + "_" + row];
    // Add this row's value to the array for this field
    arFieldData.push(fieldValue);
   }

   // Add array of values to the object we're returning
   result[fieldName] = arFieldData;
  }

  // Return the final result
  return result;
 }
}
```

The first line declares that this new class, `LoadVarsExtended`, will extend (or, if you prefer, inherits from) the built-in `LoadVars` class. The next line declares two string properties called `numRecords` and `fieldNames`, which correspond to the name/value pairs of the same names that your server will provide (see Listings 6.1, 6.2, and 6.3). The values of these two properties will be populated automatically during a `load()` or `sendAndLoad()` operation, just as they would when using a normal `LoadVars` object (as you learned in Chapter 2).

> **NOTE**
>
> Listing 6.4 would work without declaring the `numRecords` and `fieldNames` properties because the built-in `LoadVars` class is a dynamic class, meaning that the compiler won't complain if you use a property name that hasn't been specifically declared. However, it makes sense to declare any properties that your code is going to depend on anyway, for the sake of clarity. See Chapter 4 for information about dynamic classes.

Aside from the two properties, the only other addition we are making is the `getRecordsetValues()` method. Let's take a look at what happens inside the body of the method. First, a number of local variables are declared. Note that `arFieldNames` is populated by using the `String.split()` method to create a new array of field names from the comma-separated list in the `this.fieldNames` property returned by your server.

The `result` variable holds a fresh, empty `Object` object, which the method will populate with information and returns as its return value. When used in this way, an ActionScript `Object` object is similar to a HashTable (or similar class) in Java, a CFML structure in ColdFusion, or one of the various name/value containers in the `System.Collections` namespace under .NET.

The actual work of making sense out of the recordset-style values is done using two nested `for` loops. The outer `for` loops over each value in the `arFieldNames` array (that is, over each column name in the recordset). Within the loop, a convenience variable `fieldName` is created to hold the name of the field currently being looped over, and a fresh one-dimensional array called `arFieldData` is created to hold the field's values (that is, the rows of that column in the recordset).

> **NOTE**
>
> I use the term "convenience variable" to refer to any variable that I create for no other reason than to end up with code that is a bit easier to type and read (especially when I'm expecting someone to be reading and learning from the code, as in this book). One could argue that it is a tiny bit more efficient to not create a `fieldName` variable and instead use `arFieldNames[i]` in its place throughout. Feel free to make that change after you understand what's going on in the code.

The inner loop loops over the number of rows in the recordset. For each row, the value of the corresponding name/value pair from the server (age_1, age_2, or whatever) is placed into a convenience variable called fieldValue; this value is then added to the arFieldData array using the Array.push() method.

After the inner loop, the arFieldData array (which should now hold all the values for the rows in the current recordset column) is added to the result object as a property with the same name as the name of the current column. Finally, after both loops have completed their work, the result object is returned as the method's return value. Any code that calls this method will now be able to work with the recordset values by column name and row number.

> **NOTE**
>
> It's worth noting that this strategy involves your server sending all its data to the client in one chunk. That could be a bit of a problem if you are trying to send thousands of records to Flash. One advantage of using Macromedia's Flash Remoting Gateway on the server side is that it is capable of sending query recordsets to Flash in smaller chunks (these are called pageable recordsets); the rows are made available to ActionScript as they arrive.

Testing the New LoadVarsExtended Class

To test this new class, you can use the recordsetTest.fla document provided with this chapter's examples. This is nothing but an empty document with the ActionScript code in Frame 1 (see Listing 6.5):

LISTING 6.5   ActionScript Code in Frame 1 of recordsetTest.fla

```
var lv = new LoadVarsExtended;
lv.onLoad = onVarsLoaded;
lv.load("http://localhost/venue/Chapter06/newsVarSource.aspx");

function onVarsLoaded() {
  // Get loaded values, in form of object full of arrays
  var values = this.getRecordsetValues();

  // Use some debug statements to prove we retrieved data
  trace(values.headline[0]);
  trace(values.summary[0]);
  trace(values.headline[1]);
  trace(values.summary[1]);
}
```

As you can see, the basic usage of the new `LoadVarsExtended` subclass is not much different from the way you use `LoadVars` itself. You create an instance of the class, set up an `onLoad` event handler that works with the retrieved data, and then start the data-fetching process in motion with a call to `load()`. Within the `onLoad` handler (or in any other function, as long as the `onLoad` event has occurred), you can use the new `getRecordsetValues()` method to get an object full of values that can be accessed using column names and row numbers as coordinates. When you test this movie using Control > Test Movie in the Flash IDE, you should see some article headlines and summaries in the Output window (see Figure 6.1).

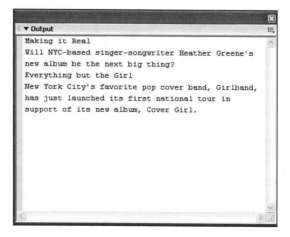

FIGURE 6.1   Output generated by `trace` statements in Listing 6.5.

NOTE

Feel free to experiment with extending the functionality of the `LoadVarsExtended` class further. You might, for instance, allow more than one recordset to be returned at a time. You can also allow the transport of other structured information (such as arrays) by adding additional methods, such as `getArrayData()` or the like.

Showing Structured Data in a Sliding Ticker

Let's do something interesting with the structured data you've retrieved with `LoadVarsExtended`. This example is a news ticker that displays a "teaser" headline and brief summary for current news articles. These teasers are presented as a kind of slideshow, where each article slides into view, is displayed for a few seconds, and then fades away to be replaced by the next teaser. Of course, this is just one example; you can do just about anything you want to with the data you've retrieved.

In some ways, this example is similar to the `artistWidget` example from Chapter 2. Like that example, this one displays retrieved information in a couple of simple text fields in a movie clip, and the movie clip is animated so that it slides in and slides out (or fades out, in this new case). The overall effect is of a ticker or slideshow (see Figures 6.2 and 6.3). The user can pause the slideshow by hovering his or her mouse over the movie; the slideshow will resume if the user moves the mouse away from the movie. The user can read the full article by clicking the movie.

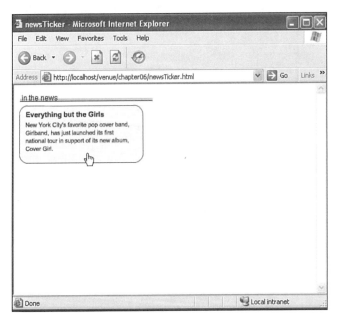

FIGURE 6.2   This news ticker shows database records one at a time.

FIGURE 6.3   The next news item slides in from the right as the existing item fades away.

Examining the newsTicker.fla Example Document

Open the newsTicker.fla document, which is included with this chapter's examples. At this point, you've already had some experience with creating a Flash example from scratch, so I won't ask you to go through the individual steps again. Just take a look at the file and explore its contents for a couple of minutes. Some items of note are as follows:

- The main timeline contains hardly anything except ActionScript code. A layer called Actions contains the code to set up and run the movie (you'll see the code in the next listing). A layer called Decoration contains a couple of visual lines and the phrase "in the news."

- If you look at the Library, you'll find a movie called InfoDisplayClip. If you double-click this symbol in the Library, you'll see that it contains five layers. The Actions layer has a stop() command in its last frame.

- Within the InfoDisplayClip are two text fields called txtHeadline and txtSummary. The former moves around a bit through some simple animation on the timeline (just move the playhead on the clip's timeline to see the movement). Note that Flash put the txtHeadline field in a separate Graphic symbol when I tweened it; I named the new symbol

HeadlineTween. There is also an instance of an empty movie clip called LoaderClip, which will be used to load an image at runtime. (I could have used a Loader component just as easily, which is what the artist widget example in Chapter 2 uses for loading images.)

- The Library also contains a clip called SlideClip, which contains three layers. The Info Display layer contains an instance of InfoDisplayClip called mcInfoDisplay. The clip slides into view during the first 15 frames of the timeline, and fades out of view from Frames 16 to 30. The start of the slide-in animation is labeled slideIn, and the start of the fade-out animation is labeled slideOut.

To create the fade-out effect, I created a new keyframe at Frame 30 and created a motion tween (the same steps I would have performed if I wanted the clip to move around on the stage). Instead of changing the clip's position in the new keyframe, I changed its transparency by adjusting its Alpha color value in the Properties panel. An Alpha value of 0 percent means that the item is essentially invisible, and an Alpha value of 100 percent means that the item displays normally; anything in between means the item displays with the corresponding amount of transparency. Thus, the motion tween between Frames 16 and 30 is about changing the clip's transparency over time, rather than changing its position over time. It's worth noting that you can also adjust an instance's Alpha value programmatically by setting its _alpha property via ActionScript; consult the Flash documentation for details.

In an effort to organize the Library for this document a little, I created a folder in the Library called InfoDisplayClip to hold the InfoDisplayClip clip, as well as the symbols found within the clip. The folder has no bearing on the way the movie behaves or is programmed.

Let's take a look at the ActionScript code in this movie. Most of the code has been collected together in Frame 1 of the main timeline's Actions layer, as shown in Listing 6.6.

Note that attaching most of a movie's ActionScript code to Frame 1 of a layer called Actions is a customary way to make it easy to predict where the important parts of a document's code can be found. If you follow this practice when you can, you will probably find your movies are a bit easier to maintain over time. That said, different people have different preferences and ideas about "best practices" when it comes to this kind of thing. You might want to do a quick search on the web for "ActionScript Best Practices" for suggestions.

Also note that Flash MX 2004 introduces the ability to create ActionScript 2.0 classes that contain all or most of the script code for a particular movie clip, thereby keeping the code out of the timeline altogether. See Chapter 4 for details about creating such classes.

LISTING 6.6   ActionScript Code in Frame 1 of newsTicker.fla

```
// These variables are global within this timeline
var millisecondInterval: Number = 2500;
var sourceURL: String =
"http://localhost/venue/Chapter06/newsVarSource.aspx";
var curSlide = -1;
var numSlides, intervalID: Number;
var newsValues: Object;


// When this movie loads, start retrieving data
this.onLoad = function() {
  var lv = new LoadVarsExtended;
  lv.onLoad = onVarsLoaded;
  lv.load(sourceURL);
}

// When the data has been retrieved
function onVarsLoaded() {
  // Remember how many records were returned by server
  numSlides = this.numRecords;
  // Get loaded values, in form of object full of arrays
  newsValues = this.getRecordsetValues();

  // Create the slides and start the slideshow
  createSlides();
  startSlideshow();
}


// This function creates the movie clips for each Slide
function createSlides() {

  // Loop over the number of desired Slides
  // (go through loop backwards, down to 0)
  for (var i = numSlides - 1; i >= 0; i--) {

    //Create new instance of clip from the library
    this.attachMovie("SlideClip", "mcSlide" + i, i);
    var mcNew = eval("mcSlide" + i);
    mcNew._y = 20;
```

continues

LISTING 6.6   ActionScript Code in Frame 1 of newsTicker.fla (Continued)

```
    // Set data in new clip
    mcNew.mcInfoDisplay.txtHeadline.text = newsValues.headline[i];
    mcNew.mcInfoDisplay.txtSummary.text = newsValues.summary[i];
    mcNew.articleURL = newsValues.filename[i];
  }
}

// This function starts the timer on the slideshow
function startSlideshow() {
  intervalID = setInterval(nextSlide, millisecondInterval);
}

// This function pauses slideshow by clearing its timer
function pauseSlideshow() {
  clearInterval(intervalID);
}


// This function advances the current slide
function nextSlide() {
  // Determine which Slide we want to show next
  var nextSlide = curSlide + 1;
  if (nextSlide == numSlides) {
    nextSlide = 0;
  }

  // Rotate the levels of existing clip instances
  // (top clip to back, next clip to front, etc)
  rotateClipDepths(_level, 0, numSlides - 1);

  // These variables hold references to old and new clips
  var mcCurrent = eval("mcSlide" + curSlide);
  var mcNew = eval("mcSlide" + nextSlide);

  // Play "animation" that brings new slide into view
  mcNew.gotoAndPlay("slideIn");
  mcNew.mcInfoDisplay.gotoAndPlay("slideIn")
  // Play "animation" that slides old slide out of view
  mcCurrent.gotoAndPlay("slideOut");

  // Remember that the new clip is now the "current" one
  // This new value is used next time this function runs
  curSlide = nextSlide;
}
```

```
// This is a utility method for rotating movie clip depths
function rotateClipDepths(mcParent, fromLevel, toLevel) {
  for (var i = fromLevel; i < toLevel; i++) {
    mcParent.getInstanceAtDepth(i).swapDepths(i+1);
  }
}
```

The first new lines set up some variables in the main timeline's variable scope. Remember that because these variables are established in the main timeline (and outside any functions), they can be accessed by any code within the main timeline. Other timelines could access these variables by targeting the main timeline with _parent or _root syntax. The millisecondInterval variable represents the number of milliseconds that each slide should remain visible as the ticker runs; a value of 2500 here means 2.5 seconds. You'll see where this value is used shortly. The sourceURL variable is the URL for the page on your server that will return the recordset data about articles; you can change the file extension so that this variable points to the ColdFusion, ASP.NET, or Java version of the news source page.

Next comes the this.onLoad code that runs when the movie first loads, telling Flash to contact your server and start retrieving the recordset data (this is nothing new, and is essentially the same as what you saw in Listing 6.5).

Then comes the onVarsLoaded() code that executes when Flash has finished retrieving the data from your server. The numSlides variable is filled with the number of records returned by the server, and newsValues is filled with the actual recordset data. Then a function called createSlides() is called (the guts of which you'll see next), which sets up the individual slides in the slideshow. Finally, another function called startSlideshow() is called, which starts the actual one-at-a-time display of the slides.

The createSlides() function is similar conceptually to the code in the artistMenu.fla document in Chapter 2 that created buttons for each artist. A for block is used to loop over the number of records returned by the server. For each record, the MovieClip.attachMovie() method is used to create a fresh copy of the SlideClip movie clip and populate its text fields with data from the current record from the server.

It's worth noting that this for loop counts backwards, so that the slide that represents the first record is at the first level (level 0). Although the clips will all be positioned at x/y position 0/0 when they are created, each clip is on its own level, with the clip for the first record directly "under" the second one and so on. The rotateClipDepths() function will be used later to shuffle the clips at runtime so that the current slide is on top of the others.

NOTE

Remember that to use `attachMovie()`, you have to give the movie clip a "linkage identifier," which is a unique name for use in scripting. To assign a linkage identifier, right-click the clip in the Library and choose Linkage. Check the Export for ActionScript option and provide a name in the Identifier field. By default, the clip's symbol name is used, which is usually as sensible a name to use as any. You can now use this identifier with `attachMovie()` to create fresh instances of the clip at runtime.

Next comes the `startSlideshow()` function, which uses ActionScript's built-in `setInterval()` function to schedule the rotation of the "slides" participating in the ticker. The goal here is to make the `nextSlide()` function get executed every 2500 milliseconds (or whatever interval is specified by `millisecondInterval`). The `setInterval()` function creates an in-memory timer that executes any other function at a specified interval. It returns a number that can be thought of as an ID number for the scheduled task that has been established. You can use the ID number later to cancel the timer (with ActionScript's `clearInterval()` method). Here, the ID number is stored at the timeline level in the `intervalID` variable.

The `pauseSlideshow()` function stops the `nextSlide()` method from being called every few seconds by deactivating the in-memory timer that was established with `setInterval()`. In this example, the `nextSlide()` method won't be called automatically again unless the `startSlideshow()` method is called again (which will create a new in-memory timer and returns a new `intervalID`). See the Flash documentation for more information about `setInterval()` and `clearInterval()`.

NOTE

The `setInterval()` function is one way to make something happen at set periods. Another way is to use the timeline of a movie clip as a timer (perhaps putting the code you want to be executed on Frame 1, and then putting enough subsequent frames on the timeline to cause the delay that you wish). Stopping such a timeline with `MovieClip.stop()` would pause this type of timer, and `MovieClip.play()` would start it up again.

Continuing in Listing 6.6, the `nextSlide()` function is what does the work of making the next slide appear in the news ticker. This function is pretty straightforward. The first thing it does is to choose which slide is next by adding 1 to the number of the current slide (if the last slide has been reached, the code starts over at the first one). Then it uses a custom function called `rotateClipDepths()`, discussed next, to make sure that the current slide is on top of the others. Then it starts the animation for the sliding-in of the new slide and the fading-out of the old slide. The animations will run their course on their own; in the meantime, the last line in this function remembers that the "new" slide should now be considered to be the current one.

Finally comes the `rotateClipDepths()` function. This function uses two methods of the `MovieClip` class to create a simple utility that accepts a range of movie clip depths and rearranges them so that the one on the bottom (that is, the one with the lowest depth number) becomes the one on the top, the one on the top becomes the second from the top, the second from the top becomes the third, and so on. As you can see, this function is really quite simple. It just loops through the specified set of levels, swapping each level's depth with the one right above it. The result is the desired reshuffling of depths (if you want to prove it to yourself, stack numbered pieces of paper on top of one another, and then swap them with each other from the bottom up—um, I may have needed to do this myself to figure out what I needed the code to do). See Chapter 5, "Movie Clips as Objects," or the Flash documentation for more information about the `MovieClip.getInstanceAtLevel()` and `MovieClip.swapDepths()` methods.

Listing 6.7 shows the only other ActionScript of any importance in the newsTicker.fla example document. This code is attached to Frame 1 of the `SlideClip` movie clip (the clip that is duplicated for each news article). This catches various mouse events, pausing the slideshow when the user hovers the mouse over the movie clip for a slide, starting it up again when the user stops hovering over the slide, and navigating the browser to the appropriate article if the user clicks the slide.

NOTE

There are a few other frames that have a bit of ActionScript code throughout this example FLA. For the most part, these frames just contain a single `stop()` command so that the various animations don't continue playing repeatedly. Just look for the little "a" icon in the timelines of the document's movie clips. That will help you find the frames that contain snippets of ActionScript code.

LISTING 6.7   ActionScript in Frame 1 of the `SlideClip` Symbol

```
// Stop timeline (until it is played programmatically)
stop();

// Pause slideshow if mouse hovers over this clip
this.onRollOver = function() {
  _parent.pauseSlideshow();
}
```

continues

LISTING 6.7   ActionScript in Frame 1 of the `SlideClip` Symbol (Continued)

```
// Then resume slideshow when mouse leaves this clip
this.onRollOut = function() {
  _parent.startSlideshow();
}

// Navigate to appropriate page if user clicks this clip
this.onRelease = function () {
  _parent.getURL(this.articleURL);
}
```

Intercepting and Parsing Raw Text Data Yourself

As you've seen in this chapter and in Chapter 2, you can use `LoadVars` to send variables from your server to Flash. The underlying assumption is that your server will be providing the variables in the form of `url`-encoded name/value pairs. This assumption is what makes it possible for the Flash Player to understand what part of your server's response represents the name of each variable, which represents the value, and so on.

If you wish, you can intercept the raw text of your server's response before Flash attempts to understand it as a set of name/value pairs. It's then up to you to either parse the text in whatever way you see fit (most likely using the string-manipulation functions provided by ActionScript's `String` class) or simply display or use the text in its raw form.

Understanding the onData *and* onLoad *Events*

The basic idea is this: the `LoadVars` class supports an event called `onData`. This event is fired when your server's response has been received in its entirety. The `LoadVars` object provides a default handler for this event, which does the work of splitting the text from the server into name/value pairs and setting string properties for each pair along the way. When that work is done, the default handler sets the `LoadVars` object's `loaded` property and fires its `onData` event, which, as you well know by now, is generally where your ActionScript does something with the received string variables.

If you create your own event handler function and attach it to the `onData` event, you will effectively "hijack" the text parsing step. The Flash Player will pass one argument to your handler function: a string value that represents the entirety of the content that was returned by your server. It is your function's responsibility to do whatever is appropriate with the text. Your function should also set the `loaded` property and fire the `onLoad` event when it is done doing whatever it needs to do. If it doesn't, `onLoad` will never fire.

The rawTextDemo1.fla document included with this chapter's examples is a bare-bones illustration of this use of `onData`. This movie contains a single text field named `txtFileContent`, which is populated with the contents of the `myTextFile.htm` at runtime (see Figure 6.4). (The text field contains some simple HTML markup, which Flash text fields can display.) Listing 6.8 shows the code used in the movie. Although this is a very simple example, it is interesting because it opens up the possibility of feeding simple text or HTML files to Flash for display—perhaps the same files that are used elsewhere in your web applications.

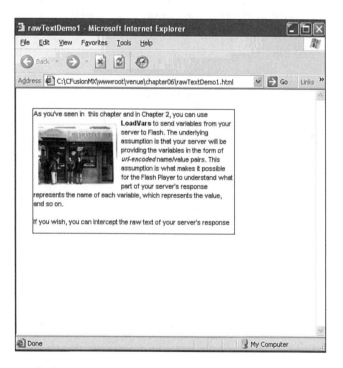

FIGURE 6.4   Retrieving and displaying raw text or HTML file content.

LISTING 6.8   ActionScript Code in Frame 1 of rawTextDemo1.fla

```
var lv = new LoadVars;
// This code executes when text is received from server
lv.onData = function(data) {
  txtFileContent.htmlText = data;
};
// Begin the download process
lv.load("myTextFile.htm");
```

Although the code in Listing 6.8 will work, it does so by updating the visual text field during the onData event. It would be more consistent with normal LoadVars usage to fire the onLoad event from within the onData handler, and take care of any user-interface updates within the onLoad handler. This makes for a cleaner, more respectful hijacking of the usual LoadVars behavior. Listing 6.9 shows the code from a second version of this simple example, rawTextDemo2.fla. This version gets the same thing done, but keeps the text-handling code in onData and the text-display code in onLoad.

LISTING 6.9   ActionScript Code in Frame 1 of rawTextDemo2.fla

```
var lv = new LoadVars;
// This code fires when text is received from server
lv.onData = function(data) {
  this.text = data;
  this.loaded = true;
  this.onLoad(true);
};
// This code fires after onData receives the text
lv.onLoad = function() {
  txtFileContent.htmlText = this.text;
}
// Begin the download process
lv.load("myTextFile.htm");
```

Just to follow this example out for one more iteration, if you plan on using a particular type of special-text-handling logic more than once, it would be in the spirit of ActionScript 2.0 principles to create a subclass of LoadVars that encapsulates the new logic. Listing 6.10 creates a new class called LoadText that overrides the default onData event with its own method. After a successful load, the complete text of the server's response is available in the text property. In addition, this subclass defines a stripCRs property that, if true (the default), removes all instances of ASCII character 13 from the received text. This makes it easier to work with text files that might have originated in Windows or UNIX/Linux environments.

LISTING 6.10   LoadText.as—Creating the *LoadText* Subclass

```
class LoadText extends LoadVars {
  // Properties specific to this subclass
  var text: String;
  var stripCRs: Boolean = true;

  // Override the default onData event handler
  function onData(data: String) {
    if (this.stripCRs) {
      data = removeCharCode(13, data);
    }
    this.text = data;
    this.loaded = true;
    this.onLoad(this.loaded);
  }

  private function removeCharCode(code: Number, fromString: String) {
    return fromString.split(String.fromCharCode(code)).join("");
  }
}
```

Listing 6.11 shows how this new LoadText subclass can be used in a movie. Note that the basic usage pattern is essentially the same as the way the built-in LoadVars class is used.

LISTING 6.11   ActionScript Code in Frame 1 of rawTextDemo3.fla

```
var lv = new LoadText;
lv.onLoad = onTextLoaded;
lv.load("myTextFile.txt");

function onTextLoaded() {
  txtFileContent.htmlText = this.text;
}
```

Retrieving and Parsing Delimited Text Files

After you have intercepted the raw text of your server's response with the onData event, you can split it or parse it up in any way that you please. Just to get you thinking about how you might approach text-parsing code of your own, let's try building a quick subclass of LoadVars that knows how to work with simple delimited text files.

Listing 6.12 is the code for a new class called LoadVarsDelimText, which extends LoadVars by replacing the support for name/value pairs with basic support for tab-delimited text files (you can use other delimiters too). During the onData event, this subclass looks at the first line of received text and uses it to determine the column names in the file. It then creates a one-dimensional array for each column, placing the values from the remaining lines of text into the arrays. In other words, the end result is similar to how the getRecordsetValues() function from earlier in this chapter works. However, whereas that function assembled the column arrays after the fact (using a potentially large number of separate name/value pairs), this version skips the whole name/value pair business altogether. You can export tab-delimited files straight from your database software, which this subclass will be able to consume on its own (in fact, this strategy works without the intervention of a server-side product such as ColdFusion, ASP.NET, or Java).

LISTING 6.12   LoadVarsDelimText.as—The *LoadVarsDelimText* Class

```
class LoadVarsDelimText extends LoadVars {
  var delimiter:String = "\t";
  var fields:Array;
  var numRecords:Number;

  function onData (data:String) {
    this.parseLines(data, this.delimiter);
    this.loaded = true;
    this.onLoad(true);
  }

  private function parseLines(text:String, delim:String) {
    var col, row: Number;
    var name: String;
    var arLines, arLine: Array;

    // Split text into lines, using ASCII 10 as separator
    // (remove ASCII 13 chars first to avoid CRLF problems)
    text = text.split(String.fromCharCode(13)).join("");
    arLines = text.split(newline);

    // Get array of column names from first line of text
    this.fields = arLines[0].split(delim);
```

```
// Store the number of lines in numRecords property
this.numRecords = arLines.length - 1;

// Create a 1D array for each column in data
for (col=0; col < this.fields.length; col++) {
  name = this.fields[col];
  this[name] = new Array();
}

// For each row of data (starting at second row)...
for (row=1; row <= this.numRecords; row++) {
  // Array of values in this line
  arLine = arLines[row].split(delim);

  // For each column, append value to this field's array
  for (col=0; col < this.fields.length; col++) {
    name = this.fields[col];
    this[name].push(arLine[col]);
  }
}
}
}
}
```

Much of this code is structured similarly to other examples in this chapter, so I'm not going to go through each line of code here. Much of the work is done by ActionScript's `String.split()` method, which will take any string and convert it into an array, using any given character as a delimiter. First, `split()` is used to separate the whole chunk of text from the server into individual lines, using the newline character (ASCII 10) as the delimiter. Then the text on the first line is split into an array of column names, using the tab character (or whatever the `delim` property is set to) as the delimiter. The `split()` method is used again inside the loop to split each remaining row into columns.

> **NOTE**
>
> This implementation of the `LoadVarsDelimText` class is far from perfect. In particular, it does not support the escaping of literal delimiter characters, which means that text that contains tab characters (or commas, or whatever delimiter you choose to use) will lead to incorrect results. In addition, it assumes that every newline character represents a new record, which means that any records that contain newlines within an actual data cell will also cause problems. It really wouldn't be terribly hard to create a more sophisticated version of this example that overcame these two limitations, but it wouldn't make a good example for a book of this scope. Tackling a better version would make a good learning exercise.

The remainder of the code is fairly similar to the `LoadVarsExtended` subclass we created earlier in this chapter. To see it in action, open up the newsTickerDelim.fla document, which is nearly identical to the newsTicker.fla document we discussed earlier. The difference, as you might expect, is that instead of connecting to one of the `articleListSource` pages (which supplied recordset-style information as a set of name/value pairs with special names), this version connects to a tab-separated file called artists.txt (which contains the same columns as the Artists table in our example database). If you compare the code in Frame 1 of the two files, you will find that very few changes needed to be made, because both subclasses expose the retrieved columns as simple one-dimensional arrays, where the array is stored as a property with the appropriate column name. The main difference, conceptually, is that with this new version, the arrays are properties of the `LoadVarsDelimText` instance itself, rather than properties of a separate object returned by a method.

Round Trips: Sending Variables to the Server

So far, you have seen Flash examples that exchange data with your server in only one direction: from your server to your Flash movies. It is, of course, also possible to send values from Flash to your server. Your server will be able to work with values provided by Flash in the same basic way that it works with values posted by HTML forms or provided in URL query strings.

The `LoadVars` class provides two methods for sending variables to your web server:

- The `LoadVars.sendAndLoad()` method, which is used by the Flash Player to send variables to your server without reloading the current web page. You can choose to have your variables sent to the server as part of an HTTP GET or POST operation; if GET, the web server receives your variables as if they were in the query string portion of a URL; if POST, the web server receives them as if they were posted by a form. In any case, this is a silent operation that takes place in the background, and the user won't see a "round trip" to the server taking place. Your movie can continue showing animations or doing whatever it needs to do while the information is being sent to your server. You will see this method in action in this section's example.

- The `LoadVars.send()` method, which is used for launching a new browser window while at the same time sending variables to the server. Again, you can specify that you want an HTTP GET or POST operation; if GET, the browser responds exactly as if you clicked a normal HTML link with your variables included in the query string portion of the URL; if POST, the browser responds exactly as if you submitted an HTML form with your variables included as form elements.

Exploring the Comment Widget Example

Let's take a look at an example that uses LoadVars.sendAndLoad() to send a value to your server for processing. This example creates a small widget for adding comments about web pages (or other online elements). The widget enables users to add new comments or to review existing comments, and either can be done without leaving the page the user is already on.

To test out the movie, visit the commentWidgetDemo.html page using your web server (that is, access it using an http:// URL instead of browsing for the file locally). The widget appears at the bottom of this fictional page (see Figure 6.5). If you type a message into the comment field and click the Save button (the green checkmark), the comment is sent to your server (see Figure 6.6), which stores the comment in the PageComments table in the example database. If you click the History button at top right, you will see all comments that have been posted to date about the current page (see Figure 6.7).

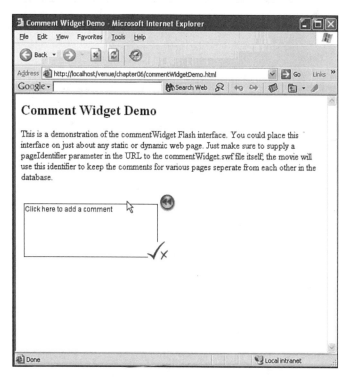

FIGURE 6.5   The comment widget can be placed on nearly any page.

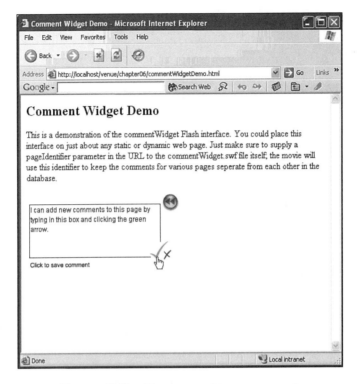

FIGURE 6.6   Users can add new comments.

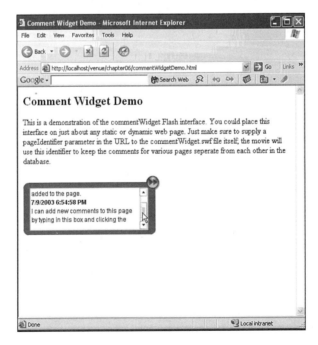

FIGURE 6.7   Users can also review existing comments.

This example relies on the PageComments table in the example database, which contains these columns:

- `idComment`, which is a simple auto-incrementing identity value.
- `sCommentText`, which holds the actual text of each comment.
- `sPageIdentifier`, which holds a string that is meant to identify each page for which this widget is collecting comments. You supply this identifier to the widget when you embed it on a page; the widget provides it to the server when new comments are added, and the server uses the identifier to query the database for existing comments if the user decides to review the comment history.
- `dCommentDate`, which records a date and time for each comment.

Go ahead and open the commentWidget.fla document, which is included with this chapter's examples. This example uses the `LoadVars.sendAndLoad()` method in two different places to exchange data with the server.

About the Server-Side Scripts to Which This Example Connects

This comment widget example connects to two different server-side scripts, which are included with this chapter's example files:

- A comment-posting page for creating new comment records in the example database. This page is called commentPost.cfm, commentPost.aspx, or commentPost.jsp, depending on your server software of choice. The page accepts two form field parameters called `pageIdentifier` and `commentText`, and it uses a simple SQL INSERT statement to insert a corresponding record into the PageComments table. It responds with a single name/value pair called `idComment`, which holds the ID number of the just-inserted comment record.
- A history-providing page for retrieving existing comment records from the database. Depending on the server you're using, this page is called commentHistorySource.cfm, commentHistorySource.aspx, or commentHistorySource.jsp. It accepts a single URL parameter called `pageIdentifier`, queries the database for all matching records, and responds with name/value pairs that follow the naming conventions expected by `LoadVarsExtended` from earlier in this chapter. The columns returned are named `date` and `text`, which correspond to the `dCommentDate` and `sCommentText` columns in the database.

Because these server-side scripts are both very simple and very similar to other examples that you have already seen, there is little point in reproducing them in print here. You are encouraged to take a quick look at the appropriate version of each page now, just to make yourself familiar with what's going on server-side.

Understanding the Comment Widget's ActionScript Code

Like most Flash movies, this example includes a number of different movie clips that work together, mostly to show different things to the user at different times. I'm not going to walk you through the construction of this document step by step. You can explore the various symbols in its Library to get an understanding of how it works. That said, nearly all of the ActionScript for this movie has been kept together in the first frame of the movie clip symbol called CommentEntryClip. As you can see in Listing 6.13, I wrote a number of functions for this example, but none of them are very long or complicated.

LISTING 6.13   ActionScript Code in Frame 1 of the CommentEntryClip Symbol

```
// These variables are global to this clip's timeline
var initialMessage = "Click here to add a comment";
var baseURL = "http://localhost/venue/chapter06/";
var commentSaveURL = baseURL + "commentPost.cfm";
var commentHistoryURL = baseURL + "commentHistorySource.cfm";
var pageIdentifier;

// Stop this movie clip's timeline for good measure
stop();

// Initialize the movie clip's contents
initUI();

// This function executes when the movie first loads
function initUI() {

  // Default identifier if not provided to root timeline
  if (_root.pageIdentifier != undefined) {
    pageIdentifier = _root.pageIdentifier;
  } else {
    pageIdentifier = "test/debug";
  }

  // Erase text in comment field when user enters it
  txtComment.onSetFocus = onCommentFieldFocused;
```

```
  // Set comment field's contents to initial message
  resetComment();
}

// This function sends a user's comment to the server
// It executes when user clicks the "save comment" button
function saveComment() {
  var text = txtComment.text;

  // Make sure user has actually typed something
  if (text == initialMessage || text == "") {
    setStatus("Please type a comment first.");

  } else {
    setStatus("Saving comment...");

    // This operation uses two LoadVars instances
    // Set up the saver
    var lvReceiver = new LoadVars;
    lvReceiver["commentText"] = text;
    lvReceiver["pageIdentifier"] = pageIdentifier;

    // Set up the loader
    var lvLoader = new LoadVars;
    lvLoader.onLoad = onSaveResponseLoaded;

    // Go ahead and start the exchange of information
    lvReceiver.sendAndLoad(commentSaveURL, lvLoader, "POST");
  }
}

// This function fires when comment has been sent to
// the server, and the server has responded.
function onSaveResponseLoaded(success) {
  if (success  && this.idComment != undefined) {
    setStatus("Your comment was saved with ID " + this.idComment);
    resetComment();
  } else {
    setStatus("Error: your comment was not saved.");
  }
}

// This function loads existing records and shows history panel
function loadHistory() {
  var lvReceiver = new LoadVarsExtended;
  lvReceiver.onLoad = onHistoryLoaded;
```

continues

LISTING 6.13   ActionScript Code in Frame 1 of the CommentEntryClip Symbol (Continued)

```
  // Contact server and begin fetching data
  var lvSender = new LoadVars;
  lvSender.pageIdentifier = pageIdentifier;
  lvSender.sendAndLoad(commentHistoryURL, lvReceiver, "GET");

  // (You could use this instead of the lvSender lines above)
  // lvReceiver.load(commentHistoryURL + "?pageIdentifier=" +
escape(pageIdentifier));

  // Provide some visual feedback for user
  setStatus("Retrieving history...");
  //mcHistory.txtHistory.text = "";
}

// This function displays history data in history panel
function onHistoryLoaded() {
  var html = "";

  // Grab all name/value pairs in recordset-style object
  var historyData = this.getRecordsetValues();
  setStatus("History records retrieved: " + this.numRecords);

  // Assemble HTML that includes info from each record
  for (var i = 0; i < this.numRecords; i++) {
    html += "<p><b>" + historyData.date[i] + "</b></p>"
      + newline + "<p>" + historyData.text[i] + "</p>";
  }

  // Display assembled HTML text in scrolling region
  mcHistory.txtHistory.text = html;

  // Slide the history panel into place
  gotoAndPlay("showHistory");
}

// ** The remainder of these functions perform minor UI tasks
// This function hides the history panel
function hideHistory() {
  gotoAndPlay("hideHistory");
}

// This function shows a status message at bottom of SWF
function setStatus(message) {
  mcStatus.txtStatus.text = message;
  mcStatus.gotoAndPlay("showMessage");
```

```
}

function onCommentFieldFocused() {
   if (txtComment.text == initialMessage) {
      txtComment.text = "";
   }
}

// Sets comment field's contents to initial message
function resetComment() {
   txtComment.text = initialMessage;
}
```

After establishing some variables in the movie clip's timeline scope, the first thing this code does is call the initUI() function, which is simply some code that executes when the movie first loads. The clip's timeline is halted with stop(). Then the function checks to see if the pageIdentifier timeline variable has a value. You'll note that one of the first lines in this listing gets the value of pageIdentifier from the root timeline; if no such variable in the root timeline exists, the local pageIdentifier variable is undefined. Thus, this code sets the local variable to test/debug if no pageIdentifier is provided to the movie when it is embedded on a web page (you'll see how this works shortly). The rest of initUI() just performs some other basic initialization tasks, such as telling the txtComment text field (where the user enters a new comment) to execute the onCommentFieldFocused() function when the user enters the field.

The most interesting lines of code are in the saveComment() function, which is obviously where a user's comment gets sent to the server for insertion into the database. The first thing this function does is to set a local text variable that holds the current contents of the text field; if the user hasn't typed anything yet, a validation message is displayed with setStatus().

NOTE

The setStatus() function, which appears toward the end of the listing, simply places the specified message onscreen by populating a text field, which is in a separate movie clip. It then animates the message by playing that movie clip. The result is a status-bar-like hint that gently fades in and out of view.

Assuming that the user has provided a comment to post, the saveComment() function continues, doing the following:

- Creates an instance of LoadVars called lvSender. This instance represents the outgoing variables that should be sent to the server. In this instance, we want to provide the server with form-style values called pageIdentifier and commentText, so string properties with those names are set on the lvSender instance.

- Creates a second instance of LoadVars, called lvReceiver. This instance represents any incoming variables that might be sent back from the server (in the usual form of name/value pairs). The onLoad event of this second instance is set to a responder function called onSaveResponseLoaded, which automatically executes when the server's response to our comment post has been received by the Flash Player.

- Performs the actual exchange of data by calling the sendAndLoad() method. As soon as this code executes, the Flash Player sends the variables in lvSender to the page at the specified URL (in this case, the URL to the commentPost page on your server). The server page receives form-style parameters named pageIdentifer and commentText, which it uses internally to store a new record in the database. The server's response is handled by lvReceiver, which fires its onLoad event as soon as the response has been completely downloaded. After the onLoad event fires, you can access the variables the server sends back using the usual technique (that is, by accessing the corresponding string properties of the lvReceiver object).

This use of sendAndLoad() specifies POST for the third argument. You can omit the POST argument if you want unless you specifically want a GET operation, because LoadVars uses POST operations by default anyway. I like to specify it explicitly just to keep things clear.

The onSaveResponseLoaded() function executes when the round trip to the server has been completed. Of course, you are free to do anything you want with any variables that the server might send back in response to your post. In this case, only one variable name/value pair is being sent back to Flash (idComment), which is simply displayed as part of a "success" type of status message. If, for some reason, the LoadVars object reports an error while contacting the server over HTTP, or if the server fails to respond with an idComment variable (perhaps because of an error message being generated on the server side), an error message is displayed to the user instead.

So, that's the basic idea: create sender and receiver instances of LoadVars (or subclasses thereof); call the sendAndLoad() method of the sender, passing the URL to send to as the first argument and the receiver instance as the second argument; and respond to any data when the receiver's onLoad event fires. The next function, loadHistory(), follows this same basic pattern: it sends the pageIdentifier value to the comment-history page on the server, telling the Flash Player to execute the onHistoryLoaded() function when the server responds. Note that in this case, the receiver is an instance of LoadVarsExtended rather than LoadVars, which means that as long as the server responds with name/value pairs that follow our special naming conventions, we can use our getRecordsetValues() method to access the text and date of each comment.

NOTE

The sendAndLoad() call in to loadHistory() uses a GET operation when communicating with your server. Variables are provided to GET operations with Flash as they are when GET (as opposed to POST) is used in a HTML form: the names and values of each variable are appended to the query string portion of the URL. If you wish, you could get rid of the lvSender instance of LoadVars, appending the pageIdentifier variable to the URL yourself instead. All that said, you should always use POST when updating or posting any new information to a server; consult an HTTP specification or reference document for details about the difference between GET and POST and when it is appropriate to use each.

If you glance at the onHistoryLoaded() function, you'll see that it does just that. It loops through the one-dimensional arrays that represent the columns from the database, creating a simple HTML string as it goes (where the date of each comment is in bold, with the actual comment just beneath it as shown in Figure 6.7). The completed HTML string is placed into the scrollable text area within the HistoryClip movie clip, which is then slid into view with a gotoAndPlay() call.

I created the scrollable text area by dragging an instance of the TextArea component from the Flash IDE's Components panel on to the Stage. Then I used the Properties panel to set its instance name to txtHistory, its editable parameter to false, and its html parameter to true. The result is a scrolling region for displaying text (not unlike a <textarea> on a normal web page), except that the text can't be edited and can include simple HTML markup, such as <b> and <p> tags. Consult the Flash documentation for more information on the simplified subset of HTML that you can use in text fields and TextArea components.

The remainder of the code in Listing 6.13 is simply about completing minor UI tasks such as sliding the History panel in and out of view, showing status messages, and so on. If you explore the commentWidget.fla document a bit, you can see the timeline variables and instance names to which the code is referring.

Specifying the pageIdentifier *When Embedding the Comment Widget in a Web Page*

The code in Listing 6.13 refers to a variable called pageIdentifier in the root timeline (_root.pageIdentifier, near the top of the listing). This identifier is sent to the server during the two sendAndLoad() calls made by the comment widget example. Presumably, you might want to place the widget on a number of different pages, or next to a number of different images. The pageIdentifier is what the widget uses to keep the comments separate from each other.

You might be wondering how to tell the SWF which pageIdentifier to use. It turns out that you can populate the main timeline with variables by including name/value pairs in the URL for the SWF when embedding a movie on a web page.

Here's how it works: as you learned in Chapter 2, you embed movies on web pages using HTML <embed>, <object>, and <param> syntax. The most important piece of information you provide to these tags is the URL for the actual .swf file you want the Flash Player to display. If you provide additional information after the .swf part of the URL, in the form of a standard query string, the Flash Player uses the name/value pairs in the query string to create string variables in the main timeline of the movie. This makes it possible to provide your movies with simple initialization values (such as the ID number of a particular artist, person, or customer—or, in this case, the pageIdentifier value to use).

If you look at the HTML source code for the commentWidgetDemo.html page (shown in Figure 6.5), you can find that the URL for the SWF is provided like this (as opposed to just commentWidget.swf):

```
commentWidget.swf?pageIdentifier=demo
```

If you don't provide a pageIdentifier in the URL query string, the _root.pageIdentifier variable is undefined at runtime. The code near the top of Listing 6.13 provides a default value of test/debug when this is the case. So, if you view the movie using File > Publish or Control > Test Movie instead of viewing it on commentWidgetDemo.html or some other web page that provides a `pageIdentifier` in the URL, `test/debug` is used for the `sPageIdentifier` column when inserting new comments or querying for existing ones.

NOTE

Another way to pass variables to a movie while embedding it in an HTML page is with a special parameter called `FLASHVARS`, instead of including it in the URL for the SWF. For details, see the "Passing URL and Form Variables" section in Chapter 10, "Flash and Sessions."

Other Means of Sending and Loading Variables

This chapter has filled you in on most of the details surrounding use of the `LoadVars` class. Flash also provides a number of other methods for retrieving or sending variables to a web server. In my opinion, these methods are generally less flexible and a bit clumsier than the `LoadVars` class, mainly because each `LoadVars` instance has its own "namespace" for variables being exchanged with a server. The variables that you want to send or retrieve must be set or accessed as named properties on the `LoadVars` instance.

The following alternative methods, on the other hand, are all based on the notion of sending or loading variables directly from a movie clip's timeline (or a movie's main timeline). These methods can come in handy in certain situations, especially if you need compatibility with older versions of the Flash Player:

- **The `MovieClip.loadVariables()` method.** This method is similar to the `load()` method of the `LoadVars` class, except that it sets variables directly in the movie clip's namespace, instead of as named properties of a separate `LoadVars` instance. You can also use the standalone `loadVariables()` or `loadVariablesNum()` commands similarly (they are compatible with Flash Players all the way back to version 4, and are not methods of any object per se). In general, it usually makes sense to use `LoadVars.load()` or `LoadVars.sendAndLoad()` instead.

- **The `MovieClip.loadMovie()` method.** You have already seen how `loadMovie()` can be used to load external content into a movie clip. If you wish, you can specify either `"GET"` or `"POST"` as the method's second argument; if you do, all variables in the movie clip's timeline will be included in the request to your web server. You can also use the standalone `loadMovie()` or `loadMovieNum()` commands similarly (they are compatible with Flash Players all the way back to version 4, and are not methods of any object per se).

- **The `MovieClip.getURL()` method.** You have seen how `getURL()` can be used to navigate the browser to a different web page. If you wish, you can specify either `"GET"` or `"POST"` as the method's second argument; if you do, all variables in the movie clip's timeline are included in the request to your web server. You can also use the standalone `getURL()` command similarly (it is compatible with Flash Players all the way back to version 4, and it is not a method of any object per se). In general, you are encouraged to consider using `LoadVars.send()` instead.

Unless a good reason exists to use one of these methods, I generally consider `LoadVars` to be a cleaner, more modern way of getting the job done. Consult the Flash documentation for more information about these methods.

Summary

This chapter dove headlong into the various nooks and crannies of the `LoadVars` object and how to use it in a variety of situations. You had seen it in action previously in Chapter 2 and Chapter 3, "Digging a Bit Deeper"—where it was used to retrieve simple text values—but this chapter explored using the object to retrieve structured, database style information—using several different techniques. You also learned about retrieving raw text from a server that hasn't been separated into name/value pairs. Finally, you learned about returning information to the server, thereby facilitating the creation of interfaces that create or edit database records on the server.

The next three chapters will introduce you to other means of exchanging data with your servers—via XML, Flash Remoting, and Web Services, respectively. After you see Flash's rather robust support for these other means of client-server communication, you may or may not come back to this chapter's comparatively primitive solutions. That said, there will always be times when you want a really simple, lightweight, easy to understand solution to a problem. My guess is that you will eventually come to think of `LoadVars` as at least a friendly acquaintance, if not a close buddy.

CHAPTER 7

CONNECTING TO SERVERS WITH XML

In Chapter 6, "Connecting to Servers with Plain Text," you learned how to work with the LoadVars class, which makes it easy to exchange data with your server in the form of simple name/value pairs. You also learned that while LoadVars doesn't provide built-in support for the exchange of structured information such as arrays or query recordsets, it is easy enough to "fake" such support by using special variable names or by overriding the default string-parsing routine with your own.

Of course, when you start thinking about exchanging structured information between two different environments (in this case, your server and the Flash Player), it's natural for XML to come to mind. Given the important role that XML tends to play in today's web applications, it should come as no surprise that Flash includes built-in XML parsing support.

You already got a taste of how to work with Macromedia Flash and XML in Chapter 2, "Your First Flash Interface." This chapter fleshes out your understanding of the XML support in the current version of Flash. First, we'll discuss the XML class, which is the classic, tried-and-true way to exchange XML with the Flash Player. Then it explores the XMLConnector component, which is a brand-new way to "draw" XML-powered interfaces that display information retrieved from your server.

> **NOTE**
>
> If you will be creating Flash movies that exchange data with other servers (that is, if the web server that serves the SWF file is not the same as the server that exposes the data from your databases and so on), you should refer to Appendix B, "Cross-Domain Data Access Policies in Flash Player 7," for important information about the new cross-domain data access policies in Flash Player 7.

Using the *XML* Class

This section provides detailed information about using ActionScript's XML class. You can think of the XML class as being a special version of the LoadVars class that you learned about in Chapter 6, except that instead of parsing the text your server sends back as name/value pairs, it parses the text as XML.

Quick Review of Basic XML Terminology

Let's take a moment to remind ourselves of some key XML terminology. I'm going to assume that you know something about XML already (if not, you need to do some research elsewhere before you proceed, or just be open-minded as you read on).

This discussion will be short and sweet. I just want to make sure that we understand each other with regard to a few terms and concepts because Flash's XML support uses a few of the terms—especially *node*—in slightly different ways than usual.

Take a look at the sample document shown in Listing 7.1, which shows one way that artist information can be presented as XML. Very similar output is produced by the server-side code that accompanies this chapter (see the "The Server-Side Code" section later in this chapter).

> **NOTE**
>
> I've added whitespace and indentation to this XML content to make it easier to read. In addition, I've abbreviated the descriptions with [...] to save space. Of course, the actual content returned by the server-side examples doesn't include the [...] characters.

LISTING 7.1   Sample XML Document

```xml
<?xml version="1.0" encoding="UTF-8"?>
<site-nav>
   <article id="3" filename="BigPlans.htm">
     <headline>Big Plans for the Future</headline>
     <summary>We will be beginning renovations here[...]</summary>
   </article>
   <article id="2" filename="MakingReal.htm">
     <headline>Making it Real</headline>
     <summary>Will NYC-based singer-songwriter Heather[...]</summary>
   </article>
   <article id="1" filename="Girlbandtour.htm">
     <headline>Everything but the Girls</headline>
     <summary>New York City's favorite pop cover band[...]</summary>
   </article>
   <artist id="1" image="girlband.jpg">
     <name>Girlband</name>
     <description>Girlband has been tuning guitars[...]</description>
   </artist>
   <artist id="5" image="nervousmen.jpg">
     <name>Nervous Men</name>
     <description>Equal parts Kraftwerk and Duran[...]</description>
   </artist>
   <artist id="3" image="roombyriver.jpg">
     <name>Room by River</name>
     <description>Room by River emerged during the[...]</description>
   </artist>
   <artist id="4" image="swim.jpg">
     <name>Swim</name>
     <description>Truly a rock and roll powerhouse[...]</description>
   </artist>
   <artist id="2" image="newoldies.jpg">
     <name>The New Oldies</name>
     <description>Something borrowed, something new[...]</description>
   </artist>
   <event id="2" ticket-price="8.00" date="01-Feb-04" time="7:30 PM">
     <name>The New Oldies</name>
   </event>
   <event id="4" ticket-price="7.00" date="20-Jan-04" time="10:00 PM">
     <name>Nervous Men</name>
   </event>
   <event id="3" ticket-price="18.50" date="12-Jan-04" time="8:00 PM">
     <name>Swim</name>
   </event>
   <event id="1" ticket-price="13.50" date="04-Jan-04" time="8:00 PM">
     <name>Girlband</name>
   </event>
</site-nav>
```

With this sample document in mind, review the following terms:

- **Declaration.** The first line of Listing 7.1 is the *XML declaration*. It specifies the XML version and character encoding for the document. The declaration rarely changes unless you are using documents written in many (human) languages.

- **Element.** In Listing 7.1, the elements are `<site-nav>`, `<article>`, `<headline>`, `<event>`, and so on. In other words, *element* is XML lingo for what we used to call a *tag*. In XML, all tags must be paired or explicitly identified as unpaired with a trailing slash (as in `<img/>` rather than just `<img>`, and so on).

- **Attribute.** In Listing 7.1, the attributes are `id`, `filename`, `image`, `ticket-price`, and so on. The XML standard says that you must always use quotes around attribute names (unquoted attributes were allowed in HTML).

- **Node.** The notion of a node is a bit more theoretical; strictly speaking, every discrete piece of information in an XML document is called a *node*. All the elements are nodes, all the attributes are nodes, all the text within elements are nodes, and all the comments are nodes—even the whitespace that you might use to indent your XML code count as nodes. However, for simplicity's sake, Flash creates `XMLNode` objects only for two types of nodes: element nodes and text nodes. Simpler support is provided for other types of nodes (such as attributes).

- **Text node.** Take a look at the `<headline>` parts of Listing 7.1. The opening `<headline>` tag represents an element node; the closing `</headline>` tag is the end of the element. Note that the text between the tags is a *text node*. Intuitively, we might glance at the whole `<headline>` section and call it one node, but as far as Flash and XML are concerned there are two nodes there: (1) a text node nested within (2) an element node.

- **Root node.** The XML specification says that every XML document must have one (and only one) root node, which is the element node at the top of the document tree. All other nodes are contained within the root node. In Listing 7.1, the root node is the `<site-nav>` element that begins and ends the document.

- **Parent, child, and sibling nodes.** People use family-style terminology when referring to the relationship between nodes in an XML document. In Listing 7.1, the `<name>` element is a child of the `<artist>` element; conversely, `<artist>` is the parent of `<name>`. In addition, `<article>`

has two child nodes: `<headline>` and `<summary>` (and each node, in turn, has exactly one child: the text node that contains the actual text of the headline or summary, respectively). It's worth noting that every single node (except the root) has exactly one parent. It's also worth noting that text nodes never have any children. Whew. Family life is so complicated.

Okay, that should do it for our purposes in this book. If you need more information about XML, take a quick visit to www.xml.com or some other online resource. New Riders has many good books about XML, too!

XML Class Members

The XML class actually has a partner class, called XMLNode. The two classes are related as follows:

- The XMLNode class contains methods and properties related to reading (or changing) the contents of a node within an XML document. As you know, each part of an XML document is called a node; in Flash, each element or text node is represented by one of these XMLNode objects. When you have your hands on an XMLNode object, you can access the node's child elements, attributes, text between the element pairs, and so on.

- The XML class contains methods, properties, and events related to loading XML from (or sending XML to) an external source, such as a URL on your server. Again, in this sense, it's a lot like the LoadVars class.

- The XML class also provides all the same methods and properties provided by the XMLNode class. When you use these methods and properties on an XML object, you are referring to an XML document's root node. When you use them on an XMLNode object, you are referring to some other node within the document.

> **NOTE**
>
> The XML and XMLNode classes have been available since version 5.0 of the Flash Player. Their performance has been improved over the years, but the basic API has remained essentially unchanged.

In other words, the XMLNode class's methods and properties are a subset of what's provided by the XML class. Table 7.1 shows the methods, properties, and events provided by the XML class only. Tables 7.2 and 7.3 show the methods and properties provided by the XMLNode class. That is, Table 7.2 shows the members related to reading the information in an XML document; Table 7.3 shows the members related to changing the structure of a document. Just keep in mind that the latter two tables apply to both the XML and the XMLNode classes.

TABLE 7.1   XML Class Members

MEMBER	DESCRIPTION
addRequestHeader (name, value)	Method. The name and value of an HTTP header to send to the server along with the XML content currently set on the XML object. The header will be sent when the send() or sendAndLoad() method is next used.
getBytesLoaded()	Method. Returns the number of bytes that have actually been received by the server. This number increases during a load() or sendAndLoad() operation; when the operation is complete, this number should equal the number returned by getBytesTotal().
getBytesTotal()	Method. Returns the number of bytes that will be returned by the server during the current load() or sendAndLoad() operation.
load(url)	Method. Begins the fetching of an XML document from a server. The url argument is the URL from which to fetch data. The XML object will continue to fetch the document in a separate thread; the onLoad event will fire when the data has been completely received. If you want, you can monitor the download progress using the getBytesLoaded() method.
parseXML(source)	Method. You don't normally need to call this method yourself. It is called internally during the default processing for the onData event. If you decide to implement your own onData event-handling code, it is your responsibility to call parseXML() in your code.
send(url [, targetWin])	Method. Navigates the browser to a new URL, removing the current page from view and sending a XML document to that URL as a part of the process. The url argument is the URL to which to send the document. The optional targetWin argument is the HTML-style window target name (you can use the same magic target names, such as _self and _parent, as you can in the TARGET attribute of an HTML link). Note that all send() calls are performed using HTTP POST operations; GET is not an option as it is with LoadVars.

MEMBER	DESCRIPTION
sendAndLoad (url, targetObj)	Method. Silently sends an XML document to a web server, without navigating the browser to a different page. The url argument is the URL to which to send the document. If you want to receive any XML content with which the server might respond, set the targetObj argument to a second XML object; the onLoad event of the second object will fire when the server's response document has been received. Note that all sendAndLoad() calls are performed using HTTP POST operations; GET is not an option as it is with LoadVars.
toString()	Method. Returns the XML-encoded version of the current contents of the XML document. In other words, this is the way to get the actual XML code for a particular document.
contentType	Property. The MIME content type that is sent to the server along with the next send() or sendAndLoad() operation. By default, this property is set to application/x-www-form-urlencoded. It's relatively unlikely that you would change this property in your day-to-day work.
docTypeDecl	Property. The DOCTYPE declaration part of the XML document. If no DOCTYPE declaration exists, this property is set to undefined.
ignoreWhite	Property. This Boolean property indicates whether nodes (within an incoming XML document) that contain only whitespace should be ignored. You should set this property to true in most situations, assuming that you are working with XML documents that contain "pure data" (as opposed to marked-up text, such as XHTML content). Otherwise, the XML object will end up holding a lot of extraneous text nodes that represent the indenting and newlines that XML documents typically contain to make them more human-readable.
loaded	Property. After a fetching operation has been started with load() or sendAndLoad(), this property is set to false. It remains false until the data has been fetched completely.

continues

TABLE 7.1   XML Class Members (Continued)

MEMBER	DESCRIPTION
status	Property. A numeric value that indicates whether an incoming XML document was parsed properly. Assuming that the received XML was well formed and parsed successfully, this property will hold a value of 0. If an error was encountered during parsing, the status will be a numeric code that indicates what type of problem was encountered. Search for `XML.status` in the Flash IDE's Help panel for the error codes.
xmlDecl	Property. The XML declaration part (the <?xml> line) of the XML document, as a string. If there is no declaration, this property is set to `undefined`.
onData	Event. Fires when data has been completely retrieved from the server, but before it has been parsed as XML. Flash passes one argument to this event, which is the raw text of the server's response (as a string). See the "Intercepting and Parsing Raw Text Data Yourself" section in Chapter 6 for details.
onLoad	Event. Fires when data has been completely retrieved from the server, and after the data has been parsed as XML. Flash passes one argument to this event, which is a Boolean value that indicates whether the operation completed successfully.

TABLE 7.2   *XMLNode* Class Members for Accessing XML Data

MEMBER	DESCRIPTION
attributes	Property. An associative array that represents the attributes of the current node (assuming that the node is an element node). If the current node has an `age` attribute, you can access it as `myNode.attributes.age` or `myNode.attributes["age"]`.
childNodes	Property. An array of the child nodes of the current node. You can loop through this array to discover or read an element's contents. Text nodes don't have children, so this property has meaning only for element nodes (that is, nodes of `nodeType 1`); this property is undefined for text nodes.

MEMBER	DESCRIPTION
firstChild	Property. Returns the first child node of the current node. Equivalent to accessing `childNodes[0]`. If no child node exists, this property is null.
hasChildNodes()	Method. Returns a Boolean value that indicates whether the current node has any children.
lastChild	Property. Returns the last child node of the current node. Equivalent to accessing `childNodes[childNodes.length-1]`. If no child node exists, this property is `null`.
nextSibling	Property. Returns the next sibling of the current node (that is, the next node that has the same parent as the current node). If no such node exists, this property returns `null`.
nodeName	Property. For element nodes, the name of the element (`tag`). Thus, if the current node is an `<artist>` element, this property returns `artist` (as a string).
nodeType	Property. Indicates whether the current node is an element node or text node. If it's an element, this property returns 1; if it's a text node, this property is 3. (In current versions of Flash, this property is never 2 or any other value.)
nodeValue	Property. For text nodes, returns the actual text contained within the node (as a string). If the current node is an element node rather than a text node, this property is null.
parentNode	Property. Returns the parent of the current node. If the current node has no parent (probably because it is the top-level element in the XML document), this property returns `null`.
previousSibling	Property. Returns the previous sibling of the current node (that is, the prior node that has the same parent as the current node). If no such node exists, this property returns `null`.
toString()	Method. Returns the actual XML code for the current node or document. If you call this method on an `XML` object, you get the complete XML for the whole document (as a string). If you call it on an `XMLNode`, you get the portion of the XML code that makes up the current node and its children.

TABLE 7.3   *XMLNode* Class Members for Changing XML Document Structures

Member	Description
appendChild(newNode)	Method. Adds the specified new node to the XML document structure, as a child of the node that you call the method on. The newNode argument must be an XMLNode object and is most likely an object that you recently created with createElement(), createTextNode(), or cloneNode().
cloneNode(deep)	Method. Returns a copy of the current node. If you set the deep argument to true, the current node's children are also copied; otherwise, the node's children are not included. The cloned node does not have a position in the XML document until you place it somewhere with appendChild(); thus, its nextSibling, previousSibling, and parentNode properties are all set to null.
insertBefore(newNode)	Method. Inserts a node just before the current node. The newNode argument must be an XMLNode object and is most likely an object that you recently created with createElement(), createTextNode(), or cloneNode().
removeNode()	Method. Removes the current node from the XML document.

Typical Usage Pattern

Assuming that your intention is to pass XML from the server to Flash, the typical usage pattern for the XML object is similar to that of LoadVars. First, you create an instance of the XML class; then you connect its onLoad event to a responder function that will process the XML document after it is received. You then call the XML object's load() method to begin the actual communication with your server. The Flash Player will contact your server, download the XML content, parse it as XML, and then call your responder function. The main difference is that your responder code will use methods and properties pertaining to the XML document's structure, as listed in Table 7.2 (as opposed to simply accessing string properties, as you do with LoadVars).

Populating a Gesture-Driven Scroller with XML

If you recall, one of the examples we explored in Chapter 5, "Movie Clips as Objects," was the creation of a gesture-driven scroller widget. The scroller enables users to easily scroll through a set of information, where each piece of information is represented by an individual movie clip within the scroller. To the user, the individual movie clips appear to be a kind of filmstrip that can be moved through or rewound with the mouse.

As a navigation element, this type of scroller is a nifty way to present an arbitrary amount of information in a fixed amount of screen real estate, so it's a natural for working with dynamic, data-driven websites. In Chapter 5, we created the scroller, but didn't do much exploration of what it would take to populate it dynamically with dynamic information at runtime. That's what we'll do now—take the scroller from Chapter 5 and populate it with movie clips that represent information received from the server. That information will come from the server in the form of XML; we use the XML class to grab the data, parse it, and massage it into the scroller. Users see information about artists, news articles, and upcoming music events in the widget, and they can scroll through the information easily (see Figure 7.1). Each item in the scroller is "hot"; clicking the item brings the user to a (fictional) detail page that displays more details.

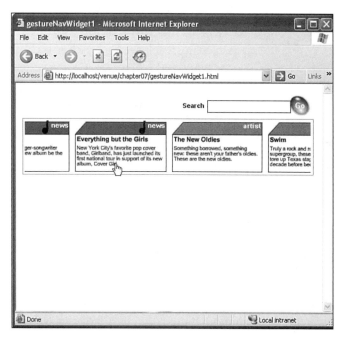

FIGURE 7.1   Gesture-driven scroller widget, powered by XML.

Table 7.4 lists the most important methods of the GestureMovieClip subclass, which was created in Chapter 5. This table is provided just as a quick reminder; please refer back to Chapter 5 for a full explanation.

TABLE 7.4   Key *GestureMovieClip* Subclass Methods

METHOD	DESCRIPTION
addClip(idName [, initObject, newName])	Adds a slide clip to the scroller. idName is the linkage identifier of the clip in the Library. The optional initObject argument can be used to supply parameters (variables) to the new clip. The optional newName argument is the instance name for the new clip; if this argument isn't provided, a default name is created by concatenating mcSlide with the new slide's index position (mcSlide0, mcSlide1, and so on).
disableGestures()	Disables (turns off) the mouse-gesture scrolling functionality.
enableGestures()	Enables the mouse-gesture scrolling functionality. The functionality is disabled when the scroller first appears so that you have a chance to add clips to the widget before users can start scrolling through it. When you are done adding clips by means of addClip(), call this method to enable the scroller.
removeAllClips()	Removes all clips from the scroller. Use this method if you want to clear the scroller so that a new set of slides can be added to it. Note that no method is provided for removing one clip at a time (although it wouldn't be so hard to create such a method).

The Server-Side Code

The Flash example in this section will connect to a page on your server that supplies information about items of interest within our fictional website. The server-side code queries the Articles, Artists, and Events tables and merges the information into an XML document like the one that was shown previously in Listing 7.1.

The name of the page that returns this content is navigationXmlSource.cfm, navigationXmlSource.aspx, or navigationXmlSource.jsp, depending on your server environment of choice. Naturally, these pages all query the example database in real time, so any changes to the database will be reflected in the XML content as well.

Because the three versions of this server-side page are all pretty similar to the XML-serving examples from Chapter 2 and Chapter 3, "Digging a Bit Deeper," the actual ColdFusion, ASP.NET, and Java code is not included as printed listings here. Take a quick look at the code for your server environment so that you can get a quick idea of what's going on. I think you'll find the code to be familiar and self-explanatory.

To support simple text-based searches, each navigationXmlSource page supports a parameter called `SearchWords` (which can be provided in the URL or as a form field). If this parameter is provided, only the records with matching text are included in the returned XML (see Figure 7.2); if the parameter is omitted, all records are included.

FIGURE 7.2   Matching records are returned if search words are provided.

The searching is performed simply, using SQL's LIKE keyword. For instance, if you include a SearchWords=girlband parameter in the URL, the page will query the Articles table using this SQL statement:

```
SELECT idArticle, sHeadline, sSummary, sFilename
FROM Articles
WHERE (sHeadline LIKE '%girlband%' OR
       sSummary LIKE '%girlband%')
ORDER BY dPublishDate DESC
```

When no SearchWords parameter is passed, this SQL is used:

```
SELECT idArticle, sHeadline, sSummary, sFilename
FROM Articles
ORDER BY dPublishDate DESC
```

Again, I encourage you to glance at navigationXmlSource.cfm, navigationXmlSource.aspx, or navigationXmlSource.jsp before proceeding, just to get an idea of what the server is up to.

NOTE

Of course, in practice you would probably use something more sophisticated to perform the searches on the server side. You might use the full-text search functionality found in many database products, such as Oracle or SQLServer. You also might use a separate full-text catalog API, such as the open source Lucene package from the Apache Jakarta Project or the built-in Verity functionality included with ColdFusion. The mechanics of fully featured text searching on the server is not what this book is focused on, so I'm just using the good old LIKE keyword in this chapter's examples. However, it would be easy to adapt the navigationXmlSource pages to use your favorite search functionality behind the scenes. All that matters is that the page produces XML with the expected tag and attribute names.

The Client-Side Code

Okay, now that you understand what the server is doing in this example, let's take a look at what's required on the client side (that is, in Flash). Go ahead and open the gestureNavWidget1.fla document that is included with this chapter's examples. If you take a quick look around, you'll find the following:

- An instance of the ScrollerClip symbol that we developed in Chapter 5. The scroller has an instance name of mcScroller.
- A layer called Search, which contains a text field called txtSearchWords for entering search criteria and a button for executing the search.

> **NOTE**
>
> By the way, the green oval button used in this example is included with one of the common Libraries that ships with Flash. To check out the button symbols that are available in this common Library, choose Window > Other Panels > Common Libraries > Buttons. You can drag any of the included symbols into your own Flash documents, or alter them to suit your needs. They also make for good learning tools—you can examine the use of layers and keyframes within these symbols for ideas and inspiration. Of course, you can always make your own buttons, as explained in Chapters 2 and 3.

- A layer called Actions, which contains a bit of ActionScript code that kicks off the retrieval of data from the server (see Listing 7.2). An `#include` statement is used to include a separate ActionScript file that contains the bulk of the code for connecting to the server and retrieving the appropriate XML data. The ActionScript file also takes care of populating the scroller with individual clips that represent information from the returned XML document.

- Three movie clips in the Library, called `NavArticleClip`, `NavArtistClip`, and `NavEventClip`. Instances of these clips will be added to the scroller for each article, artist, and event found in the XML at runtime. Each clip has a few text fields that display the name of the artist, the text in the article, and so on. Each clip has been given a linkage identifier that is the same as the symbol name, so they can be instantiated using `attachMovie()`. The three slide clips are in a Library folder named Slide Clips to keep the Library organized, but the use of the folder has no bearing on how the movie is coded or how it behaves.

Listing 7.2 shows the ActionScript code in Frame 1 of this example's Action layer.

LISTING 7.2   ActionScript in Frame 1 of gestureNavWidget1.fla

```
// The base URL for all communications with server
var _baseURL = "http://localhost/venue/chapter07/";

// Include main ActionScript code that powers this Flash movie
#include "gestureNavActions1.as"

// Populate the scroller when this movie first loads
// (the getAndDisplayNavInfo() function is in just-included file)
this.onLoad = getAndDisplayNavInfo;
```

As you can see, the first line creates a global variable called `baseURL`; this will be used throughout the rest of the example's code as the base URL for all communications with the server. Next, an `#include` statement is used to include an ActionScript file called gestureNavActions1.as, which includes the bulk of the code for the example. The last line of code sets the movie's `onLoad` handler so that the `getAndDisplayNavInfo()` function (which appears in the included ActionScript file) is called when the movie first appears in the Flash Player.

> **TIP**
>
> This `baseURL` variable technique is handy during testing and development because it gives Flash fully qualified URLs to use while you are developing and testing the movie within the Flash IDE. When you are ready to use relative URLs when contacting the server, just set `baseURL` to an empty string.

This chapter presents three versions of the included ActionScript file (gestureNavActions1.as, gestureNavActions2.as, and gestureNavActions3.as) to showcase a few different topics and techniques you'll probably find handy. Listing 7.3 is the code for the first version. It defines two functions: `getAndDisplayNavInfo()`, which is called when the movie first loads, and `fillScrollerWithClips()`, which is called when the Flash Player receives XML from your server.

> **NOTE**
>
> Make sure to adjust the extension part of the `pageURL` variable (at the top of this listing) to reflect whether you want the movie to connect to the ColdFusion, ASP.NET, or JSP versions of the XML-serving page.

LISTING 7.3   gestureNavActions1.as—XML Retrieval Code (First Version)

```
// Reference to the scroller instance on the Stage
// This line is optional; it enables the compiler to syntax-check
// method calls against the GestureMovieClip.as class file
var mcScroller:GestureMovieClip;


// This function kicks off process of fetching/displaying XML info
function getAndDisplayNavInfo(searchWords:String) {

  // Customize the scroller
  mcScroller.bgColor = 0xFFFFFF;
  mcScroller.areaHeight = 85;
  mcScroller.refreshInterval = 30;
  mcScroller.maxSpeed = 20;
```

```
  // This is the source of the XML on the server
  var pageURL = baseURL + "navigationXmlSource.aspx";

  // If search words are provided, include them as a URL parameter
  if (searchWords != null) {
    pageURL = pageURL + "?SearchWords=" + escape(searchWords);
  }

  // Create new XML instance and get it set up
  var xmlLoader = new XML;
  xmlLoader.ignoreWhite = true;
  xmlLoader.onLoad = function(success) {
    if (success) {
      // Fill the scroller with info from XML
      // (pass this XML object, so function can use its contents)
      fillScrollerWithClips(this);
    } else {
      trace("A problem occurred while retrieving XML");
    }
  }

  // Go ahead and begin contacting the server
  xmlLoader.load(pageURL);
}


// This function fills the scroller with info from XML
function fillScrollerWithClips(xml) {
  // These variables are local to this function
  var mcNew: MovieClip;
  var oVars: Object;
  var xnCurrent: XMLNode;
  // The number of child nodes within the root <site-nav> element
  var navCount:Number = xml.firstChild.childNodes.length;

  // First, turn off the scroller and remove any existing content
  mcScroller.disableGestures();
  mcScroller.removeAllClips();

  // For each of the child elements within the root
  for (var i = 0; i < navCount; i++) {
    // Convenience variable for accessing the "current" child
    xnCurrent = xml.firstChild.childNodes[i];

    // Different code for <artist>, <article>, or <event> children:
    switch(xnCurrent.nodeName) {
```

continues

LISTING 7.3   gestureNavActions1.as—XML Retrieval Code (First Version) (Continued)

```
    // For <artist> child elements
    case "artist":
      // Create movie clip within scroller to represent this child
      mcNew = mcScroller.addClip("NavArtistClip");
      mcNew.idArtist    = xnCurrent.attributes.id;
      mcNew.artistName  = xnCurrent.childNodes[0].firstChild.nodeValue;
      mcNew.description = xnCurrent.childNodes[1].firstChild.nodeValue;
      break;

    // For <article> child elements
    case "article":
      // Create movie clip within scroller to represent this child
      mcNew = mcScroller.addClip("NavArticleClip");
      mcNew.headline = xnCurrent.childNodes[0].firstChild.nodeValue;
      mcNew.summary  = xnCurrent.childNodes[1].firstChild.nodeValue;
      break;

    // For <event> child elements
    case "event":
      // Create movie clip within scroller to represent this child
      mcNew = mcScroller.addClip("NavEventClip");
      mcNew.idEvent    = xnCurrent.attributes.id;
      mcNew.eventName = xnCurrent.childNodes[0].firstChild.nodeValue;
      mcNew.price     = xnCurrent.attributes["ticket-price"];
      mcNew.dateTime  = xnCurrent.attributes["date"] + " " +
                        xnCurrent.attributes["time"];
      break;
    }
  }


// Now that all the content has been added, enable the scroller
  mcScroller.enableGestures();
}
```

The first function, getAndDisplayNavInfo(), is fairly straightforward. First, it customizes the appearance of the scroller a bit by tweaking a few of its properties (see Table 5.7 in Chapter 5 for details about the properties). Next, it creates a variable called pageURL, which is the XML-supplying page on your server. If a searchString argument was provided to the function, it is added to pageURL as a URL parameter (if the argument was not provided, searchString will be null and this if block will be skipped).

> **NOTE**
>
> The next version of this script uses a `LoadVars` object to post the `SearchString` value, instead of including it in the URL. You can use either method depending on your needs.

Then the function creates a new XML class instance called `xmlLoader` and sets its `ignoreWhite` property to `true` so that any whitespace between elements (such as the indenting and newlines that are typically added to XML documents to make them more human-readable) are ignored.

You almost always want to set `ignoreWhite` to `true`, unless you are working with documents that have elements embedded within blocks of character data (text). That typically happens only in XML that represents marked-up documents (such as XHTML), which you are relatively unlikely to be parsing in Flash. My guess is that you are more likely to be parsing XML where text is always bracketed by opening and closing elements (tags), but where the text itself is not interrupted by other elements.

Next, a function is created to handle the `onLoad` event that the XML object will fire when it receives XML from your server. Within the event function, a simple test is performed to see if the XML was received successfully. If so, the `fillScrollerWithClips()` function is called, passing the XML object itself along to the function as an argument. If the XML download and parsing process was not successful, `success` will be `false` and nothing will happen.

> **NOTE**
>
> In other situations, you might want to show an error message or take some other action when `success` is `false`. In this case, we are just catching the event silently, which means that the user will simply see nothing (a white area where the scroller would be) rather than any kind of error message.

The next function, `fillScrollerWithClips()`, is where we access the information returned by the server. The XML object that was used to communicate with the server is passed to this function as an argument called `xml`, so we can access the methods and properties of the XML class by referring to the `xml` variable. Because this function is mostly interested in reading the data from the XML document's nodes, its most interesting points are its use of the XMLNode class's properties (as listed back in Table 7.2).

Here are some items of interest within the body of the
`fillScrollerWithClips()` function:

> **Note**
>
> You might find it helpful to flip back to the sample XML document (Listing 7.1) as you look through this list.

- The `firstChild` and `childNodes` properties are used together to create a convenience variable called `navCount` that contains the number of child nodes within the `<site-nav>` root element. Because `xml` represents the document itself, `firstChild` represents the `<site-nav>` node, and `childNodes` represents all the children of `<site-nav>` (in this case, any `<artist>`, `<article>`, and `<event>` elements). The `childNodes` property is returned as a normal ActionScript array, so it has a `length` property that indicates the number of items in the array. The resulting `navCount` variable is used in a `for` block to loop over each `<artist>`, `<article>`, and `<event>` element.
- Within the `for` block, a convenience variable called `xnCurrent` is created that represents the "current" node. So, within the loop, `xnCurrent` is the `XMLNode` object that holds the artist, article, or event data in which we are interested.
- The `nodeName` property of the `xnCurrent` node object forms the basis of the large `switch` block that makes up the bulk of the function. For an `<artist>` element, `nodeName` will return the string `artist`, and so on.
- Within the `case` for each expected type of child element, the `addClip()` method is called to create a new movie clip of the appropriate type (`NavArtistClip` for artists, `NavEventClip` for events, and so on). Then some variables are set within the new clip's timeline, using values from the current XML node. The `attributes` property is used to grab the values of the current element's attributes, and the `childNodes` property is used to grab text from child elements (such as `<headline>`, `<summary>`, and so on) of the current node.

The result is a movie that displays current information from the database. One thing I like about this example is that it's pretty flexible—you could redesign any individual clip symbols within the scroller so they look however you want.

To grab the text from a child element such as `<headline>` or `<summary>`, you use `firstChild.nodeValue`, rather than just `nodeValue`, as you might expect. This is because there are really two nodes involved for each of these children:

first, the child element node, returned by `firstChild`, and a text node within the child element, returned by `nodeValue`. Flip back to the "Quick Review of Basic XML Terminology" section earlier in this chapter for details.

It's worth noting that the child elements of the current node (again, `<headline>`, `<summary>`, and so on) are accessed here by index position. For instance, in the "artist" case, this code is depending on the fact that the `<name>` element comes first within the `<artist>` block (again, glance back at Listing 7.1 if you need to) and is thus accessible at array position 0. The `<description>` element comes second and is thus accessible at position 1. If the position of `<name>` and `<description>` were to change within `<artist>`, perhaps because some other child element were added before `<name>`, this code would cease to work properly. This potential drawback is addressed in the second version of this script.

NOTE

When you're working with the `attributes` property of an element node, it's helpful to remember that ActionScript allows you to access the members of an associative array using either dot or bracket notation. Both notations are used in this example: The dot notation is handy when the attribute names are simple because there's a bit less typing; the bracket notation is needed when the attribute names contain dashes or other "funny" characters that might have special meaning to ActionScript (such as `ticket-price`, referenced near the bottom of Listing 7.2).

Adding Some Simple Extensions to the XMLNode Class

One of the Flash Player's distinguishing characteristics is that it is lean and mean. It contains very little "feature bloat," which keeps its footprint small and its downloads quick and relatively painless. I personally find it to be pretty impressive that the Flash Player contains what is essentially a whole XML parser within its guts—exposed to us as the XML class.

In general, the API for working with the contents of an XML document (that is, the XMLNode members listed in Table 7.2) is just right. It's like a lightweight version of the W3C's XML Document Object Model (DOM) specification. You can look back and forth between standardized DOM reference and Flash's XMLNode reference and see that the latter was clearly based on the former: `attributes`, `childNodes`, `nodeValue`, `nodeType`, `createElement()`, and so on...all that stuff comes straight from the DOM.

All that said, there's one DOM-style method that wasn't implemented in Flash: the `getElementsByTagName()` method. In Java, for instance, I could call `artistNode.getElementsByTagName("headline")` to get the `<headline>`

child element of an `<artist>` element. In Flash, there is no correspondingly easy way to refer to a child element by name, which is why Listing 7.3 is forced to refer to `<headline>`, `<summary>`, and similar elements by index position.

I thought it would be useful to add a few simple methods to the `XMLNode` class, in addition to the built-in ones listed in Table 7.2. In particular, I wanted something that would offer similar behavior to `getElementsByTagName()`. In addition, I felt the exercise would provide a good example of when ActionScript's ability to extend built-in classes (via prototypes) can come in handy.

The result is an ActionScript file called XMLExtensions.as, which can be included via `#include` when you need the additional methods that it defines. Table 7.5 provides a quick summary of what's included in this file.

TABLE 7.5   Additional XMLNode Members Defined in XMLExtensions.as

MEMBER	DESCRIPTION
`node.getChild(name)`	Method. Returns the first child element of the current node with the specified name. If there is no child element with the specified name, the function returns undefined.
`node.getElementsByTagName(name)`	Method. Returns all child elements of the current node that have the specified name, as an array. Like any other ActionScript array, the returned value has a `length` property that indicates the number of relevant children. If there are no child elements with the specified name, the array is empty.
`node.getText()`	Method. Assuming that `node` is an element node that contains a text node, this method returns the actual value of the text node, as a string. In other words, `getText()` is just a shortcut for `firstChild.nodeValue`.
`node.getChildText(name)`	Method. Returns the text within the first child element that has the specified name, if possible. In other words, `getText("name")` is a shortcut for `getChild("name").firstChild.nodeValue` or `getChild("name").getText()`.

MEMBER	DESCRIPTION
node.NODETYPE_ELEMENT	Constant. This property always returns 1, which is the nodeType value for an element node. This property simply provides a way to test the value of a node's nodeType value (see Table 7.2) using a named constant rather than the numeric value of 1. Using a constant rather than a number throughout your code can make the code more self-documenting.
node.NODETYPE_TEXT	Constant. This property always returns 3, which is the nodeType value for a text node.

Listing 7.4 shows the code needed to create the additional members listed in Table 7.5. The functions are not complicated at all; they simply use a few of the XMLNode methods and properties you have already seen to create a bit of new functionality.

> **NOTE**
>
> As you recall from Chapter 4, "ActionScript: A Primer," Flash MX 2004 offers two ways to extend an existing class: the older, ActionScript 1.0 way is to add items to the existing object's prototype property; the modern, ActionScript 2.0 way is to create new class files that use the class and extends keywords. In general, the latter is the better approach because it is more formalized and rigorous. However, in this situation, the classic prototype-based approach is better because we want all XMLNode instances to have the new methods, not just instances of some new subclass. Refer back to Chapter 4 for details and recommendations regarding the two methods.

LISTING 7.4   XMLExtensions.as—Extensions to the XMLNode Class

```
// Add two named constants to the built-in XMLNode class
XMLNode.prototype.NODETYPE_ELEMENT = 1;
XMLNode.prototype.NODETYPE_TEXT = 3;

// Adds new method to built-in class: XMLNode.getChild(name)
// Returns the first child element of the current node with
// the specified name; returns null if no such node exists
XMLNode.prototype.getChild = function(name:String):XMLNode {

  // Skip if no children, or if a null name was provided
  if (this.hasChildNodes() && name != null) {
    // For each child of the current node...
    for (var i:Number = 0; i < this.childNodes.length; i++) {
```

continues

LISTING 7.4   XMLExtensions.as—Extensions to the XMLNode Class (Continued)

```
      // If this child has the specified name, return it and be done!
      if (this.nodeType==this.NODETYPE_ELEMENT &&
      ➥this.childNodes[i].nodeName==name) {
        return this.childNodes[i];
      }
    }
  }

  // If we make it down here, there was nothing to be found,
  // so return undefined (would happen anyway but might as well)
  return undefined;
}

// Adds to built-in class: XMLNode.getElementsByTagName(name)
// Returns child elements with the specified name, as an array
XMLNode.prototype.getElementsByTagName = function(name:String):Array {
  // This is the array that this function will return
  var arResult = new Array;

  // Skip if no children, or if a null name was provided
  if (this.hasChildNodes() && name != null) {
    // For each child of the current node...
    for (var i:Number = 0; i < this.childNodes.length; i++) {
      // If this child has specified name, add it to result array
      if (this.nodeType==this.NODETYPE_ELEMENT &&
      ➥this.childNodes[i].nodeName==name) {
        arResult.push(this.childNodes[i]);
      }
    }
  }

  // Return the resulting array of XMLNode objects
  return arResult;
}

// Adds new method to built-in class: XMLNode.getText()
// Returns value of text node within current element
// So, node.getText() is same as node.firstChild.nodeValue
XMLNode.prototype.getText = function():String {
  // If this node's immediate child is a text node, return its value
  // Otherwise, return undefined
  if (this.firstChild.nodeType == this.NODETYPE_TEXT) {
    return this.firstChild.nodeValue;
  } else {
    return undefined;
```

```
    }
}

// Adds new method to built-in class: XMLNode.getChildText(name)
// Returns text within child node of the given name
// So, node.getChildText("a") same as node.getChild("a").getText()
XMLNode.prototype.getChildText = function(name:String):String {
    return this.getChild(name).getText();
}

// Make methods added to XMLNode should also apply to XML class
XML.prototype.getChild = XMLNode.prototype.getChild;
XML.prototype.getElementsByTagName =
➡XMLNode.prototype.getElementsByTagName;
XML.prototype.getText = XMLNode.prototype.getText;
XML.prototype.getChildText = XMLNode.prototype.getChildText;
```

As you can see, each new function in this listing is written with the special prototype property of the built-in XMLNode class object. When this code is encountered by the ActionScript interpreter, the functions will be available as methods of all XMLNode instances. Within the body of the functions, the this keyword refers to whichever XMLNode instance these methods get called on in the future.

The guts of the functions aren't very complicated. For instance, within the getChild() method, the code calls XMLNode.hasChildNodes() to make sure there are child nodes to look for in the first place. Then, a for loop is used to loop through the child nodes, checking each node's type and name inside the loop. If the type is 1 (for element) and the name matches the one passed to the function, the current child is returned. The getElementsByTagName() method is pretty similar, except that it populates and returns an array of XMLNode objects rather than a single XMLNode. The other two methods are just simple wrappers that enable you to access text node values with less typing.

Second Version of the Client-Side Code

Listing 7.5 is a revised version of Listing 7.3. You can use this version of the code by changing the #include line in gestureNavWidget.fla (Listing 7.2) to gestureNavActions2.as rather than gestureNavActions1.as. As far as your users are concerned, this version of the code operates identically to the first. However, this version is a bit cleaner from a coding perspective.

LISTING 7.5   gestureNavActions2.as—XML Retrieval Code (Second Version)

```
// Reference to the scroller instance on the Stage
// This line is optional; it enables the compiler to syntax-check
// method calls against the GestureMovieClip.as class file
var mcScroller:GestureMovieClip;

// Include "XML extensions" library, which adds convenience methods
// like getChild() to all XML/XMLNode objects, via their prototypes
#include "XMLExtensions.as"

// This function kicks off process of fetching/displaying XML info
function getAndDisplayNavInfo(searchWords:String) {

  // Customize the scroller
  mcScroller.bgColor = 0xFFFFFF;
  mcScroller.areaHeight = 85;
  mcScroller.refreshInterval = 30;
  mcScroller.maxSpeed = 20;

  // This is the source of the XML on the server
  var pageURL = baseURL + "navigationXmlSource.aspx";

  // This LoadVars object will post our request for XML
  // It will include a mock form field called SearchWords
  var lvSender = new LoadVars;
  lvSender.SearchWords = searchWords == null ? "" : searchWords;

  // Create new XML instance and get it set up
  var xmlLoader = new XML;
  xmlLoader.ignoreWhite = true;
  xmlLoader.onLoad = function(success) {
    if (success) {
      // Fill the scroller with info from XML
      // (pass this XML object, so function can use its contents)
      fillScrollerWithClips(this);
    }
  }

  // Go ahead and begin contacting the server
  lvSender.sendAndLoad(pageURL, xmlLoader, "POST");
}


// This function fills the scroller with info from XML
function fillScrollerWithClips(xml) {
```

```
// These variables are local to this function
var mcNew: MovieClip;
var oVars: Object;
var xnCurrent;
var linkageID: String;
// The number of child nodes within the root <site-nav> element
var navCount:Number = xml.firstChild.childNodes.length;

// First, turn off the scroller and remove any existing content
mcScroller.disableGestures();
mcScroller.removeAllClips();

// For each of the child elements within the root
for (var i = 0; i < navCount; i++) {
  // Convenience variable for accessing the "current" child
  xnCurrent = xml.firstChild.childNodes[i];

  // Different code for <artist>, <article>, or <event> children:
  switch(xnCurrent.nodeName) {

    // For <artist> child elements
    case "artist":
      // Create an initializer object for attachMovie()
      oVars = {
        idArtist: xnCurrent.attributes.id,
        artistName: xnCurrent.getChildText("name"),
        description: xnCurrent.getChildText("description")
      };

      // We'll use this symbol from the Library to represent
      // this child
      linkageID = "NavArtistClip";
      break;

    // For <event> child elements
    case "event":
      // Create an initializer object for attachMovie()
      oVars = {
        idEvent: xnCurrent.attributes.id,
        eventName: xnCurrent.getChildText("name"),
        price: xnCurrent.attributes["ticket-price"],
        dateTime: xnCurrent.attributes["date"] + " " +
                  xnCurrent.attributes["time"]
      };
```

continues

Listing 7.5   gestureNavActions2.as—XML Retrieval Code (Second Version) (Continued)

```
// We'll use this symbol from the Library to represent this child
        linkageID = "NavEventClip";
        break;

    // For <article> child elements
    case "article":
        // Create an initializer object for attachMovie()
        oVars = {
            idArticle: xnCurrent.attributes.id,
            headline: xnCurrent.getChildText("headline"),
            summary: xnCurrent.getChildText("summary")
        };

        // We'll use this symbol from the Library to represent this child
        linkageID = "NavArticleClip";
        break;
    }

    // Create movie clip within scroller to represent this child
    mcNew = mcScroller.addClip(linkageID, oVars);
    }

    // Now that all the content has been added, enable the scroller
    mcScroller.enableGestures();
}
```

As you can see, the basic flow and structure of this code is similar to the first version. Here are the ways in which it differs:

- This version includes the XMLUtilities.as ActionScript file, using an `#include` line. This enables the rest of the code to use any of the new XMLNode methods that were created in Listing 7.4.

- Within each `case` block, this version uses the new `getChildText()` method to access child text nodes by name. The previous version simply accessed the nodes by index position, which could cause problems if the child nodes were rearranged within each <artist>, <article>, or <event>.

- Within each `case`, this version creates an initialization object named oVars, which contains names and values for variables that should be populated in each clip's timeline. The object is then passed to the second argument (the initObject argument) of the addClip() method. Refer to the attachMovie() discussions in Chapter 5 for more information about initialization objects.

- This version uses a `LoadVars` object to send the `SearchWords` parameter to the server, instead of including it as a URL parameter. You can use this strategy whenever it's appropriate to send values to the server using POST operations rather than GET operations.

The use of `LoadVars` in Listing 7.5 is worthy of a bit more discussion. Because the `LoadVars` and `XML` classes share a large part of their API (that is, because most of their property and method names are the same and serve the same purposes), you can use them interchangeably with the `sendAndLoad()` method, as shown in this example. Thus, if you want to send normal form or URL variables to a server and get an XML document in return, you create a `LoadVars` object and call its `sendAndLoad()` method, passing an `XML` object as the second argument. When the Flash Player receives your server's response, it will pass the response to the `XML` object, which will then fire its `onData` and `onLoad` events as usual.

NOTE

You could also do the inverse (sending an XML document to the server and receiving name/value pairs in response), but you are unlikely to run into such a scenario in the near future.

It's worth noting that the Flash documentation tends to emphasize the idea of exchanging XML documents between the Flash Player and your server. That is, the documentation's examples tend to show Flash interfaces that retrieve XML from a server and then allow the user to edit the XML document in the interface (often by interacting with databound UI controls). The edited version of the document can then be easily sent back to the server with an instance of the `XML` class or an `XMLConnector` component. This book tries to present slightly different use-cases from the documentation whenever it can.

Using XPath in Flash

Believe it or not, Flash MX 2004 includes a simple XPath implementation that enables you to "query" any XML node using XPath expressions. The XPath functionality is currently exposed by a special object called `XPathAPI`. This very cool object exposes two methods for performing XPath searches, as listed in Table 7.6.

> **NOTE**
>
> These two methods are static methods, which means that you access them directly from the `XPathAPI` class object (as opposed to creating new instances of `XPathAPI` with the `new` keyword). Static methods were discussed in Chapter 4.

TABLE 7.6   Methods Provided by the mx.xpath.XPathAPI Class

METHOD	DESCRIPTION
`selectNodeList(node, path)`	Static method. The node argument is any `XMLNode` object; `path` is an `XPath` expression string. The result is an array of nodes that match the criteria specified in `path`. Like any other ActionScript array, the result has a length property that indicates the number of matching nodes. If no nodes match, the array is empty.
`selectSingleNode(node, path)`	Static method. The node argument is any `XMLNode` object; `path` is an `XPath` expression string. The result is the first node that matches the criteria specified in `path`. If no nodes match, this method returns `null`.

If you're not familiar with XPath, you'll need to read up about it online or in a reference book. A full discussion of XPath concepts and expressions just isn't within the scope of this book. Just about any book about XML will cover XPath; even better would be a book about XSLT. You can start at www.xml.com for the basics.

Making the *XPathAPI* Class Available to Your Document

The `XPathAPI` class is not an intrinsic class, which means that it is not one of the classes that is built into the Flash Player 7 executable. Instead, the class is found in a special Library object called `DataBindingClasses`. As the name implies, this object contains a number of runtime classes related to databinding (the `XPathAPI` class is just one of these special classes). Before you use the `XPathAPI` class in your code, you must add the `DataBindingClasses` object to your document's library. This makes the classes it contains available at compile time. The classes will be included in the SWF file for your movie when it is published, which in turn makes them available to the Flash Player.

To use the `DataBindingClasses` object in a Flash document, follow these steps:

1. Use Window > Other Panels > Common Libraries > Classes to open the common Classes Library.

2. Drag the `DataBindingClasses` object onto your document's Stage; this simultaneously adds the object to your document's Library.

3. Delete the instance of the `DataBindingClasses` object from the Stage. The symbol remains in your document's Library, which is all that is needed.

4. Use an `import` line to import the `mx.xpath.XPathAPI` class into the ActionScript file or frame in which you want to use XPath functionality.

5. Now you are free to use the methods listed in Table 7.6 by calling them as static methods of the `XPathAPI` class object.

NOTE

The classes contained by the `DataBindingClasses` object are included automatically whenever you create a document that uses databinding. Therefore, you don't have to perform these steps if your document already contains one of the connector components or otherwise takes advantages the databinding features in Flash MX 2004 Professional. You only need to add it to the Library yourself when you want to use the `XPathAPI` class in a document that does not use other databinding-related features.

XPathAPI Usage Basics

Now you can use the methods in Table 7.6 with any `XMLNode` object. As a very quick example, suppose for the moment that you are working with the following bit of XML:

```
<employees>
   <person gender="m">Matt</person>
   <person gender="f">Heather</person>
   <person gender="m">Tucker</person>
   <person gender="f">Apple</person>
   <person gender="m">Nate</person>
</employees>
```

Then you might use the following code snippet to get an array of all the person elements, assuming that `myXML` is an XML object that has just retrieved the `<employees>` snippet shown in the preceding code:

```
myXML.onLoad = function(success) {
  path = "/employees/person";
  arNodes = mx.xpath.XPathAPI.selectNodeList(this.firstChild, path);
}
```

You could also replace the path line with the following, which would return an array of the female employees:

```
path = "/employees/person[@gender='f']";
```

Flash's `XPathAPI` functionality currently supports just the basics and not a full implementation of the XPath standard. Here's a quick list of what you can expect to use in your XPath path expressions:

- Absolute paths, as in `/employees/person`
- Relative paths, as in `person` if the context node is `<employees>`
- The * wildcard, as in `/*/person` to retrieve all `<person>` elements, regardless of the parent
- Simple predicate conditions with the = conditional operator, such as `/employees/person[@gender='f']`
- The AND and OR keywords in predicate conditions, as in `/employees/person[@gender='f' AND @age='30']`

The following are not supported:

- Conditional operators other than =, meaning that >, <, >=, and other similar operators are not supported
- XPath's string-manipulation, numeric, and other functions
- Axes, such as `parent`, `descendant`, `following-sibling`, and `ancestor`
- Node tests such as `node()` and `text()`
- Everything else in the current XPath specifications

A Concrete Example

So far, you've been working with the XML content returned by the navigationXmlSource server-side examples, as shown back in Listing 7.1. That XML content is designed to describe information about artists, articles, and events, and it doesn't really have anything to do with the way the information is presented. That is, the XML schema shown in Listing 7.1 is fairly application-specific; it is linked conceptually to the example database for this book. That XML content is likely to be usable by any number of different applications, built with Flash or not. This is a perfectly reasonable approach and mirrors the type of application-specific XML content that you are fairly likely to encounter in practice.

There are many other ways that the same information could be represented in XML form, however. For instance, what if the XML schema had less to do with the application-specific notions of artists, articles, and events, and had more to do with the scroller functionality provided by our `GestureMovieClip` subclass?

The scrollerXmlSource.cfm, scrollerXmlSource.aspx, and scrollerXmlSource.jsp pages included with this chapter's examples create XML content that contains the same basic information that Listing 7.1 does, except in different form. If you visit one of these pages with your browser, you'll see that the top-level element is `<movie-clips>` rather than `<site-nav>`, and each item that is to appear within the scroller is represented by a `<clip>` element rather than application-specific elements (see Figure 7.3).

Listing 7.6 is an abbreviated version of the XML content returned by the scrollerXmlSource pages. As you can see, each `<clip>` has a `linkage-id` attribute that indicates which movie clip should be attached to the scroller. Within each `<clip>`, there are multiple `<var>` elements, where each `<var>` represents the name and value of the variables (or parameters) that are expected or displayed by the corresponding movie clip symbol in Flash's Library panel.

FIGURE 7.3   XML content tailored for use by GestureMovieClips.

LISTING 7.6   Sample XML Returned by scrollerXmlSource Pages

```xml
<?xml version="1.0" encoding="UTF-8"?>
<movie-clips>
  <clip linkage-id="NavArticleClip">
    <var name="idArticle">3</var>
    <var name="headline">Big Plans for the Future</var>
    <var name="summary">We will be beginning renovations[...]</var>
  </clip>
  <clip linkage-id="NavArtistClip">
    <var name="idArtist">1</var>
    <var name="artistName">Girlband</var>
    <var name="description">Girlband has been tuning[...]</var>
    <var name="image">girlband.jpg</var>
  </clip>
  <clip linkage-id="NavEventClip">
    <var name="idEvent">4</var>
    <var name="eventName">Nervous Men</var>
    <var name="price">7.00</var>
    <var name="dateTime">Tue, Jan 20 10:00 PM</var>
  </clip>
</movie-clips>
```

Now let's use the `XPathAPI` methods described in Table 7.6 to work with this new XML content. The gestureNavActions3.as ActionScript file (included with this chapter's examples) is similar to the two versions that you've seen so far (Listing 7.3 and Listing 7.5), except for the following:

- This version consumes the new version of the XML content.
- This version uses XPath to access the various child nodes within the XML document, instead of "walking" through the document's tree structure via the `firstChild`, `childNodes`, and related properties.

Listing 7.7 shows the `fillScrollerWithClips()` function as implemented in this third version of the script file. As you can see, this version doesn't have any code that is specific to the ideas of artists, events, or anything else having to do with our music venue example. The server is now in charge of populating the scroller with whatever content is appropriate. As long as there is a movie clip in the SWF's Library with the appropriate linkage name, it can be instantiated and populated with whatever data it needs (kind of by remote control).

> **NOTE**
>
> The `getAndDisplayNavInfo()` function in Listing 7.7 is essentially unchanged from the last version of the file (Listing 7.5). The changes are in the `fillScrollerWithClips()` function.

LISTING 7.7 gestureNavActions3.as—XML Retrieval Code (Third Version)

```
// This function fills the scroller with info from XML
// Reference to the scroller instance on the Stage
// This line is optional; it enables the compiler to syntax-check
// method calls against the GestureMovieClip.as class file
var mcScroller:GestureMovieClip;

// Import the XPathAPI class (it's not intrinsic)
// Alternatively, you can omit this line and refer to the class
// by its full name when you call its selectNodeList() method
import mx.xpath.XPathAPI;


// This function kicks off process of fetching/displaying XML info
function getAndDisplayNavInfo(searchWords:String) {
```

continues

LISTING 7.7 gestureNavActions3.as—XML Retrieval Code (Third Version) (Continued)

```
// Customize the scroller
mcScroller.bgColor = 0xFFFFFF;
mcScroller.areaHeight = 85;
mcScroller.refreshInterval = 30;
mcScroller.maxSpeed = 20;

// This is the source of the XML on the server
var pageURL = baseURL + "scrollerXmlSource.aspx";

// This LoadVars object will post our request for XML
// It will include a mock form field called SearchWords
var lvSender = new LoadVars;
lvSender.SearchWords = searchWords == null ? "" : searchWords;

// Create new XML instance and get it set up
var xmlLoader = new XML;
xmlLoader.ignoreWhite = true;
xmlLoader.onLoad = function(success) {
  if (success) {
    // Fill the scroller with info from XML
    // (pass this XML object, so function can use its contents)
    fillScrollerWithClips(this);
  }
}

  // Go ahead and begin contacting the server
  lvSender.sendAndLoad(pageURL, xmlLoader, "POST");
}


// This function fills the scroller with info from XML
function fillScrollerWithClips(xml) {
  // These variables are local to this function
  var mcNew: MovieClip;
  var oVars: Object;
  var arClips:Array;
  var arVars:Array;
  var xnClip:XMLNode;
  var linkageID: String;

  // Array of child nodes within root <movie-clips> element
  arClips = XPathAPI.selectNodeList(xml.firstChild, "movie-clips/clip");
```

```
// First, turn off the scroller and remove any existing content
mcScroller.disableGestures();
mcScroller.removeAllClips();

// For each of the child elements within the root
for (var i = 0; i < arClips.length; i++) {
  // Convenience variable for accessing the "current" <clip>
  xnClip = arClips[i];
  // Use linkage-id attribute of <clip> element to attach new clip
  linkageID = xnClip.attributes["linkage-id"];
  // Fresh initialization object for new clip's parameters
  oVars = new Object;
  // Array of <var> elements within this <clip> element
  arVars = XPathAPI.selectNodeList(xnClip, "clip/var");

  // For each <var> element...
  for (var j = 0; j < arVars.length; j++) {
    oVars[arVars[j].attributes["name"]] =
    ➥arVars[j].firstChild.nodeValue;
  }

  // Create movie clip within scroller to represent this <clip>
  mcNew = mcScroller.addClip(linkageID, oVars);
}

// Now that all the content has been added, enable the scroller
mcScroller.enableGestures();
}
```

This code uses the `mx.xpath.XPathAPI.selectNodeList()` method twice. The first time is near the top of the listing, where it is used to select an array of all `<clip>` elements that sit within the top-level `<movie-clip>` element, using `/movie-clip/clip` as the XPath expression. This array is looped over in the outer `for` loop, which is similar conceptually to the `for` loops in the previous versions of this script.

The second use of `selectNodeList()` appears within the outer `for` loop, to select an array of `<var>` elements within the `<clip>` element that the loop is currently processing. This time, `clip/var` is used as the XPath expression. Note that the XPath expression is evaluated relative to the node passed as the method's first argument. (In XPath terminology, then, the first argument is the *context node*.)

I think this code will be mostly clear to you, with the possible exception of the following line, which is perhaps a bit terse:

```
oVars[arVars[j].attributes["name"]]=arVars[j].firstChild.nodeValue;
```

If it helps, this one line could have been written using the following three lines. In theory, using three lines rather than one means a bit more work for the Flash Player at runtime, but in practice, any difference in performance will be extremely slight:

```
var sName = arVars[j].attributes["name"];
var sValue = arVars[j].firstChild.nodeValue;
oVars[sName] = sValue;
```

The result is that the name and value contained within the `<var>` element is added as a named string property to the `oVars` object. Because `oVars` is then passed to the `addClip()` method as the initialization object for the movie clip being added to the scroller, the values become available as timeline variables within each clip as soon as it is attached.

> **NOTE**
>
> If you would like to prove to yourself that this code behaves the same way as the previous versions, just change the `#include` line in Frame 1 of gestureNavWidget1.fla so that it refers to gestureNavActions3.as.

Using the *XMLConnector* Component

As you have learned in this chapter (and in Chapter 2), the XML class provides an easy way to get XML data from a server. The XML class is always instantiated in ActionScript code; it is never visible on the Stage. The XML class has been around since version 5 of the Flash Player (an eternity for Internet-based products), and it is the classic, tried-and-true method for working with XML in Flash projects.

Flash MX 2004 also includes a new XMLConnector component, which is found in the Components panel of the Flash IDE. Think of the XMLConnector component as a concrete, visual wrapper around the invisible XML class. The primary purpose of the XMLConnector is to supply data to Flash's form-style components (text entry boxes, drop-down lists, trees, and so on), which we explore in Chapter 11, "Building Better Forms with Flash."

Briefly, the idea is that you drag your form elements onto the Stage and then drag a XMLConnector onto the Stage as well. Then you use the Component Inspector panel to create bindings between the XMLConnector and your form elements. At runtime, Flash takes care of populating your form elements with the data retrieved by the XMLConnector (or vice versa). In other words, XMLConnector makes it possible to create data-aware interfaces with little or no ActionScript coding. You do all the work with the Component Inspector. Depending on the situation, that can make your work a lot easier, and it helps to cleanly separate data retrieval from presentation.

So, if the main benefit of the XMLConnector component is its relationship to data-bound components, why am I bringing it up in this chapter? The answer is that you can still use XMLConnector as an alternative to the XML class, if you find it easier or more convenient. In general, using XMLConnector will require a bit less coding on your part.

On the other hand, XMLConnector adds a bit of weight (file size) to your SWFs and isn't quite as flexible as the normal XML class. As a broad rule of thumb, I would generally advise against using XMLConnector unless you were planning to use some of the data-bound components. Still, I think it makes sense to show you one example that uses XMLConnector for the retrieval of an ad-hoc XML document from a server. You might like the somewhat-simplified API that it offers.

Take a look at Table 7.7, which briefly explains the most important methods, properties, and events supported by each XMLConnector component.

TABLE 7.7   Selected Members of the *XMLConnector* Class

Member	Description
direction	Property. Can be set to receive, which means that XML is downloaded from the server; send, which means that XML is sent to the server; or send/receive, which means that XML content is exchanged in both directions. This chapter deals only with the receive direction.
ignoreWhite	Property. Equivalent to the ignoreWhite property of the XML class, except that the property defaults to true (the XML class's version of the property defaults to false).
result	Event. Fires when an XML exchange has been completed. Similar conceptually to the onLoad event of the XML class.

continues

TABLE 7.7   Selected Members of the *XMLConnector* Class (Continued)

MEMBER	DESCRIPTION
results	Property. Assuming that you are using the component to retrieve an XML document (as opposed to only sending one to the server), this property will be populated with an XML object that contains the retrieved data. You can then use any of the methods and properties listed in Table 7.1 and Table 7.2 to access the data in the document.
send	Event. Fires just before an XML exchange takes place.
status	Event. Fires during an XML retrieval process. You can create an event handler that displays a status message during the retrieval process, or that takes appropriate action if a problem occurs. See the Flash documentation for a list of the status messages that may be passed to handlers of this event.
trigger()	Method. Begins the exchange of XML from a server. Assuming that the direction property is currently set to receive (as it is in this chapter's example), the component will download the XML, parse it, place the parsed XML object into the results property, and then fire the onResult result event to let your code know the download is complete.
URL	Property. The URL with which you want the component to communicate. \

If the direction property is set to receive, the trigger() method is comparable to the load() method of the XML class. If the direction is send, this method is comparable to sendAndLoad() (without a targetObj argument). If the direction is send/receive, it's comparable to sendAndLoad() with a second XML object as the targetObj argument.

Go ahead and open the gestureNavWidget2.fla document included with this chapter's example files. This document is identical to the gestureNavWidget1.fla with which you have been working, except that it uses an XMLConnector component rather than XML class instances to fetch XML from your server.

If you are interested in the additional steps involved in creating this document, you can do the following:

1. Open the original document (gestureNavWidget1.fla) and save it with the new filename (gestureNavWidget2.fla).

2. Change the #include line of the ActionScript code in Frame 1 of the main timeline so that it uses the gestureNavActions4.as file.

3. Make sure the Components panel is showing (Window > Development Panels > Components), and then drag an instance of the XMLConnector component onto the Stage (see Figure 7.4). It doesn't matter where you place the component on the Stage because it won't appear when your movie is viewed at runtime.

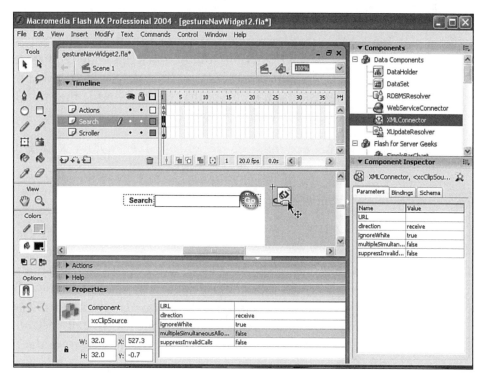

FIGURE 7.4   The XMLConnector component is like a visual wrapper around the XML class.

4. Using the Properties panel, give the component an Instance Name of xcClipSource.

5. Also in the Properties panel (under the Parameters tab), set the direction parameter to receive and the multipleSimultaneousAllowed parameter to false.

6. Click once on the `XMLConnector` component on the Stage to make sure it's selected, and then add the following code to the Actions panel:

```
on(result) {
  _parent.fillScrollerWithClips(this.results);
}
```

This code tells the component to call the `fillScrollerWithClips()` method in the parent timeline (that is, the main timeline) when results are received from the server. It passes the `results` property of the component to the function as an argument, which the function uses internally to access the retrieved data. This part hasn't changed; all the versions of `fillScrollerWithClips()` have required an XML instance to be passed in as an argument.

Now that you've done that bit of visual work to add the `XMLConnector` component and have gotten it all wired up, the ActionScript code required to actually kick of the XML retrieval process is very brief. If you look inside the navGestureActions4.as file, you will find that the code inside the `getAndDisplayNavInfo()` method is now reduced to just two lines:

```
// This function kicks off process of fetching/displaying XML info
function getAndDisplayNavInfo(searchWords:String) {
  xcClipSource.URL = baseURL + "scrollerXmlSource.cfm?SearchWords=" +
➥escape(txtSearchWords.text);
  xcClipSource.trigger();
}
```

As you can see, it takes just a single call to `trigger()` to set everything in motion. The component will then contact the server, place the retrieved XML content into the results property, and fire the `onResult` event when its done. The event-handling code you added to the component then calls `fillScrollerWithClips()`, which is essentially unchanged from the previous version (Listing 7.7).

Summary

This chapter has provided further information about the XML class to which you were introduced in Chapter 2. Several versions of a scroller interface for displaying information from the example database were presented. The first used Flash's built-in XMLNode class members to access the retrieved data; the second used a set of homemade methods to make the data even easier to access. The third used XPath to access the various data nodes and attributes within the XML code returned by the server. The fourth and final version used an XMLConnector component rather than ad-hoc XML class objects to perform the connection.

You're now well on your way to creating Flash applications that work with arbitrarily structured, multifaceted data from your server. In the next two chapters, we will marry Flash even more closely to your server via Flash Remoting and Web Services.

NOTE

Remember that if you will be creating Flash movies that exchange data with other servers (that is, if the web server that serves the SWF file is not the same as the server that exposes the data from your databases and so on), you should refer to Appendix B for important information about the new cross-domain data access policies in Flash Player 7.

CHAPTER 8

CONNECTING TO SERVERS WITH FLASH REMOTING

In Chapters 6 and 7, "Connecting to Servers with Plain Text" and "Connecting to Servers with XML," you learned how to exchange data with your server through plain text variables and XML, respectively. Both techniques are simple to use, open, and powerful—if used creatively. We still have two other means of connecting to your servers to discuss: Flash Remoting and Web Services.

This chapter introduces Flash Remoting, which was introduced with the last version of Macromedia Flash. Chapter 9, "Connecting to Servers with Web Services," introduces Flash's support for Web Services, most of which is entirely new for this version of the product.

Introducing Flash Remoting

When Macromedia released the original version of Flash MX in 2002 (corresponding to Flash Player 6), they also delivered a companion technology called *Flash Remoting*. Flash Remoting provides a simple and powerful means to exchange data on your server with the Flash Player. Suddenly, it was ridiculously easy (and efficient) to create data-aware applications with Flash.

Flash Remoting provided a clean and well-defined mechanism for interacting with pieces of programs on the server. By "pieces of programs," I mean server-resident elements such as ASP.NET pages, ADO recordsets, ColdFusion pages and Components (CFCs), Java classes, servlets, Enterprise Java Beans (EJBs), and more.

Rather than having to return the data in a specific "serialized" format (XML or URL-encoded text), you could write the server-side code without hardly any regard for how it was going to get to the Flash Player. Something called the Flash Remoting Gateway sat on the server, brokering and optimizing the interaction between the Flash Player and your pieces of programs. That all adds up to the ability to call your beans, components, servlets, and pages using a remote procedure call (RPC) metaphor.

Hmm…client-server development, using what is perhaps the ultimate thin client for the web: the Flash Player. Sounds pretty neat, eh? Well, it is. Unfortunately, I'm only going to be able to scratch the surface in this chapter. So many ways to use Remoting exist that it would be impossible to discuss them all here. However, I will get you on the road to understanding what Remoting has to offer, how it fits in with other options for exchanging data, and how to use it to pull off its neatest trick: seamlessly passing query-style recordsets from your server environment to Flash, lickety split.

Flash Remoting Versus Web Services

To recap a bit, in 2002, you had the choice between the following options for exchanging data with a server:

- Plain text variables (as discussed in Chapter 6), which was fine for simple projects or projects that needed complete compatibility with then-old (now ancient) versions of the Flash Player.
- XML documents (as discussed in Chapter 7), which are better for exchanging structured data with the Flash Player; they can be created or consumed by just about any application.

- Flash Remoting (as discussed in this chapter), which added sophisticated support for sending query recordsets to the Flash Player, potentially better performance than the XML option, and more.

Now that Flash MX 2004 is here, you also have the option of connecting to services through Web Services (as discussed in Chapter 9), which in turn enables you to use the new UI components for displaying and editing data from a Web Service. In other words, the Flash Player now supports two different mechanisms for performing RPC-style calls to server-side processes: Flash Remoting and Web Services.

The two mechanisms can solve the same sorts of problems, but are pretty different behind the scenes. Flash Remoting exchanges information with your server using something called the Action Message Format (AMF), a binary format that is generally much more compact than SOAP. You generally don't need to know anything about AMF because the conversion to and from AMF is handled behind the scenes for you; just think of it as a "compressed" or "optimized" way to exchange data through a SOAP-like mechanism. The Flash Player's support for Web Services, on the other hand, is about the player behaving as a SOAP client, communicating with Web Services providers via XML (just like any other client would).

If you and your organization are committed to adopting Web Services as an overall strategy going forward, or if you already have some Web Services ready and waiting to supply data to clients such as Flash, then you will probably be more interested in Chapter 9. You'll be particularly interested in this route if the Web Services you want to consume are publicly available services hosted by third parties.

If, however, you like the idea of a mechanism that enables you to connect Flash to your code without your necessarily having to create a Web Service, then you will probably want to consider using Flash Remoting.

To put it another way, the Flash Remoting route gets Flash closer to your server-side code. Rather than having to expose your data or functionality as a Web Service, you need only expose it in the same way that you would normally expose it to other pieces of your application (if you're working with Java, that means a EJB, a class, a servlet, or something similar; if you're working with ASP.NET, that means a ASP.NET page, a ADO.NET recordset, or an assembly; if you're working with ColdFusion, that means a ColdFusion page or a CFC).

> **NOTE**
>
> Flash Remoting is a great technology. It's worth noting, however, that while Macromedia didn't add new Remoting features for this version of Flash, they did add many new features in support of Web Services. Some people read a lot into that, seeing it as a de facto sunsetting of the Remoting framework. Others simply view it as proof that Remoting was already working well and didn't need a major update this time around.

Which Application Servers are Supported?

Unlike the other data-exchange mechanisms we're discussing in this book, the Flash Remoting framework requires the presence of a special server-side process that performs the translation and exchange of data between Flash and your code. This server-side piece is called the *Flash Remoting Gateway*; the Flash Player talks to the gateway, which talks to your code and sends back whatever results your code produces.

As of this writing, Macromedia has gateways available for the following:

- **ColdFusion MX.** As of the MX release of ColdFusion, a Flash Remoting Gateway is included in the box and installed when you install ColdFusion. You don't have to buy, install, or configure anything.

- **JRun.** Similarly, as of version 4, a remoting gateway is included with JRun, Macromedia's J2EE server. You don't have to buy or install anything special.

- **J2EE servers.** If you use a J2EE application server other than JRun, you can purchase and install Macromedia Flash MX Remoting for J2EE, a separate product available from Macromedia.

- **.NET servers.** If you use ASP.NET, or just .NET in general, you can purchase and install Macromedia Flash Remoting MX for ASP.NET, which is also a separate product available from Macromedia.

> **NOTE**
>
> As of this writing, there are several open source alternatives to Macromedia's own remoting gateways. The goal of each alternative is more or less the same: to provide an open source implementation of the server part of the Flash Remoting framework. You continue to use the client side (NetServices.as and related ActionScript libraries) as you would with one of Macromedia's own gateways. Here are some sites you can visit, which were current at the time of this writing: `www.amfphp.org`, `www.opemamf.org`, and `www.simonf.com/flap`. They provide at least partial implementations of Java, PHP, and Perl, respectively.

Some Remoting Terminology

You'll see the following list of words over and over in this chapter as well as in Macromedia's own Flash Remoting documentation, so it makes sense to start getting used to them now:

- **Flash Remoting Gateway.** Again, the gateway is the process that the Flash Player uses to talk to your code on the server. It's like an intermediary (or broker, or traffic cop) that sits between your server-side and client-side code.

- **Gateway URL.** The gateway URL is, quite simply, the URL used to connect to the remoting gateway that's been installed on your server. It's a standard HTTP (or HTTPS) URL.

- **Remote service.** The remote service is a collection of pages or methods that you would like to call from Flash. As you'll learn in the next bullet point, this is basically just a fancy name for the server-side directory or object that exposes whatever functionality you want to use.

- **Service name.** The name of the remoting service to which you want to connect. If you're connecting to pages (a ASP.NET page, a ColdFusion page, or a JSP page or Java Servlet), the service name is the path to the web server directory in which those pages are sitting. If you're connecting to an object, such as a ColdFusion Component (CFC), Enterprise JavaBean (EJB), regular JavaBean, or .NET assembly, the service name is the path to the object itself.

- **Service function.** Each page or object method that you want to call on the server is called a service function (or, if you prefer, *service method*). If you're calling a page, the name of the service function is the name of the page (without the file extension). If you're calling the method of an object, the name of the service function is the same as the name of the method.

NOTE

Sometimes people say "service method" or "remote function" or "remote method" rather than "service function." Clearly, they all mean the same thing. I tend to use the terms interchangeably.

So, the notion of a remoting service is just a metaphor that enables you to treat server-side pages and server-side objects similarly, using the same object/method type of thinking. For purposes of Flash Remoting, a directory of pages is treated like an object, and the individual pages are treated like methods. The metaphor usually holds up pretty well.

Getting Set Up

There are two different parts of the Flash Remoting framework: the server part and the client part. Before you can work with Flash Remoting, you need to have both parts installed and available, as follows:

- For the client part, you need to add the Flash Remoting Components to your Flash IDE. This quick installation process provides you with a small set of additional ActionScript objects that enable your Flash applications to connect to remoting gateways. You also get a special debugging panel that helps speed application development.
- For the server part, you need to have a Flash Remoting Gateway installed on your web application server. If you use ColdFusion MX or JRun 4 (or later), the gateway has already been installed for you. If you use ASP.NET or some other Java/J2EE server, you just need to download and install the appropriate product from Macromedia.

Installing the Client-Side Components to the Flash IDE

No matter what type of server you'll be connecting to, you first need to install a set of add-ons to your Flash IDE. This set of add-ons is called the Flash Remoting Components, and it is available for free download from Macromedia's website. At the time of this writing, the download URL was www.macromedia.com/software/flashremoting/downloads/components/.

After you install the components, you'll have a few additional items at your disposal in the Flash IDE:

- **Documentation and reference information for Flash Remoting, available through Help > Welcome to Flash Remoting > Using Flash Remoting.** This documentation set provides general how-to information about creating remoting-powered projects. It also contains essential reference information about the ActionScript objects and methods you'll be using (see Figure 8.1).

- **Context-sensitive code hints**. These pop up as you type the various methods of ActionScript remoting objects in the Actions panel or the Script window (the window where you edit external .as files).

- **The NetConnection Debugger panel, available through Window > Other Panels > NetConnection Debugger.** This panel enables you to watch the interactions between your SWFs and the remoting gateway on your server, including the information being passed back and forth. You'll learn more about this useful tool in the "Using the Special Flash Remoting Debugger" section later in this chapter.

- **You won't see these in the IDE, but an additional set of ActionScript files have been installed to the FirstRun\Include folder within Flash's program directory.** These include the following: NetServices.as, which you'll reference with an #include line in each of your Flash-powered FLAs; NetDebug.as, which you'll include when you want to use the special NetConnection Debugger tool that was just mentioned; and a bunch of other helper files that are used internally by NetServices.as and NetDebug.as.

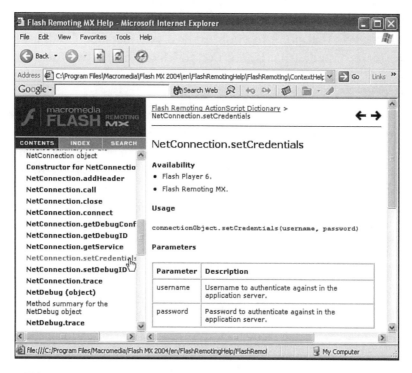

FIGURE 8.1 Help and reference documentation is always available.

Like any other external ActionScript file that you include in a Flash project, the contents of NetServices.as and related ActionScript files get incorporated into your SWF as you publish your movie. Thus, you don't need to worry about making the various .as files available on your web server.

Go ahead and download and install the Flash Remoting Components now. The installation process is straightforward, so just follow the instructions and you'll be fine.

Installing the Server-Side Components

Now that you have the client-side piece set up in the Flash IDE, you just need to set up the corresponding server-side piece on your application server. Depending on your server of choice, that might or might not be done for you already. The following subsections give the details.

ColdFusion

Flash Remoting Gateway functionality is built into ColdFusion MX and later, so you don't need to do or buy anything special if you're working with ColdFusion. The only fact to note is that you'll probably need to refer to port 8500 in URLs that point to your server if you installed ColdFusion in "stand-alone server" mode (that is, not tied to IIS or another web server).

ASP.NET

You need to obtain and install the Flash Remoting for the .NET product from Macromedia. At the time of this writing, a 30-day evaluation version is freely available from www.macromedia.com/software/flashremoting. After the 30 days are up, you will need to purchase the product; the cost is currently about $1,000 per CPU, but the price could easily change after this book goes to press. The product reverts to a single-IP developer mode after the original 30 days, which means that you can continue to use it free of charge for learning, development, or testing purposes.

If you're using ASP.NET, go ahead and install the server-side piece now. Installation is fairly painless, and it is more or less what you would expect for an application that sits on top of .NET; just follow the instructions and you should be fine.

Java-Based Servers (Other Than JRun)

You need to obtain and install the Flash Remoting for the J2EE product from Macromedia. At the time of this writing, a 30-day evaluation version is freely available from `www.macromedia.com/software/flashremoting`. After the 30 days are up, you will need to purchase the product; the cost is currently about $1,000 per CPU, but the price could easily change after this book goes to press. The product reverts to a single-IP developer mode after the original 30 days, which means that you can continue to use it free of charge for learning, development, or testing purposes.

NOTE

Again, if you happen to use JRun 4 or later as your Java/J2EE application server, Flash Remoting functionality is included, so you don't need to buy or install anything special.

So, if you're using Java, go ahead and install the server-side piece now. Installation is fairly painless, and it is more or less what you would expect for an application that sits on top of J2EE; just follow the instructions and you should be fine.

Your First Remoting Project

How many times have you wanted to show some information from a database on a web page in a tabular format? You know, where the data is shown in rows and columns, with a header row at the top of the table, and where the user is able to click the header to change the sort order? About a billion times, right?

The usual, tried-and-true approach to such a task is to generate HTML tables on the fly, where a `<tr>` is produced for each row of data. If the data might contain many rows, the usual solution is to use Next 10 and Previous 10 (or similar) links to enable the user to navigate through the data without having to effectively download the entire data set at once.

This example will show you how to use Flash's `DataGrid` control to easily produce a nice-looking display of tabular data. The control supports all the
niceties you would expect in a well-implemented HTML table version of the
display, plus some features that would be very tricky to pull off using HTML
(or DHTML or XHTML). These features include allowing the user to resize the
columns by dragging the header (see Figure 8.2) and allowing the user to scroll
through and even re-sort the data without, um, resorting to a round trip to the
server.

As you'll soon see, this is a very simple widget to create using Flash and Flash
Remoting. Technically speaking, it's really not much more than a "Hello,
World" example, but the cool thing is that this example is actually useful.
Personally, I think that says a lot about the technology.

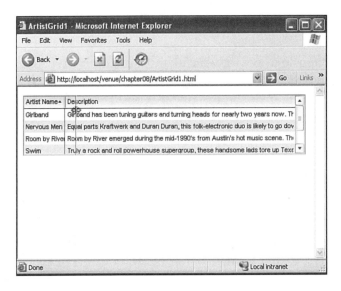

FIGURE 8.2   Users can sort, scroll, and re-sort the grid locally.

The Server-Side Code

First, let's take a look at the code needed to supply recordset data to Flash from
your application server of choice. The following sections show you the
ColdFusion, ASP.NET, and Java code needed to provide information from the
example database. For each server example, the following SQL is used to fetch
the data:

```
SELECT idArtist, sArtistName, sImageName, sDescription
FROM Artists
ORDER BY sArtistName
```

Of course, the code you use to return the data to Flash is different depending on the server you're using. The next three sections discuss the ColdFusion, .NET, and Java versions of the code, respectively. Feel free to skip ahead to the appropriate section now.

ColdFusion

To supply data to ColdFusion, all you need to do is set a special variable called FLASH.Result to whatever value you want to send to Flash. You can send just about any datatype you want—arrays, structures, query result sets, and so on. Listing 8.1 shows one of the simplest possible listings for passing data back to Flash. It queries the example database and passes the results back unmodified.

LISTING 8.1   getArtists.cfm—Supplying Data to Flash from ColdFusion Land

```
<!--- Get information from database --->
<cfquery name="DataQuery" datasource="VenueDB">
   SELECT idArtist, sArtistName, sImageName, sDescription
   FROM Artists
   ORDER BY sArtistName
</cfquery>

<!--- Provide the data to Flash --->
<cfset FLASH.Result = DataQuery>
```

> **NOTE**
>
> This listing is a normal CFML (.cfm) page. You can also use CFCs to exchange information with Flash. See the Song Rater example in the later section "A More Sophisticated Example."

ASP.NET

For ASP.NET, you can send back a query result set using the special DataSource and DataBind() members exposed by the <Macromedia:Flash> server control (from the FlashGateway namespace, which was installed when you installed the Flash Remoting for .NET software). First, you set the DataSource property to any instance of System.Data.DataTable (called data here), which has presumably been filled with rows from a System.Data.Common.DbDataAdapter of some kind (here, it's the OdbcDataAdapter called adapter). This tells the server-side Flash object what you want to send to the Flash Player. Then you call `DataBind()`, which is what does the work of actually making the data available to the player.

Listing 8.2 shows the code that supplies data to the scrolling grid. This listing was coded using C#, but you are of course free to code it with VBScript or any other scripting language supported by ASP.NET.

LISTING 8.2   getArtists.aspx—Supplying Data to Flash from .NET Land

```
<%@ Page Language="c#" Debug="true" %>
<%@ Import Namespace = "System.Data" %>
<%@ Import Namespace = "System.Data.Odbc" %>

<%@ Register TagPrefix="Macromedia" Namespace="FlashGateway"
Assembly="flashgateway" %>

<Macromedia:Flash ID="Flash" Runat="Server"/>
<%
// Open a connection to the example database
OdbcConnection conn = new OdbcConnection("DSN=VenueDB");
conn.Open();

// Query the database for information
String sql = "SELECT * FROM Artists ORDER BY sArtistName";
OdbcDataAdapter adapter= new OdbcDataAdapter(sql, conn);

// Create a DataTable to hold the data from the database
DataTable data = new DataTable();

// Fill the DataTable with query results
adapter.Fill(data);

// Assign the DataTable to the Flash.DataSource property
Flash.DataSource = data;

// Bind the DataTable, this is what gets the results to Flash
Flash.DataBind();

// close the SQL connection
conn.Close();
%>
```

This listing is a normal ASP.NET (.aspx) page. You have a number of other options for exchanging data with Flash under .NET. You can return data from assemblies, from .NET Web Services, or from code-behind files, and of course, you can use any of the usual scripting languages (C#, VB, and so on).

Java

Listing 8.3 shows one way to write the equivalent code using Java. This creates a simple bean class called `ArtistsBean`, with one public method called `getArtists()`. The method returns a `java.sql.ResultSet` object, which the Flash Remoting Gateway takes care of getting to Flash in a form that you can access through ActionScript. Note that the SQL statement is executed using a read-only, insensitively scrolling cursor.

LISTING 8.3 ArtistsBean.java—Supplying Data to Flash from Java Land

```
package venue.chapter08;

import java.sql.*;
import java.io.Serializable;

public class ArtistsBean implements Serializable {

  public ResultSet getArtists()
    throws java.sql.SQLException, java.lang.ClassNotFoundException {

    // This is the SQL query statement we will use to fetch data
    String sql = "SELECT idArtist, sArtistName, sImageName, sDescription"
     +" FROM Artists"
     +" ORDER BY sArtistName ";

    // Execute the SQL query against the example database
    Class.forName("sun.jdbc.odbc.JdbcOdbcDriver");
    Connection con = DriverManager.getConnection("jdbc:odbc:VenueDB");
    Statement stmt = con.createStatement(
     ResultSet.TYPE_SCROLL_INSENSITIVE,
     ResultSet.CONCUR_READ_ONLY);
    ResultSet rs = stmt.executeQuery(sql);

    // Return result set to Flash (or whoever calls this function)
    return rs;
  };
};
```

To make this bean visible to the Flash Remoting Gateway, place the file in a location visible to the classpath in effect for your server. In a typical JRun installation, that means placing the ArtistsBean.java file at servers\default\ SERVER-INF\classes\venue\chapter08 (the server will compile the class file for you). If you are using a different J2EE server, you will need to consult the Flash Remoting documentation (and possibly the documentation for your server) to determine the correct place to put the file. Assuming that you have been working with your server for some time, the location will most likely be quite obvious to you.

> **NOTE**
>
> This is just a simple Java class (which happens to be a bean) that uses just about the simplest code possible to query a database and return the results. You can also exchange data with EJBs, servlets, JSP pages, and more. You will need to consult the Flash Remoting documentation for details about connecting to each type of server-side object. Don't worry—the basic steps are the same for each type of object. The Flash Remoting gateway does a good job of standardizing their usages.

The Client-Side Work

Now that you've seen the simple server-side code used by our grid example, let's take a look at what you need to do in Flash to grab the query recordset returned by the server. Basically, you just build a normal Flash interface and then add a few lines of ActionScript code that calls whatever methods or pages you want to access on the server.

Go ahead and open up the ArtistGrid.fla document, which is included with this chapter's example files. You can also create the interface yourself by following these easy steps:

1. Create a new Flash document and save it as ArtistGrid.fla.
2. Drag a DataGrid component from the Components panel onto the Stage, and give it an instance name of `gridArtists`. While you're in the Properties panel, change the width and height properties to 500 and 100, and the X and Y coordinates to 0,0 (you can do the sizing and positioning through Modify > Transform > Free Transform, if you prefer).
3. Choose Modify > Document to bring up the Document Properties dialog and then use the Contents button to resize your movie to the size of the grid and click OK.
4. Add the code shown in Listing 8.4 to the Actions panel for Frame 1.

Listing 8.4 shows the ActionScript code for Frame 1 of this simple example file. As you can see, there are a few elements that you're not familiar with yet, but the code is short and easy to understand.

> **NOTE**
>
> There are several different versions of the lines that define the `frGatewayURL` and `frServiceName` variables in this listing. There's one set of lines for use with ColdFusion, a slightly different set of lines for ASP.NET, and a third version if you're using JRun. Uncomment the two lines that are relevant to your server and make sure the other lines are commented out (or just delete the lines altogether if you want).

LISTING 8.4 ActionScript Code to Show Recordset Data in a DataGrid

```
// Include the client-side Flash Remoting functionality
#include "NetServices.as"

// These 2 values change a bit depending on the server we're using
// For ColdFusion
var frGatewayURL = "http://localhost/flashservices/gateway";
var frServiceName = "venue.chapter08";
// For ASP.NET
// var frGatewayURL = "http://localhost/flashremoting/gateway.aspx";
// var frServiceName = "venue.chapter08";
// For JRun
// var frGatewayURL = "http://localhost:8100/flashservices/gateway";
// var frServiceName = "venue.chapter08.ArtistsBean";

this.onLoad = function() {
  // Here are the standard lines that get us connected to the server
  NetServices.setDefaultGatewayUrl(frGatewayURL);
  var frConnection = NetServices.createGatewayConnection();
  var frService = frConnection.getService(frServiceName, this);

  // Set up the visual look of the grid
  gridArtists.alternatingRowColors = [0xFFFFFF, 0xEEEEFF];
  gridArtists.columnNames = ["sArtistName", "sDescription"];
  gridArtists.getColumnAt(0).headerText = "Artist Name";
  gridArtists.getColumnAt(0).width = 150;
  gridArtists.getColumnAt(1).headerText = "Description";
  gridArtists.getColumnAt(1).width = 350;

  // Call our "service method" on the server
  frService.getArtists();
}

// Event: executes upon successful receipt of data from server
function getArtists_Result(result) {
  gridArtists.dataProvider = result;
}

// Event: execution if a problem occurs during remote method call
function getArtists_Status(error) {
  trace("-------- Remoting Error ---------");
  trace(error.type);
  trace(error.description);
  trace("------------------------------");
}
```

NOTE

Again, you only want to use one of the sets of lines at the top of the listing (the lines that set the `frGatewayURL` and `frServiceName` variables). Uncomment the two lines that are appropriate for the server you're accessing, and make sure the other lines are commented out (or just delete them).

The most important line in Listing 8.4 is probably the very first one: the `#include` line that includes a special ActionScript file called NetServices.as. This file was installed for you when you added the Flash Remoting Components to your Flash IDE (if you haven't done that yet, go back to the "Installing the Client-Side Components to the Flash IDE" section now for instructions and details). The NetServices.as file is what implements all the special remoting-related classes and methods that you see in this listing and throughout the ActionScript code in this chapter. The remoting classes are not intrinsic (not built into the player), so without this `#include`, the references to the `NetServices` and any related classes would fail. You'll be seeing this line in any Flash document that uses remoting.

The next few lines set up two variables called `frGatewayURL` and `frServiceName`, which refer to the *gateway URL* and *service name* that will be used to connect to the server. You'll learn more about these items in the next two sections, respectively, but for now it's enough to understand the following:

- The gateway URL specifies the server to which you want to connect.
- The service name specifies what part of the server you want to access (usually the path to a folder in your server's document root).

The next three lines use the `frGatewayURL` and `frServiceName` variables to actually set up a connection to the server. First, a static method called `NetServices.setDefaultGatewayUrl()` is used to specify the server to which to connect. Next, another static method, called `NetServices.createGatewayConnection()`, is used to create an object that represents the desired connection (I've named the object `frConnection` here). Then a method called `getService()` is called to specify what part of the server you want to access; the result is an object that represents the desired part of the server (or, in remoting terminology, the desired *service*). The end result is a variable called `frService` that can be used throughout the rest of the code to call methods and pages on the server. I call this the *service object*.

Don't worry too much about understanding these methods right this minute. For now, it's enough to understand that they are what get you connected to the correct server. You will see lines very much like these in nearly any document that uses remoting.

Next, a few members of the `DataGrid` class are used to set up the visual presentation of the grid on the Stage. First, the `alternatingRowColors` property is used to establish that the rows of the grid should alternate between white and a light gray. Next the grid is told what columns to display (and in what order) via the `columnNames` property. Then the header and width of each column is set via the `headerText` and `width` properties of the `DataGridColumn` class.

The next line is probably the most fun and interesting (come on, we can think of this stuff as fun, can't we?). This is where you get to call a page or function or object on your server by name. You can call any function of a particular service, using the service object as a kind of proxy. Here, we're interested in calling the `getArtists()` service function (which maps to the getArtists.cfm page if you're using ColdFusion, getArtists.aspx for ASP.NET, or `Artists.getArtists()` for the Java version), so we call it as a method of the service object: `frService.getArtists()`. Like magic, the Flash Player will contact the Flash Remoting Gateway on your server, invoke the appropriate code or process, and return the result (if any) to Flash. Pretty cool, eh?

> **NOTE**
>
> It's at this moment (the moment when you call a service method) that the connection to your server actually happens, not when you specify the connection attributes with `createGatewayConnection()` and `getService()`. To put it another way, remoting requests are just as stateless as normal HTTP requests; each call is a short burst of activity that stands on its own. It is not part of a true client/server style connection that persists between calls.

Like the other client-server communications you've been learning about in this book (that is, the plain-text and XML interactions covered in Chapters 6 and 7), remote service calls are handled asynchronously. This simply reflects the real-world fact that the player may have to wait for an unknown amount of time to get the results because factors such as network congestion, connection speed, and server load might affect the amount of time a function actually takes to get information back to Flash. What this means in practice is that the next line of ActionScript will likely be executed before the service function is done doing its work, so you can't start working with the results on the line right after the service call. Instead, you need to set up a responder function, which Flash will automatically call when it gets a response from the server. Conceptually, this is no different from the fact that you needed to set up a responder function for the `onLoad` event of the `LoadVars` and `XML` classes that you've already worked with in earlier chapters.

That's what the last lines of code are about. They create a responder function called `getArtists_Result()` that Flash will execute when the `getArtists()` method call has completed successfully. Flash always supplies one argument to the responder function, which is whatever value was returned by the server. Inside the responder function, you can refer to `result` (or whatever you choose to name the argument) to access the returned value. In this case, `result` is the query-style recordset returned by the SQL `SELECT` statement executed against the example database in Listing 8.1, 8.2, or 8.3, which means that it will be an instance of the special Flash Remoting `RecordSet` class (see the "The *RecordSet* Class: Accessing Query Results" section, later in this chapter, for details).

In this simple example, all we want to do is display the data in the recordset in the `DataGrid` named `gridArtists`, which is easily accomplished using the grid's `dataProvider` property. The `DataGrid` component exposes too many methods and properties to explain here, but for now it's enough to know that it accepts any array of objects and displays each item in the array as a row in the grid (assuming that the array contains objects that have properties that match up to the grid's column names). Luckily, the `items` property of the `RecordSet` class is exactly that, so we can fill the grid with the query results quickly and easily.

In addition to the `_Result` responder function, you can also create a similar `_Status` function that displays debugging information for your own use or that performs some sort of graceful fallback operation. In this example, the `getArtists_Status()` function just outputs some trace statements about the nature of the error (Figure 8.3 shows what might happen if your database becomes unavailable for some reason), but you can take whatever action you feel is appropriate. For details about handling status events, see the "More Details about Responding to Status Events" section later in this chapter.

FIGURE 8.3   Use `Status` functions to respond to problems on the server.

That's all there is to it! I know it took a while to explain, but if you'll look back at Listing 8.4 now, I think you'll agree that it makes sense and gets a lot done with just a few lines of code. (It's only about 15 lines long if you don't count the comments and error-tracing code.)

Some More Details About Gateway URLs

A few words are in order about the correct gateway URL to use for your server. The code in Listing 8.4 provided three different `frGatewayURL` lines to use for ColdFusion, ASP.NET, and JRun. The following sections provide additional notes about each of these servers, respectively.

For ColdFusion

To connect to a ColdFusion server, you use this gateway URL:

```
http://localhost/flashservices/gateway
```

If you're using the standalone version of ColdFusion on port 8500, you'll need to add the port number, like so:

```
http://localhost:8500/flashservices/gateway
```

For .NET

To connect to a gateway installed on a .NET server, you can generally use this gateway URL:

```
http://localhost/flashremoting/gateway.aspx
```

This assumes that a `flashremoting` application folder has been set up for the site you're accessing, with a `bin` folder that includes the `flashgateway.dll` assembly, and that the `flashremoting` folder also contains a `gateway.aspx` file (which can just be an empty file). This should have been set up for the Default site when you installed Flash Remoting for .NET. To use remoting for sites other than the Default site, you will likely need to copy these items to a `flashremoting` folder in the other site's document root. Consult the Flash Remoting for .NET documentation for complete installation details.

For JRun

To connect to the gateway included with JRun 4, you use this gateway URL (it's the same as the ColdFusion URL):

```
http://localhost/flashservices/gateway
```

If you installed JRun on a machine that already had another web server running, JRun is probably listening for HTTP requests on a port other than the usual 80 (most likely 8100). If so, just add the port number as you would normally, like so:

```
http://localhost:8100/flashservices/gateway
```

If you create other JRun server instances, it might be necessary to deploy or redeploy the EAR for Flash Remoting MX. You can do so easily using the JRun console.

> **NOTE**
>
> During development, you might want to consider checking the Enable Dynamic Reload and Enable Dynamic Compile options for the Macromedia Flash Remoting web application (this is within the Enterprise Application of the same name). This will allow you to make changes to your Java files without having to cycle the server between edits.

For Other Java/J2EE Servers

For Java/J2EE servers other than JRun, the exact gateway URL might be slightly different, depending on how you've configured your server and deployed the Flash Remoting EAR. It won't be hard to figure out the correct URL to use. Consult the Flash Remoting for J2EE documentation for details.

Using localhost in Gateway URLs

You may use `localhost` as long as the Flash Remoting Gateway is on the same machine from which the SWF is being served. At runtime, the `localhost` portion of the URL will be replaced with the hostname or IP address from which the Flash Player downloads your movie (the value of `_root._url` is used internally to pull this off).

Of course, you are free to replace `localhost` with the hostname or IP address of another server, although you may have to place a cross-domain policy file on the gateway server. See Appendix B, "Cross-Domain Data Access Policies in Flash Player 7," for details about policy files and related security policies in Flash Player 7.

Overriding the Gateway URL in your HTML

You've seen how to specify the gateway URL for your server: you just pass it as a string to the `setDefaultGatewayUrl()` method, which tells the client-side remoting classes the server to which to connect. One potential problem is that the gateway URL is now hardcoded into the movie; if you wanted to use a different gateway later (perhaps you moved from ASP.NET to ColdFusion or vice versa), you would need to change the URL in your ActionScript and republish the movie.

Remoting enables you to work around such a situation by overriding the default URL when you add a Flash widget to your own web pages. Just add an additional parameter called FLASHVARS to the `<object>` / `<param>` / `<embded>` HTML that includes your SWF. The value of the parameter should be a name/value pair, where the name of the pair is `gatewayUrl` and the value is the actual gateway URL that you want to use when the movie actually runs on the current page.

So, the `<object>` block would contain a new `<param>` tag that might look like the code following this paragraph, where `myserver` is the server to which you want your Flash movie to connect. This FLASHVARS value overrides the default gateway URL you provided to `setDefaultGatewayUrl()` in your ActionScript code:

```
<param name="FLASHVARS"
value="gatewayUrl=http://myserver/flashservices/gateway">
```

In addition, the `<embed>` tag would contain a FLASHVARS attribute, like so:

```
FLASHVARS="gatewayUrl=http://myserver/flashservices/gateway"
```

Remember that ActionScript variable names are case-sensitive, so make sure to spell `gatewayUrl` exactly as shown. On the other hand, attribute names aren't case-sensitive in HTML, so you could use FLASHVARS or flashvars.

> **NOTE**
>
> You can also use FLASHVARS to set other variables in the main timeline, not just the special `gatewayUrl` variable. See the "HTML *<object>* and *<embed>* Parameters" section in Chapter 2, "Your First Flash Interface," for details.
>
> Alternatively, you can include the `gatewayUrl` variable in the URL for your .swf file, using the usual name/value pair syntax that you would use to pass URL parameters to web pages. The FLASHVARS parameter is essentially just an alternative syntax for specifying variables in a SWF's URL.
>
> See the "Step 1: Passing the Variables to Flash" section in Chapter 10, "Flash and Sessions," for details about FLASHVARS and variables in SWF URLs.

More Details About Responder Functions

In Listing 8.4, you saw how to create a responder function for a remote service call. You just use the simple `_Result` naming convention to tell Flash which function to execute when the remote call is complete. Flash will execute the function, passing whatever value the server-side code returns as the function's only argument. It's tradition to name this argument `result`, which means that the returned value is available within the body of your responder function as `result`.

> **NOTE**
>
> If the server-side code doesn't return a value, `result` will be undefined.

Responder Functions in Other Movie Clips and Timelines

If, for whatever reason, you want to place the `_Result` functions in a different timeline, you can do so by providing the path to the appropriate movie clip when you call the `getService()` method.

So, instead of this line:

```
var frService = frConnection.getService(frServiceName, this);
```

You might use this line, if you had a movie clip with the instance name `mcDisplay` and if that clip contained responder functions in Frame 1 of its timeline:

```
var frService = frConnection.getService(frServiceName, mcDisplay);
```

Responder Functions as onResult *Event Handlers*

There's a whole different way to create responder functions, if you want. Instead of creating a `_Result` function that corresponds with each remote call (as in `getArtists_Result`, or `createArtistRecord_Result()`, or whatever), you can create an event handler called `onResult` that responds to all remote calls performed on the service object, regardless of the name of the remote function. You might define such a function like so:

```
this.onResult = function(result) {
  // ...your code here...
}
```

Or, alternatively, like so:

```
function myResponderFunction(result) {
  // ...your code here...
}
this.onResult = myResponderFunction;
```

There's more, actually. If you want, you can create a custom object that contains an `onResult()` method and pass that object to `getService()` rather than `this`. When the remote call is complete, your object's method will be called; within the body of the method, `this` refers to the custom object and `result` refers to the remote function's return value. You can also create an ActionScript 2.0 style class that exposes a public `onResult()` method and then passes an instance of that class rather than `this` to the `getService()` function. See the Flash Remoting documentation for details.

Confused yet? I realize that all these different means of creating responder functions might be a bit baffling at this point. Nine times out of ten, it's sufficient (and easiest, and clearest) to use the simple _Result naming convention as originally shown in Listing 8.4. Just keep in mind that other options are available if you should ever need them. You can read up on these options in Macromedia's Flash Remoting documentation if the need should arise.

By the way, if you don't specify a responder function at all, nothing will happen when your service function returns a value. This is fine when you're calling a remote function that doesn't return a value, but you might want to consider creating an empty responder function just for consistency's sake.

NOTE

When you test a movie in the Flash IDE using Control > Test Movie, you will see a friendly warning message in the Output (tracing) window whenever you call a remote function that doesn't have a responder function. You can ignore the message if you want—it won't be visible when your movie is viewed normally.

More Details About Responding to Status Events

To respond to problems that might occur during the processing of a remote function, you can create functions that respond to status events. You just create a function that ends in _Status in much the same way as you create functions that end in _Result to handle successes. In Listing 8.4, a simple set of trace() statements is used to display information about the error (refer back to Figure 8.3), but you could choose to respond differently, perhaps by providing a simpler interface when problems occur or by asking the user to try again at a different time.

When a problem occurs, Flash checks whether a _Status function or onStatus handler is available. If there is, Flash executes the function, passing a special error object to the function as its only argument. The error object contains several string properties that provide information about what went wrong. Assuming that you name this argument error, you can access these properties within the body of your status function as follows:

- error.type
- error.description
- error.details

The exact text that each property contains depends, of course, on the nature of the problem that occurred. The text is often passed through without modification from a database driver or other process on the server. If you wanted your end users to be able to see the error information, you might do something like the following:

```
myTextField.text = status.type + "; " + status.description;
```

On the other hand, if you wanted to respond to different error messages in different ways, you might use a construct like this one:

```
if (status.description.toLowerCase().indexOf('file not found') > -1) {
  // ...your code here...
}
```

NOTE

Instead of creating functions whose names end in _Status, you can create an onStatus event handler. The onStatus handler will fire whenever a problem arises during any remote function call on a given service object (as opposed to creating _Status functions to handle each remote method call). To implement such handlers, you can use the same techniques that are allowed for onResult (as described in the previous section of this chapter).

Using the Special Flash Remoting Debugger

A special debugging panel called the NetConnection Debugger is available for "spying" on the interactions between the Flash Player and the remoting gateway. You can use this panel to troubleshoot or debug your remoting-powered applications, or just to watch what happens when you execute a service method.

To use the NetConnection Debugger, do the following:

1. Add an #include line to your project that includes the NetDebug.as file. The best place to put the line is right after the #include for NetServices.as. In Listing 8.4, the new NetDebug.as line would be the second line of code.

2. Make the NetConnection Debugger panel visible by choosing Window > Other Panels > NetConnection Debugger.

3. Preview your SWF in test mode using Control > Test Movie.

The debugger panel will include all kinds of helpful information about Flash's interaction with your server, including the name of each service function called, the argument values passed to the function (if any), and the value returned by each function. For instance, if you click the line for the result of the getArtists() call in our simple grid example, you see the actual values of each cell of the returned recordset (see Figure 8.4).

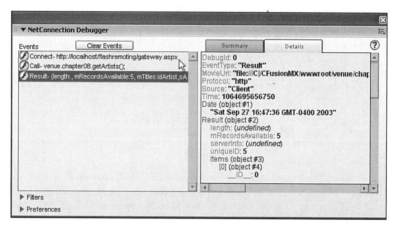

FIGURE 8.4   The NetConnection Debugger lets you inspect the data exchanged with each service function call.

NOTE

Make sure to remove or comment out the #include for NetDebug.as when you publish the final version of the movie. There's no reason why a publicly available movie should include the functionality, and leaving it out will cut down on the file size of the SWF by about 6K.

Remoting Classes: A Mini-Reference

You've gotten a quick introduction-by-example to the three important ActionScript classes related to Flash Remoting: NetServices, NetConnection, and RecordSet. Tables 8.1, 8.2, and 8.3 provide a listing of the important methods of these three classes, respectively. All three classes are made available to ActionScript when you use #include to include the NetServices.as file in your Flash projects.

The *NetServices* Class: Connecting to a Remote Server

First up is `NetServices`, which you use to set up a connection to the server. Note that these are static methods, which means that you call the methods on the `NetServices` class object itself, rather than creating an instance of the class with the `new` keyword.

TABLE 8.1 *NetServices* Class Methods

METHOD	DESCRIPTION
`setDefaultGatewayUrl(url)`	Static method. Sets the default gateway URL, which will be used whenever a specific URL is not provided to the `createGatewayConnection()` method. You can override this by providing a `gatewayUrl` parameter to the movie. See the "Some More Details about Gateway URLs" section, earlier in this chapter, for details.
`createGatewayConnection([url])`	Static method. Creates a new `NetConnection` instance (see Table 8.2). The optional `url` argument may be used to provide a gateway URL, but the standard practice is to omit this argument and use the `setDefaultGatewayUrl()` method instead.

The *NetConnection* Class: Connecting to a Specific Service

Table 8.2 shows the important methods for the `NetConnection` class. You call these methods on an instance of the class, which you create using `createGatewayConnection()` (see Table 8.1).

Only those `NetConnection` methods that you are likely to actually need are listed here. The complete list of methods (most of which are used internally by the Flash Remoting framework) is available in the ActionScript Dictionary part of the Flash Remoting documentation.

TABLE 8.2   Key *NetConnection* Class Methods

METHOD	DESCRIPTION
`myConn.setCredentials` `(username, password)`	Method. Specifies a username and password for accessing a remote method that requires such credentials. See Chapter 10 for details.
`myConn.getService(name, client)`	Method. Creates a service object with which you can call specific remote functions. The `name` argument is the name of the service. The client argument is the movie clip or object that contains responder functions.

The *RecordSet* Class: Accessing Query Results

Table 8.3 shows the members of the `RecordSet` class that you are most likely to use in your applications. Many of these methods are applicable only when you are working with a *pageable recordset*, which just means a recordset that is being received from the server in small chunks of rows rather than all at once.

TABLE 8.3   Key *RecordSet* Class Members

METHOD	DESCRIPTION
`getItemAt(index)`	Method. Returns the contents of the specified record (row) from the recordset, where an index of 0 means the first row, 1 means the second row, and so on. The row is returned as an associative array (that is, an instance of the `Object` class) that contains properties named after each column in the recordset.
`getLength()`	Method. Returns the number of rows in the recordset. It's important to understand that in the case of a pageable recordset, this value indicates the number of records in the server-side recordset, even though they might not all have been delivered to Flash yet.
`getNumberAvailable()`	Method. Returns the number of rows that have been received from the server. Important only when working with a pageable result set. For normal, non-pageable result sets, this method is synonymous with `getLength()`.

METHOD	DESCRIPTION
isFullyPopulated()	Method. Returns a Boolean value that indicates whether all rows have been received from the server. Important only when working with a pageable result set.
isLocal()	Method. Returns a Boolean value that indicates whether the recordset came from a server through Flash Remoting or was constructed locally through scripting. This value would be true for all recordset objects used in this chapter's examples.
setDeliveryMode(mode [, pagesize, numprefetchpages])	Method. Sets the delivery mode for a pageable recordset, which determines how and when the remaining records (after the initial set of records) should be fetched from the server. The mode argument can be ondemand, fetchall, and page. The pagesize and numprefetchpages arguments are applicable only in page mode.
items	Property. The actual data contained within the recordset, as an array. Within the array, each item is an object that represents a database-style data row (record). Each object contains properties that match the column names. When you want to access the data in your code, it is generally better to use the getItemAt(), getLength(), and related methods, instead of accessing the items property directly. However, you might want to assign the entire items property to data-bound components such as TextInput, Label, and DataSet. See the "Flash Remoting and Data Binding" section, later in this chapter, for details.

Table 8.4 lists the remaining `RecordSet` class members, which you are less likely to need often but might find handy every once in a while. In general, these methods have counterparts in the new `DataSet` component API, which will probably be more flexible, powerful, and easier to use and work with. (`RecordSet` has been around for years, whereas `DataSet` was just introduced for Flash MX 2004.) See the "Flash Remoting and Data Binding" section for details about `DataSet` and its relationship to `RecordSet`.

So, generally speaking, it probably makes sense to use `DataSet` components (which you can easily fill with records from a remoting `RecordSet`) to provide data-editing, sorting, and filtering functionality that the following methods would otherwise provide. That said, these methods are here for your use if you need them. Although no examples in this book use them, they are fairly straightforward and are explained more completely in the Flash Remoting documentation.

TABLE 8.4   Additional *RecordSet* Class Methods

METHOD	DESCRIPTION
`addItem(record)`	Method. Adds a new record to the recordset; the new record becomes the recordset's last row. It is assumed that record is an object (associative array) that contains properties whose names are the same as the recordset's column names.
`addItemAt(index, record)`	Method. Like `addItem()`, except that the new record is added at the index position you specify rather than at the end.
`addView(object)`	Method. Specifies that `object` should receive notification when the contents of the recordset change, are resorted, and so on. In general, now that we have the data-bound components in Flash MX 2004, it probably makes sense to use `DataSet` components to handle things like notifications, filtering, and sorting.
`removeAll()`	Method. Empties the recordset of all records (rows). The column name and other definitional properties of the recordset remain.

METHOD	DESCRIPTION
`removeItemAt(index)`	Method. Removes a single record from the recordset.
`replaceItemAt(index, record)`	Method. Replaces a record (row) with a new one. Equivalent to a `removeItemAt()` call, followed by `addItemAt()`.
`setField(index, fieldName, value)`	Method. Replaces the value in a particular column and row position with a new value.
`sort(compareFunction)`	Method. Sorts the recordset using a custom sorting function that you create. The sorting function needs to return –1, 0, or 1 when passed any two records (just like JavaScript's `Array.sort()` method). See the Flash documentation for details.
`sortItemsBy(fieldName, direction)`	Method. Sorts the recordset by whatever field you specify. The direction can be specified as `"DESC"` (case-sensitive); otherwise, the sort is in ascending order.

A More Sophisticated Example

Now that you've gotten a handle on the basics of Flash Remoting, let's take a look at a more sophisticated example. This section discusses the creation of a Flash-based "Song Rater" interface for our fictional music venue. The Song Rater enables users to listen to songs in MP3 format and rate the songs (see Figure 8.5). The song ratings are kept in a database, with each rating being stored immediately when the user casts his or her vote. A display at the bottom-right corner of the movie shows the average rating for the song, as well as the number of votes that have been cast so far (this display updates itself every few seconds so that users can see the overall ratings change as people cast their opinions about songs).

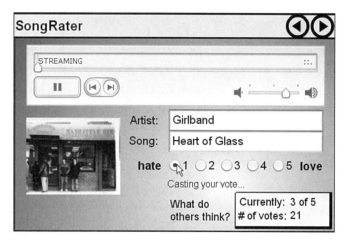

FIGURE 8.5   The Song Rater example uses several Flash Remoting features together.

This example exhibits a number of Flash Remoting concepts, including the following:

- Calling multiple remote functions within the same SWF
- Calling remote functions that accept arguments
- Looping through and working with data from recordset on the client, including making changes to the local version of the data
- Calling remote functions that return values other than recordsets
- Calling remote functions repeatedly on a schedule to reflect changes in data in real time (or what at least appears to be real time to your users).

In addition, this example shows you how to work with some additional Flash concepts and components, including the following:

- The `MediaPlayback` component, which is used to play MP3 song files. The component includes buttons for pausing and playing the MP3, as well as a volume control, rewind button, and other simple navigation controls. The component can play streaming video files, too, so this example could easily be adapted for working with video rather than audio.
- The `RadioButton` component, which is similar to an `<input>` of `type="radio"` in an HTML form. A series of `RadioButtons` is used in this example to enable the user to rate a song on a scale from 1 ("hate it") to 5 ("love it").

> **NOTE**
>
> Of course, you can apply the same basic logic and techniques to most of the other components that ship with Flash. You are in no way restricted to using `MediaPlayback` and `RadioButton` components when using Flash Remoting.

On the Server

As usual, the example files for this chapter include three versions of the server-side part of this example.

- The ColdFusion version is implemented as a CFC called SongRatings.cfc.
- The .NET version is implemented as ASP.NET pages called getSongs.aspx, rateSong.aspx, and getAvgRating.aspx.
- The Java version is implemented as a bean called `SongRatingsBean`.

Because the listings are simple and similar to the first set of examples in this chapter, they aren't printed here—for the sake of brevity. Go ahead and open up the appropriate file(s) for your application server of choice now. I promise that you won't find anything surprising in there—it's straightforward server-side code.

Each version of the server-side code creates three remote service functions that can be called from a SWF through Flash Remoting. Table 8.5 describes the functions and their arguments.

TABLE 8.5   Methods Exposed by the Remote *SongRatings* Service

METHOD	DESCRIPTION
`getSongs()`	Returns a query-style recordset of information about songs in the `Songs` table from the example database.
`rateSong(idSong, nRating)`	Inserts a new record into the `SongRatings` database table for the song and rating provided.
`getAvgRating(idSong)`	Queries the database for statistics about ratings for a particular song. Returns an associative array (or structure, or object, or whatever you want to call it) with two values: AVGRATING, which is the average rating the song has gotten over time; and NUMRATINGS, which is the number of rating records (votes) in the database so far.

Each function is really just a logical wrapper around a SQL statement that queries the example database for this book. For instance, if you examine the example code for your server, you'll find that the getSongs() function executes the following SELECT statement, exposing the result to Flash as a recordset:

```
SELECT
  Songs.idSong, Songs.sSongName, Songs.sFileName,
  Artists.sImageName, Artists.sArtistName,
  0 as nRating
FROM Songs, Artists
WHERE Songs.idArtist = Artists.idArtist
ORDER BY sSongName
```

The rateSong() function inserts a new record into the SongsRatings table, based on the idSong and idRating arguments, like so:

```
INSERT INTO SongRatings (idSong, nRating)
VALUES (%idSong%, %nRating%)
```

Of course, the words %idSong% and %nRating% are placeholders for the arguments provided to the function by the Flash movie. The actual syntax used in the VALUES part of the query varies depending on the server (you'll see the actual syntax in the example files).

The getAvgRating() function queries the database for aggregated statistics about the existing ratings for a particular song, like so:

```
SELECT
  COUNT(*) AS NUMRATINGS,
  AVG(nRating) AS AVGRATING
FROM SongRatings
WHERE idSong = %idSong%
```

> **NOTE**
>
> You aren't limited to database queries when you create your own functions for use with Flash Remoting. Queries are used in this example simply because they are so ubiquitous and easy to understand.

On the Client

Now that you've gotten an idea of what the server is up to (and I do encourage you to look at the server-side files for your server before proceeding), let's take a look at what's involved on the client.

The Visual Elements

Go ahead and open up the SongRater.fla file in Flash and take a look around, making yourself a bit familiar with the elements on the Stage, in the Library, and on the Timeline. I'm not going to bore you with step-by-step instructions on how to create this file because you've gone through that type of exercise a few times by now. Instead, I'll list the important elements in the document, which are as follows:

- The Timeline contains a number of layers, with labels like Actions, Realtime Display, Voting UI, and so on. The layers are used purely for organization; you could create this movie (and most movies that don't contain animation) without using layers at all.

- The Player layer contains a `MediaPlayback` component named `mpSongPlayer`. In the Component Inspector, the MP3 option has been selected to indicate that the component will be playing audio files at runtime (the other option is FLV, which is for playing video files—see the Flash documentation for details about the FLV video file format). The URL parameter has been left empty (the actual MP3 file to play will be set at runtime via script).

- The Voting UI layer contains a series of `RadioButton` components, which are similar to HTML radio inputs. If you look in the Parameters section of the Properties panel, you'll see that each radio button has been given a `groupName` parameter of `rgSongRating`, which causes them to behave as a group of mutually exclusive choices. You'll also see that they've been labeled from 1 to 5, but the `data` properties range from –2 to 2. So, if the user clicks the button marked "3" (which is in the middle of the range), his or her choice is actually recorded as 0 (to indicate neither a love nor hate of the song). In addition, you'll see that the Actions panel contains a few lines of code that call a method called `rateSong()` (look ahead to Listing 8.6) when each radio button is clicked.

- The Clip Info layer contains a Loader component called `ldrImageLoader`, which will be populated with an image to display at runtime through script. The layer also contains two text fields named `txtArtistName` and `txtSongName`, which will display the artist and title of each song at runtime.

- The Title Bar layer contains some simple graphics, plus round "Back" and "Next" buttons that the user can use to navigate from song to song. If you look at the ActionScript attached to these buttons, you'll see that they call the `prevClip()` and `nextClip()` functions, respectively (the code for which you'll see in Listing 8.6), when clicked.

> **NOTE**
>
> By the way, I added the two navigation buttons (visible at the top-right corner of Figure 8.5) by opening the common buttons library (Window > Other Panels > Common Libraries > Buttons), and then dragging the buttons from the Circle Buttons folder onto the Stage.

- The Realtime Display layer contains an instance of a movie clip named `RatingClip` (visible at the bottom-right corner of Figure 8.5). The instance name of the clip is `mcRating`.

- In the Library for this document, the `RatingClip` symbol has been associated with the ActionScript 2.0 class called `RatingMovieClip`. The class extends the built-in MovieClip class; you'll see the code in Listing 8.6.

- The Actions layer contains just a few lines of code—mostly `#include` statements that include external ActionScript files.

The ActionScript Code

Listing 8.5 shows the ActionScript code in Frame 1 of the Actions layer of SongRater.fla:

LISTING 8.5   ActionScript Code in Frame 1 of SongRater.fla

```
// Include the client-side Flash Remoting functionality
#include "NetServices.as"
#include "NetDebug.as"

// Include the ActionScript code that powers this specific SWF
#include "SongRaterMainCode.as"

// Call our "service method" on the server
frService.getSongs();
```

As you can see, this part of the code is extremely brief. It simply includes the usual `NetServices.as` and `NetDebug.as` files, the latter of which can be removed or commented out when you no longer want to be able to use the NetConnection Debugger window. A new file called `SongRaterMainCode.as`, which you will see in a moment, is included next. This file contains all the non-trivial ActionScript code for the movie, including setting up the Flash Remoting service object called `frService`. The last line uses that service object to call the `getSongs()` remote method on the server.

NOTE

There are any number of ways to handle the `#include` lines and corresponding files. You could move the first two `#include` lines into the SongRaterMainCode.as file, leaving just the third `#include` line in Frame 1 of the FLA. You could put the call to `getSongs()` in SongRaterMainCode.as, too. This organization seemed the most clear to me, but you might have different preferences.

Listing 8.6 shows the ActionScript code in the SongRaterMainCode.as file, which is included in Frame 1 of the SongRater.fla document (see Listing 8.5). This is where all the important code for the Song Rater example can be found.

If you want, you are free to move this code to Frame 1 of the FLA (where the `#include` line is now) instead of keeping it in a separate file. I find it handy to use separate files when the amount of ActionScript gets to be a bit long, but you are free to organize your files in whatever way you please. You might have a policy of using external .as files whenever there are more than 20 lines of code, say, or you might decide that you should never use external .as files unless the same code is going to be used by more than one FLA.

LISTING 8.6   SongRaterMainCode.as—ActionScript File Included by Frame 1

```
// Timeline-resident vars to retain recordset, selected row number
var rsSongs;
var nCurRow;

// These 2 values change a bit depending on the server we're using
// For ColdFusion
var frGatewayURL = "http://localhost/flashservices/gateway";
var frServiceName = "venue.chapter08.SongRatings";
// For ASP.NET
// var frGatewayURL = "http://localhost/flashremoting/gateway.aspx";
// var frServiceName = "venue.chapter08.SongRatings";
// For JRun
// var frGatewayURL = "http://localhost:8100/flashservices/gateway";
```

continues

LISTING 8.6 SongRaterMainCode.as—ActionScript File Included by Frame 1 (Continued)

```
// var frServiceName = "venue.chapter08.SongRatingsBean";

// Here are the standard lines that get us connected to the server
NetServices.setDefaultGatewayUrl(frGatewayURL);
var frConnection = NetServices.createGatewayConnection();
var frService = frConnection.getService(frServiceName, this);

// Fires upon successful receipt of data from server
function getSongs_Result(result) {
  // Retain returned recordset in rsSongs variable in timeline
  rsSongs = result;
  // Show the first clip
  navigateToSong(0);
}

function navigateToSong(row) {
  // Get pointer to appropriate row in the recordset
  var oCurrentSong = rsSongs.getItemAt(row);
  // Remember this row number as the current row
  nCurRow = row;

  // Set contents of visual controls
  txtSongName.text = oCurrentSong.sSongName;
  txtArtistName.text = oCurrentSong.sArtistName;
  rgSongRating.selectedData = oCurrentSong.nRating;

  // Load and show appropriate artist photo
  ldrImageLoader.contentPath = "../images/artists/" +
oCurrentSong.sImageName;

  // Load and play appropriate MP3 sound clip
  mpSongPlayer.setMedia("../clips/" + oCurrentSong.sFileName);

  // Set the idSong property in the realtime-rating-display clip
  mcRating.idSong = oCurrentSong.idSong;
}

// Function to save a rating to the server via Flash Remoting
function rateSong(rating) {
  // Feedback for user
  txtStatus.text = "Casting your vote...";

  // Get data from current row of recordset
  var oCurrentSong = rsSongs.getItemAt(nCurRow);
  frService.rateSong(oCurrentSong.idSong, rating);
```

```
  // Keep new value in local version of recordset
  rsSongs.setField(nCurRow, "nRating", rating);
}

// Fires when a rating is successfully committed to server
function rateSong_Result(result) {
  txtStatus.text = "";
}

// Fires when a rating can't be successfully committed to server
function rateSong_Status(error) {
  txtStatus.text = "Sorry, your vote could not be cast.";
  trace(error.type)
  trace(error.description)
  trace(error.details)
}

// Function to advance to next row of clip recordset
function nextSong() {
  var newRow = nCurRow >= rsSongs.getLength() - 1 ? 0 : nCurRow + 1;
  navigateToSong(newRow);
}

// Function to advance to previous row of clip recordset
function prevSong() {
  var newRow = nCurRow <= 0 ? rsSongs.getLength() - 1 : nCurRow - 1;
  navigateToSong(newRow);
}
```

The first two lines establish two variables that will be used to track the state of recordset data from the server. The query-style recordset returned by the getSongs() remote function will be stored in the rsSongs variable, and nCurRow will keep track of which record within the recordset is currently being displayed to the user. Both variables are declared with var outside of any function blocks, so they persist between and are available to all function calls.

NOTE

It's also worth noting that both variables will be stored in the main timeline's variable scope, just as if the var lines appeared in Frame 1 of the FLA itself. They could also be targeted through a target path (such as _parent, if you wanted to access the variables from a movie clip sitting within the main timeline).

The next few lines set up the Flash Remoting connection and service objects, just like the first example in this chapter. The only thing that's changed is the service name, to indicate that we want to connect to different code examples on the server.

> **NOTE**
>
> The code in Listing 8.6 shows the frGateway value appropriate for ColdFusion. If you're using ASP.NET or Java, change the frGatewayURL to the appropriate value from Listing 8.4.

Next comes a function called getSongs_Result(). If you recall, Frame 1 of the FLA contains a call to the getSongs() remote function through Flash Remoting. This result function will get executed automatically when the call is completed successfully (because of the special _Result naming convention). Within the result function, the most important line is the first one, which assigns the result value (which we know is a recordset because that's what the server-side code returns) to the rsSongs timeline variable. This enables us to refer to the recordset outside of the context of the result function; without it, the recordset object would cease to exist after the result function finished executing. The next line calls a function called navigateToSong(), passing 0 as an argument to indicate that the first song should be navigated to (that is, shown to the user).

Within the navigateToSong() function, the getItemAt() method from Table 8.4 is used to grab the record indicated by the row argument. The result is stored in the oCurrentSong variable. Next, the nCurRow variable is set to the value of the row argument so that the movie will remember which record is currently being shown after this function finishes its work. Now all the function needs to do is to tell Flash to display the values from the current record. This is easily done by setting various properties to the value of the appropriate query column within the oCurrentSong record, as follows:

- For the text fields that show the song title and artist name, that simply means setting their text properties.
- To display the correct love/hate radio button as currently selected, that means setting the selectedData property of the rgSongRating object.
- To show the appropriate artist photo in the Loader component, that means setting the contentPath property of the loader to the appropriate URL (here, the relative path to the images/artists folder, plus the value of the sImageName column from the server-side database).

- To play the appropriate MP3 file in the `MediaPlayback` component, that means calling the component's `setMedia()` method with the MP3 file's URL. See the Components Dictionary for related `MediaPlayback` class members, such as the read-only `contentPath` property and the `stop()`, `play()`, and `pause()` methods.

- To show the up-to-date statistics for the song's current rating status, that means calling the `setSongID()` method of the custom `RatingMovieClip` subclass (see Listing 8.7).

NOTE

The `rgSongRating` object exists because the `groupName` parameters of each radio button has been set to `rgSongRating`. Flash creates an object at runtime that represents each group of radio buttons; the object exposes a `selectedData` property that can be used to get or set which of the buttons is currently selected. Two other properties to deal with radio button selections are as follows: `selected` and `selection`. See the Flash documentation for details.

When a user clicks one of the radio buttons to rate a song, the ActionScript code attached to each radio button calls the `rateSong()` function, passing the value of the radio button (-2, -1, 0, 1, or 2) as the function's `rating` argument. As you can see, `rateSong()` is a local function (that is, part of Listing 8.6) that is primarily a wrapper around the remote function of the same name. First, a status message is displayed to the user in a simple text field, and then the current record from the query is placed into the local `oCurrentSong` variable (just as in the previous `function` block). Then the remote `rateSong()` method is called, supplying the ID number of the currently playing song as the first argument and the user's `rating` choice as the second argument. Finally, the `RecordSet.setField()` method (see Table 8.4) is used to store the user's choice of ratings into the local version of the `RecordSet`. Without this last step, the user's rating would reset to 0 if he or she navigated to the next song and then returned to the current one.

The rest of the code is elementary. The `_Result` and `_Status` responders for the `rateSongs()` remote function call are extremely simple because the remote function doesn't return any data with which the application needs to work. Finally, the `nextSong()` and `prevSong()` methods (which execute when the user clicks the navigation buttons at the top-right corner of the interface) simply increment or decrement the current row number as appropriate. The `RecordSet.getLength()` method (see Table 8.3) is used together with some simple math to determine if the user is already looking at the last (or first) song, in which case, he or she is sent back around to the first (or last) song.

Using Flash Remoting in ActionScript 2.0 Classes

The one remaining piece of the Song Rater example is the part that displays running statistics about each song's overall rating. This part of the example has been implemented as an independent movie clip that is linked to an ActionScript 2.0 class. The class file contains all the code needed to retrieve and display the rating information; you'll find no ActionScript at all in the movie clip itself.

You might be wondering why an ActionScript 2.0 class was used for part of the Song Rater example, whereas traditional ActionScript 1.0-style coding techniques (with code attached to frames and so on) were used for the main part of the example. Well, the ActionScript classes for Flash Remoting were developed during the 1.0 era, so I wanted to make sure that you had a complete example that used the classes in the way they were originally intended to be used. At the same time, I wanted to make sure you could see that Flash Remoting can be used with 2.0-style coding techniques. Additionally, I wanted you to see that you can easily mix and match the two styles of coding in the same project as you wish.

Listing 8.7 shows the class file for the `RatingMovieClip` class, to which the `RatingClip` movie clip symbol in the Library is linked. The symbol contains two text fields, named `txtRealtimeRating` and `txtRealtimeCount`. There's a single instance of this clip on the Stage, with an instance name of `mcRating`.

LISTING 8.7   RatingMovieClip.as—ActionScript 2.0 Class File for `RatingClip` Symbol

```
class RatingMovieClip extends MovieClip {

  // Properties for scheduling getRating() calls via setInterval()
  public var refreshInterval:Number = 5000;
  private var intervalID:Number;

  // These 2 properties change depending on the server we're using
  // Here we inherit the values at runtime from the parent timeline,
  // But you could hardcode them here instead if you wanted to use
  // a different gateway or service for this part of the application
  public var frGatewayURL:String;
  public var frServiceName:String;

  // More properties, related to Flash Remoting
  private var NetServices;
  private var frConnection;
  private var frService;
```

```
// More private properties
private var _idSong:Number;
private var txtRealtimeRating:TextField;
private var txtRealtimeCount:TextField;

// This event fires when the clip first loads/appears
private function onLoad() {
  // Initialize NetServices (workaround for AS 1.0/2.0 disparity)
  NetServices = _global.NetServices;
  frGatewayURL = _parent.frGatewayURL;
  frServiceName = _parent.frServiceName;

  // This clip shall be invisible at first
  this._visible = false;

  // Here are the standard lines that get us connected to the server
  NetServices.setDefaultGatewayUrl(frGatewayURL);
  frConnection = NetServices.createGatewayConnection();
  frService = frConnection.getService(frServiceName, this);
}

// Public function to set the idSong property
public function set idSong(idSong:Number):Void {
  this._idSong = idSong;
  this._visible = false;

  // Call the getRealtimeRating() method now
  getRealtimeRating();

  // Also schedule getRealtimeRating() method for repeated calls
  clearInterval(this.intervalID); // clears existing timer, if any
  this.intervalID =
    ➥setInterval(this, "getRealtimeRating", this.refreshInterval);
}

// Public function to get the _idSong property
public function get idSong():Number {
  return this._idSong;
}

// This function executes repeatedly on a schedule
public function getRealtimeRating() {
  // Call our "service method" on the server
  frService.getAvgRating(this._idSong);
}
```

continues

LISTING 8.7   RatingMovieClip.as—ActionScript 2.0 Class File for `RatingClip` Symbol (Continued)

```
// Fires when remote function succeeds
private function onResult(result:Object) {
  // Round rating value to 1 decimal point, then offset by 3 stars
  // (will be NaN here if database returned NULL on server)
  var rating:Number = (Math.round(result.AVGRATING * 10)/10) + 3;
  txtRealtimeRating.text = rating + " of 5";
  txtRealtimeCount.text = result.NUMRATINGS;

  // Hide the clip if no rating is available
  this._visible = isNaN(result.AVGRATING) == false;
}

// Fires when remote function fails
private function onStatus(error:Object) {
  trace("Could not retrieve 'realtime rating'");
  trace(error.type);
  trace(error.description);
}
}
```

The first few lines of this class file use the `var` keyword to set up a number of properties for the class, most of which are `private`. One of the public properties is `refreshInterval`, which represents how frequently the rating display should be refreshed.

One property of note here is the `NetServices` property. Because this is an ActionScript 2.0 class, you can't include the NetServices.as script file with an `#include` line (`#include` isn't allowed in class files). Therefore, NetServices.as needs to be included elsewhere in the movie (it can be anywhere, as long as it will be encountered before the code in this class executes). One of the things that NetServices.as does internally is to create a variable called `_global.NetServices`, which is the object you are working with when you refer to the `NetServices` object normally (such as in Listings 8.4 and 8.6). To be able to refer to `NetServices` within this class file, you need to establish a class property (most likely with the same name, though you could use a different name if you wished) to hold a reference to the global object. The property's value should be set to `_global.NetServices` before any remoting calls are attempted (here, this assignment occurs in the `onLoad` event handler).

> **NOTE**
>
> If all this business about the `_global` object and the local property sounds complicated to you, just go ahead and ignore the explanation for now if you want. The point is that the two lines of extra code for the local `NetServices` property are what's needed to work around the fact that NetServices.as is implemented as a ActionScript 1.0 pseudo-class, whereas the example code we're actually looking at is a true ActionScript 2.0 class. You can refer to Chapter 4, "ActionScript: A Primer," for some details about the differences between ActionScript 1.0 and 2.0 classes. There's also some good information in the Flash documentation on the subject (search the Help files for **object-oriented**).

Because of its name, the code in the `onLoad()` function will execute automatically when the movie first loads. This function sets up the connection to the Flash Remoting gateway, using the same `createGatewayConnection()` and related methods you've seen in the other listings in this chapter. Because `frService` has been declared as an instance-level property, its value will persist after the `onLoad` function finishes doing its work. This function also sets the `_visible` property of the movie clip to `false`, so that the clip is invisible when the rest of the SWF first loads and appears in the Flash Player.

> **NOTE**
>
> Remember that in a class file, `this` always refers to the current instance of the class. Because this class extends the built-in `MovieClip` class, you can set any of the usual properties for visibility, position, width, height, and so on (see Table 5.1 in Chapter 5, "Movie Clips as Objects").
>
> The word `this` is also always implied in a class file, so you can actually omit it anywhere you see it in Listing 8.7. That said, I personally find it to be much clearer to include the explicit `this` reference in most situations, especially when referring to a property of the class (or any of its superclasses/ancestors).

The `set idSong()` setter function executes when the clip's `idSong` property is set (at the end of `navigateToSong()` from Listing 8.6). It sets the internal `_idSong` property to whatever value has been provided to the argument, makes sure the current movie clip is invisible, and then calls the `getRealtimeRating()` method (discussed next), which kicks off the process of retrieving information from the server.

> **NOTE**
>
> A getter function for the `idSong` property is also included in this listing for consistency's sake, although it is not actually used in this example. For more information about getters and setters (that is, the use of the `get` and `set` keywords in function declarations), refer back to Chapter 4.

The setter then schedules the `getRealtimeRating()` method for repeated executions every five seconds thereafter (by default, though you could change the interval by adjusting the public `refreshInterval` property that this subclass exposes). The `clearInterval()` method is also used here, to clear any scheduled executions that might have been established during previous calls to this function. The net effect is that the function executes every five seconds after the user navigates to a new song.

NOTE

You saw `clearInterval()`, `setInterval()`, `intervalID`, and `refreshInterval` used in a similar way in the News Ticker example from Chapter 6. Flip back to that chapter for a more detailed explanation of their use.

The actual `getRealtimeRating()` method is extremely simple, just a one-line wrapper around the remote `getAvgRating()` method on the server. When the remote method returns its values successfully, Flash automatically executes the `onResult()` function.

NOTE

Remember that you can create responders in two ways: by using the special `_Result` naming convention; or by handling the `onResult` event. Listing 8.6 used the former; Listing 8.7 uses the latter. See the "More Details About Responder Functions" sections, earlier in this chapter, for details.

Within `onResult()`, the `result` variable will hold the object (or, if you prefer, associative array) that was returned by the server. In this case, the object will include properties named AVGRATING and NUMRATINGS (see Table 8.5). You can refer to these properties using either dot notation as shown (`result.AVGRATING`) or by using bracket notation such as `result["AVGRATING"]`.

Some simple math is performed on the AVGRATING property to round it off to the nearest single decimal point (1.58743 will be rounded to 1.6, for instance) and store the result in a local variable called `rating`. If, on the server side, the value for AVGRATING is returned as NULL (which will happen if there are no votes for the current song in the database), `result.AVGRATING` will be a non-numeric value when it gets to Flash.

The easiest way to test for a non-numeric value is to use the built-in `isNaN()` function, which returns `true` if a value is not numeric (and can't be converted to a number). In this case, the `_visible` property is set to the inverse of what `isNaN()` returns, which means that the current movie clip will be visible when the value is numeric and invisible when the value is NULL on the server. See the Flash documentation for further details about `isNaN()` and the related `Number.NaN` constant.

> **NOTE**
>
> The server-side and client-side code for the `getAvgRating()` function uses all capital letters for the property names. This is for compatibility with the ColdFusion version of the server-side code. (ColdFusion stores all structure key names in uppercase, which is usually fine because CFML is case-insensitive; ActionScript, however, is not, so you have to use capital letters on the client side regardless of the capitalization used on the server.) If you are using a different application server, you can use any capitalization you want; just make sure to use the same capitalization in your server- and client-side code.

Flash Remoting and Data Binding

Macromedia's development tools have long provided strong support for recordset-style data. As you have already seen, Flash Remoting is no exception. It's very easy to pass query-style recordsets from your server to the Flash Player, enabling all sorts of clever and sophisticated interfaces.

Although the Flash Remoting `RecordSet` support has been around since the original release of Flash MX, Macromedia Flash MX Professional 2004 includes new support for recordset-style data in the form of the new `DataSet` component. This section will explore the use of `RecordSet` data with the `DataSet` component in this latest and greatest version of Flash.

> **NOTE**
>
> Don't get the wrong idea here. Flash Remoting is not only—or even primarily—about recordsets. In fact, Flash Remoting makes it easy to return just about any type of information from your server, be it an associative array (such as the one returned by the `getAvgRating()` remote method in the Song Rater example), a normal array (which you haven't seen in action but behaves just as you'd expect), or a simple scalar value such as a number or string. That said, recordset data deserves special attention because it's so uniquely useful when building data-aware applications and because the Flash Remoting Components include a number of special features related only to recordsets.

Using RecordSet and DataSet Together

If you have Flash MX Professional 2004, you might have already played around a bit with the databound components that were introduced in this version of Flash. This section will introduce you to some of the databinding features, concentrating on how they can be used together with recordsets retrieved through Flash Remoting.

Before we get started, I want to take a moment to discuss why I haven't been using the databound components all along in this chapter (and in this book in general). There are three main reasons:

- This version of Flash contains a great many databound components, and the framework and classes that surround the databinding concept are numerous and relatively complex, with lots and lots of properties, methods, and events. Far too many, in fact, to cover in this chapter, or even in this book (without changing its scope and nature).

- The databound components are available only in the Professional version of Flash MX 2004. I wanted to make sure that this book is relatively useful, regardless of whether you happen to be using the Professional version.

- The databound components are clearly designed for use in what Macromedia calls Rich Internet Applications (RIAs), where the entire user interface for an application is designed more or less (the idea is more) with Flash. This book isn't about RIAs per se—it's about many different ways (both big and small) to use Flash within the context of a dynamic web application.

- It is my belief that you will find the databound components to be helpful time savers in some situations, but unnecessarily complex for others. Databinding generally means fewer lines of code, but more fiddling and clicking around in the IDE. You'll get an idea for the nature of this tradeoff and whether it makes sense for you in the "Adding Databound Components to the Song Rater Example" section, which is coming up shortly.

In other words, it is this book's intention to steer you neither toward nor away from the new databound components in Flash MX Professional 2004. You will, however, learn enough about basic databinding principles and the overall architecture to be able to use most of the related components and features with little fuss.

Introduction to the *DataSet* Component

As you've learned, the `RecordSet` object available in client-side Flash Remoting projects represents a recordset, similar in structure and function as a database table, or the results of a SQL `SELECT` statement. It contains rows and columns of data, accessible either through the `items` property or through the API described in Tables 8.3 and 8.4. However, you never see it on the Stage. `RecordSet` objects are a purely code-resident concept; you cannot click them or work with them interactively in the Flash IDE.

The `DataSet` component is similar, except that it *does* appear on the Stage at design time. You can adjust its properties in the Properties panel and Component Inspector, and you can use the Flash IDE to bind the data it holds to visual user interface controls such as text entry fields, drop-down boxes, image loaders, data grids, and more. Although the component appears on the Stage at design time, it does not appear at runtime. That is, your users never see it. It exists visually only for you and your team of developers.

Key `DataSet` features include the following:

- The ability to be *bound* to visual user interface components (such as `TextBox`, `DateField`, `Loader`, `ComboBox`, and `DataGrid`). The components automatically show whatever data is placed into the `DataSet`, with absolutely no scripting (you'll see this in action in the next example). The binding can be two-way so that edits made in the controls are persisted in the local `DataSet`.
- The concept of a *current row*, which is a row whose data will be reflected in databound controls such as `TextInput`, `Label`, and so on. Only one row will be considered current at any given time. You can change the current row through script using methods such as `next()`, `previous()`, `first()`, `last()`, and `skip()`; you can move to a particular row number using the `selectedIndex` property. As the current row changes, the values in any data-bound controls change automatically.

NOTE

Unfortunately, not all of Flash MX 2004 Professional's UI components support databinding in a straightforward manner. For instance, `RadioButton` components can't be bound to datasets as of this writing because they don't support any bindable properties. Furthermore, there is little consistency with respect to which components support databinding and which do not. It would be hard to anticipate, for instance, that `Label` components can be bound but that `RadioButton` components cannot. It is possible that this situation will have changed by the time you read this book.

- The ability to be *sorted* on the client (that is, without re-fetching data from the server) through methods such as `addSort()`, `useSort()`, `hasSort()`, and `removeSort()`.

- The ability to be *filtered*, such that only matching records are displayed or iterated through until further notice. The `filtered` and `filterFunc` properties control this behavior. You can also set *ranges*, which are similar (but more efficient if the desired rows are contiguous).

- The ability to be connected to *resolver* components such as RDBMSResolver and XUpdateResolver, which make it easy to send the contents of the dataset back to a server so that the data can be updated on the server side. The resolvers don't send the whole dataset to the server. They send only the actual changes that were made to the data on the client.

NOTE

The `DataSet` is not the only component that can be bound to the databound UI controls. You can also bind controls to connector components such as `XMLConnector` and `WebServiceConnector`, and you can even bind controls to each other. There is plenty of information about databinding in the Flash documentation.

Adding Databound Components to the Song Rater Example

As a learning exercise, let's try creating a second version of the Song Rater example movie, except this time using the databound components to hook data from the server up to the text fields, image `Loader`, and `MediaPlayback` components. Instead of using "old school" ActionScript to keep track of the current row and to populate the controls with the correct data, we'll place the data into a `DataSet`, bind the `DataSet` to the controls, and let Flash's databinding features do the rest.

Go ahead and open up the SongRaterBound.fla document, which is included with this chapter's examples. At first glance, it looks nearly identical to the original version. If you look more closely, however, you'll see that a few changes have been made:

- A `DataSet` component sits just off the Stage, at the top-right corner (see Figure 8.6). (It doesn't matter where the `DataSet` is placed because it doesn't appear at runtime.)

- The areas where the artist name and song title appear used to be ordinary text fields, but now they are `Label` components. (Ordinary Text fields don't support data binding.)

- The `RatingClip` symbol in the Library, which used to be an ordinary movie clip, is now listed as a component.

- The `DataSet` has been bound to the `Loader` and `Label` components. It has also been bound to the custom `mcRating` movie clip/component. You can see the bindings under the Bindings tab of the Component Inspector panel.

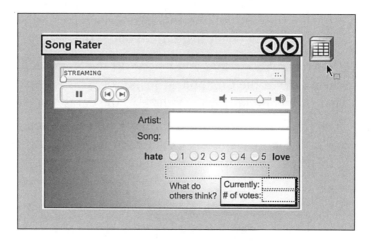

FIGURE 8.6   The new version of the Song Rater uses a `DataSet` to hold recordset-style data at runtime.

Setting up the Components

If you want to know exactly how this document was set up for databinding, you can follow these steps:

1. Start with the original SongRater.fla document and rename it as SongRaterBound.fla.

2. Change the `#include` line in Frame 1 from SongRaterMainCode.as to SongRaterBoundMainCode.as (the new file is shown in Listing 8.8).

3. Drag a `DataSet` from the Components panel onto the work area that surrounds the Stage (as was shown in Figure 8.6). Give it an instance name of `dsSongs`.

4. Delete the `txtArtistName` and `txtSongName` text fields and replace them with `Label` components with instance names of `lblArtistName` and `lblSongName`, respectively.

5. Right-click the `RatingClip` symbol in the Library, select Component Definition, and then add a parameter named `idSong` with a default Value of `0` and a Type of `Number`. When you click OK, you should see that the symbol is now being listed as a component (for details, see the "Turning Clips into Components" section at the end of Chapter 5.

Binding the UI Components to the DataSet

Now that the appropriate components have been added, you can bind them together using the Component Inspector. Follow these steps:

1. Select the `DataSet` that you placed off the Stage, and then click the Schema tab in the Component Inspector. This is where you tell Flash what data columns (fields) will be in the dataset at runtime.

2. Click the Add a Component Property button, which is the large plus sign at the left edge of the Component Inspector. A new field appears in the list below, with a default name of `new field` (see Figure 8.7).

FIGURE 8.7 Add fields to the `DataSet`'s schema to make them available for binding.

3. Change the new field's name from *new field* to sArtistName. Note that the data type is set to String, which is fine for this field (because the sArtistName column in our example database contains character-type data).

4. Add similar fields for sFileName, sImageName, sSongName, idSong, and nRating. Change the data type property for the latter two fields to Number because the corresponding database columns are numeric. Now the Flash IDE is aware of the fields (columns) that we'll be retrieving through Flash Remoting, and it can present the field names in dialog boxes as we proceed.

5. With the `DataSet` component still selected, click the Bindings tab in the Component Inspector. This is where you specify which visual controls (on the Stage) should be bound to which fields (that you just created).

6. Click the Add Binding button (which is the plus sign, similar to the one in Figure 8.7) to bring up the Add Binding dialog box. Select the sArtistName field you created earlier (see Figure 8.8), and then click OK. The new binding appears in the list in the Component Inspector.

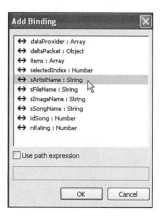

FIGURE 8.8   You can bind controls to any of the `DataSet`'s fields.

7. Change the new binding's direction property from `in/out` to `out` (see Figure 8.9). This tells the databinding framework that you want data only from the dataset to get to the bound UI control, rather than going in both directions (you would use `in/out` if you wanted the user to be able to edit the data with the bound control).

FIGURE 8.9   The direction should be set to `out` unless you want the data to be editable.

8. Still in the properties for the new binding, double-click the magnifying glass icon for the bound to property to bring up the Bound To dialog box. Select the entry for the `Label` named lblArtistName (see Figure 8.10). Note that the Schema location option is set to text:String, which is the only option available. Click OK to complete the binding.

9. Repeat the last three steps for the sSongName field, binding it to the `Label` named lblSongName.

10. Bind the sImageName field to the `ldrImageLoader` component (this time it's the *contentPath* field that's available under the Schema location option, rather than *text*).

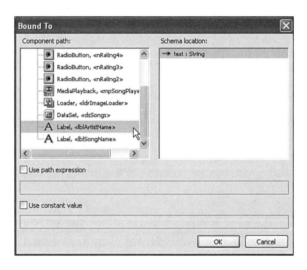

FIGURE 8.10   Each field can be bound to any UI component in the current document.

11. Add a Number-type field for our custom `mcRating` component (using the Schema tab), and then go back to the `DataSet` and bind its idSong field to `mcRating`'s idSong field (whew!).

12. Still in the Bindings tab for the `DataSet`, select the binding for sImageName. Change the formatter property to Compose String, and then double-click the magnifying glass icon for the formatter options property, which brings up the Compose String dialog box. Type **../images/artists/<.>** for the String template, and then click OK (the <.> part represents the actual value of the sImageName column at runtime).

Examining the Code Changes

Now that the data bindings have been set up, some of the ActionScript from the original version of the movie (Listing 8.6) can be removed. Listing 8.8 shows the revised ActionScript file included by the databound version of the Song Rater example FLA.

LISTING 8.8　SongRaterBoundMainCode.as—Revised ActionScript Code for Song Rater Example (Databound Version)

```
// These 2 values change a bit depending on the server we're using
var frGatewayURL = "http://localhost/flashservices/gateway";
var frServiceName = "venue.chapter08.SongRatings";
// For ASP.NET
// var frGatewayURL = "http://localhost/flashremoting/gateway.aspx";
// var frServiceName = "venue.chapter08.SongRatings";
// For JRun
// var frGatewayURL = "http://localhost:8100/flashservices/gateway";
// var frServiceName = "venue.chapter08.SongRatingsBean";

// Here are the standard lines that get us connected to the server
NetServices.setDefaultGatewayUrl(frGatewayURL);
var frConnection = NetServices.createGatewayConnection();
var frService = frConnection.getService(frServiceName, this);

// Fires upon successful receipt of data from server
function getSongs_Result(result) {
  // Assign items in recordset to the DataSet component
  dsSongs.dataProvider = result;
}

// Function to save a rating to the server via Flash Remoting
function rateSong(rating) {
  // Feedback for user
  txtStatus.text = "Casting your vote...";

  // Get data from current row of recordset
  frService.rateSong(dsSongs.idSong, rating);

  // Place the user's rating choice in the local dataset
  dsSongs.currentItem.nRating = rating;
}

// Fires when a rating is successfully committed to server
function rateSong_Result(result) {
  txtStatus.text = "";
}
```

continues

LISTING 8.8   SongRaterBoundMainCode.as—Revised ActionScript Code for Song Rater Example
(Databound Version) (Continued)

```
// Fires when a rating can't be successfully committed to server
function rateSong_Status(error) {
  txtStatus.text = "Sorry, your vote could not be cast.";
  trace(error.type)
  trace(error.description)
  trace(error.details)
}


// Fires when the current song has changed
// This is a good opportunity to handle any processing that
// Flash's databinding features aren't able to handle easily
function whenSongChanges() {
  mpSongPlayer.setMedia("../clips/" + dsSongs.currentItem.sFileName);
  rgSongRating.selectedData = dsSongs.currentItem.nRating;
}


// Execute the whenCurrentSongChanges() function when the song data
// is first loaded into DataSet, or when user navigates to new song
dsSongs.addEventListener("iteratorScrolled", whenSongChanges);
dsSongs.addEventListener("afterLoaded", whenSongChanges);
```

As you can see, the amount of ActionScript needed to power the movie has been cut down somewhat. One significant change is in the `getSongs_Result()` responder function, where the `result` recordset is assigned to the `dataProvider` property of the `dsSongs` dataset. It is at this moment that the data returned by the server becomes available to the `DataSet` component (and thus to the UI controls to which the dataset is bound).

The `navigateToSong()` method, which did the work of placing the data from the records into the appropriate visual controls, has been eliminated. For the most part, the databinding steps that were discussed in the "Binding the UI Components to the DataSet" section have taken the place of the code that was in `navigateToSong()`.

A new event handler function called `whenSongChanges()` has been created to take care of the tasks that the databinding framework is currently not capable of. Because the display of the artist name, song title, artist photo, and current rating are all handled via databinding, the only components that this function needs to update are the `MediaPlayback` and the `RadioButton` components. These components are easily updated using one line of code each (a call to setMedia() for the song player, and updating the selectedData property for the radio buttons). Note that the data associated with the currently selected song is easily accessible via the currentItem property of the dataset (see Table 8.6).

NOTE

You, of course, are free to replace the radio buttons with a component that does support straightforward data binding, such as the NumericStepper (spin control) component.

The addEventListener() function is used to hook the whenSongChanges() function up to the iteratorScrolled and afterLoaded events emitted by the dataset. The function will now execute when data is loaded into the dataset—which, in this case, happens through Flash Remoting—or whenever the user navigates to a different song record.

NOTE

You may be wondering why the mpSongPlayer part of the whenSongChanges() function can't be handled via databinding. After all, the contentPath property of the component appears to be bindable via the Component Inspector (just like the ldrImageLoader component). That's true, but if you consult the Components Dictionary portion of the Flash documentation about contentPath, you'll see that its value can be changed only at runtime via setMedia(). It is thus somewhat unclear why contentPath is exposed as a bindable property (or why it is not at least flagged as a read-only bindable property). Perhaps this inconsistency will be addressed in a future release—it may have already been addressed by the time you read this book.

All that's left is the ActionScript code that powers the song-navigation buttons. In the non-databound version of the Song Rater example, the code for the Next button looked like this, which called a separate nextSong() function in the main script file:

```
on(release) {
   _root.nextSong();
}
```

The new script file doesn't have a nextSong() function and doesn't really need one. Instead, we can instruct the button to move the current record of the dataset ahead by one row, using a method called next() (provided by the DataSet component class) like so:

```
on(release) {
   _root.dsSongs.next();
}
```

As soon as the next() method is called, the dsSongs dataset moves its internal cursor so that the next record becomes the current record. It then broadcasts the change to the UI controls that it is bound to, and their values are automatically updated accordingly.

To enable the users to loop back around to the first record after they have reached the last one, we use two additional DataSet methods: hasNext() and first():

```
on(release) {
  if ( _root.dsSongs.hasNext() ) {
    root.dsSongs.next();
    } else {
    root.dsSongs.first();
  }
}
```

Basic *DataSet* Class Members

The DataSet component has a rather extensive API of methods, properties, and events that enable you to control the data-holding, record-navigation, and other services that the component provides through script. Unfortunately, they can't all be discussed in this chapter. Table 8.6 is a listing of the most basic DataSet class members, including the methods for controlling the current row position that you saw in the last section.

> **NOTE**
>
> This is not an exhaustive reference. Many other methods, properties, and events are available, including methods for sorting, filtering, and searching. See the Flash documentation for the complete list.

TABLE 8.6 Basic *DataSet* Class Members

MEMBER	DESCRIPTION
ds.first()	Method. Moves the cursor to the first row in the dataset.
ds.last()	Method. Moves the cursor to the last row in the dataset.
ds.next()	Method. Moves the cursor to the next row (if possible).
ds.previous()	Method. Moves the cursor to the previous row (if possible).
ds.hasNext()	Method. Returns a Boolean value that indicates whether another record exists after the current one.

`ds.hasPrevious()`	Method. Returns a Boolean value that indicates whether another record exists before the current one.
`ds.isEmpty()`	Method. Returns a Boolean value that indicates whether any rows exist in the dataset. It is equivalent to testing whether the length property is 0.
`ds.selectedIndex`	Property. Returns the current row number.
`ds.length`	Property. Returns the number of rows in the dataset.
`ds.dataProvider`	Property. Provides access to the dataset through the `DataProvider` API. Used for binding the dataset to visual controls that also have concepts of columns and rows (notably the `DataGrid`, `List`, and `ComboBox`). Consult the ActionScript Dictionary for details about the `DataProvider` API.
`ds.items`	Property. Provides direct access to records stored in the dataset, as an array of objects. (Each object in the array is a *transfer object*, the definition of which is beyond the scope of this book. Please consult the Flash documentation for details.)
`ds.properties`	Property. An object (associative array) that contains information about each column (field) in the dataset. Among other things, you could discover the column names dynamically using a `for(name in properties)` loop; within the loop, `name` would indicate the name of a column.
`ds.currentItem`	Property. An object (associative array) that represents the current record within the dataset. Equivalent to `ds.items[ds.selectedIndex]`.
`afterLoaded`	Event. Fired when data has been loaded into the dataset, generally by setting the value of the `dataProvider` property.
`iteratorScrolled`	Event. Fired when the value of `currentItem` changes, usually in response to a call to one of the navigation methods such as `next()` or `previous()`.
`modelChanged`	Event. Fired when the contents of the dataset change. This event may be caused by the insertion of a new record, an edit to an existing record, the application of a new sort or filter, and so on.

> **NOTE**
>
> After you become familiar with the basic usage of Flash Professional's `DataSet` and databinding features, you are encouraged to consult the ActionScript Dictionary part of the Flash documentation for a full listing of the `DataSet` class's methods, properties, and events.

What You Haven't Learned About Flash Remoting

This chapter has introduced you to Flash Remoting and shown you how to use it to create a working example that calls a remote function, passes data to the server (in the form of remote function arguments), and receives data from the server (in the form of associative array-like objects and query-style recordsets). There is more to Flash Remoting that just wasn't possible to cover in these pages.

A quick rundown of additional Flash Remoting features and capabilities follows. Keep these items in mind and check them out further if the need arises. Flash documentation contains plenty of information about these topics.

Incrementally Loading Recordsets

You've seen how easy it is to pass a recordset from your server to Flash. You might be wondering what happens if you pass back a large recordset, with thousands and thousands of records. Wouldn't it take a long time for the recordset data to be received by the Flash Player?

The Flash Remoting framework provides for the concept of a *pageable* recordset, which simply means that the recordset will be retrieved from the server in chunks (pages) of, say, 25 rows each. Conceptually, the concept of a pageable recordset is similar to that of a streaming audio or video file; Flash can start displaying or working with the first rows of the recordset right away, even though the rest of the data is still being received.

If you are using ColdFusion, you can see how this works right now by going back to the getArtists.cfm page (Listing 8.1) and changing this line:

```
<!--- Provide the data to Flash --->
<cfset FLASH.Result = DataQuery>
```

To this:

```
<!--- Provide the data to Flash --->
<cfset FLASH.PageSize = 2>
<cfset FLASH.Result = DataQuery>
```

Now revisit the ArtistGrid.html example page. If you look closely, you will see that the records stream into the grid in sets of two records each. Clearly, if there were many, many records, this would enable the user to start looking through the data right away, while the remaining records continued to download in the background.

Consult the Flash Remoting documentation for your server for details about pageable recordsets.

NOTE

To use pageable recordsets with the Flash Remoting Gateway for J2EE servers, you need to apply Macromedia Flash Remoting Updater 1. Consult Macromedia's website for specific Release Notes and download instructions.

Server-Side Details

As we've discussed, Flash Remoting Gateways have been built into ColdFusion MX and JRun 4, and additional gateways are available for ASP.NET and J2EE servers. Each gateway enables you to connect to different types of pages and objects within your server environment; the result is a tight fit between Flash Remoting and your development platform of choice.

Depending on what server you're using, I invite you to take a look at the specific capabilities of the corresponding Flash Gateway, as follows:

- If you're using ColdFusion, you've already seen the two basic types of objects Flash Remoting can access (CFML pages and CFCs), so you have the least amount of additional learning ahead of you.

- If you're using Microsoft .NET, you can access .NET assemblies and .NET Web Services (in addition to ASP.NET pages, which you've already learned about) through Flash Remoting. All can be made available as remote services and functions accessible by the Flash Player through script.

- If you're using JRun or another J2EE server, you can use Flash Remoting to access many different types of objects and services on the server: Servlets, EJBs (even stateful ones), JSP pages, and more. This is all in addition to ad-hoc, stateless classes and beans that you saw used in this chapter's examples.

Arrays and Other Datatypes

Because they are the most interesting and flexible, this chapter focused on received query-style recordsets and associative arrays (objects) from the server. It is, however, possible to receive other datatypes from the server through Flash Remoting, including normal arrays, dates, and plain old numbers and strings.

The Flash Remoting Gateway on your server takes care of converting each type of data to the type that is appropriate for ActionScript. Consult the Flash Remoting documentation for details about which server-side datatypes will be mapped to which ActionScript datatypes. For the most part, the conversion is straightforward and exactly what you would expect.

Client-Side Recordset Filtering and Sorting

The Flash Remoting `RecordSet` object supports a number of methods for changing the sort order of a local recordset or filtering its contents. You can use these methods to create SWFs that let users navigate through and locate records in just about any way you feel is appropriate. These additional methods are listed briefly in Table 8.4; see the Flash Remoting documentation for full details.

If you're using Flash MX Professional 2004, the `DataSet` component provides similar (but even more sophisticated) functionality. See the Flash documentation for details (in particular, the `DataSet` class in the ActionScript Dictionary).

Open Source Remoting, Alternative Implementations, and Other Third-Party Tools

As you have learned in this chapter, the Flash Remoting functionality is implemented in two pieces: the server part (the Flash Remoting Gateway that is appropriate for your server) and the client part (the Flash Remoting Components, which are ActionScript classes). Actually, if you think about it, there is a third part, which is the Flash Player itself.

Various parties, both commercial and non-commercial, have come up with their own implementations, replacements, or extensions of either the server or client parts of Flash Remoting. While none of these implementations are supported, guided, or recommended by Macromedia as of this writing, you might want to look into the alternatives.

Here is a list of alternate implementations of the server-side piece of Flash Remoting. Each provides Flash Remoting Gateway functionality, and some add additional features and support not available in Macromedia's own gateways:

- **FlashORB.** A commercial Java implementation (`www.flashorb.com`)
- **OpenAMF.** A free, open-source implementation for Java (`www.openamf.org`)
- **The AMFPHP Project.** A free, open-source implementation for PHP (`www.amfphp.org`)
- **FLAP.** A free, open-source implementation for Perl (`www.simonf.com/flap`)

Here is a list of other interesting tools and Libraries related to the client-side part of Flash Remoting development:

- Joey Lott's ActionScript 2.0 implementation of the Flash Remoting Components (`www.person13.com/flashremoting`)
- Branden Hall's Community MX Tester panel, a debugging tool (`www.communitymx.com`)

Summary

You learned a lot about Flash Remoting in this chapter. First, we created a movie that contained only a data grid. Then we created a Song Rater example that retrieves information from a server and enables the user to navigate through the data and insert new database records on the server. Then you learned how to use Flash Remoting together with Flash MX 2004 Professional's new databinding features, through the new `DataSet` component.

Next, you'll learn about connecting Flash movies to Web Services. Flash's Web Services support is similar conceptually to its support for Flash Remoting. Both enable a SWF to call remote methods on a server. Rather than using a Flash Remoting Gateway in between, however, the Web Services support has your SWFs talking directly to servers through SOAP, WSDL, and HTTP.

CHAPTER 9

CONNECTING TO SERVERS WITH WEB SERVICES

With the introduction of Macromedia Flash MX Professional 2004, there is now a second means for getting RPC-style access to server-side functionality: via Web Services. Instead of a Flash Remoting Gateway behaving as the go-between between Flash and your code, any compliant implementation of the Web Services standards behaves as the go-between.

NOTE

The Web Services functionality discussed in this chapter is available in the Professional version of Flash MX 2004 only. If you are not using the Professional version but still want to connect to existing Web Services, you might want to explore using Flash Remoting as an alternative. The Flash Remoting Gateway on your server can behave as a proxy, connecting to a web service on another server on your Flash movie's behalf. See Chapter 8, "Connecting to Servers with Flash Remoting," and your Flash Remoting documentation for details. See also the "Options for Connecting to Web Services" section in this chapter.

Overview of Flash's Support for Web Services

Before we get started with some concrete examples, a few words are in order to help you understand the Web Services features available in Flash MX 2004. This section will provide an overview of Flash's new Web Services support. It will also give you a very quick crash course about what Web Services are and what they mean to you.

What Are Web Services?

Wow, you ask the best questions! For the purposes of our discussion here, Web Services are special objects that reside, metaphorically, on a web server. Like the objects in most programming languages, these objects can have any number of methods and properties. The neat trick is that the methods and properties are made available according to an open, standard specification of simple languages and protocols. The result is that any given web service can be accessed and used by any client that understands the specification. It doesn't matter if the service and client are on the same local network, whether they were created with the same programming language, or whether they are running on the same operating system (OS) or platform.

> **NOTE**
>
> Okay, complete platform neutrality is still a work in progress. As you probably know, there are two main flavors of Web Services in common use today. To say that one is Sun's and the other is Microsoft's is perhaps an over-generalization, but it is a useful one. In any case, the two flavors aren't necessarily good at talking to each other. Most third-party tool developers—like the good folks at Macromedia—make sure that their tools work the same way with either flavor.

This is not the time or place to get into a theoretical discussion about the history of Web Services, the kinds of problems that Web Services are best at solving, or where they fit in the ever-advancing evolution of distributed computing. This is, after all, not a book about Web Services. If you want to learn more, I invite you to get a book about building Web Services with your application server of choice, or to do some research online (www.xml.com is as good a place to start as any).

How Does One Create a Web Service?

Another great question! The answer is that it depends on the application server or programming environment that you are using. Each application server that is being covered explicitly in this book—ColdFusion, ASP.NET, and J2EE—provides at least one means for creating a web service with a minimum of fuss and bother. In general, you write the same sort of server-side code that you would normally. You just save it with a special file extension, place it in a special directory, or register it with some kind of configuration file or visual interface.

You'll see some simple examples within this chapter, but it's up to you to learn how to create and set up Web Services on your own server. To put it another way, this chapter is interested in teaching you how to connect to Web Services that already exist on your servers, not how to create the services from scratch. There are plenty of other books and resources available for the latter.

Some Quick Definitions

Like any other modern Internet-related technology, Web Services comes with its own set of acronyms and terminology. Here's a quick rundown of the specific terms you'll be seeing throughout this chapter, just in case you're new to Web Services. This is by no means an exhaustive set of definitions, but it should be enough to keep you from being completely baffled as you work through the remainder of this chapter.

- **Web Services Description Language (WSDL).** WSDL is an XML-based format for describing the methods and properties that a particular web service provides. All web services clients—of which Flash is one—use the WSDL description of a service to figure out what arguments are required for each method, what the datatypes of the arguments and properties are, and so on. The Flash Player uses this information at runtime to connect to a server; the Flash IDE uses it at design time to show you the methods and properties available for scripting or binding. Depending on your background, you may be used to referring to this kind of process as component "discovery" or "introspection."

- **WSDL URL.** The WSDL description for a particular web service is traditionally made available at an HTTP URL so that it can be easily accessed by clients interested in using the service. This URL is generally called the *WDSL URL*, which is sensible enough. As a developer or programmer, the WSDL URL is usually the only thing you need to know ahead of time to use a web service in a particular project.

Your programming or development environment—in this case, the Flash IDE—will take it from there, making the methods and properties available to you either in code or in some kind of visual display. In Flash, the methods and properties become visible in the Web Services panel and in the Component Inspector. You'll see how as you work through this chapter.

- **Simple Object Access Protocol (SOAP).** SOAP is the specification that is used when a web services client wants to use an actual method or property of a particular web service. SOAP defines, primarily, an XML format that contains information about what the client wants to access (which method it wants to call, for instance, or which property it wants to get or set) as well as any data that goes along with the request (such as the values for each of a method's arguments). The same basic format is used by the server to send a response back to the client. I'm obviously leaving out some of the technical details—there are some special HTTP headers used and so on—but the basic idea is that these "packets" of XML-encoded information are sent back and forth over HTTP, and that's essentially how the client and server communicate.

- **Universal Description, Discovery and Integration (UDDI).** When you hear someone speak about WSDL and SOAP, you often hear about UDDI in the same breath. UDDI is used to create "directories" that people or processes can use to find WSDL URLs for Web Services. It's kind of like the DNS (or the 411, maybe) of Web Services land. In any case, Flash's Web Services implementation has no need to support UDDI. The assumption, and it's a fair one, is that you'll already know to which web service you want to connect. More than likely, you created it yourself.

- **Web services client or consumer.** Any software that knows how to talk to a web service and call its methods is a web services *client* (also called a web services *consumer*). Often times, the client is another server that is either on the same local network or elsewhere on the Internet. Other times, the client is a standalone application installed on a user's machine. Of course, the web services clients we'll be discussing in this book are SWFs, which connect directly to Web Services as clients (you'll learn more about the specifics in the next section).

Okay, that should be enough to get you through the rest of this chapter. Consult the documentation for your application server of choice for more information about these terms and concepts. That documentation should also provide information about how to construct your own Web Services, which you can then access from Flash or any other web services client.

Flash as a Web Service Client

Again, Flash MX 2004 (the Professional version only) is a web services consumer. That functionality is built right into the Flash IDE and gets compiled into your SWF files upon publication. Indeed, it's helpful to keep in mind that you are working with two different clients as you work with Web Services in Flash, as follows:

- At design time, the Flash IDE can behave as a client to Web Services you want your movies to access. Each service's methods then become available to you in various drop-down lists and parameter choosers in the Component Inspector and Properties panels, and in the new Web Services panel. The purpose of this functionality is to make your life easier as a developer. Rather than having to remember each method name and argument (and type them over and over), you can lean on the Flash IDE to keep track of that stuff for you.

- At runtime, your SWFs also behave as web services clients so that the various UI elements and script code in your movie can interact with your servers (or the servers of third parties). The runtime functionality knows how to download and interpret WSDL descriptions of services, just as the Flash IDE does. More importantly, it also knows how to execute actual web service methods so that actual server-side data or logic can be accessed.

Thus, whereas the Flash IDE is mostly interested in a web service's metadata (the WSDL part), your SWFs are mostly interested in actual method calls (the SOAP part).

Options for Connecting to Web Services

You have a few different options for working with Web Services in Flash MX 2004. The first option in the following bulleted list is the most obvious and the easiest to use. For those reasons, it is also the option that most people will choose to use most often. The last two options are of note because they doesn't require the Professional version of Flash.

- A **WebServiceConnector** component. This is the option that is most visible in the Flash IDE, the Flash documentation, and the new features list. You just drag a WebServiceConnector onto the Stage, give it a WSDL URL to which to connect, and then add one line of script that calls its trigger() method. The component supports databinding, so you can use it to update UI controls without additional scripting if you choose to do so. Because it is flexible, relatively easy to use, and appropriate for use with or without Flash's new databinding framework, most of the discussion in this chapter will be based on using this component. You will learn all about this in the next section, "Using the *WebServiceConnector* Component."

- **A `WebService` class instance.** If you prefer to connect to a web service without using any design-time components at all, you can create an instance of the `WebService` class via script at runtime. You might choose to use this option if you want your movie to be able to connect to Web Services dynamically (that is, where the web service or its methods and properties are not known at design time). This option is covered in the "Connecting to a Web Service Using Script Alone" section later in this chapter.

- **Via Flash Remoting.** Most Flash Remoting Gateway implementations (including the one included with ColdFusion, and the gateway for ASP.NET) provide built-in support for connecting to Web Services on the server side. The web service becomes visible to Flash as a Remoting-style remote service, which in turn means that the methods of the service become available to Flash as remote methods (which can be accessed just like any other remote service function). See Chapter 8 for details about Flash Remoting.

- **Via any of the other techniques discussed in this book.** The new Web Services features in Flash are neat because the Flash IDE and the Flash Player now have built-in understanding of WSDL and SOAP, so you can connect to Web Services directly. However, there is no law that says you can't connect to your own pages on the server using any technique you please and have your server-side pages talk to Web Services behind the scenes. You could go back to Chapters 6, 7, or 8—the plain text, XML, and Remoting chapters, respectively—and use the same basic techniques used in those chapters. You would replace the queries in the server-side examples with calls to Web Services (using whatever syntax is appropriate for the server you are using). Sure, Flash won't know that it's talking to a web service. It thinks it's just talking to an ad-hoc page on your server. That's not necessarily a bad thing, depending on how you like to think about the overall architecture of your web applications. I encourage you to keep this option in mind as you read through this chapter.

Using the *WebServiceConnector* Component

The next few sections will introduce you to the `WebServiceConnector` component. You'll be working with an example Flash document that I call the Rating
Chart example, which allows users to display information about the current
rating of a song (as rated by users of the Song Rater example from Chapter 8).
Up-to-the-minute song rating data is provided by a web service, which is then
accessed by Flash and displayed as a simple bar chart (see Figure 9.1).

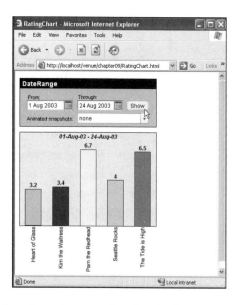

FIGURE 9.1   Current song rating data is displayed as a bar chart.

Users can specify the range of dates for which they would like to see song rating information. This is done by typing in the From and Through fields or by
using the date picker widgets provided (see Figure 9.2).

Users can also specify that they would like to see a series of dates by picking
daily, *weekly*, or *monthly* from the drop-down menu provided (see Figure 9.3).
If, for instance, the user picks *weekly*, he or she will see an animated chart that
reflects changes in each song's ratings over time. The information for the first
week appears first, followed by a short pause, and then the information for the
second week, and so on.

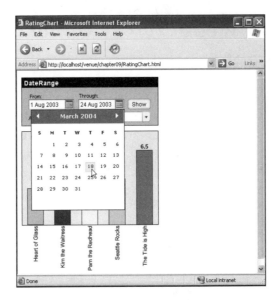

FIGURE 9.2   Users select a range of dates to report on the chart.

The user can hover the mouse over any bar to pause the display; when he or she moves the mouse away from the bar, the step-by-step display resumes.

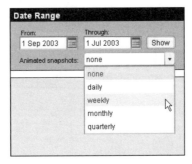

FIGURE 9.3   Users get animated charts if they choose a snapshot option.

The Server-Side Code

As usual, we'll first take a look at the server-side code that's powering this example. Listings 9.1, 9.2, and 9.3 each create a web service that exposes the same set of methods to Flash (or to whatever web services client that wishes to access them) using ColdFusion, .NET, and Java, respectively. Although the code and other implementation details are different for each listing—probably the most different of the listings you've seen in this book—they all provide equivalent functionality from Flash's point of view.

Table 9.1 shows the methods exposed publicly by this web service, regardless of which application server is being used. (Each individual implementation may have other methods that are used internally.)

TABLE 9.1   Methods Exposed by this Section's Web Service Examples

METHOD	DESCRIPTION
getSongs()	Returns information about songs. The method returns an array of objects, one for each song record in the database. Each object contains two properties: idSong and sSongName.
getSongRatings (dStartDate, dEndDate, spanDivider)	Returns information about song ratings. The dStartDate and dEndDate arguments define the span of time for which to return information. The spanDivider argument tells the method whether the span of time should be broken down into smaller spans: it can be set to d, ww, m, or q for spans of days, weeks, months, or quarters; if set to none or any other value, just one set of data is returned.
	The method returns an array of objects, one for each span of time. There will be one such object if spanDivider is none, or several such objects if spanDivider is d, ww, m, or q. Each object contains three properties: dStartDate and dEndDate, which indicate the dates for the current span of time; and songs, which is an array of songs from the database. Each song is represented by another object, with three properties: idSong, AvgRating, and NumRatings.

The ColdFusion Version

Listing 9.1 shows the ColdFusion version of the web service used by the Rating Chart example. It creates a ColdFusion Component (CFC) called SongRatingWebService. The CFC includes two functions: the publicly accessible getSongs() and getSongRatings() methods listed in Table 9.1, and an internal worker function called getSeriesData(), which does the work of querying the database for a given date range.

> **NOTE**
>
> You don't have to end the names of your own CFCs with `WebService`. I'm just doing that here to keep things clear for purposes of this book.

LISTING 9.1   SongRatingWebService.cfc—ColdFusion Version of the Web Service

```coldfusion
<cfcomponent>

  <!--- This function is exposed via web services --->
  <cffunction name="getSongs" access="remote" returntype="query">
    <!--- Local variables --->
    <cfset var result = "">

    <!--- Retrieve song information from database --->
    <cfquery name="result" datasource="VenueDB">
      SELECT idSong, sSongName
      FROM Songs
      ORDER BY sSongName
    </cfquery>

    <!--- Return the result --->
    <cfreturn result>
  </cffunction>


  <!--- This function is exposed via web services --->
  <cffunction name="getSongRatings" access="remote" returntype="array">
    <cfargument name="dStartDate" type="date" required="Yes">
    <cfargument name="dEndDate" type="date" required="Yes">
    <cfargument name="spanDivider" type="string" required="Yes">

    <!--- Local variables --->
    <cfset var result = ArrayNew(1)>
    <cfset var tempEndDate = "">
    <cfset var seriesData = "">


    <!--- Different modes, depending on spanDivider argument --->
    <cfswitch expression="#spanDivider#">

      <!--- If "none" or other non-recognized divider specified --->
      <cfdefaultcase>
        <!--- Get data for this range, append to result array --->
        <cfset seriesData = getSeriesData(dStartDate, dEndDate)>
        <cfset ArrayAppend(result, seriesData)>
```

```
      </cfdefaultcase>

      <!--- If valid divider specified, return multiple ranges --->
      <cfcase value="m,d,ww,q" delimiters=",">
        <!--- Loop until we reach the last of the date ranges --->
        <cfloop condition="dStartDate lte dEndDate">
          <!--- This is the end date for this date range --->
          <cfset tempEndDate = DateAdd(spanDivider, 1, dStartDate)>
          <!--- Get data for this range, append to result array --->
          <cfset seriesData = getSeriesData(dStartDate, tempEndDate)>
          <cfset ArrayAppend(result, seriesData)>
          <!--- This is the start date for the next date range --->
          <cfset dStartDate = tempEndDate>
        </cfloop>
      </cfcase>
    </cfswitch>

    <!--- Return the result --->
    <cfreturn result>
</cffunction>


<!--- Internal function: returns data for a single date range --->
<cffunction name="getSeriesData" access="private" returntype=
"Struct">
  <cfargument name="dStartDate" type="date" required="Yes">
  <cfargument name="dEndDate" type="date" required="Yes">

  <!--- Local variables --->
  <cfset var result = StructNew()>
  <cfset var RatingsQuery = "">

  <!--- Query database for song and rating information --->
  <cfquery name="RatingsQuery" datasource="VenueDB">
    SELECT
      s.idSong,
      AVG(sr.nRating) AS AvgRating,
      COUNT(*) AS NumRatings
    FROM
      Songs s LEFT OUTER JOIN
      SongRatings sr ON s.idSong = sr.idSong
      AND
        sr.dRatingDate >=
        <cfqueryparam value="#dStartDate#" cfsqltype="CF_SQL_TIMESTAMP">
        AND sr.dRatingDate <=
```

continues

```
        <cfqueryparam value="#dEndDate#" cfsqltype="CF_SQL_TIMESTAMP">
    GROUP BY
        s.idSong
    </cfquery>

    <!--- Populate data structure to represent this series --->
    <cfset result["startDate"] = dStartDate>
    <cfset result["endDate"] = dEndDate>
    <cfset result["songs"] = RatingsQuery>

    <!--- Return the result--->
    <cfreturn result>
  </cffunction>

</cfcomponent>
```

> **NOTE**
>
> Unfortunately, ColdFusion does not maintain the case of column names. Instead of storing them internally using the same capitalization that they have when they come from the database, ColdFusion stores the column names internally in all uppercase. This means that the column names will be transferred to Flash in all uppercase, which means that you must use all uppercase in your ActionScript code.

As you can see, this listing is fairly simple. Because the getSongs() method has been marked with an access="remote" attribute, it becomes available when the CFC is accessed as a web service. The guts of the function are extremely simple: A query named result is executed against the database. It is then returned to Flash (or whatever client is requesting the information) as a query-style recordset.

Within the getSongRatings() method (which is also enabled for remote access), two different types of processing are used, depending on the spanDivider argument. If spanDivider is none (or any other non-functional value), the function simply calls the internal getSeriesData() method and appends it to the result array. If spanDivider is specifying a recognized time span (day, week, month, or quarter), a simple loop is used to iterate through the time spans, calling getSeriesData() for each span along the way. By the time the public function is done doing its work, its result array contains an object (which in turn contains an array of song-related objects) for each time span requested.

> **NOTE**
>
> There are many, many ways one could write this code. This is not necessarily the most efficient (mainly because it requires a separate query for each time span), but it is easy to understand and it is supported by most database systems. In actual practice, you could probably write a clever SQL statement or stored procedure that retrieved all the information in one go.

You should now be able to verify that the web service is available by visiting the following URL with your browser: `http://localhost/venue/ chapter09/SongRatingWebService.cfc` (assuming a typical ColdFusion installation on your local machine). After you provide your password (use the same one you use for the ColdFusion Administrator), the server will respond with a documentation page that lists the names and arguments for each method (see Figure 9.4).

FIGURE 9.4   ColdFusion provides this automatic documentation page for CFCs.

The Microsoft .NET Version

Listing 9.2 shows the .NET version of the web service used by the Rating Chart example. This web service was written as a single Active Server Methods (.asmx) file for simplicity's sake. The functions marked with a `[WebService]` line will be publicly available as web service methods. In actual practice, you might choose to use a separate code-behind file to contain your actual code.

Consult the .NET Framework SDK documentation set for details about constructing XML Web Services with ASP.NET.

LISTING 9.2   SongRatingWebService.asmx—Microsoft .NET Version of the Web Service

```csharp
<%@ WebService Language="C#" Class="SongRatingWebService2" %>

using System.Web.Services;
using System;
using System.Data;
using System.Data.Odbc;
using System.Collections;
using System.Xml.Serialization;

[WebService(Namespace="http://nateweiss.com/fsg/webservices")]
public class SongRatingWebService2 : WebService {

  [WebMethod(Description="Returns IDs and names of songs")]
  public Song[] getSongs() {

    // Query the database for song data
    string sql = "SELECT idSong, sSongName " +
      "FROM Songs ORDER BY sSongName";
    OdbcConnection connection = new OdbcConnection("DSN=VenueDB");
    OdbcCommand command = new OdbcCommand(sql, connection);
    connection.Open();
    OdbcDataReader reader = command.ExecuteReader();

    // Fill an ArrayList with song instances
    ArrayList list = new ArrayList();

    // For each record from the database, create a Song struct
    while(reader.Read()) {
      Song song = new Song();
      song.IDSONG = reader.GetInt32(0);
      song.SSONGNAME = reader.GetString(1);
      list.Add(song);
    }

    // Covert the ArrayList into a normal C# array
    Song[] result = new Song[list.Count];
    list.CopyTo(result);

    // Return the array
    return result;
  }
}
```

```
[WebMethod(Description="Returns aggregated ratings for songs")]
public SongRatingSeries[] getSongRatings(
  DateTime dStartDate,
  DateTime dEndDate,
  string spanDivider)
{

  // Use a resizeable array to hold series data
  ArrayList list = new ArrayList();

  // If no span divider is desired
  if (spanDivider == "none") {
    // Get series data for the time span
    list.Add(getSeriesData(dStartDate, dEndDate));

  // If a span divider was specified
  } else {
    DateTime dTempEnd = new DateTime();

    // Loop until we reach the last of the date ranges
    while(dStartDate <= dEndDate) {
      // Compute end date for this date range
      switch(spanDivider) {
        case "d":  dTempEnd = dStartDate.AddDays(1);    break;
        case "ww": dTempEnd = dStartDate.AddDays(7);    break;
        case "m":  dTempEnd = dStartDate.AddMonths(1);  break;
        case "q":  dTempEnd = dStartDate.AddMonths(3);  break;
      }

      // Get series data for the time span, append to array
      list.Add(getSeriesData(dStartDate, dTempEnd));
      // This is the start date for the next date range
      dStartDate = dTempEnd;
    }
  }

  // Covert the ArrayList into a normal C# array
  SongRatingSeries[] result = new SongRatingSeries[list.Count];
  list.CopyTo(result);

  // Return the result
  return result;
}
```

continues

LISTING 9.2   SongRatingWebService.asmx—Microsoft .NET Version of the Web Service (Continued)

```
// Internal function: returns data for a single date range
private SongRatingSeries getSeriesData(
  DateTime startDate,
  DateTime endDate)
{
  // SQL code to query database for song and rating information
  string sql = "SELECT s.idSong, AVG(sr.nRating) AS AvgRating, " +
    "COUNT(sr.idSongRating) AS NumRatings " +
    "FROM Songs s LEFT OUTER JOIN SongRatings sr  " +
    "ON s.idSong = sr.idSong " +
    "AND sr.dRatingDate >= ? "+
    "AND sr.dRatingDate <= ? " +
    "GROUP BY s.idSong";

  // Define a database connection
  // (In practice you wouldn't create a new connection each time)
  OdbcConnection connection = new OdbcConnection("DSN=VenueDB");
  OdbcCommand command = new OdbcCommand(sql, connection);

  // Fill date placeholders in database-independent fashion
  command.Parameters.Add("dRatingDate", OdbcType.DateTime);
  command.Parameters.Add("dRatingDate", OdbcType.DateTime);
  command.Parameters[0].Value = startDate;
  command.Parameters[1].Value = endDate;

  // Query the database
  connection.Open();
  OdbcDataReader reader = command.ExecuteReader();

  // Populate data structure to represent this series
  SongRatingSeries result = new SongRatingSeries();
  result.startDate = startDate;
  result.endDate = endDate;

  // Use a resizeable array to hold data records
  ArrayList list = new ArrayList();

  // Fill the array with data
  while(reader.Read()) {
    SongRating rec = new SongRating();
    rec.IDSONG = reader.GetInt32(0);
    rec.NUMRATINGS = reader.GetInt32(2);
    // GetDecimal() will throw an error if a null is retrieved
    if (! reader.IsDBNull(1)) {
      rec.AVGRATING = reader.GetDecimal(1);
```

```
    }
    list.Add(rec);
  }

  // Convert the ArrayList to a real C# array
  result.songs = new SongRating[list.Count];
  if (list.Count > 0) {
    list.CopyTo(result.songs);
  }

  // Return the result
  return result;
}



// The getSongs() method returns an array of this struct
public struct Song {
  public int IDSONG;
  public string SSONGNAME;
}

// The getSeriesData() method returns an array of this struct
public struct SongRatingSeries {
  public DateTime startDate;
  public DateTime endDate;
  public SongRating[] songs;
}

// The SongRatingSeries.song property is an array of this struct
public struct SongRating {
  public int IDSONG;
  public decimal AVGRATING;
  public int NUMRATINGS;
}

}
```

Unfortunately, the .NET version of this web service requires a bit more code than you may have anticipated. As of this writing, the WebServicesConnector component that shipped with the initial release of Flash MX Professional 2004 does not provide direct support for web service methods that return .NET DataSet instances. The alternative is to return an array of objects, as discussed in the "Query-Style Recordsets and Arrays of Objects" section, which is coming up shortly in this chapter.

Normally, one might expect to be able to use hashtables or another similar type as the objects in the array. However, .NET Web Services cannot return hashtables (at least not at the time of this writing); you must use an object type with a stronger definition. The most direct solution is to define a custom `struct` type for each combination of database columns that you want to return from Web Services. (Of course, you could define the `struct` classes in a separate namespace for easier reuse.)

In addition, if you are using a `DataReader` to populate the array of objects, it is often necessary to use an `ArrayList` rather than a regular fixed-length array (as shown in Listing 9.2) because the number of database records fetched by a reader is not known until the end of the recordset has been reached. After the `ArrayList` has been populated, you can convert it to an ordinary array using the `ArrayList.CopyTo()` method. This will allow the array of objects to be consumed by Flash as if it were a query recordset.

You should be able to verify that the web service is operational by visiting the following URL with your browser: `http://localhost/venue/chapter09/SongRatingWebService.asmx` (assuming a typical.NET installation on your local machine). Internet Information Server (IIS) should respond with a simple web page that lists the service's public methods. You can click a method name to bring up a page that allows you to test each method from your browser (as shown in Figure 9.5).

FIGURE 9.5   IIS provides this automatic documentation and testing page for each web service.

The Java/J2EE Version

Listing 9.3 shows the Java version of the web service used by the Rating Chart example. The listing is a fairly straightforward implementation of the methods listed previously. One item of note is the private `makeArrayList()` utility function, which takes a `java.sql.ResultSet` and converts it into a `java.util.ArrayList` filled with `java.util.Hashtable` instances, where each hashtable represents a row of data from the database. This step is necessary because `ResultSet` is not directly serializable via Web Services.

> **NOTE**
>
> An alternative would be to return an object that supports the `javax.sql.WebRowSet` interface, which is expected to be supported by Flash's `WebServiceConnector` component. This alternative will likely be more efficient, but it was not possible to put together a straightforward example for this book because the current Java distribution does not include an actual implementation of `WebRowSet` (it only defines the interface). At the time of this writing, version 1.5 of the Java 2 JRE was expected to include standard reference implementations of the various `RowSet` interfaces, so it is likely that more information will be available by the time you read this book.

LISTING 9.3   SongRatingWebService.jws—Java Version of the Web Service

```
/*
   If this file is saved as a .jws file, it will be exposed as an
   "instant" web service by many engines. Alternatively, it can be
   saved and compiled as an ordinary Java class, then configured
   to be exposed as a web service with a <service> element in your
   JSP/J2EE server's WEB-INF/server-config.wsdd configuration file.
*/

import java.sql.*;
import java.util.*;

public class SongRatingWebService {

   private String dbDriver = "sun.jdbc.odbc.JdbcOdbcDriver";
   private String dbURL = "jdbc:odbc:VenueDB";


   // This function is exposed via Web Services
   public ArrayList getSongs()
     throws java.lang.ClassNotFoundException, java.sql.SQLException
   {
     // This is the SQL query statement we will use to fetch data
     String sql = "SELECT idSong AS IDSONG, sSongName AS SSONGNAME" +
       " FROM Songs ORDER BY sSongName";
```

continues

```java
    // Execute the SQL query against the example database
    Class.forName(dbDriver);
    Connection con=DriverManager.getConnection(dbURL);
    ResultSet rs = con.createStatement().executeQuery(sql);

    return makeArrayList(rs);
  }


  // This function is exposed via Web Services
  public ArrayList getSongRatings(
    java.util.Date dStartDate,
    java.util.Date dEndDate,
    String spanDivider)
    throws java.lang.ClassNotFoundException, java.sql.SQLException
  {
    // Use a resizeable array to hold series data
    ArrayList result = new ArrayList();

    // If no span divider is desired
    if (spanDivider.equals("none")) {
      result.add(getSeriesData(dStartDate, dEndDate));

    // If a span divider was specified
    } else {
      // Get instance of Calendar class for adding dates
      GregorianCalendar cal = new GregorianCalendar();

      // Loop until we reach the last of the date ranges
      while(dStartDate.compareTo(dEndDate) <= 0) {
        // Compute end date for this date range
        cal.setTime(dStartDate);
        if (spanDivider.equals("ww")) cal.add(cal.WEEK_OF_YEAR, 1);
        else if (spanDivider.equals("d")) cal.add(cal.DATE, 1);
        else if (spanDivider.equals("m")) cal.add(cal.MONTH, 1);
        else if (spanDivider.equals("q")) cal.add(cal.MONTH, 3);

        // Get series data for the time span, append to array
        result.add(getSeriesData(dStartDate, cal.getTime()));
        dStartDate = cal.getTime();
      }
    }

    // Return the result
    return result;
  }
```

```
// Internal function: returns data for a single date range
private Hashtable getSeriesData(
  java.util.Date dStartDate,
  java.util.Date dEndDate)
  throws java.lang.ClassNotFoundException, java.sql.SQLException
{
  // Get database connection
  Class.forName(dbDriver);
  Connection con = DriverManager.getConnection(dbURL);

  // SQL code to database for song and rating information
  String sql = "SELECT s.idSong AS IDSONG, " +
    "AVG(sr.nRating) AS AVGRATING, " +
    "COUNT(sr.idSongRating) AS NUMRATINGS " +
    "FROM Songs s LEFT OUTER JOIN SongRatings sr " +
    "ON s.idSong = sr.idSong " +
    "AND sr.dRatingDate >= ? "+
    "AND sr.dRatingDate <= ? " +
    "GROUP BY s.idSong";

  // Set date parameters and execute query
  PreparedStatement statement = con.prepareStatement(sql);
  statement.setTimestamp(1, new Timestamp(dStartDate.getTime()));
  statement.setTimestamp(2, new Timestamp(dEndDate.getTime()));
  ResultSet rs = statement.executeQuery();

  // Populate hash to represent this series
  Hashtable result = new Hashtable();
  result.put("startDate", dStartDate);
  result.put("endDate", dEndDate);
  result.put("songs", makeArrayList(rs));

  // Return the result
  return result;
}


// Convenience function for getting a java.util.ArrayList, filled
// with java.util.Hashtable instances for each row in a ResultSet
private ArrayList makeArrayList(ResultSet rs)
  throws java.sql.SQLException
{
  // This is the resizeable array that will be returned
  ArrayList result = new ArrayList();
```

continues

```java
    // Get the metadata (column names and such) for the ResultSet
    ResultSetMetaData meta = rs.getMetaData();

    // For each row in the ResultSet
    while (rs.next()) {

      // New hashtable for this row
      Hashtable hash = new Hashtable();

      // For each column in ResultSet, add a name/value pair to hash
      for (int i = 1; i <= meta.getColumnCount(); i++) {
        Object val = rs.getObject(i);
        if (val == null) val = "";
        hash.put(meta.getColumnName(i), val);
      }

      // Append the hash to the array
      result.add(hash);
    }

    // Return the result
    return result;
  }
```

Many Java Web Services engines support two different means of creating a web service. The first way is to save the Java source code for an ordinary class as a Java Web Service (.jws) file. The server will compile the class on the fly and expose its public methods as web service methods. The second way is to save the class in the server's classpath and then add a <service> element to the server-config.wsdd file in your WEB-INF folder.

Listing 9.3 assumes that you are using a web service engine that supports the simpler .jws method. JRun 4, ColdFusion MX 6.1, and other J2EE servers powered by the Apache AXIS engine support .jws files. If your Java server does not support .jws files, you should still be able to make the example work by saving Listing 9.3 with a .java extension, compiling it, adding the class to the classpath, and then adding the following <service> element (or similar) to server-config.wsdd:

```xml
<service name="SongRatingWebService" provider="java:RPC">
  <parameter name="methodName" value="getSongs getSongRatings"/>
  <parameter name="className" value="venue.chapter09.SongRatingWebService"/>
</service>
```

You should be able to verify that the web service is operational by visiting the following URL with your browser: `http://localhost/venue/chapter09/` `SongRatingWebService.jws` (assuming a typical JRun or other AXIS-powered installation on your local machine). Your server should respond with a simple web page that shows the service's name (as shown in Figure 9.6). Depending on your server, the page may include links to automatic documentation or testing pages.

FIGURE 9.6   Most Java implementations will provide an HTML page for the web service.

If you are not using .jws files, the URL for the page shown in Figure 9.6 will be different and may vary depending on the Java server you are using. Try `http://localhost/services/SongRatingWebService` as a starting point.

Query-Style Recordsets and Arrays of Objects

As of this writing, the Web Services functionality that ships with Flash can directly consume recordset data from ColdFusion. Java and .NET may require a bit more work, as follows:

- A ColdFusion-based web service method that returns a query-style recordset will send the data to Flash using the `QueryBean` datatype. Within ActionScript, this type is treated just like an array of objects (where each object in the array has a name/value pair for each column and where each item in the array represents a row). In fact, you can change the output of such a method from one return type to the other (to a query or to an array of structures, for example) without changing your ActionScript code at all.

- A Java-based web service method that returns an implementation of `javax.sql.WebRowSet` should be able to be consumed by Flash without much special consideration. Because no such implementations were part of a typical Java distribution at the time of this writing, the examples in this book do not take advantage of this feature. The alternative is to code the server-side method so that it returns an array of objects (hashtables, for instance), and Flash will treat it the same way.

- A .NET web service method that returns an ADO.NET style recordset *cannot* be consumed directly by the Web Services components that shipped with the initial version of Flash MX 2004. You must convert the data into an array of objects and return the array instead. That said, it is certainly possible that an interim update to the Flash components will change this fact after this book goes to print.

Because ColdFusion will always return column names in uppercase (see the note after Listing 9.1), column names are specified in uppercase throughout all the code in this chapter. In addition, the .NET and Java versions (Listing 9.2 and 9.3) use `AS` statements in their database queries to force the column names to come back in uppercase. These unusual measures are merely to make it easier to use the same SWFs with each type of server. If you are not using ColdFusion, you can skip the `AS` renaming on the server side and use your usual mixed-case column names (`sSongName` rather than `SSONGNAME`) in your ActionScript code.

Testing the Server-Side Code

To test that the server-side code from Listing 9.1, Listing 9.2, or Listing 9.3 is working correctly, you can visit the WSDL URL for the new web service on your server. The exact WSDL URL will vary a bit depending on the application server you are using, whether it is installed on your local machine, and how it is configured.

Table 9.2 shows the WSDL URL that you will most likely use to access the new web service on your own server. As usual, replace the `localhost` with the actual name or IP address of your server if it is not installed on your local machine. In addition, make sure to add the HTTP port number if your server is listening on a port other than the default port (80).

TABLE 9.2   Typical WSDL URLs for the Example Web Services

SERVER	WSDL URL
ColdFusion MX	`http://localhost/venue/chapter09/SongRatingWebService.cfc?WSDL`
Microsoft .NET	`http://localhost/venue/chapter09/SongRatingWebService.asmx?WSDL`
JRun 4	`http://localhost/venue/chapter09/SongRatingWebService.jws?WSDL`

Other J2EE	The exact URL will vary depending on the web service engine you are using (Tomcat/AXIS, WebSphere, and so on). Likely candidates include the following two URLs:
	
	`http://localhost/venue/chapter09/SongRatingWebService.jws?WSDL`
	
	`http://localhost/services/SongRatingWebService?WSDL`

When you visit the appropriate URL from Table 9.2 with your web browser, you should get back WSDL content that describes the new web service. The exact WSDL will vary slightly depending on the server you are using, but it should clearly contain references to the `getSongRatings()` method and its arguments (see Figure 9.7). If the proper WSDL content does not seem to appear, or if you get error messages from your application server, you may need to consult your server's documentation to determine whatever additional configuration steps are necessary.

FIGURE 9.7   Your server should now be able to return WSDL content that describes the new service.

NOTE

Don't worry; it's not important for you to understand what all the elements, attributes, and namespace references in the WSDL do. Only Flash—or whichever web services client wants to access the service—needs to understand that stuff. If you want to learn more, a few quick searches online will bring you to WSDL references that explain it all in detail. It's not exactly light bedtime reading, but you might find it interesting.

Components Used in the Rating Chart Example

Go ahead and open up the RatingChart.fla document now (it's included with this chapter's example files). You'll see that it is a relatively simple document, with four layers:

- The Actions layer contains just a single line of code: an `#include` directive that includes an external file called RatingChartMainCode.as. This is where the actual ActionScript code for the document is located.

- The UI Elements layer contains the user interface controls for the selection of date ranges and so on (visible in Figure 9.3). The layer also contains two `WebServiceConnector` components instance names of `wsGetSongs` and `wsGetSongRatings`.

- The UI Background layer simply contains some shading and text to make the interface look reasonably nice.

- The Bar Chart layer contains an instance of a component called `SimpleBarChart`. As the name implies, the component is capable of producing simple bar charts (more on that in a moment). The instance on the stage has been given an instance name of `bcChart`.

Some of these components haven't been discussed in this book yet. For the most part, their behavior and usage is self-explanatory, so complete introductions and class references are not provided here for each component. You can find out more about the specific properties, methods, and events supported by each component in the Flash documentation, but most of the time, you'll be able to drag them onto the Stage and alter just a few properties in the Component Inspector.

That said, a quick rundown of the components used in this example is in order so that you understand what's going on in the rest of this section. The following list shows the components you'll find in the RatingChart.fla document, with a few quick notes for each:

- Two `DateField` components, named `dfStartDate` and `dfEndDate`. `DateField` components are great whenever you want the user to be able to specify a date quickly and easily. Users can type the date themselves or click the icon provided to choose from a pop-up calendar (visible in Figure 9.2).

- A `ComboBox` component, named `dbSpanDivider`. Its `data` property has been set in the Component Inspector as `[0,1,7,30]`, and its `labels` property has been set with corresponding labels (for none, daily, weekly, and so on). If the user chooses the weekly option from the combo box, for instance, its value will be `7`. The value of the user's current selection is available via ActionScript as the `value` property.

- A `Button` component, with a visible label of `Show`. The button has one line of code attached to its `click` event in the Actions panel. The line of code simply executes the `trigger()` method (see Table 9.3 in the next section) of the `WebServiceConnector` component on the Stage. Note that `Button` components fire `click` events, whereas button symbols that you make yourself fire `onRelease` events. As always, you are free to create an event handler in a frame or ActionScript 2.0 class and hook it up to the button with `addEventListener()` (instead of placing the code in the Actions panel for the button object itself). See Chapter 4, "ActionScript: A Primer," for details about the various ways of responding to an event.

- A `SimpleBarChart` component, named `bcChart`. The `SimpleBarChart` component is not one of the components that ships with Flash. It was created for use in this example and is discussed briefly in Appendix A, "Notes on Building the `SimpleBarChart` Component." It exposes a small set of properties and methods for telling the chart what data to display and how to tweak its presentation.

NOTE

The `SimpleBarChart` component being used in this chapter is relatively simple and has only a few features. It was written especially for this book so that you would have an in-depth, working example of what it takes to create your own visualizations for data. If you want a more fully featured bar, line, or other type of chart or graph (without writing your own), you should visit the Macromedia Flash Exchange at `www.macromedia.com`. There are a number of sophisticated, component-based, third-party solutions there (generally for a small price). Another great place to look for components is `www.flashcomponents.net`.

WebServiceConnector Component Reference

Now that you've become familiar with the server-side code used to supply data to the Rating Chart example, it's time to take a closer look at the Flash component used to connect to the server: the WebServiceConnector component. This sophisticated component makes it remarkably easy to build Flash movies that consume (that is, use) Web Services. As you will see in the next section, it generally requires only a few quick steps to get everything set up to call any given web service method.

Table 9.3 shows the methods, properties, and events supported by the WebServiceConnector component.

TABLE 9.3   *WebServiceConnector* Component Members

MEMBER	DESCRIPTION
WSDLURL	Property. The WDSL URL of the web service that you would like to access. Note that the name of this property is in all uppercase letters (somewhat of an anomaly). Refer back to Table 9.2 for the WSDL URL you will likely use to connect to your own server for the Rating Chart example.
operation	Property. The name of the web service method that you would like to call as a string (for instance, getSongRatings to call the getSongRatings() method described in Table 9.1). Please note that the specified web service method will not be called until the component's trigger() method is executed via script at runtime.
suppressInvalidCalls	Property. Determines whether the call to the web service method should be suppressed if the values provided for the method's parameters are invalid (for instance, of the wrong datatype). If false (the default), the web service method is called anyway, which may mean that the web service will throw an error message (depending on how the server-side language handles datatype conversions and so on). If true, the web service method does not actually get called; instead, the component fires its status event with a code property of InvalidParams.

MEMBER	DESCRIPTION
multipleSimultaneousAllowed	Property. Determines whether the component will be willing to execute more than one web service call at the same time. If `true` (the default), multiple calls are allowed; if `false`, a second call will fire a `status` event with a `code` property of `CallAlreadyInProgress` if the first call is not yet complete. It's worth noting that there is no first in first out (FIFO) stack or queue in place, so there is no guarantee that the server will not respond to a second or third call before the first one is complete. The component will fire its `result` events in the order that the server's responses are received, which may or may not be the same order in which the calls were initiated.
params	Property. The parameters (arguments) to supply to the web service method, as an array. You must provide the parameters in the same order that they are defined in the server-side implementation of the method (and thus, the same order described in the WSDL for the service). Often, you will use data-binding to provide the parameters, instead of providing an array to `params` yourself.
trigger()	Method. Executes the web service method. The component will fire its `result` event when the server's response is received. Depending on the `suppressInvalidCalls` and `multipleSimultaneousAllowed` properties, it is possible that the call will be suppressed; if so, the component will fire its status event with an appropriate `code` value.
status	Event. Fires when the status of the component changes. Flash will pass a single argument to the event, which is a status object. The status object contains `code`, `target`, and `data` properties. Of these, the `code` property is the most interesting: it will be set to the strings `StatusChange` (indicating normal operation), `CallAlreadyInProgress`

continues

TABLE 9.3   *WebServiceConnector* Component Members (Continued)

MEMBER	DESCRIPTION
	(which may happen if `multipleSimultaneousAllowed` is `false`), `InvalidParams` (which may happen if `suppressInvalidCalls` is `true`), or `WebServiceFault` (which indicates an error condition). The `target` property is a reference to the `WebServiceConnector` that fired the event. The `data` property contains additional information about the status of the web service call, and it will contain different information depending on the `code`. See the Flash documentation for the specific data values that Flash will provide under different circumstances.
results	Property. The data, if any, that is returned by the web service method. The datatype of this property depends on the web service method (`results` will be a string if the method returns a string, an instance of the `Array` class if the method returns an array, and so on).
result	Event. Fires when the web service method call is completed successfully. Flash will pass a single argument (known as the *event object)* to any event handler you provide. The `result` object contains `type` and `target` properties. The `type` property is always set to the string `result`; `target` is a reference to the `WebServiceConnector` that fired the event. You can refer to the data returned by the remote method as `target.results` or *connector_name*`.results` (where *connector_name* is the instance name of the component).
send	Event. Fires as a result of a call to the `trigger()` method, just before the server is contacted to execute the web service method. An event object will be passed to any event handlers you provide for this event; the object contains type and target properties (see the `result` event in the preceding row of this table).

> **NOTE**
>
> The `WebServiceConnector` component members listed in Table 9.3 also apply to instances of the `WebService` class that you create at runtime using new `WebService()` syntax. See the "Connecting to a Web Service Using Script Alone" section, later in this chapter, for details.

Basic Usage of the *WebServiceConnector* Component

Now that you have a familiarity with the methods, properties, and events provided by the `WebServiceConnector` component, let's see how some of those members can be used in practice.

Take a look at the topmost `WebServiceConnector` on the Stage in RatingChart.fla (the component has an instance name of `wsGetSongRatings`). Select the component, and then open the Component Inspector panel. Under the Parameters tab, you'll notice that the `WSDLURL` property has been set to one of the URLs listed in Table 9.2 and that the `operation` property has been set to `getSongRatings` (see Table 9.1). Under the Schema tab, the `params` property has been filled in with the arguments of the `getSongRatings()` method (`dStartDate`, `dEndDate`, and `spanDivider`). Under the Bindings tab, those three parameters have been bound to the `dfStartDate`, `dfEndDate`, and `cbSpanDivider` controls, respectively.

If you are interested in familiarizing yourself with the process of setting up the `WebServiceConnector` component as used in this example, delete the one that's on the Stage now and re-create it by going through the following steps:

> **NOTE**
>
> These steps walk you through the process of binding the two date-picker controls and the one drop-down control to the `WebServiceConnector`. Depending on how you like to work, you may prefer to use scripting to copy the values from the controls to the web service arguments (instead of allowing databinding to copy the values for you). If so, you can skip this whole process and add a few lines of code in place of the bindings (see the "Connecting to a Web Service Using Script Alone" section, later in this chapter, for an example).

1. Drag a new `WebServiceConnector` from the Components panel onto the stage, and then give it an instance name of `wsGetSongRatings`. It doesn't matter where you place the component because it won't be visible when your movie is actually viewed. I usually place it in the gray work area that surrounds the white portion of the Stage.

2. Under the Parameters tab of the Properties or Component Inspector panel, fill in the WSDLURL setting with whatever URL is appropriate for your server (refer back to Table 9.2 for details). When you press Enter, you will probably notice that Flash whirrs around a bit in the background for a moment. That's the IDE contacting your server for the WSDL code that describes your server (refer back to Figure 9.7).

3. Also under the Parameters tab, enter **getSongRatings** for the operation setting. You can type the operation in manually or choose it from the drop-down menu provided (see Figure 9.8).

FIGURE 9.8   The methods provided by the web service are available in the operation drop-down menu.

NOTE

Hmm, how did Flash populate that drop-down menu? It got the available operation (method) names from the WSDL content it downloaded from your server. If you're not excited at this point, you might want to check your pulse.

---

4. Still under the Parameters tab, set multipleSimultaneousAllowed to false (see Table 9.3 for details).

5. Activate the Schema tab in the Component Inspector, and note that schema elements have been populated for you. Under the params element—which represents the web service method's arguments—you should see elements called dStartDate, dEndDate, and spanDivider (see Figure 9.9). Also note that the datatypes for each argument have been set appropriately (the dStartDate and dEndDate arguments take date values, whereas spanDivider is a string). In addition, the datatype of the results element has been set to Array (the [n] element underneath is a placeholder for the items in the array). All this happened automatically when you selected getSongRatings for the operation setting (as shown previously in Figure 9.8). You don't have to adjust any of the schema elements; just make a note that Flash is aware of what your web service needs and returns for each method.

NOTE

Many times, you will not have to manually adjust any setting for individual schema items for a web service method. That said, there are quite a few settings available, which you might want to explore on your own. In particular, the `formatter` and `encoder` settings can be of use when you want to display typed information (such as dates) in `TextInput` or `Label` controls as formatted strings. In addition, the `validation options` setting can be helpful when using databound UI controls to create data-entry interfaces. Some of these options will be covered in Chapter 11, "Building Better Forms with Flash," and you can refer to the Flash documentation for complete setting-by-setting explanations.

FIGURE 9.9   Web service argument and return metadata is populated for you in the component's Schema tab.

6. Click the Bindings tab in the Component Inspector. Click the Add Binding button (the plus sign), and then choose the `dStartDate` parameter from the Add Binding dialog box (see Figure 9.10). Click OK to add the binding.

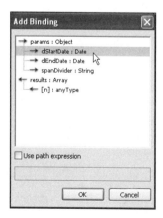

FIGURE 9.10   You can add bindings for each argument expected by a web service method.

7. Click the `bound to` option for the new binding, and then click the magnifying glass icon (see Figure 9.11) to bring up the Bound To dialog box.

FIGURE 9.11   After adding an argument binding, you need to specify the control to which it should be bound.

8. Select the `dfStartDate` control in the left side of the Bound To dialog box, and then verify that the `selectedDate` property is selected on the right side (see Figure 9.12). Some UI controls have multiple items from which to choose on the right side, but `DateField` controls have only the `selectedDate` item (which, clearly, represents the date the user has selected at runtime).

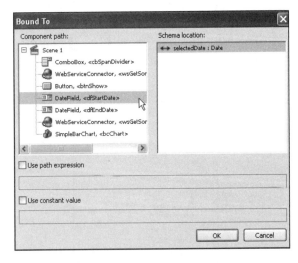

FIGURE 9.12   The binding's endpoint is the `DateField`'s `selectedDate` property.

9. Repeat Steps 6–8, this time for the `dEndDate` parameter and the `dfEndDate` component.

10. Repeat Steps 6–8 again, this time for the `spanDivider` parameter and the `cbSpanDivider` control. When you get to the Bound To dialog box (see Figure 9.12), choose the `value` property (as opposed to `selectedDate`). For a `ComboBox` control, the value of the user's selection is available as `value`; the control does not, of course, expose a `selectedDate` property.

> **NOTE**
>
> There are some additional bindable properties available for the `ComboBox` component (`dataProvider`, `selectedIndex`, and `selectedItem`). Each type of component exposes different bindable properties. Explore these properties on your own or consult the Flash documentation for the complete list for each component.

A Few Words About the *SimpleBarChart* Component

Before we take a look at the ActionScript code for the Rating Chart example, you need to understand the methods exposed by the `SimpleBarChart` component. Table 9.4 lists the component members used by this chapter's example. You will find further discussion of this component—including the parameters you can set via the Properties panel or the Component Inspector—in Appendix A.

> **NOTE**
>
> Remember that this component is not something that ships with Flash. It was written for this book as an example of the types of data visualization components you or your team could consider building from scratch.

TABLE 9.4   *SimpleBarChart* Component Members

MEMBER	DESCRIPTION
`addField(name, label)`	Method. Adds a field (which will be represented by a bar) to the bar chart. The `name` is any string or ID number that will uniquely identify the field; it does not appear visually on the chart. The `label` is a label to display at the bottom of the chart.

continues

TABLE 9.4   *SimpleBarChart* Component Members (Continued)

MEMBER	DESCRIPTION
addSeries(data, title)	Method. Adds a set of data points to the bar chart. The data argument is an object (associative array) that contains properties for each field added via addField(). The value of each property is the number to represent in the chart. The title argument is a string to display as the chart's title when this series is showing.
clearAll()	Method. Removes all fields and series data from the chart, effectively resetting it.
draw()	Method. Causes the chart to display the first data series in bar chart form.
refreshInterval	Property. The number of milliseconds that should lapse between the display of one series and the next. A value of 2000 means that the chart will pause for 2 seconds after showing each series. If there is only one series, this property has no effect. If this property is set to 0, the display will not automatically advance from series to series; however, you can still navigate through the series using the next() and previous() methods (see Appendix A).

So, if you have a SimpleBarChart component on the Stage with an instance name of bcChart, you could display some information in the chart like so:

```
bcChart.addField("lp", "Liz Phair");
bcChart.addField("nw", "Nate Weiss");
bcChart.addSeries({nw:34, lp:36}, "Ages in 2003");
bcChart.addSeries({nw:35, lp:36}, "Ages in 2004");
bcChart.addSeries({nw:36, lp:36}, "Ages in 2005");
bcChart.draw();
```

The result would be a bar chart with two bars. The chart will display three snapshots of data, one after another. One bar remains the same from series to series; the other's value climbs by 1 for each year.

> **NOTE**
>
> Again, see Appendix A for more details about `SimpleBarChart`. If you want a more fully featured chart component, you may want to explore the Flash Charting Components from the Macromedia Flash Exchange at `www.macromedia.com`.

The ActionScript Code

With all the various controls in place, it's time to take a look at the ActionScript code that powers the Rating Chart example. Like the Song Rater example from Chapter 8, most of the ActionScript code for this example is contained within a single, external ActionScript file called RatingChartMainCode.as. The file is included in Frame 1 of the RatingChart.fla document with this include line:

```
#include "RatingChartMainCode.as"
```

Listing 9.4 shows the contents of the RatingChartMainCode.as file.

LISTING 9.4   RatingChartMainCode.as—Main ActionScript Code for the Rating Chart Example

```
// Turns on trace statements for data binding events
// (comment or uncomment this line as needed)
//_global.__dataLogger = new mx.data.binding.Log();


// This function executes when the movie first appears
this.onLoad = function() {

  // Set initial values of DateField components
  var today = new Date;
  this.dfStartDate.selectedDate = new Date(2003, 7, 1);
  this.dfEndDate.selectedDate = new Date(2003, 9, 1);

  // Call clearAllFromChart() function before getSongs() call
  wsGetSongs.addEventListener("send", clearAllFromChart);

  // Call addSongsToChart() function when getSongs() call done
  wsGetSongs.addEventListener("result", addSongsToChart);

  // Call addDataToChart() function when getSongRatings() call done
  wsGetSongRatings.addEventListener("result", addDataToChart);

  // Call webServiceConnector_Status() function in case of errors
  wsGetSongs.addEventListener("status", webServiceConnector_Status);
```

continues

LISTING 9.4   RatingChartMainCode.as—Main ActionScript Code for the Rating Chart Example

```
    wsGetSongRatings.addEventListener("status", webServiceConnector_Status;
}

// This function executes when user clicks "Show" button
function getSongsFromServer() {
    // Call the getSongs() web service method
    wsGetSongs.trigger();
}


// This function fires if a WebServiceConnector runs into a problem
function webServiceConnector_Status(ev) {
    if (ev.data.faultcode != undefined) {
        trace("----- problem with web service call -----");
        trace("connector: " + ev.code);
        trace("ws method: " + ev.target.operation);
        trace("fault code: " + ev.data.faultcode);
        trace("fault string: " + ev.data.faultstring);
        trace("-------------------------------------");
    }
}


// This function executes when addSongsToChart() is done
function getRatingsFromServer() {
    // Call the getSongRatings() web service method
    wsGetSongRatings.trigger();
}

// This function will fire before getSongs() web service call
function clearAllFromChart() {
    // Remove existing fields/data/series (if any) from chart
    bcChart.clearAll();
    // Disable the Show button temporarily
    btnShow.enabled = false;
}

// This executes when data received by wsGetSongs connector component
// Within this function, "ev.target" is same as "wsGetSongs"
function addSongsToChart(ev) {
    var i:Number;
    var thisSong:Object;
```

```
  // For each row of song data...
  for (i = 0; i < wsGetSongs.results.length; i++) {
    // Within this loop, thisSong is the current data object
    thisSong = wsGetSongs.results[i];
    // Add the song as a field to the bar chart
    bcChart.addField(thisSong["IDSONG"], thisSong["SSONGNAME"]);
  }

  // Kick off second method call
  getRatingsFromServer();
}

// This function will fire when data is received from web service
// Within this function, "ev.target" is same as "wsGetSongRatings"
function addDataToChart(ev) {
  var thisSeries:Object;
  var seriesData:Object;
  var seriesTitle:String;
  var thisValue:Number;

  // For each "series" of data (each represents a range of dates)
  for (var i = 0; i < wsGetSongRatings.results.length; i++) {
    // Within this loop, this is the current series
    thisSeries = wsGetSongRatings.results[i];
    // This object gets filled with data points to show in bars
    seriesData = new Object;


    // For each song within this series
    for (var j = 0; j < thisSeries.songs.length; j++) {
      // Within this loop, this is the current song
      var thisSong = thisSeries.songs[j];

      // This is the value that we want to plot on chart
      thisValue = (Math.round(thisSong["AVGRATING"] * 10) / 10) + 3;

      // Add value to seriesData as a name/value pair
      seriesData[thisSong["IDSONG"]] = isNaN(thisValue)? 3 : thisValue;
    }

    // Add the data for this series to the chart now
    seriesTitle = dateFormat(thisSeries.startDate) + " - " +
dateFormat(thisSeries.endDate);
    bcChart.addSeries(seriesData, seriesTitle);
  }
```

continues

LISTING 9.4   RatingChartMainCode.as—Main ActionScript Code for the Rating Chart Example (Continued)

```
  // Now that the chart has been populated
  bcChart.draw();
  btnShow.enabled = true;
}


function dateFormat(date) {
  return date.getDate() + " "
  + dfStartDate.monthNames[date.getMonth()] + " "
  + date.getFullYear();
}
```

The specific sequence of events that occurs in this example is as follows:

1. The user clicks the Show button on the chart, which executes the getSongsFromServer() function, which in turn triggers the wsGetSongs component.

2. In response to the trigger() call, wsGetSongs component fires its send event, which executes the clearAllFromChart() function (discussed next).

3. The wsGetSongs component contacts the server, asking it to execute the getSongs() web service method.

4. When the getSongs() method is complete (the amount of time being dependant on network traffic, server performance, and so on), the server returns the result to Flash.

5. In response to the server's reply, the wsGetSongs component fires its result event, which executes the addSongsToChart() function. This function adds fields to the bar chart for each song. After this is done, it calls the getRatingsFromServer() function, which in turn triggers the wsGetSongRatings component.

6. The wsGetSongRatings component contacts the server, asking it to execute the getSongRatings() web service method. The server queries the database and sends back its reply.

7. In response to the server's reply, the wsGetSongRatings component fires its result event, which executes the addDataToChart() function. This function adds the actual data series to display on the chart.

With this sequence of events in mind, let's take a look at the actual code in Listing 9.4. The first thing this code does is to set up a handler that executes when the movie first loads in the Flash Player. Within this `onLoad` handler, the two `DateField` controls are given default values by setting their `selectedDate` properties.

NOTE

I have hard-coded the default date range into the example to correspond with the actual data records in the database. If you want the date pickers to default to the current date, just use `new Date()` (without any arguments). See the ActionScript Dictionary in the Flash documentation for information about the `Date` class's constructor.

Next, `addEventListener()` is used to tell Flash to execute the `clearAllFromChart()` function when the `WebServiceConnector` called `wsGetSongs` fires its `send` event (say that 10 times fast). In other words, we want `clearAllFromChart()` to execute just before the `getSongs()` web service method is executed on the server. Two more `addEventListener()` calls hook the `addSongsToChart()` and `addDataToChart()` functions up to the `result` event of the `getSongs()` and `getSongRatings()` web service calls, respectively. As you will soon see, all this means is that a single call to `wsGetSongs.trigger()` will set off a chain reaction of events that lead to the display of data on the bar chart.

The next two functions are `getSongsFromServer()` and `getRatingsFromServer()`, which are one-line wrappers around the `trigger()` method (see Table 9.3) of the `wsGetSongs` and `wsGetSongRatings` components, respectively. Calling one of these wrapper functions tells Flash to contact the server and ask it to perform the remote method specified by the component's `operation` property. Flash will fire the `send` event just before contacting the server and the `result` event after the server's response has been successfully received.

The `clearAllFromChart()` function, which is called just before the first web service call (to the `getSongs()` method), removes any existing data from the bar chart using the `clearAll()` method (see Table 9.4). It also disables the Show button by setting its `enabled` property to `false`. The button will remain grayed out until the service calls are complete. This gives the user some indication that something is happening, and it also prevents the user from making multiple calls to the server simultaneously (which might make sense in some contexts but would serve no purpose for this example).

Next up is the `addSongsToChart()` function, which fires when the `getSongs()` web service method has been called successfully. Because `getSongs()` returns an array (see Table 9.1), the `wsGetSongs.results` property (see Table 9.3) will hold an array at runtime. This array is a standard ActionScript `Array` object, and it can be looped over with a standard `for` loop. In this case, each item in the array is an object that represents a song, with properties called `IDSONG` and `SSONGTITLE`. Within the `for` loop, the `addField()` method of the `SimpleBarChart` component (see Table 9.4) is called to add a field to the chart for each song. The song's ID number is used as the field's unique name, and the song's title is used as the field's bar label.

> **NOTE**
>
> By the way, within the `addSongsToChart()` function, you can refer to `ev.target` instead of `wsGetSongs` if you wish. Flash will pass an event object to the function as the component's `result` event fires. (You can name this argument anything you like—the name `ev` is often used in the Flash documentation, so I'm using it here for consistency.) One of the properties of any event object is `target`, which is a reference back to the object that is firing the event. Depending on the situation, using `ev.target` generally makes it more reusable, abstract, and self-contained (often at the cost of being somewhat less clear). For details, see the "Responding to Events" section in Chapter 4.

The last function in Listing 9.4 is the `addDataToChart()` function, which is really quite similar to `addSongsToChart()`. The outer `for` loops over the array returned by the `getSongRatings()` web service function (each item in this array represents a data series). The inner `for` loops over the array of song-information objects within the `songs` property of each series. Basically, the outer loop creates an associative array object called `seriesData`, and the inner loop fills it with name/value pairs (where the name is the ID number of the song and the value is the rating to show in the bar chart). Then, the outer loop adds the series to the chart using the `SimpleBarChart.addSeries()` method (see Table 9.4). Finally, the `SimpleBarChart.draw()` method is used to display the chart to the user, and the Show button is re-enabled by setting its `enabled` property to `true`.

The Web Services Panel

The Flash IDE includes a Web Services panel, which you can use to keep track of the various WSDL URLs you are using in your Flash movies. It gives you a quick overview of each web service you have used in the past, along with each service's methods, arguments, datatypes, and so on.

To open the Web Services panel, choose Window > Development Panels > Web Services from Flash's main menu. The panel contains an item for each WSDL URL you have provided to a `WebServiceConnector` component in the current document or any other Flash document. (Flash appends the word "Service" onto the actual name of the web service, which is usually the same as the filename part of the WSDL URL.) You can expand each web service item to see each of its methods, and you can expand the methods to view its arguments and what kind of data it returns (see Figure 9.13).

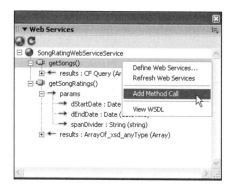

FIGURE 9.13   You can use the Web Services panel as a mini-reference for the Web Services you use often.

The Web Services panel provides a number of additional features in addition to the display of methods and properties:

- If you right-click any web service method and choose Add Method Call, Flash will place a new Web Services connector onto the Stage, with the WSDL URL and `operation` property already filled in for you.

- Also from the right-click menu, you can choose Refresh Web Services, which causes Flash to redownload the WSDL definition for each service in the list. Use this option if the methods or arguments of a web service have changed recently; refreshing the list will also cause the `operation` drop-down list in the Component Inspector to be updated accordingly. You can also use the Refresh Web Services button at the top-left corner of the panel to do the same thing.

- The right-click menu also provides a View WSDL option, which will open the actual WSDL content for the service in a new browser window.

- You can choose Define Web Services to add new WSDL URLs to the list or to remove services you're not interested in using anymore.

Viewing Trace Statements from the Data Logger

If you would like to monitor the work that the `WebServiceConnector` compo-nents are doing at runtime, you can enable the data logger facility included with Flash MX Professional 2004 . When the data logger is enabled, a series of trace messages appears in the Output window—the messages appear as each web service or data binding operation occurs (see Figure 9.14). You can use these messages to time how long web service methods take to execute, to debug bindings between databound components, and more.

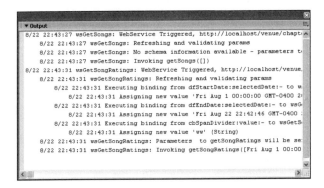

FIGURE 9.14   The trace statements emitted by the data logger are useful for optimization and troubleshooting.

To enable the data logger functionality, you just add a single line of code to your project, as follows (note the two underscores before `dataLogger`):

```
_global.__dataLogger = new mx.data.binding.Log();
```

> **NOTE**
>
> Okay, it's not an easy line of code to remember. I'm not exactly sure what to tell you about the syntax. Just try to memorize it, I guess, because the functionality sure comes in handy!

To disable the data logger, just remove the line from your code (or comment it out), or turn the behavior off programmatically by setting the `_global.__dataLogger` property to `null`, like so:

```
_global.__dataLogger = null;
```

Connecting to a Web Service Using Script Alone

As we discussed earlier in this chapter, the RatingChart.fla example uses two `WebServicesConnector` components to connect to the `getSongs()` and `getSongRatings()` web service methods. The components are the design-time representation of the web service you want to access.

If, for whatever reason, you would rather connect to a web service using ActionScript code only (that is, without any design-time elements on the Stage), you can do so by creating instances of the `WebService` class. The RatingChartScriptOnly.fla and RatingChartScriptOnlyMainCode.as files (included with this chapter's examples) show you how to make this happen.

The only difference between the two .fla files is the absence of `WebServiceConnector` components on the Stage. The differences between the main ActionScript files are more numerous, but most of them are in the first few functions. Listing 9.5 shows the code for the RatingChartScriptOnlyMainCode.as file.

NOTE

Because the remainder of this code is identical to Listing 9.4, only the first few functions are printed here. The complete code is included with this chapter's example files.

LISTING 9.5   RatingChartScriptOnlyMainCode.as—Making Web Service Calls Without Connectors

```
// Turns on trace statments for data binding events
// (comment or uncomment this line as needed)
//_global.__dataLogger = new mx.data.binding.Log();

// These variables exist for all code in this timeline
var wsRatingService;
// WSDL URL for ColdFusion
var myServiceURL =
"http://localhost/venue/chapter09/SongRatingWebService.cfc?WSDL";
// WSDL URL for ASP.NET
//var myServiceURL =
"http://localhost/venue/chapter09/SongRatingWebService.asmx?WSDL";
// WSDL URL for Java
//var myServiceURL =
"http://localhost/venue/chapter09/SongRatingWebService.jws?WSDL";


// This function executes when the movie first appears
this.onLoad = function() {

  // Set initial values of DateField components
  var today = new Date;
  this.dfStartDate.selectedDate = new Date(2003, 7, 1);
  this.dfEndDate.selectedDate = new Date(2003, 9, 1);

  // Instantiate WebService object for web service method calls
  wsRatingService = new mx.services.WebService(myServiceURL);
}

// This function executes when user clicks "Show" button
function getSongsFromServer() {
  // Call clearAllFromChart() function before getSongs() call
  clearAllFromChart();
  // Call the getSongs() web service method
  var callback = wsRatingService.getSongs();
  callback.onResult = addSongsToChart;
  callback.onFault = webServiceConnector_Status;
}


// This function fires if a WebServiceConnector runs into a problem
function webServiceConnector_Status(fault) {
  trace("----- problem with web service call -----");
  trace("fault code: " + fault.faultcode);
```

```
    trace("fault string: " + fault.faultstring);
    trace("-------------------------------------");
}


// This function executes when addSongsToChart() is done
function getRatingsFromServer() {
    // Call the getSongRatings() web service method
    //wsGetSongRatings.trigger();
    var callback =
wsRatingService.getSongRatings(this.dfStartDate.selectedDate,
this.dfEndDate.selectedDate, this.cbSpanDivider.value);
    callback.onResult = addDataToChart;
    callback.onFault = webServiceConnector_Status;
}


// This function will fire before getSongs() web service call
function clearAllFromChart() {
    // Remove existing fields/data/series (if any) from chart
    bcChart.clearAll();
    // Disable the Show button temporarily
    btnShow.enabled = false;
}


// This executes when data received by wsRatingService connector
// component
// Within this function, "ev.target" is same as "wsRatingService"
function addSongsToChart(result) {
    var i:Number;
    var thisSong:Object;

    // For each row of song data...
    for (i = 0; i < result.length; i++) {
        // Within this loop, thisSong is the current data object
        thisSong = result[i];
        // Add the song as a field to the bar chart
        bcChart.addField(thisSong["IDSONG"], thisSong["SSONGNAME"]);
    }

    // Kick off second method call
    getRatingsFromServer();
}


// This function will fire when data is received from web service
// Within this function, "ev.target" is same as "wsGetSongRatings"
function addDataToChart(result) {
```

continues

LISTING 9.5   RatingChartScriptOnlyMainCode.as—Making Web Service Calls Without Connectors
(Continued)

```
var thisSeries:Object;
var seriesData:Object;
var seriesTitle:String;
var thisValue:Number;

// For each "series" of data (each represents a range of dates)
for (var i = 0; i < result.length; i++) {
  // Within this loop, this is the current series
  thisSeries = result[i];
  // This object gets filled with data points to show in bars
  seriesData = new Object;

  // For each song within this series
  for (var j = 0; j < thisSeries.songs.length; j++) {
    // Within this loop, this is the current song
    var thisSong = thisSeries.songs[j];

    // This is the value that we want to plot on chart
    thisValue = (Math.round(thisSong["AVGRATING"] * 10) / 10) + 3;

    // Add value to seriesData as a name/value pair
    seriesData[thisSong["IDSONG"]] = isNaN(thisValue)? 3 : thisValue;
  }

  // Add the data for this series to the chart now
  seriesTitle = dateFormat(thisSeries.startDate) + " - " +
  ➥dateFormat(thisSeries.endDate);
  bcChart.addSeries(seriesData, seriesTitle);
}

// Now that the chart has been populated
bcChart.draw();
btnShow.enabled = true;
}


function dateFormat(date) {
  return date.getDate() + " "
  + dfStartDate.monthNames[date.getMonth()] + " "
  + date.getFullYear();
}
```

As you can see, the process for calling web service methods using script code alone is slightly different from the other approach you've seen in this chapter (using `WebServiceConnector` components). The basic usage steps are as follows:

1. Create an instance of the `mx.services.WebService` class, passing the WSDL URL for the desired web service to the class's constructor. In Listing 9.5, the instance is stored in the timeline variable called `wsRatingService`.

2. Code your calls to the web service using ordinary method-calling syntax, as in `wsRatingService.getSongs()` to call the `getSongs()` method on the server. This step takes the place of the `WebServiceConnector.trigger()` method that you learned about earlier in this chapter. If the web service method accepts arguments, include them (in the order defined on the server) between the parentheses, just as you would for an ordinary ActionScript method. Listing 9.5 shows how to provide arguments to the `getSongRatings()` method.

3. Each call to a web service method returns a callback object. Assign a function reference to the `onResult` property of the callback object; this function will be called as an event handler when the web service method completes successfully. Flash will pass a single argument to your handler function, which is the value returned by the web service method. You can name the argument anything you want, but it's traditional to name it `result`.

4. Within the body of the handler function, refer to the `result` argument to refer to the values returned by the server.

5. Similarly, you can create an `onFault` handler; the handler will receive a fault object as its only argument when a problem occurs. You can refer to the `faultcode`, `faultstring`, and other properties of this object to display debugging information or take other action.

NOTE

The implementation of the `mx.services.WebService` class is provided in a separate class library called `WebServiceClasses`. To use the class, you must add `WebServiceClasses` to your document's Library. To do so, open the Classes Library panel by choosing Window > Other Panels > Common Libraries > Classes. Drag the `WebServiceClasses` item on to your document's Stage, and then delete the instance from the Stage. The `WebServiceClasses` Library will now appear in your document's Library panel, which makes the `mx.services` package available to the ActionScript code in your document. This step is necessary only if your document does not contain any `WebServiceConnector` components (adding the component adds the class Library to your document implicitly).

Similarly, if you want to use the data logger, you must include the `mx.data` package by dragging the `DataBindingClasses` Library object into your document. If you fail to do so, and your document doesn't use any design-time databinding features, the call to `mx.data.binding.Log()` will fail to compile.

In some respects, this means that calling web service methods is more straight-forward than the use of visual `WebServiceConnectors`, especially if you plan to call many different service methods and don't plan on using databinding. I personally find it simpler and more intuitive to call the methods by name, for instance, rather than via the `trigger()` method of the connector class. Consult the Flash documentation for further details about the `mx.services.WebService` class, as well as the related `PendingCall` and `SOAPCall` classes.

So, whereas the first version of this example (Listing 9.4) used Flash MX 2004 Professional's databinding and component framework to make web service calls and to provide the user's selections into method arguments, Listing 9.5 uses ActionScript alone to create web service connections and provide the server with the user's selections. The first approach requires a bit more clicking around in the Flash IDE, and the second approach requires a few more lines of code. You can choose to use either approach (or a mix of the two) in your own projects.

Web Services and Data Binding

As discussed at the end of Chapter 8, the Professional version of Flash MX 2004 includes a comprehensive databinding framework for binding controls to sources of data. The SongRaterBound.fla example in Chapter 8 uses a `DataSet` component as the data source, but there are other ones too: `DataHolder`, `XMLConnector`, and—you guessed it—`WebServiceConnector`.

The example files for this chapter include a modified version of the SongRaterBound.fla document which uses Web Services instead of Flash Remoting to connect to the server. The example works in exactly the same way as the user is concerned, but uses a series of WebServiceConnector components to communicate with the corresponding server-side methods.

The Server-Side Code

Of course, to be able to do its work, the example needs to be able to talk to a web service that provides equivalent methods to the ones exposed by Flash Remoting in Chapter 8's examples. Those Web Services examples have been provided along with this chapter's example files, as follows:

- For ColdFusion, we can just use the same SongRatings.cfc file that was used in Chapter 8. (Any CFC method that is marked with `access="remote"` is automatically exposed to both Flash Remoting and web services clients.) The file has been renamed to SongRaterBackendService.cfc to avoid confusion with the other CFC example for this chapter (SongRatingWebService.cfc).
- For .NET, we will use a Active Server Methods file called SongRaterBackendService.asmx.
- For Java, we will use a Java Web Services file called SongRaterBackendService.jws.

Each server implementation exposes `getSongs()`, `rateSong()`, and `getAvgRating()` methods, just like the Remoting-ready versions in Chapter 8 did. (Please refer back to Table 8.5 in Chapter 8 for details about the arguments and data returned by each of these methods.)

WebServiceConnectors, DataSets, and UI Controls

Go ahead and open up the SongRaterBound.fla example file now. You'll notice that it is largely identical to the version from Chapter 8 (you can open them both to compare them if you wish). The most immediately noticeable difference is the presence of three `WebServiceConnector` controls named `wsGetSongs`, `wsRateSong`, and `wsGetAvgRating`, which have their `operation` parameters set to call the `getSongs()`, `rateSong()`, and `getAvgRating()` web service methods, respectively.

NOTE

One of the three connectors (`wsGetAvgRating`) is actually part of the `RatingClip` component movie clip. The other two are on the main timeline's Stage.

Because the `getSongs()` web service method returns a recordset-like array of objects, it can be easily hooked up to the `DataSet` that powers the UI controls in the Song Rater. All that's needed is to set up a binding between the `results` property of the `wsGetSongs` component and the `dataProvider` property of the `dsSongs` dataset (this binding has been set up already, visible in the Component Inspector). The databinding framework will take care of filling the dataset with the data that comes back from the server each time the web service method is triggered and called successfully.

Because the UI controls (the labels that display the artist name and song title, the loader that displays the artist's photo, the media player that plays the current song, and so on), are all bound to the DataSet component, hardly anything else needs to be changed. This is one of the greatest benefits of the way datasets fit into Flash's databinding framework: the dataset acts as an abstraction layer between your controls and the actual source of your data. The actual data source can be swapped out easily (in this case, we switched from a Flash Remoting style RecordSet to a WebServiceConnector) without anyone having to revisit the way the UI controls are updated, or how people navigate from record to record. In this respect, DataSet components can be thought of as shields between your application logic and its presentation.

Changes to the ActionScript Code

Listing 9.6 shows the version of the SongRaterBoundMainCode.as file used by this chapter's version of the Song Rater example. This code is quite a bit shorter than the original version from Chapter 8 because the mechanics of making the calls to the server-side methods are now being handled by the WebServiceConnector components.

LISTING 9.6   SongRaterBoundMainCode.as—Using Web Services in the Song Rater Example

```
// This line can be commented/uncommented for data logging/tracing
_global.__dataLogger = new mx.data.binding.Log();

// This code executes when this movie first loads
this.onLoad = function() {
  // Hook up web services events to responder functions
  wsRateSong.addEventListener("result", rateSong_Result);
  wsRateSong.addEventListener("status", webServiceConnector_Status);
  wsRateSong.addEventListener("status", webServiceConnector_Status);
  wsGetSongs.trigger();
}

// This function fires if a WebServiceConnector runs into a problem
function webServiceConnector_Status(ev) {
  if (ev.data.faultcode != undefined) {
    trace("----- problem with web service call -----");
    trace("connector: " + ev.code);
    trace("ws method: " + ev.target.operation);
    trace("fault code: " + ev.data.faultcode);
    trace("fault string: " + ev.data.faultstring);
    trace("-------------------------------------------");
  }
}
```

```
}

// Function to save a rating to the server via Flash Remoting
function rateSong(rating) {
  // Feedback for user
  txtStatus.text = "Casting your vote...";

  // Get data from current row of recordset
  wsRateSong.params = [dsSongs.currentItem.IDSONG,
  ➥rgSongRating.selectedData];
  wsRateSong.trigger();

  // Place the user's rating choice in the local dataset
  dsSongs.currentItem.nRating = rating;
}

// Fires when a rating is successfully committed to server
function rateSong_Result(result) {
  txtStatus.text = "";
}

// Fires when the current song has changed
// This is a good opportunity to handle any processing that
// Flash's databinding features aren't able to handle easily
function whenSongChanges() {
  mpSongPlayer.setMedia("../clips/" + dsSongs.currentItem.SFILENAME);
  rgSongRating.selectedData = dsSongs.currentItem.NRATING;
}

// Execute the whenCurrentSongChanges() function when the song data
// is first loaded into DataSet, or when user navigates to new song
dsSongs.addEventListener("iteratorScrolled", whenSongChanges);
dsSongs.addEventListener("afterLoaded", whenSongChanges);
```

When the movie first loads, the onLoad handler hooks the result and status events of the wsRateSong connector to the appropriate responder functions. Then the wsGetSongs connector's trigger() method is called to kick off the actual retrieval of songs from the server. Assuming the call is successful, the retrieved data will be sent to the DataSet and thus appear in the UI controls; if not, the webServiceConnector_Status() function will execute and output some trace statements for troubleshooting purposes. The guts of the rateSong() function has been adjusted similarly, with the original call to Flash Remoting being replaced with a call to wsRateSong.trigger().

> **NOTE**
>
> Ending a function name with `_Result` or `_Status` doesn't have any special meaning when using Web Services (as it does when using Flash Remoting), but I decided to use the same function names as the original version from Chapter 8 for consistency's sake. You might consider using a similar naming convention when creating listener functions for events, even though it's not required.

The only other change of any significance is within the code for the `RatingClip` component movie clip, which is attached to an ActionScript 2.0 class named `RatingMovieClip`. Listing 9.7 shows the code for this `MovieClip` subclass, which is largely unchanged from the original version in Chapter 8.

LISTING 9.7   RatingMovieClip.as—Accessing Structured Data from a Web Service

```
class RatingMovieClip extends MovieClip {

  // Properties for scheduling getRating() calls via setInterval()
  public var refreshInterval:Number = 5000;
  private var intervalID:Number;

  // More private properties
  private var _idSong:Number;
  private var txtRealtimeRating:TextField;
  private var txtRealtimeCount:TextField;
  private var wsGetAvgRating;

  // This event fires when the clip first loads/appears
  private function onLoad() {
    // This clip shall be invisible at first
    this._visible = false;

    // Add listeners to the WebServiceConnector's events
    wsGetAvgRating.addEventListener("result", onResult);
    wsGetAvgRating.addEventListener("status", onStatus);
  }

  // Public function to set the idSong property
  public function set idSong(idSong:Number):Void {
    this._idSong = idSong;
    this._visible = false;

    // Call the getRealtimeRating() method now
    getRealtimeRating();

    // Also schedule getRealtimeRating() method for repeated calls
    clearInterval(this.intervalID); // clears existing timer, if any
```

```
    this.intervalID =
       setInterval(this, "getRealtimeRating", this.refreshInterval);
}

// Public function to get the _idSong property
public function get idSong():Number {
    return this._idSong;
}

// This function executes repeatedly on a schedule
public function getRealtimeRating() {
    // Call our "service method" on the server
    wsGetAvgRating.trigger();
}

// Fires when remote function succeeds
private function onResult(ev) {
    var result = ev.target.results;

    // Round rating value to 1 decimal point, then offset by 3 stars
    // (will be NaN here if database returned NULL on server)
    var rating:Number = (Math.round(result.avgRating * 10)/10) + 3;
    _parent.txtRealtimeRating.text = rating + " of 5";
    _parent.txtRealtimeCount.text = result.numRatings;

    // Hide the clip if no rating is available
    _parent._visible = isNaN(result.avgRating) == false;
    _parent._visible = !isNaN(result.avgRating);
}

// Fires when remote function fails
private function onStatus(status) {
    if (status.code == "WebServiceFault") {
       trace("Could not retrieve 'realtime rating'");
       trace(status.data.faultcode);
       trace(status.data.faultstring);
    }
}
}
}
```

The private wsGetAvgRating property corresponds to the wsGetAvgRating connector on the RatingClip clip's Stage. When the clip first loads, its result and status events are hooked up to the onResult and onStatus methods. Then, within the getRealtimeRating() method, a single call to the connector's trigger() method is all that's needed to kick off the process of connecting to the actual web service.

Because there isn't anything in this listing that provides a value to the method's `idSong` argument, you may be wondering how the `getAvgRating()` web service method knows the song about which to return statistics. Well, if you look in the Component Inspector for the connector, you'll see that its `idSong` parameter has been bound to the movie clip's `idSong` property. The binding ensures that the current value will always be sent to the server when the connector's `trigger()` method is called.

Alternatively, you could remove the binding and set the parameter yourself, just before the call to `trigger()`, like so:

```
wsGetAvgRating.params = [this.idSong];
```

> **NOTE**
>
> In this case, there is only one parameter to provide (the `idSong` argument), but it still must be expressed using array notation. If there was more than one parameter, you would simply separate the values with commas (within the square brackets). You must provide the arguments in the same order as they are declared in the WSDL (in other words, in the same order as they appear in your server-side code).

In any case, when the web service replies, the `onResult()` function will execute because it has been set up as a listener of the connector's `result` event. Within the body of the function, the `ev` argument represents the actual event that occurred, and `ev.target` is synonymous with the `wsGetAvgRating` connector (because it fired the event). A convenience variable called `result` is created to refer to the `results` property of the connector; from that point on, the code can refer to `result.avgRating` and `result.numRatings` (because those are the properties of the object returned by the web service method), just as the original version of the code did.

Flash's Security Policies and Third-Party Web Services

The examples in this chapter all assume that you want to access a web service running on the same server that is hosting the SWF file. If you want to use a web service that resides on another server on your network, or a publicly available web service provided by a third party, then the Flash Player's cross-domain security policies will need to be considered and worked around.

By default, the Flash Player will allow a movie to access Web Services only if the hostname portion of the WSDL URL is on the same server (or at least in the same domain) from which the SWF was loaded. If not, any web service method calls will fail unless a cross-domain policy file has been placed on the target server (which is the server hosting the web service).

If your intention is to access a web service hosted by a third party, you might want to consider creating a proxy web service on one of your own servers that connects to the third party's service. You can then have your SWFs connect to the proxy. This way, the Flash Player won't be worried about security. In addition, because your server would then be sitting between your SWFs and the third party, you would be able to create a workaround if the third party's service changes, goes down, or ceases to exist. The code needed to create such a proxy web service will differ depending on the application server and language with which you are working; consult your server's documentation for details.

> **NOTE**
>
> By "proxy web service," I just mean a web service that has the same methods as the third party's service and that calls the other service's methods internally. Other people might refer to such a monster as a "stub" or a "wrapper."

See Appendix B, "Cross-Domain Data Access Policies in Flash Player 7" for details about creating policy files.

Summary

This chapter has explored how to use the new Web Services components, tools, and panels in the Flash IDE to create SWFs that call web service methods. `WebServiceConnnector` components were used to provide the connectivity in most of the examples, but you also learned how to use `WebService` class instances to create new connections at runtime. You also learned how data-bound controls can be used to provide arguments to—or display data retrieved from—web service methods.

You have now gotten solid introductions to all four means of exchanging data with servers in Flash: plain text, XML, Flash Remoting, and Web Services. Most people would probably consider the first to be the simplest and least sophisticated—and the last as the most modern and evolved—but the truth is that they are all valuable and they can be mixed and matched at will within the same project (or even the same movie).

PART IV
USING FLASH FOR
DATA COLLECTION

10 Flash and Sessions   439

11 Building Better Forms with Flash   489

CHAPTER 10

FLASH AND SESSIONS

In the preceding four chapters, you learned how to integrate Flash with your server using the four major means of integration: plain text variables, XML, Flash Remoting, and Web Services. As you have seen, one cool aspect of each of these techniques is that you get to keep writing your server-side code using the same languages and basic techniques that you're already familiar with. The proof, as the saying goes, is in the pudding: none of the server-side examples have been difficult or contained anything surprising. In fact, there is hardly anything Flash-specific in the ColdFusion, .NET, or Java examples throughout this book as a whole. That's been good news overall, eh?

Here's more good news: that basic story doesn't change much when you start thinking about applications that need to maintain session state. For the most part, you can maintain session-level (or user-level) information using the same techniques you use today.

This chapter will briefly discuss the following:

- Where Flash sits in a session-aware application and what needs to happen to make session-resident variables visible to Flash. There's really not much to it.

- Scenarios regarding user logins that might arise as you are developing your applications.

- The use of *local shared objects* in Flash, which are basically a fancier, more modern version of browser-style cookies.

You will find that Flash fits in rather neatly with your application server's notion of sessions. Thus, if you are already building session-aware applications without Flash, adding some Flash elements isn't going to make your session-tracking efforts any more painful.

In fact, you may find that implementing certain user interfaces with Flash (as opposed to traditional server-powered web pages) can make state-related matters simpler and more elegant. Why? Because whereas traditional pages are stateless, Flash movies can be considered to be stateful because the same SWF can contact a server again and again without reloading (and thus reinstantiating) itself.

Session State Concepts—A Quick Recap

Most web applications of any complexity need to track some kind of session state—sometimes called client state—as users move from page to page. There is usually at least one piece of information—the contents of a shopping cart, perhaps, or the fact that a user has logged in—that must be remembered by the application as the user navigates between URLs.

This is not a book about general web session management techniques, so this is not the time or the place to teach you how to track state in your web applications. There are details galore in your application server's documentation, and you probably know how to do this stuff with dynamic web pages anyway. Just to jog your memory, then, the basic facts of life are these (proprietary extensions notwithstanding):

- HTTP and the web are *stateless*, meaning that a bare-bones HTTP server has no understanding that two consecutive page requests from the same user have anything to do with one another.

- As far as a bare-bones server is concerned, both requests appear out of thin air, are completely anonymous, and might as well be coming from two different users on opposite sides of the globe.
- If your application needs to be able to follow a user as he or she moves from page to page—and it probably does—it needs to employ some kind of server-powered means to connect the dots.

So, assuming that you need to maintain the state of a user's session in your application, you need to do something to pass at least one piece of information from the server to the client—and back again—with each page request. Depending on the application server you are using, your options may have slightly different names, but they generally boil down to the following:

- Passing values from page to page as URL or hidden form parameters
- Asking the browser to remember a cookie, which the browser then echoes back to the server with each subsequent request
- Using session-tracking features built into the application server (the server uses one or both of the first two techniques internally to provide this functionality)
- Creating a unique identifier, storing it in a database, and then using one of the other techniques (usually the first) to keep the identifier associated with the session

You can keep using any of these techniques with Flash. By the end of this chapter, you'll understand how.

Passing URL and Form Variables

The tried-and-true, brute force method for maintaining the state of information between dynamic web pages is to use URL and hidden form fields. A good example of this method is the creation of a "Next N" user interface for search results (you know, where the user clicks links for the next 10 or previous 10 records and so on).

For instance, let's assume we're studying a simple search mechanism, where the user gets to search a product catalog (or something similar). If the user searched for the word Oranges, and there were three pages of results with up to 20 items per page, your application might generate links for the three pages that look something like the <a> links that follow. These links pass values called `criteria` and `startrow` back to the server when the user clicks them, thereby creating a sort of poor-man's memory of what the user originally searched for:

```
<a href="search.jsp?criteria=Oranges&startrow=1">Page 1</a>

<a href="search.jsp?criteria=Oranges&startrow=21">Page 2</a>

<a href="search.jsp?criteria=Oranges&startrow=31">Page 3</a>
```

Similarly, if there is a need for the `criteria` and `startrow` values to survive another form submission, the values can be passed as hidden form fields. It's a bit of a silly example, but the code following this paragraph would create a form that allows the user to type the desired results page in a text field; the state of her search criteria is preserved using the `type="hidden"` field:

```
<form method="post" action="search.jsp">
  <input type="hidden" name="criteria" value="Oranges" />
  Go to page:
  <input type="text" name="startrow" value="1" size="2" />
  <input type="submit" value="OK" />
</form>
```

As you know, you have to be careful when using this technique, because any link or form that does not pass the `criteria` value will "break the chain" and cause the user's original search criteria to be "forgotten." Regardless of whether you are using this simple technique for a search interface, a shopping cart, or an account management page, the basic lesson is the same: any value that you want to preserve must be passed every single time the server is contacted. If you forget, or if your page contains some kind of plug-in–rendered content that doesn't help you pass the information, all is then basically lost.

Step 1: Passing the Variables to Flash

Say you have a Flash movie that you want to place on Page A. The Flash movie needs to load data from—or direct the user to—Page B. Page B depends on a passed parameter (similar to the `criteria` samples in the previous section). In other words, the Flash movie needs to maintain the "chain" of parameter passing. Is all lost?

Nope. Just pass the value to the SWF when you include the SWF in a web page, using one of the following two techniques in the `<embed>` and `<object>` code:

- Include the values you want to pass in the URL for the .swf file
- Include a `flashvars` parameter in the `<embed>` and `<object>` code itself

As you learned in the "Adding the Interface to a Web Page" section in Chapter 2, "Your First Flash Interface," a typical block of HTML code for embedding a movie onto a page looks like this:

> **NOTE**
>
> This HTML snippet has whitespace and indenting added for clarity. I've also truncated the `codebase` attribute to make the snippet easier to read. The complete snippet is automatically generated and included in the accompanying HTML file whenever you publish a movie, so you can always cut and paste from there. See Chapter 2 for details.

```
<object
  classid="clsid:D27CDB6E-AE6D-11CF-96B8-444553540000"
  codebase="http://download.macromedia.com/pub/..."
  width="350"
  height="132"
  align="middle"
  id="artistWidget">
  <param name="movie" value="artistWidget.swf">
  <param name="quality" value="high">
  <param name="bgcolor" value="#FFFFFF">
  <param name="allowScriptAccess" value="sameDomain">

  <embed
    width="350"
    height="132"
    align="middle"
    name="artistWidget"
    src="artistWidget.swf"
    quality="high"
    bgcolor="#FFFFFF"
    allowScriptAccess="sameDomain"
    TYPE="application/x-shockwave-flash"
    pluginspage="http://www.macromedia.com/go/getflashplayer">
  </embed>
</object>
```

In the URL for the SWF

To pass the `criteria` value to this Flash movie in the URL for the .swf file, you would simply adjust the two `artistWidget.swf` references so that they include a name/value pair for `criteria`. Thus, the `<param>` tag for movie would be the following:

```
<PARAM NAME="movie" VALUE="artistWidget.swf?criteria=Oranges">
```

You would also need to include the value in the `src` attribute of the `<embed>` tag, like so:

```
src="artistWidget.swf?criteria=Oranges"
```

Values passed in a SWF's URL become available as variables in the root timeline. For instance, within artistWidget.swf, the value of `_root.criteria` (or `_root["criteria"]`) would be set to the string `Oranges`.

In a flashvars Parameter

The other way to pass a value to the Flash movie is to use a `flashvars` parameter. Add a `<param>` for the `<object>` tag and an attribute to the `<embed>` tag, where the name for both is `flashvars`. The value of the parameter is the variable you want to pass, formatted as a url-encoded name/value pair.

Thus, you would have your dynamic page generate an additional `<param>` tag within the snippet from the last section, which would look like this:

```
<param name="flashvars" value="criteria=Oranges">
```

You would also add a corresponding attribute to the `<embed>` tag, which would look like this:

```
flashvars="criteria=Oranges"
```

If you have more than one variable to pass, simply separate them with `&` characters as you would in a URL (make sure to do this in both the `<param>` and `<embed>` sections):

```
flashvars="criteria=Oranges&startrow=1"
```

> **NOTE**
>
> If the value part of a name/value pair may contain spaces, slashes, or any other non-alphanumeric characters, you must encode the value using the usual url-encoded format. Just use the encoding function provided by your server.

Values passed via `flashvars` become available as variables in the root timeline, just like values passed in the SWF's URL. For instance, within artistWidget.swf, the value of `_root.criteria` (or `_root["criteria"]`) would be set to the string `Orange`.

The `flashvars` technique can be more efficient with respect to network traffic than the URL technique. Browsers cache downloaded items based on their URLs (including the query string portion of the URL, where variables are passed). Therefore, a single SWF that is accessed several times by the same client machine will be downloaded anew if any variable names or values in the SWF's URL change. However, if the same values are passed via the `flashvars` technique, the browser will be able to supply a cached version of the SWF to the Flash Player (if one is available, according to the user's cache preferences), even if the names or values of the variables change.

NOTE

In fact, you can use the URL trick in reverse if you have a SWF that should always be downloaded afresh with each page view. By adding a unique (or close to unique) value to the URL for the SWF when embedding the movie in your pages, you can circumvent the browser's usual behavior, which would be to reuse a cached version of the SWF, if available (according to the user's cache preferences). To generate the pseudo-unique value, developers often use a random number, a GUID or UUID, the millisecond portion of the current time, or any other value that is extremely likely to be different (at a per-user level) for each page refresh.

Step 2: Passing the Variables Back to the Server

After you've passed variables to Flash in the SWF's URL or in a `flashvars` parameter, it's easy to pass them back as part of an interaction with the server. Just include the variable whenever you use any of these methods, most of which have been discussed in this book (particularly in Chapters 2, 3, 6, and 7):

- `MovieClip.getURL()`
- `MovieClip.loadVariables()`
- `MovieClip.loadMovie()`
- `LoadVars.load()` or `XML.load()`
- `LoadVars.send()` or `XML.send()`
- `LoadVars.sendAndLoad()` or `XML.sendAndLoad()`
- Just about any other method that accepts the URL for a dynamic page on your server.

For any of the preceding methods, you can simply add the variable to the URL, making sure to escape any non-alphanumeric characters with ActionScript's `escape()` function. For instance, the following line would navigate the browser to the `search.jsp` page, passing a name/value pair for the `criteria` variable as it goes:

```
this.getURL("search.jsp?criteria=" + escape(_root.criteria));
```

When using the methods of the `LoadVars` or `XML` classes, you can add the name/value pair to the object before calling the method. Here's an example that passes the value of `_root.criteria` (which, according to the snippets in the previous sections, was passed from the server) back to the server:

```
lvServerPage = new LoadVars;
lv.criteria = _root.criteria;
lv.load("search.jsp");
```

> **NOTE**
>
> You could create a subclass that extends the `LoadVars` or `XML` class, which automatically adds the variables you commonly use. For instance, the subclass could contain its own `load()` method. Within the method, an `if (_root.criteria != undefined)` test could determine if the variable exists in the root timeline. If it does, the variable can be added to the object using `this["criteria"] = _root.criteria`. Then your method would call `super()` to perform the actual loading. See Chapter 4, "ActionScript: A Primer," for details about creating ActionScript 2.0 subclasses and the use of the `super()` keyword.

If you are using `loadVariables()` or `loadMovie()`, and the `criteria` variable already exists on the timeline from which you are calling the method, you can just specify GET or POST for the `variables` argument. The `criteria` variable (along with all other variables in the timeline) will be sent to the server as part of the request. The following line would send all variables in the root timeline—which includes any variables that were passed *to* the movie via the URL or `flashvars` technique—from the movie to a JSP page on the server:

```
_root.loadVariables("search.jsp", "POST");
```

> **NOTE**
>
> See Chapter 6, "Connecting to Servers with Plain Text," for a discussion of the various methods that were mentioned in this section.

Some Potential "Gotchas" When Accessing Passed-In Variables

Keep the following points in mind when working with variables that have been passed to Flash via the URL or flashvars technique:

- The name of the passed-in variables are case-sensitive after they reach ActionScript, regardless of whether variable names are case-sensitive in your server environment. The word flashvars, however, is not case-sensitive—flashvars or FLASHVARS will work equivalently.

- All variables passed via the URL or flashvars technique are received by ActionScript as string variables (that is, they are accessible as instances of the String class). If you want to treat the value of one of these variables as a numeric, Boolean, or other datatype, you need to convert the string to the desired value yourself.

As an example, say you have a server-side Boolean variable called isFirstTimeVisit, and you pass it to Flash using either the URL or flashvars technique. Depending on what server you are using, the value of the variable will most likely be True or true or YES or 1—as a string—when it appears in the HTML code that embeds the movie in your pages. The value of the ActionScript _root.isFirstTimeVisit variable will therefore be True or true or YES or 1—again, as a string—when your movie loads. Due to the way that ActionScript performs runtime type conversions, simple conditional tests against the _root.isFirstTimeVisit variable will evaluate to the Boolean value true even when the variable holds a string value of "false". (Basically, the rule is that any non-empty string will evaluate to true when accessed in a Boolean context.) For instance, the following if block would not behave as expected:

```
if (_root.isFirstTimeVisit) {
  // Code here executes even if the value is "False" or "false"
}
```

To get the desired behavior, you need to test against the string True or true (using the capitalization that your server uses when converting a Boolean to a string). The following snippet would work correctly for a variable that was being passed by an ASP.NET page that was coded using the Visual Basic script language:

```
if (_root.isFirstTimeVisit == "True") {
  // Code here executes even if the value is "False"
}
```

If you don't want to have to remember to compare the value against the string value every time, you could convert the variable in the `_root` timeline when the movie first loads, by including the following line in the first frame or `onLoad` handler of your SWF:

```
_root.isFirstTimeVisit = (_root.isFirstTimeVisit == "True");
```

The following line is an alterative way to code the same logic:

```
_root.isFirstTimeVisit = _root.isFirstTimeVisit == "True" ? true :
false;
```

Because the case and value of the passed-in variable might differ depending on the type of server you are using—YES for ColdFusion, `True` for Visual Basic, `true` for Java, and `1` for most databases—you might want to create a simple function that accepts a string value and returns the appropriate Boolean value. Such a function could take care of checking for each likely value from a server, thus enabling you to change servers later without changing your ActionScript code. Here is a simple ActionScript function that does just that:

```
function convertStrToBool(val:String):Boolean {
  val = val.toLowerCase();
  return (val == "1" || val == "true" || val == "yes");
}
```

With this function in place, you could convert the passed-in `_root.isFirstTimeVisit` variable to the appropriate Boolean value using the following line (again, at the top of Frame 1 or in the `onLoad` handler for your SWF):

```
_root.isFirstTimeVisit = convertStrToBool(_root.isFirstTimeVisit);
```

Numeric datatypes are easier. If you have a server-side numeric variable called `hitCount`, it will be available as `_root.hitCount` within ActionScript, assuming that you pass it using either the URL or `flashvars` technique. It will be a string variable when it first gets to ActionScript, but you can convert it easily to a proper number with the help of ActionScript's `Number` function, like so:

```
_root.hitCount = Number(_root.hitCount);
```

See the ActionScript Reference Guide portion of the Flash documentation for details about datatype conversions.

Sharing Session Variables with Flash

All three of the application servers covered in this book include session management features that make it easy to work with user sessions. The exact mechanics vary a bit from server to server, but the basic idea is similar: the application server provides a session scope, in which you can store variables and objects that will remain associated with each user's visit to your pages. The variables remain on the server side (usually in the server's RAM by default) and are never passed to or made visible to the client (unless your code does so explicitly).

Of course, the server needs some way to keep track of which user is which. By default, the server does so by setting a cookie on the user's browser. The cookie is subsequently used to map each of the user's page requests to the correct set of session variables on the server.

- For ColdFusion, the name of the cookie is `jsessionid` if the "Use J2EE Session Variables" option is checked in the ColdFusion Administrator. Otherwise, two cookies called `CFID` and `CFTOKEN` are used.
- For ASP.NET, the name of the cookie is `ASP.NET_SessionID`.
- For J2EE applications, the name of the cookie is `jsessionid`.

Making Flash a Participant in the Session

So, assuming that you are using your server's session variables in an application, how do you let Flash participate in the session? How do you arrange things so that session variables set during the execution of a normal dynamic page are shared with requests initiated by Flash (via methods such as `LoadVars.load()`, `XML.sendAndLoad()`, `MovieClip.getURL()`, and so on)?

Believe it or not, you don't have to do anything special. When your ActionScript code uses a method that causes Flash to contact your server, the actual HTTP request is performed by the guts of the browser that is hosting the SWF. (Basic HTTP request functionality is one of the services that browsers must provide to any plug-in.) As such, the browser will include any cookie information that it would normally include when interacting with a server for a normal web page request.

NOTE

Another side effect of the fact that the HTTP request goes through the browser is that the `HTTP_USER_AGENT` CGI variable reflects the name and version of the browser, not the Flash Player (which, arguably, would normally be considered to be the user agent). If you want to create a web page that detects the user's Flash Player version, you can use the Detect Flash Version option in the HTML tab of Flash's Publish Settings dialog box (File > Publish Settings). Detection scripts (sometimes called "sniffers") are also available from Macromedia's web site and from third-party solutions, such as BrowserHawk.

So, assuming that the server has issued a session-tracking cookie previously, the request from Flash will be identified correctly and all will be well in session land. If, by chance, the request from the Flash movie is the first request of the user's session—which may happen if the SWF is on a static page but accesses a data-driven URL internally—the server will start a new session for the user, which will then be shared among subsequent Flash and normal page requests.

NOTE

Session variables will not work "automagically," as described here, if the browser has been configured not to accept cookies, or if you have configured your server not to issue cookies for session tracking. See the next section of this chapter for details.

Of course, just because server-side session variables work with Flash requests doesn't mean that you can refer to the session variables in your ActionScript code. Flash, as a client, is no more privy to the internal goings-on of your server than a traditional browser client is. Thus, just as you have to explicitly pass session variables to JavaScript if you want them to be available to the browser, you have to explicitly pass session variables to ActionScript to make them available to a Flash movie.

It's not hard to pass a session variable to a Flash movie. You can go back to Chapters 6–9 and add session variables to the server-side examples. Doing so makes them return the current values of whatever session variables you want to make available to Flash. Conversely, your server-side code can accept arguments or parameters from Flash, which can then be stored in session variables.

> **NOTE**
>
> You could also pass the current value of a session variable in the URL of the SWF, or in a `flashvars` parameter. See the "Passing URL and Form Variables" section, earlier in this chapter, for details.

To sum up, your server doesn't know the difference between a normal page request from your browser and a request initiated by Flash. This means that you can use session variables just as you do now, regardless of whether you are creating a normal dynamic page or a page for Flash's consumption. If you want a SWF to know or change the value of a session variable, you need to create a page or remote function that passes the data back and forth.

Maintaining Session State Without Cookies

All is well and good unless the user's browser (or a firewall or proxy between the user and your server) has been configured to disallow cookies. In that case, the requests coming from Flash will not contain the session identifier that your server needs to map the request to the session scope in its memory. Thus, the server will be forced into treating every page request as if it were coming from a brand new user session, which means that session variables will no longer work as advertised.

> **NOTE**
>
> This is not a particular problem with Flash. It's a fact of life when using any browser (or other client) that doesn't accept cookies. If you look in your server's documentation, there will be a whole section devoted to making session variables work without cookies.

If you want Flash-initiated requests to participate in server-managed sessions in a cookieless environment, you need to make sure that the session ID is provided to the server along with each Flash-initiated request (that is, to each ActionScript call to `getURL()`, `XML.load()`, `LoadVars.send()`, and so on).

The exact steps required to pass the session ID back to the server vary a bit from server to server. The steps for ColdFusion and Java are conceptually similar, while the steps for ASP.NET use a different strategy.

> **NOTE**
>
> I encourage you to skip the following sections unless you need to use session variables without cookies. The only reason I suggest skipping ahead is because the discussion may be a bit discouraging, making the requirements sound more complicated than they actually are. Just keep in mind that everything is really quite simple and elegant if cookies are allowed.

Cookieless Sessions with ColdFusion

For ColdFusion, you need to pass the `Session.CFID` and `Session.CFTOKEN` values to the Flash movie (or the `Session.jsessionid` value if you are in Use J2EE Sessions mode) and then back to the server with each ActionScript request. The easiest way to pass the values to Flash is to use CFML's `URLSessionFormat()` function around the URL for the .swf file when embedding the movie on your ColdFusion-generated web pages; this will ensure that the correct values are added to the URL for you if the client does not accept cookies.

See the "Passing URL and Form Variables" section earlier in this chapter for details about the mechanics of passing the values from the server to Flash and back again.

Cookieless Sessions with ASP.NET

For ASP.NET, you need to make sure that the web application is configured to manage sessions in cookieless mode. You do this by adding a `cookieless="true"` attribute to the `<sessionState>` element in your application's Web.config file. ASP.NET will then begin rewriting the URLs of page requests for you, inserting the session identifier after the server name.

Now simply make sure that your ActionScript calls use relative URLs when accessing server-side resources. That is, don't hardcode the full URL (with the `http://` and all) into your movies when you are done testing them. Instead, use relative URLs so that the session portion of the URL is preserved when Flash makes its requests. As long as you use relative URLs, sessions will be maintained correctly and all will be well.

If your Flash movie must access an absolute URL (perhaps on a different physical server), but still needs to participate in cookieless sessions, you could use the methods of the `String` class to parse the session ID out of the SWF's URL (available as `_root._url` in ActionScript). You would then reinsert the ID into the URLs you want to access.

> **NOTE**
>
> If you are using classic ASP (.asp) pages rather than ASP.NET (.aspx) pages, the procedure will be different (more similar to the ColdFusion or Java procedure). Consult your ASP documentation for what's needed for cookieless sessions.

Cookieless Sessions with Java/J2EE

For Java/J2EE servers, you need to pass the `jsessionid` to the Flash movie and then back to the server with each ActionScript request. This is the same information that the `HttpServletResponse.encodeURL()` method adds to URLs, but you shouldn't actually use that method in .swf URLs because the method adds a semicolon that Flash won't be able to understand. As long as every request from Flash includes the `jsessionid`, session information will be preserved.

See the "Passing URL and Form Variables" section earlier in this chapter for details about the mechanics of passing the values from the server to Flash and back again.

Sharing Cookies with Flash

As explained in the "Making Flash a Participant in the Session" section earlier in this chapter, requests initiated by Flash will provide any existing cookies to the server, just like a normal page request. This means that server-side pages or remote methods that rely on cookies will continue to work if they are accessed by Flash.

Flash does not, however, provide a programming hook for getting or setting cookie values. (JavaScript code in web pages can access the `document.cookie` object to get or set cookies; there is no corresponding object available to ActionScript.) Thus, if you want a cookie to be available to ActionScript, you need to pass it to the movie using one of the techniques in the "Passing URL and Form Variables" section of this chapter. If you want the movie to be able to set a cookie, you need to create a server-side page or method that does the cookie-setting. You then call that server-side resource from within your SWF.

Alternatively, you could create a JavaScript function on the containing web page called `setCookie()`. Inside the body of the JavaScript function, you would use the `document.cookie` object to set the desired cookie. With most browser and Flash Player versions, you would then be able to call the JavaScript function using the following syntax in your ActionScript code, assuming that the function accepts two arguments (for the name and value of the desired cookie, respectively):

```
getURL("javascript:setCookie('faveArtist',
"+_root.txtFaveArtist.text+");");.
```

See the Flash documentation for the browser and Flash Player version limitations for the use of `javascript:` URLs in ActionScript code. Keep in mind that your movie's behavior will now be dependant upon whether JavaScript is enabled in the browser. In addition, for compatibility with Netscape 6.1 and earlier, you will need to set `swLiveConnect` parameter to `true` when you embed the movie in your pages.

Persisting Data with Local Shared Objects

As you learned earlier in the "Sharing Cookies with Flash" section, ActionScript does not have direct access to the cookie headers that are used to get and set cookies in the browser. You can explicitly pass cookie values from the server as URL or `flashvars` parameters, and you can pass information back to the server. The server is then free to set the passed-back value as a cookie, but the Flash client has no straightforward way to get or set the values without "round trips" to the server. (This is somewhat ironic because the cookies are actually stored on the client machine, where Flash is running.)

So, does the lack of cookie support mean that you have no way to remember bits and pieces of information on the client machine? Absolutely not. Instead of cookies, Flash provides support for something it calls *local shared objects*. Local shared objects are similar to cookies, except that they can store typed and structured data (arrays, objects, dates, numbers, and so on) in addition to strings. Additionally, local shared objects can hold significant amounts of data (the contents of a dataset, say), as long as the user has authorized your server domain to use the corresponding amount of disk space on his or her local drive. Cookies, in contrast, can store only very limited amounts of information.

> **NOTE**
>
> For details about the size and other limitations of cookies—and in fairness, the limitations are by design—please refer to the original HTTP cookie specification at `www.netscape.com/newsref/std/cookie_spec.html`. I find this document to be a bit of an interesting read, both for its technical content and as an artifact of the simple but powerful innovations that Netscape made during its early years.

The *SharedObject* Class

Table 10.1 shows the members of the `SharedObject` class, which provides the API for saving and retrieving bits and pieces of information on the user's machine.

> **NOTE**
>
> In Table 10.1, so is a placeholder for any instance of the `SharedObject` class. As you can see, most of the members pertain to instances of the class. There is one method, `getLocal()`, that is a static method (meaning that you call it as a method of the `SharedObject` class itself, rather than as an instance). You will see how this works in the next example.

TABLE 10.1   *SharedObject* Class Members

MEMBER	DESCRIPTION
`SharedObject.getLocal (name, [path])`	Static method. Creates a new `SharedObject` instance with the given `name`. Any existing data associated with the name will be read from the user's drive and made available in the new instance's `data` property. You may also specify a `path`, which allows you to share the local shared object with other Flash movies from the same domain.
`so.clear()`	Method. Removes all data from the shared object and deletes the object from the user's drive. If you wish, you can then add new data to the object using the `data` property.
`so.data`	Property. An object (associative array) that contains the actual information to be associated with the shared object on the user's drive. You can add as many items to the data object as you wish. The data will be saved to disk when you call the `flush()` method and will be read in from disk the next time the shared object is loaded with `getLocal()`.

continues

TABLE 10.1   *SharedObject* Class Members (Continued)

MEMBER	DESCRIPTION
so.flush ([minimumDiskSpace])	Method. Attempts to save all the data in the local object to disk. In other words, this is your "save" command. The method will return true if the save was successful, false if it was unsuccessful, or the string value pending if the user is being prompted to accept or deny the use of disk space on his or her local drive. If you anticipate storing a large amount of data in the shared object over time, you can provide a value to the minimumDiskSpace property.
so.getSize()	Method. Returns an approximation of the shared object's current size (that is, the size of all the names and values stored in its data property) in bytes. This can be a costly operation if the object contains a large amount of data.
so.onStatus	Event. This event fires as a shared object is loaded or flushed, and it can provide information about whether the data was saved successfully. The main reason it would not be saved successfully is if the amount of data in the object would exceed the amount of storage the user has authorized for local objects. See the Flash documentation for details about this event.

> **NOTE**
>
> The data in local shared objects is stored on the user's drive in clear text. Anyone who has access to the drive will be able to view the information if they know where to look. (This is no different from how cookies are implemented in today's browsers.) Therefore, you must not use local shared objects to save confidential or valuable information.

Basic *SharedObject* Usage

The code snippet after this paragraph exhibits a typical use of the SharedObject class. Say you have a login form with text input fields for the user's username and password, and you would like to remember the username part in a local shared object so that the user doesn't have to retype it next time. While you are at it, you wouldn't mind saving the current date and time so that your Flash movie can be aware of when the user last logged in. The following lines of code would get the job done:

```
var so = SharedObject.getLocal("lastLogin");
so.clear();
so.data.username = tiUsername.text;
so.data.loginDate = new Date;
so.flush();
```

Assuming that the preceding code executes when the user successfully logs in, you could use the following code to prefill the username text field when the login form first appears:

```
var so = SharedObject.getLocal("lastLogin");
if (so.data.username != undefined) {
  tiUsername.text = so.data.username;
}
```

If you need to remove a single item from the data property, you can use ActionScript's delete keyword. The following code loads the lastLogin local shared object, removes its username data, and resaves it to the user's drive:

```
var so = SharedObject.getLocal("lastLogin");
delete so.data.username;
so.flush();
```

Allowing SWFs to Share the Same Local Shared Objects

By default, every SWF uses its own space on your server's drive to store any local shared objects that it creates. If you save a value in a local shared object from within one SWF, it will not be accessible by another SWF, even if both SWFs are on the same server (or even the same folder) and use the same name in the getLocal() method. In other words, each Flash movie effectively has its own namespace for local shared objects.

If you want two different SWFs to be able to share the same local shared object data, you can specify a common path in the optional path argument of the getLocal() method (see Table 10.1). As you might expect, the sharing will work only if the two SWFs were downloaded from the same server domain. See the Flash documentation for details.

> **NOTE**
>
> If you are interested in sharing shared objects between SWFs that come from different locations, I encourage you to check out John Grden's in-depth article on the subject at `www.acmewebworks.com/default.asp?ID=85`

Local Shared Objects and Size Limitations

Because you can store any number of items in a local shared object's `data` property, and because the items can in turn be arrays or objects filled with other objects, it is possible for a local shared object to get fairly large. Naturally, there needs to be some limitations set on the total size of shared objects (otherwise, you could maliciously fill up a user's drive with dummy information). The Flash Player allows the user to specify how much space can be used for local shared objects, on a domain-by-domain basis.

To view or change the settings, right-click any Flash movie on any web page, and then choose Settings from the context menu. The second tab (the one marked with a file folder) is where you can adjust the Local Storage settings for the server domain from which the SWF was downloaded (see Figure 10.1). By moving the slider, the user can allocate a given amount of space for shared objects. If the user moves the slider all the way to zero, your SWFs will not be able to save any local shared objects, regardless of their size.

FIGURE 10.1   Users can limit the amount of disk space your servers can use for local shared objects.

If the user has specified that your server may not store any information at all, any calls to `flush()` will simply return `false` and no prompting or saving will take place. If the user has specified some other limit, and if your code attempts to save a local shared object that would exceed that limit, calls to the `flush()` method (see Table 10.1) will cause the user to be automatically prompted with the settings dialog (see Figure 10.1). In such a case, the object will be saved if the user ups the limit; otherwise, it will not be saved. In addition, the `flush()` method returns the string `pending` to indicate that the user is being prompted.

NOTE

Code execution does not stop while the dialog box is being displayed; if your movie needs to react to whether the user approves or denies the request for more space, you need to create an event handler for the `onStatus` event (see Table 10.1).

Also, note that the size of your SWF as it is displayed in the Flash Player must be at least 215 wide by 138 pixels high; otherwise; the Flash Player will not be able to display the prompt to the user. Don't worry about the size of the SWF if your movie is unlikely to need to prompt the user.

The examples in this chapter assume that the data stored by a local shared object will be relatively trivial—just a few bytes here or there for a username or preference of some kind—and non-critical (that is, where the application will not fail to operate if the shared object cannot be saved). Please consult the Flash documentation for details and usage examples related to the storage of potentially large or complex data structures in shared objects (specifically the `onStatus` event, the `getSize()` method, and the optional `minimumDiskSpace` argument of the `flush()` method).

Putting It Together: Tracking User Logins

The example files for this chapter include an example that I call the Secured Content Demo, which uses server-side session variables to track user logins. There is an HTML-based login form (see Figure 10.2) and a Flash movie that contains its own login form (see Figure 10.3). Both versions of the form use a common set of methods to perform the actual login operation, and both track the login using the same session variables.

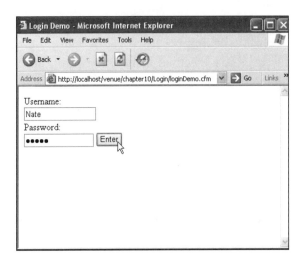

FIGURE 10.2   Users can log in using an HTML-based form.

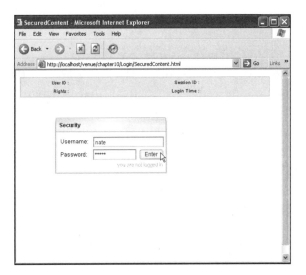

FIGURE 10.3   Users can also log in using a form within Flash.

The result is a simple implementation of a "single sign-on" system. If a user logs in using the HTML-based form and then proceeds to the Flash-enabled page, the Flash movie will understand that the user has already authenticated and will not reprompt him or her for a username and password. The reverse is also true; if a user logs in via the Flash movie first, he or she will not be reprompted to sign in when he or she later navigates to the non-Flash page.

The Server-Side Code

As usual, three versions of the server-side code are included with the example files for this chapter. Each version implements the following:

- A web page entitled Login Demo, which presents an HTML-based login form (and continues to present it until the user logs in with a valid username and password). After the user logs in, the page displays a welcome message. The page is named loginDemo.cfm, loginDemo.aspx, and loginDemo.jsp for the ColdFusion, ASP.NET, and Java versions, respectively.

- A second web page that exchanges XML data with Flash. The page accepts a single URL parameter called `action`, which can be set to `getUserInfo`, `attemptLogin`, or `logout`. The page responds with XML that contains a single `<response>` element. Flash uses the information in the `<response>` element to decide whether to prompt the user for a username and password, which content to show the user, and so on. This page is named LoginXmlSource.cfm, LoginXmlSource.aspx, and LoginXmlSource.jsp for the ColdFusion, ASP.NET, and Java versions, respectively.

- A class called `LoginManager`, which is used internally by the two pages already mentioned. The implementation of the class is somewhat different for the three types of servers, but in each case, it exposes methods called `getUserInfo()`, `attemptLogin()` and `logout()` (as listed in Table 10.2). The methods take care of verifying whether a username and password have a matching record in the database and storing each user's login status in the server's session scope. The class is implemented in LoginManager.cfc, LoginManager.cs, and LoginManager.java for the ColdFusion, ASP.NET, and Java versions, respectively.

- A class called `LoginInfoObject`, which is also used internally by the other items in this bulleted list. This is just a simple data structure object, with named properties related to a user's login status (`isLoggedIn`, `idLogin`, `sessionID`, `rightList`, and `loggedInSince`). This helper class is implemented in LoginInfoObject.cfc and LoginInfoObject.java for the ColdFusion and Java versions, respectively. The ASP.NET version of this class is nested within the LoginManager.cs file (together with the previous item in this bulleted list).

Table 10.2 details the actions exposed by the `LoginManager` class used by this section's example. The code for the ColdFusion, ASP.NET, and Java implementations of these methods is provided in the next three sections, respectively.

TABLE 10.2   Methods Exposed by the *LoginManager* Class

METHOD	DESCRIPTION
`attemptLogin` `(username, password)`	Attempts to log in the user with the specified username and password. If a matching record is found in the Users table in the example database, the user's information is stored in a `LoginInfoObject` instance (in the server's session scope) to remember that the user has logged in. Returns a Boolean value that indicates whether the login was successful.
`getUserInfo()`	Returns a `LoginInfoObject` object that contains four properties about the current session's login status: `isLoggedIn`, `idUser`, `rightList`, and `loggedInSince`. The returned value reflects the state of the `LoginInfoObject` in the server's session scope.
`logout()`	Resets the login information in the server's session scope, thereby logging the current user out.

> **NOTE**
>
> The ASP.NET and Java versions each pass an additional argument to the methods listed in Table 10.2. The ASP.NET versions of the methods expect the user's `HttpSessionState` object to be provided (in addition to the arguments listed in Table 10.2). The Java versions expect a `LoginInfoObject` to be provided (the calling page is expected to store the object in the session scope).
>
> I varied the implementations a bit to keep the code simple for each version and also to reflect the notion that there are often multiple ways to skin any given cat. By reviewing the code for each implementation, you can see how session values can be passed to Flash, regardless of whether they are passed internally by reference or passed internally by value.

The server-side implementations of these methods rely on a table called Users, which is part of the example database for this book. The Users table contains the following columns:

- `idUser`, which is an auto-incrementing ID number
- `sUsername`, for logging in with
- `sPassword`, also for logging in with

- sRightList, which is a comma-separated list of rights that the user has been granted. If you prefer, you can think of the rights as being like privileges, or roles, or user groups. The idea is to provide a simple way to give some users more access than others. You can adapt or normalize this aspect of the database structure to suit your needs.

> **NOTE**
>
> You can log in to this chapter's examples using nate as a username and flash as a password. You can also log in using winona as a username and flash as a password; this user has a different list of rights than nate (it seems the second user isn't as trusted). Feel free to change the passwords or to add additional users within the database table.

Understanding How the XML-Serving Pages Work

As mentioned in the previous section, this chapter's example includes a page that serves XML data about a user's current login status. The page is named LoginXmlSource.cfm, LoginXmlSource.aspx, or LoginXmlSource.jsp, depending on which server you are using. Internally, the page calls the methods provided by the LoginManager class (see Table 10.2) to carry out the mechanics of logging the user in or out. The page, then, can be seen as a thin wrapper that exposes the LoginManager methods to a URL (using XML as the communication language).

> **NOTE**
>
> Conceptually, this is very similar to how Web Services work, so you could easily reengineer this chapter's example to use Web Services instead of an ad-hoc XML exchange. See Chapter 9, "Connecting to Servers with Web Services," for details.

If the LoginXmlSource page is called with an action=attemptLogin parameter in the URL, the page expects that a username and password has been provided to the page—in XML form—as the body of the incoming HTTP request. The page expects the credentials to be supplied as a very simple XML document that contains just one element, as follows:

```
<credentials username="nate" password="flash"/>
```

The page uses the XML parsing functionality provided by your server to extract the username and password from the <credentials> packet; it then calls the LoginManager.attemptLogin() method that was listed in Table 10.2. If the login is successful—that is, if the username and password

match a record in the database—the page responds with another very simple
XML packet, as follows:

```
<response isLoggedIn="true"/>
```

If the login is not successful, the page responds with this packet, which should
come as no surprise:

```
<response isLoggedIn="false"/>
```

If the LoginXmlSource page is called with an action=logout parameter in the
URL, it calls LoginManager.logout() internally and responds with the same
isLoggedIn="false" packet that accompanies an unsuccessful login.

If the LoginXmlSource page is called with an action=getUserInfo parameter
in the URL, it responds with a slightly larger packet with information about the
user's login status. Assuming that the user is currently logged in, the packet will
look similar to the following:

```
<response isLoggedIn="true">
  <idUser>1</idUser>
  <rightList>secureItem1,secureItem2</rightList>
  <loggedInSince>3/18/2004 1:41 PM</loggedInSince>
  <session-id>dekafsmew3yirgrjl3m1e2if</session-id>
</response>
```

The <idUser> and <rightList> elements are the user's idUser value and
rightList values from the database. The <loggedInSince> element indicates
when the user's attemptLogin() call succeeded, and the <session-id> is the
server-specific ID for the user's current web session. (The format of the session
ID will vary depending on which server you are using.)

The ColdFusion Version

Listing 10.1 shows the ColdFusion code for the LoginManager class that was
described in Table 10.2. The class is implemented as a ColdFusion Component
(CFC). It maintains an instance of LoginInfoObject (also implemented as a
CFC) in the session scope, filling it with data or reinstantiating it as necessary.

LISTING 10.1   LoginManager.cfc—ColdFusion Version of LoginManager

```
<cfcomponent>

  <!--- Constructor section --->
  <!--- Keep a LoginInfoObject instance in the session scope --->
  <!--- Put an empty one there now if none exists already --->
```

```
<cfif not IsDefined("Session.LoginInfo")>
  <cfset Session.LoginInfo = CreateObject("component",
  ➡"LoginInfoObject")>
</cfif>

<!--- Method: Attempts login with username/password --->
<cffunction name="attemptLogin" access="public" returntype="boolean">
  <cfargument name="username" type="string" required="Yes">
  <cfargument name="password" type="string" required="Yes">

  <!--- This function's result shall indicate success/failure --->
  <cfset var result = false>

  <!--- Query the database for matching user records --->
  <cfquery name="LoginQuery" datasource="VenueDB">
    SELECT idUser, sRightList
    FROM Users
    WHERE sUsername = '#username#'
    AND sPassword = '#password#'
  </cfquery>

  <!--- If the login is successful, keep login info in session --->
  <cfif LoginQuery.RecordCount eq 1>
    <cfset Session.LoginInfo = CreateObject("component",
    ➡"LoginInfoObject")>
    <cfset Session.LoginInfo.isLoggedIn = True>
    <cfset Session.LoginInfo.idUser = LoginQuery.idUser>
    <cfset Session.LoginInfo.rightList = LoginQuery.sRightList>
    <cfset Session.LoginInfo.loggedInSince = TimeFormat(Now())>
    <cfset Session.LoginInfo.sessionID = Session.SessionID>
    <cfset result = true>
  <cfelse>
    <cfset this.logout()>
  </cfif>

  <!--- Return the result --->
  <cfreturn result>
</cffunction>


<!--- Method: returns the login info for current user --->
<cffunction name="getUserInfo" access="public"
➡returntype="LoginInfoObject">
  <cfreturn Session.LoginInfo>
</cffunction>
```

continues

```
<!--- Method: logs the user out --->
<cffunction name="logout" access="public" returntype="void">
  <cfset Session.LoginInfo = CreateObject("component",
  ➥"LoginInfoObject")>
</cffunction>

</cfcomponent>
```

Listing 10.1 relies on a very short helper CFC called `LoginInfoObject`, which simply declares the properties returned by the `getUserInfo()` method. The contents of `LoginInfoObject.cfc` are as follows:

```
<cfcomponent>
  <!--- Component properties --->
  <cfproperty name="isLoggedIn" type="boolean">
  <cfproperty name="idUser" type="numeric">
  <cfproperty name="rightList" type="string">
  <cfproperty name="loggedInSince" type="string">
  <cfproperty name="sessionID" type="string">

  <!--- Populate properties with default values --->
  <cfset this.isLoggedIn = false>
  <cfset this.idUser = -1>
  <cfset this.rightList = "">
  <cfset this.loggedInSince = "">
  <cfset this.sessionID = "">
</cfcomponent>
```

Listing 10.2 shows the code for the ColdFusion version of the LoginXmlSource page. It calls the methods created in Listing 10.1 internally, exposing the results as `<response>` packets, as discussed in the previous section.

LISTING 10.2   LoginXmlSource.cfm—XML Serving Page (ColdFusion Version)

```
<!--- URL "action" may be getUserInfo, attemptLogin, or logout --->
<cfparam name="action" type="string" default="getUserInfo">

<!--- Create instance of LoginManager class --->
<cfset lm = CreateObject("component", "LoginManager")>

<!--- Different processing depending on processing --->
<cfswitch expression="#action#">

  <!--- If user is attempting to log in --->
```

```
  <cfcase value="attemptLogin">
    <!--- Get username/password from incoming <credentials/> --->
    <cfset credentialXML = XmlParse(GetHttpRequestData().content)>
    <cfset username = credentialXML.XmlRoot.XmlAttributes.username>
    <cfset password = credentialXML.XmlRoot.XmlAttributes.password>
    <!--- Attempt actual login operation --->
    <cfset success = lm.attemptLogin(username, password)>
    <!--- Compose XML reply --->
    <cfxml variable="resultXML">
      <cfoutput>
        <response isLoggedIn="#success#"/>
      </cfoutput>
    </cfxml>
  </cfcase>

  <!--- If the user is logging out --->
  <cfcase value="logout">
    <!--- Perform actual logout operation --->
    <cfset lm.logout()>
    <!--- Compose XML reply --->
    <cfxml variable="resultXML">
      <response isLoggedIn="false"/>
    </cfxml>
  </cfcase>

  <!--- If the user's current login status is being requested --->
  <cfcase value="getUserInfo">
    <!--- Get current login status --->
    <cfset info = lm.getUserInfo()>

    <!--- Compose XML reply --->
    <cfxml variable="resultXML">
      <cfoutput>
        <response isLoggedIn="#info.isLoggedIn#">
          <idUser>#info.idUser#</idUser>
          <rightList>#info.rightList#</rightList>
          <loggedInSince>#info.loggedInSince#</loggedInSince>
          <session-id>#info.sessionID#</session-id>
        </response>
      </cfoutput>
    </cfxml>
  </cfcase>
</cfswitch>

<!--- Turn off debugging output if appropriate --->
<cfsetting showdebugoutput="No" enablecfoutputonly="Yes">
```

continues

LISTING 10.2   LoginXmlSource.cfm—XML Serving Page (ColdFusion Version) (Continued)

```
<!--- Set content type for our response to the client (Flash) --->
<cfcontent type="text/xml" reset="yes">
<!--- Return the composed XML to the client --->
<cfoutput>#ToString(resultXML)#</cfoutput>
```

The ASP.NET Version

Listing 10.3 shows the ASP.NET code for the `LoginManager` class that was described in Table 10.2. The class is implemented using the C# language (though it could have been coded with VBScript just as easily). It also contains the declaration for `LoginInfoObject` as a nested class.

> **NOTE**
>
> If you are using ASP.NET, you must set up this chapter's folder as an application, using the IIS Manager console. Right-click the folder (`chapter10`) in the IIS Manager, choose Properties, and then press the Create button next to Application Name (under the Directory tab). Use `chapter10` as the application name. This will cause IIS to see the web.config file in this folder, which turns on session variables.
>
> IIS will also see the `bin` folder, which contains a DLL for the `LoginManager` and `LoginInfoObject` classes discussed in this section. If you make change to this file, you will need to recompile the corresponding LoginManager.dll file in the `bin` folder for this chapter.

LISTING 10.3   LoginManager.cs—.NET Version of LoginManager

```
using System;
using System.Data;
using System.Data.Odbc;
using System.Web.Services;
using System.Web.SessionState;

public class LoginManager {

  public bool attemptLogin(HttpSessionState Session, string username,
string password) {

    // This is the result value that will be passed back
    bool result = false;

    // Open a connection to the example database
    OdbcConnection conn = new OdbcConnection("DSN=VenueDB");
    conn.Open();

    // Query the database for information
    string sql = "SELECT idUser, sRightList, idUser" +
      " FROM Users " +
```

```
        " WHERE sUsername = '" + username + "'" +
        " AND sPassword = '" + password + "'";
    OdbcCommand cmd = new OdbcCommand(sql, conn);
    OdbcDataReader reader = cmd.ExecuteReader();

    // If a record was returned
    if (reader.Read()) {
      // Create a new LoginInfoObject
      LoginInfoObject loginInfo = new LoginInfoObject();
      loginInfo.isLoggedIn = true;
      loginInfo.idUser = reader.GetInt32(0);
      loginInfo.rightList = reader.GetString(1);
      loginInfo.loggedInSince = DateTime.Now;
      loginInfo.sessionID = Session.SessionID;

      // Store the object in the session scope
      Session["LoginInfo"] = loginInfo;

      // Consider the user logged-in
      result = true;
    } else {
      // Login failed--log any existing users out too
      logout(Session);
    }

    // Done with the database connection
    conn.Close();

    // Return the result
    return result;
  }

  public LoginInfoObject getUserInfo(HttpSessionState Session) {
    // If the user is currently logged in
    if (Session["LoginInfo"] != null) {
      return (LoginInfoObject)Session["LoginInfo"];

    // If user is not logged in, return a dummy info object
    } else {
      LoginInfoObject temp = new LoginInfoObject();
      temp.isLoggedIn = false;
      temp.sessionID = Session.SessionID;
      return temp;
    }
  }
```

continues

LISTING 10.3   LoginManager.cs—.NET Version of LoginManager (Continued)

```
  public void logout(HttpSessionState Session) {
    Session.Remove("LoginInfo");
  }
}

public class LoginInfoObject {
  public bool isLoggedIn = false;
  public int idUser = -1;
  public string rightList = "";
  public DateTime loggedInSince;
  public string sessionID = "";
}
```

Listing 10.4 shows the code for the ASP.NET version of the XML-serving page that was discussed in the "Understanding How the XML-Serving Pages Work" section earlier in this chapter. The page is coded with Visual Basic syntax for the sake of variety; you could use C#, JScript.NET, or another language just as easily.

LISTING 10.4   LoginXmlSource.aspx—XML Serving Page (ASP.NET Version)

```
<%@ page
  language="VBScript"
  contentType="text/xml"
  debug="true" %>

<%@ import namespace="System.Xml" %>

<%
  ' URL "action" may be getUserInfo, attemptLogin, or logout
  Dim action As String = Request.Params("action")
  If action = "" Then action = "getUserInfo"

  ' Create instance of LoginManager class
  Dim lm As LoginManager = new LoginManager()

  ' If user is attempting to log in
  If action = "attemptLogin" Then
    ' Get username/password from incoming <credentials/>
    Dim reader As XmlTextReader = new
    ➥XmlTextReader(request.InputStream)
    reader.MoveToContent()
    reader.MoveToAttribute("username")
    Dim username = reader.Value
    reader.MoveToAttribute("password")
    Dim password = reader.Value
```

```
    ' Attempt actual login operation
    Dim success As Boolean = lm.attemptLogin(Session, username, pass-
word)
    Response.write("<response isLoggedIn=""" + LCase(success) + """/>")

  ' If the user's current login status is being requested
  ElseIf action = "getUserInfo" Then
    ' Get current login status
    Dim info As LoginInfoObject = lm.getUserInfo(Session)

    ' Compose XML reply
    Response.write("<response isLoggedIn=""" + LCase(info.isLoggedIn) +
    ➥""" >")
    Response.write("<idUser>" + info.idUser.toString() + "</idUser>")
    Response.write("<rightList>" + info.rightList + "</rightList>")
    Response.write("<loggedInSince>" +
    ➥info.loggedInSince.toLongTimeString() + "</loggedInSince>")
    Response.write("<session-id>" + info.sessionID + "</session-id>")
    Response.write("</response>")

  ' If the user is logging out
  ElseIf action = "logout" Then
    lm.logout(Session)
    Response.write("<response isLoggedIn=""false""/>")

  End If
%>
```

The Java Version

Listing 10.5 shows the ASP.NET code for the `LoginManager` class that was described in Table 10.2. If your JSP engine does not provide dynamic compilation, you will need to recompile the corresponding LoginManager.class file if you make any changes to this listing.

NOTE

If you are using Java, you may need to add the Login folder to your JSP/Servlet engine's classpath so that the `LoginInfoObject.class` and `LoginManager.class` classes are visible to your JSP compiler. Some JSP engines might compile the classes for you automatically from the Java source files; adjust the classpath if you get error messages about the classes not being found. (If you are using JRun, you can adjust the classpath in the Settings page of the JRun Management Console.) Alternatively, you can copy the classes to a folder that is already in the engine's classpath.

LISTING 10.5   LoginManager.java—Java Version of LoginManager

```java
import java.sql.*;
import java.text.DateFormat;

public class LoginManager {

  public boolean attemptLogin(LoginInfoObject info, String username,
String password)
     throws java.sql.SQLException, java.lang.ClassNotFoundException {

     // This is the value that we will return to caller
     boolean result = false;

     // This is the SQL query statement we will use to fetch data
     String sql = " SELECT idUser, sRightList FROM Users" +
       " WHERE sUsername = '" + username + "' " +
       " AND sPassword = '" + password + "' ";

     // Execute the SQL query against the example database
     Class.forName("sun.jdbc.odbc.JdbcOdbcDriver");
     Connection con = DriverManager.getConnection("jdbc:odbc:VenueDB");
     ResultSet rs  = con.createStatement().executeQuery(sql);

     // If a record was retrieved from the database
     if (rs.next()) {
       // Place relevant data in LoginInfoObject structure
       info.isLoggedIn = true;
       info.idUser = rs.getInt(1);
       info.rightList = rs.getString(2);
       java.util.Date now = new java.util.Date();
       info.loggedInSince =
DateFormat.getTimeInstance(DateFormat.LONG).format(now);
       // Consider user logged in
       result = true;

     // If the login fails
     } else {
       // Consider any previously-logged-in user invalid
       logout(info);
     }

     // Return the result
     return result;
  }
```

```
  // This method simply returns its argument
  // It is provided for consistency with other servers's versions
  public LoginInfoObject getUserInfo(LoginInfoObject info) {
    return info;
  }


  public void logout(LoginInfoObject info) {
    info.isLoggedIn = false;
    info.idUser = -1;
    info.rightList = null;
    info.loggedInSince = "";
    info.sessionID = null;
  }
}
```

Listing 10.6 shows the code for a JSP version of the XML-serving page that was discussed in the "Understanding How the XML-Serving Pages Work" section earlier in this chapter. This implementation makes itself responsible for maintaining an instance of the LoginInfoObject class in the session scope, passing the instance to the LoginManager class with each method call:

LISTING 10.6   LoginXmlSource.jsp—XML Serving Page (JSP Version)

```
<%@ page
  import="java.sql.*,javax.xml.parsers.*,org.w3c.dom.*"
  contentType="text/xml"
%>

<%
  // URL "action" var may be getUserInfo, attemptLogin, or logout
  String action = request.getParameter("action");
  if (action == null) action = "getUserInfo";

  // Keep an instance of LoginInfoObject in the session scope
  // Put a fresh one there now if it doesn't exist already
  if (session.getAttribute("loginInfo") ==  null) {
    session.setAttribute("loginInfo", new LoginInfoObject());
  }
  LoginInfoObject info =
(LoginInfoObject)session.getAttribute("loginInfo");

  // Create instance of LoginManager class
  LoginManager lm = new LoginManager();

  // *** action=getUserInfo ***
```

continues

LISTING 10.6 LoginXmlSource.jsp—XML Serving Page (JSP Version) (Continued)

```
if (action.compareTo("getUserInfo") == 0) {
  out.write("<response isLoggedIn=\"" + info.isLoggedIn + "\" >");
  out.write("<idUser>" + info.idUser + "</idUser>");
  out.write("<rightList>" + info.rightList + "</rightList>");
  out.write("<loggedInSince>" + info.loggedInSince +
  ➥"</loggedInSince>");
  out.write("<session-id>" + info.rightList + "</session-id>");
  out.write("</response>");

// *** action=attemptLogin ***
} else if (action.compareTo("attemptLogin") == 0) {
  // Parse the incoming <credentials/> element
  DocumentBuilderFactory df = DocumentBuilderFactory.newInstance();
  DocumentBuilder builder = df.newDocumentBuilder();
  Document doc = builder.parse(request.getInputStream());
  // Perform actual login attempt operation
  String user = doc.getDocumentElement().getAttribute("username");
  String pswd = doc.getDocumentElement().getAttribute("password");
  boolean success = lm.attemptLogin(info, user, pswd);
  // Return XML fragment reflecting whether user is now logged in
  out.write("<response isLoggedIn=\"" + success + "\" />");

// *** action=logout ***
} else if (action.compareTo("logout") == 0) {
  // Log the user out
  lm.logout(info);
  // Return XML fragment reflecting whether user is now logged in
  out.write("<response isLoggedIn=\"false\" />");

}
%>
```

The code for the helper `LoginInfoObject` class is extremely simple, as follows:

```
public class LoginInfoObject {
  public boolean isLoggedIn = false;
  public int idUser = -1;
  public String rightList = null;
  public String loggedInSince = null;
  public String sessionID = null;
}
```

The Web-Based Login Form Pages

This chapter's example files include ColdFusion, ASP.NET, and Java implementations of a web-based login page, named loginDemo.cfm, loginDemo.aspx, and loginDemo.jsp, respectively. Each version uses the `LoginManager` class internally to check whether the current user has logged in previously. If not, it displays a web-based form by including a static HTML file called WebBasedLoginForm.html, which uses standard `<form>` syntax to collect a username and password from the user. When the user logs in successfully, the login demo page includes SecuredContent.html, which displays the SecuredContent.swf movie that will be discussed in the next section of this chapter.

For the most part, the server-side code for this page is self-explanatory, using the same `LoginManager` calls internally as the XML-server pages that were shown in the previous three sections of this chapter. Because they are largely redundant, they aren't shown in printed form in this book. Feel free to take a look at the files themselves if you are interested in how they work.

The Client-Side Code

Now that you are familiar with the server-side code used for the login example, let's take a look at what's involved on the client. Go ahead and open up the SecuredContent.fla document, which is included with this chapter's example files. You'll see that the example contains hardly anything at all. There are a few text fields on the Stage for displaying information about the user's login status. The fields are named `txtUserID`, `txtRightList`, `txtSessionID`, and `txtLoggedInSince`.

The document's Library contains two movie clip symbols called `SecureItem1` and `SecureItem2`, which are placeholders for some kind of sensitive content that should be shown only to authorized users. The symbols each have linkage identifiers so that they can be instantiated through script at runtime. These simple symbols don't provide any interactivity or anything fun or interesting at this point, but they could obviously be replaced with anything you want. You could also choose to load external SWFs instead of using linked symbols from the library.

The only ActionScript in the movie is in Frame 1, as shown in Listing 10.7.

> **NOTE**
>
> The ActionScript listings in this section are a bit more challenging that the ones you've seen in preceding chapters. Don't be discouraged. As usual, when you break it down line by line, this code turns out to be pretty simple conceptually.

LISTING 10.7   ActionScript Code in Frame 1 of SecuredContent.fla

```
import mx.managers.PopUpManager;
import mx.containers.Window;

// This function executes when this SWF first loads
this.onLoad = function() {
  // Create new popup window, with login form movie as its content
  var loginPopup = PopUpManager.createPopUp(_root, Window, true,
    {contentPath:"loginForm.swf",
     title:"Security",
     _x:100,
     _y:100,
     _width:250,
     _height:120});

  // This function fires when the user is confirmed as logged in
  // (the onLogin mock-event is fired by the LoginMovieClip class)
  loginPopup.onLogin = function(userInfo) {

    // If the user has the right to see certain content...
    if (userInfo.hasRight("secureItem1")) {
      PopUpManager.createPopUp(_root, Window, false,
      {contentPath:"SecureItem1",
       title:"Secure Item #1",
       _x:100,
       _y:50,
       _width:292,
       _height:175});
    }

    // If the user has the right to see certain content...
    if (userInfo.hasRight("secureItem2")) {
      PopUpManager.createPopUp(_root, Window, false,
      {contentPath:"SecureItem2",
       title:"Secure Item #2",
       _x:200,
       _y:100,
       _width:292,
       _height:175});
```

```
   }

   // Display information about logged-in user session
   _root.txtUserID.text = userInfo.idUser;
   _root.txtRightList.text = userInfo.rightList;
   _root.txtSessionID.text = userInfo.sessionID;
   _root.txtLoggedInSince.text = userInfo.loggedInSince;

 };
}
```

Because it's attached to the movie's `onLoad` event, this code will execute when the SWF first loads in the Flash Player. The first action this code takes is to display a modal dialog box window with the static `PopupManager.createPopup()` method. An external movie called loginForm.swf is displayed within the dialog box; it's this external movie that contains the actual username and password fields. (You will see the code for this movie shortly.)

This is the first time you're seeing the `createPopup()` method, which is new in Flash MX 2004. As you can see, the syntax is somewhat bizarre, but it's a very useful method nonetheless. The first three arguments represent the parent for the window object (which is a movie clip at the end of the day), the class to use for the new window (which could be a subclass of your own creation if you wished), and a Boolean value that indicates whether the pop-up window should be modal. The fourth argument is a set of initialization properties, which you can use to specify any of the properties of the `Window` class. The code in Listing 10.7 sets the `contentPath` (the relative path to the external SWF to display in the pop-up) and `title` (a string to display in the pop-up's title bar) properties. It also sets the `_x`, `_y`, `_width`, and `_height` properties, which control the pop-up's size and position on the Stage.

NOTE

The `Window` class also provides `x`, `y`, `width`, and `height` properties (which inherit from the `mx.core.UIObject` class that ships with Flash), which are roughly equivalent to the `_x`, `_y`, `_width`, and `_height` properties (which are properties of the intrinsic `MovieClip` class exposed by the Flash Player). The idea behind the new properties is to put a more developer-friendly face on the classic `MovieClip` properties. Feel free to use them when working with components such as `Window` if you find them easier to work with or remember.

Personally, I prefer to use the underscored properties because they can be used consistently with components and regular movie clips, but the nonunderscored properties have certain advantages that are too subtle to discuss here. Consult the Components Dictionary portion of the Flash documentation for details.

When you put all that together, you get one odd-looking line of code, but it sure packs a punch. The result is a modal pop-up window within the main movie. The pop-up behaves much like a regular operating system dialog box. You can drag it around by its title bar, it floats above any other content in the Flash Player, and nothing else in the movie can be interacted with until the window is closed.

NOTE

Before you can use the `Window` class, you must add the `Window` component to your document's library. To do so, drag an instance of the component from the Components panel onto your document's Stage, and then delete the instance. The component will now show up in your document's Library, which is what is needed for instances of the `Window` class to be created successfully at runtime.

For details about the `Window` class and the `PopupManager.createPopup()` method, refer to the ActionScript Dictionary portion of the Flash documentation.

The rest of Listing 10.7 creates a handler for an event called `onLogin`, which will be fired by the loginForm.swf movie when the user successfully logs in. The event will pass a single argument to the handler, which is an instance of the custom `UserInfo` class. You'll see the code for `UserInfo` shortly (when you get to the UserInfo.as file later in this chapter), but for now, all you need to know is that it exposes a method called `hasRight()`. This method returns a Boolean value that indicates whether the current user has the specified right (or, if you prefer, privilege or role).

In this case, the `hasRight()` method is used to display the `SecureItem1` and `SecureItem2` movie clips from the document's Library if the user has rights named `secureItem1` and `secureItem2`, respectively, in the Users table of the example database. These placeholders for secure content are displayed in their own windows, again via the `PopUpManager.createPopUp()` method. These windows are specified as non-modal (by specifying `false` as the method's first argument), which means that the user can interact with either window as he or she wishes. The user can click each window's title bar to bring it to the forefront and can drag the title bar to move the window around on the Stage. The end result is similar to a multiple document interface (MDI) application in a native Windows application.

The `UserInfo` class also exposes properties called `idUser`, `rightList`, `sessionID`, and `loggedInSince`, which correspond to the properties exposed by the `LoginInfoObject` data structure class on the server side. In this example, these properties are simply displayed in corresponding text fields at the top of the Stage to prove that the session-based information can be retrieved successfully by Flash.

Next, take a look at the loginForm.fla document. The document's Library contains a movie clip symbol called `LoginClip`. The clip contains two `XMLConnector` components named `xcGetUserInfo` and `xcAttemptLogin`, each of which has been configured to contact the XML-serving pages that were discussed earlier in this chapter. The clip also contains a text field named `txtStatus`, which is used to display status messages to the user. There isn't any ActionScript code in this clip, but it is linked to an ActionScript 2.0 class called `LoginMovieClip`. A single instance of this clip has been placed on the main Stage for the document, with an instance name of `mcLogin`.

The `LoginClip` symbol contains an instance of a second movie clip called `LoginFormClip`, with an instance name of `mcForm`. This second clip contains two `TextInput` components, called `tiUsername` and `tiPassword`, and a button named `btnEnter`. These components have been placed in their own movie clip so that their visibility can be easily turned on and off by setting the nested clip's `_visible` property.

Listing 10.8 shows the code for the `LoginMovieClip` class, which is a descendant of the built-in `MovieClip` class. This class powers the text fields and components in the `LoginClip` and `LoginFormClip` symbols.

LISTING 10.8   LoginMovieClip.as—The LoginMovieClip ActionScript 2.0 Class

```
import mx.controls.Alert;

dynamic class LoginMovieClip extends MovieClip {

    // Base URL for XML exchanges
    // Can be set to empty string if testing in Flash IDE not needed
    var urlBase = "http://localhost/venue/chapter10/Login/";
    // For ColdFusion
    var urlGetUserInfo:String  = urlBase +
    ➥"LoginXmlSource.cfm?action=getUserInfo";
    var urlAttemptLogin:String = urlBase +
    ➥"LoginXmlSource.cfm?action=attemptLogin";
    // For ASP.NET
    //var urlGetUserInfo:String  = urlBase +
    ➥"LoginXmlSource.aspx?action=getUserInfo";
    //var urlAttemptLogin:String = urlBase +
    ➥"LoginXmlSource.aspx?action=attemptLogin";
    // For Java/JSP
```

continues

```
//var urlGetUserInfo:String  = urlBase +
➥"LoginXmlSource.jsp?action=getUserInfo";
//var urlAttemptLogin:String = urlBase +
➥"LoginXmlSource.jsp?action=attemptLogin";

// This function executes when the movie clip first loads
function onLoad() {
  // Make this movie be invisible when it first loads
  // (the surrounding popup window box will still be visible)
  this.mcForm._visible = false;

  // Set up XMLConnector components
  this.xcGetUserInfo.URL = urlGetUserInfo;
  this.xcAttemptLogin.URL = urlAttemptLogin;
  // Hook up event listeners
  this.xcGetUserInfo.addEventListener("result", getUserInfo_Result);
  this.xcGetUserInfo.addEventListener("status", xmlConnector_Status);
  this.xcAttemptLogin.addEventListener("result",
  ➥attemptLogin_Result);
  this.xcAttemptLogin.addEventListener("status",
  ➥xmlConnector_Status);
  this.mcForm.btnEnter.addEventListener("click", btnEnter_Click);

  // Prefill the username field with the last username, if available
  var so = SharedObject.getLocal("loginPopup");
  if (so.data.lastUsername != undefined) {
    this.mcForm.tiUsername.text = so.data.lastUsername;
  }

  // Get user's current info, including whether they are logged in
  trace('Triggering getUserInfo() on the server');
   showStatus("checking your status...");
  this.xcGetUserInfo.trigger();
}


// This function fires when XML is received from the server
function getUserInfo_Result(ev) {
  // This is the XMLNode for the <response/> element from server
  var xnResponse = ev.target.results.firstChild;

  // If server reports that the user is currently logged in
  if (xnResponse.attributes.isLoggedIn.toLowerCase() == "true") {
    // Construct new UserInfo object
```

```
      // The object exposes a hasRight() method
      var userInfo:UserInfo = new UserInfo(xnResponse);

      // Call the onLogin() function (if any) attached to popup window
      // The function can do whatever it wants with the user info
      this._parent._parent._parent.onLogin(userInfo);

      // Close the popup window that contains this movie
      // (this movie instance will also be destroyed)
      trace("User is logged in; closing popup window.");
       _parent.showStatus("you are logged in");
      this._parent._parent._parent.deletePopUp();

  // If the user is not currently logged in
  } else {
      // Make this movie visible, so user can enter username/password
      trace("The user is not logged in; showing login form");
       _parent.showStatus("you are not logged in");
      _parent.mcForm._visible = true;

  }
}


// This function fires when the user clicks the Enter button
function btnEnter_Click() {
  // Compose a XML packet that contains username and password
  var username:String = _parent.tiUsername.text;
  var password:String = _parent.tiPassword.text;
  var xmlParams = new XML('<credentials username="'
    + username + '" password="' + password + '"/>');

  // Send the packet to the server for user verification
   _parent._parent.showStatus("sending your credentials...");
  _parent._parent.xcAttemptLogin.params = xmlParams;
  _parent._parent.xcAttemptLogin.trigger();
}


// This function picks up errors in XML exchanges
function xmlConnector_Status(ev) {
  if (ev.code == "Fault") {
    _parent.showStatus("error: " + ev.code.faultcode);
  }
}
```

continues

```
// This function fires when XML for a login attempt is received
function attemptLogin_Result(ev) {
  // This is the XMLNode for the <response/> element from server
  var xnResponse = ev.target.results.firstChild;

  // If the server reports that the login was successful
  if (xnResponse.attributes["isLoggedIn"].toLowerCase() == "true") {
    // Persist the credentials in a local shared object
    var so = SharedObject.getLocal("loginPopup");
    so.clear();
    so.data.lastUsername = _parent.mcForm.tiUsername.text;
    so.flush();

    // Trigger getUserInfo() on server
    trace("Login successful; re-triggering getUserInfo() method");
    _parent.showStatus("login successful");
    _parent.xcGetUserInfo.trigger();

  // If the server reports that the login was unsuccessful
  } else {
    _parent.showStatus("login failed");
    trace("Login failed:" + xnResponse.attributes["isLoggedIn"]);
    Alert.show("Verify password and try again.", "Login Failed");

  }
}

// Simple function to display a status message on-screen
function showStatus(msg:String) {
  this.txtStatus.text = msg;
}
}
```

The first lines of this listing establish string properties called urlBase, urlGetUserInfo, and urlAttemptLogin, which are used to provide the appropriate URL for the XML-serving page on your server. Three sets of lines are provided for ColdFusion, ASP.NET, and Java; comment out the lines that don't pertain to the server you are using.

The onLoad function executes when the clip first loads (as used in this chapter, that means when the loginForm.swf movie appears in the pop-up window spawned by Listing 10.7). Within the onLoad block, the _visible property of the mcForm clip is set to false, which means that the user-interface elements (the username and password fields and so on) will not appear right away. The pop-up window is still visible; it just appears to be mostly empty for a moment as this listing performs its initial tasks.

Next, the `addEventListener()` method is used to hook up some of the other functions in this listing to various events. The `btnEnter_Click` method will execute when the Enter button in the login form is clicked (visible in Figure 10.3), and the `getUserInfo_Result` and `attemptLogin_Result` methods will execute each time the `getUserInfo()` and `attemptLogin()` methods are called on the server (via the XML-serving page discussed earlier in this chapter), respectively.

Next, a local shared object instance is used to prefill the username field with the user's last entries, if available. This portion of the listing is very similar to the code snippets in the "Persisting Data with Local Shared Objects" section earlier in this chapter. Finally, the `trigger()` method of the `xcGetUserInfo` connector is called, which causes the Flash player to contact the server for information about the user's current login status.

> **NOTE**
>
> Remember that local shared objects are stored in plain text on the client's drive. Only you can decide whether it is appropriate to store a username or password as a local shared object for your application.

When the `xcGetUserInfo` call completes, the `getUserInfo_Result()` method will execute automatically. Within this function block, `ev.target` refers to the connector that is firing the `result` event (in this case, the `xcGetUserInfo` component). Therefore, `ev.target.results` refers to the XML document that was returned by the server, which in turn means that `ev.target.results. firstChild.attributes.isLoggedIn` will be a `true` or `false` value (as a string) that indicates whether the user has already logged in at some prior moment during the web session. A convenience variable called `xnResponse` is used in this part of the code to make it easier to refer to `ev.target.results. firstChild` (which corresponds to the `<response>` element returned by the server).

If the user is already logged in, a new `UserInfo` object is created using the `new` keyword. The result is an object that holds the data about the user contained within the `<response>` element from the server, with the addition of a method called `hasRight()` that can be used by whatever Flash movie is making use of the login form (see Listing 10.7). You will see the source code for the `UserInfo` object in a moment (see Listing 10.9).

The next line might look a bit strange to you because of the three `_parent` references in a row. Because this function is an event handler for `xcGetUserInfo`, `this` refers to the connector, `this._parent` refers to the `LoginClip` movie clip, `this._parent._parent` refers to the main timeline of loginForm.swf, and `this._parent._parent._parent` refers to the pop-up window that loaded the SWF (whew!). The end result is that this is the syntax needed to call the `onLogin()` function that was attached to the pop-up window in Listing 10.7.

NOTE

If you remove the `onLogin` function from Listing 10.7, your action won't cause Listing 10.8 to stop working. If there is no `onLogin` function attached to the pop-up window, `this._parent._parent._parent.onLogin` will resolve to `undefined`, which just means that nothing will happen when this line is encountered. This behavior gives you a simple but effective technique for firing your own events from within the code for a class.

There are other, more sophisticated means of firing your own events; refer to the `dispatchEvent()` method in the Flash documentation for details.

The final line of code in this `if` block calls the `deletePopUp()` method of the pop-up window. This method is available for any window that was originally created with `PopUpManager.createPopUp()`. Please refer to the ActionScript Dictionary for details about the `createPopUp()` and `deletePopUp()` methods.

If the user is not currently logged in, the `else` condition kicks in, which makes the actual login UI elements visible. The user can now enter his or her username and password. When the user clicks the Enter button, the `xcAttemptLogin` connector is triggered, which causes the username and password to be sent to the server for validation. The server will respond with a `<response>` element that contains `true` if the user was logged in successfully and `false` if not (see the "Understanding How the XML-Serving Pages Work" section earlier in this chapter for details).

NOTE

The username and password are passed to the server in XML form as a simple packet that contains a single `<credentials/>` element. If the username and password might contain quotation marks, ampersands, or other characters that have special meaning to XML, they would need to be escaped properly; that step is skipped here for simplicity's sake.

When the server responds with its answer, the `attemptLogin_Result()` function executes; within the body of the function, `ev.target.results.firstChild` will hold the `<response>` element from the server, which in turn contains the Boolean value returned by the server. If the user was logged in successfully, the user's username is saved in a local shared object so that it can be prefilled automatically the next time the user needs to log in. Then the `xcGetUserInfo` connector is triggered (for the second time), which should cause the pop-up window to fire its `onLoad` pseudo-event and then close.

If the username and password were not valid, the `mx.controls.Alert` class is used to display a Login Failed message to the user (see Figure 10.4). The `Alert` class is similar to the `PopUpManager` class that was used in Listing 10.7; you can read all about it in the ActionScript Dictionary portion of the Flash Documentation. That said, its use is self-explanatory when your intention is to display a simple message with an OK button, which is all that is needed in this case.

NOTE

Before you can use the `Alert` class, you must add the Alert component to your document's Library. To do so, drag an instance of the component from the Components panel onto your document's Stage, and then delete the instance. The component will now show up in your document's Library, which is what is needed for the `Alert.show()` method to work properly at runtime.

FIGURE 10.4   The `Alert` class provides a simple means to display pop-up messages.

The final listing for this chapter (Listing 10.9) is the ActionScript class file for the `UserInfo` class. This custom class was designed to be the client-side counterpart to the `LoginInfoObject` data structure class that is used on the server side to track the user's login status at the session level (see Table 10.2). Its constructor accepts a single argument, which is assumed to be a reference to the `<response>` XML packet method result from the server. The `isLoggedIn`, `idUser`, `loggedInSince`, and `sessionID` properties are copied verbatim from the XML to the new instance of the class.

Rather than merely storing the `rightList` property as a comma-separated string (which is how it is received from the server), the property is split into an array and then looped over in a `for` loop. The result is that the class's private `rights` property will end up holding a property for each right that the user has been granted. Therefore, the `hasRight()` method—which is used by Listing 10.7—can execute quickly and easily because all it needs to do is test for the existence of the corresponding property within `this.rights`. This chapter's example calls `hasRight()` only once after each login, but in a movie that needed to check for a number of different rights (potentially over and over again), it becomes efficient to convert the comma-separated list into an associative array in this manner.

Listing 10.9   UserInfo.as—The `UserInfo` ActionScript 2.0 Class

```
class UserInfo {
  public var isLoggedIn:Boolean;
  public var idUser:Number;
  public var loggedInSince:String;
  public var sessionID:String;
  public var rightList:String;
  private var rights:Object = new Object;

  // Constructor
  public function UserInfo(xnResponse) {
    // Assume that the object from the server has these properties
    this.isLoggedIn = xnResponse.attributes["isLoggedIn"];
    this.idUser = xnResponse.getChildText("idUser");
    this.rightList = xnResponse.getChildText("rightList");
    this.loggedInSince = xnResponse.getChildText("loggedInSince");
    this.sessionID = xnResponse.getChildText("session-id");

    // Split the rightList from the server into an array
    var arRights:Array = this.rightList.split(",");
    // For each right, create property on this object's rights object
    for (var i:Number = 0; i < arRights.length; i++) {
      this.rights[arRights[i]] = true;
    }
  }

  // Returns whether the user has the right with the given name
  public function hasRight(rightName:String):Boolean {
    return this.rights[rightName] != undefined;
  }
}
```

Testing It Out

You can now test out the example for this chapter using your browser. To prove that the example works correctly, follow these steps:

1. Open the login demo page in your browser by navigating to `http://localhost/venue/chapter10/Login/loginDemo.aspx` (replacing the file extension with .cfm or .jsp as appropriate).

2. Log in using the web-based form (shown previously in Figure 10.2). Unless you have edited the data in the Users table, you can use either **nate** or **winona** as the username and **flash** as the password.

3. After you log in with the web-based form, the SecuredContent.swf movie displays. Its own Security pop-up dialog box will display momentarily as the movie verifies your login status with the server. The pop-up should then close, replaced with new windows that display whatever content you are privy to (based on your username). Information about your login status is also displayed across the top of the user interface (see Figure 10.5).

4. Use the File > New Window command in your browser to open a new window, and navigate the new window to `http://localhost/venue/chapter10/Login/SecuredContent.html`. Note that you are still considered logged in by Flash, even though this is a static HTML page.

5. Return to the first browser window and log out by adding a `logout=yes` parameter to the URL in your browser's address bar. The application should respond by redisplaying the web-based login form. Don't log back in.

6. Go back to the second browser window (the static page with the Flash movie on it) and reload the page. Note that Flash now knows that you are logged out, and it presents its own login dialog box. Go ahead and log in.

7. Return to the first browser window, remove the `logout=yes` parameter from the URL, and reload the page. Note that this page understands that you have logged in again, even though you did so through a static page.

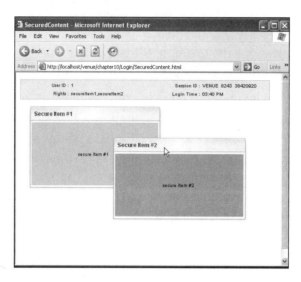

FIGURE 10.5   Session variables on the server power this Flash-based interface on the client.

Feel free to play around with logging in and out. The example simply proves that session data can be shared between Flash and your dynamic, server-side code, even if the Flash movies reside on static HTML pages.

Summary

This chapter discussed a variety of methods and techniques related to session and client state management. First, you learned how to pass values through Flash in the same basic way you pass values through links and form values in traditional web pages. Next, you learned how Flash movies and traditional web pages can share the same per-session scope offered by your server's session management features. After a brief discussion of the role of browser cookies in Flash-enabled applications, you learned about local shared objects, which are similar to (but more powerful than) browser cookies. Finally, you took a look at how several of the stateful techniques that were discussed can be combined to track the login status of your users.

CHAPTER 11

BUILDING BETTER FORMS WITH FLASH

I'm sure you are familiar with building web-based forms with HTML. You know the drill: set up a form container with a pair of `<form>` tags, add visual data-entry elements with tags such as `<input>`, `<textarea>`, and `<select>`, and add a Submit button so that the user can post the form. You then build a server-side page that validates the submissions and processes them accordingly.

They may not be fancy, but the amazing thing about HTML-based forms is that they are perfectly adequate for many, many situations. That's really kind of amazing, given their age. After all, HTML forms have barely changed at all since their introduction way back when. Think about it—we've all been using the same basic form elements for years now, via the same HTML tags that were supported by the very earliest web browsers. That's proof that plain old HTML forms must be at least reasonably suited to the task.

But let's face it—HTML forms don't work well all the time. I mean, how many times have you wanted to add one of the following to a form:

- A tree control, like the one in your native operating system that represents your computer's directory structure
- A calendar control that allows the user to pick a date quickly and easily
- A drop-down list that fills itself with values from the server in real time, based on some kind of criteria
- A text field that restricts the user to typing a phone number or email address with the proper formatting and without any illegal characters
- A spin control that allows the users to select a whole number, but limits them to a minimum or maximum value and doesn't allow them to type letters or some other junk instead
- A combo box that lets the user pick from a drop-down list of values, or—get this—*type a new value* (Ugh, if I could count the times I've been forced to use a <select> box with a text input field marked "Other" next to it....)
- Or, more simply, how about a text area that doesn't let the user type an unlimited number of characters?

Sure, some of the preceding control types can be created using a mix of the standard form elements, JavaScript, and so-called Dynamic HTML (DHTML). But some can't. Even the ones that can are subject to the usual concerns about browser and version compatibility, and they can more or less be counted on to break if the user's browser (or firewall) has been configured to disallow JavaScript code.

NOTE

The XForms specification might change the basic set of form controls available to non-Flash web pages, but none of the major browsers support XForms at the time of this writing. It's worth noting that one could create a Flash-based implementation of XForms that would work in any browser that supports Flash; building such a creature would be an interesting learning exercise. See www.w3.org for details about XForms.

Flash as Form Presentation Engine

You guessed it. Flash can be an ideal mechanism for designing better, more sophisticated data-entry forms and delivering them to users.

As usual, this book isn't going to try to convince you to use Flash just for the sake of using it. If a form would actually provide a better experience for your users if it were free of the limitations of the basic HTML form elements, then by all means use Flash. It is very likely to solve whatever usability or flow problem you are having. However, if there is no need to use Flash for a particular form, stick to HTML. To put it another way: If it ain't broke, don't fix it.

Advantages and Disadvantages of Flash-Based Forms

Flash-based forms offer a number of specific advantages over traditional HTML forms, each of which may or may not apply to a particular project. Here are some of the advantages:

- **Statefulness.** As you know, Flash makes it easy to show or hide different pieces of content at runtime and switch between them without resetting their state. Multi-step, wizard-style forms can therefore be presented to the user and navigated between without costly and cumbersome round-trips to the server.

- **Ease of development.** Depending on the situation, Flash-based forms can actually be easier to develop and integrate into your web applications. The more complex the data-entry task, the more likely it is that you would have to jump through crazy hoops if using HTML alone (simple HTML forms are really quick to put together, but complex ones can take forever). Flash-based forms, on the other hand, generally don't get harder to develop as they get more complex.

- **Robust client-side validation.** With Flash, your script code is compiled into your SWF at publish time. There is no way for users to see your forms while also disabling ActionScript. This means that you can count on any client-side validation to actually occur at runtime. In contrast, a user who has JavaScript disabled will still be able to see your HTML forms, effectively allowing them to sidestep any browser-based validation.

- **Cross-platform reliability.** Because they are rendered by the Flash plug-in rather than the user's browser, you can depend on Flash-based forms to look and behave very, very close to identically on all platforms and in all browsers.

- **Freedom to innovate.** Flash forms, by their very nature, give you more flexibility to create the form of your (or your designer's or your boss's) dreams. You can use any of the extensive set of form controls that ship with Flash. If you don't like them, you can download others from the Macromedia Flash Exchange site or from third parties. If you don't like any of those, you can create your own (without resorting to the platform dependence of ActiveX or the runtime cost of applets).

There are a few disadvantages to using Flash-based forms over straight HTML, which also will vary in importance depending on the situation:

- **Download size.** If you are creating a form with the UI components that ship with Flash MX Professional 2004—and chances are you will if you build forms with Flash at all—your SWFs can get fairly large. It won't be uncommon to end up with a file size that is over 100KB in size. The good news is that the SWF will generally only have to be downloaded once (rather than multiple times for an HTML form that requires round trips to the server for validation and so on), but it's still somewhat likely that a Flash form will be heavier than an HTML-only counterpart. File size may not matter much—if at all—when building intranet/extranet applications, but may be an important factor when building applications for the general public.

- **Flash 7 player required in many cases.** Again, assuming that you are using the form controls that ship with Flash MX Professional 2004, your users might need the Flash 7 player to view your Flash-based forms. Not all special, forms-related features in Flash MX 2004 require Flash Player 7 (many will work with Flash Player 6, as long as it's release version R79 or later). But certain key features—such as the DataSet component—do require version 7. Again, this is likely not to be a problem with intranet/extranet applications, but may be a bit of a barrier when creating applications for the general public, at least until version 7 of the player becomes widely deployed.

NOTE

You can have the Flash IDE automatically create a page that lets the users know if they don't have the correct version of Flash. Just check the Detect Flash Version checkbox under the HTML tab of the Publish Settings dialog box (File > Publish Settings, or Shift+Ctrl+F12).

Controls at Your Disposal

As you well know by now, the Components panel in Flash MX Professional 2004 contains a large number of user interface components that are clearly geared toward creating forms and form-like interfaces (see Figure 11.1). You have already seen and used a few of these controls in earlier chapters, but its time we considered them as a set, for it is the greater sum of their parts that this chapter is interested in.

NOTE

I often refer to the form-like components as "controls" or "UI controls." The Flash documentation tends to simply call them components, but I find it useful to use a different word for this subset of the component set, to differentiate them from the non-visual data access components and the media components.

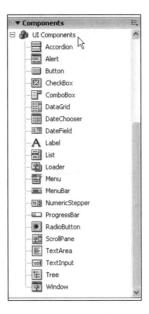

FIGURE 11.1   Form-related components available in Flash MX Professional 2004.

Table 11.1 lists the form-related controls that ship with this version of Flash, along with the HTML counterpart—if there is one—for each.

> **NOTE**
>
> In addition to the components listed in Table 11.1, you can also use normal text fields when creating forms. See the "Basic Form Submissions" section, later in this chapter, for details.

TABLE 11.1   Forms-Related Components in Flash MX Professional 2004

FLASH UI COMPONENT	HTML FORMS COUNTERPART
Alert	None, but similar conceptually to `window.alert()` or `window.confirm()` in JavaScript-enabled browsers.
Button	An `<input>` tag with a `type` of `submit` or `button`, or a `<button>` element.
CheckBox	`<input type="checkbox">`
ComboBox	`<select size="1">`, except that `ComboBox` components can be editable (allowing users to type a new value).
DataGrid	None, unless you count an HTML table filled with rows of text input fields.
DateChooser	None.
DateField	None.
Label	None, although people often use a text `<input>` with read-only or `disabled` flags—or a `<span>` that accepts dynamic `innerText` via script—to emulate label-like behavior.
List	`<select>`
Loader	An `<img>` tag whose `src` attribute is being manipulated via JavaScript.
NumericStepper	None.
RadioButton	`<input type="radio">`
ScrollPane	`<iframe>` (or a `<div>` that provides scrollbars on browsers that support that).
TextArea	`<textarea>`
TextInput	`<input type="text">` or `<input type="password">`
Tree	None.
Window	None, but similar conceptually to `window.open()` in JavaScript.

Rich Internet Applications

Many of the form-related features in this version of Flash were clearly developed to help developers of what Macromedia calls Rich Internet Applications (RIAs). As noted in the introduction, this book is not trying to sell the RIA story in particular. Instead, this book has been encouraging you to see Flash as being useful in a larger set of situations. It can be a tool for adding bits and pieces of well-placed interactivity and richness throughout traditional web-based applications. It doesn't have to be seen as an opportunity for rethinking what it means to create a web-based application. That said, if you start creating sophisticated forms with Flash, you may end up creating an RIA even if you're not so interested in the concept yourself.

More information about Macromedia's vision for RIAs is available at the company's website. At the time of this writing, quite a few RIA-related articles, presentations, and other resources were available at the Rich Internet Applications Topic Center, located at `www.macromedia.com/devnet/ria`.

Basic Form Submissions

I'm one of these people that tends to find the simplest solution to be the best one. So, before we get started with building fancy forms with the new UI controls in Flash MX Professional 2004, I'd like to take a moment to discuss the fact that you can build perfectly serviceable forms using ordinary Flash text fields. Text fields (which you create using the Text Tool in the Tools bar, not with the Components panel) have been around since the earliest days of Flash. As such, they are simple—perhaps even more primitive than HTML-based text inputs—but can still be used creatively. You have all the animation, layering, and other tools in Flash's arsenal at your disposal to dress up such a form and make it behave the way you want it to.

The absolute easiest, thinnest, lightest way to create a Flash-based form would be like this:

1. Create a new Flash document, and add as many editable text fields as you need.

2. Using the Properties panel, assign a variable name to each text field (by typing a name in the field marked *Var*).

3. Add a button for submitting the form, and add a line of code to call the `getURL()` method when the button is clicked.

Make sure to specify POST for getURL()'s *variables* argument (the third argument), and use _self for the second argument unless you want the server's response to appear in a different window. A typical code snippet might look like this:

```
on(release) {
  _root.getURL("postForm.aspx", "_self", "POST");
}
```

Flash will contact the server, posting all variables in the main timeline to the specified URL. Your server will receive the names and values of each variable in exactly the same way as it would receive form field values from an ordinary HTML form. In fact, your server won't have any way of differentiating the incoming submission as being from Flash as opposed to a straightforward web page.

> **NOTE**
>
> Assigning a variable name to a text field is kind of like a poor man's databinding. Changing the value of the timeline variable via script also changes the value in the text field. In addition, any changes the user makes to the value in the text field will also change the value of the timeline variable. The text field is, effectively, a window onto the current value of the variable (as a string). In fact, some developers will place text fields in a movie temporarily as a quick and dirty means of watching how a variable's value changes over time.

If you want to get a bit more sophisticated, give each text field an instance name instead of a variable name, and then post their values by adding them to a LoadVars object on your own, as shown in the following snippet. This way requires a few more lines of code, but you won't be inadvertently posting any variables that you aren't specifically intending to post, and it gives you an opportunity to add conditional or other processing before the information is posted. The following snippet would submit the user's first and last name entries to the server as form-style POST data:

```
on(release) {
  var lv = LoadVars;
  lv.firstname = txtFirstName.text;
  lv.lastname = txtLastName.text;
  lv.send("postForm.aspx", "_self", "POST")
}
```

Regardless of how you write your ActionScript code, using ordinary text fields—instead of the more sophisticated component-based controls—has two principal advantages:

- **File size.** Flash-based forms that contain classic text fields are likely to be very small in terms of file size. It's quite possible to end up with SWFs whose kilobyte count is in the single digits, which is likely to be lighter than the equivalent HTML version of a form page.
- **Version compatibility.** As long as you use classic text fields for data entry and the `getURL()` method for posting their values, just about any version of the Flash Player will be able to display your Flash-based forms. See the "Writing Scripts for Earlier Versions of Flash Player" section in the ActionScript Reference Guide portion of the Flash documentation for details.

Please refer back to Chapter 2, "Your First Flash Interface," and Chapter 6, "Connecting to Servers with Plain Text," for more information about posting simple variables with the `LoadVars` object, details about the `MovieClip.getURL()` method, and related topics.

> **NOTE**
>
> The `LoadVars` object requires Flash Player 6. Please consult the Flash documentation for complete details about player version compatibility issues. In general, the safest thing to do is to publish your SWF for the minimum player version you want to support. The Flash IDE will warn you at publish time if you are using any ActionScript features that aren't available in the version for which you are publishing.

Introducing Form Screens

Okay, take a deep breath here. Flash MX Professional 2004 provides a second authoring mode that we haven't explored in this book up until this point. By now you are familiar with creating normal Flash documents, where you start off with a blank stage and the main timeline. If you want to create a movie that shows different content at different moments—different steps in a multi-step signup form, for instance—you would generally place the content changes in different keyframes. You would then use ActionScript methods such as `gotoAndStop()` to navigate between the keyframes. A variation on this technique would be to place the steps in separate movie clips and then toggle their `_visible` properties as the user moves from step to step.

You also have a new second option in Flash Professional: Screens mode. This mode refashions the Flash IDE a bit, hiding the timeline by default. Instead of the timeline, you have a new outline-like interface for adding content to your SWFs. Instead of thinking in terms of frames, where the current frame contains the currently displayed content, you think in terms of *screens*. Each screen has its own Stage, in which you place components, shapes, and other content. To switch what's being displayed at runtime, you show or hide the screens via script.

The whole idea with screens is that today's Flash is often used to create movies that don't contain any animation and thus never really use the timeline for what it was originally intended: real-time movement. In these movies, the timeline is basically ignored, with content sitting in only the first frame of the movie. (If the movie is meant to present or collect different information at different moments, it might have several frames with different content in each, but even then the timeline is generally never told to "play" through the frames at the movie's frame rate.) The new Screens mode is meant to make it easier to create this type of interface.

> **NOTE**
>
> Don't get the wrong idea. You do not need to use the Screens mode to create forms with Flash MX Professional. You can create forms using the classic Timeline mode as well. The inverse is also true. If you find that you love the Screens mode, use it to create other types of Flash movies as well (not just forms).

The Two Types of Screen-Based Documents

There are actually two types of documents you can create in Screens mode:

- A *Flash Form Application*, which, as the name indicates, is obviously meant to be well suited for creating forms. Each screen within the document is a *Form Screen*, which can be hidden or shown at runtime via script. This is the type of document we'll be working with in this chapter.
- A *Flash Slide Presentation*, which is meant to be well suited for sequential, slide-by-slide presentations (such as those made with presentation software such as Microsoft PowerPoint). Each screen within the document is a *Slide Screen*, and it's particularly easy to add buttons or timers that advance the user to the next or previous screen.

The two types of screen-based documents are actually quite similar. You work with them in the Flash IDE in the same way, and they behave similarly at runtime. The main differences are as follows:

- Only one screen in a slide-based document is visible at any given time (having been designed with slide-show style delivery in mind), whereas multiple screens in a form-based document can be visible at once (the form screens overlay one another, as if they were in separate layers).

- Because there is an assumption that the screens in a slide-based document will be viewed in a sequence, Flash provides convenient methods such as gotoNextSlide() and gotoFirstSlide() for navigating among the slides. With form-based documents, the assumption is that you may want to push the users through a non-sequential path as they complete a data-entry process so that there is no built-in concept of a "next" or "previous" screen.

> **NOTE**
>
> You can even create hybrid documents that contain some form screens and some slide screens by using the Insert Screen Type command in the Screen Outline pane's context menu.

Creating Screen-Based Documents

It's easy to create a screen-based document in Flash Professional. This quick exercise will show you how and will also familiarize you with the two different types of screen-based documents (Form Application documents and Slide Presentation documents).

Creating a Slide Presentation

Let's start with the Slide Presentation type first. Follow these steps to create the new document:

1. Choose File > New, and then choose Flash Slide Presentation for the new document type (see Figure 11.2) and click OK. A new document appears, with two screens shown in the Screen Outline pane on the left side of the stage (see Figure 11.3). Note that the screens are labeled presentation and slide1 by default.

2. Click the Insert Screen button at the top of the outline pane. This adds a new screen to the bottom of the outline, labeled `slide2` (see Figure 11.4).

3. Select the `presentation` screen in the outline, and then add some content—it doesn't matter what—to the Stage.

4. Select the `slide1` screen in the outline, and then add some more content to the Stage. Note that the content in both the `presentation` slide and the `slide1` slide are visible.

5. Now select the `slide2` screen in the outline, noting that the content in `slide1` disappears as you do so (but that the content in the `presentation` screen is still visible). Now add some more content to the Stage.

6. Click back and forth between the `slide1` and `slide2` screens in the outline, noting either slide's content is visible only when it is selected, but that the content in the `presentation` slide is always visible.

7. Test the movie using the usual Control > Test Movie command (or Ctrl+Enter). Note that when the movie appears, the content in the `presentation` and `slide1` screens is showing.

8. Still in test mode, press the right-arrow key on your keyboard. The content from `slide1` disappears, replaced by the content in `slide2`. Note that you can also navigate back to `slide1` using the left-arrow key.

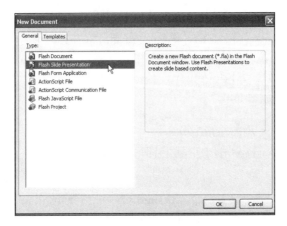

Figure 11.2   Screen-based documents offer a choice between slide and form metaphors.

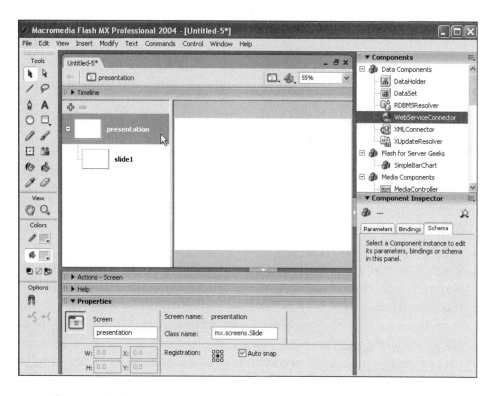

FIGURE 11.3   Screen-based documents contain two screens by default.

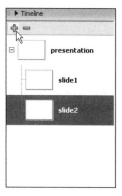

FIGURE 11.4   You can add as many screens to your document as you need.

As you can see, the slides in a Slide Presentation document comprise a simple hierarchy. There is always one *top-level* slide (or, if you prefer, *root slide*) at the top of the hierarchy. The top-level slide is called `presentation` by default, though you can change the name if you wish. The content in this slide is always visible, which makes it good for including background artwork, a toolbar, or any other content that should be visible at all times.

Within the top-level slide, there can be any number of *child slides*. Only one child slide is visible at any given time. As you noted in the last step, the user can navigate among the slides with the arrow keys (just as with most presentation software), though you can turn this behavior off if you wish. Of course, you can add buttons or other navigation elements for navigating among the slides as well.

Clearly, the Slide Presentation type of document has been included in Flash as a way to create PowerPoint-style presentations using the Flash IDE. Although this type of document may be targeted more toward business users, you will soon find that it is nearly identical to the Form Application type of document, which is clearly targeted more toward application developers such as us. It's my belief that you may want to use both types of documents in your applications— even mixing and matching a bit from time to time—depending on the context.

Creating a Form Application

Now let's try creating the type of screen-based document that is geared more toward developers: the Flash Form Application document type. The procedure is basically the same:

1. Choose File > New to create another new document, this time selecting the Flash Form Application document type (visible in Figure 11.2).
2. Note that the new document has two screens—just like the slide presentation you created in the last section, except now the screens are called `application` and `form1` instead of `presentation` and `slide1`.
3. Add another screen using the Insert Screen button (visible in Figure 11.3), noting that the new screen is called `form2`.
4. Add some content to all three slides, noting that the content from all of them is always visible. If you test the movie, you will find that the everything-visible rule also applies at runtime. Also note that the arrow keys have no effect.

As you can see, the two types of screen-based documents are very similar. Slide Presentation documents provide a bit more runtime functionality out of the box (the keyboard navigation and the rule that only one screen appears at a time) so that they will be navigable without any ActionScript code added at all. Form Application documents assume that you will want more granular control over what happens at runtime, so there is no default behavior regarding screen navigation (or visibility). You can add navigation behavior very easily using ActionScript.

Rearranging Screens in the Screen Outline Pane

You can move screens around in the Screen Outline pane to rearrange their position in the application. Just click the screen and drag it to the desired position. If you drag to the right side of a screen (where its name is), the screen you are dragging will become a child of the screen you drop it on. If you drag to the left side of the screen (where its preview is), the dragged screen is inserted under the screen you drop it on. Depending on where you move a screen to, you may be implicitly changing its index position for ActionScript methods such as getChildScreen() (see Table 11.2). You may also be implicitly changing its parent, as reflected by properties such as indexInParent and parentIsScreen.

You can also insert screens and nested screens via the context menu in the Screen Outline pane (see Figure 11.5). The commands available in the context menu are straightforward; check them out at your leisure.

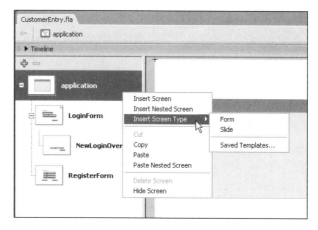

FIGURE 11.5   You can cut, paste, insert, and nest screens as you wish.

WHY HERE? WHY NOW?

Now that you've gotten a taste of what screen-based documents are all about, you may be wondering why this new mode wasn't used in earlier chapters—especially because the new mode deemphasizes the timeline, which is generally of little use to non-designers such as ourselves.

The fact that there are now two entry points to the IDE makes the work of this kind of book somewhat tough, and I'm not sure that there is a perfect way to introduce them both in a relatively short volume. In the end, I chose to leave the discussion out of earlier chapters because screen-based documents do the following:

- **Tend to obfuscate certain Flash concepts.** As I've mentioned, screen-based documents deemphasize the timeline and many important Flash concepts that go along with it. It is my belief that you are better off understanding the Timeline mode first, and then adopting the Form/Screen mode later if you like it.

- **Is as-yet-unproven in the Flash community.** Because it's an entirely new way of working in the Flash IDE, it remains to be seen to what extent the Flash community embraces the new Form/Slide framework.

- **Is not ubiquitous among Flash developers.** If you understand the Timeline mode, you'll be able to chat freely with Flash people everywhere. If you understand only the new mode, you'll be able to chat only with Flash people who have upgraded to Flash MX 2004, bought the Professional version, and choose to use the new mode.

- **Can be slower at publish time.** At the time of this writing, documents created with screens took longer to create, open, and publish than traditional timeline-based movies. Runtime performance is fine, though, so the performance affects only you, not your users. It is more than possible that this performance problem will be rectified by the time you read this.

Scripting Form Screens

Each screen in a Form Application document (or Slide Presentation document) is scriptable. The screens are exposed to ActionScript as nested objects in a manner that is very similar to the way nested movie clips are exposed in a regular Flash document. Each screen is a descendant of the usual `MovieClip` class, so you can use most of the same methods and properties that you are used to using with movie clips in your script code.

Referencing Screens in ActionScript Code

Each screen can be referenced in script by the screen name shown in the Screen Outline pane to the left of the Stage. For instance, in a Form Application document, the top-level screen is called `application` by default; therefore, you may refer to the screen in your ActionScript code as `_root.application`. (You can leave off the `_root` part if the script you are writing is executing in the context of `_root` already; this is no different from how the relative referencing of normal movie clips works.)

For instance, the following line would set the `visible` property of the top-level screen to `false`, thereby making the root screen (and all the other screens as well because they are all contained within the top-level screen) invisible at run-time:

```
_root.application.visible = false;
```

Nested screens can be referenced using dot notation, just like nested movie clips. For instance, the following line would set the `visible` property of the `form1` screen to `false`, thereby making it invisible (but leaving the visibility of other slides alone):

```
_root.application.form1.visible = false;
```

> **NOTE**
>
> You can also use the usual `_parent` property to refer to the parent of a form or a slide screen. In a default Form Application document, for instance, the `_parent` property of the `form1` screen object resolves to the `application` screen object. See also the `parentIsScreen` and `parentIsSlide` properties listed in Tables 11.2 and 11.3 (in the next section of this chapter).

To change a screen's name, double-click the screen in the Screen Outline pane and type the new name (you will, of course, need to change any existing references in your ActionScript code accordingly). You can also rename a screen by selecting it in the outline, and then typing the new name in the Properties pane. Either method changes the screen's instance name, which means that you'll need to adjust any ActionScript code that refers to the slide by name accordingly.

The ActionScript Screens API

By default, each screen in a Form Application document is an instance of the `mx.screens.Form` class; screens in a Slide Presentation document are instances of `mx.screens.Slide`. Both are descendants of a common class called `mx.screens.Screen`. This common `Screen` class, in turn, extends `mx.controls.Loader`, which descends from `MovieClip`.

> **NOTE**
>
> To be precise, the complete class hierarchy for the Form class would be as follows: `mx.screens.Form` > `mx.screens.Screen` > `mx.controls.Loader` > `mx.core.View` > `mx.core.UIComponent` > `mx.core.UIObject` > `MovieClip`. But who's counting? Seriously, you might find it interesting to take a look through the `classes\mx` folder within Flash MX's `Configuration` directory to get a sense of what extends what. Reference information for each of the intermediary classes is available in the ActionScript Dictionary portion of the Flash documentation. At the time of this writing, a helpful class hierarchy chart was at `www.macromedia.com/devnet/mx/flash/articles/component_architecture_03.html`.

Sound complicated? Don't be intimidated. All this means in practice is that every screen has all the methods, properties, and events that a normal movie clip has. In addition, it has all the methods and properties defined by the `Loader` and `Screen` classes. The result is the baseline functionality of any screen, regardless of whether it's a form or a slide. On top of that baseline, a form gets a few more items from the `Form` class, and slides get a few more from `Slide`.

> **NOTE**
>
> We've done some relatively simple class extending in this book, but nothing as extensive as what Macromedia has done with the classes in the `mx` package. It's nice to see that the ActionScript 2.0 class and extension framework is solid and flexible enough to provide much of the functionality that ships with the product.

Table 11.2 shows the methods, properties, and events of the `mx.screens.Screen` class.

TABLE 11.2   *mx.screens.Screen* Class Members

MEMBER	DESCRIPTION
`getChildScreen(index)`	Method. Returns the child screen at the given index. Returns `undefined` if there is no such screen.
`currentFocusedScreen`	Static property. Use `Screen.currentFocusedScreen` to refer to the screen object that currently has focus in the movie. Note that you call this property statically on the `Screen` class itself, not on an actual screen instance in your movie.
`indexInParent`	Property. Returns the index position of the screen within its parent, where the first child is `0`.

MEMBER	DESCRIPTION
numChildScreens	Property. The number of child screens that are nested within the current screen. You can use this property to set up a `for` loop that loops over each of a particular screen's children; within the loop, you would use `getChildScreen()` to get a reference to the current screen for the loop.
parentIsScreen	Property. A Boolean value that indicates whether the current screen's parent is also a screen. For the top-level screen, this property is `false`; it is `true` for all other screens visible at design time.
rootScreen	Property. A reference to the top-level screen that contains the current screen. This property provides an alternative to referring to the top-level screen (`_root.application`, for instance).
allTransitionsInDone	Event. If you have set up a screen transition to occur when this screen appears, this event fires when the transition is complete. See the Flash documentation for information about screen transitions, which cause screens to appear with animated effects (such as fading or sliding in or out).
allTransitionsOutDone	Event. If you have set up a screen transition to occur when this screen is hidden, this event fires when the transition is complete. See the Flash documentation for details.
mouseDown	Event. Fires when the user clicks the mouse button over the screen.
mouseDownSomewhere	Event. Fires when the user clicks the mouse button somewhere in the movie, but not necessarily on the screen in question.
mouseMove	Event. Fires when the user moves the mouse while within the screen's bounding box.
mouseOut	Event. Fires when the user moves the mouse out of the screen's bounding box.
mouseOver	Event. Fires when the user moves the mouse into the screen's bounding box.

continues

TABLE 11.2   *mx.screens.Screen* Class Members (Continued)

MEMBER	DESCRIPTION
mouseUp	Event. Fires when the user releases the mouse button over the screen.
mouseUpSomewhere	Event. Fires when the user releases the mouse button somewhere in the movie, but not necessarily the screen in question.
reveal	Event (inherited from UIObject). Fires when the screen's visible property changes from false to true.
hide	Event (inherited from UIObject). Fires when the screen's visible property changes from true to false.
focusIn	Event (inherited from UIComponent). Fires when the screen receives focus.
focusOut	Event (inherited from UIComponent). Fires when the screen loses focus.
load	Event (inherited from UIObject). Fires when the screen is first created (loaded).
unload	Event (inherited from UIObject). Fires when the screen is being destroyed (unloaded).

> **NOTE**
>
> The mouse-related events listed in Table 11.2 work similarly to the mouse-related events for the normal MovieClip class. For details, see Chapter 5, "Movie Clips as Objects," or the ActionScript Dictionary part of the Flash documentation.
>
> The members in Table 11.2 that are inherited from UIComponent or UIObject are also supported by most of the components in the Components panel. See the Components Dictionary portion of the Flash documentation for details.

Table 11.3 lists the methods, properties, and events of the mx.screens.Form class. Remember that all form slides inherit all the members of mx.screens.Screen (listed in Table 11.2), as well as the usual MovieClip members.

> **NOTE**
>
> All but one of these members performs the same basic function as the similarly named member in Table 11.2, except that they reflect form screens only (not slide screens) in your document. In contrast, the members in Table 11.2 reflect both types of screens. To put it another way, the similarly named members in these two tables are synonymous if your document contains only form screens. The only time when there is any need to distinguish between them is when you are using a mixture of form and slide screens in the same document.

TABLE 11.3   *mx.screens.Form* Class Members

MEMBER	DESCRIPTION
getChildForm(index)	See Table 11.2.
currentFocusedForm	See Table 11.2.
indexinParentForm	See Table 11.2.
visible	Property. Indicates whether the form is visible. Setting this property to false makes the form screen invisible; setting it to true makes it visible again.
numChildForms	See Table 11.2.
parentIsForm	See Table 11.2.
rootForm	See Table 11.2.

As mentioned, all screens are descendants of the Loader class, which means that screens have some built-in abilities with regard to loading external content. Table 11.4 shows the methods, properties and events exposed by Loader.

> **NOTE**
>
> This same set of methods and properties applies to any Loader components that you drag onto the Stage from the Components panel.

TABLE 11.4   *mx.controls.Loader* Class Members

MEMBER	DESCRIPTION
load([url])	Method. Loads content into the loader; the content will be displayed visually as soon as it loads. You may provide a URL for the content with the optional url argument, which is simply shorthand for setting contentPath and then load() on two separate lines of code. If you don't provide a url argument, the current value of contentPath is used to load the content.

continues

TABLE 11.4   *mx.controls.Loader* Class Members (Continued)

MEMBER	DESCRIPTION
autoLoad	Property. A Boolean value that indicates whether the loader should load its content when the movie first loads (or whenever contentPath changes). The default is true. If you change this property to false, the loader will not actually load any content until you call the load() method.
bytesLoaded	Property. A number that indicates the number of bytes that the loader has loaded so far. You would typically use this value when responding to a progress event, to show a status indicator to the user.
bytesTotal	Property. A number that indicates the total file size of the content that the loader is loading. You would typically use this value when responding to a progress event, to show a status indicator to the user.
content	Property. A reference to the actual content that has been loaded. Thus, if you have told a form screen (which is a loader subclass) called form1 to load a SWF, and the SWF includes a nested movie clip called mcMyClip, you could change the clip's visibility via _root.application.form1.content.mcMyClip._visible.
contentPath	Property. The relative or absolute URL for the content you want to appear in the loader. The content can be an external SWF file or a JPEG image (as long as it's not a progressive JPEG). You can also provide the linkage name of a symbol in the document's Library; at runtime, a new instance of the symbol will be created and displayed in the loader.
percentLoaded	Property. A number that indicates how much of the content has been loaded, as a percentage. You would typically use this value when responding to a progress event, to show a status indicator to the user.
scaleContent	Property. A Boolean value that indicates whether the content should be scaled to fit the loader.
complete	Event. Fires when a piece of content has been loaded completely by the loader. If you are displaying a status indicator about the load process, this event is a good moment to hide the status indicator, display a *download complete* message, or whatever is appropriate.
progress	Event. Fires repeatedly as the loader loads its content. Typically, this event is used as an opportunity to display the current value of the bytesLoaded, bytesTotal, or percentLoaded properties.

Attaching ActionScript Code to Screens

You can add ActionScript code to a screen in any of the following places:

- In the Actions Panel for a screen
- In a screen's timeline, which is hidden by default
- In a custom ActionScript 2.0 class file

The following sections will briefly explain each of these methods.

Attaching Code to Screen Events in the Actions Panel

You can attach code to specific screen events using on(event) syntax by clicking a screen in the Screen Outline and then typing the desired event handler in the Actions panel (see Figure 11.6). Within the handler, the this keyword will refer to the screen. For instance, assuming that a screen contains a TextInput component named tiPasswordConfirm, the following code would set the component's visibility to false each time the screen was revealed (shown after having been hidden):

```
on(reveal) {
   this.tiPasswordConfirm.visible = false;
}
```

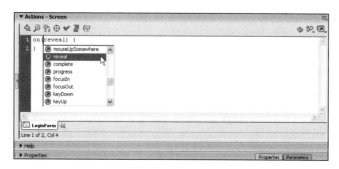

FIGURE 11.6   You can write screen event handlers in the Actions panel.

Attaching Code to a Screen's Underlying Timeline

Although the new screen-based authoring mode deemphasizes the timeline (and associated concepts such as frames and layers), the truth is that screens are, at the end of the day, descendants of MovieClip. That means that every screen has a timeline, even though the authoring environment hides it from you by default. You can add additional frames to the screen's timeline, create tweened animations, add layers and labels—basically anything you can do with a normal movie or movie clip's timeline.

That said, the new screen-based authoring mode was designed specifically to make the timeline less necessary. You are encouraged to try to avoid using a screen's timeline. For instance, if you want to create a visual overlay of some kind, you could usually add a nested Form screen instead of adding a layer to the screen's timeline. Similarly, if you want some animation to occur within a screen, you could usually place a separate movie clip on the screen's Stage (or load an external SWF) instead of adding animation-related frames to the screen's timeline.

One good reason to access a screen's timeline is to add custom functions that will be called from elsewhere in the screen (or elsewhere in the SWF). As you will learn in the next section, a particularly clean way to add functions to a screen is to create an ActionScript 2.0 class that contains the functions. You then attach the screen to the new class. However, if you don't want to create an ActionScript 2.0 class for some reason, you can define your functions in Frame 1 of the screen's timeline instead.

To add code to a screen's underlying timeline, do the following:

1. Select the desired screen in the Screen Outline pane.
2. Expand the Timeline panel, which appears above the Screen Outline in a minimized state by default (visible at the top of Figure 11.4).
3. Attach code to the timeline as you would normally (by clicking one of its frames and then typing code in the Actions panel).

It's worth noting that all the events for the Screen, Form, and Slide classes are exposed using the event listener system (as opposed to the event callback system). This applies even to the load and unload events, even though the inherited onLoad and onUnload events (from MovieClip) are implemented as callbacks.

NOTE

See Chapter 4, "ActionScript: A Primer," for a discussion about events that use listeners versus callbacks.

For instance, the following code will not execute when the screen first loads, even though the same code would work in the timeline of a regular movie or movie clip:

```
this.onLoad = function() {
  this.tiPasswordConfirm.visible = false;
}
```

Instead, you would need to implement your event handler using the listener technique instead. The following code snippet shows how to re-cast the preceding snippet using a listener:

```
function whenLoaded() {
  this.tiPasswordConfirm.visible = false;
}
this.addEventListener("load", whenLoaded);
```

Attaching Code to Screens via Custom Classes

You can create an ActionScript 2.0 class that contains all or most of the script code to make a particular screen do whatever it is supposed to do.

This is very similar conceptually to creating an ActionScript 2.0 class that powers a movie clip symbol in the Library (such as the GestureMovieClip class from Chapter 5, the RatingMovieClip class from Chapter 8, "Connecting to Servers with Flash Remoting," or the LoginMovieClip class from Chapter 10, "Flash and Sessions"). The main difference is that instead of extending the built-in, intrinsic MovieClip class, you will extend the mx.screens.Form or mx.screens.Slide class, depending on the type of screen with which you are working.

1. Create an ActionScript 2.0 class file that extends the mx.screens.Form or mx.screens.Slide class, depending on the type of screen with which you are working.
2. Click the slide in the Screen Outline pane, and then open the Properties panel and select its Properties tab (as opposed to the Parameters tab).
3. Type the name of the class (without the .as extension) in the Class name field (see Figure 11.7).

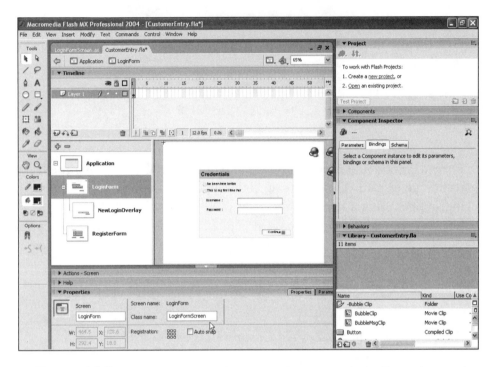

FIGURE 11.7   Specify the ActionScript class for a screen in the Properties panel.

For instance, here is the ActionScript 2.0 class-based equivalent of the event-handling snippets shown in the previous two sections:

```
class LoginFormScreen extends mx.screens.Form {
  function onLoad() {
    this.tiPasswordConfirm.visible = false;
  }
}
```

You will see some examples of ActionScript 2.0 classes for specific screens later in this chapter.

Some Thoughts on Form Validation

In my view, one of the greatest potential benefits of building forms with Flash instead of ordinary HTML is the ability to add different types of relatively reliable validation. There are a few reasons why a Flash-based form may be better suited for robust validation than an equivalent HTML-based form:

- You can you take advantage of Flash's ActionScript support, which is generally far better at behaving exactly the same way across browser products and versions than JavaScript implementations are. In addition, it can't be disabled by the end user or stripped out by a firewall or proxy server. (In fairness, it is possible that you will need to consider which version of the Flash Player is being used, but it's a lot less obtrusive to ask a user to upgrade their Flash Player than to switch browsers or operating systems. Plus, most examples in this book can be used with Flash Player 6 or 7, so anyone who has updated their Flash Player in the past few years will be able to access your Flash-based forms.)

- Because you have all of Flash's animation, layering, and other dynamic presentation tools at your disposal, you can create dynamic, user-friendly, unobtrusive ways of alerting the user when an entry has failed a validation test. In contrast, an HTML-based form generally needs to create a pop-up window, perform a round-trip to the server, or use some kind of DHTML-based widget that is unlikely to work correctly with all browsers.

- Flash MX Professional 2004 ships with a set of built-in validation features as a part of its databinding framework. You can use these features to create client-side validation with just a few lines of code. If you use these features, you'll also get the added benefit of knowing that you are using relatively standard practices in your movies.

Because Flash is so flexible and can connect to servers in so many different ways, there are many ways that you can approach the validation of Flash-based form data. For the purpose of this discussion, I'd like to address these broad categories of validation techniques:

- **Simple script-based validation.** Where you write ad-hoc ActionScript code that tests a user's entry against some kind of business rule.
- **Databound validation.** Where you use the built-in validation features included with the databinding features in Flash MX Professional 2004.

- **Realtime server-side validation.** Where you connect to a server to validate a user's entry, presumably because only the server can determine whether the entry is acceptable (for instance, whether a just-entered username has already been taken by another user).

The following sections will discuss each of these broad techniques, respectively. Please keep in mind that any of these techniques could be coded in a variety of ways. For instance, the realtime server-side validation technique could be implemented using XML, or Flash Remoting, or Web Services, or just plain-text variables. Therefore, try to absorb the basic principles being demonstrated (rather than focusing only on the code) as you look through the next three sections.

Simple Script-Based Validation

You are always free to add any type of ad-hoc validation script to your movies, regardless of whether you are using the screen-based authoring mode and regardless of whether you are using the databinding features in the Professional version of Flash. This method will probably be the most familiar if you have worked with JavaScript in HTML forms in the past, and you can always return to it if the more structured databinding features fail you for any reason.

The Basics

In a way, this type of validation is so simple that you've probably already guessed how it works. You just write a simple `if` block that tests whether the value of a text field—or any other form control, for that matter—contains a value that you consider acceptable. If the value is acceptable, you allow your code to continue on to the next task (most likely sending the data to the server). If the value is not acceptable, you let the user know by presenting some sort or (usually visual) feedback. You then use `return` or a similar statement to stop your script before it proceeds to the next task.

For instance, the following code snippet—which would likely appear within a larger chunk of code, such as the handler for a button's click event—would display a simple error message (see Figure 11.8) if the user left the text field or text input named `txtPassword` empty:

```
if (txtPassword.text == "") {
  mx.controls.Alert.show("Type your password first", "No Password");
  return;
}
```

FIGURE 11.8   The user is notified about the invalid entry via an alert.

NOTE

For this snippet to work, you would first need to make sure there is an Alert symbol in your document's Library (by dragging an Alert component from the Components panel onto the Stage and then deleting it). Also, you can leave out the `mx.controls.` part of the `Alert` class's name if you add an `import` line that imports the `mx.controls.Alert` class. See the code for the `LoginMovieClip` class in Chapter 10 for a complete example that uses the `Alert` class.

The other `Alert`-based snippets in this section assume that you have imported `mx.controls.Alert` with an `import` line.

Of course, you aren't limited to testing only for an empty string. You can use any of ActionScript's string-manipulation functions to check for certain characters, enforce a minimum length, or perform just about any other validation test you can dream up. For instance, the following snippet would ensure that the user's password entry is at least five characters long:

```
if (txtPassword.text.length < 5) {
  Alert.show("Passwords must be 5 characters long", "No Password");
  return;
}
```

Similarly, the following snippet uses the `indexOf()` and `lastIndexOf()` methods of the ActionScript `String` class to determine whether the value entered in the `TextInput` component named `tiEmail` appears to be a valid email address. If the user's value contains an @ sign and a dot, and the dot is after the @ sign, the email address is considered to be valid. This isn't a perfect test because the user could still enter multiple @ signs (or spaces or other invalid characters), but it's a sensible starting point that you could perfect on your own:

```
var pw = tiEmail.text;
if ( (pw.indexOf("@") < 1) || (pw.lastIndexOf(".") < pw.indexOf("@")))
{
  Alert.show("Please enter a real email address!", "Invalid Email");
  return;
}
```

> **NOTE**
>
> I know what you're thinking. Unfortunately, ActionScript does not provide regular expression support at this time. Sure would be nice, eh? Maybe in the next version.

Setting Focus to the Invalid Control

If you want to set focus to the UI control that contains the invalid entry (so that the user doesn't have to click it herself to fix the problem), you can use the `setFocus()` method exposed by all visual components. The following snippet would set focus to the `tiPassword` control if the user's entry is determined to be invalid:

```
if (tiPassword.text == "") {
  tiPassword.setFocus();
  Alert.show("Please type your password first!", "No Password");
  return;
}
```

> **NOTE**
>
> This `setFocus()` method is supported by each UI control's class. The actual implementation is in the `UIComponent` class, from which all components descend. See the ActionScript Dictionary for details.

The intrinsic `TextField` class doesn't expose a `setFocus()` method. To set focus to a normal text field (as opposed to a component), use the `setFocus()` method provided by the static `Selection` class. The following snippet would set focus to the text field named `tiPassword` when the user provided an invalid entry:

```
if (tiPassword.text == "") {
  Selection.setFocus("tiPassword");
  Alert.show("Please type your password first!", "No Password");
  return;
}
```

Notifying the User Without Alerts

While the `Alert` component is certainly effective, it has the potential disadvantage of being modal (that is, the alert dialog steals the focus away from the form). The user must dismiss the alert by clicking the OK button before continuing, which can be a drag after a while. You may want to take advantage of

Flash's considerable presentation skills to alert your users to validation problems in a more subtle or user-friendly fashion.

For instance, the Login Form example that you will see later in this chapter contains a movie clip symbol called `BubbleClip`, which looks a bit like a speech bubble in a cartoon. A single instance of the clip is created in the root timeline, with an instance name of `mcBubble`. The clip's class exposes a single public method called `showMessage()`, which displays the message in the speech bubble and positions the bubble next to the offending UI control (see Figure 11.9). The bubble also contains a fade-in effect that makes its appearance feel more like a helpful reminder than a direct order.

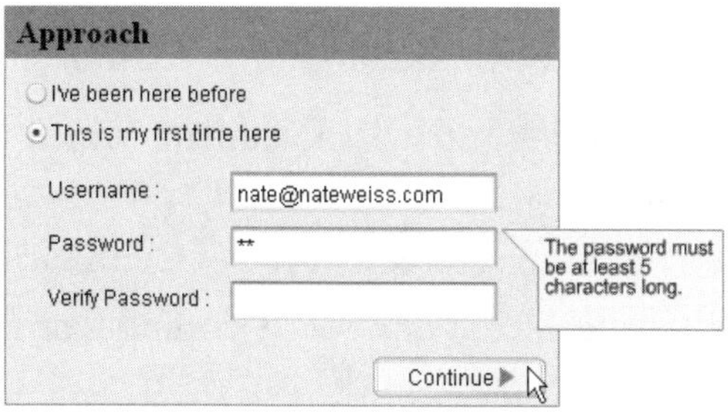

FIGURE 11.9   You can create unobtrusive ways to let the user know an entry is invalid.

Here is a snippet from that example (you can see it in context by looking ahead to Listing 11.2), which is very similar to the snippets you have seen in the preceding pages. The only difference is that the bubble widget, rather than the `Alert` component that ships with Flash, is used to display the error message:

```
if (tiUsername.text == '') {
  mcBubble.showMessage("Please type a username.", tiUsername);
  return false;
};
```

As you will see in Listing 11.4 (later in this chapter), the `showMessage()` method accepts two arguments. The first is the message to display in the bubble. The second is the control that the bubble should point to (the bubble will position itself next to the top-right corner of the specified control).

Databound Validation

The simple techniques—if you can even call them that—shown in the previous sections use ad-hoc tests to determine whether a field is currently valid. That approach works fine, but it adheres to no particular structure, standard practice, or methodology.

An alternative is to use the validation mechanisms provided by the databinding framework in the Professional version of Flash. Let's call this technique *databound validation*. There is quite a bit to the databound validation features in Flash MX Professional 2004, but the basics are easy to understand by example.

The Basics

Please do the following to see databound validation in action:

1. Open the CustomerEntry.fla document, which is included with this chapter's examples.

2. Click the `LoginForm` screen in the Screen Outline pane.

3. Click the `WebServiceConnector` component named `wsCreateNewCustomer` in the top-right corner. This connector has been set up to call a web service method called `createNewCustomer()`, which accepts some customer information (username, password, first and last names, telephone number, and email address) and uses it to create a new customer record in the example database.

4. With the connector component still selected, open the Component Inspector panel (Window > Development Panels > Component Inspector) if it's not visible already.

5. Click the Parameters tab and note that the `suppressInvalidCalls` property has been set to `true` (see Figure 11.10). This tells the `WebServiceConnector` to abort a call to `trigger()` if any of the corresponding web service method's parameters are missing or invalid. See Chapter 9, "Connecting to Servers with Web Services," for reference information about this property.

> **NOTE**
>
> The `XMLConnector` component also has a `suppressInvalidCalls` property, so you can use this same technique with pages that exchange regular XML documents. See Chapter 7, "Connecting to Servers with XML."

FIGURE 11.10 The `suppressInvalidCalls` option tells Flash to insist upon valid entries before contacting the server.

6. Click the Bindings tab and note that a binding has been set up between each of the web service method's parameters and the corresponding UI controls (see Figure 11.11). Four of the controls (`email`, `telephone`, `lastName`, and `firstName`) are bound to controls in the current screen (the `RegisterForm` screen). The other two (`username` and `password`) are bound to controls in the `LoginForm` screen.

FIGURE 11.11 The web service method's arguments have been bound to UI controls in the movie.

7. Click the Schema tab and note that the data type field for four of the method's arguments (`username`, `password`, `firstName`, and `lastName`) remains set to the basic data type dictated by the web service's Web Services Description Language (WSDL) document. In this case, the basic data type is `String` for all the parameters. Note that the required field is set to `true` for each of these parameters because the web service method considers them to be required arguments (see Figure 11.12).

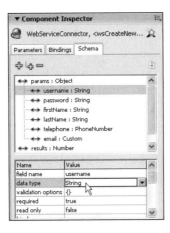

FIGURE 11.12   Each argument has its required field set to `true`.

> **NOTE**
>
> For a different web service method, the types might have been set to `Boolean`, `Number`, or some other basic data type. This type-setting happens automatically when you select the `operation` parameter for the connector (see Figure 11.10).

8. Still in the Schema tab, select the `phoneNumber` argument and note that its data type has been set to PhoneNumber (see Figure 11.13). PhoneNumber is one of the built-in validation rules that ship with this version of Flash. Similar types include SocialSecurity and ZipCode.

9. Still in the Schema tab, select the `email` argument and note that its data type has been set to Custom. Additionally, the validation options field has been set to specify a classname of `EmailValidator`, which refers to an ActionScript 2.0 class that knows how to determine whether a string contains a valid email address. You can double-click the validation options field to bring up the Custom Validation Settings dialog box (see Figure 11.14), which allows you to specify a different custom validation class of your own devising. See the "Creating Your Own Custom Validation Classes" section (coming up shortly) for details.

FIGURE 11.13   Flash knows how to validate phone numbers out of the box.

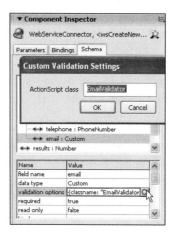

FIGURE 11.14   You can provide your own classes that implement custom validation rules.

Handling valid *and* invalid *Events*

Because the `suppressInvalidCalls` property of the `WebServiceConnector` component has been set to `true`, Flash will perform validation on each parameter just before each attempt to contact the server. That is, the user's entries are tested for validity just after each call to the connector's `trigger()` method, but before the web service method is actually invoked.

In the CustomerEntry.fla example, validation will fail if any of the following are true:

- Any of the controls bound to required arguments have been left empty (actually, all the arguments are required in this example).

- The control bound to the `phoneNumber` parameter (in this case, a `TextInput` named `tiPhoneNumber`) does not contain a valid phone number, as determined by the built-in PhoneNumber validation included with Flash Professional.

- The control bound to the `email` parameter (in this case, `tiEmail`) does not contain a valid email address, as determined by the custom `EmailValidator` class that will be discussed in the next section of this chapter.

The connector will emit a `valid` or `invalid` event at the moment that it determines whether all arguments have been provided correctly. If all arguments are valid, the connector emits a `valid` event. It then immediately continues on to the task of contacting the server and invoking the actual web service method. If any of the arguments are found not to be valid, the connector emits an `invalid` event and stops without contacting the server.

It is relatively unlikely that you would want your movie to pay attention to the `valid` event, except perhaps to display a message of some kind in a status bar within your movie. In contrast, it is extremely likely that you will want to write handlers for `invalid` events. It is in these handlers that you will display an alert or some other visual indication that the user's entry was unacceptable.

Each databound control that is participating in the method call will also emit `valid` or `invalid` events as appropriate. Whereas the events fired by the connector indicate whether the set of arguments as a whole were found to be valid, the events fired by the individual UI controls indicate whether the specific arguments to which they are bound were found to be valid. Because they are more specific, it may be easier to write code that responds to the control-specific events, rather than to the events fired by the connector.

> **NOTE**
>
> If you set up your connector's schema to perform validation but don't write any `invalid` event handlers that tell the user what went wrong, the user may not have any idea what to do to fix the problem. The call to the server will simply fail, silently, like so many trees in Californian forests.

For instance, the following code snippet (paraphrased from Listing 11.2, later in this chapter) creates a handler function for the `tiFirstName` component, which is bound to the `firstName` argument of the `createNewCustomer()` web service method:

```
function firstName_Invalid(ev) {
  _root.mcBubble.showMessage("Please provide a first name.", this);
}
tiFirstName.addEventListener("invalid", firstName_Invalid);
```

Within the body of the handler function, the `BubbleMovieClip.showMessage()` method is called to provide some feedback to the user, displaying an error message and pointing to the problem.

NOTE

The event object passed to your handler contains two helpful properties, in addition to the properties that are normally present in an event object: `message`, which is a canned message that could be displayed to the user in lieu of your own; and `field`, which is the name of the bound argument or property (such as `firstName` in this example). See the Flash documentation for details about these properties.

As usual, you are free to create event handlers using `on(event)` syntax in the Actions panel for the object in question. Thus, as an alternative to the preceding snippet, you could set up the same functionality by adding the following lines to the Actions panel for the `tiFirstName` component:

```
on(invalid) {
    _root.mcBubble.showMessage("Please provide a first name.", this);
}
```

NOTE

As mentioned at beginning of this section, the `WebServiceConnector` will also be firing `valid` and `invalid` events, which you can respond to by writing similar handlers. The main difference is that the `this` keyword will then refer to the connector rather than the input control.

Creating Your Own Custom Validation Classes

As you learned in the previous section, it is possible to create custom validation classes to supplement the ones that ship with Flash (`PhoneNumber`, `SocialSecurity`, `ZipCode`, and so on). Such classes are easy to write.

Simply create an ActionScript 2.0 class file that extends a special class called `mx.data.binding.CustomValidator`. Within the class, implement a public method called `validate()` that accepts one argument (the databinding framework will pass the value being validated to this argument). Within the body of the `validate()` function, add whatever code you need to determine the validity of the value. If at any point you find that the value is not valid, use the special `validationError()` method (inherited from `CustomValidator`) to tell the databinding framework not to accept the value.

If your function throws one of these errors, the value will be considered invalid and the server connection process will be aborted (assuming you are binding to a connector with `suppressInvalidCalls` set to `true`). Whatever message you supply to the `validationError()` method will be passed to any `invalid` event handlers as the event object's `message` property. If your function finishes its work without throwing a `validationError()` message, the value is considered to be valid and the process of connecting to the server is allowed to continue (assuming all other bound values are valid as well, of course).

Listing 11.1 is an example of a custom validation class, upon which you can model similar classes. This class is called EmailValidator, and it is used in the CustomerEntry.fla example to provide basic email address validation (refer back to Figure 11.14).

LISTING 11.1   EmailValidator.as—An Example of a Custom Validation Class

```
class EmailValidator extends mx.data.binding.CustomValidator {
  public function validate(value:String) {
    if (value.indexOf("@") < 1) {
      this.validationError("Email addresses must contain an @ sign.");
    }
    if (  value.lastIndexOf("@") > value.lastIndexOf(".")  ) {
      this.validationError("There must be a dot after the @ sign.");
    }
  }
}
```

After you have created such a class, you use it by specifying its name (without the .as extension) in the Custom Validation Settings dialog box for any schema field that has its data type option set to Custom (as shown back in Figure 11.14). You can use the class name alone if the class file is in the same folder as your FLA.

> **NOTE**
>
> If you want to store the class file in a common location where it can be stored by other FLAs, make it part of a package (perhaps venue.validation) available to Flash's classpath (the full path might be Classes/venue/validation/EmailValidator.as, within Flash's Configuration directory). Then include the package name in the Custom Validation Settings dialog. An example would be venue.validation.EmailValidator.

Realtime Server-Side Validation

Although the client-side-only techniques we've discussed so far in this chapter (simple script-based validation and databound validation) give you a lot of flexibility, there will be times when you will need to consult with a server to determine whether a given value can be considered valid. For instance, if you wanted to check the actual validity of a credit card number, that's something you might be able to do only with the help of a server-side process. Similarly, if you are asking a new user to choose a username, only the server will be able to determine if the username has already been taken by someone else.

To perform this type of validation, just create a page or remote method that can be accessed by Flash via any of the connection methods discussed in this book (see Chapters 6–9). When it comes time to check whether a user's entry is valid, call the server-side code, passing the user's entry to the server as you do so. If the server reports that the value is invalid, let the user know via an error message or some other type of feedback (just like any other type of validation).

For example, the CustomerEntry.fla example for this chapter uses a web services method called `isUsernameAvailable()` that accepts a single string argument (the desired username) and returns a Boolean value that indicates whether the username is available (`true`) or has already been taken by another user (`false`). In the Flash document, a `WebServiceConnector` component named `wsIsUsernameAvailable` is used to connect to the server and invoke the remote method. After the client-side-only validation steps have passed, the remote method is called via the connector's `trigger()` method.

The following code snippet, paraphrased from Listing 11.2 (which appears later in this chapter if you want to see it in context), uses the `BubbleMovieClip.showMessage()` method once again to display feedback to the user if the server reports that the username is already taken:

```
function isUsernameAvailable_Result() {
  // If server reports that the username is already taken
  if (this.results == false) {
    var msg = ("Username is already taken. Please choose another.";
  _root.mcBubble.showMessage(msg, _parent.tiUsername);
    return;
}
```

The Customer Entry Example

You have been seeing bits and pieces of an example called CustomerEntry.fla throughout the preceding sections. You may have already tested it out. Let's take a look at that example now.

On the Server

This example interacts with a web service that exposes a small set of methods related to creating and returning customer records. As usual, this chapter's example files include three versions of the web service, implemented with ColdFusion, ASP.NET, and Java, respectively. Table 11.5 lists the methods provided by each version.

TABLE 11.5   Methods Exposed by This Chapter's Web Service Example

WEB SERVICE METHOD	DESCRIPTION
`createNewCustomer(username, password, firstName, lastName, telephone, email)`	Creates a new customer record, storing the username, password, and contact information in the Customers table in the example database. Returns the newly created customer ID number.
`getCustomerID(username, password)`	Returns the customer ID number associated with the specified username and password. If there is no such customer record (which probably means that a user is providing an incorrect username or password), this method returns `-1`.
`isUsernameAvailable(username)`	Returns a Boolean value that indicates whether the specified username has already been taken. It returns `true` if there is a record in the Customers table with the given username, and `false` if there is no such record.

The code for each version of this web service is straightforward and contain no surprises, so they are not shown as printed listings in the chapter. You can pull them up in your favorite editor if you are curious about the server-side code. Here are the files that you would look at:

- The ColdFusion version is implemented as a CFC called UserCheck.cfc.
- The ASP.NET version is implemented as an Active Server Methods file called UserCheck.asmx.
- The Java version is implemented as an "instant" Java Web Service file called UserCheck.jws. The same code could also be compiled as a standard Java class, and then exposed as a web service by adding a <service> element to WEB-INF/server-config.wsdd (or through a similar configuration step).

Refer to Chapter 9 for details about connecting to web service methods from your Flash movies.

Examining the Document in the Flash IDE

Go ahead and open up that example now, and make a note of the following:

- The example was created via the Flash Form Application document type, and it now contains four screens: the top-level screen is called `application`; the second screen is called `LoginForm`; the third screen is nested within `LoginForm` and is called `NewLoginOverlay`; the fourth screen is nested within the top level and is called `RegisterForm` (see Figure 11.15).

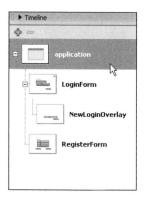

FIGURE 11.15   The document contains four screens, arranged in a simple hierarchy.

- The `application` screen contains nothing but some rectangular shapes and shading for visual effect. Because this is the top-level screen, the content in all other screens will appear on top of the shapes and shading.
- The `LoginForm` screen contains text fields for a username and password (see Figure 11.16). It also contains two radio buttons marked *I've been here before* and *This is my first time here*. At runtime, the options cause a third text field—for confirming a new password—to appear or disappear (see Figure 11.17). The idea is that an existing user need only enter her username and password, but that a new user is instead supplying new credentials (and thus should be asked to confirm the password).

FIGURE 11.16   Existing users are prompted for their credentials.

FIGURE 11.17   New users are ask to supply new credentials.

- The `LoginForm` screen has been attached to the ActionScript 2.0 class called `LoginFormScreen`, which you will see shortly in Listing 11.2. Refer to the "Attaching Code to Screens via Custom Classes" section, earlier in this chapter, for details about creating custom ActionScript classes for specific screens.

- The third text field is actually in the nested NewLoginOverlay screen. This screen is invisible by default because its `visible` parameter has been set to `false` in the Properties panel. The radio buttons in the `LoginForm` screen turn its visibility on and off at runtime by adjusting the visible property to `true` or `false` (see Figure 11.18).

NOTE

As I've pointed out a number of times in this book, some developers frown on the practice of attaching code directly to objects in the Actions panel. These developers prefer to keep all code in one central location, preferably in an external ActionScript file that is included with an #include in Frame 1 of a document (or screen). Better yet, they might even place all the code in an ActionScript 2.0 class file.

Either alternative can make it easier to see all the code for a movie at once, and either can make it easier to track changes with source control software. That being said, there is a case to be made for placing small snippets of code in the Actions panel for a specific object—it's often simpler and it can keep the connection between a particular cause and effect more clear. See Chapter 4 for details about the various ways to respond to events fired by buttons, radio buttons, and other types of objects.

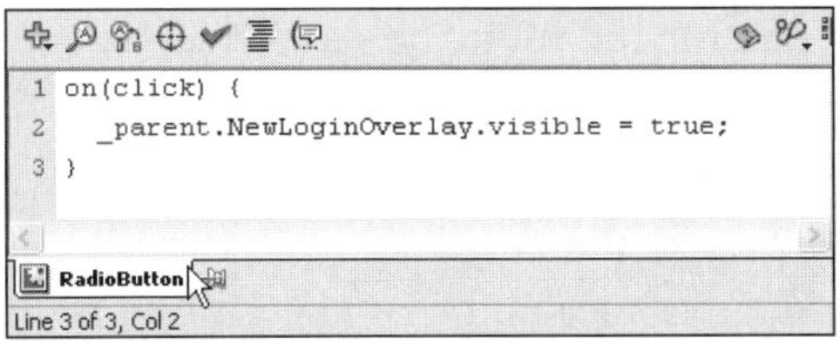

```
1  on(click) {
2      _parent.NewLoginOverlay.visible = true;
3  }
```

RadioButton
Line 3 of 3, Col 2

FIGURE 11.18   New customers are asked to supply new and unique credentials.

- There are two versions of the Continue button that are visible in the username/password screen (visible in Figures 11.16 and 11.17). The first one is in LoginForm and executes a function called continueExisting() when clicked. The second one is in NewLoginOverlay, which executes a function called continueNew() instead (you will see both methods in Listing 11.2). Because the two buttons are at the same X/Y position, they appear to be the same button to the end user.

- The RegisterForm screen contains four text fields, for a new user's first name, last name, telephone number, and email address (see Figure 11.19).

- There are three WebServiceConnectors on the Stage. They call web service methods named getCustomerID(), isUsernameAvailable(), and createNewCustomer(). The first method is used when the user is an existing customer; the second two are used for new customer registrations.

- Each argument for the web service methods is bound to the appropriate text input fields. Note that it's perfectly acceptable for a single UI control to be bound to more than one WebServiceConnector. For instance, the tiUsername control is bound to username arguments for all three connectors.

Registration

First Name	Nate
Last Name	Weiss
Telephone	718-555-1212
Email :	nate@nateweiss.com

Back   Continue ▶

FIGURE 11.19   New customers fill in contact details on a separate screen.

- The bindings for the input fields in the RegisterForm screen have validation options applied to them, as described in the "Databound Validation" section earlier in this chapter.

- If the user gets to the RegisterForm screen and clicks the Back button (visible in Figure 11.19), he or she will be returned to the LoginForm screen. This is accomplished by setting the visible properties for the two screens when the button is clicked (see Figure 11.20). If the user clicks the Continue button on this screen, a new user record is created on the server via the createNewCustomer() web service method (see Figure 11.21).

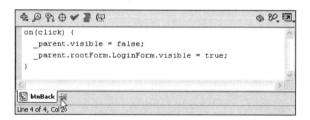

```
on(click) {
    _parent.visible = false;
    _parent.rootForm.LoginForm.visible = true;
}
```

btnBack
Line 4 of 4, Col

FIGURE 11.20   The user can go back to LoginForm from RegisterForm.

Listing 11.2 is the class file for the ActionScript 2.0 LoginFormScreen class that powers the LoginForm screen in the CustomerEntry.fla example document. Except for very short snippets of code attached to buttons (most of which is shown in this section's figures), all the ActionScript code for this example is here.

FIGURE 11.21   Users click Continue on this form to create a new customer record.

> **NOTE**
>
> For this listing to work, you must uncomment the appropriate `ServiceWSDLURL` line near the top of this listing to indicate the server to which you want the example to connect. In an actual, deployed application, you would use a relative URL instead of an absolute URL (that is, without the `http://` part). Doing so keeps you from hardcoding the server name into the movie.

LISTING 11.2   LoginFormScreen.as—ActionScript Code Used by the CustomerEntry.fla Example

```
// Import the Messages class, which declares constant properties
// such as CUST_BAD_CREDENTIALS and CUST_DUPLICATE_UNAME
import venue.constants.Msgs;

dynamic class LoginFormScreen extends mx.screens.Form {

  // Declare constants
  static var NO_RECORD_FOUND:Number = -1;

  // Uncomment one of these lines to use the desired server
  // ColdFusion Version
  var ServiceWSDLURL =
➥"http://localhost/venue/chapter11/UserCheck.cfc?WSDL";
  // ASP.NET Version
  //var ServiceWSDLURL =
➥"http://localhost/venue/chapter11/UserCheck.asmx?WSDL";
  // Java Version
  //var ServiceWSDLURL =
➥"http://localhost/venue/chapter11/UserCheck.jws?WSDL";


  // This function fires when this screen first loads
  function onLoad() {

    // Turn on data logging to monitor web service calls
    // (you can comment this out when no longer needed)
    //_global.__dataLogger = new mx.data.binding.Log();
```

continues

LISTING 11.2   LoginFormScreen.as—ActionScript Code Used by the CustomerEntry.fla Example
(Continued)

```
// Force the "_root" keyword to always refer to this SWF
// (never another SWF that loaded this one externally)
this._lockroot = true;

// Make the other form invisible
rootForm.RegisterForm.visible = false;

// Create an instance of the BubbleMovieClip, named mcBubble
_root.attachMovie("BubbleMovieClip", "mcBubble", 1000);

// Set the WSDLURL of the WebServiceConnector components
this.wsGetCustomerID.WSDLURL = ServiceWSDLURL;
this.wsIsUsernameAvailable.WSDLURL = ServiceWSDLURL;
this.wsCreateNewCustomer.WSDLURL = ServiceWSDLURL;

// Hook up event listeners to web service connectors
this.wsGetCustomerID.addEventListener("result",
➥getCustomerID_Result);
this.wsIsUsernameAvailable.addEventListener("result",
➥isUsernameAvailable_Result);
this.wsCreateNewCustomer.addEventListener("result",
➥createNewCustomer_Result);

// Hook up validation event listeners to form input fields
this.parentForm.RegisterForm.tiFirstName.addEventListener("invalid",
this.firstName_Invalid);
    this.parentForm.RegisterForm.tiLastName.addEventListener("invalid",
    ➥lastName_Invalid);

this.parentForm.RegisterForm.tiTelephone.addEventListener("invalid",
telephone_Invalid);
    this.parentForm.RegisterForm.tiEmail.addEventListener("invalid",
    ➥email_Invalid);
}

// Executes when the user clicks continue and is existing user
function continueExisting() {
  if (validateUsernameAndPassword()) {
    this.wsGetCustomerID.trigger();
  }
}

// Executes when the user clicks continue and is existing user
function continueNew() {
```

```
    if (validateUsernameAndPassword()) {
      this.wsIsUsernameAvailable.trigger();
    }
}


// Executes when server responds to a login attempt
function getCustomerID_Result() {
  if (this.results == NO_RECORD_FOUND) {
    _root.mcBubble.showMessage(Msgs.CUST_BAD_CREDENTIALS,
    ➥_parent.tiUsername);
  } else {
    _parent.returnCustomerID(this.results);
    return;
  }
}


// Executes when server responds to a "is username unique" request
function isUsernameAvailable_Result() {
  // If server reports that the username is already taken
  if (this.results == false) {
    _root.mcBubble.showMessage(Msgs.CUST_DUPLICATE_UNAME,
    ➥_parent.tiUsername);
    return;

  // If the server reports that the username is available
  } else {
    // Send user to new-account-entry form
    _parent.visible = false;
    _parent.rootForm.RegisterForm.visible = true;
  }
}


// Executes when server responds to a create-new-user request
function createNewCustomer_Result() {
  trace("got it " + this.results);
  _parent.returnCustomerID(this.results);
}


// Returns a customer ID to the root form
// The root form can do whatever it wants with the ID
function returnCustomerID(id) {
  trace("Returning customer ID: " + id);
  this.rootForm.visible = false;
```

continues

```
    _root.setCustomerID(id);
}


// Validates user entries on the first (login) form
function validateUsernameAndPassword():Boolean {
  // Validate text field
  if (this.tiUsername.text == '') {
    _root.mcBubble.showMessage(Msgs.CUST_MISSING_UNAME,
    ➥this.tiUsername);
    return false;
  };

  // Validate text field
  if (this.tiUsername.text.length < 5) {
    _root.mcBubble.showMessage(Msgs.CUST_INVALID_UNAME,
    ➥this.tiUsername);
    return false;
  };

  // Validate text field
  if (this.tiPassword.text == '') {
    _root.mcBubble.showMessage(Msgs.CUST_MISSING_PSSWD,
    ➥this.tiPassword);
    return false;
  };

  // Validate text field
  if (this.tiPassword.text.length < 5) {
    _root.mcBubble.showMessage(Msgs.CUST_INVALID_PSSWD,
    ➥this.tiPassword);
    return false;
  };

  // If "new username" (as opposed to existing user) form is showing
  if (this.NewLoginOverlay.visible) {
    if (this.tiPassword.text != this.NewLoginOverlay.tiPassword.text)
{
      _root.mcBubble.showMessage(Msgs.CUST_CONFIRM_PSSWD,
      ➥this.NewLoginOverlay.tiPassword);
      return false;
    }
  };
```

```
  // Return true if all entries are valid
  return true;
}


// Validation event handlers for the form input fields
function firstName_Invalid() {
  _root.mcBubble.showMessage(Msgs.CUST_MISSING_FNAME, this);
}
function lastName_Invalid() {
  _root.mcBubble.showMessage(Msgs.CUST_MISSING_LNAME, this);
}
function telephone_Invalid() {
  _root.mcBubble.showMessage(Msgs.CUST_INVALID_PHONE, this);
}
function email_Invalid() {
  _root.mcBubble.showMessage(Msgs.CUST_INVALID_EMAIL, this);
}

}
```

> **NOTE**
>
> See the next section, "A Short Digression About Constants," for an explanation of the variables (such as NO_RECORD_FOUND and Msgs.CUST_BAD_CREDENTIALS) that appear in capital letters in this listing.

You have already several portions of this code, in slightly different form, in various snippets and figures in this chapter. This listing uses a number of the properties of the Screen class that were listed in Table 11.2 to access the various screens in the example document.

Because this ActionScript 2.0 class is attached to the LoginForm screen in the FLA, the this keyword usually refers to the LoginForm screen. The exception is in the event handlers for the Button and WebServiceConnector components, within the bodies of which the this keyword refers to the button or connector.

So, event handlers for other components aside, the current context is the LoginForm screen, which means that this.NewLoginOverlay—or just NewLoginOverlay—refers to the NewLoginOverlay screen that is nested within LoginForm (as shown back in Figure 11.15). Similarly, this.parentForm (or this.rootForm) refers to the application screen, and this.parentForm.RegisterForm refers to the RegisterForm screen that is a child of application.

If you test this example out in a browser, you will find that the following are true:

- You can indicate that you are either an existing customer or a new customer.

- If you are an existing customer, you must enter a username and password of at least five characters each. This is an example of simple, script-based validation.

- If you are an existing customer, you will receive an error message if you provide an incorrect username or password. This is an example of real-time, server-side validation.

- If you are a new customer, the `NewLoginOverlay` screen appears, forcing you to provide your password for a second time. If the passwords don't match, you are notified with an error message. This is another example of simple, script-based validation.

- If you are a new customer, you will receive an error message if the username you choose has already been taken. This is another example of realtime, server-side validation.

- If you are a new customer, you will also have to fill out the controls on the `RegisterForm` screen. This is an example of databound validation.

A Short Digression About Constants

The strange-looking `NO_RECORD_FOUND` variable at the top of Listing 11.2 is what's known as a *constant* or *class constant*. You are probably already familiar with the concept of a constant, so I won't go into a lengthy explanation here. Basically, any variable whose value will probably never change—and should not be changed at runtime—is a constant. Different programming languages provide different ways of declaring constants. In ActionScript, you declare constants by coding an ordinary `var` line and then adding the `static` keyword, as shown in Listing 11.2.

The whole idea with constants is to give a name to some value that otherwise has little meaning to human readers. For instance, the purpose of the `NO_RECORD_FOUND` constant in this example is to represent the special value of −1 that is returned by the `getCustomerID()` web service method (see Table 11.5). Rather than having the special value of −1 turn up here and there in your code, you can declare a constant for it, which makes your code more readable.

Note

It's traditional to use all capital letters and underscores (instead of mixed case) for variables that are to be used as constants. You are, of course, free to use a variable name such as `NoRecordFound` instead of `NO_RECORD_FOUND`; the capital letters don't signify anything special to Flash. However, the use of capital letters will help others understand that the value of the variable is not meant to be manipulated via script.

This may all may seem silly when there is just one value to consider, but it would make a lot more sense if there were other special values to consider for each customer record. You might, perhaps, have the database return a –2 for an account that has been closed and a –3 for an account that has been put on hold. Then, in your code, you could create constants called `ACCT_CLOSED` and `ACCT_ON_HOLD` and use them instead of using –2 and –3 over and over again.

So, what makes a constant different from an ordinary variable? Nothing, really, except for how you use them as a programmer.

Just for the heck of it, I created a separate ActionScript 2.0 class file to hold some string constants that represent certain messages for the user. The class is called `Msgs`, and it simply declares a number of constants using the same `static` syntax shown in Listing 11.2. The constants can then be used by importing this class with the `import` keyword and then referring to the constants by name as static properties of the class itself (as shown in Listing 11.2). Listing 11.3 shows the code for the `Msgs` class.

Listing 11.3 Msgs.as—Defining Message Constants in a Separate ActionScript 2.0 Class

```
class venue.constants.Msgs {
  static var CUST_MISSING_UNAME:String = "Please provide a username.";
  static var CUST_INVALID_UNAME:String = "The username must be at least
➥5 characters";
  static var CUST_MISSING_PSSWD:String = "Please provide a password.";
  static var CUST_INVALID_PSSWD:String = "The password must be at least
➥5 characters";
  static var CUST_CONFIRM_PSSWD:String = "You must re-type the password
➥correctly.";
  static var CUST_MISSING_FNAME:String = "Please provide a first name.";
  static var CUST_MISSING_LNAME:String = "Please provide a first name.";
  static var CUST_INVALID_PHONE:String = "Please provide a phone number.";
  static var CUST_INVALID_EMAIL:String = "Please provide a valid email.";
  static var CUST_BAD_CREDENTIALS:String = "That username or password
➥is invalid.";
  static var CUST_DUPLICATE_UNAME:String = "This username is already
➥taken. Please choose another.";
}
```

It's worth noting that because a package name of venue.constants is used in the class at the top of this listing, the file must be placed within a folder named constants within another folder named venue. The venue folder needs to be in the same directory as the FLA that is using the class or at some other location in Flash's classpath. See Chapter 4 for details about the classpath.

> **NOTE**
>
> Actually, it's more traditional—and makes a lot more sense—to use constants to represent arbitrary numbers (rather than using them to represent strings). The DB_NO_RECORD_FOUND constant in Listing 11.2 is an example of a constant that represents an arbitrary number. I just wanted to show you how constants can be defined in a separate class file and made easily reusable.

A Few Words on Organization

Take a quick glance back at Figure 11.2. It could be argued that it would make more sense to create two ActionScript class files for this example, one for the LoginForm screen and one for the RegisterForm screen, because both screens contain elements that rely on scripting. I chose to use one class file so that you would see how components in one screen can be referenced from the context of another screen.

In contrast, you might decide to have a general policy of always creating a class for every screen that requires scripting. Or you could decide not to use class files at all, instead putting your custom functions on a screen's underlying timeline. As usual, Flash offers a number of different ways to organize your code. Use whatever system or methodology makes sense to you and your team for a particular project.

> **NOTE**
>
> Similarly, some people might vote for putting the nonvisual, data-access components (in this case, the three WebServiceConnector instances) in the root slide, or perhaps in a separate slide altogether. It's up to you to decide whether to keep your connectors—and other data-related components such as DataSet—close to the controls to which they are bound.

Source Code for the BubbleMovieClip Class

Listing 11.4 is the ActionScript 2.0 class file that powers the "speech bubble" widget shown back in Figure 11.9. This code is fairly straightforward. It assumes that it is attached to a movie clip symbol, an instance of which has been placed on the Stage. The clip contains another movie clip, with an instance name of mcBubbleMsg. The mcBubbleMsg clip contains a simple text field named `txtMessage`, plus the artwork for the speech bubble itself. The `onLoad` handler in this listing makes sure that the whole contraption is invisible when the SWF first loads.

LISTING 11.4 BubbleMovieClip.as—Code for the Speech-Bubble Movie Clip

```
class BubbleMovieClip extends MovieClip {

  // Declare props to reflect expected contents of this movie clip
  public var mcBubbleMsg:MovieClip;

  // Executes when this clip first loads
  public function onLoad() {
    // Start off invisible
    this._visible = false;
  }

  // Public function to show a message
  public function showMessage(message:String,
  ➥pointTo:mx.core.UIComponent, focus:Boolean) {
    // Place the message in the text field within this clip
    mcBubbleMsg.txtMessage.text = message;

    // Position this clip on the Stage
    this._y = pointTo.y;
    this._x = pointTo._x + pointTo.width;

    // Set focus to the item we're pointing at, if called for
    if (focus) {
      pointTo.setFocus();
    }

    // Make this clip visible
    this._visible = true;

    // Play fade-in animation
    this.gotoAndPlay("fade in");
  }

  // Public function to hide the message
  public function hideMessage() {
    this._visible = false;
  }
}
```

As you can see, this class exposes one public method called `showMessage()`, which is used several times within Listing 11.2. The method accepts three arguments: `message`, which is displayed in the text field within the `mcBubbleMsg` instance; `pointTo`, which indicates the UI control that the speech bubble should point to; and `focus`, which is a Boolean value that indicates whether the `pointTo` control should be focused via its `setFocus()` method.

After the specified message has been placed into the text field, and after the speech bubble has been positioned next to the appropriate control, the movie clip is made visible, and a simple fade in animation is played via the usual `MovieClip.gotoAndPlay()` method. You can take a look at the `BubbleClip` symbol in the Library to examine the animation; it just uses the `mcBubbleMsg` clip's `_alpha` property to make the clip fade in over the span of a few frames.

Loading External Content into Screens

The example you have been working with in this chapter (CustomerEntry.fla) contains several screens, with each screen containing its own components, labels, shapes, or other content. When the movie is published, all the content gets compiled into the generated SWF.

Every screen is also capable of loading external content at runtime. The screen can load an external SWF or JPEG image, using either an absolute or relative URL. The screen can also load a symbol—most likely a movie clip symbol—from the Library, as long as the symbol has been given a linkage identifier. These abilities are inherited from the Loader class (refer to Table 11.4). It's almost as if there was an invisible Loader component built on the Stage of every screen, just waiting to be used.

Conceptually, loading content into a screen is not much different from loading external content into an empty movie clip with the `MovieClip.loadMovie()` method, which has been used in a number of examples throughout this book. Loading the content via a screen (or a `Loader` component) is just a slightly more structured and managed way to do so.

Specifying External Content at Design Time

To construct a quick example that demonstrates how to load external content into screens, do the following:

1. Use File > New to create a new Flash Slide Application document. The document will have two slides when it first appears. They are named `presentation` and `slide1`.

2. Use File > Save to save the new document as ExternalContent.fla.

3. Click slide1 in the Screen Outline pane, and then use the Properties panel to set the `contentPath` property to CustomerEntry.swf, which is the SWF file from the previous example from this chapter (see Figure 11.22).

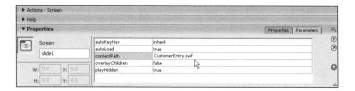

FIGURE 11.22   It's easy to load external content into a screen.

NOTE

The external content is not visible in the screen while you are authoring in the Flash IDE. It's loaded at runtime, not design time.

---

4. Add another slide to the document; it will probably be named `slide2`.

5. Set the new slide's `contentPath` property to ../chapter09/RatingChart.swf (the Ratings Chart example from Chapter 9). You could use the URL for any other SWF if you prefer, or the URL for a JPEG.

6. Now go ahead and Test the movie via Control > Test Movie. You'll see the CustomerEntry.swf example. If you press the right arrow key, you'll see the second example. If you press the left arrow key, you'll come back to the first example. Simple, eh?

Loading External Content via ActionScript

You can set the content to be loaded via script just as easily by setting the contentPath property in response to whatever event is appropriate. For instance, you could place a button in the top-level screen and then load content into the slide1 screen by adding the following lines to the Actions panel for the button:

```
on(click) {
   _parent.slide1.contentPath = "CustomerEntry.swf";
}
```

Or, you could set the screen's autoLoad property to false in the Properties panel and then use the load() method to load the external content, like so:

```
on(click) {
   _parent.slide1.load("CustomerEntry.swf");
}
```

Accessing the External Content After It Loads

After an external SWF loads into a screen, the document that loaded it can access its contents via the content property of the screen. Thus, if a screen named form1 has loaded an external SWF, and the external SWF contains a movie clip with an instance name of mcPhoto, the visibility of the clip could be controlled with the following line:

```
_root.form1.content.mcPhoto._visibility = false;
```

Adding a *ProgressBar* Component

It is particularly easy to add a progress bar that displays the download progress of a screen's external content. To give this a try, follow these steps:

1. Go back to the ExternalContent.fla document that you created a few moments ago in the "Specifying External Content at Design Time" section.

2. Click the slide1 screen in the Screen Outline pane.

3. Drag a ProgressBar component onto the Stage from the Components panel, positioning it near the center of the Stage, and give it an instance name of pbLoadProgress.

4. Using the Properties panel, set the `mode` property to `polled` (see Figure 11.23). You should use `polled` whenever you want the progress bar to monitor the download progress of a `MovieClip` object. See the Flash documentation for information about the other two options (`event` and `manual`).

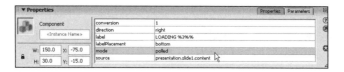

FIGURE 11.23   It's easy to create a download progress bar for a screen's content.

5. Also using the Properties panel, set the `source` property to `presentation.slide1.content`.

6. With the `ProgressBar` still selected, open the Actions panel and add an `on(complete)` handler that sets the components `visible` property to `false` (see Figure 11.24).

FIGURE 11.24   The progress bar will disappear when the content finishes loading.

7. Copy and paste the `ProgressBar` into the `slide2` screen, and change its source property to `presentation.slide2.content`. Also change the word LOADING in the `label` property to LOADING MORE (but leave the `%3%%` part at the end alone).

To test out the progress bars, do the following:

1. Use Control > Test Movie to preview the movie in the Flash IDE. You will probably see the progress bars for a moment, but they will disappear almost immediately because the external SWF is on your local drive.

2. Still in Preview mode, choose View > Download Settings > DSL (or any of the other speeds listed).

3. Choose View > Simulate Download (or just press Ctrl+Enter). Now you will see the progress bar move as an actual user would see it if he or she were using a medium-speed Internet connection. When the progress bar reaches 100 percent, it disappears and the external content appears, just as expected.

After you start the simulated download (that is, while the progress bar is moving), you can press the left and right arrow keys to switch between the two slides in the main document, thereby switching between the two progress bars. (You'll be able to tell them apart because one is labeled LOADING and the other is labeled LOADING MORE.) The two progress bars operate independently.

> **NOTE**
>
> Consult the Using Components portion of the Flash Documentation for complete reference information about the label, source, mode, and other properties of the ProgressBar component.

Depending on the situation, you may not want all pieces of external content to be downloaded at the same time, especially if the first screen is one of the screens that gets its content externally. It may make more sense for the first screen to download its content first so that it gets the full bandwidth of the user's connection. Then the other screens can begin downloading their external content while the user is interacting with (or is at least distracted by) the first screen.

To make this change, do the following:

1. Still in the ExternalContent.fla document, click the slide2 screen and use the Properties panel to set its autoLoad property (see Table 11.4) to false.

2. Go to the Actions panel for the first slide's progress bar (not the second slide's) and change the code to the following (the last two lines are new):

```
on(complete) {
  this.visible = false;
  _parent.rootSlide.slide2.load();
  _parent.rootSlide.slide2.pbLoadProgress.source =
"presentation.slide2.content";
}
```

> **NOTE**
>
> It is necessary to reset the value of the source property after telling the screen to load an external URL via script.

Now if you test the movie using the Simulate Download option, switching back and forth between the slides during the download progress, you will find that the first slide gets all the download attention until it is fully loaded. Only then does the second slide begin loading.

Ironically enough, the ExternalContent.swf file itself is now likely to be 30–40KB, which means that the progress bar won't appear until the user's connection has already pulled down nearly all of the first 30–40KB worth of Flash content. The fact that the progress bar does not appear right away defeats some of the purpose for having a progress bar in the first place. This is an unfortunate fact of life when using the Flash MX 2004 components (screens included). The use of just about any component guarantees that the file size of the SWF will be at least 25–30KB; the combination of screens plus any one component is likely to add another 5–10KB. The good news is that the size doesn't keep increasing at nearly the same rate for each component you add to a movie.

An Aside: Preloader Documents

If you don't necessarily want the functionality of screens, but still want to display a movie's download progress, you might want to consider using an extremely small preloader movie instead of a screen-based document. Any number of examples of preloader SWFs can be found online or in other books. I have provided a basic preloader movie with this chapter's example files. The document is named Preloader.fla, and there are some accompanying instructions in the PreloaderDiscussion.html file.

The example uses the new `MovieClipLoader` API—which is new for this version of Flash—to load your main movie. Many other techniques have been developed over the years to deal with the problem of preloading movies. You are encouraged to explore other solutions online.

Summary

This chapter has covered a lot of ground, building upon the knowledge you have gained in prior chapters. First, we talked a bit about the potential advantages of Flash-based forms. Then you learned about the new screen-based authoring mode in Flash MX Professional 2004, which is particularly well suited for creating Flash-based forms. Then you explored a number of ways to enforce validation rules, both with and without realtime support from the server. Next, you learned about loading screen content at runtime, and how to display a progress bar as the screen content is loading.

With the basics of Flash-based form building under your belt, you can explore some of the other components in Flash's Components panel. The `Tree`, `Grid`, `Checkbox`, and `TextArea` components are all very useful for creating slick, interactive forms for your web applications. In addition, although they aren't data-entry controls per se, the `Accordian`, `MenuBar`, and `ScrollPane` components are interesting indeed and can augment the usability of a Flash-based form. Extensive documentation and examples for all these components are available in the Flash documentation and online. All can be scripted and connected to server-side data and logic using any of the server-integration techniques discussed in this book.

Have fun!

PART V
APPENDIXES

A   Notes on Building the
    SimpleBarChart Component   551

B   Cross-Domain Data Access Policies in
    Flash Player 7   583

NOTES ON BUILDING THE SIMPLEBARCHART COMPONENT

In Chapter 9, "Connecting to Servers with Web Services," a simple component named SimpleBarChart was used to create a bar chart that displays information about song ratings. This appendix provides some further information about the component, some notes on the steps needed to put it together, and a annotated look at the source code.

Although this short appendix does not come close to covering everything there is to know about creating components with Macromedia Flash MX 2004, it may nonetheless prove useful to you as an example of relatively complex ActionScript code. The source code for this component shows you how to do the following:

- Create a working component, complete with useful properties, methods, and events.

- Mark properties as *inspectable*, meaning that they can be set in the Properties panel or the Component Inspector.

- Draw shapes at runtime, using the drawing-related methods of the `MovieClip` class (see Chapter 5, "Movie Clips as Objects," for reference information about the drawing methods).
- Use ActionScript 2.0 inheritance to create a simple "chain" of classes and subclasses (see Chapter 4, "ActionScript: A Primer," for more information about the `extends` keyword and class inheritance).
- Design and implement an API for the visualization of data (most likely from a server).

I encourage you to play around with this example on your own, perhaps improving on its (admittedly imperfect) API design, or perhaps pillaging some of the code for your own projects.

About Flash MX 2004 Components

The first version of Flash that supported a component-like concept was Flash 5, which introduced a feature called SmartClips that can be seen as a precursor to today's components. The next version, Flash MX, was the first version to use the word *component* to describe independent, fully encapsulated objects for Flash developers. Flash MX 2004 introduces a third system for creating components, which Macromedia calls the V2 component architecture.

NOTE

This appendix demonstrates how to create V2 components, which are new for Flash MX 2004. In Chapter 5, you learned that it is also possible to quickly turn a movie clip into a simple component using the Component Definition dialog box for the clip symbol in the Library. That is the first step in creating the older, V1 type of components (which is still supported in Flash MX 2004). Consult the Flash documentation or the Macromedia website for more information about the differences between the component architectures. In general, you are encouraged to use the V2 system when you can.

Differences Between Components and Ordinary Movie Clips

To build a component, you start with a movie clip symbol and then create an ActionScript 2.0 class that defines the clip's behavior. In other words, components are not much different from ordinary movie clips that have ActionScript 2.0 classes associated with them. The main differences are as follows:

- Components can appear in the Components panel of the Flash IDE and can be dragged into new documents just like the components that ship with Flash MX 2004.

- Components have metadata embedded within the corresponding ActionScript 2.0 class file that describes the properties and events that should appear in the Properties panel and Component Inspector.

- A completed component is assembled into a special type of file called a *SWC file*. The SWC file contains all the bits and pieces that the component was made with, including the elements and compiled versions of each ActionScript class used throughout. An SWC file is self-contained and can be distributed to third parties without the source ActionScript or Flash document (.fla) files.

NOTE

SWC files are similar conceptually to JAR (Java archive) files, in that they are based on the PKZIP archive format and contain a manifest that enumerates the contents of the archive. You can open an SWC with any ZIP-compatible program, such as WinZip.

Of course, it takes a bit of extra work to create a component, but you may be pleasantly surprised at how little extra work it really turns out to be in practice. This appendix presents an example component that you can use to jumpstart the process of learning how to make your own components. You will, however, probably need to consult the Creating Components portion of the Flash documentation for a thorough overview of the process.

About the *SimpleBarChart* Component

As you learned in Chapter 9, the SimpleBarChart component is relatively easy to use. First, you drag an instance of the component onto the Stage and give it an instance name. You can set many of the component's properties at design time, including its background color and other visual characteristics (see Table A.1). Then you add one or more *fields* to the instance via script, using the addField() method (see Table A.2). Each field will be represented by a bar when the chart is displayed. Next, you add one or more *data series* to the instance, using the addSeries() method; each series represents the state of the fields at a particular moment in time. Then you call the draw() method, which causes the chart to display the bars for the first series. If you have set the refreshInterval property, the data series will be displayed one after the other, with a pause between each series.

For instance, if you have an instance of the component called bcChart, the following code snippet would cause three bars to be displayed between the chart. Every 1.5 seconds, the data reflected by the bars would change (displaying the 2003, 2004, and 2005 states of the data, respectively).

```
bcChart.refreshInterval = 1500;
bcChart.addField("nw", "Nate Weiss");
bcChart.addField("jl", "Jennifer Lopez");
bcChart.addField("ba", "Ben Affleck");
bcChart.addSeries({nw:20, jl:12, ba:45}, "Fans in 2003");
bcChart.addSeries({nw:17, jl:24, ba:13}, "Fans in 2004");
bcChart.addSeries({nw:34, jl:36, ba:21}, "Fans in 2005");
bcChart.draw();
```

The examples for this chapter include a Flash document called UseChart.fla, which contains this code snippet in its first frame. You can open and test the document to see the bar chart in action.

> **NOTE**
>
> Please refer back to Chapter 9 for an example of using data from a server with the component.

SimpleBarChart Reference

Table A.1 shows the public properties supported by the `SimpleBarChart` component. All these properties are inspectable, meaning that they can be set either at design time (via the Properties panel or the Component Inspector) or at runtime (via ActionScript).

TABLE A.1 *SimpleBarChart* Component Properties

PROPERTY	DESCRIPTION
barColors	Array. An array of colors to use for the bars in the chart. The first bar will have the first color, the second bar will have the second color, and so on. If there are more bars than there are specified colors, the colors will repeat. The default is a set of six assorted colors.
barSpacing	Numeric. The amount of horizontal space between each bar. The default is 30 pixels.
bgColor	Numeric. The color of the chart's background, expressed as a hexadecimal number (such as 0xFF0000 for red). The default is 0xEFEFEF, a light gray.
borderColor	Numeric. The color of the chart's border. The default is 0x000000 (black).
borderWidth	Numeric. The line width used for the chart's border, in pixels. The default is 0 (hairline). Refer back to Chapter 5 for information about line widths and hairlines.
labelWidth	Numeric. The width of the text fields that display the current value represented by each bar. The default is 150 pixels.
refreshInterval	Numeric. The number of milliseconds that you would like the chart to pause between data series. If this property is set to 0 (the default), the chart will not switch between the series automatically. If there is only one data series, this property is effectively ignored.
subRefreshNumSteps	Numeric. If `useAnimation` is `true` (the default), this value indicates how many animated steps should occur after each change to the data series. The default is 10.

continues

TABLE A.1 *SimpleBarChart* Component Properties (Continued)

PROPERTY	DESCRIPTION
subRefreshInterval	Numeric. If useAnimation is true, this value indicates how many milliseconds should elapse between each step of the animation process. The default is 20 milliseconds, which means that the total length of the animation is 200 milliseconds (10 steps times 20 milliseconds), or one-fifth of a second.
useAnimation	Boolean. Whether an animated effect is used when the data series changes in the bar chart. If false, the bars jump abruptly from one value to the next. If true, the bars grow or shrink smoothly from one value to the next. This property defaults to true.
yScaleMax	Numeric. The value at which the chart's y scale should end. If the chart is asked to display a value that is more than this property, the property will automatically be increased to accommodate the value. In other words, you can leave the value at 0 (the default) if you want the chart to scale automatically.
yScaleMin	Numeric. The value at which the chart's y scale should begin. The default is 0, meaning that a value of 0 will be plotted at the very bottom of the chart. If the chart is asked to display a value that is less than this property, the property will automatically be decreased to accommodate the value.

Table A.2 shows the public methods exposed by the SimpleBarChart component. Please refer back to Chapter 9 to see these methods used in an actual example.

TABLE A.2 *SimpleBarChart* Component Methods

Method	Description
addField(name, label)	Method. Adds a field (which will be represented by a bar) to the bar chart. The name is any string or ID number that will uniquely identify the field; it does not appear visually on the chart. The label is a label to display at the bottom of the chart.
addSeries(data, title)	Method. Adds a set of data points to the bar chart. The data argument is an object (associative array) that contains properties for each field added via addField(). The value of each property is the number to represent in the

Method	Description
	chart. The `title` argument is a string to display as the chart's title when this series is showing.
`clearAll()`	Method. Removes all fields and series data from the chart, effectively resetting it.
`draw()`	Method. Causes the chart to display the first data series in bar chart form.

Creating the *SimpleBarChart* Component

This section will explain the steps that were necessary to create the `SimpleBarChart` component. First we will take a look at the items in the movie clip symbol that represents the visual aspect of the component. Then we will review the ActionScript code that makes the component do its job at runtime.

What to Look for in the Source Document

Open the SimpleBarChart_Source.fla document, which is included with this chapter's examples. The document itself was created normally, by choosing Flash Document in the New Document dialog box.

Please note the following:

- There is absolutely nothing on the main document's Stage, though if there were, it wouldn't make any difference. The only items that matter in this document are its Library symbols.
- The Library contains two symbols: a component symbol called `SimpleBarChart` (which represents the finished component), and a bare-bones movie clip called `BackgroundClip`.
- The `SimpleBarChart` symbol was created by creating a new movie clip symbol and then setting both the Name and Linkage Identifier to `SimpleBarChart` (see Figure A.1). Note that the "Export in first frame" option has been disabled in the symbol's Properties dialog box, per Macromedia's recommendations for creating components.
- The AS 2.0 Class field for the `SimpleBarChart` symbol has also been set to the string `venue.simplecharts.SimpleBarChart`, which corresponds to the ActionScript 2.0 class file called SimpleBarChart.as (the source code for which you will see shortly in Listing A.2).

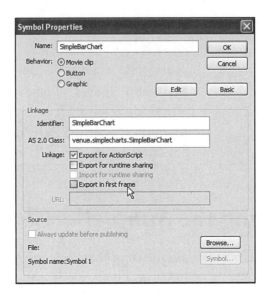

FIGURE A.1   The properties of the `SimpleBarChart` symbol.

- The AS 2.0 Class field has also been set to `venue.simplecharts.`
  `SimpleBarChart` in the component symbol's Component Definition
  dialog box (see Figure A.2). Note that the component's parameters (as
  listed in Table A.1) are listed in the top part of the dialog box. The
  parameters were not entered into the dialog box by hand, however.
  The parameters are read automatically from the ActionScript 2.0 class
  file (which you'll see in Listing A.2).

- The `SimpleBarChart` symbol's timeline contains three layers: Actions,
  Assets, and Background. Any ActionScript code that needs to be placed
  in the timeline—and a few lines are required—should be in the Actions
  layer. Any additional symbols that might be instantiated via script at
  runtime should be placed in Frame 2 of the assets layer, which ensures
  that the symbols are included with the final SWC file. (In this case,
  there are no such symbols, so the Assets layer is empty.)

- Whatever is in Frame 1 determines the initial size of the component
  when it is first dragged onto the Stage at design time; it is not displayed
  at runtime. In this case, Frame 1 of the Background layer contains an
  instance of the `BackgroundClip` movie clip. The clip contains a single
  rectangle shape, which is exactly 300 pixels wide and 200 pixels high
  and is aligned exactly with the clip's registration point (that is, its X/Y
  position is 0,0). The clip instance's Alpha property has been set to 0 in
  the Properties panel, which makes it invisible at both runtime and

design time. The main purpose of BackgroundClip in this document is to establish the initial size of the component at design time. There has to be something in Frame 1; in a case such as this (where the component is going to draw itself from scratch, rather than relying on visual elements on the stage), it can just be something invisible.

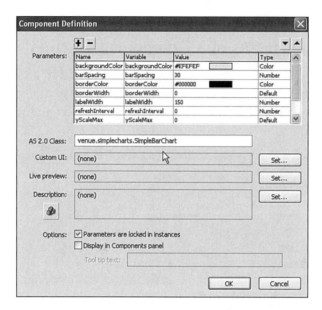

FIGURE A.2   Flash reads the component's parameters from the ActionScript 2.0 class file.

- The BackgroundClip symbol also contains a text field that includes font outlines for the Arial font (click the Character button in the Properties panel for the text field). This ensures that the font outlines will be included in the final SWC for the component; the outlines will in turn be included in SWFs that use the component. Font outlines are needed whenever rotated text will be displayed, and this component needs to display rotated text labels that appear under each bar. If the document that is using the component wants to use a different fort for the labels, it will need to include the appropriate font outlines on its own. Refer to the Flash documentation about the TextField. embedFonts property for details.

- The Actions layer for Frame 1 has one line of code: `import SimpleBarChart`, which ensures that the ActionScript 2.0 class file is included with the final SWC file. Frame 2 also contains one line of code: `stop()`, which keeps the movie from looping back to Frame 1. There is no other ActionScript code in the FLA; everything else is in separate ActionScript 2.0 class files.

Required Elements in a Component's ActionScript File

There are a few basic elements that you should add to a class file for a component. Listing A.1 shows a skeletal ActionScript class that shows how to place these elements in a class file. You can use this file as a guide for creating new components.

LISTING A.1   ClassSkeleton.as—Skeletal ActionScript Class File for a Component

```
import mx.core.UIComponent;

class mypackage.MyComponent extends mx.core.UIComponent {

  // These properties should be declared for any component
  static var symbolName:String = "MyComponent";
  static var symbolOwner:Object = mypackage.MyComponent;
  static var version:String = "1.0.0.0";
  var className:String = "MyComponent";

  // Constructor
  public function MyComponent() {
  }

  // Implement init() method
  public function init() {
    // Call the superclass's init() method
    super.init()
  }

  // Implement size() method
  public function size() {
    // Call the superclass's size() method
    super.size();
  }
}
```

This is, in most respects, an ordinary ActionScript 2.0 class file. The only thing special about it is that it implements a few special methods and properties that are used internally by Flash's component architecture (both at design time and runtime). You will need to consult the Flash documentation for a complete explanation of these elements, but consider the following as a brief introduction:

- A component class should extend `mx.core.UIComponent` or `mx.Core.UIObject`. Both descend from `MovieClip` and offer all the inherited methods and properties that would be available if you extended `MovieClip` directly. Consult the Flash documentation for an explanation of which class to extend from in which situations.

- You must include an `import` line for the `UIComponent` or `UIObject` class that you choose to extend. This forces the base class to be included in the SWC file for your component. You must also include `import` lines for any additional classes that you refer to in the class file (not including built-in intrinsic classes such as `MovieClip` or `TextField`).

- You should declare the four variables shown near the top of Listing A.1 (of course replacing the actual version number, package, and component names with your own). These values are used internally to implement certain component features.

- You should implement a constructor function. Macromedia recommends that you leave the constructor empty when possible; instead, put any initialization code in the `init()` method. See Chapter 4 for details about constructors.

- You should implement an `init()` method, which at a minimum calls the superclass's `init()` method via the `super` keyword. This method will be called automatically at runtime when your component is instantiated; it is also called at design time when you drag an instance of the component onto the Stage or open a document that contains the component. Any initialization code (code that would ordinarily go in a constructor) is usually placed here.

- You should implement a `size()` method, which at a minimum calls the superclass's `size()` method (again, via the `super` keyword). This method will be called automatically at runtime if the component's size is changed via script; it is also at design time if you change the size of a component instance on the Stage. You may wish to have the component redraw or rearrange its visual elements within this method.

Marking Properties as Inspectable

You can add special *metadata tags* to a component's ActionScript 2.0 class file to allow the component to describe itself to the Flash IDE. Flash MX 2004 supports a number of different metadata tags, but the most important one is `[Inspectable]`. The `[Inspectable]` tag tells Flash that a particular property should appear in the Properties or Component Inspector panels at design time. You—or other Flash developers—can then use the panels to quickly make changes to the component without ActionScript (of course, you are still free to set the properties via script when you want to).

To use the `[Inspectable]` tag, simply place it on its own line above the public property that you want to be inspectable at design time. You can place the tag above simple property declarations (that is, `var` lines within the `class` block but outside of any `function` blocks) or above the property's setter if you are using getters and setters. (See Chapter 4 for information about getters and setters.)

NOTE

The Flash IDE will be able to show changes in the component's live preview only for properties that have setters.

The `[Inspectable]` tag supports a number of attributes that you can add for further control over how each property is represented in the Flash IDE at design time:

- **name.** For providing a descriptive name to show at design time (if not provided, the actual property name is used).
- **type.** For specifying the property's datatype, which allows the Flash IDE to show convenient pickers or drop-downs as appropriate (if not provided, the actual property's datatype is used).
- **defaultValue.** For specifying a default value for the property in the Flash IDE. You should provide a default value for setters. For simple `var` declarations, Flash will pick up the actual default from the right side of the declaration (if any) if this attribute is not provided.
- **enumeration.** For providing a fixed set of acceptable property values for developers to choose from in the Flash IDE.
- **verbose.** For specifying that a property should show up in the Component Inspector but not the Properties panel.

You can see the `type` and `defaultValue` attributes in use by looking ahead to Listing A.3.

NOTE

There are three additional attributes, called `category`, `listOffset`, and `variable`, but you are relatively unlikely to need them in practice. See the Flash documentation for details.

Flash MX 2004 supports the following metadata tags in addition to `[Inspectable]`. Please see the Creating Components portion of the Flash documentation for details about these tags:

- **[InspectableList]**. For controlling which of a superclass's inspectable properties are exposed at design time.
- **[Event]**. For declaring any custom events that the component may throw (via the `dispatchEvent()` method, as discussed in the Flash documentation).
- **[Bindable]**. For creating properties that can be bound to via databinding.
- **[ChangeEvent]**. For telling Flash which events can trigger changes via databinding.
- **[ComponentTask]**. For creating design-time behavior that makes it easier for developers to configure or use your component (advanced).
- **[IconFile]**. For providing a custom icon to represent your component in the Components panel.

ActionScript Source Code for *SimpleBarChart*

Now that you've gotten a general understanding of what goes into the ActionScript class files for a component, let's take a look at the three classes used by the `SimpleBarChart` example:

- DrawingUIComponent.as, which provides some basic drawing functionality. This class extends the `mx.core.UIComponent` class, from which most components are derived. Alternatively, this component could have been derived from `mx.core.UIObject` instead. See the Flash documentation for an explanation of the differences between these two core classes.

- SimpleBarChart.as, which is the main class file for the component. It extends `DrawingUIComponent`, adding all of the public properties and methods listed in Tables A.1 and A.2. The class also contains some additional private members that are used internally.
- BarChartField.as, which is a very basic class for tracking the data in each of the chart's fields. It is a simple descendant of `Object` and is little more than a declaration of a few properties.

These three classes are all members of a custom ActionScript package called `venue.simplecharts`, which means that they will compile properly only if they are in a folder called simplecharts, which is in a folder called venue, which in turn is in the classpath.

Therefore, if you want to experiment with the classes, you will need to do *one* of the following:

- Copy the venue folder (included with this appendix's example files) to the Classes folder within Flash's configuration folder.
- Add the folder for this appendix's example files to the global classpath, via Edit > Preferences > ActionScript > ActionScript 2.0 Settings.

NOTE

See Chapter 4 for details about classpaths.

The DrawingUIComponent *Class*

Listing A.2 is the source code for the `venue.simplecharts.DrawingUIComponent` class. It contains just one method, `drawBox()`, which is nearly identical to the method of the same name that was included in the `GestureMovieClip` class from Chapter 5.

LISTING A.2   DrawingUIComponent.as—Source Code for the `DrawingUIComponent` Class

```
import mx.core.UIComponent;

class venue.simplecharts.DrawingUIComponent extends UIComponent {

   // These properties should be declared for any component
   static var symbolName:String = "DrawingUIComponent";
   static var symbolOwner:Object = venue.simplecharts.DrawingUIComponent;
   static var version:String = "1.0.0.0";
   var className:String = "DrawingUIComponent";
```

```
public function DrawingUIComponent() {
}

public function init() {
   super.init();
}

public function size() {
   super.size();
}


// This method draws a box within any clip
// (The implementation is generic and could be reused elsewhere)
private function drawBox(mcOn:MovieClip, x:Number, y:Number,
w:Number, h:Number, bgColor, bgAlpha:Number, lineColor:Number,
lineThickness:Number):Void {
   // Coordinates of lower-right corner
   var x2:Number = x + w;
   var y2:Number = y + h;

   // Get ready to start drawing
   mcOn.moveTo(x, y);
   mcOn.lineStyle(lineThickness, lineColor);
   mcOn.beginFill(bgColor, bgAlpha);

   // Draw the four lines
   mcOn.lineTo(x2, y);   // top side
   mcOn.lineTo(x2, y2); // right side
   mcOn.lineTo(x, y2);  // bottom
   mcOn.lineTo(x, y);   // left side

   // Fill the box in
   mcOn.endFill();
}
}
```

The SimpleBarChart Class

Listing A.3 is the source code for the venue.simplecharts.SimpleBarChart class. This is the class that actually implements the bar charting functionality. The SimpleBarChart symbol in the source FLA's library has been set to use this class in its AS 2.0 fields (see Figures A.1 and A.2).

This listing contains a number of ActionScript methods, objects, and techniques that you haven't seen elsewhere in this book. Here's a quick rundown of some of the new concepts, which happen to be related to creating text labels via script (consult the ActionScript Dictionary portion of the Flash Documentation for details):

- The `MovieClip.createTextField()` method provides a way to create new text fields dynamically via script.

- You can specify the formatting in the new text fields by creating `TextFormat` objects and applying the formatting to text fields via the `TextField.setNewTextFormat()` method.

- You can determine the amount of physical space needed to display a particular string in a text field by calling the `TextFormat.getTextExtent()` method. The method is used in this example to determine how much space to leave for the title at the top of the chart.

> **NOTE**
>
> This listing is long, and some of the code is potentially confusing. Don't be discouraged. Most of the methods shown here are simply using the same kinds of movie-clip creation and other techniques that you've seen elsewhere in this book.

LISTING A.3   SimpleBarChart.as—Source code for the `SimpleBarChart` Component Class

```
/*
  SimpleBarChart class
  An ActionScript 2.0-based class for simple bar charting

  Presented as a learning exercise for:
  - Creating components
  - Marking component properties as Inspectable
  - Drawing shapes at runtime
  - Creating text fields at runtime
  - Using ActionScript 2.0 inheritance

  Author: Nate "Server Geek" Weiss (nate@nateweiss.com)
  Modified: September, 2003
*/
import venue.simplecharts.DrawingMovieClip;
import venue.simplecharts.BarChartField;

// This class inherits all members of my DrawingMovieClip class
// (see DrawingMovieClip.as for details)
```

```
class venue.simplecharts.SimpleBarChart extends
venue.simplecharts.DrawingUIComponent {

  // These properties should be declared for any component
  static var symbolName:String = "SimpleBarChart";
  static var symbolOwner:Object = venue.simplecharts.SimpleBarChart;
  static var version:String = "1.0.0.0";
  var className:String = "SimpleBarChart";

  // Public properties: dimensions
  [Inspectable]
  public var barSpacing:Number = 30;
  [Inspectable]
  public var labelWidth:Number = 150;
  [Inspectable]
  public var refreshInterval:Number = 0;
  // Public properties: formatting
  [Inspectable]
  public var yScaleMax:Number = 0;
  [Inspectable]
  public var yScaleMin:Number = 0;
  [Inspectable]
  public var useAnimation:Boolean = true;
  [Inspectable]
  public var subRefreshInterval:Number = 20;
  [Inspectable]
  public var subRefreshNumSteps:Number = 10;

  // Public properties: not inspectable
  public var barColors:Array =
[0xFF0000,0x00FF00,0x0000FF,0xFFFF00,0x00FFFF,0xFF00FF];
  public var tfValueFormat:TextFormat;
  public var tfTitleFormat:TextFormat;
  public var tfLabelFormat:TextFormat;

  // Private properties
  private var _chartFields:Array = new Array;
  private var _chartData:Array = new Array;
  private var _currentIndex:Number = -1;
  private var _paused:Boolean = false;
  private var _intervalID:Number;
  private var _subIntervalID:Number;
  private var _txtTitle:TextField;
  private var _yScaleMax:Number;
  private var _yScaleMin:Number;
  private var _bgColor:Number;
```

continues

LISTING A.3   SimpleBarChart.as—Source code for the `SimpleBarChart` Component Class (Continued)

```
private var _borderColor:Number;
private var _borderWidth:Number;
private var _subIntervalCount:Number;
private var mcBackground:MovieClip;

// Constructor
// Macromedia recommends that component constructors be left empty
// if possible. Put initialization code in init() method instead.
public function SimpleBarChart() {
}


// Implement init() method
// All components should implement, calling super.init() within
// Flash calls this method automatically at design time or runtime
public function init() {

  // Set private scale variables that from public scale properties
  this._yScaleMin = this.yScaleMin;
  this._yScaleMax = this.yScaleMax;

  // Call the superclass's init() method
  super.init()

  // Draw border and background
  drawBackground();

  // Set up a default text format for labels
  if (this.tfValueFormat == undefined) {
   this.tfValueFormat = new TextFormat("Arial", 12, 0x000000, true);
   this.tfValueFormat.align = "center";
  }

  // Set up a default text format for labels
  if (this.tfLabelFormat == undefined) {
   this.tfLabelFormat = new TextFormat("Arial", 12, 0x000000, false);
   this.tfLabelFormat.align = "right";
  }

  // Set up a default text format for titles
  if (this.tfTitleFormat == undefined) {
   this.tfTitleFormat = new TextFormat("Arial", 12, 0x000000, true, true);
```

```
        this.tfTitleFormat.align = "center";
    }

    // Create a new text field object for the chart title
    var textHeight:Number =
this.tfTitleFormat.getTextExtent("X").textFieldHeight;
    this.createTextField("_txtTitle", this.getNextHighestDepth(), 0, 0,
this.width, 20);
    // Apply appropriate text formatting attributes
    this._txtTitle.selectable = false;
    this._txtTitle.setNewTextFormat(this.tfTitleFormat);

  }


  // Implement size() method
  // All components should implement, calling super.size() within
  // Flash calls this method automatically at design time or runtime
  public function size() {

    // Why do I feel like I'm at McDonald's right now?
    super.size();

    // Resize the background movie clip
    this.mcBackground._width = this.width;
    this.mcBackground._height = this.height;
  }


  private function drawBackground() {
    // Draw a border and background
    this.createEmptyMovieClip("mcBackground", this.getNextHighestDepth());
    this.drawBox(this.mcBackground, 0, 0, this.width, this.height,
this._bgColor, 100, this._borderColor, this.borderWidth);
  }


  // Adds a field (which will be visible as a bar) to the chart
  public function addField(name:String, label:String):Number {
    // Rotate the bar colors, then grab a color for this bar
    this.barColors.push(this.barColors.shift());
    var thisBarColor:Number = this.barColors[0];
```

continues

```
    // Construct new field "object"
    var field:BarChartField = new BarChartField(name, label, thisBarColor);

    // Add field object to internal array of fields
    _chartFields.push(field);

    // Return the position of the new field object
    return _chartFields.length - 1;
  }




  // This method creates visual bars for each field (as movie clips)
  public function draw() {
    var i:Number;
    var field:BarChartField;
    var xPosition:Number;
    var numberOfBars = this._chartFields.length;

    // Determine where to place the first bar (its X position)
    var barWidth = (this.width / numberOfBars) - this.barSpacing;
    var spaceForEachBar =(barWidth + this.barSpacing);
    var spaceForAllBars = (numberOfBars * spaceForEachBar) +
(this.barSpacing);
    var firstBarAt = ((this.width - spaceForAllBars) / 2) +
(this.barSpacing);

    // Determine the height of text fields for bar labels
    // Use that to compute an X offset for labels (for centering)
    var labelTextMetrics = this.tfLabelFormat.getTextExtent("X");
    var labelOffset = (barWidth / 2) - (labelTextMetrics.height / 2) - 1;

    // For each field (bar) in chart...
    for (i = 0; i < numberOfBars; i++) {
      // This is the current field in the loop
      field = this._chartFields[i];

      // Calculate x position of new bar
      xPosition = (i * spaceForEachBar) + firstBarAt;

      // ****** create data bar *******
      // Create new movie clip to hold the bar for this field
      this.createEmptyMovieClip("mcBar"+i, this.getNextHighestDepth());
      field.mcBar = this["mcBar"+i];
      // Draw a colored bar on the new clip's canvas
```

```
    this.drawBox(field.mcBar, 0, 0, barWidth, 1, field.bgColor,
    ➥100, 0x000000, 0);
    // Position the bar clip on this movie clip's stage
    field.mcBar._x = xPosition;
    field.mcBar._alpha = 90;
    // Attach mouse events to data bar
    field.mcBar.onRollOver = onBarOver;
    field.mcBar.onRollOut = onBarOut;

    // Create a text label object for this field
    this.createTextField("txtValue"+i, this.getNextHighestDepth(),
    ➥0, 0, barWidth, 18);
    field.txtValue = this["txtValue"+i];
    // Apply appropriate text formatting attributes
    field.txtValue.selectable = false;
    field.txtValue.setNewTextFormat(this.tfValueFormat);
    // Position the text field on this movie clip's stage
    field.txtValue._x = xPosition;
    field.txtValue._y = height - field.txtValue._height;

    // Create a text label object for this field
    this.createTextField("txtLabel"+i, this.getNextHighestDepth(),
    ➥0, 0, this.labelWidth, barWidth);
    field.txtLabel = this["txtLabel"+i];
    // Apply appropriate text formatting attributes
    field.txtLabel.selectable = false;
    field.txtLabel.embedFonts = true;
    field.txtLabel._rotation = -90;
    field.txtLabel.setNewTextFormat(this.tfLabelFormat);
    // Actual text for the label
    field.txtLabel.text = field.label;
    // Position the text field on this movie clip's stage
    field.txtLabel._x = xPosition + labelOffset;
    field.txtLabel._y = height + field.txtLabel._height;
  }

  // Show the first series
  showSeries(0);

  // Begin animation between series, if applicable
  resume();
}


// Displays a data series in the chart
public function showSeries(index:Number) {
```

continues

LISTING A.3   SimpleBarChart.as—Source code for the `SimpleBarChart` Component Class
(Continued)

```
var i:Number;
var field:BarChartField;
var fieldValue:Number;
var yScale = (_yScaleMax - _yScaleMin);

// For each field...
for (i = 0; i < this._chartFields.length; i++) {
  // Within this loop, this is the "current" field object
  field = this._chartFields[i];

  // Determine the correct value to show for this field
  field.value = this._chartData[index][field.name];
  field.txtValue.text = field.value.toString();

  // Calculate the height of the bar, relative to the scale
  field.targetHeight = (field.value / yScale) *
➥(this.height - 18 - this._txtTitle._height);

  // Go ahead and resize the bar to the correct height
  // If we aren't animating the changes between the series,
  // Then just resize the bar to the new value now
  if (this.useAnimation == false) {
     resizeField(field, field.targetHeight, true);

  // If we are animating the changes between the series,
  // Schedule subIntervalAnimate() function to execute repeatedtly
  } else {
    // Reset the previous sub-interval schedule, if any
    this._subIntervalCount = 0;
    clearInterval(this._subIntervalID);
    // How much should bar change its height at each sub-interval?
    field.subIntervalChange = (field.targetHeight -
➥field.mcBar._height) this.subRefreshNumSteps;
    // Schedule the repeated executions
    this._subIntervalID = setInterval(this, "subIntervalAnimate",
➥this.subRefreshInterval);
  }
}

// If there is a title to display for this series, display it
if (this._chartData[index]._title != undefined) {
  this._txtTitle.text = this._chartData[index]._title;
}
```

```
      // Remember that this is the current position
      this._currentIndex = index;

      // Ask Flash to redraw screen now (depending on movie's fps)
      updateAfterEvent();
   }


   // This function fires repeatedly after each data-series change,
   // Resulting in an animated (tweened) effect from series to series
   private function subIntervalAnimate() {
      var i:Number;
      var field:BarChartField;

      // For each field...
      for (i = 0; i < this._chartFields.length; i++) {
         field = this._chartFields[i];

         // Keep track of how many times this function executes
         this._subIntervalCount++;

         // If it has already executed the desired number of times
         if (this._subIntervalCount >= this.subRefreshNumSteps) {
            // Stop executing this function repeatedly, for the moment
            clearInterval(this._subIntervalID);
            // Set the bar to its final, correct size
            resizeField(field, field.targetHeight, true);

         // Otherwise, we should change the bar's size by a small amount
         } else {
            // This is the current height of the bar
            var curHeight:Number = field.mcBar._height;
            // Change the bar's size now
            resizeField(field, curHeight + field.subIntervalChange, true);
         }
      }
   }


   // This function resizes the visual bar for a particular field
   private function resizeField(field:Object, height:Number,
moveLabel:Boolean) {
      // Make bar be invisible if there is no numeric value for field
      field.mcBar._visible = isNaN(field.value) == false;
      field.txtValue._visible = isNaN(field.value) == false;
```

continues

```
    // Set the bar clip's height and position to reflect the value
    field.mcBar._height = height;
    field.mcBar._y = this.height - height;

    // Position this field's label appropriately
    if (moveLabel) {
      field.txtValue._y = field.mcBar._y - field.txtValue._height;
    }

    // Remember that this field is now this tall
    field.currentHeight = height;
  }


  // This method adds a series (set of actual data points) to chart
  public function addSeries(data:Object, title:String):Number {
    // Do any of the values in this series go beyond current scale?
    for (var name in data) {
     if (data[name] > this._yScaleMax) {
        this._yScaleMax = data[name];
      }
      if (data[name] < this._yScaleMin) {
        this._yScaleMin = data[name];
      }
    }

    // Store the label as a property of the series
    data._title = title;

    // Add new series to internal data array
    _chartData.push(data);
    // Return the assigned index position for the series
    return _chartData.length - 1;
  }


  public function resume() {
    // Clear any existing schedules (if any)
    pause();
    // Schedule next() function to execute repeatedly, if appropriate
    if (this.refreshInterval > 0) {
      this._intervalID = setInterval(this, "next", refreshInterval);
    }
  }
```

```
public function pause() {
  clearInterval(this._intervalID);
}


public function next() {
  // New index position
  var index = this._currentIndex + 1;
  // Allow for going around the horn
  if (index >= this._chartData.length) {
    index = 0;
  }

  // Go to that index position
  showSeries(index);
}


public function previous() {
  // New index position
  var index = this._currentIndex - 1;
  // Allow for going around the horn
  if (index < 0) {
    index = this._chartData.length - 1;
  }
  // Go to that index position
  showSeries(index);
}



// This method removes all information from chart
public function clearAll() {
  // For each existing field/bar, remove visual items
  for (var i = 0; i < this._chartFields.length; i++) {
    this._chartFields[i].mcBar.removeMovieClip();
    this._chartFields[i].txtValue.removeTextField();
    this._chartFields[i].txtLabel.removeTextField();
  }

  // Reset the internal arrays, discarding all data
  this._chartData = new Array;
  this._chartFields = new Array;
```

continues

LISTING A.3   SimpleBarChart.as—Source code for the `SimpleBarChart` Component Class
(Continued)

```
  // Reset the scale
  this._yScaleMin = this.yScaleMin;
  this._yScaleMax = this.yScaleMax;
}



// Setter for bgColor property
[Inspectable(defaultValue="#EFEFEF", type=Color)]
public function set backgroundColor(val:Number):Void {
  this._bgColor = val;
  drawBackground();
}

// Getter for bgColor property
public function get backgroundColor():Number {
  return this._bgColor;
}



// Setter for borderColor property
[Inspectable(defaultValue="#000000", type=Color)]
public function set borderColor(val:Number):Void {
  this._borderColor = val;
  drawBackground();
}

// Getter for borderColor property
public function get borderColor():Number {
  return this._borderColor;
}



// Setter for borderWidth property
[Inspectable(defaultValue=0)]
public function set borderWidth(val:Number):Void {
  this._borderWidth = val;
  drawBackground();
}

// Getter for borderWidth property
public function get borderWidth():Number {
  return this._borderWidth;
}
```

```
  // This fires when user hovers over a bar
  private function onBarOver() {
    this._alpha = 100;
    _parent.pause();
  }

  // This fires when a user rolls away from a bar
  private function onBarOut() {
    this._alpha = 90;
    _parent.resume();
  }
}
```

Unfortunately, it's not possible to go into a line-by-line explanation of this listing in the space remaining in this book. It has been commented fairly extensively, however, and I think you'll find that you can follow the code fairly easily if you spend a bit of time playing around with it.

As you look through the listing, keep your eyes out for the following variables and other items:

- The chart's fields are stored in a private array called _chartFields. The public addField() method constructs a new instance of BarChartField (see Listing A.4) and then adds the new field object to the _chartFields array.

- Similarly, the chart's data series are stored in the private _chartSeries array. The addSeries() method adds the series object to the array via Array.push().

- The most complex method in this listing is the public draw() method, which creates the visual elements for each of the chart's fields. For the first field, a movie clip named mcBar0 is created for the field's actual bar. A text field named txtValue0 is created to display the current value of the bar, and a second text field called txtLabel0 is created for the label under the bar. For the second series, these items will be called mcBar1, txtValue1, and txtLabel1, and so on. References to these items are stored in the field object's mcBar, txtValue, and txtLabel properties, which makes them easy to refer to later.

- The showSeries() method takes care of displaying a particular data series in the chart. It changes the text shown in the txtValue label for each field and then calculates how high each bar should be (in pixels) based on the value of each field in the specified series. The desired height is stored in the field's targetHeight property.

- The private _currentIndex property keeps track of which data series the chart is currently displaying. This value will get incremented by the next() method every refreshInterval milliseconds.

- If the useAnimations property is true, the private subIntervalAnimate() method is scheduled for repeated execution every subRefreshInterval milliseconds. This method calls resizeField() internally to take care of the actual resizing of the bars. The schedule is cancelled after the method executes subRefreshNumSteps times.

The BarChartField Class

Listing A.4 is the source code for the venue.simplecharts.BarChartField class. This class is a very simple extension of the intrinsic Object class. Its only purpose here is to formalize the properties of each field that is stored in the _chartData array within SimpleBarChart (Listing A.3).

LISTING A.4   BarChartField.as—Source Code for the BarChartField Class

```
class venue.simplecharts.BarChartField extends Object {

  // Simple properties
  public var name:String;
  public var label:String;
  public var value:Number;
  public var bgColor:Number;
  public var targetHeight:Number;
  public var subIntervalChange:Number;

  // These properties represent visual elements for this field
  public var mcBar:MovieClip;
  public var txtValue:TextField;
  public var txtLabel:TextField;

  // Constructor
  function BarChartField(name:String, label:String, bgColor:Number) {
    this.name = name;
    this.label = label;
    this.bgColor = bgColor;
  };
}
```

If you wanted to make the overall organization of this chart example more modular and object-oriented in nature, you could move some of the field-specific functionality to this class. For instance, you could create a `BarChartField.drawBar()` method that would take care of drawing the bar for the field, rather than having the `SimpleBarChart` class draw the bar in its `draw()` method.

Recompiling the Component After Making Changes

If you make a change to the component (either in the component symbol's timeline or stage, or in one of the ActionScript files), you will need to recompile the SWC file so that it can be tested or used in a regular Flash document. To recompile the SWC, do the following:

1. Right-click on the component symbol in the Library, and then choose Export SWC file. The Export File dialog box appears, prompting you for a name and folder for the SWC file.

2. Specify the folder where you would like Flash to place the new version of the SWC file. In most situations, you will want this to be a subfolder of the Components folder, within Flash's Configuration directory. The subfolder name will determine how the component appears in the Components panel. For instance, I created a subfolder called Flash for Server Geeks, which causes the component to show up in the Components panel in a category of the same name (see Figure A.3).

3. Regardless of the folder location you choose, make sure to type `SimpleBarChart.swc` for the filename.

4. Click Save to create the SWC file.

> **NOTE**
>
> Remember, the ActionScript class files can't be recompiled unless you make sure the `venue.simplecharts` package can be found in Flash's global classpath. See the beginning of this section for details.

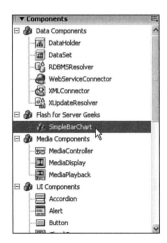

FIGURE A.3   Your own components can be visible in the Components panel.

Now that the SWC file has been created, follow these steps to try out the new version in a normal Flash document:

1. Choose Reload from the Components panel menu (at the top-right corner of the panel) to force Flash to see the new version of the component.

2. Drag the component from the Components panel onto the Stage of a normal Flash document. If an older version of the component was already in the document's library, Flash will ask you if you want to use the existing version or update the component; choose the Replace existing component option and click OK (see Figure A.4) to update your document's Library (you can then delete the new instance that you just dragged onto the Stage).

3. Test the component in whatever manner is appropriate. If you have changed the component's inspectable properties, the changes should now be reflected in the Properties panel or Component Inspector.

FIGURE A.4   It's easy to replace an existing component with an updated version.

Summary

This appendix has introduced you to many of the basic concepts involved in creating a new component from scratch. You will need to consult the Flash documentation for a complete discussion of all the ins and outs of component development for Flash MX 2004, but the annotated code presented in this appendix should nonetheless prove to be a helpful learning tool. Have fun!

CROSS-DOMAIN DATA ACCESS POLICIES IN FLASH PLAYER 7

Macromedia Flash Player 7 introduces a new policy regarding what URLs a SWF is allowed to access at runtime. In a nutshell, the new policy makes the following two assertions:

- A Flash movie may access data only from the same server (based on the domain name) from which it was downloaded. That is, if a SWF lives on Server A, it can access data only on Server A. Any other attempt to access data will fail, even if the server that has the data is in the same domain.

- If a movie wants to break this rule, it is up to the domain providing the data to allow the rule to be broken. So, if a movie from Domain A wants to access data from a server in Domain B, the server in Domain B must be configured to allow it. The configuration must also be performed for two servers in the same domain that want to work together.

> **NOTE**
>
> The policy is not enforced while you are testing a movie in the Flash IDE. It's therefore easy to forget about the restrictions until you are done testing.

The new policy affects all the data-access techniques discussed in this book, including all attempts to access the following:

- Pages that accept or return plain-text variables (as discussed in Chapter 6, "Connecting to Servers with Plain Text")
- Pages that accept or return XML data (as discussed in Chapter 7, "Connecting to Servers with XML")
- Remote service methods via Flash Remoting (as discussed in Chapter 8, "Connecting to Servers with Flash Remoting")
- Remote service methods via Web Services (as discussed in Chapter 9, "Connecting to Servers with Web Services")

> **NOTE**
>
> The new policy also affects runtime shared objects, a Flash feature that has not been discussed in this book. Runtime shared objects are symbols that can be accessed by the Flash Player at runtime, rather than being compiled into a SWF. See the Flash documentation for details about runtime shared objects.

> **NOTE**
>
> There are slightly different rules for whether a movie can load an external SWF from a different server (for instance, via `loadMovie()`). Basically, Flash Player 7's policy is that SWFs can be loaded only from the same server (the same domain name) that provided the original SWF. If they don't, the loaded SWF cannot communicate with the SWF that loaded it (or vice versa). This rule is slightly different than the rule that existed for previous versions of Flash Player (which allowed communications between SWFs that came from different server names within the same domain). See the Flash documentation for details.

How the Policy Is Enforced

First, just to make this discussion a bit easier to follow, let's define a few terms. These are my own terms, by the way, not Macromedia's:

- **Data-access call.** A *data-access call* is any ActionScript function or method that provides access to data on a server. This includes `XML.load()`, `XML.sendAndLoad()`, `LoadVars.load()`, `LoadVars.sendAndLoad()`, `loadVariables()`, `loadVariablesNum()`, and all Flash Remoting and Web Services method calls.

- **Source server.** The *source server* is the server from which a SWF was downloaded by the Flash Player. Note that this is not necessarily the same server that provided the page on which the SWF appears.
- **Target server.** The *target server* is the server from which a SWF wants to access external data.

Before the Flash Player 7 allows a data-access call to take place, it checks for the presence of a special file called crossdomain.xml at the target server's document root. This XML file is called a *cross-domain policy file*, the purpose of which is to specify which SWFs should be able to access the data on the server.

For instance, suppose that a SWF wants to access data at the following URL:

```
http://www.orangewhipstudios.com/newsfeeds/todaysnews.xml
```

The Flash Player will first attempt to access a crossdomain.xml file, using this URL:

```
http://www.orangewhipstudios.com/crossdomain.xml
```

One of two things will happen:

- If the server responds with a valid crossdomain.xml file, the instructions in the file will be used to determine whether the data-access call will be allowed to execute.
- If there is no such crossdomain.xml file—that is, if the server responds with HTTP status code 404 (not found) or if the file is invalid—then the default rule will be used. In other words, only data-access calls where the source and target servers are the same will be allowed to execute.

Creating a Cross-Domain Policy File

If you want SWFs from other domains—or from other servers in the same domain—to be able to access the data on your server, you need to create a crossdomain.xml file and place it in the *data-serving server's* document root. This section will explain how.

> **NOTE**
>
> Again, there is no need to create a cross-domain policy file if the SWFs and the data you want to access are on the same server. You need to worry about policy files only if you want to supply data to SWFs from other servers in your domain or other domains, or if you are creating SWFs that need to access data from other servers or domains.

It's very easy to create a cross-domain policy file. You start off with an XML file that contains a pair of `<cross-domain-policy>` tags, and then you add one or more `<allow-access-from>` elements that describe which SWFs should be able to access the data on the server. Each `<allow-access-from>` element must have a `domain` attribute, which can specify any of the following:

- **A single domain name.** For instance, `domain="www.nateweiss.com"` allows access from SWFs that were loaded from `www.nateweiss.com`. It would have no bearing on whether SWFs that were loaded from `private.nateweiss.com` would have access.

- **An IP address.** For instance, `domain="192.168.0.1"` allows access from SWFs that were loaded from the IP address 192.168.0.1. Please note that there is no way to specify a range of IP addresses; you must specify each address with a separate `<allow-access-from>` element. Also note that the Flash Player is not in the business of resolving DNS hostnames, so allowing access to 192.168.0.1 has no bearing on whether SWFs from `www.nateweiss.com` will be allowed access, even if DNS reports that `www.nateweiss.com` resolves to 192.168.0.1.

- **A single asterisk character** (`*`). An asterisk used alone allows access from all SWFs, regardless of the domain name or IP address from which the Flash Player loaded them. After you add an `<allow-access-from>` element that specifies `domain="*"`, any other elements are extraneous and are effectively ignored.

- **A single asterisk followed by a domain suffix.** The asterisk behaves as a wildcard that matches all hostnames (or subdomains) within the specified domain. The asterisk may appear only at the beginning of the domain attribute, and it must be followed by a dot (`.`) character. For instance, `domain="*.nateweiss.com"` will allow access from SWFs that are loaded from `www.nateweiss.com`, `data.nateweiss.com`, `services.data.nateweiss.com`, or `nateweiss.com`. Similarly, `domain="*.data.nateweiss.com"` will allow access from `data.nateweiss.com` or `services.data.nateweiss.com`.

NOTE

It's worth noting that there is no `<deny-access-from>` element. There is no way to create a policy file that allows access from all domains except a select few. Your choices are to specify each allowed domain separately, or to accept them all.

For instance, suppose that you have created a data-access page or Web Service on a server called `publicdata.nateweiss.com`, and you want all Flash movies everywhere to be able to access your data. You would simply save the following XML as a file called crossdomain.xml, in your HTTP server's document root, thereby exposing your data or services to the general Flash-using public:

```
<cross-domain-policy>
  <allow-access-from domain="*" />
</cross-domain-policy>
```

NOTE

If you have only data-access pages set up on your local machine right now, you might be wondering how to test whether policy files work as advertised. Just create a SWF that accesses data from localhost (as every example in this book does), and then pull up the test page for the SWF using your browser. Now edit the URL in your browser's Address bar, replacing the localhost part with 127.0.0.1 (or your computer's actual IP address). The request should fail—unless you have created a policy file that allows access from all computers or your specific IP address.

Now suppose that you create a different set of data-access pages or Web Services at `privatedata.nateweiss.com`. You don't want this data to be exposed to the public, but you do want it to be available to SWFs that you place on `www.nateweiss.com` or `nateweiss.com`. To do so, you would save the crossdomain.xml file in privatedata.nateweiss.com's document root:

```
<cross-domain-policy>
  <allow-access-from domain="www.nateweiss.com" />
  <allow-access-from domain="nateweiss.com" />
</cross-domain-policy>
```

Issues to Keep in Mind

You now know how to create cross-domain policy files for your server. For the most part, that's all you really need to know. The following sections list a few other considerations to keep in mind with regard to the new cross-domain security policy. For further details, consult the Flash documentation.

General Policy File Considerations

Here are some general considerations to keep in mind:

- Cross-domain policy files are a Macromedia invention that currently apply only to Flash Player 7 (and later). They have absolutely no bearing on whether other HTTP clients (including plain old web browsers) can access the data on your servers.

- If you create a SWF that accesses a publicly available Web Service or XML feed hosted by a third party, you are at the mercy of the third party to add a policy file that allows SWFs from your domain to access it. Until the third party does so, your SWF will not be able to access the data.

- Even though cross-domain policy files are able to successfully control direct access by SWFs (as long as Flash Player 7 or later is being used), they have no bearing over whether another server is able to access the data and expose it to SWFs at its own URLs. In such a case, the other server's policy file would affect Flash's ability to access the data (rather than the original server's policy file, if any).

- A cross-domain policy file affects all data-access pages or services on that server. If you want one set of pages or services to use one policy file and another set to use a different policy file, you must place the two sets on two different servers. (Of course, the two servers don't need to be on separate physical machines; they need only be on separate virtual servers, such that they have different document roots for placing the policy files in.)

- A cross-domain policy file at an HTTP URL does not have any bearing on requests for an HTTPS URL, or vice versa. For instance, consider a SWF that was loaded by the Flash player from `http://www.nateweiss.com/movie.swf` and is trying to access data at `https://data.nateweiss.com/news.xml` via `XML.load()`. There must be a policy file at `https://data.nateweiss.com/crossdomain.xml` that permits access from `www.nateweiss.com`.

Policy Files and Flash Player Versions

It's also important to keep in mind that the new cross-domain policy is new for Flash Player 7 (the version that corresponds with the release of the Flash MX 2004 development tool). Previous versions of Flash Player used a fixed security policy, where data was allowed to be downloaded from any server within the same domain as the SWF. That is, under Flash Player 6, a SWF that was downloaded from www.nateweiss.com could access data from data.nateweiss.com, but not from www.lizweiss.com.

The Flash documentation provides lots of details about the effect this difference makes under various scenarios, but here are the basic concepts to keep in mind:

- The new cross-domain policy is enforced by the Flash Player, not by the SWF. This means that if you publish a movie as Flash 6, it may behave differently with respect to cross-domain access data, depending on whether the user is using Flash Player 6 or 7.

- If Flash Player 7 loads a SWF that was published for Flash 6 or earlier, it attempts to use the same cross-domain policy file that is used for version 7 content (even though the same SWF will not be beholden to the policy if played back on Flash Player 6). That is, the player will check for a policy file at the target server's root URL and will use the policy file to determine what should be allowed.

- If, however, Flash Player 7 loads a version 6 SWF and there is no corresponding policy file, and the access would have been allowed by Flash Player 6, the player will prompt the user for permission to access the remote data. The purpose of the prompt is to make sure that Flash 6 applications can still run under Flash Player 7. To circumvent the prompt, provide a policy file. Further details are available in the Flash documentation.

INDEX

Symbols

{ } (curly braces), 132

; (semicolon), 131

: operator, 139-140

? operator, 139-140

A

absolute URLs, 74

access

    cross-domain data policies, 583-584

        creating, 585-587

        documenting, 588-589

        enforcing, 584-585

    event objects, 179

    forms, 544

    passed-in variables, 447

    movies, 44-46

    queries, 342-345

Action Message Format (AMF), 317

Actions panel

    customizing, 128

    navigating, 17

    screens, 511

    troubleshooting, 121-124

    undocking, 119-120

    variables, 125-128

ActionScript, 6, 116-117

    buttons, 63-65

    classes, 157

        creating, 158-172

        inheritance, 172-173

    datatypes, 146

        arrays, 149-150

        associative arrays, 150-151

dates, 148

numbers, 146

strings, 147

elements, 130

comments, 130-131

conditional statements, 137-140

expressions, 140-143

loops, 143-146

syntax, 131-133

variables, 133-137

events, 174-180

Flash Remoting, 340. *See also* Flash Remoting

forms, 544

functions, 151

arguments, 152-153

returning values, 154

storing, 156-157

strict typing, 155

syntax, 152

history of, 118

IDE, 119

customizing, 128

Help panel, 129

troubleshooting, 121-124

typing variables, 125-128

undocking, 119-120

interfaces, 35-42

Library

adding clips, 202-206

applying linkage identifiers, 206-209

deleting movie clips, 211-212

modifying movie clips, 209-211

MovieClip class, 182-189

gesture-based scroller widgets, 190-196

GestureMovieClip class, 197-200

reviewing GestureMovieClip class, 200-202

new features, 118-119

playback, 92-94

relationship to ECMAScript/JavaScript, 117

screens, 505

attaching to, 511-514

referencing, 504

SimpleBarChart component, 560-577

Web services, 415-428

XML class, 272-275

members, 275-280

populating gesture-driven scrollers, 281-299

usage patterns, 280

addEventListener() method, 178

adding

ActionScript, 63-65

animation, 87-92

clips

applying Library linkage identifiers, 206-209

deleting, 211-212

Library, 202-206

modifying, 209-211

comments, 130-131

databound components, 364-374

extensions, 291-295

interfaces, 69-75

keyframes, 90

LoadVars object, 39-40

metatags, 562-563

movie clip content at runtime, 218

private/public keywords, 162

ProgressBar component, 544-547

properties, 162

special comments, 128

visual elements to interfaces, 31-34

addresses, 441-448. *See also* gateways; URLs

alerts, 518

alignment
Actions panel, 119-120
mouse scrolling functionality, 212-218
movie clips, 209-211
screens, 503-504

AMF (Action Message Format), 317

animation, 87-92

API (Application Programming Interface), 505

applications
Flash Remoting, 318
forms
creating, 502
RIAs, 495
NetConnection Debugger, 339-340
selecting, 20-21
sessions
sharing variables, 449-453
states, 440-441

applying linkage identifiers, 206-209

arguments, ActionScript functions, 152-153

arrays
ActionScript, 149-151
Flash Remoting, 376
LoadVars class
newsTicker.fla document, 245-251
parsing, 252-258
retrieving, 234-243
viewing, 244
local shared data, 454-456
Web services, 401-402

ArtistButtonClip, creating, 65-67

artists, selecting, 40-42

ASP.NET
configuring, 20
cookieless sessions with, 452. *See also* cookies
Flash Remoting, 322, 326
logins, 468-471
supplying data as plain text, 28-30

associative arrays, ActionScript, 150-151

attaching ActionScript code to screens, 511-514

attributes, XML, 274

B

bar charts, 551-554
creating, 557-579
recompiling, 579-580
references, 555-557

BarChartField class, 578-579

binding
Flash Remoting, 361
adding databound components, 364-374
applying DataSet/RecordSet classes, 362-364
UI components, 366-368
Web services, 428-434

break statement, 145-146

BubbleMovieClip class, 540-542

building
components, 553
LoadVarsExtended class, 239-242
SimpleBarChart component, 557-579

built-in classes
ActionScript, 157
creating, 158-172
inheritance, 172-173

Button component, 405

buttons, 98
components, 180
events, 100-103
invisible, 103-104
modifying, 99-100
navigation
adding ActionScript, 63-65
ArtistButtonClip, 65-67
creating with XML, 46-63
testing, 68-69
rollover, 59-63

C

calling methods
NetConnection class, 341
NetServices class, 341
scheduling, 213-214

case statements, 138

CFC (ColdFusion Component), 464

charts
creating, 557-579
recompiling, 579-580
references, 555-557
SimpleBarChart component, 551-554

child nodes, XML, 274

children, 106-108

classes
ActionScript, 157
adding clips to Library, 202-206
applying Library linkage identifiers, 206-209
creating, 158-172
deleting movie clips, 211-212
Flash Remoting, 340. See also Flash Remoting
inheritance, 172-173
modifying movie clips, 209-211
BarChartField, 578-579
BubbleMovieClip, 540-542
custom
attaching code to, 513
validating, 525
DataSet
binding UI components, 366-368
Flash Remoting, 362-364
members, 372-374
DrawingUIComponent, 564
LoadVars, 231-234
newsTicker.fla document, 245-251
parsing structured data, 252-258
retrieving structured data, 234-243
sending variables, 258-270
viewing structured data, 244
LoadVarsExtended
building, 239-242
testing, 242-243
LoginManager, 462
MovieClip, 182-189
gesture-based scroller widgets, 190-196
GestureMovieClip class, 197-200
reviewing GestureMovieClip class, 200-202

NetServices
   accessing queries, 342-345
   connecting, 341
  properties, 167
  RecordSet, 362
  SharedObject, 455-456
  SimpleBarChart, 565. *See also*
   SimpleBarChart component
  XML, 272, 275
   members, 275-280
   populating gesture-driven scrollers,
    281-299
   usage patterns, 280
  XMLConnector, 308-312
  XMLNode, 291-295
  XPathAPI, 300-308

classpaths, 165

client-side code
  Flash Remoting, 328-333
  gesture-driven scrollers, 284-291, 295-299
  logins, 475-486

clients
  Flash Remoting, 322
   capabilities, 374-376
   configuring, 320-324, 345-361
   data binding, 361-374
   installing components, 320-323
   third-party implementations, 377
  Web services, 382-383

clips, 9, 104
  components
   comparing to, 553
   converting, 223-226
  content, 218
  events, 109

Library, 202-206
  applying linkage identifiers, 206-209
  deleting, 211-212
  modifying, 209-211
mask, 221-223
MovieClip class, 182-189
  gesture-based scroller widgets, 190-196
  GestureMovieClip class, 197-200
  reviewing GestureMovieClip class,
   200-202
movies
  creating, 35-36
  publishing, 42-46
responder functions, 337
slide, 192
this keyword, 109
timeline, 104-106
targets, 106-108

code, 6-7
  ActionScript, 116. *See also* ActionScript
   attaching to screens, 511-514
   connecting Web services, 423-428
   interfaces, 35-42
   loading external content, 544
   referencing screens, 504
   screens API, 505
   Web services, 415-420
  Flash Remoting
   client-side code, 328-333
   server-side code, 324-327
  gesture-driven scrollers, 282-291, 295-299
  hints, 124
  HTML, 70-74
  inserting, 122-123
  LoadVars class, 236

logins, 461-486

mask clips, 221-223

server-side, 386-404

shapes, 219-220

supplying data to, 24-25

variables

ASP.NET, 28-30

ColdFusion, 26-27

encoding, 25-26

Java, 30

viewing, 369-372

ColdFusion

configuring, 21

cookieless sessions, 452. *See also* cookies

Flash Remoting, 322

gateways, 334

server-side code, 325

logins, 464-467

supplying data as plain text, 26-27

Web services, 387-391

ColdFusion Component (CFC), 464

ComboBox component, 405

commands

gotoAndPlay(), 94

stop(), 94

comments

ActionScript, 130-131

variables, 128

comparisons

components/movie clips, 553

Flash Remoting/Web services, 316-317

Component Definition dialog box, 224

components, 110, 552

building, 553

buttons, 180, 405

clips, 223-226

ComboBox, 405

databound, 364-374

DataSet, 363-364

DateField, 405

Flash Remoting, 320-323

forms, 493-494

ProgressBar, 544-547

SimpleBarChart, 405, 551-554

creating, 557-579

recompiling, 579-580

references, 555-557

Web services

ActionScript code, 415-420

connecting, 423-428

monitoring WebServiceConnector component, 422

panel, 420-421

RatingChart.fla document, 404-405

server-side code, 386-404

SimpleBarChart component, 413-415

WebServiceConnector component, 385, 406-413

XMLConnector, 308-312

Components panel, navigating, 16

conditional expressions, 140-143

conditional statements, 137

?/: operators, 139-140

case/switch statements, 138

if/else statements, 138

configuration

ASP.NET, 20

classes, 158-172

ColdFusion, 21

cookies, 453-454

Flash Remoting, 320-324, 345-361
   capabilities, 374-376
   client-side code, 328-333
   components, 365-368
   data binding, 361-374
   debugging, 339-340
   gateways, 333-336
   installing components, 320-323
   NetConnection class, 341
   NetServices class, 341
   RecordSet class, 342-345
   responder functions, 336-338
   server-side code, 324-327
   third-party implementations, 377
   troubleshooting, 338-339
focus, 518
forms, 491-492
   attaching ActionScript code to, 511-514
   controls, 493-494
   creating screen-based documents, 499-504
   CustomerEntry.fla document, 527-542
   loading external content, 542-547
   realtime server-side validation, 526-527
   RIAs, 495
   screens, 497-499
   scripting, 504-510
   submitting, 495-497
   validating, 515-526
interfaces, 31
   adding visual elements, 31-34
   coding ActionScript, 35-42
   publishing, 42-46
Java, 21
mask clips, 221-223

navigation buttons
   adding ActionScript, 63-65
   ArtistButtonClip, 65-67
   testing, 68-69
   with XML, 46-63
rollover buttons, 59-63
servers, 19
   formatting databases, 19-20
   placing example files (document root), 22
   selecting applications, 20-21
setInterval() method, 213-214
shapes, 219-220
variables
   ActionScript, 134-136
   datatypes, 136
   strict typing, 136-137
Web services, 381
   ActionScript code, 415-420
   clients, 383
   components, 404-405
   connecting, 423-428
   customizing, 383-384
   data binding, 428-434
   defining, 381-382
   monitoring WebServiceConnector component, 422
   panel, 420-421
   security, 434-435
   server-side code, 386-404
   SimpleBarChart component, 413-415
   WebServiceConnector component, 385, 406-413

connections, 5-6
Flash Remoting, 316
   binding data, 361-374
   capabilities, 374-376

client-side code, 328-333

comparing to Web services, 316-317

configuring, 320-324, 345-361

debugging, 339-340

gateways, 318, 333-336

NetConnection class, 341

NetServices class, 341

RecordSet class, 342-345

responder functions, 336-338

server-side code, 324-327

terminology, 319

third-party implementations, 377

troubleshooting, 338-339

servers

configuring, 19

formatting databases, 19-20

placing example files (document root), 22

selecting applications, 20-21

Web services, 380, 423-428

ActionScript code, 415-420

clients, 383

components, 404-405

creating, 381

customizing, 383-384

data binding, 428-434

defining, 381-382

monitoring WebServiceConnector component, 422

panel, 420-421

security, 434-435

server-side code, 386-404

SimpleBarChart component, 413-415

WebServiceConnector component, 385, 406-413

XML

applying XMLConnector component, 308-312

members (XML class), 275-280

populating gesture-driven scrollers, 281-299

usage patterns, 280

XML class, 272, 275

constants, 538-540

constructors

functions, 158

MovieClip class, 205-206

consumer Web services, 382

content, adding at runtime, 218

continue statement, 145-146

controlling playback (ActionScript), 92-94

controls

forms, 493-494

invalid, 518

conventions, naming, 125

converting clips to components, 223-226

cookies

session state, 451-453

sharing, 453-454

copying

HTML, 70-74

symbols, 80-84

Create New Symbol dialog box, 203

createMaskClip() method, 221

cross-domain data access policies, 583-584

creating, 585-587

documenting, 588-589

enforcing, 584-585

curly braces ({ }), 132

custom classes
screens, 513
validation, 525

customization
Actions panel, 128
ASP.NET, 20
classes, 158-172
ColdFusion, 21
cookies, 453-454
Flash Remoting, 320-324, 345-361
   capabilities, 374-376
   client-side code, 328-333
   components, 365-368
   data binding, 361-374
   debugging, 339-340
   gateways, 333-336
   installing components, 320-323
   NetConnection class, 341
   NetServices class, 341
   RecordSet class, 342-345
   responder functions, 336-338
   server-side code, 324-327
   third-party implementations, 377
   troubleshooting, 338-339
focus, 518
forms, 491-492
   attaching ActionScript code to, 511-514
   controls, 493-494
   creating screen-based documents, 499-504
   CustomerEntry.fla document, 527-542
   loading external content, 542-547
   realtime server-side validation, 526-527
   RIAs, 495
   screens, 497-499
   scripting, 504-510
   submitting, 495-497
   validating, 515-526
interfaces, 31
   adding visual elements, 31-34
   coding ActionScript, 35-42
   publishing, 42-46
Java, 21
mask clips, 221-223
navigation buttons
   adding ActionScript, 63-65
   ArtistButtonClip, 65-67
   testing, 68-69
   with XML, 46-63
rollover buttons, 59-63
servers, 19
   formatting databases, 19-20
   placing example files (document root), 22
   selecting applications, 20-21
setInterval() method, 213-214
shapes, 219-220
variables
   ActionScript, 134-136
   datatypes, 136
   strict typing, 136-137
Web services, 383-384
   ActionScript code, 415-420
   clients, 383
   components, 404-405
   connecting, 423-428
   customizing, 383-384
   data binding, 428-434
   defining, 381-382
   monitoring WebServiceConnector component, 422
   panel, 420-421
   security, 434-435

server-side code, 386-404

SimpleBarChart component, 413-415

WebServiceConnector component, 385, 406-413

D

data binding

Flash Remoting, 361

adding databound components, 364-374

applying DataSet/RecordSet classes, 362-364

Web services, 428-434

Data Logger Web services, 422

databases, formatting, 19-20

databound components, adding, 364-374

databound validation, 520

DataSet class

Flash Remoting, 362-364

members, 372-374

UI components, 366-368

datatypes

ActionScript, 146

arrays, 149-150

associative arrays, 150-151

dates, 148

numbers, 146

strings, 147

variables, 136

DateField component, 405

dates

ActionScript, 148

local shared data, 454-456

declarations, XML, 274

defining Web services, 381-382

deleting movie clips , 211-212

delimited text files, parsing, 255-258

design

Actions panel, 128

ASP.NET, 20

classes, 158-166, 168-172

ColdFusion, 21

cookies, 453-454

forms, 491-492

attaching ActionScript code to, 511-514

controls, 493-494

creating screen-based documents, 499-504

CustomerEntry.fla document, 527-542

loading external content, 542-547

realtime server-side validation, 526-527

RIAs, 495

screens, 497-499

scripting, 504-510

submitting, 495-497

validating, 515-526

Flash Remoting, 320-324, 345-361

capabilities, 374-376

client-side code, 328-333

components, 365-368

data binding, 361-374

debugging, 339-340

gateways, 333-336

installing components, 320-323

NetConnection class, 341

NetServices class, 341

RecordSet class, 342-345

responder functions, 336-338

server-side code, 324-327

third-party implementations, 377

troubleshooting, 338-339

focus, 518

forms, 491-492

  attaching ActionScript code to, 511-514

  controls, 493-494

  creating screen-based documents, 499-504

  CustomerEntry.fla document, 527-542

  loading external content, 542-547

  realtime server-side validation, 526-527

  RIAs, 495

  screens, 497-499

  scripting, 504-510

  submitting, 495-497

  validating, 515-526

interfaces, 31

  adding visual elements, 31-34

  coding ActionScript, 35-42

  publishing, 42-46

Java, 21

mask clips, 221-223

navigation buttons

  adding ActionScript, 63-65

  ArtistButtonClip, 65-67

  testing, 68-69

  with XML, 46-63

rollover buttons, 59-63

servers, 19

  formatting databases, 19-20

  placing example files (document root), 22

  selecting applications, 20-21

setInterval() method, 213-214

shapes, 219-220

variables

  ActionScript, 134-136

  datatypes, 136

  strict typing, 136-137

Web services, 383-384

  ActionScript code, 415-420

  clients, 383

  components, 404-405

  connecting, 423-428

  customizing, 383-384

  data binding, 428-434

  defining, 381-382

  monitoring WebServiceConnector component, 422

  panel, 420-421

  security, 434-435

  server-side code, 386-404

  SimpleBarChart component, 413-415

  WebServiceConnector component, 385, 406-413

development

  ActionScript, 119

    customizing Actions panel, 128

    Help panel, 129

    troubleshooting Actions panel, 121-124

    typing variables (Actions panel), 125-128

    undocking Actions panel, 119-120

  IDE

    Actions panel, 17

    adding animation, 87-92

    buttons, 98

    Components panel, 16

    controlling playback (ActionScript), 92-94

    erasing tweaned motion, 96

    events (buttons), 100-103

    Help panel, 18

    invisible buttons, 103-104

    jumping frames, 95-98

    Library panel, 80-86

modifying buttons, 99-100

navigating, 11-13

Properties panel, 18

Stage, 16

Timeline, 14, 86

Tools bar, 15

dialog boxes

Component Definition, 224

Create New Symbol, 203

documentation

cross-domain data access policies, 588-589

session state, 440-441

documents, 22

forms, 491-492

attaching ActionScript code to, 511-514

controls, 493-494

creating, 495-497

CustomerEntry.fla document, 527-542

formatting screen-based documents, 499-504

loading external content, 542-547

realtime server-side validation, 526-527

RIAs, 495

screens, 497-499

scripting, 504-510

validating, 515-526

Library

adding clips to, 202-206

applying linkage identifiers, 206-209

deleting movie clips, 211-212

modifying movie clips, 209-211

newsTicker.fla document, 245-251

preloader, 547

RatingChart.fla, 404-405

SimpleBarChart component, 557

XML, 272

domains, 583-584

creating, 585-587

documenting, 588-589

enforcing, 584-585

drawBox() method, 220

drawing

objects, 15

shapes, 219-220

DrawingUIComponent class, 564

E

ECMAScript, 117

elements

ActionScript, 130

comments, 130-131

conditional statements, 137-140

expressions, 140-143

loops, 143-146

syntax, 131-133

variables, 133-137

SimpleBarChart component, 560-577

XML, 274

else statements, 138

encoding variables, 25-26

ASP.NET, 28-30

ColdFusion, 26-27

Java, 30

enforcing cross-domain data access policies, 584-585

environments

ActionScript, 119

customizing Actions panel, 128

Help panel, 129

troubleshooting Actions panel, 121-124

typing variables (Actions panel),
125-128
undocking Actions panel, 119-120
IDE
Actions panel, 17
adding animation, 87-92
buttons, 98
Components panel, 16
controlling animation (ActionScript),
92-94
erasing tweaned motion, 96
events (buttons), 100-103
Help panel, 18
invisible buttons, 103-104
jumping frames, 95-98
Library panel, 80-86
modifying buttons, 99-100
navigating, 11-13
Properties panel, 18
Stage, 16
Timeline, 14, 86
Tools bar, 15

erasing tweaned motion, 96

events

ActionScript, 174-180
buttons, 63-65, 100-103
invalid/valid, 523
movie clips, 109
MovieClip class, 182-189
gesture-based scroller widgets, 190-196
GestureMovieClip class, 197-200
reviewing GestureMovieClip class,
200-202
onData, 252
onLoad, 252
OnResult event handlers, 337-338
screens, 511

status, 338-339
updateAfterEvent() method, 217-218

example files, placing in document root, 22

execution of XPathAPI class, 300-308

expressions
ActionScript, 140
conditional, 140-143

extensions, XMLNode class, 291-295

external content, loading, 542-544

external SWF, loading at runtime, 56-59

F

false operator, 141

fetching
ActionScript, 35-42
server data, 74

fields, hiding, 441-448

files. *See also* clips; documents
ActionScript, 560-577
classes, 165
cross-domain policies
creating, 585-587
documenting, 588-589
sizing, 75
text, 255-258

filtering recordsets, 376

FLA, 9

Flash, 8
interfaces
adding visual elements, 31-34
building, 31
coding ActionScript, 35-42
publishing, 42-46

navigating, 4-5

versions, 10-11

Flash Player, 8

Flash Remoting, 316

capabilities, 374-376

configuring, 320-324, 345-361

binding data, 361-374

client-side code, 328-333

debugging, 339-340

gateways, 333-336

installing components, 320-323

NetConnection class, 341

NetServices class, 341

RecordSet class, 342-345

responder functions, 336-338

server-side code, 324-327

troubleshooting, 338-339

gateways, 318

supplying data as, 24

terminology, 319

third-party implementations, 377

Web services, 316-317

flashvars parameter, 444

focus, configuring, 518

for in loops, 144

for loops, 143-144

formatting. *See also* **configuration**

classes, 158-166, 168-172

cookies, 453-454

cross-domain data access policies, 585-587

databases, 19-20

forms, 491-492

attaching ActionScript code to, 511-514

controls, 493-494

creating, 495-504

CustomerEntry.fla document, 527-542

loading external content, 542-547

realtime server-side validation, 526-527

RIAs, 495

screens, 497-499

scripting, 504-510

validating, 515-526

mask clips, 221-223

setInterval() method, 213-214

shapes, 219-220

SimpleBarChart component, 557-579

slide presentations, 499-502

variables

ActionScript, 134-136

datatypes, 136

strict typing, 136-137

Web services, 381

ActionScript code, 415-420

clients, 383

components, 404-405

connecting, 423-428

customizing, 383-384

data binding, 428-434

defining, 381-382

monitoring WebServiceConnector component, 422

panel, 420-421

security, 434-435

server-side code, 386-404

SimpleBarChart component, 413-415

WebServiceConnector component, 385, 406-413

forms, 491-492

controls, 493-494

creating, 495-497

CustomerEntry.fla document, 527-542

logins
  testing, 487-488
  tracking, 459-486

RIAs, 495

screens, 497-499
  attaching ActionScript code to, 511-514
  creating screen-based documents, 499-504
  loading external content, 542-547
  scripting, 504-510

validating, 515-527

variables, 441-448

frames
  Hit, 103-104
  jumping, 95-98

functionality, scrolling, 212-218

functions. *See also* **commands**
  ActionScript, 151
    arguments, 152-153
    returning values, 154
    storing, 156-157
    strict typing, 155
    syntax, 152
  getter/setter, 169-172
  loadArtist(), 40-42
  responder, 336-338

G

gateways (Flash Remoting), 318, 333
  ColdFusion, 334
  gateways, 335
  JRun, 334
  localhost, 335

.NET, 334
  overriding, 335-336

gesture-based scroller widgets, 190-196
  GestureMovieClip class, 197-200
  reviewing, 200-202

gesture-driven scrollers, populating, 281-299

GestureMovieClip class, 197-202

getter functions, 169-172

gotoAndPlay() command, 94

H

handling events, invalid/valid, 523

Help panel
  ActionScript, 129
  navigating, 18

hiding fields, 441-448

hints, code, 124

histories, ActionScript, 118

Hit frames, invisible buttons, 103-104

Hosts, localhost gateways, 335

HTML (Hypertext Markup Language), 7.
  See also **code**
  copying/pasting, 70-74
  gateways, 335-336

I

IDE (Integrated Development Environment)
  Actions panel, 17
  ActionScript, 119
    customizing Actions panels, 128
    Help panel, 129

troubleshooting Actions panels, 121-124

typing variables (Actions panels), 125-128

undocking Actions panels, 119-120

buttons, 98

  events, 100-104

  modifying, 99-100

Components panel, 16

Flash Remoting, 320-323

Help panel, 18

Library panel, 80-86

navigating, 11-13

Properties panel, 18

Stage, 16

Timeline, 14, 86

  adding animation, 87-92

  controlling playback (ActionScript), 92-94

  erasing tweened motion, 96

  jumping frames, 95-98

Tools bar, 15

XMLConnector component, 308-312

if statements, 138

implementation of XPath, 299-308

inheritance, 172-173

initialization of movie clips with parameters, 208-209

initializeVisuals() method, 219

inserting code, 122-123

installation (Flash Remoting), 320-324, 345-361

  capabilities, 374-376

  client-side code, 328-333

  client-side components, 320-322

  data binding, 361-374

  debugging, 339-340

  gateways, 333-336

  NetConnection class, 341

  NetServices class, 341

  RecordSet class, 342-345

  responder functions, 336-338

  server-side code, 324-327

  server-side components, 322-323

  third-party implementations, 377

  troubleshooting, 338-339

instances, symbols, 80-84

integration

  IDE. *See* IDE

  servers, 5-6

intercepting raw data, 252-258

interfaces

  ActionScript, 35-42

  API ActionScript screens, 505

  ASP.NET, 28-30

  building, 31

  ColdFusion, 26-27

  forms, 493-494

  gesture-based scroller widgets, 190-196

    GestureMovieClip class, 197-200

    reviewing GestureMovieClip class, 200-202

  Java, 30

  navigation buttons

    adding ActionScript, 63-65

    ArtistButtonClip, 65-67

    creating with XML, 46-63

    testing, 68-69

  publishing, 42-46

  supplying data to, 24-25

  variables, 25-26

  visual elements, 31-34

Web pages, 69-75

Web services, 420-421

Internet forms, RIAs, 495

intervals, setInterval() method, 213-214

invalid control, configuring, 518

invalid events, 523

invisible buttons, 103-104

J

J2EE (Java 2 Enterprise Edition)
cookieless sessions with, 453
Web services, 397-401

Java
configuring, 21
cookies sessions with, 453. *See also* cookies
Flash Remoting
gateways, 335
server-side code, 326-327
logins, 471-474
servers, 323
supplying data as plain text, 30
Web services, 397-401

JavaScript, relationship to ActionScript, 117

JRun, Flash Remoting gateways, 334

jumping frames, 95-98

K

Keyframes, adding, 90

keywords, 154
private/public, 162
this, 109
var, 134-136

L

languages, 6-7
ActionScript, 116. *See also* ActionScript
HTML, 70-74

Library, 202-206
applying Library linkage identifiers, 206-209
deleting, 211-212
modifying, 209-211
panel, 84-86
symbols, 80-84

limitations, sizing local shared objects, 458-459

lines, drawing, 219-220

linkage identifiers, 83, 206-209

listener event mode, responding to events, 178

loadArtists() function, 40-42

loading
external SWF at runtime, 56-59
forms, 542-544
recordsets, 374-375
variables, 269-270

LoadVars class, 231-234
structured data
newsTicker.fla document, 245-251
parsing, 252-258
retrieving, 234-243
viewing, 244
variables, 258-270

LoadVars object, 39-42, 497

LoadVarsExtended class
building, 239-242
testing, 242-243

localhost, applying in gateway URLs, 335

LoginManager class, 462

logins

testing, 487-488

tracking, 459-486

logs, Data Logger Web services, 422

loops

ActionScript, 143

break statement/continue statement,
145-146

for, 143-144

for in, 144

while, 145

parameters, 74

M

maintenance, session state without cookies,
451-453

management

forms, 540

sessions, 440-441

sharing variables, 449-453

testing logins, 487-488

tracking logins, 459-486

margins, 133

markup, 6-7

mask clips, programming, 221-223

members

DataSet class, 372-374

LoadVars class, 231-234

newsTicker.fla document, 245-251

parsing structured data, 252-258

retrieving structured data, 234-243

viewing structured data, 244

MovieClip class, 182-189

gesture-based scroller widgets, 190-196

GestureMovieClip class, 197-200

reviewing GestureMovieClip class,
200-202

RecordSet class, 342-345

WebServiceConnector component, 406-413

XML class, 275-280

metatags, adding, 562-563

methods

addEventListener(), 178

calls, 213-214

classes, 167

createMaskClip(), 221

drawBox(), 220

initializeVisuals(), 219

logins

testing, 487-488

tracking, 459-486

MovieClip class, 182-189

gesture-based scroller widgets, 190-196

GestureMovieClip class, 197-200

reviewing GestureMovieClip class,
200-202

NetConnection class, 341

NetServices class, 341

RecordSet class, 344-345

respondToMouseGestures(), 214-217

setInterval(), 213-214

SimpleBarChart component, 556-557

updateAfterEvent(), 217-218

modifying

Actions panel, 119-120

buttons on rollover, 99-100

code, 369-372

movie clips, 209-211

screens, 503-504

monitoring WebServiceConnector component, 422

motion, erasing, 96

mouse

gesture-based scroller widgets, 190-196

GestureMovieClip class, 197-200

reviewing GestureMovieClip class, 200-202

scrolling functionality, 212-218

MovieClip class, 182-189

constructors

applying Library linkage identifiers, 206-209

symbols, 205-206

deleting, 211-212

modifying, 209-211

properties, 204-205

movies, 7-8

clips, 9, 104

applying Library linkage identifiers, 206-209

comparing to components, 553

deleting, 211-212

events, 109

Library, 202-206

modifying, 209-211

responder functions, 337

state mechanisms, 105-106

targets, 106-108

this keyword, 109

timeline, 104-105

components, 223-226

content, 218

creating, 35-36

MovieClip class, 182-189

gesture-based scroller widgets, 190-196

GestureMovieClip class, 197-200

reviewing GestureMovieClip class, 200-202

publishing, 42-46

Timeline, 44-46

moving

ActionScript functions, 156-157

gesture-based scroller widgets, 190-196

GestureMovieClip class, 197-200

reviewing GestureMovieClip class, 200-202

HTML, 70-74

movie clips, 209-211

N

naming

conventions, 125

frames, 95-96

symbols, 83-84

navigation, 4-5

buttons, 98

adding ActionScript, 63-65

ArtistButtonClip, 65-67

creating with XML, 46-63

events, 100-103

invisible, 103-104

modifying, 99-100

testing, 68-69

functionality, 212-218

gesture-based scroller widgets, 190-196

GestureMovieClip class, 197-200

reviewing GestureMovieClip class, 200-202

gesture-driven scrollers, 281-299

IDE, 11-13

   Actions panel, 17

   Components panel, 16

   Help panel, 18

   Properties panel, 18

   Stage, 16

   Timeline, 14

   Tools bar, 15

   Web services, 420-421

.NET

   Flash Remoting, 334

   Web services, 391-396

NetConnection class, connecting, 341

NetConnection Debugger, 339-340

NetServices class, connecting, 341

Networks

   Flash Remoting, 316

     binding data, 361-374

     capabilities, 374-376

     client-side code, 328-333

     comparing to Web services, 316-317

     configuring, 320-324, 345-361

     debugging, 339-340

     gateways, 318, 333-336

     NetConnection class, 341

     NetServices class, 341

     RecordSet class, 342-345

     responder functions, 336-338

     server-side code, 324-327

     terminology, 319

     third-party implementations, 377

     troubleshooting, 338-339

   servers

     configuring, 19

     formatting databases, 19-20

     placing example files (document root), 22

     selecting applications, 20-21

   Web services, 380, 423-428

     ActionScript code, 415-420

     clients, 383

     components, 404-405

     creating, 381

     customizing, 383-384

     data binding, 428-434

     defining, 381-382

     monitoring WebServiceConnector component, 422

     panel, 420-421

     security, 434-435

     server-side code, 386-404

     SimpleBarChart component, 413-415

     WebServiceConnector component, 385, 406-413

   XML

     applying XMLConnector component, 308-312

     members (XML class), 275-280

     populating gesture-driven scrollers, 281-299

     usage patterns, 280

     XML class, 272, 275

new features, ActionScript, 118-119

newlines, 131

newsTicker.fla document, 245-251

nodes, 272

   child, 274

   executing XPathAPI class, 300-308

   parent, 274

   root, 274

   text, 274

   XML, 274

   XPath, 299-300

notification of users without alerts, 518

null operators, 142

numbers
    ActionScript, 146
    frames, 95-96
    local shared data, 454-456

O

objects
    events
        accessing, 179
        ActionScript, 174-180
    LoadVars, 39-40, 497
        newsTicker.fla document, 245-251
        parsing, 252-258
        retrieving, 234-243
        viewing, 244
    local shared, 454
        SharedObject class, 455-456
        sizing, 458-459
        SWFs, 457
    MovieClip class, 182-189
        gesture-based scroller widgets, 190-196
        GestureMovieClip class, 197-200
        reviewing GestureMovieClip class, 200-202
    movies, 35-36
    Tools bar, 15
    Web services, 401-402
    XML, 51-54
    XPath, 299-308

on (event) syntax, 177, 180

onData events, 252

onLoad events, 252

onResult event handlers, 337-338

operators
    :/?, 139-140
    expressions. *See* expressions
    false, 141
    null, 142
    true, 141
    undefined, 142

options
    Actions panel, 128
    ASP.NET, 20
    classes, 158-172
    ColdFusion, 21
    cookies, 453-454
    Flash Remoting, 320-324, 345-361
        capabilities, 374-376
        client-side code, 328-333
        components, 365-368
        data binding, 361-374
        debugging, 339-340
        gateways, 333-336
        installing components, 320-323
        NetConnection class, 341
        NetServices class, 341
        RecordSet class, 342-345
        responder functions, 336-338
        server-side code, 324-327
        third-party implementations, 377
        troubleshooting, 338-339
    focus, 518
    forms, 491-492
        attaching ActionScript code to, 511-514
        controls, 493-494
        creating screen-based documents, 499-504
        CustomerEntry.fla document, 527-542
        loading external content, 542-547

realtime server-side validation, 526-527

RIAs, 495

screens, 497-499

scripting, 504-510

submitting, 495-497

validating, 515-526

interfaces, 31

  adding visual elements, 31-34

  coding ActionScript, 35-42

  publishing, 42-46

Java, 21

mask clips, 221-223

navigation buttons

  adding ActionScript, 63-65

  ArtistButtonClip, 65-67

  testing, 68-69

  with XML, 46-63

rollover buttons, 59-63

servers, 19

  formatting databases, 19-20

  placing example files (document root), 22

  selecting applications, 20-21

setInterval() method, 213-214

shapes, 219-220

variables

  ActionScript, 134-136

  datatypes, 136

  strict typing, 136-137

Web services, 383-384

  ActionScript code, 415-420

  clients, 383

  components, 404-405

  connecting, 423-428

  customizing, 383-384

  data binding, 428-434

  defining, 381-382

  monitoring WebServiceConnector component, 422

  panel, 420-421

  security, 434-435

  server-side code, 386-404

  SimpleBarChart component, 413-415

  WebServiceConnector component, 385, 406-413

output, viewing, 54-56

overriding gateways, 335-336

P

packages, 166. *See also* classes

pageable recordsets, 374

panels, Web services, 420-421

parameters

  flashvars, 444

  loop, 74

  movie clips, 208-209

  play, 74

parent nodes, XML, 274

parents, 106-108

parsing

  delimited text files, 255-258

  structured data, 252-258

passed-in variables, accessing, 447

passing

  URLs, 441-448

  variables, 441-448

  XML, 280

pasting HTML, 70-74

paths

  classpaths, 165

  targets, 106-108

persistence, 454
    SharedObject class, 455-456
    sizing, 458-459
    SWFs, 457

plain text
    ASP.NET, 28-30
    ColdFusion, 26-27
    Java, 30
    supplying data as, 24

playback, controlling, 92-94

policies
    cross-domain data access, 583-584
        creating, 585-587
        documenting, 588-589
        enforcing, 584-585
    security, 434-435

populating gesture-driven scrollers, 281-299

positioning
    Actions panel, 119-120
    mouse scrolling functionality, 212-218
    movie clips, 209-211
    screens, 503-504

preferences
    Actions panel, 128
    ASP.NET, 20
    classes, 158-172
    ColdFusion, 21
    cookies, 453-454
    Flash Remoting, 320-324, 345-361
        capabilities, 374-376
        client-side code, 328-333
        components, 365-368
        data binding, 361-374
        debugging, 339-340

    gateways, 333-336
    installing components, 320-323
    NetConnection class, 341
    NetServices class, 341
    RecordSet class, 342-345
    responder functions, 336-338
    server-side code, 324-327
    third-party implementations, 377
    troubleshooting, 338-339
focus, 518
forms, 491-492
    attaching ActionScript code to, 511-514
    controls, 493-494
    creating screen-based documents, 499-504
    CustomerEntry.fla document, 527-542
    loading external content, 542-547
    realtime server-side validation, 526-527
    RIAs, 495
    screens, 497-499
    scripting, 504-510
    submitting, 495-497
    validating, 515-526
interfaces, 31
    adding visual elements, 31-34
    coding ActionScript, 35-42
    publishing, 42-46
Java, 21
mask clips, 221-223
navigation buttons
    adding ActionScript, 63-65
    ArtistButtonClip, 65-67
    testing, 68-69
    with XML, 46-63
rollover buttons, 59-63

servers, 19
>
> formatting databases, 19-20
>
> placing example files (document root), 22
>
> selecting applications, 20-21

setInterval() method, 213-214

shapes, 219-220

variables
>
> ActionScript, 134-136
>
> datatypes, 136
>
> strict typing, 136-137

Web services, 383-384
>
> ActionScript code, 415-420
>
> clients, 383
>
> components, 404-405
>
> connecting, 423-428
>
> customizing, 383-384
>
> data binding, 428-434
>
> defining, 381-382
>
> monitoring WebServiceConnector component, 422
>
> panel, 420-421
>
> security, 434-435
>
> server-side code, 386-404
>
> SimpleBarChart component, 413-415
>
> WebServiceConnector component, 385, 406-413

preloader documents, 547

presentation engines, 491-492

> attaching ActionScript code to, 511-514
>
> controls, 493-494
>
> creating, 495-497
>
> creating screen-based documents, 499-504
>
> CustomerEntry.fla document, 527-542
>
> loading external content, 542-547
>
> realtime server-side validation, 526-527
>
> RIAs, 495
>
> screens, 497-499
>
> scripting, 504-510
>
> validating, 515-526

presentations. *See* **movies**

private keywords, adding, 162

programming, 6-7

> ActionScript
>
> > connecting Web services, 423-428
> >
> > interfaces, 35-42
> >
> > Web services, 415-420
>
> ActionScript, 116. *See also* ActionScript
>
> cookies, 453-454
>
> Flash Remoting
>
> > client-side code, 328-333
> >
> > debugging, 339-340
> >
> > gateways, 333-336
> >
> > NetConnection class, 341
> >
> > NetServices class, 341
> >
> > RecordSet class, 342-345
> >
> > responder functions, 336-338
> >
> > server-side code, 324-327
> >
> > troubleshooting, 338-339
>
> gesture-driven scrollers
>
> > populating, 282-291, 295-299
>
> HTML, 70-74
>
> logins, 461-486
>
> mask clips, 221-223
>
> shapes, 219-220
>
> supplying data to, 24-25
>
> variables
>
> > ASP.NET, 28-30
> >
> > ColdFusion, 26-27
> >
> > encoding, 25-26
> >
> > Java, 30
>
> viewing, 369-372
>
> Web services, 386-404

ProgressBar component, adding, 544-547

properties
adding, 162
classes, 167
getter/setter functions, 169-172
MovieClip class, 182-189
gesture-based scroller widgets, 190-196
GestureMovieClip class, 197-200
reviewing GestureMovieClip class, 200-202
symbols, 204-205
SimpleBarChart component, *555-556*

Properties panel, navigating, 18

protocols, SOAP, 382

prototype-based classes, 158

public keywords, adding, 162

publishing, 9, 42-46

Q

queries
RecordSet class, 342-345
recordsets, 401-402
strings, 25
XPath, 299-308

R

ratingChart.fla document, 404-405

raw data, intercepting, 252-258

realtime server-side validation, 526-527

rearranging screens, 503-504

recompiling SimpleBarChart component, 579-580

RecordSet class
Flash Remoting, 362
queries, 342-345

recordsets
filtering, 376
loading, 374-375
LoadVars class
newsTicker.fla document, 245-251
parsing, 252-258
retrieving, 234-243
viewing, 244
Web services, 401-402

references
screens (ActionScript), 504
SimpleBarChart component, *555-557*
WebServiceConnector component, 406-409

registration points, 211. *See also* positioning

relationships, ECMAScript/JavaScript, 117

relative URLs, 74

remote procedure call (RPC), 316

reports, Data Logger Web services, 422

responder functions, Flash Remoting, 336-338

responding to events (ActionScript), 175-180

respondToMouseGestures() method, 214-217

results
OnResult event handlers, 337-338
queries, 342-345

retrieving
delimited text files, 255-258
structured data, 234-243

returning values, 154

reviewing GestureMovieClip class, 200-202

RIAs (Rich Internet Applications), 495

rollover buttons, 99-100

    creating, 59-63

root nodes, XML, 274

root slides, 502

RPC (remote procedure call), 316

runtime

    ArtistButtonClip, 65-67

    conditional statements, 137

        ?/: operators, 139-140

        case/switch, 138

        if/else, 138

    external SWF, 56-59

    frames, 97-98

S

saving ActionScript functions, 156-157

scheduling method calls, 213-214

screens. *See also* interfaces

    forms, 497-499

        attaching ActionScript code to, 511-514

        creating screen-based documents, 499-504

        scripting, 504-510

    referencing, 504

scripting, 6-7

    form screens, 504-510

    validation, 516-526

ScrollerClip, 224

scrolling

    functionality, 212-218

    gesture-based scroller widgets, 190-196

        GestureMovieClip class, 197-200

        reviewing GestureMovieClip class, 200-202

    gesture-driven scrollers, 281-299

searching

    executing XPathAPI class, 300-308

    XPath, 299-300

security, 434-435

selecting

    applications, 20-21

    artists, 40-42

    objects, 15

semicolon (;), 131

sending variables to servers, 258-270

server-side code

    gesture-driven scrollers, 282-284

    logins, 461-475

    Web services, 386-404

server-side languages, 6

servers

    configuring, 19

        formatting databases, 19-20

        placing example files (document root), 22

        selecting applications, 20-21

    connecting, 5-6

    cookies, 453-454

    Flash Remoting, 316

        binding data, 361-374

        capabilities, 374-376

        client-side code, 328-333

comparing to Web services, 316-317
configuring, 320-324, 345-361
debugging, 339-340
gateways, 318, 333-336
installing components, 320-323
NetConnection class, 341
NetServices class, 341
RecordSet class, 342-345
responder functions, 336-338
server-side code, 324-327
terminology, 319
third-party implementations, 377
troubleshooting, 338-339
realtime server-side validation, 526-527
sessions, 440-441, 449-453
supplying data to, 24-25
variables, 258-270
XML
  members (XML class), 275-280
  populating gesture-driven scrollers, 281-299
  usage patterns (XML class), 280
  XML class, 272-275

services
NetConnection class, 341
Web
  ActionScript code, 415-420
  clients, 383
  comparing to, 316-317
  components, 404-405
  connecting, 380, 423-428
  creating, 381
  customizing, 383-384
  data binding, 428-434
  defining, 381-382

monitoring WebServiceConnector component, 422
panel, 420-421
security, 434-435
server-side code, 386-404
SimpleBarChart component, 413-415
WebServiceConnector component, 385, 406-413

sessions
login
  testing, 487-488
  tracking, 459-486
states, 440-441, 451-453
variables, 449-453

setInterval() method, 213-214

setter functions, 169-172

shapes, drawing, 219-220

sharing
cookies, 453-454
local shared objects, 454
  SharedObject class, 455-456
  sizing, 458-459
  SWFs, 457
session variables, 449-453

Simple Object Access Protocol (SOAP), 382

SimpleBarChart component, 405-415, 551-554
creating, 557-579
recompiling, 579-580
references, 555-557

sizing
files, 75
local shared data, 458-459

slide clips, 192

slide presentations, creating, 499-502

sliding tickers
newsTicker.fla document, 245-251
viewing structured data, 244

SOAP (Simple Object Access Protocol), 382

sorting recordsets, 376

source documents, 557. *See also* documents

special comments, variables, 128

spin control, 44

SQL (Structured Query Language), 7

Stage, navigating, 16

starting
Actions panel, 119-120
logins
testing, 487-488
tracking, 459-486

state
sessions, 440-441
maintaining without cookies, 451-453
testing logins, 487-488
tracking logins, 459-486
timelines, 105-106
web pages, 441-448

statements
ActionScript, 137
?/: operators, 139-140
case/switch, 138
if/else, 138
break, 145-146
continue, 145-146
trace
viewing output, 54-56
Web services, 422

static methods, classes, 167

status events, Remote Flashing, 338-339

stop() command, 94

storing ActionScript functions, 156-157

strict variable typing, 136-137
classes, 162
functions, 155

strings
ActionScript, 147
local shared data, 454
SharedObject class, 455-456
SWFs, 457
queries, 25

structured data
LoadVars class
newsTicker.fla document, 245-251
parsing, 252-258
retrieving, 234-243
viewing, 244
local shared objects, 454
SharedObject class, 455-456
sizing, 458-459
SWFs, 457

Structured Query Language (SQL), 7

subclasses, 172-173
GestureMovieClip class, 197-202
MovieClip class
applying Library linkage identifiers, 206-209
constructors, 205-206
deleting movie clips, 211-212
modifying movie clips, 209-211
properties, 204-205

submissions, forms, 495-497

supplying data to, 24-25

support
applications, 318
Web services, 380
clients, 383
creating, 381
customizing, 383-384
defining, 381-382

.swf files, 8
local shared objects, 457
runtime, 56-59
URLs, 444

switch statements, 138

symbols
Create New Symbol dialog box, 203
Library, 202-206
applying Library linkage identifiers, 206-209
deleting movie clips, 211-212
modifying movie clips, 209-211
Library panel, 80-84
naming, 84

syntax. *See also* **programming**
ActionScript, 131-133, 152
on (event), 177, 180

T

targets, path, 106-108

terminology, 7-9

testing
interfaces, 42-46
LoadVarsExtended class, 242-243
logins, 487-488
navigation buttons, 68-69
Web services, 402-404

text
comments, 130-131
delimited, 255-258
nodes, 274
plain
ASP.NET, 28-30
ColdFusion, 26-27
Java, 30
supplying data as, 24
special comments, 128
syntax, 131-133

third-party Flash Remoting implementations, 377

third-party Web services, security policies, 434-435

this keyword, 109

timeline, 9, 86
animation
adding, 87-92
controlling playback (ActionScript), 92-94
erasing tweaned motion, 96
jumping frames, 95-98
movie clips, 104-105
accessing, 44-46
state mechanisms, 105-106
targets, 106-108
this keyword, 109
navigating, 14
responder functions, 337

times, attaching code to screens, 511

tools, Actions panel, 121-124

Tools bar, navigating, 15

trace statements
output, 54-56
Web services, 422

tracking
logins, 459-486
testing, 487-488

troubleshooting
Actions panel, 121-124, 129
Flash Remoting, 338-340
logins, 487-488
Web services, 402-404

tru operator, 141

tweaned motion, erasing, 96

types
of screen-based documents, 498-499
of symbols, 82

typing variables
Actions panel, 125-128
classes, 162
functions, 155
strict, 136-137

U

UDDI (Universal Description, Discovery and Integration), 382

UI components, binding, 366-368

undefined operators, 142

undocking Actions panel, 119-120

Universal Description, Discovery and Integration (UDDI), 382

updateAfterEvent() method, 217-218

URLs (Uniform Resource Locators)
absolute, 74
passing, 441-448
relative, 74
WDSL, 381

users
alerts, 518
login
testing, 487-488
tracking, 459-486

V

valid events, 523

validation
custom classes, 525
databound, 520
forms, 515-526
CustomerEntry.fla document, 527-542
realtime server-side, 526-527

values
ActionScript, 154
cookies, 453-454

var keyword, creating variables, 134-136

variables
Actions panel, 125-128
ActionScript, 133
creating, 134-136
datatypes, 136
expressions, 140-143
strict typing, 136-137
ASP.NET, 28-30
ColdFusion, 26-27

encoding, 25-26

loading, 269-270

LoadVars class, 231-234

newsTicker.fla document, 245-251

parsing structured data, 252-258

retrieving structured data, 234-243

sending, 258-270

viewing structured data, 244

LoadVars object, 39-40

logins

testing, 487-488

tracking, 459-486

passing, 447

sessions, 449-453

strict typing

classes, 162

functions, 155

versions, 10-11

ActionScript, 118-119

cross-domain data access policies, 589

viewing

code, 369-372

interfaces, 35-42

output, 54-56

structured data, 244

visual elements, adding, 31-34

visual language elements, 7

W

Web pages

interfaces, 69-75

login form pages, 475

state, 441-448

Web services

ActionScript code, 415-420

clients, 383

components, 404-405

connecting, 380, 423-428

creating, 381

customizing, 383-384

data binding, 428-434

defining, 381-382

Flash Remoting, 316-317

panel, 420-421

security, 434-435

server-side code, 386-404

SimpleBarChart component, 413-415

supplying data as, 24

WebServiceConnector component, 385, 406-413, 422

Web Services Description Language (WSDL), 381

Web Services panel, 420-421

WebServiceConnector component, 385

members, 406-413

monitoring, 422

while loops, 145

whitespace, 133

widgets, 190-196

GestureMovieClip class, 197-200

reviewing GestureMovieClip class, 200-202

writing, 175, 180. *See also* code; responding

WSDL (Web Services Description Language), 381

X-Z

XML (Extensible Markup Language), 7

attributes, 274

class, 272, 275

members, 275-280

populating gesture-driven scrollers, 281-299

usage patterns, 280

declarations, 274

elements, 274

logins, 463

navigation buttons

adding ActionScript, 63-65

ArtistButtonClip, 65-67

creating, 46-63

testing, 68-69

nodes, 274

child, 274

parent, 274

root, 274

text, 274

objects, 51-54

supplying data as, 24

XPath, 299-308

XMLConnector component, 308-312

XMLNode class, adding extensions, 291-295

XPath, 299-308

www.informit.com

YOUR GUIDE TO IT REFERENCE

New Riders has partnered with **InformIT.com** to bring technical information to your desktop. Drawing from New Riders authors and reviewers to provide additional information on topics of interest to you, **InformIT.com** provides free, in-depth information you won't find anywhere else.

Articles

Keep your edge with thousands of free articles, in-depth features, interviews, and IT reference recommendations— all written by experts you know and trust.

Online Books

Answers in an instant from **InformIT Online Books'** 600+ fully searchable online books.

POWERED BY

Catalog

Review online sample chapters, author biographies, and customer rankings and choose exactly the right book from a selection of more than 5,000 titles.

VOICES THAT MATTER

HOW TO CONTACT US

VISIT OUR WEB SITE AT WWW.NEWRIDERS.COM

On our web site, you'll find information about our other books, authors, tables of contents, and book errata. You will also find information about book registration and how to purchase our books, both domestically and internationally.

EMAIL US

Contact us at: **nrfeedback@newriders.com**

- If you have comments or questions about this book
- To report errors that you have found in this book
- If you have a book proposal to submit or are interested in writing for New Riders
- If you are an expert in a computer topic or technology and are interested in being a technical editor who reviews manuscripts for technical accuracy

Contact us at: **nreducation@newriders.com**

- If you are an instructor from an educational institution who wants to preview New Riders books for classroom use. Email should include your name, title, school, department, address, phone number, office days/hours, text in use, and enrollment, along with your request for desk/examination copies and/or additional information.

Contact us at: **nrmedia@newriders.com**

- If you are a member of the media who is interested in reviewing copies of New Riders books. Send your name, mailing address, and email address, along with the name of the publication or Web site you work for.

BULK PURCHASES/CORPORATE SALES

The publisher offers discounts on this book when ordered in quantity for bulk purchases and special sales. For sales within the U.S., please contact: Corporate and Government Sales (800) 382-3419 or **corpsales@pearsontechgroup.com**. Outside of the U.S., please contact: International Sales (317) 428-3341 or **international@pearsontechgroup.com**.

WRITE TO US

New Riders Publishing
800 East 96th Street, 3rd Floor
Indianapolis, IN 46240

CALL/FAX US

Toll-free (800) 571-5840
If outside U.S. (317) 428-3000
Ask for New Riders
FAX: (317) 428-3280

New Riders

Voices that Matter™

OUR AUTHORS

PRESS ROOM

| web development | design | photoshop | new media | 3-D | server technologies |

EDUCATORS

ABOUT US

CONTACT US

You already know that New Riders brings you the **Voices That Matter**.

But what does that mean? It means that New Riders brings you the

Voices that challenge your assumptions, take your talents to the next

level, or simply help you better understand the complex technical world

we're all navigating.

Visit **www.newriders.com** to find:

- ▸ **10% discount** and **free shipping** on all book purchases
- ▸ Never-before-published chapters
- ▸ Sample chapters and excerpts
- ▸ Author bios and interviews
- ▸ Contests and enter-to-wins
- ▸ Up-to-date industry event information
- ▸ Book reviews
- ▸ Special offers from our friends and partners
- ▸ Info on how to join our User Group program
- ▸ Ways to have your Voice heard

New Riders

WWW.NEWRIDERS.COM